PERSONAL FINANCE

FOURTH CANADIAN EDITION

PERSONAL FINANCE

JEFF MADURA
Florida Atlantic University

HARDEEP SINGH GILL
Northern Alberta Institute of Technology (NAIT)

Pearson

To Mary

VICE PRESIDENT, EDITORIAL: Anne Williams
ACQUISITIONS EDITOR: Keara Emmett
MARKETING MANAGER: Spencer Snell
CONTENT MANAGER: Emily Dill
PROJECT MANAGER: Sarah Gallagher
CONTENT DEVELOPER: Patti Sayle
MEDIA CONTENT MANAGER: Nicole Mellow
MEDIA CONTENT DEVELOPER: Toni Chahley
MEDIA DEVELOPER: Olga Avdyeyeva

PRODUCTION SERVICES: Cenveo® Publisher Services
PERMISSIONS PROJECT MANAGER: Joanne Tang
PHOTO PERMISSIONS RESEARCH: Integra Publishing Services
TEXT PERMISSIONS RESEARCH: Integra Publishing Services
INTERIOR DESIGNER: Anthony Leung
COVER DESIGNER: Alex Li
COVER IMAGE: GolubaPhoto/Shutterstock and 3DProfi/Shutterstock
VICE-PRESIDENT, DIGITAL STUDIO: Gary Bennett

Pearson Canada Inc., 26 Prince Andrew Place, North York, Ontario M3C 2H4.

9780134724713

1 18

Library and Archives Canada Cataloguing in Publication

Madura, Jeff, author
    Personal finance / Jeff Madura, Florida Atlantic University, Hardeep Singh Gill, Northern Alberta Institute of Technology (NAIT).—Fourth Canadian edition.

Includes index.
ISBN 978-0-13-472471-3 (hardcover)

    1. Finance, Personal—Canada—Textbooks. I. Gill, Hardeep, 1972-, author II. Title.

HG179.M254 2018   332.02400971   C2017-903202-X

BRIEF CONTENTS

CONTENTS

**PART 2 MANAGING YOUR
FINANCIAL RESOURCES**

Chapter 5
**Banking Services and
Managing Your Money** 134

PART 4 PERSONAL INVESTING

PART 5 RETIREMENT AND ESTATE PLANNING

PART 6 SYNTHESIS OF FINANCIAL PLANNING

Chapter 16
Integrating the Components
of a Financial Plan.............................. 462

PREFACE

When will you be able to buy a home? Can you afford a new car or a vacation? How can you pay off your credit card balance? What should you invest in?

The answers to these questions are tied directly to how you, as a **student,** manage your finances. Managing your finances wisely will bring a sense of security and freedom that you can enjoy for years to come. Very few courses you will take throughout your post-secondary career will have the potential to profoundly shape your future like a personal finance course. Taking this course is your first step on the path toward a stable financial future.

With *Personal Finance*, Fourth Canadian Edition, as your guide, you will master key concepts that will aid you in managing and increasing your personal wealth. The aim of this textbook is to equip you with knowledge and decision-making tools to help you make sound financial decisions.

New to the Fourth Canadian Edition

Revised Chapter Introduction Cases

Each chapter opens with a chapter introduction, with student-centric scenarios that include at least two discussion questions designed to introduce important concepts and themes covered in the chapter.

Free Apps for Personal Finance

Throughout each chapter, students are advised of a variety of useful applications that they can download to their smartphones, for free, that apply to many of the key concepts covered in the chapter.

Psychology of Personal Finance

Personal finance behaviour is influenced by psychology. For example, some spending decisions are made on impulse due to the desire for immediate satisfaction. A feature called Psychology of Personal Finance explains how financial planning decisions are affected by psychology. At the end of every chapter, there is also an accompanying section that tests students' understanding of how psychological forces influence personal finance decisions.

End-of-Chapter *Challenge Questions*

Multi-step financial planning problems called Challenge Questions require deeper analysis, inviting students to apply knowledge and demonstrate chapter material comprehension.

End-of-Chapter *Mini-Cases*

At the end of each chapter, new mini-cases provide students with an opportunity to synthesize and to apply a number of concepts from each chapter in a practical manner. There are one to two mini-cases per chapter.

More Visual Exhibits

More exhibits appear throughout the entire book to enhance concept retention and to provide a visual representation of facts and figures.

Improved *Ethical Dilemmas*

End-of-chapter ethical scenarios focus on topics of student interest to engage the reader. Designed to help students apply ethical principles to financial situations and problems, these real-life ethical situations are presented along with critical thinking questions.

Key Chapter Updates

Chapter 1: In addition to being SMART (specific, measurable, action-oriented, realistic, and time bound), goals must be prioritized. The idea of prioritizing your goals is introduced through a new mini case and the use of an online tool that helps students understand that goals need to be considered in terms of their priority relative to your personal situation.

Chapter 2: The discussion of the simple interest formula, $I = P \times r \times t$, has been expanded to include variations of this formula that allow students to solve for P, r, and t. In addition, a new learning outcome provides a brief discussion and example calculations for solving for the number of compounding periods (N) and the nominal annual interest rate (I/Y). At the end of the chapter, a revised and expanded list of financial planning problems provides students with an opportunity to use their financial calculator to solve for all time value of money variables.

Chapter 3: A summary of the budgeting steps covered in Learning Outcome 3, Creating a Budget, is provided at the end of the section. This summary will help reinforce the actions that are required in this critical component of personal financial planning.

Chapter 5: The topic of Interac e-transfers is introduced for the first time in this edition as a new banking service available to Canadians.

Chapter 6: A new table summarizing the advantages and disadvantages of using credit is introduced in this edition. The home equity loan has been reintroduced as the home equity line of credit, HELOC, in order to better reflect how these types of secured credit facilities are set up in Canada. The section on negotiating the price of a car has been expanded so as to provide further guidance to those students who are in the market for a car—now or in the future.

Chapter 7: The section on mortgage refinancing is now complemented by a new example calculation for a blend-and-extend mortgage refinancing.

Chapter 8: The concept of maintaining a minimum amount of coverage on a homeowner's insurance policy that provides replacement cost coverage is clarified with the use of a detailed example.

Chapter 11: The topic of electronic trading systems is expanded with a discussion of the bid price, ask price, and the bid–ask spread, including definitions and examples. Learning Outcome 4 has been better organized, updated, and renamed *How to Analyze Stocks*. Learning Outcome 5 on *Stock Valuation* has been updated to include a discussion on the two main methods to value a stock—the intrinsic valuation mode and the relative valuation model.

TRIED AND TRUE LEARNING TOOLS IN THE FOURTH CANADIAN EDITION

Learning Objectives

Corresponding to the main headings in each chapter, and indicated by marginal callouts throughout the chapter, the list of learning objectives guides students through the material.

Marginal Glossary

Throughout the text, key terms and their definitions appear in the text margin where they are first discussed.

Explanation by Example

Practical examples applying concepts in realistic scenarios throughout the chapters help cement student understanding of key concepts.

Myth or Fact

Throughout the text, "Myth or Fact" features highlight popular misconceptions about financial planning; providing students with an opportunity to reinforce key ideas from the chapter and/or to use their intuition to determine whether a statement is a myth or a fact.

Summary

In bullet form, the summaries correlate the key points from each chapter with the learning objectives provided at the beginning of the chapter.

Review Questions

The Review Questions test students' understanding by asking them to compare and contrast concepts, interpret financial quotations, and decide how financial data can be used to make personal finance decisions.

Financial Planning Problems

At the end of each chapter, Financial Planning Problems require students to demonstrate knowledge of mathematically based concepts to perform computations in order to make well-informed personal finance decisions.

End-of-Chapter Study Guide

Each chapter concludes with 10 multiple-choice and 10 true/false study questions for extra review.

AN INTERACTIVE APPROACH

Personal Finance's interactive approach incorporates online resources along with many examples, problems, and ongoing case studies, all of which focus on providing students with hands-on practice applying financial concepts.

MyLab Finance

This integrated online homework tool gives students the hands-on practice and tutorial assistance they need to learn skills efficiently. Ample opportunities for online practice and assessment in MyLab™ Finance are seamlessly integrated into the content of each chapter and organized by section within the chapter summaries. Select Financial Planning Problems and Bonus questions are available in the Study Plan, and select Review Questions, new Chapter Test questions, and new Financial Literacy Test questions are available for instructors to assign. MyLab Finance also includes helpful financial planning tools such as financial calculators and tutorials and glossary flashcards. Please visit MyLab Finance for more information and to register.

Build Your Own Financial Plan

Personal Finance's structure mirrors a comprehensive financial plan. In each chapter, students learn the skills they need to build their own financial plan. The Build Your Own Financial Plan exercises are an integrated series of problems and worksheets that present a portion of a financial plan based on the concepts presented in each chapter. The exercises and associated worksheets are available on MyLab Finance. At the end of the course, students will have completed a financial plan that they can continue to implement beyond the school term.

Financial Planning Weblinks

In every chapter, marginal weblinks highlight useful internet resources. You will find a website address and a description of what type of information the website provides.

Financial Planning Online Exercises

At the end of each chapter, Financial Planning Online Exercises show students how to obtain, critically evaluate, and use internet-based resources in making personal finance decisions.

Build a Financial Plan for the Sampson family

The parents of two children, Dave and Sharon Sampson, have made few plans regarding their financial future. They are eager to start saving toward a new car, their children's post-secondary education, and their retirement. Students apply chapter concepts to counsel the Sampsons. The Sampsons—A Continuing Case chapter-end cases and accompanying worksheets are provided on MyLab Finance.

Appendix A: Projects

Appendix A provides a number of projects for students to complete relating to specific aspects of personal finance. The list of projects includes:

- Assessing Your Credit
- Career Planning Project

- Leasing an Apartment
- Stock Market Project
- Comparison Shopping: Online versus Local Purchases
- Mortgage Case Project
- Mutual Fund Comparison Project

Appendix B: Your Career

Appendix B provides direction on determining and managing your career. Topics include:

- Determining Your Career Path
- Getting the Skills You Need
- Changing Your Career

Real-Life Scenarios

Students are prompted to **build a financial plan for Brad MacDonald** using the Brad MacDonald—A Continuing Case scenarios that are provided at the end of each part of the text. Brad has expensive tastes—as evidenced by his soaring credit card balance—and he needs assistance in gaining control over his finances. The accompanying worksheets for Brad MacDonald—A Continuing Case are available on MyLab Finance.

HALLMARKS OF *PERSONAL FINANCE,* FOURTH CANADIAN EDITION

We recognize that students who decide to take a course in personal finance have a variety of academic backgrounds, interests, and personal goals. For some, such a course might be a prerequisite to a future in finance or business. Others may decide to take the course because they want to learn more about how to create a budget or to plan for a large purchase such as a car on their current income. Our aim with this text is to provide students with all the tools they need to fully understand and plan their personal finances in a way that is useful, engaging, and rewarding.

Textbook Content and Organization

We have organized this text into a logical chapter order. The first chapter establishes the text's organization by introducing students to the key components of a financial plan. The text is then organized into six parts, beginning with Chapter 2, which are keyed to the components of a comprehensive financial plan.

Part 1: Tools for Financial Planning

Part 2: Managing Your Financial Resources

Part 3: Protecting Your Wealth

Part 4: Personal Investing

Part 5: Retirement and Estate Planning

Part 6: Synthesis of Financial Planning

Key Topics in the Fourth Canadian Edition of *Personal Finance*

We have included several important topics for Canadian students in this edition. You will find some examples of these key discussions in the following chapters:

Chapter 2: In Chapter 2, we discuss the importance of the time value of money (TVM) concept and provide a step-by-step introduction to the calculator steps, using the TI BA II Plus calculator, used to perform TVM calculations.

Chapter 4: In Chapter 4, we provide background on taxes and tax planning strategies, and then provide an appendix that guides students step by step through the process of completing a tax return.

Chapter 6: In Chapter 6, we discuss identity theft, different identity theft tactics, and ways to protect against this kind of theft.

Chapter 9: In Chapter 9, we discuss the various levels of health and life insurance coverage available to Canadians, including disability, critical illness, and long-term care.

Chapter 10: In Chapter 10, we examine different types of investments and the trade-offs that need to be considered when examining investment return and risk.

Chapter 11: In Chapter 11, we show students how to complete an analysis of a firm, an economic analysis of stocks, and an industry analysis of stocks in order to determine an investment strategy.

Chapter 14: In Chapter 14, we present a comprehensive review of public and private retirement options, including the process of converting retirement assets to income.

Decision-Making Emphasis

All of the information presented in this book is geared toward equipping students with the expertise they need to make informed financial decisions. Each chapter establishes a foundation for the decisions that form the basis of a financial plan. When students complete each chapter, they are, therefore, prepared to complete the related financial plan subsection provided on MyLab Finance. Key to understanding personal finance is knowing how to apply concepts to real-life planning scenarios. The many examples, financial planning problems, exercises, and cases place students in the role of the decision-maker and planner.

Focus on Opportunity Costs

Personal Finance calls attention to the trade-offs involved in financial decisions. The decision to buy a new car affects the amount of funds available for recreation, rent, insurance, and investments. The text uses numerous examples and exercises to illustrate and teach students about the interdependence of personal finance decisions.

The quantitative side of financial planning intimidates many students. *Personal Finance* simplifies the mathematics of personal finance by explaining its underlying logic. Formulas and calculations are explained in the text and then illustrated in examples. Examples that can be solved using a financial calculator are depicted with a keypad illustration. Students are referred to websites with online calculators whenever pertinent. The Financial Planning Problems and Financial Planning Online Exercises provide students with ample opportunity to practise applying math-based concepts.

INSTRUCTOR AND STUDENT SUPPORT PACKAGE

The following array of supplementary materials is available to help busy instructors teach more effectively and to allow busy students to learn more efficiently.

For Instructors

- *Instructor's Resource and Solutions Manual*—This comprehensive manual pulls together a wide variety of teaching tools and resources. Each chapter contains a chapter overview, chapter objectives, teaching tips, and detailed answers and step-by-step solutions to the Chapter Overview Questions, Review Questions, Financial Planning Problems, Challenge Questions, Ethical Dilemma Questions, Mini-Case Questions, Sampson family case questions, and Myth or Fact Margin Questions. Each part concludes with solutions to the Brad MacDonald case questions.

- *Computerized Test Bank*—Pearson's computerized test banks allow instructors to filter and select questions to create quizzes, tests, or homework. Instructors can revise questions or add their own, and may be able to choose print or online options. These questions are also available in Microsoft Word format.

- *PowerPoint Slides®*—This useful tool provides PowerPoint slides illustrating key points from each chapter. Instructors can easily convert the slides to transparencies or view them electronically in the classroom during lectures.

Learning Solutions Managers

Learning Solutions Managers work with faculty and campus course designers to ensure that Pearson technology products, assessment tools, and online course materials are tailored to meet your specific needs. This highly qualified team is dedicated to helping schools take full advantage of a wide range of educational resources, by assisting in the integration of a variety of instructional materials and media formats. Your local Pearson Education sales representative can provide you with more details on this service program.

For Students
MyLab Finance

MyLab Finance provides students with personalized Study Plans and the opportunity for additional practice. MyLab Finance also includes the Pearson eText. The Pearson eText gives students access to their textbook anytime, anywhere. In addition to note taking, highlighting, and bookmarking, the Pearson eText offers interactive and sharing features. Instructors can share their comments or highlights, and students can add their own, creating a tight community of learners within the class.

Financial Planning Problems are available in the Study Plan, and the following resources are also available:

- Build Your Own Financial Plan exercises and worksheets

- Brad MacDonald—Continuing Case

- The Sampson Family—Continuing Case

- Financial calculators and calculator tutorials

- Interactive Glossary Flashcards for all of the key terms in the text

Read the Build Your Own Financial Plan exercises, then use the worksheets to generate a personal cash flow statement, create a personal balance sheet, and set personal financial goals. After reading the case study, use the Continuing Case worksheets to prepare cash flow statements and balance sheets for Brad MacDonald and for the Sampsons.

ACKNOWLEDGMENTS

I wish to acknowledge the help and support of the many people associated with Pearson Canada who made this textbook possible, including Keara Emmett, Acquisitions Editor; Patti Sayle, Developmental Editor; Sarah Gallagher, Project Manager; Revathi Viswanathan, Production Editor; Heather MacDougall, Copy Editor; Joel Gladstone, Proofreader; and Charmaine Felder, Technical Checker. I also wish to thank Cecile Wendlandt, who provided the initial spark that gave me the energy to work on this project.

—Hardeep Gill

Overview of a Financial Plan

After a long semester that ended with their graduation from college, Mo (age 23) and Farah (age 23) could not help but feel an overwhelming sense of satisfaction as they enjoyed the sand and surf on their post-graduation beach vacation. Now that they were moving on with their respective careers, the soon-to-be-married couple faced a new set of financial challenges.

As they imagined their financial futures, the young couple had to think about a number of financial choices, some of which could only be accomplished at the expense of not reaching other goals immediately. Should they buy a new car now? If they did buy a new car, how would this decision impact their plans for their wedding and honeymoon? The couple also had to consider whether they should move out of their apartment and buy a house. How would home ownership impact their cash flow? Although it was a long way off, Mo and Farah were also wondering when they should start thinking about retirement. All of these decisions require detailed planning, but the idea of establishing personal and financial goals for their futures seemed like a difficult task. There was so much they wanted to do and they were not sure if they would ever have the financial resources to do it all.

In a world where there are few guarantees, thorough financial planning, prudent financial management, and careful spending can help you achieve your financial goals.

The personal financial planning process enables you to understand a financial plan and to develop a personal financial plan. The simple objective of financial planning is to make the best use of your resources to achieve your financial goals. The sooner you develop your goals and a financial plan to achieve those goals, the easier it will be to achieve them.

QUESTIONS:

1. What are some of the important financial decisions that Mo and Farah should consider at this stage of their lives?
2. What steps should Mo and Farah take in order to establish their goals?
3. If they wanted professional advice, how should they go about finding a financial adviser?

THE LEARNING OBJECTIVES OF THIS CHAPTER ARE TO:

1. Explain how you could benefit from personal financial planning
2. Identify the key components of a financial plan
3. Outline the steps involved in developing a financial plan

L.O.1

HOW YOU BENEFIT FROM AN UNDERSTANDING OF PERSONAL FINANCE

personal finance (personal financial planning)
The process of planning your spending, financing, and investing activities, while taking into account uncontrollable events, such as death or disability, in order to optimize your financial situation over time.

personal financial plan
A plan that specifies your financial goals and describes the spending, financing, and investing activities that are intended to achieve those goals and the risk management strategies that are required to protect against uncontrollable events, such as death or disability.

per capita debt
The amount of debt each individual in Canada would have if total debt (consumer debt plus mortgages) was spread equally across the population.

Personal finance, also referred to as **personal financial planning**, is the process of planning your spending, financing, and investing activities, while taking into account uncontrollable events such as death or disability, in order to optimize your financial situation over time. A **personal financial plan** specifies your financial goals and describes the spending, financing, and investing activities that are intended to achieve those goals and the risk management strategies that are required to protect against uncontrollable events such as death or disability. Although Canada is one of the world's wealthier countries, many Canadians do not manage their financial situations well. Consequently, they tend to rely too much on credit and have excessive debt. Excessive debt levels affect your ability to achieve important financial goals. Consider the following statistics:

- As of June 2015, total consumer bankruptcies increased by 4.2 percent over the previous year.
- The personal savings rate has been decreasing for the past 30 years and was estimated to be at 4.2 percent as of the third quarter of 2015.
- The delinquency rate on personal loans for youth aged 18 to 25 increased by 11.7 percent from 2015 to 2016.
- From 2000 to 2014, the level of household debt relative to income has increased from 110.1 percent to 166.1 percent, making Canadians the most indebted householders among G7 countries.
- As of May 2016, the per capita debt of Canadians has increased to $17 995. **Per capita debt** represents the amount of debt each individual in Canada would have if total debt (consumer debt plus mortgages) were spread equally across the population.

You have numerous options regarding the choice of bank deposits, credit cards, loans, insurance policies, investments, and retirement plans. All of these options involve decisions you will have to make for yourself. Relying on government benefits alone may not provide you with the financial future you imagine for yourself. With an understanding of personal finance, you will be able to make decisions that can enhance your financial situation. How much do you know about personal finance? Various government agencies of various countries have attempted to assess financial literacy in recent years. Surveys have documented that people tend to have very limited personal finance skills. In addition, surveys have found that many people who believe they have strong personal finance skills do not really understand some basic personal finance concepts.

Do you consider yourself financially literate? Try the financial literacy/knowledge quiz of the Canadian Financial Capability Survey located on the Statistics Canada website at www.statcan.gc.ca/pub/11-008-x/2011001/article/11413-eng.htm#a11. Even if your knowledge of personal finance is limited, you can substantially increase your knowledge and improve your financial planning skills by reading this text. An understanding of personal finance is beneficial to you in many ways.

Make Your Own Financial Decisions

An understanding of personal finance enables you to make informed decisions about your financial situation. Each of your spending decisions has an **opportunity cost**, which represents what you give up as a result of that decision. By spending money for a specific purpose, you forgo alternative ways that you could have spent the money and also forgo saving the money for a future purpose. For example, if your decision to use your cellphone costs $100 per month, you have forgone the possibility of using that money to buy new clothes or to save for a new car. Informed financial decisions increase the amount of money that you accumulate over time and give you more flexibility to purchase the products and services you want in the future.

opportunity cost
What you give up as a result of a decision.

myth or **fact** Financial planners and advisers are registered with a provincial financial planning regulatory agency.

Opportunity cost will also affect your savings decisions. In Chapter 3, we will discuss how you can use budgeting tools to increase your savings. Savings can then be used toward short-, medium-, or long-term goals. Generally, the savings in an emergency fund—a short-term goal—will earn less interest than will your investments in a retirement plan—a long-term goal. Although an emergency fund is very important to your personal financial plan, saving too much for short-term needs does limit your opportunity for long-term growth. You should strive to balance your savings goals among short-, medium-, and long-term goals.

Judge the Advice of Financial Advisers

The personal financial planning process will enable you to make informed decisions about your spending, saving, financing, and investing. Nevertheless, you may prefer to rely on advice from various types of financial advisers. An understanding of personal finance allows you to judge the guidance of financial advisers and to determine whether their advice is in your best interest rather than in their best interest.

EXAMPLE

You want to invest $10 000 of your savings. A financial adviser guarantees that your investment will increase in value by 20 percent ($2000) this year, but he will charge you 4 percent of the investment ($400) for his advice. If you had a background in personal finance, you would know that no investment can be guaranteed to increase in value. Therefore, you would realize that you should not trust this financial adviser. You could either hire a more reputable financial adviser or review investment recommendations made by financial advisers on the internet (often at no cost).

The **Financial Planning Standards Council (FPSC)** is a not-for-profit organization that was created to benefit the public through the development, enforcement, and promotion of the highest competency and ethical standards in financial planning. It provides a series of questions that you can ask a financial adviser, also known as a financial planner. The answers that you receive to these questions will help you evaluate whether or not you are comfortable with the perspective and business approach of a potential financial adviser. You can access these questions through the FPSC website at financialplanningforcanadians.ca/financial-planning/10-questions-to-ask-your-planner. Each question comes with some hints and tips so that you can get the most benefit from the responses you receive.

Financial Planning Standards Council (FPSC)
A not-for-profit organization that was created to benefit the public through the development, enforcement, and promotion of the highest competency and ethical standards in financial planning.

Become a Financial Adviser

Although a single course such as this is not sufficient to become a financial adviser, an interest in and aptitude for the number of products and ideas discussed in this text may lead you to consider a career in the financial services sector. Financial advisers are in demand because many people lack an understanding of personal finance, are not interested in making their own financial decisions, or simply do not have the time necessary to research and educate themselves on financial issues in order to make informed decisions. (It should be clearly stated, though, that most advisers cannot make decisions for their clients. An individual must give permission to the financial adviser before any action can be taken.)

The FPSC website provides a description of the six steps that must be completed in order to earn the Certified Financial Planner (CFP)® designation. Obtaining this credential is a significant step toward building a successful career as a financial adviser because it indicates that you have met the education, examination, experience, and ethical requirements set by the FPSC. Step 1 involves the successful completion of an approved core curriculum program. Step 2 involves successful completion of the FPSC Level 1® Examination in Financial Planning; upon completing this exam, a candidate moves to Step 3 and becomes an FPSC Level 1 certificant. Step 4 involves completing an FPSC-Approved Capstone Course. At Step 5, a candidate will complete their final exam on the path to CFP® certification. After completing this exam and obtaining three years of qualifying work experience in a financial planning–related position, the candidate is eligible to complete their final step by applying for CFP® certification. In order to maintain their certification, a CFP® professional must adhere to the FPSC Standards of Professional Responsibility, complete 25 hours of continuing education requirements, and renew their CFP® certification on an annual basis. Additional information describing the path to CFP® certification may be found at www.fpsc.ca/beaplanner/path-to-certification. The CFP® examinations cover fundamental financial planning practices, financial management, investment planning, insurance and risk management, tax planning, retirement planning, and estate planning and legal aspects. Obtaining and maintaining CFP® certification allows you to be identified by potential clients as a financial adviser who is dedicated to a high level of professionalism in providing financial planning advice.

COMPONENTS OF A FINANCIAL PLAN

L.O.2

A complete financial plan contains your personal finance decisions related to five key components:

1. Budgeting and tax planning
2. Financing your purchases
3. Protecting your assets and income (insurance)
4. Investing your money
5. Planning your retirement and estate

These five components are very different; decisions concerning each component are captured in separate plans that, taken together, form your overall financial plan. To begin your introduction to the financial planning process, let's briefly explore each component.

A Plan for Your Budgeting and Tax Planning

budget planning (budgeting)
The process of forecasting future income, expenses, and savings goals.

Budget planning (also referred to as **budgeting**) is the process of forecasting future income, expenses, and savings goals. That is, it requires you to decide whether to spend or save money. If you receive $750 in income during one month, the amount you save is the amount of money (say, $100) that you do not spend. The relationship between income after taxes, spending, and saving is illustrated in Exhibit 1.1. Some individuals are "big spenders": they focus their budget decisions on how to spend most or all of their income and therefore

EXHIBIT 1.1 How a Budget Plan Affects Savings

BIG SPENDER

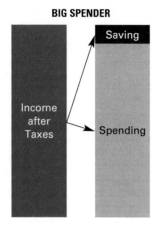

BIG SAVER

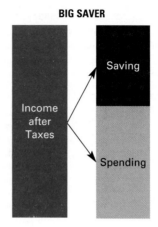

have little or no money left for saving. Others are "big savers": they set a savings goal and consider spending their income after taxes only after allocating a portion of it toward saving. Budgeting can help you estimate how much of your income will be required to cover monthly expenses so that you can set a reasonable and practical goal for saving each month.

A first step in budgeting should be to evaluate your current financial position by assessing your income, your expenses, your **assets** (what you own), and your **liabilities** (debt, or what you owe). Your **net worth** (or wealth) is the value of what you own minus the value of what you owe. You can measure your wealth by your net worth. As you save money, you increase your assets and therefore increase your net worth. Budgeting enables you to build your net worth by setting aside part of your income to either invest in additional assets or reduce your liabilities.

assets
What you own.

liabilities
What you owe; your debt.

net worth
The value of what you own minus the value of what you owe.

myth or **fact** Budgeting is more important for individuals who have trouble covering their monthly expenses.

Your budget is influenced by your income, which in turn is influenced by your life stage. Exhibit 1.2 provides an overview of the six major life stages and the key financial considerations you will make at each of those stages. Individuals who are pursuing post-secondary education during their education stage of life tend to have smaller incomes, usually from part-time jobs, and thus smaller budgets. At this stage, it is important to establish good saving and spending habits—consider saving money inside a TFSA—and begin establishing a credit rating. After completing their education, individuals advance to the early career stage of life and are able to obtain jobs that pay higher salaries, which result in larger budgets. Adopting the pay-yourself-first principle, managing your debt, buying furnishings for your own place or a car for your first job, and building your investment portfolio by starting with a mutual fund are important considerations for someone at this life stage.

FREE APPS for Personal Finance

Your Spending Decisions

Application:

Use iSpending by Hana Mobile LLC to keep track of your income and expenses. You can add transactions under different categories, such as income, food, and entertainment. Summaries for today/week/month/year are also available.

EXHIBIT 1.2 Typical Financial Planning Life Stages

Life Stages

	Education	Early Career	Family and Mid-Career	Prime Earning	Early Retirement	Late Retirement
Age Group	0–22	23–30	31–49	50–64	65–74	75+
Consider Your Current Financial Position	• Establish good saving and spending habits • Consider saving money inside a TFSA • Establish a credit rating	• Follow the pay-yourself-first principle • Pay off student loans and other short-term debt • Buy furnishings for a home • Buy a car • Consider a mutual fund, inside or outside an RRSP	• Buy a home and review insurance needs (health, life, disability, critical illness) • Start a family • Open an RESP account • Continue with your RRSPs • Reduce/minimize taxes • Have a will and power of attorney • Investigate employer-based savings options • Start a business	• Are all debts paid? • Have taxes been minimized? • Adequate savings? • Children's education fund? • Weddings? • Job security? • Elder care?	• What can you expect from OAS/CPP programs? • RRSP/LIRA/work place pension maturity options? • Account for all your assets • Retirement income distribution patterns • What happens if a spouse dies? • Changes to your will and power of attorney	• RRSP/LIRA maturity options? • Annuitize assets? • Reverse mortgage? • Wealth management: how, who, where? • Estate planning
Milestones	• Graduation	• First job • New job/Raise	• Marriage • First house • First baby • Divorce	• Empty nest • Parental care • Close to retirement	• Retirement • Empty nest • Travel • Parental care	

As you progress through the next three life stages, you may experience various milestones. Milestones, such as getting married, having children, or starting a new job, will often result in a need or desire to update your personal financial plan. However, waiting for milestones before creating a personal financial plan can be very dangerous because you may not have any time to prepare. For example, when you reach the milestone of marriage, you may find that the expense of planning a wedding requires you to change your spending habits. At that point, you will have to ask yourself how much you can afford to spend on a wedding. If you have not been planning ahead, you may have to scale back on your wedding plans. As a student, not planning ahead for a milestone would be the same as not studying for your final exam until the day before you are supposed to write it—not a good idea! Budget planning is the first step in building a successful plan so that you do not have to sacrifice what you really want when the time comes.

Although the majority of your personal financial plan will be in place by the time you reach the late retirement life stage, it is still important to be aware of any issues that are outstanding. In particular, you may need to review your wealth management options and your estate plan. Managing your money will become more difficult as you move through this life stage. Therefore, it is important to understand what wealth management options are available and to plan accordingly. In addition, your estate plan should be reviewed to ensure that it reflects your wishes at death. As you can see, personal finance is a subject that you will encounter throughout your life. Refer back to Exhibit 1.2 as you read this textbook. The alternatives you will consider at each life stage and/or milestone will be discussed at various points in the textbook.

Another key part of budgeting is estimating the typical expenses that you will incur each month. If you underestimate expenses, you will not achieve your savings goals. Achieving future wealth requires you to sacrifice by moderating your spending today.

Many financial decisions are affected by tax laws, as some forms of income are taxed at a higher rate than others. By understanding how your varying financial choices would be affected by taxes, you can make financial decisions that have the most favourable effect on your after-tax cash flows. Budgeting and tax planning are discussed in Part 1 because they underpin decisions about all other parts of your financial plan.

A Plan to Manage Your Financial Resources

Short-term cash needs and unexpected expenses, such as emergencies, are a fact of life, and you must plan how you will cover them. Your ability to cover these expenses depends on your liquidity. **Liquidity** refers to your access to ready cash, including savings and credit, to cover short-term or unexpected expenses. The budget planning process described above will help you reach your savings goals. Your liquidity can be allocated to short-term needs, such as a cup of coffee or an unexpected car repair, or to long-term needs, such as retirement. You can enhance your liquidity through money management and credit management.

Money management involves decisions regarding how much money to retain in liquid form and how to allocate the funds among short-term investment instruments. If you do not have access to money to cover short-term needs, you may have insufficient liquidity. As a result, it is important to set up an emergency fund to cover short-term needs. An **emergency fund** contains the portion of savings that you have allocated to short-term needs such as unexpected expenses in order to maintain adequate liquidity. Finding an effective liquidity level involves deciding how to invest your money so that you can earn a return but also have easy access to cash if needed. Money management is discussed in Chapter 5.

As an alternative to establishing an emergency fund by investing some of their savings for short-term needs, many individuals rely on credit to supplement their liquidity. As a result, credit and credit management are important aspects of liquidity. **Credit management** involves decisions regarding how much credit to obtain to support your spending and which sources of credit to use. Credit is commonly used to cover both large and small expenses when you are short on cash, so it enhances your liquidity. Credit should be used only when necessary since you must repay borrowed funds with interest (and the interest expenses may be very high). Unfortunately, the use of consumer credit has steadily increased since 1980. As of 2005, consumer credit represented 38 cents of each dollar of personal spending in Canada. Combined with the steady decline in the personal savings rate mentioned earlier in this chapter, it is clear that credit management has become a very important part of liquidity for many Canadians. Credit management is discussed in Chapter 6. The use of money management and credit management to manage your liquidity is illustrated in Exhibit 1.3.

Loans are typically needed to finance large expenditures, such as university or college tuition, a car, or a home. The amount of financing needed is the difference between the amount of the purchase and the amount of money you have available, as illustrated in Exhibit 1.4. Managing loans includes determining how much you can afford to borrow, deciding on the maturity (length of time) of the loan, and selecting a loan that charges an appropriate interest rate.

liquidity
Access to ready cash, including savings and credit, to cover short-term or unexpected expenses; also, the ease with which an investor can convert an investment into cash without a loss of capital.

money management
Decisions regarding how much money to retain in liquid form and how to allocate the funds among short-term investment instruments.

emergency fund
A portion of savings that you have allocated to short-term needs such as unexpected expenses in order to maintain adequate liquidity.

credit management
Decisions regarding how much credit to obtain to support your spending and which sources of credit to use.

EXHIBIT 1.3 Managing Your Liquidity

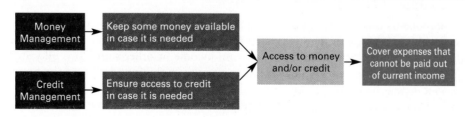

EXHIBIT 1.4   Financing Process

A Plan for Protecting Your Assets and Income

risk
Exposure to events (or perils) that can cause a financial loss.

risk management
Decisions about whether and how to protect against risk.

insurance planning
Determining the types and amount of insurance needed to protect your assets.

In the context of insurance, the term **risk** can be defined as exposure to events (or perils) that can cause a financial loss. **Risk management** represents decisions about whether and how to protect against risk. Individuals may avoid, reduce, accept, or share (insure) their exposure to risk. Insuring against risk involves insurance planning.

To protect your assets, you can conduct **insurance planning**, which determines the types and amount of insurance that you need. In particular, automobile insurance and homeowner's insurance protect your assets, while health insurance and life insurance protect your income. In general, it is important to insure risks that would result in either a significant loss of income for a long period of time or an unplanned use of your financial resources.

A Plan for Your Investing

investment risk
Uncertainty surrounding not only the potential return on an investment but also its future potential value.

risk tolerance
A person's ability to accept risk, usually defined as a potential loss of return and/or loss of capital.

Any savings that you have beyond what you need to maintain liquidity should be invested. Because these funds normally are not used to satisfy your liquidity needs, they can be invested with the primary objective of earning a return. Potential investments include stocks, bonds, mutual funds, and real estate. You must determine how much you wish to allocate toward investments and what types of investments you wish to consider. Since investments are subject to **investment risk** (uncertainty surrounding their potential return and future potential value), you need to understand your personal tolerance to risk in order to manage it. There are many different kinds of risk; however, at this point in our discussion, risk can most easily be defined as a potential loss of return and/or loss of capital. Your ability to accept such potential losses is your **risk tolerance**.

A Plan for Your Retirement and Estate

retirement planning
Determining how much money you should set aside each year for retirement and how you should invest those funds.

estate planning
Determining how your wealth will be distributed before and/or after your death.

Retirement planning involves determining how much money you should set aside each year for retirement and how you should invest those funds. Retirement planning must begin well before you retire so that you can accumulate sufficient money to invest and support yourself after you retire. Money contributed to various kinds of retirement plans, with the exception of tax-free savings accounts (TFSAs), is sheltered from taxes until it is withdrawn from the retirement account. Money contributed to a TFSA is not only tax sheltered, but also tax free when it is withdrawn.

Estate planning is the act of determining how your wealth will be distributed before and/or after your death. Effective estate planning protects your wealth against unnecessary taxes and ensures that your wealth is distributed in a timely and orderly manner.

The Components of a Financial Plan

The components of a financial plan are illustrated in Exhibit 1.5. Each part is shown as a step in the exhibit, with the lower step serving as a foundation for the higher steps. Budgeting focuses on how cash received (from income or other sources) is allocated to savings, spending, and taxes. Budget planning serves as the foundation of the financial plan, as it is your base for making personal financial decisions.

The next component is managing your financial resources because you must have adequate liquidity and a plan for financing your major purchases such as a new car or a home. Insurance is used to protect your wealth. Next, you can consider investment

EXHIBIT 1.5 Components of a Financial Plan

alternatives such as stocks, bonds, and mutual funds. Finally, planning for retirement and estate planning focuses on the wealth that you will accumulate by the time you retire.

An effective financial plan builds your wealth and therefore enhances your net worth. In this text you will have the opportunity to develop the components of your financial plan. By completing the Building Your Own Financial Plan exercises, you will build a personal financial plan by the end of the school term. Exhibit 1.6 lists examples of the decisions you will make in each component.

EXHIBIT 1.6 Example of Decision Made in Each Component of a Financial Plan

A Plan for:	Types of Decisions
1. Managing your income	What expenses should you anticipate?
	How much money should you attempt to save each month?
	How much money must you save each month toward a specific purchase?
	What debt payments must you make each month?
2. Managing your financial resources	How much money should you maintain in your bank account?
	Should you use credit cards as a means of borrowing money?
	How much money can you borrow to purchase a car?
	Should you borrow money to purchase a car or should you lease a car?
	How much money can you borrow to purchase a home?
	What type of mortgage loan should you obtain to finance the purchase of a house?
3. Protecting your assets and income	What type of insurance do you need?
	How much insurance do you need?
4. Investing	How much money should you allocate toward investments?
	What types of investments should you consider?
	How much risk can you tolerate when investing your money?
5. Planning your retirement and estate	How much money will you need for retirement?
	How much money must you save each year so that you can retire in a specific year?
	How will you allocate your estate among your heirs?

EXHIBIT 1.7   How Financial Planning Affects Your Cash Flows

```
                        ┌─────────────────────┐
                        │  1. Financial       │
                        │  Planning Tools     │
                        └─────────────────────┘
                                  │
                               $ Income
                                  │
                                  ▼
┌──────────────────┐    $ Investments for    ╭──────────╮    $ Credit     ┌──────────────────┐
│ 5. Retirement and│◄───────────────────     │   Your   │◄──────────      │  2. Financial    │
│  Estate Planning │     Retirement          │   Cash   │    $ Deposits   │  Management      │
└──────────────────┘                         ╰──────────╯    ────────►    └──────────────────┘
                          $ Investments     ╱           ╲   $ Insurance
                              ╱                            ╲  Premiums
                            ▼                                ▼
              ┌──────────────────┐              ┌──────────────────────┐
              │  4. Investing    │              │  3. Protecting Your  │
              │                  │              │  Assets and Income   │
              │                  │              │  (Insurance)         │
              └──────────────────┘              └──────────────────────┘
```

How the Components Relate to Your Cash Flows. Exhibit 1.7 illustrates the typical types of income (cash that you receive) and expenses (cash that you spend). This exhibit also shows how each component of the financial plan reflects decisions on how to obtain or use cash. You receive income in the form of a salary from your employer and use some of that cash to spend on products and services. Other examples of income include rental income from property, interest income from guaranteed investment certificates (GICs), and capital gains income from stocks that you own. Budgeting focuses on the relationship between your income and your expenses. Your budgeting decisions determine how much of your income you spend on products and services. The residual income can be allocated for your personal finance needs. Financial management focuses on depositing a portion of your excess cash in an emergency fund or obtaining credit to support your purchases. Protecting your assets and income focuses on determining your insurance needs and spending money on insurance premiums. Investing focuses on using some of your excess cash to build your wealth. Planning for your retirement and estate focuses on periodically investing cash in your retirement account and determining how you will distribute assets before and/or after your death.

If you need more cash inflows beyond your income, you may decide to rely on savings that you have already accumulated or obtain loans from creditors. If your income exceeds the amount that you wish to spend, you can use the excess funds to make more investments or to repay some or all of the principal on existing loans. Thus, your investment decisions can serve as a source of funds (selling your investments) or as a way of using additional funds (making additional investments). Your financing decisions can serve as a source of funds (obtaining additional loans) or as a use of funds (repaying existing loans).

PSYCHOLOGY of Personal Finance

How Psychology Affects Your Financial Plan

Psychology has a major impact on human behaviour and decision making. Therefore, it has a major impact on your spending behaviour and your ability to implement an effective financial plan. For this reason, the impact of psychology on financial planning is given attention in various sections, like this one, throughout the text. Consider the two completely different types of spending behaviour described here, so that you can determine which type reflects your own behaviour.

How the Components Relate to Your Cash Flows. Some people allow their desire for immediate satisfaction and their focus on peer pressure to influence most of their financial planning decisions. This causes them to spend excessively, meaning that they make purchases that are not necessary. They tend to spend every dollar they earn, without serious consideration to use any money for other purposes. They also tend to make many impulse purchases, which are purchases made on the spur of the moment, not because they needed the products or were even shopping specifically for those products. They get a strong dose of pleasure from the purchase, perhaps more so than the ultimate use of some of the products that they buy. This type of behaviour may be referred to as "shopping therapy" or "retail therapy" because the act of shopping (and buying) boosts the morale of some people. However, the boost provided by the therapy may quickly vanish, so that additional therapy (shopping) is needed. The spending can become addictive.

People who spend based on peer pressure may purchase a new car that they cannot afford, even when they already own a reliable car, just because their friends or neighbours have a new car. While they receive immediate satisfaction from having a new car, they may now also have the obligation of a $500 monthly car payment for the next four years. This decision will use up much of their monthly income, and could prevent them from allocating any funds toward all the other financial planning functions such as managing liquidity, insurance, investments, and retirement planning. Notice that all these other financial planning functions are intended to offer future benefits. Thus, the behaviour of people who spend based on immediate satisfaction and peer pressure causes them to spend excessively now, which leaves nothing for the future. They may say that all of their spending was on necessities and they did not have any extra funds to use for financial planning purposes. Their perception of necessities, however, is whatever allows them to achieve immediate satisfaction.

People with this type of mindset may make promises to themselves that they will reduce their spending in the future in order to focus on financial planning functions. But with this mindset, they may always find reasons to justify spending their entire paycheque—or more.

Another psychological force is a hopeless feeling that is used to justify spending. Some people think that if they can allocate only a small amount, such as $500 for saving or other forms of financial planning, they will never be able to achieve any long-term goals. Thus, they use this reasoning to justify spending all of their income. Their logic is that they might as well enjoy use of the money now.

Focus on the Future. Other people have more discipline when deciding whether to spend all of their income, and their decision making is influenced by other psychological forces. They may have a strong desire to avoid debt at this point in their lives because they would feel stress from the obligation of making large debt payments. For this reason, they may avoid purchasing a new car or any types of purchases that would cause large credit card payments, and this allows them to use their income for other purposes. They recognize that by spending conservatively today, they will have additional money available that they can use for financial planning functions in order to improve their financial future.

Assess Your Own Spending Behaviour. How would you describe your spending behaviour? Do you focus only on achieving immediate satisfaction, or are you disciplined so that you can improve your financial future? If you spend conservatively now so that you can improve your financial future, you'll benefit from this text, because it explains how you can conduct your financial planning. Conversely, if you spend excessively now to achieve immediate satisfaction, you have no money left to direct toward financial planning functions discussed in this text, such as managing liquidity, insurance, investing, or retirement planning. Take this brief quiz to determine which behaviour category you are in:

> Do you pay rent for a single apartment rather than share an apartment?
>
> Do you have large monthly car payments?
>
> Do you have credit card bills for which you can only make the minimum payment each month?
>
> Do you spend all of your income within the first day or two of receiving your paycheque on clothes, electronic games, or other items, even if that money is needed for rent or car loan payments?
>
> Do you always find a reason each month to spend all of your income?

If you answered "yes" to any of these questions, you might be able to reduce your spending behaviour so that you could allocate more money toward financial planning functions. This will allow you to accumulate more wealth in the future, and with that wealth, you will be able to afford more spending in the future. This text will help guide you to achieve these goals.

L.O.3

DEVELOPING THE FINANCIAL PLAN

Six steps are involved in developing each component of your financial plan.

Step 1: Establish Your Financial Goals

You must determine your financial goals. In the financial planning process, it is important to establish SMART goals. That is, goals should be specific (S), measurable (M), action-oriented (A), realistic (R), and time bound (T).

Specify Your Goals. Goals can be specified in a number of ways. One goal could be to save a specific amount of money so that you can make a down payment on a house. Another could simply be to pay down your debt and improve your creditworthiness. Goals may also be specified in the form of an amount of cash flow that you hope to have someday, such as $25 000 per year in income from your RRSP during your retirement.

Measure Your Goals. Whether you are saving a fixed dollar amount, paying down debt, or building a nest egg for retirement, you must determine how much cash you will need to accomplish each of these goals. Financial calculators available on the internet can help you plan your goals.

Act on Your Goals. A goal must include specific action steps that you will take to reach your goal. For example, do you need to contact your bank to open a savings account so that you can start putting money aside from each paycheque?

Set Realistic Goals. You need to be realistic about your goals so that you can have a strong likelihood of achieving them. A financial plan that requires you to save almost all of your income is useless if you are unable or unwilling to follow that plan. When this overly ambitious plan fails, you may become discouraged and lose interest in planning.

Timing of Goals. Financial goals can be characterized as short term (within the next year), medium term (typically between one and five years), or long term (beyond five years). For instance, a short-term financial goal may be to accumulate enough money to purchase a car within six months. A medium-term goal would be to pay off a school loan in the next three years. A long-term goal would be to save enough money so that you can maintain your lifestyle and retire in 25 to 30 years.

Maeva loves to travel; so much so that she is planning a trip to Europe after high school gradua-tion. After going online and researching the cost of her trip, she determines that she will need to save $3000 over the next two years. Next, she calculates how much she can earn if she works full time over the next two summers and part time during the school year. After speaking to her manager at work about adding shifts and discussing her travel budget with her parents to get their feedback, Maeva is confident that she can achieve her goal. She concludes that in two years' time, she will be in a position to book airfare and have enough money saved for hotels, trains, food, and shopping for her European vacation.

Maeva's goal is a SMART goal since it meets each of the criteria set out above. It is specific in that she is saving for a trip to Europe after high school graduation. It is measurable since she has specified that she needs to save $3000. It is action-oriented since she has researched the cost, calculated the additional income she needs, spoken with her manager about adding shifts, and discussed her plan with her parents. Maeva's research has led her to the conclusion that her plan is realistic. Finally, her plan is time bound since she wants to take the trip in the next two years.

FREE APPS for Personal Finance

Goal Planning

Application:

Use goalGetter, a financial goal planner by Advisor Software, Inc., to determine how much you need to save to reach your goals. Use this app to enter your current savings and to select goals and their value. goalGetter will let you know how much additional monthly savings are needed.

myth or **fact** When setting goals, it is important to share them with family members so you are motivated to achieve them.

Step 2: Consider Your Current Financial Position

Your decisions about how much money to spend next month, how much money to place in your savings account, how often to use your credit card, and how to invest your money depend on your financial position. A person with little debt and many assets will clearly make different decisions than a person with mounting debt and few assets. And a single individual without dependants will have different financial means than a couple with children, even if the individual and the couple have the same income. The appropriate plan also varies with your age and wealth. If you are 20 years old with zero funds in your bank account, your financial plan will be different than if you are 65 years old and have saved much of your income over the last 40 years.

Step 3: Identify and Evaluate Alternative Plans That Could Help You Achieve Your Goals

You must identify and evaluate the alternative financial plans that could achieve your financial goals (specified in Step 1), given your financial position (determined in Step 2). For example, to accumulate a substantial amount of money in 10 years, you could decide either to save a large portion of your income over that period or to invest your initial savings in an investment that may grow in value over time. The first plan is a more conservative approach, but requires you to save money consistently over time. The second plan does not require as much discipline because it relies on the initial investment to grow substantially over time. However, the second plan has a greater chance of failure because there is risk related to whether the value of the initial investment will increase as expected.

Step 4: Select and Implement the Best Plan for Achieving Your Goals

You need to analyze and select the plan that will be most effective in achieving your goals. Individuals in the same financial position with the same financial goals may decide on different financial plans. For example, you may be willing to save a specific amount of money every month to achieve a particular level of wealth in 10 years. Another individual may prefer to make some risky investments today (rather than save money every month) in order to achieve the same level of wealth in 10 years. The type of plan you select to achieve your financial goals is influenced by your willingness to take risk and by your self-discipline.

Using the Internet. The internet provides you with valuable information for making financial decisions. Your decision to spend money on a new music system or to save that money may depend on how much you can earn from depositing the money. Your decision to purchase a new car depends on the prices of new cars and financing rates on car loans. Your decision to purchase a home depends on the prices of homes and the financing rates on mortgages. Your decision to invest in stocks is influenced by the prices of stocks and potential returns. Your decision to purchase insurance may be influenced by the insurance premiums quoted by different insurance agencies and policy options. All of these financial decisions require knowledge of prevailing prices or interest rates, which are literally at your fingertips on the internet.

Financial Planning Online Exercises are provided at the end of each chapter so that you can practise using the internet for financial planning purposes. URLs in this text are available and updated on the text's website for easy navigation.

When you use online information for personal finance decisions, keep in mind that some information may not be accurate. Use reliable sources, such as websites of government agencies or financial media companies that have proven track records of reporting financial information. Also, recognize that free personal finance advice provided online does not necessarily apply to every person's unique situation. Get a second opinion before you follow online advice, especially when the advice recommends that you spend or invest money.

FOCUS ON ETHICS: Personal Financial Advice

Many individuals have a limited background in financial planning and rely on professionals in the financial services industry for advice when developing their financial plans. While most advisers take their responsibilities seriously and are very ethical, there are some unethical and incompetent advisers.

One facet of financial services products that creates a potential conflict of interest for your adviser is the many fee and commission structures available on even a single product such as a life insurance policy. Your objective is to get the best advice appropriate to your needs. The adviser's objective should be the same, but the method (or product) selected may be recommended because of the commission structure that the product offers. There is a potential conflict of interest any time a salesperson charges a fee or commission.

The solution to this conflict of interest is to do your homework. By being alert, asking questions, and carefully considering advice received, you may be able to avoid advisers who do not put your interests first. Check the adviser's credentials. Financial services professionals are licensed for the products they sell and they must meet continuing education requirements to maintain those licences. Throughout the textbook, you will find information that will lead you to the various self-regulatory organizations (SROs) that govern licensed financial services professionals in the financial services industry. For example, The Investor Education Fund website, **www.getsmarteraboutmoney.ca/** is dedicated to helping you improve your financial know-how and make better investing decisions.

Funding for the site is provided by the Ontario Securities Commission (OSC), so the information is objective and can be trusted.

While most financial services professionals are indeed professionals and knowledgeable in their field, it is still your responsibility to monitor your investments and to ensure that their advice serves your needs. It should be your decision which product to buy, how much insurance coverage you should have, and when you should change investments. Educating yourself on these financial products will help you make sound decisions.

Step 5: Evaluate Your Financial Plan

After you develop and implement each component of your financial plan, you must monitor your progress to ensure that the plan is working as you intended. Keep your financial plan easily accessible so that you can evaluate it over time. In general, you should review your plan annually. You should also review your plan if you experience one of the milestones listed in Exhibit 1.2 on page 6.

Step 6: Revise Your Financial Plan

If you find that you are unable or unwilling to follow the financial plan that you developed, you need to revise the plan to make it more realistic. You may need to adjust your financial goals if you are unable to maintain the plan for achieving a particular level of wealth.

As time passes, your financial position will change, especially upon specific events such as graduation from a post-secondary institution, marriage, a career change, or the birth of a child. As your financial position changes, your financial goals may change as well. You need to revise your financial plan to reflect such changes in your means and priorities.

The steps to developing a financial plan are summarized in Exhibit 1.8.

EXHIBIT 1.8 Summary of Steps Used to Develop a Financial Plan

1. Establish your SMART financial goals.

   - What are your short-term financial goals?
   - What are your medium-term financial goals?
   - What are your long-term financial goals?

2. Consider your current financial position.

   - How much money do you have in savings?
   - What is the value of your investments?
   - What is your net worth?

3. Identify and evaluate alternative plans that could achieve your goals.

   - Given your goals and existing financial position described in the previous steps, how can you obtain the necessary funds to achieve your financial goals?
   - Will you need to reduce your spending to save more money each month?
   - Will you need to make investments that generate a higher rate of return?

4. Select and implement the best plan for achieving your goals.

   - What are the advantages and disadvantages of each alternative plan that could be used to achieve your goals?

5. Evaluate your financial plan.

   - Is your financial plan working properly? That is, will it enable you to achieve your financial goals?

6. Revise your financial plan.

   - Have your financial goals changed?
   - Should parts of the financial plan be revised in order to increase the chance of achieving your financial goals? (If so, identify the parts that should be changed, and determine how they should be revised.)

MyLab Finance   Visit MyLab Finance for additional study and practice tools. Select Financial Planning Problems are available in the Study Plan. Create your own study plan, generate personal cash flow statements and balance sheets, and set personal financial goals.

SUMMARY

L.O.1   Explain how you could benefit from personal financial planning

Personal financial planning is the process of planning your income spending, financing, and investing activities, while taking into account uncontrollable events such as death or disability, in order to optimize your financial situation.

An understanding of personal finance enables you to make informed decisions about your financial situation, to judge the advice of financial advisers, and to make an informed decision on whether or not a career in financial planning is for you.

L.O.2   Identify the key components of a financial plan

A financial plan has five components: (1) budgeting and tax planning, (2) managing your financial resources, (3) protecting your assets and income, (4) investing, and (5) planning your retirement and estate.

L.O.3   Outline the steps involved in developing a financial plan

The financial planning process involves six steps: (1) establishing your financial goals, (2) considering your current financial position, (3) identifying and evaluating alternative plans that could achieve your goals, (4) selecting and implementing the best plan for achieving your financial goals, (5) evaluating the financial plan over time to ensure that you are meeting your goals, and (6) revising the financial plan when necessary.

REVIEW QUESTIONS

1. Define personal financial planning. What types of decisions are involved in a personal financial plan?

2. What is an opportunity cost? What might be some of the opportunity costs of spending $10 per week on lottery tickets?

3. How can an understanding of personal finance benefit you?

4. What are the five key components of a financial plan?

5. Define budget planning. What elements must be assessed in budget planning?

6. How is your net worth calculated? Why is it important?

7. What factors influence income? Why is an accurate estimate of expenses important in budget planning?

8. What are the key financial considerations during the early career life stage?

9. Should you wait for a milestone to be reached before creating a personal financial plan? Explain.

10. How do tax laws affect the budgeting process?

11. What is liquidity? What two factors are considered in managing liquidity? How are they used?

12. What is an emergency fund? What is an alternative to establishing an emergency fund?

13. What factors are considered in managing your financial resources?

14. What is the primary objective of investing? What else must be considered? What potential investment vehicles are available?

15. What are the three elements of planning to protect your assets? Define each element.

16. What is retirement planning? When should you begin the process of retirement planning? Explain.

17. What is the purpose of estate planning?

18. How does psychology affect your cash flow?

19. How does each element of financial planning affect your cash flows?

20. What are the six steps in developing a financial plan?

21. How do your financial goals fit into your financial plan? What is a SMART goal?

22. Name some factors that might affect your current financial position.

23. How do your current financial position and goals relate to your creation of alternative financial plans?

24. Once your financial plan has been implemented, what is the next step? Why is it important?

25. Why might you need to revise your financial plan?

26. List some information available on the internet that might be useful for financial planning. Describe one way you might use some of this information for financial planning purposes.

27. What are some of the different types of unethical behaviour financial advisers might engage in? How can an understanding of personal financial planning help you deal with this potential behaviour?

FINANCIAL PLANNING PROBLEMS

MyLab Finance Financial Planning Problems marked with a 🌐 can be found in MyLab Finance.

🌐 **1.** Julia brings home $1600 per month after taxes. Her rent is $350 per month, her utilities are $100 per month, and her car payment is $250 per month. Julia is currently paying $200 per month to her orthodontist for maintenance of her braces.

    a. If Julia's groceries cost $50 per week and she estimates her other expenses to be $150 per month, how much will she have left each month to put toward savings to reach her financial goals?

    b. Julia is considering trading in her car for a new one. Her new car payment will be $325 per month, and her insurance cost will increase by $60 per month. Julia determines that her other car-related expenses (gas, oil) will stay about the same. What is the opportunity cost if Julia purchases the new car?

🌐 **2.** Mia has $3000 in her chequing account, an auto loan for $500, and an outstanding credit card balance of $135. Mia's monthly disposable income is $2000, and she has monthly expenses of $1650. What is Mia's net worth?

🌐 **3.** At the beginning of the year, Arianne had a net worth of $5000. During the year she set aside $100 per month from her paycheque for savings and borrowed $500 from her cousin that she must pay back in January of next year. What was her net worth at the end of the year?

🌐 **4.** Anna has just received a gift of $500 for her graduation, increasing her net worth by $500. If she uses the money to purchase an HD-TV, how will her net worth be affected? If she invests the $500 at 10 percent interest per year, what will it be worth in one year?

🌐 **5.** Jason's car was just stolen and the police informed him that they will probably be unable to recover it. His insurance will not cover the theft. Jason has a net worth of $3000, all of which is easily convertible to cash. Jason requires a car for his job and his daily life. Based on Jason's net cash flow, he cannot afford more than $200 in car payments. What options does he have? How will these options affect his net worth and net cash flow?

CHALLENGE QUESTIONS

1. Jeevun is very security conscious. Now that he has finished school and has started his first job, he wants to make sure that he is smart with his money. In order to increase his net worth by 10 percent in the next year, he decides that he must increase his contributions to his RRSP by $200 per paycheque. In order to implement his plan, he contacts his benefits person at work to change his contribution plan by Friday. The next day, he contacts his financial adviser to review investment options in his RRSP for when his new contributions start. Jeevun anticipates that his new investment plan will begin in two weeks. Do you think Jeevun's goal is a SMART goal? Explain.

2. Your best friend, Eriel (age 26), has approached you for some financial advice on goal setting. Eriel started her first job three years ago and recently received a raise. Now that she is making some additional money, she is more concerned than ever about making good financial decisions. Considering her stage in life and using SMART goal planning, what suggestions would you have for Eriel with respect to what she should do with the extra money that she is now earning? For example, what would you suggest if Eriel tells you that she would like to go on a trip?

ETHICAL DILEMMA

Michael loves cars. His favourite car is the Subaru WRX STI. Recently, Michael saw a sales ad for his dream car. The price seemed too good to be true, so Michael decided to contact the seller to see if he could take it for a test drive.

After test driving the car and negotiating the price, Michael decided that this was a once-in-a-lifetime opportunity to purchase a vehicle that he had always dreamed of owning. The owner of the car, Michelle, had informed Michael that the car needed some work but that it seemed to be mechanically sound. Michael agreed that the car did run well and otherwise appeared to be in good shape. After agreeing upon a price, Michael purchased the Subaru from Michelle.

A few months later, Michael started to notice some minor problems with the vehicle. Although he was able to financially afford to pay for these repairs, he was starting to get nervous because he found that he was quickly using up money that he

had set aside for his goal of attending college full-time. In fact, Michael had already decided to drop one class so that he could pick up some extra shifts at work in order to pay for some of the vehicle problems he was having.

The following semester, Michael decided that he could no longer afford to make repairs to his Subaru. He decided to sell the car for $3000 less than what he had paid for it! To make matters worse, Michael's vehicle expenses forced him to reduce the number of courses he was taking at college. He was now a part-time student.

a. Did Michelle act ethically in her dealings with Michael?

b. What could Michael have done to avoid some of the problems that he had incurred?

c. Use the concepts of opportunity cost and SMART goal planning to explain how Michael could have made a better financial decision.

 FINANCIAL PLANNING ONLINE EXERCISES

1. Go to www.careers-in-finance.com/fpskill.htm.

   a. What are the most important skills needed to perform the job of a financial planner? Which skills are your strengths and which are your weaknesses?

   b. How can you obtain the skills you lack?

2. The purpose of this exercise is to familiarize you with two of the many financial literacy resources available on the internet.

   a. Go to www.financialmentor.com/calculator/savings-account-calculator. How many years will it take you to reach your goal of saving $100 000 if you have an initial deposit of $5000, you are able to make a monthly contribution of $200, and you expect an average annual return of 6 percent compounded annually on your investments? What if you are able to make a monthly contribution of $300 and your average annual return is 8 percent?

   b. Using the information in Financial Planning Problem 2, determine Mia's net worth using the Net Worth Calculator located at www.tdcanadatrust.com/planning/net_worth.html#tip_1.

 PSYCHOLOGY OF PERSONAL FINANCE: Your Spending Behaviour

1. This chapter explains how consumers may make purchases that they cannot afford in order to keep up with their friends. This could prevent them from allocating any funds toward any financial planning functions such as liquidity, insurance, investments, and retirement planning. Are your spending decisions influenced by the need for immediate satisfaction or by peer pressure? Or are your spending decisions influenced more by the

desire to avoid debt? What factors have the most influence on your spending behaviour?

2. Read one practical article about how psychology affects behaviour when paying taxes. You can easily retrieve possible articles by doing an online search using the terms "psychology" and "spending." Summarize the main points of the article.

MINI-CASE: SMART Goal Planning

Brittany Hartman, 22, graduated with her Marketing diploma a year ago. Almost immediately, she found a job as a salesperson for a technology company. After bonuses, she was making about $3500 per month.

Although Brittany was able to get by, she never really considered the impact of her daily spending habits on her cash flow. Now she has some financial goals and she needs help. Whenever she can, Brittany uses her credit card to make purchases. Although the balance on her credit card is a little high (the balance is $8000 and climbing), Brittany has little trouble making the minimum monthly payment of $250. Brittany would like to see the credit card balance go down. Eventually, she would like to pay it off completely. Brittany's other goal is to save $4000 a year so that she can retire 35 years from now. She indicates that she would like to start saving in five years. She feels that delaying the start of her retirement will not have a big impact on the final amount of retirement savings she will accumulate.

Do Brittany's goals meet the SMART goal criteria? If not, which aspects of SMART goal planning is she missing with respect to her goal of paying off her credit card? How about with respect to her retirement goal? What advice do you have for Brittany that would help her make her goals SMART?

MINI-CASE: The Goal Prioritizer

Randi Dallaire, 23, just graduated from college with a degree in marketing and landed her first job with a local advertising agency. Now that she has achieved her first milestone—graduation—she is ready to enter the real world and make some real money. Having finished school, Randi realizes that she has the opportunity to realize many of her goals, but she is unsure as to which ones she should pursue first.

Randi decides to randomly list all of the goals that she would like to accomplish and comes up with the following list: (1) start an emergency fund, (2) buy a computer, (3) open and contribute to an RRSP account for retirement, (4) obtain a credit card, (5) save for a vacation, (6) pay off her student loan, (7) purchase life insurance, (8) get married someday, (9) have children in the future, (10) help take care of her parents as they get older, (11) learn more about the Canada Pension Plan, (12) buy a kitchen table for her condo, and (13) minimize her taxes.

Randi is overwhelmed by all the goals that she has listed and asks you to help her prioritize them. Using the information provided in Exhibit 1.2 and the goal prioritizer calculator, located at http://cgi.money.cnn.com/tools/prioritize/prioritize_101.jsp, help Randi prioritize her goals. What assumptions did you have to make? Based on your assumptions, what goal should Randi pursue first? Second? Third? Can she pursue more than one goal at a time? Explain. NOTE: The goal prioritizer tool works best when you enter goals as one word answers. For example, enter "start an emergency fund" as "emergency."

Study Guide

Circle the correct answer and then check the answers in the back of the book to chart your progress.

Multiple Choice

1. Personal finance is:
   a. The process of planning your spending, financing, and investing activities, while taking into account controllable events such as death or disability, in order to optimize your financial situation.
   b. The process of planning your spending and investing activities, while taking into account uncontrollable events such as death or disability, in order to optimize your financial situation.
   c. The process of planning your spending, financing, and investing activities, while taking into account uncontrollable events such as death or disability, in order to optimize your financial situation.

d. The process of planning your spending and investing activities, while taking into account controllable events such as death or disability, in order to optimize your financial situation.

2. Opportunity cost represents:
   a. Short- versus long-term financial decisions.
   b. What you give up as a result of making a decision.
   c. The financial cost of any opportunity.
   d. Evaluating different alternatives for financial decisions.

3. An understanding of personal finance is beneficial to you in many ways, including the following:
   a. Helping you make informed decisions about your financial situation.
   b. Helping you judge the guidance of financial advisers.
   c. Helping you determine whether a career as a financial adviser is right for you.
   d. All of the above.

4. Which of the following individuals would be considered a "big saver"?
   a. Jill has recently inherited $20 000 from her aunt's estate. Jill is unsure whether she should use this money to pay off her student loans or buy a new car. She decides to put this money in a savings account until she can figure out what to do with it.
   b. Ted earns $1000 per month, after deductions and taxes. Before he spends any of this money, he allocates 10 percent ($100) to his savings plan and then considers spending the rest of his money.
   c. Maria earns $1200 per month, after deductions and taxes. Maria has always been nervous about spending money, fearing that she may not have enough when she needs it. She only spends money on the bare essentials of life. As a result, she is often able to save more than half of her monthly income.
   d. Frank earns $1100 per month, after deductions and taxes. He has a very active social life and spends most of his time out of the house with friends. Frank usually spends all of his take-home pay and sometimes is rejected by the ABM because he has no money in his account.

5. Olani Waters, 32, and his spouse, Vanessa, 28, are expecting their first child in a few months. David, their financial adviser, has agreed to help them determine how much life insurance they need and what their options are with respect to registered education savings plans (RESPs). What life stage would most appropriately describe the Waters' current financial position?
   a. Early career
   b. Education
   c. Family and mid-career
   d. Prime earning

6. Finding an effective liquidity level involves:
   a. Deciding how to invest your money in order to maximize your return.
   b. Deciding how to invest your money in order to maximize your return, before considering whether you need easy access to cash.
   c. Deciding how to invest your money in order to maximize your return, such that you will never have to rely on credit management to cover short-term needs.
   d. Deciding how to invest your money so that you can earn a return but also have easy access to cash if needed.

7. An emergency fund is required in financial planning to:
   a. Maintain credit rating.
   b. Maintain your standard of living.
   c. Manage risk.
   d. Maintain adequate liquidity.

8. Risk management represents decisions about whether and how to protect against risk. Individuals may ___, ___, ___, or ___ their exposure to risk.
   a. avoid, remove, accept, insure
   b. avoid, reduce, accept, insure
   c. avoid, reduce, acknowledge, insure
   d. avoid, remove, acknowledge, insure

9. Which of the following would be classified as a medium-term goal?
   a. Saving for a down payment to purchase a house in three years.
   b. Buying new clothes to begin school this month.
   c. Retiring in 10 years.
   d. Paying for your two-year-old child's college education.

10. Which of the following would defeat the efforts made in developing a successful financial plan?
    a. Establishing your financial goals.
    b. Considering your current financial position.
    c. Identifying and evaluating alternative plans that could achieve your goals.
    d. Evaluating your financial plan every five years.

11. Place the following six steps of the financial plan in the correct order.
    1. Select and implement the best plan for achieving your goals.
    2. Consider your current financial position.
    3. Evaluate your financial plan.
    4. Establish your financial goals.
    5. Revise your financial plan.
    6. Identify and evaluate alternative plans.
    a. 4, 2, 6, 1, 3, 5
    b. 2, 4, 6, 1, 3, 5
    c. 4, 2, 6, 3, 1, 5
    d. 2, 4, 6, 3, 1, 5

12. Alex has become stressed by his tight budget and is unwilling to stick to his financial plan. What action should he take?
    a. Establish his goals.
    b. Re-evaluate his goals.
    c. Implement the best plan.
    d. Revise his plan.

13. Raj and Chandan have established their financial goals. Given their current financial position, they have decided to invest $100 per month in a mutual fund at the end of every year for 10 years (Plan A). Raj's co-worker suggests that, instead of saving for 10 years, the couple should immediately contribute a large lump sum, such as $1200, into a mutual fund (Plan B). Although both plans may allow the couple to achieve their goals, which of the following statements should be considered before the couple makes a decision?
    a. Plan A is a more aggressive approach that requires them to save money consistently over time, whereas Plan B does not require as much discipline and is more likely to fail because there is risk related to whether the value of the initial investment will increase as expected.
    b. Plan A is a more conservative approach that requires them to save money consistently over time, whereas Plan B requires more discipline and is more likely to fail because there is risk related to whether the value of the initial investment will increase as expected.
    c. Plan A is a more conservative approach that requires them to save money consistently over time, whereas Plan B does not require as much discipline and is more likely to fail because there is risk related to whether the value of the initial investment will increase as expected.
    d. Plan A is a more conservative approach that requires them to save money consistently over time, whereas Plan B requires more discipline and is more likely to succeed because the value of the initial investment will increase as expected.

14. When implementing the best plan to meet your financial goals, you can use information available on the internet or the advice of a financial adviser. When deciding which products to buy, how much insurance coverage you should have, and when you should change investments, who is responsible for the plan that you implement?
    a. It is your responsibility to monitor your financial plans.
    b. If you have established a long-term relationship with your financial adviser, it is his or her responsibility to monitor your financial plans.
    c. The company whose products you have purchased should monitor your financial plans.
    d. All of the above.

15. Why might you need to revise your plan from time to time in order to make it more realistic?
    a. You are unable to follow the financial plan.
    b. You are unwilling to follow the financial plan.
    c. Your financial position has changed.
    d. All of the above.

True/False

1. True or False? The personal savings rate of Canadians has decreased for the past 30 years.

2. True or False? In order to become a financial adviser, you must meet the education, examination, and experience requirements set by the FPSC.

3. True or False? A single course in personal finance will allow you to start a career as a financial adviser.

4. True or False? Personal finance includes the process of planning your net worth.

5. True or False? Your net worth is the value of what you own (your assets) minus the value of what you owe (your liabilities).

6. True or False? Credit management is not a very important part of overall liquidity management for many Canadians.

7. True or False? Access to credit is a preferred source of liquidity when compared to an emergency fund.

8. True or False? Loans are typically needed to finance large and small expenditures.

9. True or False? The best choice for savings above and beyond what is required for liquidity purposes is low-risk, low-return investments.

10. True or False? Your personal tolerance to risk should be understood if you are considering investments such as stocks, bonds, mutual funds, and real estate.

11. True or False? When determining how to manage risk, individuals may avoid, reduce, accept, or insure their exposure to risk.

12. True or False? Estate planning describes the process of how your wealth will be distributed before and after your death.

13. True or False? Retirement planning should take place well before you retire.

14. True or False? Your financial goals must be specific, measurable, realistic, and timely if you wish to achieve them.

15. True or False? In general, you should review your financial plan once every two years.

PART 1

Tools for Financial Planning

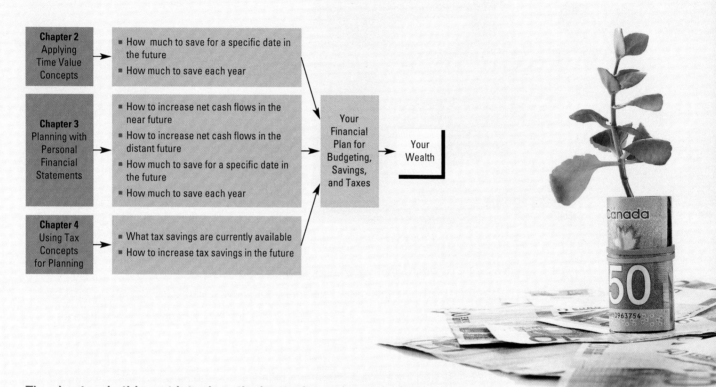

Chapter 2 Applying Time Value Concepts	▪ How much to save for a specific date in the future ▪ How much to save each year		
Chapter 3 Planning with Personal Financial Statements	▪ How to increase net cash flows in the near future ▪ How to increase net cash flows in the distant future ▪ How much to save for a specific date in the future ▪ How much to save each year	Your Financial Plan for Budgeting, Savings, and Taxes	Your Wealth
Chapter 4 Using Tax Concepts for Planning	▪ What tax savings are currently available ▪ How to increase tax savings in the future		

The chapters in this part introduce the key tools used to make financial planning decisions. Chapter 2 illustrates how you can use time value of money concepts to make decisions about saving. Chapter 3 describes the personal financial statements that help you monitor your spending and guide your budgeting and savings decisions. Chapter 4 explains how to use tax concepts to assess and minimize your tax liability. Your budget, savings, and tax plans all influence your cash flows and wealth.

Applying Time Value Concepts

Monkey Business Images/
Shutterstock

Haroon recalled what his mom had always told him, "It's the little things that count." As a star soccer player on his college team, Haroon had always applied this maxim to how he prepared for the college soccer season. He always made sure that he spent extra time on his "short game," knowing that his decision making in the immediate area would have a significant impact on what happened further down the field. He was now starting to realize that his mom's valuable lesson could also be applied to his finances.

As a busy college student, Haroon often found himself scrambling to organize his day. As such, his spending habits were not as good as they could be. On a weekly basis, Haroon spent around $125 on coffee, lunch, dinner, vending machines, and cash purchases that he did not keep track of. Harooon realized that he needed to get better at tracking, and reducing, his expenses.

Haroon's mom had also told him that money accumulates when it is invested and earns interest. Over a long period of time, money can grow substantially because interest is earned not only on the deposited funds, but also on the interest that has already accumulated. The lesson is that saving even a small amount per month or year at an early age can enhance your wealth over time.

QUESTIONS:

1. How much does Haroon spend on coffee, lunch, dinner, vending machines, and cash purchases on an annual basis?

2. If Haroon reduced his annual expenses by 25 percent, how much money would he have after 10 years if he invested this money at 7 percent compounded annually? How much would he have after 20 years?

3. Provide three suggestions that Haroon could implement now that would help him reduce his expenses.

THE LEARNING OBJECTIVES OF THIS CHAPTER ARE TO:

1. Explain the difference between simple interest and compound interest

2. Calculate the future value of a single dollar amount that you save today

3. Calculate the present value of a single dollar amount that will be received in the future

4. Calculate the future value of an annuity

5. Calculate the present value of an annuity

6. Calculate the number of compounding periods and the nominal annual interest rate

7. Convert a nominal interest rate to an effective interest rate

THE IMPORTANCE OF THE TIME VALUE OF MONEY

L.O.1

The time value of money is a powerful principle. In fact, it is so powerful that Albert Einstein stated that "Compound interest is the eighth wonder of the world. He who understands it, earns it ... he who doesn't ... pays it." The time value of money is especially important for estimating how your money may grow over time.

EXAMPLE

To show you the power of the time value of money, consider the situation in which your ancestors may have found themselves in 1694. At that time, let us assume that one of them invested $20 in a savings account at a local bank earning 5 percent interest compounded annually. Also assume that this ancestor never informed his family members of this transaction and that the money remained in the account accumulating interest of 5 percent compounded annually until 2017, when the bank locates you and informs you of the account. Over this time period, the $20 would have accumulated to approximately $140 million.

As a more realistic example, consider that an investment today of just $2000 in an account that earns 6 percent compounded annually will be worth about $11 487 in 30 years—an increase of 474 percent!

These examples show how money grows over time when you receive a return on your investment. When you spend money, you incur an opportunity cost of what you could have done with that money had you not spent it. In the previous example, if you had spent the $2000 on a vacation rather than saving or investing the money, you would have incurred an opportunity cost of the alternative ways that you could have used the money. That is, you can either have a vacation today or have that money accumulate to be worth $11 487 in 30 years (among other possible choices). Whatever decision you make, you will forgo some alternative uses of those funds.

In addition to the cost associated with a lost opportunity, time value of money also refers to the gain or loss of interest on a dollar amount. **Interest** is the rent charged for

interest
The rent charged for the use of money.

simple interest
Interest on a loan or investment computed as a percentage of the loan or investment amount, or principal.

the use of money. Depending on whether you have borrowed or loaned money, you will either pay or receive interest, respectively. There are two ways of computing interest: simple interest and compound interest. **Simple interest** is interest on a loan or investment computed as a percentage of the loan or investment amount, or the principal. The interest paid or earned is not reinvested. Simple interest is measured using the principal, the interest rate applied to the principal, and the loan's time to maturity. The amount of simple interest is determined by the relationship:

$$I = P \times r \times t$$

where I = interest earned (in dollars)
P = principal, or present value
r = annual interest rate expressed as a decimal or percent
t = time (in years)

EXAMPLE

Farah makes a deposit of $1000 in a high-interest savings account paying 3 percent simple interest annually. At the end of year one, the bank will credit Farah's chequing account with $30, calculated as:

$$I = P \times r \times t$$
$$\$30 = \$1000 \times 0.03 \times 1$$

In year two, the initial principal of $1000 will again earn $30 in interest. The $30 will be credited to Farah's chequing account. The table below displays what this process looks like over the first three years of Farah's $1000 investment.

Year	Principal	Interest	Accumulated Interest	Amount Credited to Chequing Account
1	$1000	$30	$30	30
2	1000	30	60	30
3	1000	30	90	30

The simple interest formula can be reorganized in order to solve for the other three variables: principal, interest rate, and time to maturity. The diagram below provides an easy way to remember how to set up the simple interest formula in order to solve for these other variables.

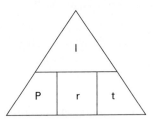

You can solve for any variable by looking at the relationship among the remaining variables. For example, in solving for principal, P, note that I is above r and t, and that r and t are on the same line. Therefore, $P = \frac{I}{rt}$. Similarly, $r = \frac{I}{Pt}$ and $t = \frac{I}{Pr}$.

compound interest
The process of earning interest on interest.

Compound interest refers to the process of earning interest on interest. In the previous example, if the bank had set up Farah's savings account such that the interest earned was not credited to her chequing account, Farah would have earned interest on her interest. The principal of compound interest can best be understood through a detailed example.

Samantha makes an initial deposit of $1000 in a compound interest savings account paying 3 percent interest annually. At the end of year one, the bank will credit Samantha's account with $30 ($1000 × 0.03 × 1). Compound interest *increases the principal amount on which Samantha earns interest in the second year, by the amount of interest that is earned in the first year.* In other words, in year two, she would earn 3 percent interest on the $1000 of original principal plus the $30 of interest earned in year one. This process will repeat itself in subsequent years.

Year	Principal	Interest	Accumulated Interest	Account Balance
1	$1000.00	$30.00	$30.00	$1030.00
2	1030.00	30.90	60.90	1060.90
3	1060.90	31.83	92.73	1092.73

Throughout this text, time value of money concepts will be applied to many types of financial planning problems. For simple problems, such as the Samantha example above, a time value of money table may be all that you need to calculate the future value of a single dollar amount. Other methods that may be used to solve time value of money problems include time value of money formulas and tables, and financial calculators. In this chapter, all three of these methods will be used to solve time value of money problems. In future chapters, we will only rely on the Texas Instruments BA II Plus financial calculator to illustrate and solve time value of money problems.

The time value of money is most commonly applied to two types of cash flows: a single dollar amount (also referred to as a lump sum) and an annuity. An **annuity** refers to the payment of a series of equal cash flow payments at equal intervals of time. We will begin our discussion with the future and present value of a single dollar amount. Later in this chapter, we will apply time value of money concepts to annuities.

annuity
The payment of a series of equal cash flow payments at equal intervals of time.

FUTURE VALUE OF A SINGLE DOLLAR AMOUNT

L.0.2

When Samantha deposited $1000 in a savings account that paid compound interest, her account balance grew to $1092.73 over three years. The results of the power of compounding are much more dramatic at higher rates of return (i) and over longer periods of time (t). The Samantha example above demonstrates the time value of money concept over a three-year period. As the time period become longer, it becomes more tedious and time-consuming to create a table. As a result, it is more practical to apply a formula to determine the future value of an investment.

Using a Formula to Determine Future Value of a Single Dollar Amount

In a compound interest rate environment, future value is determined using the formula:

$$FV = PV\left(1 + \frac{i}{n}\right)^{nt}$$

where FV = future value

PV = present value

i = annual interest rate (as a decimal)

n = number of compounding periods per year

t = time (in years)

Notice that the annual interest rate (i) has to be adjusted to reflect the correct number of compounding periods (n). The concept of compounding periods will be discussed after the example below. For now, it is important to note that the number of compounding periods in the Samantha example is one; therefore, $n = 1$. As a result, the formula above can be re-written as:

$$FV = PV(1 + i)^t$$

EXAMPLE

Based on her initial deposit of $1000, Samantha now asks you to determine how much money she would have in her compound interest savings account if she keeps it open for the next 20 years. Since it would be tedious and time consuming to create a table to calculate this amount, you have decided to use the future value formula for a single dollar amount. Using the formula above, you determine that she should have $1806.11 in her account after 20 years.

$$FV = PV(1 + i)^t = \$1000(1 + 0.03)^{20} = \$1806.11$$

In the Samantha example, interest is compounded annually ($n = 1$). The table below displays the number of compounding periods per year for different compounding periods. The amount of interest paid or earned will increase with an increase in the number of compounding periods per year.

Compounding Period	Number of Compounding Periods per Year (n)
Annually (every year)	1
Semi-annually (every 6 months)	2
Quarterly (every 3 months)	4
Monthly (every month)	12
Weekly (every week)	52
Daily (every day)	365

Using the Future Value Table

future value interest factor (FVIF)
A factor multiplied by today's savings to determine how the savings will accumulate over time.

You can also quickly determine the future value for any period of time by using the **future value interest factor (FVIF)**, which is a factor multiplied by today's savings to determine how the savings will accumulate over time. The factor depends on the interest rate and the number of years the money is invested. The factor is determined based on an annual interest rate where the number of compounding periods is one. Your deposit today is multiplied by the *FVIF* to determine the future value of the deposit.

myth or fact The interest rate that you are quoted on an investment or loan represents the amount of interest that you will earn or pay.

Table 2.1 shows the *FVIF* for various interest rates (i) and time periods (n). Each column in the table lists an interest rate and each row lists a possible time period. By reviewing any column, you will notice that as the number of years increases, the *FVIF* becomes higher. This means that the longer the time period in which your money is invested at a set rate of return, the more your money will grow.

Table 2-1 Future Value Interest Factors for $1 Compounded at i Percent for n Periods: $FV = PV \times FVIF_{i,n}$

Period	1%	2%	3%	4%	5%	6%	7%	8%	9%	10%	11%	12%	13%	14%	15%	16%	17%	18%	19%	20%
1	1.010	1.020	1.030	1.040	1.050	1.060	1.070	1.080	1.090	1.100	1.110	1.120	1.130	1.140	1.150	1.160	1.170	1.180	1.190	1.200
2	1.020	1.040	1.061	1.082	1.102	1.124	1.145	1.166	1.188	1.210	1.232	1.254	1.277	1.300	1.322	1.346	1.369	1.392	1.416	1.440
3	1.030	1.061	1.093	1.125	1.158	1.191	1.225	1.260	1.295	1.331	1.368	1.405	1.443	1.482	1.521	1.561	1.602	1.643	1.685	1.728
4	1.041	1.082	1.126	1.170	1.216	1.262	1.311	1.360	1.412	1.464	1.518	1.574	1.630	1.689	1.749	1.811	1.874	1.939	2.005	2.074
5	1.051	1.104	1.159	1.217	1.276	1.338	1.403	1.469	1.539	1.611	1.685	1.762	1.842	1.925	2.011	2.100	2.192	2.288	2.386	2.488
6	1.062	1.126	1.194	1.265	1.340	1.419	1.501	1.587	1.677	1.772	1.870	1.974	2.082	2.195	2.313	2.436	2.565	2.700	2.840	2.986
7	1.072	1.149	1.230	1.316	1.407	1.504	1.606	1.714	1.828	1.949	2.076	2.211	2.353	2.502	2.660	2.826	3.001	3.185	3.379	3.583
8	1.083	1.172	1.267	1.369	1.477	1.594	1.718	1.851	1.993	2.144	2.305	2.476	2.658	2.853	3.059	3.278	3.511	3.759	4.021	4.300
9	1.094	1.195	1.305	1.423	1.551	1.689	1.838	1.999	2.172	2.358	2.558	2.773	3.004	3.252	3.518	3.803	4.108	4.435	4.785	5.160
10	1.105	1.219	1.344	1.480	1.629	1.791	1.967	2.159	2.367	2.594	2.839	3.106	3.395	3.707	4.046	4.411	4.807	5.234	5.695	6.192
11	1.116	1.243	1.384	1.539	1.710	1.898	2.105	2.332	2.580	2.853	3.152	3.479	3.836	4.226	4.652	5.117	5.624	6.176	6.777	7.430
12	1.127	1.268	1.426	1.601	1.796	2.012	2.252	2.518	2.813	3.138	3.498	3.896	4.334	4.818	5.350	5.936	6.580	7.288	8.064	8.916
13	1.138	1.294	1.469	1.665	1.886	2.133	2.410	2.720	3.066	3.452	3.883	4.363	4.898	5.492	6.153	6.886	7.699	8.599	9.596	10.699
14	1.149	1.319	1.513	1.732	1.980	2.261	2.579	2.937	3.342	3.797	4.310	4.887	5.535	6.261	7.076	7.987	9.007	10.147	11.420	12.839
15	1.161	1.346	1.558	1.801	2.079	2.397	2.759	3.172	3.642	4.177	4.785	5.474	6.254	7.138	8.137	9.265	10.539	11.974	13.589	15.407
16	1.173	1.373	1.605	1.873	2.183	2.540	2.952	3.426	3.970	4.595	5.311	6.130	7.067	8.137	9.358	10.748	12.330	14.129	16.171	18.488
17	1.184	1.400	1.653	1.948	2.292	2.693	3.159	3.700	4.328	5.054	5.895	6.866	7.986	9.276	10.761	12.468	14.426	16.672	19.244	22.186
18	1.196	1.428	1.702	2.026	2.407	2.854	3.380	3.996	4.717	5.560	6.543	7.690	9.024	10.575	12.375	14.462	16.879	19.673	22.900	26.623
19	1.208	1.457	1.753	2.107	2.527	3.026	3.616	4.316	5.142	6.116	7.263	8.613	10.197	12.055	14.232	16.776	19.748	23.214	27.251	31.948
20	1.220	1.486	1.806	2.191	2.653	3.207	3.870	4.661	5.604	6.727	8.062	9.646	11.523	13.743	16.366	19.461	23.105	27.393	32.429	38.337
21	1.232	1.516	1.860	2.279	2.786	3.399	4.140	5.034	6.109	7.400	8.949	10.804	13.021	15.667	18.821	22.574	27.033	32.323	38.591	46.005
22	1.245	1.546	1.916	2.370	2.925	3.603	4.430	5.436	6.658	8.140	9.933	12.100	14.713	17.861	21.644	26.186	31.629	38.141	45.923	55.205
23	1.257	1.577	1.974	2.465	3.071	3.820	4.740	5.871	7.258	8.954	11.026	13.552	16.626	20.361	24.891	30.376	37.005	45.007	54.648	66.247
24	1.270	1.608	2.033	2.563	3.225	4.049	5.072	6.341	7.911	9.850	12.239	15.178	18.788	23.212	28.625	35.236	43.296	53.108	65.031	79.496
25	1.282	1.641	2.094	2.666	3.386	4.292	5.427	6.848	8.623	10.834	13.585	17.000	21.230	26.461	32.918	40.874	50.656	62.667	77.387	95.395
30	1.348	1.811	2.427	3.243	4.322	5.743	7.612	10.062	13.267	17.449	22.892	29.960	39.115	50.949	66.210	85.849	111.061	143.367	184.672	237.373
35	1.417	2.000	2.814	3.946	5.516	7.686	10.676	14.785	20.413	28.102	38.574	52.799	72.066	98.097	133.172	180.311	243.495	327.988	440.691	590.657
40	1.489	2.208	3.262	4.801	7.040	10.285	14.974	21.724	31.408	45.258	64.999	93.049	132.776	188.876	267.856	378.715	533.846	750.353	1051.642	1469.740
45	1.565	2.438	3.781	5.841	8.985	13.764	21.002	31.920	48.325	72.888	109.527	163.985	244.629	363.662	538.752	795.429	1170.425	1716.619	2509.583	3657.176
50	1.645	2.691	4.384	7.106	11.467	18.419	29.456	46.900	74.354	117.386	184.559	288.996	450.711	700.197	1083.619	1670.669	2566.080	3927.189	5988.730	9100.191

(continued)

Table 2-1   (Continued)

Period	21%	22%	23%	24%	25%	26%	27%	28%	29%	30%	31%	32%	33%	34%	35%	40%	45%	50%
1	1.210	1.220	1.230	1.240	1.250	1.260	1.270	1.280	1.290	1.300	1.310	1.320	1.330	1.340	1.350	1.400	1.450	1.500
2	1.464	1.488	1.513	1.538	1.562	1.588	1.613	1.638	1.664	1.690	1.716	1.742	1.769	1.796	1.822	1.960	2.102	2.250
3	1.772	1.816	1.861	1.907	1.953	2.000	2.048	2.097	2.147	2.197	2.248	2.300	2.353	2.406	2.460	2.744	3.049	3.375
4	2.144	2.215	2.289	2.364	2.441	2.520	2.601	2.684	2.769	2.856	2.945	3.036	3.129	3.224	3.321	3.842	4.421	5.063
5	2.594	2.703	2.815	2.932	3.052	3.176	3.304	3.436	3.572	3.713	3.858	4.007	4.162	4.320	4.484	5.378	6.410	7.594
6	3.138	3.297	3.463	3.635	3.815	4.001	4.196	4.398	4.608	4.827	5.054	5.290	5.535	5.789	6.053	7.530	9.294	11.391
7	3.797	4.023	4.259	4.508	4.768	5.042	5.329	5.629	5.945	6.275	6.621	6.983	7.361	7.758	8.172	10.541	13.476	17.086
8	4.595	4.908	5.239	5.589	5.960	6.353	6.767	7.206	7.669	8.157	8.673	9.217	9.791	10.395	11.032	14.758	19.541	25.629
9	5.560	5.987	6.444	6.931	7.451	8.004	8.595	9.223	9.893	10.604	11.362	12.166	13.022	13.930	14.894	20.661	28.334	38.443
10	6.727	7.305	7.926	8.594	9.313	10.086	10.915	11.806	12.761	13.786	14.884	16.060	17.319	18.666	20.106	28.925	41.085	57.665
11	8.140	8.912	9.749	10.657	11.642	12.708	13.862	15.112	16.462	17.921	19.498	21.199	23.034	25.012	27.144	40.495	59.573	86.498
12	9.850	10.872	11.991	13.215	14.552	16.012	17.605	19.343	21.236	23.298	25.542	27.982	30.635	33.516	36.644	56.694	86.380	129.746
13	11.918	13.264	14.749	16.386	18.190	20.175	22.359	24.759	27.395	30.287	33.460	36.937	40.745	44.912	49.469	79.371	125.251	194.620
14	14.421	16.182	18.141	20.319	22.737	25.420	28.395	31.691	35.339	39.373	43.832	48.756	54.190	60.181	66.784	111.119	181.614	291.929
15	17.449	19.742	22.314	25.195	28.422	32.030	36.062	40.565	45.587	51.185	57.420	64.358	72.073	80.643	90.158	155.567	263.341	437.894
16	21.113	24.085	27.446	31.242	35.527	40.357	45.799	51.923	58.808	66.541	75.220	84.953	95.857	108.061	121.713	217.793	381.844	656.841
17	25.547	29.384	33.758	38.740	44.409	50.850	58.165	66.461	75.862	86.503	98.539	112.138	127.490	144.802	164.312	304.911	553.674	985.261
18	30.912	35.848	41.523	48.038	55.511	64.071	73.869	85.070	97.862	112.454	129.086	148.022	169.561	194.035	221.822	426.875	802.826	1477.892
19	37.404	43.735	51.073	59.567	69.389	80.730	93.813	108.890	126.242	146.190	169.102	195.389	225.517	260.006	299.459	597.625	1164.098	2216.838
20	45.258	53.357	62.820	73.863	86.736	101.720	119.143	139.379	162.852	190.047	221.523	257.913	299.937	348.408	404.270	836.674	1687.942	3325.257
21	54.762	65.095	77.268	91.591	108.420	128.167	151.312	178.405	210.079	247.061	290.196	340.446	398.916	466.867	545.764	1171.343	2447.515	4987.883
22	66.262	79.416	95.040	113.572	135.525	161.490	192.165	228.358	271.002	321.178	380.156	449.388	530.558	625.601	736.781	1639.878	3548.896	7481.824
23	80.178	96.887	116.899	140.829	169.407	203.477	244.050	292.298	349.592	417.531	498.004	593.192	705.642	838.305	994.653	2295.829	5145.898	11222.758
24	97.015	118.203	143.786	174.628	211.758	256.381	309.943	374.141	450.974	542.791	652.385	783.013	938.504	1123.328	1342.781	3214.158	7461.547	16834.109
25	117.388	144.207	176.857	216.539	264.698	323.040	393.628	478.901	581.756	705.627	854.623	1033.577	1248.210	1505.258	1812.754	4499.816	10819.242	25251.164
30	304.471	389.748	497.904	634.810	807.793	1025.904	1300.477	1645.488	2078.208	2619.936	3297.081	4142.008	5194.516	6503.285	8128.426	24201.043	69348.375	191751.000
35	789.716	1053.370	1401.749	1861.020	2465.189	3258.053	4296.547	5653.840	7423.988	9727.598	12719.918	16598.906	21617.363	28096.695	36448.051	130158.687	*	*
40	2048.309	2846.941	3946.340	5455.797	7523.156	10346.879	14195.051	19426.418	26520.723	36117.754	49072.621	66519.313	89962.188	121388.437	163433.875	700022.688	*	*
45	5312.758	7694.418	11110.121	15994.316	22958.844	32859.457	46897.973	66748.500	94739.937	134102.187	*	*	*	*	*	*	*	*
50	13779.844	20795.680	31278.301	46889.207	70064.812	104354.562	154942.687	229345.875	338440.000	497910.125	*	*	*	*	*	*	*	*

*Not shown because of space limitations.

By reviewing any row of Table 2.1, you will notice that as the interest rate increases, the *FVIF* becomes higher. This means that the higher the rate of return, the more your money will grow over a given time period.

Suppose that you want to know how much money you will have in five years if you invest $5000 now and earn an annual return of 9 percent. The present value of money (*PV*) is the amount invested, or $5000. The *FVIF* for an interest rate of 9 percent and a time period of five years is 1.539 (look down the column for 9 percent, and across the row for five years). Thus, the future value (*FV*) of the $5000 in five years will be:

$$FV = PV \times FVIF_{i,n}$$

$$FV = PV \times FVIF_{9\%,5}$$

$$= \$5000 \times 1.539$$

$$= \$7695$$

Using a Financial Calculator

There are a variety of financial calculators available for purchase that greatly simplify time value of money (TVM) calculations. This section introduces the basic elements of the time value of money calculations and the corresponding keystrokes for the Texas Instrument BA II Plus (TI BA II Plus) calculator. The basic function keys of the TI BA II Plus calculator are located in the third row of its keyboard and include:

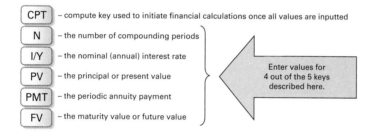

CPT – compute key used to initiate financial calculations once all values are inputted

N – the number of compounding periods

I/Y – the nominal (annual) interest rate

PV – the principal or present value

PMT – the periodic annuity payment

FV – the maturity value or future value

Enter values for 4 out of the 5 keys described here.

Before performing a TVM calculation on the TI BA II Plus, it is important to clear the existing TVM values in the calculator's TVM worksheet. This can be done by entering 2ND CLRTVM. To avoid calculation errors, you should perform this entry before beginning each new calculation. Once the calculator memory is cleared, the usual method for solving TVM problems is to enter a value for four of the five keys indicated in the diagram above.

When entering a value, it is normal practice to follow TVM cash flow sign conventions. A cash outflow occurs when money is paid out and should be entered as a negative number. A cash inflow occurs when money is received and should be entered as a positive number. For example, when you borrow money, the amount you receive is a cash inflow while the payments you make are a cash outflow. On the other hand, the lender, for example a bank, would treat the loan as a cash outflow and the payments they receive from you as a cash inflow. The +/− key on the TI BA II Plus is used to convert a positive number to a negative number, and vice versa.

In addition to setting cash outflows and inflows, it is important to recognize and specify the number of payments per year and, as discussed earlier, the number of compounding periods per year when performing a TVM calculation. To access this function on your calculator, press 2ND P/Y. After pressing these two keys, the calculator will display something like P/Y = 1.0000. This display indicates that the calculator is currently set such that there is only one payment per year. That is, payments are annual. If you wish to change the number of payments per year, enter the correct value and press ENTER. For example, if you enter P/Y = 12, you have indicated that payments are monthly. After entering P/Y, you can use the arrow keys, ↓ or ↑, to check the number of compounding periods per year, which will display something like C/Y = 1.000. Again, you can change this value by entering the correct value and pressing ENTER .

Time periods do not have to be identical. For example, when you receive a loan from the bank to buy a house, the compounding period is usually semi-annual (C/Y=2) and the payment is often monthly (P/Y=12). A larger number of compounding periods will increase the amount of interest that you earn on an investment or the amount of interest that you pay on a loan. A larger number of deposits, i.e., payments, to an investment account will increase the amount of interest you earn; however, a larger number of loan payments will decrease the amount of interest you pay. In general, a greater payment frequency always works in your favour, whereas a greater compounding frequency works in your favour with respect to investments, but not with respect to loans. Once you have completed adjusting P/Y and C/Y, press 2ND QUIT to exit this function.

TVM EXAMPLE

Suppose you have $5687 to invest in the stock market today. You like to invest for the long term and plan to choose your stocks carefully. You will invest your money for 12 years in certain stocks on which you expect a return of 10 percent compounded annually. The inputs for the TI BA II Plus are shown in the diagram in the margin. Note that other financial calculators can vary slightly in their setup.

The calculator key strokes are as follows:

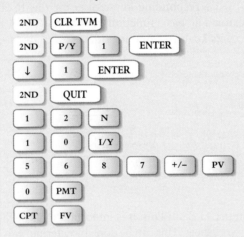

The *PV* is a negative number here, reflecting the outflow of cash to make the investment. The calculator computes the future value to be $17 848.24, which indicates that you will have $17 848.24 in your brokerage account in 12 years if you achieve a return of 10 percent compounded annually on your $5687 investment.

Use a financial calculator to determine the future value of $5000 invested at 9 percent compounded annually for five years. (This is the previous example used for the *FVIF* table.) Your answer should be $7693.12. Any difference in answers using the *FVIF* table versus using a financial calculator is due to rounding.

FREE APPS for Personal Finance

Estimating Growth in Savings

Application:

Use Future Value of Your Money by Garinet Media Network, LLC., to determine how much your money can grow, based on the amount of money you have today, the amount you plan to put away every month, and the estimated annual interest rate you expect to earn.

PRESENT VALUE OF A SINGLE DOLLAR AMOUNT

In many situations, you will want to know how much money you must deposit or invest today to accumulate a specified amount of money at a future point in time. The process of obtaining present values is referred to as **discounting**. Suppose that you want to have $20 000 for a down payment on a house in three years. You want to know how much money you need to invest today to achieve $20 000 in three years. That is, you want to know the present value of $20 000 that will be received in three years, based on some interest rate that you could earn over that period.

discounting
The process of obtaining present values.

Using a Formula to Determine Present Value of a Single Dollar Amount

To determine the present value of an amount of money received in the future, you need to know:

- The amount of money to be received in the future
- The interest rate to be earned on your deposit
- The number of years the money will be invested
- The number of compounding periods

With respect to the example above, let's say that you are able to earn 3 percent compounded annually on the amount of money that you need to invest today toward your down payment. We can determine the present value, or principal, that is needed to achieve our goal using the formula:

$$PV = \frac{FV}{\left(1 + \frac{i}{n}\right)^{nt}}$$

Similar to what we discussed with the future value formula, the present value formula can be simplified when dealing with an interest rate that compounds annually, ($n = 1$).

$$PV = \frac{FV}{(1 + i)^t}$$

Using this formula, we can determine that the amount of money you need to invest today to have $20 000 for a down payment in three years' time is $18 302.83, calculated as:

$$\$18\ 302.83 = \frac{\$20\ 000}{(1 + 0.03)^3}$$

Using the Present Value Table

The present value can also be calculated using a **present value interest factor (PVIF)**, which is a factor multiplied by the future value to determine the present value of that amount. The *PVIF* depends on the interest rate and the number of years the money is invested. The factor is determined based on an annual interest rate where the number of compounding periods is one. The future value of your investment is multiplied by the *PVIF* to determine the present value of the deposit.

present value interest factor (*PVIF*)
A factor multiplied by the future value to determine the present value of that amount.

Table 2.2 shows the *PVIF* for various interest rates (*i*) and time periods (*n*). Each column in the table lists an interest rate, while each row lists a time period.

You will notice that, in any column of the table, the *PVIF* is lower as the number of years increases. This means that less money is needed to achieve a specific future value when the money is invested for a greater number of years.

Table 2-2 Present Value Interest Factors for $1 Compounded at i Percent for n Periods: $PV = FV \times FVIF_{i,n}$

Period	1%	2%	3%	4%	5%	6%	7%	8%	9%	10%	11%	12%	13%	14%	15%	16%	17%	18%	19%	20%
1	.990	.980	.971	.962	.952	.943	.935	.926	.917	.909	.901	.893	.885	.877	.870	.862	.855	.847	.840	.833
2	.980	.961	.943	.925	.907	.890	.873	.857	.842	.826	.812	.797	.783	.769	.756	.743	.731	.718	.706	.694
3	.971	.942	.915	.889	.864	.840	.816	.794	.772	.751	.731	.712	.693	.675	.658	.641	.624	.609	.593	.579
4	.961	.924	.888	.855	.823	.792	.763	.735	.708	.683	.659	.636	.613	.592	.572	.552	.534	.516	.499	.482
5	.951	.906	.863	.822	.784	.747	.713	.681	.650	.621	.593	.567	.543	.519	.497	.476	.456	.437	.419	.402
6	.942	.888	.837	.790	.746	.705	.666	.630	.596	.564	.535	.507	.480	.456	.432	.410	.390	.370	.352	.335
7	.933	.871	.813	.760	.711	.665	.623	.583	.547	.513	.482	.452	.425	.400	.376	.354	.333	.314	.296	.279
8	.923	.853	.789	.731	.677	.627	.582	.540	.502	.467	.434	.404	.376	.351	.327	.305	.285	.266	.249	.233
9	.914	.837	.766	.703	.645	.592	.544	.500	.460	.424	.391	.361	.333	.308	.284	.263	.245	.225	.209	.194
10	.905	.820	.744	.676	.614	.558	.508	.463	.422	.386	.352	.322	.295	.270	.247	.227	.208	.191	.176	.162
11	.896	.804	.722	.650	.585	.527	.475	.429	.388	.350	.317	.287	.261	.237	.215	.195	.178	.162	.148	.135
12	.887	.789	.701	.625	.557	.497	.444	.397	.356	.319	.286	.257	.231	.208	.187	.168	.152	.137	.124	.112
13	.879	.773	.681	.601	.530	.469	.415	.368	.326	.290	.258	.229	.204	.182	.163	.145	.130	.116	.104	.093
14	.870	.758	.661	.577	.505	.442	.388	.340	.299	.263	.232	.205	.181	.160	.141	.125	.111	.099	.088	.078
15	.861	.743	.642	.555	.481	.417	.362	.315	.275	.239	.209	.183	.160	.140	.123	.108	.095	.084	.074	.065
16	.853	.728	.623	.534	.458	.394	.339	.292	.252	.218	.188	.163	.141	.123	.107	.093	.081	.071	.062	.054
17	.844	.714	.605	.513	.436	.371	.317	.270	.231	.198	.170	.146	.125	.108	.093	.080	.069	.060	.052	.045
18	.836	.700	.587	.494	.416	.350	.296	.250	.212	.180	.153	.130	.111	.095	.081	.069	.059	.051	.044	.038
19	.828	.686	.570	.475	.396	.331	.277	.232	.194	.164	.138	.116	.098	.083	.070	.060	.051	.043	.037	.031
20	.820	.673	.554	.456	.377	.312	.258	.215	.178	.149	.124	.104	.087	.073	.061	.051	.043	.037	.031	.026
21	.811	.660	.538	.439	.359	.294	.242	.199	.164	.135	.112	.093	.077	.064	.053	.044	.037	.031	.026	.022
22	.803	.647	.522	.422	.342	.278	.226	.184	.150	.123	.101	.083	.068	.056	.046	.038	.032	.026	.022	.018
23	.795	.634	.507	.406	.326	.262	.211	.170	.138	.112	.091	.074	.060	.049	.040	.033	.027	.022	.018	.015
24	.788	.622	.492	.390	.310	.247	.197	.158	.126	.102	.082	.066	.053	.043	.035	.028	.023	.019	.015	.013
25	.780	.610	.478	.375	.295	.233	.184	.146	.116	.092	.074	.059	.047	.038	.030	.024	.020	.016	.013	.010
30	.742	.552	.412	.308	.231	.174	.131	.099	.075	.057	.044	.033	.026	.020	.015	.012	.009	.007	.005	.004
35	.706	.500	.355	.253	.181	.130	.094	.068	.049	.036	.026	.019	.014	.010	.008	.006	.004	.003	.002	.002
40	.672	.453	.307	.208	.142	.097	.067	.046	.032	.022	.015	.011	.008	.005	.004	.003	.002	.001	.001	.001
45	.639	.410	.264	.171	.111	.073	.048	.031	.021	.014	.009	.006	.004	.003	.002	.001	.001	.001	*	*
50	.608	.372	.228	.141	.087	.054	.034	.021	.013	.009	.005	.003	.002	.001	.001	.001	*	*	*	*

*PVIF is zero to three decimal places.

Table 2-2 (Continued)

Period	21%	22%	23%	24%	25%	26%	27%	28%	29%	30%	31%	32%	33%	34%	35%	40%	45%	50%
1	.826	.820	.813	.806	.800	.794	.787	.781	.775	.769	.763	.758	.752	.746	.741	.714	.690	.667
2	.683	.672	.661	.650	.640	.630	.620	.610	.601	.592	.583	.574	.565	.557	.549	.510	.476	.444
3	.564	.551	.537	.524	.512	.500	.488	.477	.466	.455	.445	.435	.425	.416	.406	.364	.328	.296
4	.467	.451	.437	.423	.410	.397	.384	.373	.361	.350	.340	.329	.320	.310	.301	.260	.226	.198
5	.386	.370	.355	.341	.328	.315	.303	.291	.280	.269	.259	.250	.240	.231	.223	.186	.156	.132
6	.319	.303	.289	.275	.262	.250	.238	.227	.217	.207	.198	.189	.181	.173	.165	.133	.108	.088
7	.263	.249	.235	.222	.210	.198	.188	.178	.168	.159	.151	.143	.136	.129	.122	.095	.074	.059
8	.218	.204	.191	.179	.168	.157	.148	.139	.130	.123	.115	.108	.102	.096	.091	.068	.051	.039
9	.180	.167	.155	.144	.134	.125	.116	.108	.101	.094	.088	.082	.077	.072	.067	.048	.035	.026
10	.149	.137	.126	.116	.107	.099	.092	.085	.078	.073	.067	.062	.058	.054	.050	.035	.024	.017
11	.123	.112	.103	.094	.086	.079	.072	.066	.061	.056	.051	.047	.043	.040	.037	.025	.017	.012
12	.102	.092	.083	.076	.069	.062	.057	.052	.047	.043	.039	.036	.033	.030	.027	.018	.012	.008
13	.084	.075	.068	.061	.055	.050	.045	.040	.037	.033	.030	.027	.025	.022	.020	.013	.008	.005
14	.069	.062	.055	.049	.044	.039	.035	.032	.028	.025	.023	.021	.018	.017	.015	.009	.006	.003
15	.057	.051	.045	.040	.035	.031	.028	.025	.022	.020	.017	.016	.014	.012	.011	.006	.004	.002
16	.047	.042	.036	.032	.028	.025	.022	.019	.017	.015	.013	.012	.010	.009	.008	.005	.003	.002
17	.039	.034	.030	.026	.023	.020	.017	.015	.013	.012	.010	.009	.008	.007	.006	.003	.002	.001
18	.032	.028	.024	.021	.018	.016	.014	.012	.010	.009	.008	.007	.006	.005	.005	.003	.002	.001
19	.027	.023	.020	.017	.014	.012	.011	.009	.008	.007	.006	.005	.004	.004	.003	.002	.001	*
20	.022	.019	.016	.014	.012	.010	.008	.007	.006	.005	.005	.004	.003	.003	.002	.001	.001	*
21	.018	.015	.013	.011	.009	.008	.007	.006	.005	.004	.003	.003	.003	.002	.002	.001	*	*
22	.015	.013	.011	.009	.007	.006	.005	.004	.004	.003	.003	.002	.002	.002	.001	.001	*	*
23	.012	.010	.009	.007	.006	.005	.004	.003	.003	.002	.002	.002	.001	.001	.001	*	*	*
24	.010	.008	.007	.006	.005	.004	.003	.003	.002	.002	.002	.001	.001	.001	.001	*	*	*
25	.009	.007	.006	.005	.004	.003	.003	.002	.002	.001	.001	.001	.001	.001	.001	*	*	*
30	.003	.003	.002	.002	.001	.001	.001	.001	*	*	*	*	*	*	*	*	*	*
35	.001	.001	.001	.001	*	*	*	*	*	*	*	*	*	*	*	*	*	*
40	*	*	*	*	*	*	*	*	*	*	*	*	*	*	*	*	*	*
45	*	*	*	*	*	*	*	*	*	*	*	*	*	*	*	*	*	*
50	*	*	*	*	*	*	*	*	*	*	*	*	*	*	*	*	*	*

*PVIF is zero to three decimal places.

Similarly, an inspection of any row in the table will reveal that less money is needed to achieve a specific future value when the money is invested at a higher rate of return.

EXAMPLE

You would like to accumulate $50 000 in five years by making a single investment today. You believe you can achieve a return from your investment of 8 percent annually. What is the dollar amount you need to invest today to achieve your goal?

The *PVIF* in this example is 0.681 (look down the column for 8 percent and across the row for five years). Using the present value table, the present value (*PV*) is:

$$PV = FV \times PVIF_{i,n}$$

$$PV = FV \times PVIF_{8\%,5}$$

$$= \$50\ 000 \times 0.681$$

$$= \$34\ 050$$

Therefore, you need to invest $34 050 today to have $50 000 in five years if you expect an annual return of 8 percent.

---

myth or **fact** All financial calculators calculate the time value of money in the same manner.

Using a Financial Calculator

Using a financial calculator, present values can be obtained quickly by inputting all known variables and solving for the one unknown variable.

TVM EXAMPLE

Loretta would like to accumulate $500 000 by the time she retires in 20 years. If she can earn an 8.61 percent return compounded annually, how much must she invest today to have $500 000 in 20 years? Since the unknown variable is the present value (*PV*), the calculator input will be as shown at left.

The calculator key strokes are as follows:

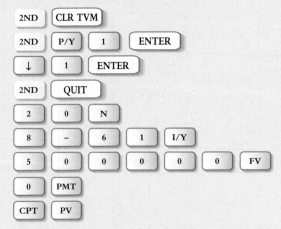

Therefore, Loretta would have to invest $95 845.94 today to accumulate $500 000 in 20 years if she does earn 8.61 percent compounded annually.

Use a financial calculator to determine the present value of a single sum by calculating the present value of $50 000 in five years if the money is invested at an interest rate of 8 percent compounded annually. This is the example used earlier to illustrate the present value tables. Your answer should be $34 029. Your answer may vary slightly due to rounding.

FUTURE VALUE OF AN ANNUITY

L.O.4

Earlier in the chapter, you saw how your money can grow from a single deposit. An alternative way to accumulate funds over time is through an annuity. Recall that an annuity refers to the payment of a series of equal cash flow payments at equal intervals of time. There are two main types of annuities: an ordinary annuity and an annuity due. An **ordinary annuity** is a stream of equal payments that are received or paid at equal intervals of time at the end of a period. An alternative to an ordinary annuity is an **annuity due**, which is a series of equal cash flow payments that occur at the beginning of each period. Thus, an annuity due differs from an ordinary annuity in that the payments occur at the beginning instead of at the end of the period. For example, a monthly deposit of $50 as new savings in a bank account at the end of every month is an ordinary annuity. If this deposit occurred at the beginning of the month, it would be an annuity due.

The most important thing to note about an annuity is that if the amount or frequency of the payment changes over time, the payment stream does not reflect an annuity. Your telephone bill is not an annuity since the payments are not the same each month.

The best way to illustrate the future value of an ordinary annuity or an annuity due is through the use of **timelines**, which show payments received or paid over time.

ordinary annuity
A stream of equal payments that are received or paid at equal intervals in time at the end of a period.

annuity due
A series of equal cash flow payments that occur at the beginning of each period.

timelines
Diagrams that show payments received or paid over time.

EXAMPLE

You plan to invest $100 at the end of every year for the next three years. You expect to earn an annual interest rate of 10 percent compounded annually on the funds you invest. Using a timeline, the cash flows from this ordinary annuity can be represented as follows:

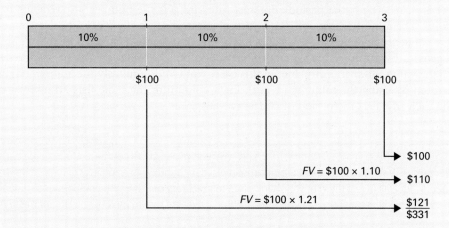

In contrast, consider the situation where you plan to invest $100 at the beginning of every year for the next three years. Assuming that you earn the same interest rate, the cash flows from this annuity due can be represented as follows:

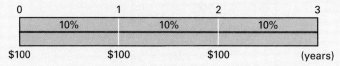

Notice from the above two diagrams that not only do payments occur at the beginning of each period with respect to an annuity due, but interest is earned for one additional period since the first $100 invested starts to earn interest immediately.

Using a Formula to Determine Future Value of an Annuity

Continuing with the example above, you would like to know how much money will be in your investment account at the end of the third year. This amount is the future value of the annuity. How much money you will have in your account will depend on whether you have invested at the end or beginning of every year during the next three years. For an ordinary annuity, the future value can be determined using the formula:

$$FV = PMT \times \left[\frac{(1 + i)^n - 1}{i} \right]$$

For an annuity due, all you have to do is adjust your answer for an ordinary annuity by multiplying it by $(1 + i)$.

Using the information provided in this example, the amount of money that will be in your investment account at the end of the third year if the investment is made as an ordinary annuity is:

$$\$331 = \$100 \times \left[\frac{(1 + 0.10)^3 - 1}{0.10} \right]$$

If the investment is made as an annuity due, you would multiply your answer for an ordinary annuity by $(1+ i)$. As a result, $\$331 \times (1 + 0.10) = 364.10$ would be the value of your investment if you invest $100 at the beginning of the year.

Using the Future Value Annuity Table

Computing the future value of an annuity by looking up each individual single-sum *FVIF* is rather tedious. Consequently, Table 2.3 lists the factors for various interest rates and periods (years). These factors are referred to as **future value interest factors for an annuity** ($FVIFA_{i,n}$), where i is the periodic interest rate and n is the number of payments in the annuity. The annuity payment (PMT) can be multiplied by the $FVIFA$ to determine the future value of the annuity ($FVA = PMT \times FVIFA$). It is important to note that Table 2.3 will provide the future value for an ordinary annuity. The table can also be used to determine the value for an annuity due. In this case, you would multiply the annuity payment generated by using the table by $(1 + i)$. Each column in the table lists an interest rate, while each row lists the period of concern.

future value interest factor for an annuity (*FVIFA*)
A factor multiplied by the periodic savings level (annuity) to determine how the savings will accumulate over time.

EXAMPLE

Suppose that you have won the lottery and will receive $150 000 at the end of every year for the next 20 years. The payments represent an ordinary annuity. As soon as you receive the payments, you will invest them at your bank at an interest rate of 7 percent compounded annually. How much will be in your account at the end of 20 years (assuming that you do not make any withdrawals)?

To find the answer, you must determine the future value of the annuity. (The stream of cash flows is in the form of an annuity since the payments are equal in value and equally spaced in time.) Using Table 2.3 to determine the factor, look in the $i = 7\%$ column and the $n = 20$ periods row. Table 2.3 shows that this factor is 40.995.

The next step is to determine the future value of your lottery annuity:

$$FVA = PMT \times FVIFA_{i,n}$$
$$= PMT \times FVIFA_{7\%,20}$$
$$= \$150\,000 \times 40.995$$
$$= \$6\,149\,250$$

Thus, after 20 years, you will have $6 149 250 if you invest all of your lottery payments in an account earning an interest rate of 7 percent. In this example, you received $150 000 at the end of the year. What if you receive this money at the beginning of the year? In this case, multiply the future value of your lottery annuity by $(1 + i)$. Your answer should be $6 579 698.

Table 2-3 Future Value Interest Factors for $1 Annuity Compounded at i Percent for n Periods: $FVA = PMT \times FVIFA_{i,n}$

Period	1%	2%	3%	4%	5%	6%	7%	8%	9%	10%	11%	12%	13%	14%	15%	16%	17%	18%	19%	20%
1	1.000	1.000	1.000	1.000	1.000	1.000	1.000	1.000	1.000	1.000	1.000	1.000	1.000	1.000	1.000	1.000	1.000	1.000	1.000	1.000
2	2.010	2.020	2.030	2.040	2.050	2.060	2.070	2.080	2.090	2.100	2.110	2.120	2.130	2.140	2.150	2.160	2.170	2.180	2.190	2.200
3	3.030	3.060	3.091	3.122	3.152	3.184	3.215	3.246	3.278	3.310	3.342	3.374	3.407	3.440	3.472	3.506	3.539	3.572	3.606	3.640
4	4.060	4.122	4.184	4.246	4.310	4.375	4.440	4.506	4.573	4.641	4.710	4.779	4.850	4.921	4.993	5.066	5.141	5.215	5.291	5.368
5	5.101	5.204	5.309	5.416	5.526	5.637	5.751	5.867	5.985	6.105	6.228	6.353	6.480	6.610	6.742	6.877	7.014	7.154	7.297	7.442
6	6.152	6.308	6.468	6.633	6.802	6.975	7.153	7.336	7.523	7.716	7.913	8.115	8.323	8.535	8.754	8.977	9.207	9.442	9.683	9.930
7	7.214	7.434	7.662	7.898	8.142	8.394	8.654	8.923	9.200	9.487	9.783	10.089	10.405	10.730	11.067	11.414	11.772	12.141	12.523	12.916
8	8.286	8.583	8.892	9.214	9.549	9.897	10.260	10.637	11.028	11.436	11.859	12.300	12.757	13.233	13.727	14.240	14.773	15.327	15.902	16.499
9	9.368	9.755	10.159	10.583	11.027	11.491	11.978	12.488	13.021	13.579	14.164	14.776	15.416	16.085	16.786	17.518	18.285	19.086	19.923	20.799
10	10.462	10.950	11.464	12.006	12.578	13.181	13.816	14.487	15.193	15.937	16.722	17.549	18.420	19.337	20.304	21.321	22.393	23.521	24.709	25.959
11	11.567	12.169	12.808	13.486	14.207	14.972	15.784	16.645	17.560	18.531	19.561	20.655	21.814	23.044	24.349	25.733	27.200	28.755	30.403	32.150
12	12.682	13.412	14.192	15.026	15.917	16.870	17.888	18.977	20.141	21.384	22.713	24.133	25.650	27.271	29.001	30.850	32.824	34.931	37.180	39.580
13	13.809	14.680	15.618	16.627	17.713	18.882	20.141	21.495	22.953	24.523	26.211	28.029	29.984	32.088	34.352	36.786	39.404	42.218	45.244	48.496
14	14.947	15.974	17.086	18.292	19.598	21.015	22.550	24.215	26.019	27.975	30.095	32.392	34.882	37.581	40.504	43.672	47.102	50.818	54.841	59.196
15	16.097	17.293	18.599	20.023	21.578	23.276	25.129	27.152	29.361	31.772	34.405	37.280	40.417	43.842	47.580	51.659	56.109	60.965	66.260	72.035
16	17.258	18.639	20.157	21.824	23.657	25.672	27.888	30.324	33.003	35.949	39.190	42.753	46.671	50.980	55.717	60.925	66.648	72.938	79.850	87.442
17	18.430	20.012	21.761	23.697	25.840	28.213	30.840	33.750	36.973	40.544	44.500	48.883	53.738	59.117	65.075	71.673	78.978	87.067	96.021	105.930
18	19.614	21.412	23.414	25.645	28.132	30.905	33.999	37.450	41.301	45.599	50.396	55.749	61.724	68.393	75.836	84.140	93.404	103.739	115.265	128.116
19	20.811	22.840	25.117	27.671	30.539	33.760	37.379	41.446	46.018	51.158	56.939	63.439	70.748	78.968	88.211	98.603	110.283	123.412	138.165	154.739
20	22.019	24.297	26.870	29.778	33.066	36.785	40.995	45.762	51.159	57.274	64.202	72.052	80.946	91.024	102.443	115.379	130.031	146.626	165.417	186.687
21	23.239	25.783	28.676	31.969	35.719	39.992	44.865	50.422	56.764	64.002	72.264	81.698	92.468	104.767	118.809	134.840	153.136	174.019	197.846	225.024
22	24.471	27.299	30.536	34.248	38.505	43.392	49.005	55.456	62.872	71.402	81.213	92.502	105.489	120.434	137.630	157.414	180.169	206.342	236.436	271.028
23	25.716	28.845	32.452	36.618	41.430	46.995	53.435	60.893	69.531	79.542	91.147	104.602	120.203	138.295	159.274	183.600	211.798	244.483	282.359	326.234
24	26.973	30.421	34.426	39.082	44.501	50.815	58.176	66.764	76.789	88.496	102.173	118.154	136.829	158.656	184.166	213.976	248.803	289.490	337.007	392.480
25	28.243	32.030	36.459	41.645	47.726	54.864	63.248	73.105	84.699	98.346	114.412	133.333	155.616	181.867	212.790	249.212	292.099	342.598	402.038	471.976
30	34.784	40.567	47.575	56.084	66.438	79.057	94.459	113.282	136.305	164.491	199.018	241.330	293.192	356.778	434.738	530.306	647.423	790.932	966.698	1181.865
35	41.659	49.994	60.461	73.651	90.318	111.432	138.234	172.314	215.705	271.018	341.583	431.658	546.663	693.552	881.152	1120.699	1426.448	1816.607	2314.173	2948.294
40	48.885	60.401	75.400	95.024	120.797	154.758	199.630	259.052	337.872	442.580	581.812	767.080	1013.667	1341.979	1779.048	2360.724	3134.412	4163.094	5529.711	7343.715
45	56.479	71.891	92.718	121.027	159.695	212.737	285.741	386.497	525.840	718.881	986.613	1358.208	1874.086	2590.464	3585.031	4965.191	6879.008	9531.258	13203.105	18280.914
50	64.461	84.577	112.794	152.664	209.341	290.325	406.516	573.756	815.051	1163.865	1668.723	2399.975	3459.344	4994.301	7217.488	10435.449	15088.805	21812.273	31514.492	45496.094

(continued)

Table 2-3   (Continued)

Period	21%	22%	23%	24%	25%	26%	27%	28%	29%	30%	31%	32%	33%	34%	35%	40%	45%	50%
1	1.000	1.000	1.000	1.000	1.000	1.000	1.000	1.000	1.000	1.000	1.000	1.000	1.000	1.000	1.000	1.000	1.000	1.000
2	2.210	2.220	2.230	2.240	2.250	2.260	2.270	2.280	2.290	2.300	2.310	2.320	2.330	2.340	2.350	2.400	2.450	2.500
3	3.674	3.708	3.743	3.778	3.813	3.848	3.883	3.918	3.954	3.990	4.026	4.062	4.099	4.136	4.172	4.360	4.552	4.750
4	5.446	5.524	5.604	5.684	5.766	5.848	5.931	6.016	6.101	6.187	6.274	6.362	6.452	6.542	6.633	7.104	7.601	8.125
5	7.589	7.740	7.893	8.048	8.207	8.368	8.533	8.700	8.870	9.043	9.219	9.398	9.581	9.766	9.954	10.946	12.022	13.188
6	10.183	10.442	10.708	10.980	11.259	11.544	11.837	12.136	12.442	12.756	13.077	13.406	13.742	14.086	14.438	16.324	18.431	20.781
7	13.321	13.740	14.171	14.615	15.073	15.546	16.032	16.534	17.051	17.583	18.131	18.696	19.277	19.876	20.492	23.853	27.725	32.172
8	17.119	17.762	18.430	19.123	19.842	20.588	21.361	22.163	22.995	23.858	24.752	25.678	26.638	27.633	28.664	34.395	41.202	49.258
9	21.714	22.670	23.669	24.712	25.802	26.940	28.129	29.369	30.664	32.015	33.425	34.895	36.429	38.028	39.696	49.152	60.743	74.887
10	27.274	28.657	30.113	31.643	33.253	34.945	36.723	38.592	40.556	42.619	44.786	47.062	49.451	51.958	54.590	69.813	89.077	113.330
11	34.001	35.962	38.039	40.238	42.566	45.030	47.639	50.398	53.318	56.405	59.670	63.121	66.769	70.624	74.696	98.739	130.161	170.995
12	42.141	44.873	47.787	50.895	54.208	57.738	61.501	65.510	69.780	74.326	79.167	84.320	89.803	95.636	101.840	139.234	189.734	257.493
13	51.991	55.745	59.778	64.109	68.760	73.750	79.106	84.853	91.016	97.624	104.709	112.302	120.438	129.152	138.484	195.928	276.114	387.239
14	63.909	69.009	74.528	80.496	86.949	93.925	101.465	109.611	118.411	127.912	138.169	149.239	161.183	174.063	187.953	275.299	401.365	581.858
15	78.330	85.191	92.669	100.815	109.687	119.346	129.860	141.302	153.750	167.285	182.001	197.996	215.373	234.245	254.737	386.418	582.980	873.788
16	95.779	104.933	114.983	126.010	138.109	151.375	165.922	181.867	199.337	218.470	239.421	262.354	287.446	314.888	344.895	541.985	846.321	1311.681
17	116.892	129.019	142.428	157.252	173.636	191.733	211.721	233.790	258.145	285.011	314.642	347.307	383.303	422.949	466.608	759.778	1228.165	1968.522
18	142.439	158.403	176.187	195.993	218.045	242.583	269.885	300.250	334.006	371.514	413.180	459.445	510.792	567.751	630.920	1064.689	1781.838	2953.783
19	173.351	194.251	217.710	244.031	273.556	306.654	343.754	385.321	431.868	483.968	542.266	607.467	680.354	761.786	852.741	1491.563	2584.665	4431.672
20	210.755	237.986	268.783	303.598	342.945	387.384	437.568	494.210	558.110	630.157	711.368	802.856	905.870	1021.792	1152.200	2089.188	3748.763	6648.508
21	256.013	291.343	331.603	377.461	429.681	489.104	556.710	633.589	720.962	820.204	932.891	1060.769	1205.807	1370.201	1556.470	2925.862	5436.703	9973.762
22	310.775	356.438	408.871	469.052	538.101	617.270	708.022	811.993	931.040	1067.265	1223.087	1401.215	1604.724	1837.068	2102.234	4097.203	7884.215	14961.645
23	377.038	435.854	503.911	582.624	673.626	778.760	900.187	1040.351	1202.042	1388.443	1603.243	1850.603	2135.282	2462.669	2839.014	5737.078	11433.109	22443.469
24	457.215	532.741	620.810	723.453	843.032	982.237	1144.237	1332.649	1551.634	1805.975	2101.247	2443.795	2840.924	3300.974	3833.667	8032.906	16579.008	33666.207
25	554.230	650.944	764.596	898.082	1054.791	1238.617	1454.180	1706.790	2002.608	2348.765	2753.631	3226.808	3779.428	4424.301	5176.445	11247.062	24040.555	50500.316
30	1445.111	1767.044	2160.459	2640.881	3227.172	3941.953	4812.891	5873.172	7162.785	8729.805	10632.543	12940.672	15737.945	19124.434	23221.258	60500.207	154105.313	383500.000
35	3755.814	4783.520	6090.227	7750.094	9856.746	12527.160	15909.480	20188.742	25596.512	32422.090	41028.887	51868.563	65504.199	82634.625	104134.500	325394.688	*	*
40	9749.141	12936.141	17153.691	22728.367	30088.621	39791.957	52570.707	69376.562	91447.375	120389.375	*	*	*	*	*	*	*	*
45	25294.223	34970.230	48300.660	66638.937	91831.312	126378.937	173692.875	238384.312	326686.375	447005.062	*	*	*	*	*	*	*	*

*Not shown because of space limitations.

As an exercise, use the future value annuity table to determine the future value of five $172 payments, received at the end of every year and earning an interest rate of 14 percent. Your answer should be $1137.

myth or **fact** Future value interest factors (*FVIF*) and a financial calculator will generate different answers to a question.

Using a Financial Calculator to Determine the Future Value of an Annuity

Using the TI BA II Plus calculator to determine the future value of an annuity is similar to using the calculator to determine the future value of a single dollar amount. As before, the known variables must be inputted in order to solve for the unknown variable.

The example below illustrates the use of the TI BA II Plus calculator to determine the future value of an annuity.

TVM EXAMPLE

You have instructed your employer to deduct $80 from your paycheque at the end of every month and automatically invest the money at an annual interest rate of 5 percent compounded annually. You intend to use this money for your retirement in 30 years. How much will be in the account at that time?

This problem differs from the others we have seen so far, in that the payments are deducted on a monthly (not annual) basis; as a result, *P/Y* = 12. You would like to obtain the future value of the annuity and consequently need the number of periods, the interest rate, the present value, and the payment. Because there are 12 months in a year, there are 30 × 12 = 360 periods. The number of compounding periods, *n*, can always be calculated as the number of years times the number of payments per year, *P/Y*. The interest rate is 5. Also, note that to determine the future value of an annuity, most financial calculators require an input of zero for the present value. The payment in this problem is −$80, since the deduction represents a cash outflow.

The calculator key strokes are as follows:

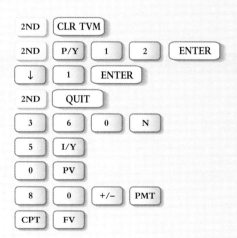

Therefore, you will have $65 230 when you retire in 30 years as a result of your monthly investment. What if you ask your employer to deduct and invest the money from your paycheque at the beginning of the month? Since the withdrawals are being made monthly and not annually, simply multiplying the answer for your ordinary annuity by (1 + *i*) will not give you the correct answer. Instead, you must adjust your financial calculator to let it know that cash flows are occurring at the beginning of the period.

Tamara is going on a vacation to Montreal exactly two years from today. As part of her shopping budget for the trip, she has decided to save $200 per month at the beginning of each month. The account into which she will be depositing money pays an interest rate of 3 percent compounded annually. How much money will Tamara have available for shopping in Montreal? This problem requires you to adjust your TI BA II Plus calculator for beginning of the month investment contributions. The calculator key strokes for this calculation are:

[2ND] [BGN]

[2ND] [SET]

[2ND] [QUIT]

After making this adjustment, you can enter the inputs for the time value of money keys:

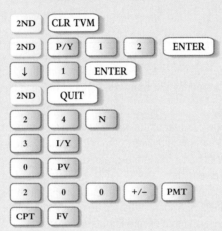

Tamara will have saved $4951 toward her shopping budget. To reset the calculator for end-of-the-period payments, repeat the three steps shown above.

FREE APPS for Personal Finance

Calculating Your Savings

Application:

Savings Calculator is a Web app you can use to calculate your savings given an initial amount, a monthly savings amount, an interest rate, and an interest accrual period. Change the values of each parameter to see the effect on your savings.

L.O.5

PRESENT VALUE OF AN ANNUITY

Just as the future value of an annuity can be obtained by compounding the individual cash flows of the annuity and then totalling them, the present value of an annuity can be obtained by discounting the individual cash flows of the annuity and totalling them.

Referring to our earlier example of an ordinary annuity with three $100 payments and an interest rate of 10 percent, we can graphically illustrate the process as follows:

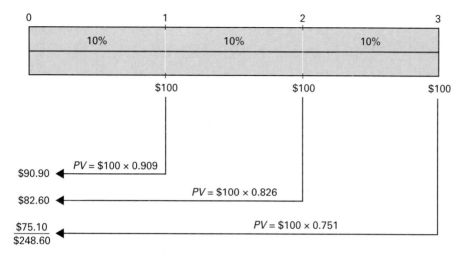

Adding up the individual present values leads to the conclusion that the present value of this annuity is $248.60. Therefore, three $100 payments received at the end of each of the next three years are worth $248.60 to you today if you can invest your money at an interest rate of 10 percent compounded annually. If this was an annuity due, you would multiply your answer by $(1 + i)$ to get $273.46.

Using a Formula to Determine Present Value of an Annuity

Continuing with the example above, you would like to determine how much three $100 payments at the end of each of the next three years will be worth today. This amount is the present value of the annuity. The present value of an annuity can be determined using the formula:

$$PV = PMT \times \left[\frac{1 - \left[\frac{1}{(1 + i)^n} \right]}{i} \right]$$

Using the information provided in this example, the amount of money that will be in your investment account at the end of the third year is:

$$\$248.69 = \$100 \times \left[\frac{1 - \left[\frac{1}{(1 + 0.10)^3} \right]}{0.10} \right]$$

The difference in the answer provided using timelines, $248.60, and the present value of an annuity formula, $248.69, can be attributed to rounding errors. Again, if these payments were at the beginning of each of the next three years, you would multiply your answer by $(1 + i)$ to get $273.56.

Using the Present Value Annuity Table

Table 2.4 shows the **present value interest factors for an annuity** ($PVIFA_{i,n}$) for various interest rates (i) and time periods (n) in the annuity. Each column in the table lists an interest rate, while each row lists a time period. The present value annuity table provides

present value interest factor for an annuity (PVIFA)

A factor multiplied by a periodic savings level (annuity) to determine the present value of the annuity.

Table 2-4 Present Value Interest Factors for $1 Annuity Discounted at i Percent for n Periods: $PVA = PMT \times PVIFA_{i,n}$

Period	1%	2%	3%	4%	5%	6%	7%	8%	9%	10%	11%	12%	13%	14%	15%	16%	17%	18%	19%	20%
1	.990	.980	.971	.962	.952	.943	.935	.926	.917	.909	.901	.893	.885	.877	.870	.862	.855	.847	.840	.833
2	1.970	1.942	1.913	1.886	1.859	1.833	1.808	1.783	1.759	1.736	1.713	1.690	1.668	1.647	1.626	1.605	1.585	1.566	1.547	1.528
3	2.941	2.884	2.829	2.775	2.723	2.673	2.624	2.577	2.531	2.487	2.444	2.402	2.361	2.322	2.283	2.246	2.210	2.174	2.140	2.106
4	3.902	3.808	3.717	3.630	3.546	3.465	3.387	3.312	3.240	3.170	3.102	3.037	2.974	2.914	2.855	2.798	2.743	2.690	2.639	2.589
5	4.853	4.713	4.580	4.452	4.329	4.212	4.100	3.993	3.890	3.791	3.696	3.605	3.517	3.433	3.352	3.274	3.199	3.127	3.058	2.991
6	5.795	5.601	5.417	5.242	5.076	4.917	4.767	4.623	4.486	4.355	4.231	4.111	3.998	3.889	3.784	3.685	3.589	3.498	3.410	3.326
7	6.728	6.472	6.230	6.002	5.786	5.582	5.389	5.206	5.033	4.868	4.712	4.564	4.423	4.288	4.160	4.039	3.922	3.812	3.706	3.605
8	7.652	7.326	7.020	6.733	6.463	6.210	5.971	5.747	5.535	5.335	5.146	4.968	4.799	4.639	4.487	4.344	4.207	4.078	3.954	3.837
9	8.566	8.162	7.786	7.435	7.108	6.802	6.515	6.247	5.995	5.759	5.537	5.328	5.132	4.946	4.772	4.607	4.451	4.303	4.163	4.031
10	9.471	8.983	8.530	8.111	7.722	7.360	7.024	6.710	6.418	6.145	5.889	5.650	5.426	5.216	5.019	4.833	4.659	4.494	4.339	4.192
11	10.368	9.787	9.253	8.760	8.306	7.887	7.499	7.139	6.805	6.495	6.207	5.938	5.687	5.453	5.234	5.029	4.836	4.656	4.486	4.327
12	11.255	10.575	9.954	9.385	8.863	8.384	7.943	7.536	7.161	6.814	6.492	6.194	5.918	5.660	5.421	5.197	4.988	4.793	4.611	4.439
13	12.134	11.348	10.635	9.986	9.394	8.853	8.358	7.904	7.487	7.013	6.750	6.424	6.122	5.842	5.583	5.342	5.118	4.910	4.715	4.533
14	13.004	12.106	11.296	10.563	9.899	9.295	8.745	8.244	7.786	7.367	6.982	6.628	6.302	6.002	5.724	5.468	5.229	5.008	4.802	4.611
15	13.865	12.849	11.938	11.118	10.380	9.712	9.108	8.560	8.061	7.606	7.191	6.811	6.462	6.142	5.847	5.575	5.324	5.092	4.876	4.675
16	14.718	13.578	12.561	11.652	10.838	10.106	9.447	8.851	8.313	7.824	7.379	6.974	6.604	6.265	5.954	5.668	5.405	5.162	4.938	4.730
17	15.562	14.292	13.166	12.166	11.274	10.477	9.763	9.122	8.544	8.022	7.549	7.120	6.729	6.373	6.047	5.749	5.475	5.222	4.990	4.775
18	16.398	14.992	13.754	12.659	11.690	10.828	10.059	9.372	8.756	8.201	7.702	7.250	6.840	6.467	6.128	5.818	5.534	5.273	5.033	4.812
19	17.226	15.679	14.324	13.134	12.085	11.158	10.336	9.604	8.950	8.365	7.839	7.366	6.938	6.550	6.198	5.877	5.584	5.316	5.070	4.843
20	18.046	16.352	14.878	13.590	12.462	11.470	10.594	9.818	9.129	8.514	7.963	7.469	7.025	6.623	6.259	5.929	5.628	5.353	5.101	4.870
21	18.857	17.011	15.415	14.029	12.821	11.764	10.836	10.017	9.292	8.649	8.075	7.562	7.102	6.687	6.312	5.973	5.665	5.384	5.127	4.891
22	19.661	17.658	15.937	14.451	13.163	12.042	11.061	10.201	9.442	8.772	8.176	7.645	7.170	6.743	6.359	6.011	5.696	5.410	5.149	4.909
23	20.456	18.292	16.444	14.857	13.489	12.303	11.272	10.371	9.580	8.883	8.266	7.718	7.230	6.792	6.399	6.044	5.723	5.432	5.167	4.925
24	21.244	18.914	16.936	15.247	13.799	12.550	11.469	10.529	9.707	8.985	8.348	7.784	7.283	6.835	6.434	6.073	5.746	5.451	5.182	4.937
25	22.023	19.524	17.413	15.622	14.094	12.783	11.654	10.675	9.823	9.077	8.422	7.843	7.330	6.873	6.464	6.097	5.766	5.467	5.195	4.948
30	25.808	22.396	19.601	17.292	15.373	13.765	12.409	11.258	10.274	9.427	8.694	8.055	7.496	7.003	6.566	6.177	5.829	5.517	5.235	4.979
35	29.409	24.999	21.487	18.665	16.374	14.498	12.948	11.655	10.567	9.644	8.855	8.176	7.586	7.070	6.617	6.215	5.858	5.539	5.251	4.992
40	32.835	27.356	23.115	19.793	17.159	15.046	13.332	11.925	10.757	9.779	8.951	8.244	7.634	7.105	6.642	6.233	5.871	5.548	5.258	4.997
45	36.095	29.490	24.519	20.720	17.774	15.456	13.606	12.108	10.881	9.863	9.008	8.283	7.661	7.123	6.654	6.242	5.877	5.552	5.261	4.999
50	39.196	31.424	25.730	21.482	18.256	15.762	13.801	12.233	10.962	9.915	9.042	8.304	7.675	7.133	6.661	6.246	5.880	5.554	5.262	4.999

Table 2-4 (Continued)

Period	21%	22%	23%	24%	25%	26%	27%	28%	29%	30%	31%	32%	33%	34%	35%	40%	45%	50%
1	.826	.820	.813	.806	.800	.794	.787	.781	.775	.769	.763	.758	.752	.746	.741	.714	.690	.667
2	1.509	1.492	1.474	1.457	1.440	1.424	1.407	1.392	1.376	1.361	1.346	1.331	1.317	1.303	1.289	1.224	1.165	1.111
3	2.074	2.042	2.011	1.981	1.952	1.923	1.896	1.868	1.842	1.816	1.791	1.766	1.742	1.719	1.696	1.589	1.493	1.407
4	2.540	2.494	2.448	2.404	2.362	2.320	2.280	2.241	2.203	2.166	2.130	2.096	2.062	2.029	1.997	1.849	1.720	1.605
5	2.926	2.864	2.803	2.745	2.689	2.635	2.583	2.532	2.483	2.436	2.390	2.345	2.302	2.260	2.220	2.035	1.876	1.737
6	3.245	3.167	3.092	3.020	2.951	2.885	2.821	2.759	2.700	2.643	2.588	2.534	2.483	2.433	2.385	2.168	1.983	1.824
7	3.508	3.416	3.327	3.242	3.161	3.083	3.009	2.937	2.868	2.802	2.739	2.677	2.619	2.562	2.508	2.263	2.057	1.883
8	3.726	3.619	3.518	3.421	3.329	3.241	3.156	3.076	2.999	2.925	2.854	2.786	2.721	2.658	2.598	2.331	2.109	1.922
9	3.905	3.786	3.673	3.566	3.463	3.366	3.273	3.184	3.100	3.019	2.942	2.868	2.798	2.730	2.665	2.379	2.144	1.948
10	4.054	3.923	3.799	3.682	3.570	3.465	3.364	3.269	3.178	3.092	3.009	2.930	2.855	2.784	2.715	2.414	2.168	1.965
11	4.177	4.035	3.902	3.776	3.656	3.544	3.437	3.335	3.239	3.147	3.060	2.978	2.899	2.824	2.752	2.438	2.185	1.977
12	4.278	4.127	3.985	3.851	3.725	3.606	3.493	3.387	3.286	3.190	3.100	3.013	2.931	2.853	2.779	2.456	2.196	1.985
13	4.362	4.203	4.053	3.912	3.780	3.656	3.538	3.427	3.322	3.223	3.129	3.040	2.956	2.876	2.799	2.469	2.204	1.990
14	4.432	4.265	4.108	3.962	3.824	3.695	3.573	3.459	3.351	3.249	3.152	3.061	2.974	2.892	2.814	2.478	2.210	1.993
15	4.489	4.315	4.153	4.001	3.859	3.726	3.601	3.483	3.373	3.268	3.170	3.076	2.988	2.905	2.825	2.484	2.214	1.995
16	4.536	4.357	4.189	4.033	3.887	3.751	3.623	3.503	3.390	3.283	3.183	3.088	2.999	2.914	2.834	2.489	2.216	1.997
17	4.576	4.391	4.219	4.059	3.910	3.771	3.640	3.518	3.403	3.295	3.193	3.097	3.007	2.921	2.840	2.492	2.218	1.998
18	4.608	4.419	4.243	4.080	3.928	3.786	3.654	3.529	3.413	3.304	3.201	3.104	3.012	2.926	2.844	2.494	2.219	1.999
19	4.635	4.442	4.263	4.097	3.942	3.799	3.664	3.539	3.421	3.311	3.207	3.109	3.017	2.930	2.848	2.496	2.220	1.999
20	4.657	4.460	4.279	4.110	3.954	3.808	3.673	3.546	3.427	3.316	3.211	3.113	3.020	2.933	2.850	2.497	2.221	1.999
21	4.675	4.476	4.292	4.121	3.963	3.816	3.679	3.551	3.432	3.320	3.215	3.116	3.023	2.935	2.852	2.498	2.221	2.000
22	4.690	4.488	4.302	4.130	3.970	3.822	3.684	3.556	3.436	3.323	3.217	3.118	3.025	2.936	2.853	2.498	2.222	2.000
23	4.703	4.499	4.311	4.137	3.976	3.827	3.689	3.559	3.438	3.325	3.219	3.120	3.026	2.938	2.854	2.499	2.222	2.000
24	4.713	4.507	4.318	4.143	3.981	3.831	3.692	3.562	3.441	3.327	3.221	3.121	3.027	2.939	2.855	2.499	2.222	2.000
25	4.721	4.514	4.323	4.147	3.985	3.834	3.694	3.564	3.442	3.329	3.222	3.122	3.028	2.939	2.856	2.499	2.222	2.000
30	4.746	4.534	4.339	4.160	3.995	3.842	3.701	3.569	3.447	3.332	3.225	3.124	3.030	2.941	2.857	2.500	2.222	2.000
35	4.756	4.541	4.345	4.164	3.998	3.845	3.703	3.571	3.448	3.333	3.226	3.125	3.030	2.941	2.857	2.500	2.222	2.000
40	4.760	4.544	4.347	4.166	3.999	3.846	3.703	3.571	3.448	3.333	3.226	3.125	3.030	2.941	2.857	2.500	2.222	2.000
45	4.761	4.545	4.347	4.166	4.000	3.846	3.704	3.571	3.448	3.333	3.226	3.125	3.030	2.941	2.857	2.500	2.222	2.000
50	4.762	4.545	4.348	4.167	4.000	3.846	3.704	3.571	3.448	3.333	3.226	3.125	3.030	2.941	2.857	2.500	2.222	2.000

the present value for an ordinary annuity. The table can also be used to determine the value for an annuity due. In this case, you would multiple the annuity payment generated by using the table by $(1 + i)$.

EXAMPLE

You have just won the lottery. As a result of your luck, you will receive $82 000 at the end of every year for the next 25 years. A financial firm offers you a lump sum of $700 000 in return for these payments. If you can invest your money at an annual interest rate of 9 percent, should you accept the offer?

This problem requires you to determine the present value of the lottery annuity. If the present value of the annuity is higher than the amount offered by the financial firm, you should reject the offer. Using Table 2.4 to determine the factor, look in the $i = 9\%$ column and the $n = 25$ periods row. Table 2.4 shows that this factor is 9.823.

The next step is to determine the present value of the annuity:

$$PVA = PMT \times PVIFA_{i,n}$$
$$= PMT \times PVIFA_{9\%,25}$$
$$= \$82\ 000 \times 9.823$$
$$= \$805\ 486$$

Thus, the 25 payments of $82 000 each are worth $805 486 to you today if you can invest your money at an interest rate of 9 percent. Consequently, you should reject the financial firm's offer to purchase your future lottery payments for $700 000. If you receive these payments at the beginning of the year, the payments would be worth $805 486 \times (1.09) = $877 980.

As an exercise, use the present value annuity table to determine the present value of eight $54 payments, received at the end of every year and earning an interest rate of 14 percent. Your answer should be $250.50, which means that the eight payments have a present value of $250.50.

Using a Financial Calculator to Determine the Present Value of an Annuity

Determining the present value of an annuity with the TI BA II Plus calculator is similar to using the calculator to determine the present value of a single-sum payment. Again, the values of known variables are inserted to solve for the unknown variable.

TVM EXAMPLE

Dave, a recent retiree, receives his $600 pension at the end of each month. He will receive this pension for 20 years. If Dave can invest his funds at an interest rate of 10 percent compounded annually, he should be just as satisfied receiving this pension as receiving a lump sum payment today of what amount?

This problem requires us to determine the present value of the pension annuity. Since payments are received monthly, $P/Y = 12$. Because there are $20 \times 12 = 240$ months in 20 years, $n = 240$. The $600 monthly pension is a cash inflow to Dave, so this amount is entered as a positive number.

The calculator key strokes are as follows:

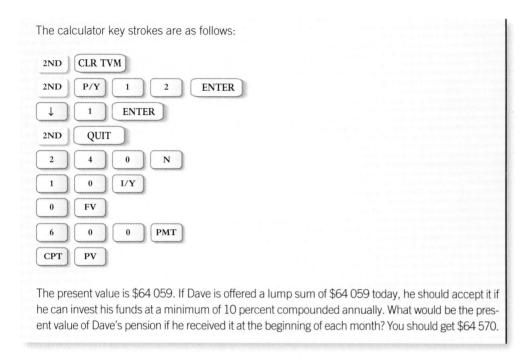

The present value is $64 059. If Dave is offered a lump sum of $64 059 today, he should accept it if he can invest his funds at a minimum of 10 percent compounded annually. What would be the present value of Dave's pension if he received it at the beginning of each month? You should get $64 570.

CALCULATE THE NUMBER OF COMPOUNDING PERIODS AND THE NOMINAL ANNUAL INTEREST RATE

L.O.6

You can also use the TI BA II Plus to determine the number of compounding periods required to grow an investment from a present value to a future value and the nominal annual interest rate earned on an investment.

Solving for Number of Compounding Periods

TVM EXAMPLE

How long would it take for $1635 to increase to $2310 if the investment earned interest at a rate of 8 percent compounded annually? The calculator key strokes are as follows:

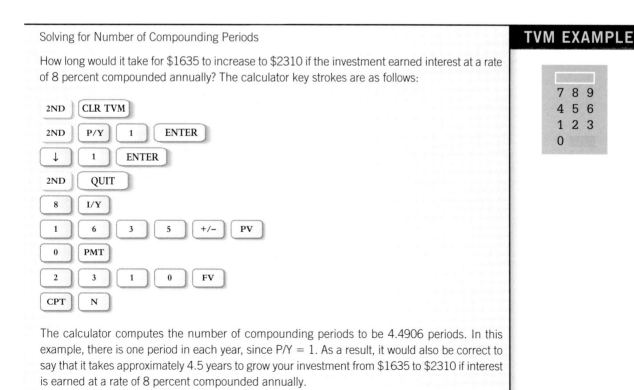

The calculator computes the number of compounding periods to be 4.4906 periods. In this example, there is one period in each year, since P/Y = 1. As a result, it would also be correct to say that it takes approximately 4.5 years to grow your investment from $1635 to $2310 if interest is earned at a rate of 8 percent compounded annually.

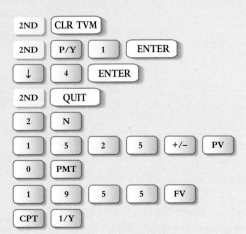

TVM EXAMPLE

Solving for Nominal Annual Interest Rate

What nominal rate of interest compounded quarterly must be earned on a savings account for it to grow from $1525 to $1955 over a period of 2 years? The calculator key strokes are as follows:

2ND	CLR TVM
2ND	P/Y	1	ENTER
↓	4	ENTER
2ND	QUIT
2	N
1	5	2	5	+/−	PV
0	PMT
1	9	5	5	FV
CPT	1/Y

The calculator computes the nominal annual interest rate to be 12.61 percent compounded quarterly.

L.O.7

INTEREST RATE CONVERSION

nominal interest rate
The stated, or quoted, rate of interest.

The interest rates used to solve questions up to now are known as nominal interest rates. A **nominal interest rate** is the stated, or quoted, rate of interest. It is also known as the annual percentage rate (APR). For example, if we compare 10 percent compounded semi-annually to 10 percent compounded monthly, it would be correct to say that the nominal interest rate in each case is 10 percent. However, we also know that investments that have a higher compounding frequency will earn more interest. Similarly, loans that have a higher compounding frequency will result in more interest paid by the borrower. When comparing two or more interest rates, the nominal interest rate is not useful because it does not take into account the effect of compounding. In order to make objective investment decisions regarding loan costs or investment returns over different compounding frequencies, the effective interest rate has to be determined. The **effective interest rate** is the actual rate of interest that you earn, or pay, over a period of time. It is also known as the effective yield (EY). The effective interest rate allows for the comparison of two or more interest rates because it reflects the effect of compound interest. When comparing investment or loan alternatives, it is often useful to convert nominal interest rates to effective interest rates using the following formula:

effective interest rate
The actual rate of interest that you earn, or pay, over a period of time.

$$EY = \left(1 + \frac{i}{n}\right)^n - 1$$

The effective yield of 10 percent compounded semi-annually is:

$$EY = \left(1 + \frac{0.10}{2}\right)^2 - 1$$
$$EY = (1.05)^2 - 1$$
$$EY = 0.1025 \ or \ 10.25\%$$

The effective yield of 10 percent compounded monthly is:

$$EY = \left(1 + \frac{0.10}{12}\right)^{12} - 1$$
$$EY = (1.0083)^{12} - 1$$
$$EY = 0.1047 \ or \ 10.47\%$$

The table below displays the equivalent effective interest rates for various nominal interest rates:

	Nominal Interest Rate	Effective Interest Rate
a.	10% compounded annually	10.00%
b.	10% compounded semiannually	10.25
c.	10% compounded quarterly	10.38
d.	10% compounded monthly	10.47
e.	10% compounded weekly	10.51
f.	10% compounded daily	10.52

These values demonstrate two important points: (1) The nominal and effective interest rates are equivalent for annual compounding, and (2) the effective annual interest rate increases with increases in compounding frequency.

The effective yield can also be calculated using the TI BA II Plus calculator.

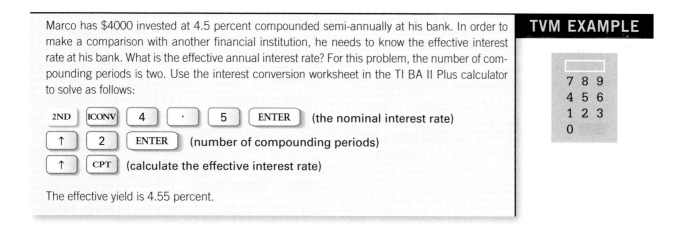

TVM EXAMPLE

Marco has $4000 invested at 4.5 percent compounded semi-annually at his bank. In order to make a comparison with another financial institution, he needs to know the effective interest rate at his bank. What is the effective annual interest rate? For this problem, the number of compounding periods is two. Use the interest conversion worksheet in the TI BA II Plus calculator to solve as follows:

2ND ICONV 4 . 5 ENTER (the nominal interest rate)

↑ 2 ENTER (number of compounding periods)

↑ CPT (calculate the effective interest rate)

The effective yield is 4.55 percent.

How Time Value Can Motivate Saving

The results from estimating the future value of an annuity may surprise you. Your money can grow substantially over time when you invest periodically and when interest is earned on your savings over time. The exercise of estimating the future value of an annuity might encourage you to develop a savings plan, because you see the reward as a result of your willingness to save. Consider how much you may be able to save over each of the next five years, and estimate the future value of an annuity over this period based on the prevailing interest rate. Then, apply it to a 10-year period and also to a 20-year period. Notice how the amount saved over 10 years is more than twice the amount saved over 5 years, and the amount saved over 20 years is more than twice the amount saved over 10 years. Your estimates might convince you to save more money each year, so that you can build your savings and wealth over time, and therefore have more money to spend in the future.

> **MyLab Finance**   Visit MyLab Finance for additional study and practice tools. Select Financial Planning Problems are available in the Study Plan. Create your own study plan, generate personal cash flow statements and balance sheets, and set personal financial goals.

SUMMARY

L.O.1   Explain the difference between simple interest and compound interest.

Interest is the rent charged for the use of money. With simple interest, the interest earned is not reinvested, whereas with compound interest, the interest earned is reinvested and earns additional interest. All else being equal, an investment that earns compound interest will earn more than an investment that earns simple interest.

L.O.2   Calculate the future value of a single dollar amount that you save today.

You can calculate the future value of a single dollar amount to determine the future value of an investment or loan. The future value can be determined by using time value of money formulas, tables, or a financial calculator. The future value of a dollar amount can be determined once you know the present value of the investment or loan, the interest rate, the number of years the money will be borrowed or invested, and the number of compounding periods.

L.O.3   Calculate the present value of a single dollar amount that will be received in the future.

You can estimate the present value of a single dollar amount so that you know what a future payment would be worth if you had it today. The present value of a single dollar amount to be received in the future is determined by discounting the future value. The present value of a future amount can be determined by using time value of money formulas, tables, or a financial calculator.

L.O.4   Calculate the future value of an annuity.

An annuity refers to a series of equal cash flow payments at equal intervals of time. An annuity where the

cash flows occur at the end of the period is referred to as an ordinary annuity. An annuity where the cash flows occur at the beginning of the period is referred to as an annuity due. Calculating the future value involves determining the future value of every single dollar amount contained within the annuity, which can be determined using time value of money formulas, a future value annuity table, or a financial calculator.

L.O.5   Calculate the present value of an annuity.

You can estimate the present value of an annuity so that you can determine how much a stream of future payments is worth today. This involves determining the present value of every single dollar amount contained within the annuity, which can be determined by using time value of money formulas, a present value annuity table, or a financial calculator.

L.O.6   Calculate the number of compounding periods and the nominal annual interest rate.

You can calculate the number of compounding periods required to grow an investment from a present value amount to a future value amount when provided with a nominal interest rate. In addition, the nominal annual interest rate earned on an investment that grows from a present value amount to a future value amount over a number of periods may also be determined.

L.O.7   Convert a nominal interest rate to an effective interest rate.

The nominal interest rate is the stated, or quoted, rate of interest, whereas the effective interest rate is the actual rate of interest that you earn, or pay, over a period of time. In order to compare two interest rates, you should compare the effective interest rate of one investment to the effective interest rate of another investment.

REVIEW QUESTIONS

1. What is the time value of money? How is it related to opportunity costs?

2. Define interest. Define and describe simple interest and compound interest.

3. List three methods that can be used to solve time value of money problems.

4. To what types of cash flows is the time value of money concept most commonly applied?

5. What inputs are required when calculating the future value of a single dollar amount using a formula?

6. How many compounding periods per year are there when interest is compounded annually? Semi-annually? Quarterly? Monthly? Weekly? Daily?

7. What is the future value interest factor? What is the formula for determining the future value of a single dollar amount when using the future value interest factor table? What information must be known in order to find the correct future value interest factor?

8. What should you do each time before you use a financial calculator to solve a time value of money problem?

9. What is the difference between a cash inflow and a cash outflow?

10. On the Texas Instruments BA II Plus calculator, what calculator keys do you have to press in order to access the number of compounding periods per year function?

11. What is discounting?

12. Describe some instances when determining the present value of an amount is useful.

13. What formula is used when determining the present value of a single dollar amount?

14. What is the present value interest factor? What is the formula for determining the present value of a single dollar amount when using the present value interest factor table?

15. Define annuity. Define and describe the two main types of annuities.

16. What formula is used to determine the future value of an annuity?

17. What is the future value interest factor for an annuity? What is the formula for determining the future value of

an annuity when using the future value interest factor for an annuity table?

18. When using a formula or annuity table, what must you do to adjust your calculation for an annuity due?

19. What formula is used to determine the present value of an annuity?

20. What is the present value interest factor for an annuity? What is the formula for determining the present value of an annuity when using the present value interest factor for an annuity table?

21. What would be the number of compounding periods (n) when determining the future value of an annuity, where money is invested monthly over a five-year period?

22. Define the terms *nominal interest rate* and *effective interest rate*. Why is it important to be able to distinguish between these two different rates?

In questions 23 through 26, indicate whether you would solve for the future value of a single sum, the present value of a single sum, the future value of an annuity, or the present value of an annuity.

23. You want to know how much you must deposit today to have $5000 in five years.

24. You plan to contribute $300 per month to your company's retirement plan and want to know how much you will have at retirement.

25. You received $500 as a gift for graduation and want to know how much it will be worth in three years if you deposit it in a savings account.

26. You must decide between accepting a lump sum settlement and annual payments.

FINANCIAL PLANNING PROBLEMS

MyLab Finance Financial Planning Problems marked with a 🌐 can be found in MyLab Finance.

Answer the following questions using time value of money formulas or the TI BA II Plus financial calculator. Unless indicated otherwise, all cash flows occur at the end of the period.

🌐 1. Earl wants to know how much he will have available to spend on his trip to Belize in three years if he deposits $3000 today at an interest rate of 9 percent compounded quarterly. (FV)

🌐 2. Rodney received a total of $1000 cash as graduation gifts from various relatives. He wants to invest it in a guaranteed investment certificate (GIC) so that he will have a down payment on a car when he graduates from university in five years. His bank will

pay 3 percent interest compounded annually for the five-year GIC. How much will Rodney have in five years to put down on his car? (FV)

🌐 3. Michelle is attending college and has a part-time job. Once she finishes college, Michelle would like to relocate to a metropolitan area. She wants to build her savings so that she will have a "nest egg" to start her off. Michelle works out her budget and decides that she can afford to set aside $50 per month for savings. Her bank will pay her 3 percent interest compounded annually on her savings account. What will Michelle's balance be in five years? (FV)

4. Farah will receive $1550 each year for 15 years from an ordinary annuity that she has recently purchased. If she earns interest at a rate of 6.6 percent compounded annually, what is the present value of the amount that she will receive? (PV)

5. Cheryl wants to have $2000 in spending money to take on a trip to Niagara Falls in three years. How much must she deposit now in a savings account that pays 4 percent interest compounded monthly to have the money she needs in three years? (PV)

6. Shania would like to finance the purchase of her car. If she borrows $20 000 as a five-year loan from the bank and the bank requires her to make end-of-month payments of $400, what is the annual interest rate on her loan if interest is compounded monthly and the loan is completely paid off at the end of the five-year period? (I/Y)

7. If Shazaad wants to save $40 000 for a down payment on a home in five years, assuming an interest rate of 4.5 percent compounded quarterly, how much money does he need to save each month? (PMT)

8. Amy and Vince want to save $7000 so they can take a trip to Prince Edward Island in four years. How much must they save each month to have the money they need if they can get 8 percent interest compounded semi-annually on their savings? (PMT)

9. Stacey would like to have $1 million available to her at retirement. If she makes contributions of $300 per month to a tax-free investment account for 30 years, what rate of return must she earn on her investments? Assume that interest is compounded quarterly. (I/Y)

10. Juan would like to give his newly born grandson a gift of $18 000 on his eighteenth birthday. Juan would like to know what rate of return, compounded monthly, he must earn on a tax-free investment account if he deposits $1000 today and makes regular monthly deposits of $50 per month at the end of each month. What is Juan's required rate of return? (I/Y)

11. Sandra deposits $2500 in her savings account. How many years will it take her savings account to increase to $5000 if she is able to earn a rate of return of 4 percent interest compounded annually? Assume Sandra will make no additional deposits to her savings account? (N)

12. Jeron invests $75 per month, at the beginning of each month, at 5 percent interest compounded

weekly. How long, in years, will it take him to accumulate $5000? (N)

13. Judith has just become eligible to participate in her company's retirement plan. Her company matches her contributions dollar for dollar. The plan averages an annual return of 12 percent interest compounded annually. Judith is 40 and plans to work until age 65. If she contributes $200 per month, at the end of each month, how much does her employer contribute per month? How much will she have in her retirement plan at retirement? (FV)

14. Twins Jessica and Joshua, both 25, graduated from college and began working in the family restaurant business. The first year, Jessica began putting $2000 per year in a registered retirement savings plan (RRSP) and contributed to it for a total of 10 years. After that time, she made no further contributions until she retired at age 65. Joshua did not start making contributions to his RRSP until he was 35, but he continued making contributions of $2000 per year until he retired at age 65. Assuming that both Jessica and Joshua receive 10 percent interest compounded annually per year, how much will Jessica have at retirement? How much did she contribute in total? How much will Joshua have at retirement? How much did he contribute in total? (FV)

15. How much money will Penny Pincher have after 40 years if she invests $500 at the beginning of each month and is able to earn a rate of return of 9 percent compounded semi-annually on her investments? (FV)

16. Jesse has just learned that she won $1 million in her provincial lottery. She has the choice of receiving a lump sum payment of $312 950 or $50 000 per year for the next 20 years. Jesse can invest the lump sum at 8 percent interest compounded monthly, or she can invest the annual payments at 6 percent interest compounded annually. Which should she choose for the greatest return after 20 years? Assume that Jesse plans on investing all of her lottery winnings for the next 20 years. (FV)

17. Winners of the Dream a Dream Lotto draw are given the choice of receiving the winning amount divided equally over 20 years or as a lump sum cash option amount. The cash option amount is determined by discounting the winning amount at 7 percent interest compounded quarterly over 20 years. This week, the lottery is worth $6 million to a single winner. What would the cash option payout be? (PV) Lucy spends $10 per week on lottery tickets. If she takes the same amount that she spends on lottery tickets and invests it each week for the next five years at 10 percent interest compounded monthly, how much will she have in five years? (FV)

18. Sufen can take his $1000 income tax refund and invest it in a three-year GIC at 5 percent interest compounded quarterly, or he can use the money to purchase a stereo system and put $30 a month in a bank savings account that will pay him 4 percent interest compounded daily. Which choice will give him more money at the end of three years? (FV)

19. You have an investment in which you earn a nominal interest rate of 8.44 percent compounded quarterly on your investments. What is the equivalent effective interest rate? (EFF)

20. The effective interest rate on your credit card is 35 percent. What is the equivalent nominal interest rate if interest compounds daily? (EFF)

CHALLENGE QUESTIONS

1. Tommy and Shan Li established a plan to save $300 per month for their children's education. Their oldest child is six years old and will begin college in 12 years. They will invest the $300 in a savings account that they expect will earn interest of about 5 percent per year, compounded monthly, over the next 12 years. The Lis wonder how much additional money they would accumulate if they could earn 7 percent a year, compounded monthly, on the savings account instead of 5 percent. They also wonder how their savings would accumulate if they could save $400 per month instead of $300 per month at either of these rates of return. The Lis have asked for you to help them determine the answers to these questions.

2. Which of the following cash flow streams, A or B, is more attractive if the appropriate discount rate is 6.5 percent, compounded quarterly?

Year	A	B
0	$0	$0
1	1500	0
2	1500	0
3	1500	2500
4	1500	2500
5	1500	2500
6	1500	2500

ETHICAL DILEMMA

Cindy and Jack have always practised good financial habits, in particular, developing and living by a budget. They are currently in the market to purchase a new car and have budgeted $300 per month for car payments.

While Cindy and Jack are visiting a local dealership, a salesman, Herb, shows them a car that meets their financial requirements. Then he insists that they look at a much more expensive car that he knows they would prefer. The more expensive car would result in payments of $500 per month.

In discussing the two cars, Cindy and Jack tell Herb that the only way they can afford a more expensive car would be to discontinue making a $200 monthly contribution to their retirement plan, which they have just begun. They plan to retire in 30 years. Herb explains that they would need to discontinue the $200 monthly payments for only five years, that

is, the length of the car loan. Herb calculates that the $12 000 in lost contributions over the next five years could be made up over the remaining 25 years by increasing their monthly contribution by only $40 per month, and they would still be able to achieve their goal.

a. Comment on the ethics of a salesperson who attempts to talk customers into spending more than they had originally planned and budgeted.

b. Is Herb correct in his calculation that Cindy and Jack can make up the difference in their retirement by increasing their monthly contributions by only $40 per month for the remaining 25 years? (Note: Assume a rate of return of 6 percent interest compounded annually on Cindy and Jack's investment and assume that they make the investments annually.)

FINANCIAL PLANNING ONLINE EXERCISES

1. Go to www.teachmefinance.com.

   a. Click on "Time Value of Money." Review the information on present value and future value and the examples. What is the relationship between present value and future value?

   b. Click on "Annuities." Review the information and examples.

   c. Click on "Perpetuities." Read the information and examples. What are perpetuities?

   d. Click on "Future Value of an Uneven Cash flow." Review the information and illustration.

2. Go to www.getsmarteraboutmoney.ca/tools-and-calculators/compound-interest-calculator/compound-interest-calculator.aspx.

   a. Use the "Compound interest calculator" to determine how much money you will save if you have nothing in your account currently and if you deposit $500 quarterly for the next 20 years. Your expected rate of return is 10 percent compounded annually.

   b. Approximately how many years would it take you to reach a savings goal of $1 million if you deposit $250 monthly and expect a rate of return of 8 percent compounded quarterly? How long, in years and months, would it take you to accumulate $1 million if you could earn 10 percent compounded quarterly instead of 8 percent compounded quarterly?

   c. How much must you contribute to your savings annually if you currently have $500 in your account, your savings goal is $1 million, and you plan to retire in 35 years? You expect a rate of return of 10 percent compounded monthly.

PSYCHOLOGY OF PERSONAL FINANCE: Future Value of Your Cash

1. This chapter explains how your cash deposited in a bank can grow over time. Some people are only willing to save if they are rewarded with a high interest rate. However, the interest rate on deposits has been relatively low lately. Does this influence your willingness to save? Would you save more money if interest rates were higher?

2. This chapter illustrates how the amount of debt you owed would not grow as quickly when interest rates are low. Since interest rates have been low lately, are you more willing to borrow money?

MINI-CASE 1: Lots of Plans

Jenny Smith, 28, just received a promotion at work. Her salary has increased to $40 000 and she is now eligible to participate in her employer's pension plan. The employer matches employee contributions up to 6 percent of their salary. Jenny wants to buy a new car in two years. The model car she wants to buy currently costs $24 000. She wants to save enough to make an $8000 down payment and plans to finance the balance. At age 30, Jenny will be eligible to receive a $50 0000 inheritance left by her late grandfather. Her trust fund is invested in bonds that pay 7 percent interest, compounded quarterly. Jenny and her boyfriend, Paul, have also set a wedding date for two years in the future, after he finishes school. Paul will have $40 000 of student loans to repay after graduation. Both Jenny and Paul want to buy a home of their own as soon as possible. Justify Jenny's participation in her employer's pension plan using time value of money concepts. Calculate the amount that Jenny needs to save each year for the down payment on a new car, assuming she can earn 6 percent, compounded annually, on her savings. What will be the value of Jenny's trust fund at age 60, assuming she takes possession of the money at age 30, uses half for a house down payment, and leaves half of the money untouched where it is currently invested? If Paul wants to repay his student loans in full within five years and pays a 7.75 percent interest rate, compounded annually, what will be his annual end of year payment?

MINI-CASE 2: Retirement Income

James Cardinal, 56, just retired after 31 years of teaching. He is a husband and father of three. Two of his children, Carl and Dan, still live at home while they are finishing college. James received a $150 000 lump sum retirement bonus and will receive $3800 per month from his retirement annuity. In addition, James has saved $150 000 in a retirement savings account and another $100 000 in a bank account. His retirement savings account earns an average return of 5 percent per year, compounded annually, while his bank account earns 2 percent per year, compounded annually. James has decided to deposit his retirement bonus in his bank account. James' current monthly expenses total $5800. James has asked for your advice in helping him determine how much he can withdraw per month from his other investments in order to supplement the income he receives from his retirement annuity. Specifically, will he be able to withdraw enough to cover off his $5800 of monthly expenses? If not, determine for how many years James will be able to withdraw income from his other investments. Assume that James will first withdraw income from his bank account. Once this account is empty he will withdraw income from his retirement savings account. Also, if James does have an income shortfall, determine what rate of return on his retirement savings account will allow him to cover his expenses during his retirement years after he has withdrawn all of his savings from his bank account. Assume that James will live for another 30 years, and that his current month-end expenses will remain at $5800 throughout his retirement. All figures are after-tax.

Study Guide

Circle the correct answer and then check the answers in the back of the book to chart your progress.

Multiple Choice

1. The accumulation of interest over time is called:
   a. An annuity.
   b. An ordinary annuity.
   c. Compounding.
   d. Present value.

2. The most important thing to note about an annuity is:
   a. That the payment must not change over time.
   b. That the payment increases according to the discount rate.
   c. That it reflects the growth of a single lump sum.
   d. That it reflects the power of simple interest.

3. Which of the following is not an example of a future value?
   a. The balance in your chequing account today
   b. A savings account balance in five years
   c. A mortgage balance in 10 years
   d. The value of a retirement account in 20 years

4. Don wants to know how much he needs to save every year to amass $15 000 in five years at a 5 percent interest rate compounded annually. What is he calculating using his financial calculator?
   a. Present value
   b. Future value
   c. Interest rate
   d. Payment

5. Everything else being equal, the ___the interest rate, the ___the final accumulation of money.
   a. higher; higher
   b. lower; lower
   c. higher; lower
   d. a and b are both correct

6. To compute how much you would need to save each year for the next 25 years to allow you to withdraw $20 000 for the following 30 years, you would need to use:
   a. The future value of an annuity formula.
   b. The present value of an annuity formula.
   c. Both the future and the present value of annuity formulas.
   d. Both the present and the future value of a single dollar amount formulas.

7. An interest rate of 10 percent compounded quarterly is ___an interest rate of 9.7 percent compounded daily on an equivalent effective interest rate basis.
   a. the same as
   b. greater than
   c. less than
   d. not comparable to

8. Present and future value concepts are not applied to which of the following?
   a. Payments on a home
   b. Calculation of withdrawals needed during retirement

c. Calculation of savings for a large purchase

d. The balance of your chequing account today

9. How much interest will you pay on a loan of $10 000 if you are paying the loan off in nine months and your loan rate is 4 percent? (rounded to the nearest dollar):

a. $200

b. $300

c. $100

d. $500

10. If Art wants $35 000 in 10 years and can earn 12 percent interest compounded monthly, how much does he need to invest today?

a. $10 538

b. $10 506

c. $10 605

d. $10 583

11. What is the future value of $200 deposited today at 8 percent interest compounded annually for three years (rounded to the nearest dollar)?

a. $252

b. $250

c. $248

d. $249

12. Carol would like to have $500 000 saved in her registered retirement savings plan (RRSP) in 30 years at an interest rate of 10 percent compounded annually. How much should she contribute at the end of each year?

a. $3039.62

b. $2000.00

c. $2182.00

d. $1956.20

13. How much will you have if you deposit $1000 at the beginning of each year for the next five years in an account paying 7 percent interest compounded daily?

a. $5751.00

b. $5779.51

c. $5002.88

d. $6198.53

14. If you borrow $20 000 as a five-year loan from the bank and the bank requires you to make end-of-year payments of $4878.05, what is the annual interest rate on this loan if interest is compounded annually (rounded to the nearest percent)?

a. 8 percent

b. 6 percent

c. 7 percent

d. 4 percent

15. What is the effective interest rate for a credit card advertised at 28 percent interest compounded daily? (rounded to one decimal)

a. 32.3 percent

b. 29.8 percent

c. 31.9 percent

d. 28.9 percent

True/False

1. True or False? Whether a dollar is received today or in the future, it will be worth about the same amount to you.

2. True or False? An annuity is a stream of equal payments that are received or paid at random periods of time.

3. True or False? An example of an opportunity cost is saving money rather than taking a vacation.

4. True or False? An investment or loan that has an interest rate of 6 percent compounded annually also has an equivalent effective interest rate of 6 percent.

5. True or False? The inputs in the time value of money formulas when calculating the present or future value of a single dollar amount are the same.

6. True or False? The process of obtaining present values is also called compounding.

7. True or False? The present value interest factor (PVIF) becomes lower as the number of years increases.

8. True or False? The cash flows of an annuity due occur at the beginning of each period.

9. True or False? On the TI BA II Plus financial calculator, the number of compounding periods (n) is determined as the number of years times the number of compounding periods per year.

10. True or False? It is always better to choose a lump sum rather than periodic payments over time.

11. True or False? Compound interest refers to the process of earning interest on interest.

12. True or False? When you borrow money, the amount you receive should be entered as a negative number on your financial calculator.

13. True or False? Investments that have a higher compounding frequency will earn more interest.

14. True or False? The future value interest factor (FVIF) becomes higher as the interest rate increases.

15. True or False? The interest rate used to solve time value of money (TVM) questions is known as the effective interest rate.

Planning with Personal Financial Statements

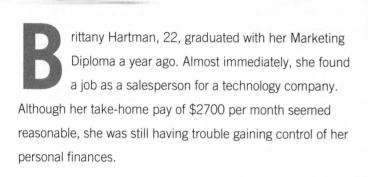

Brittany Hartman, 22, graduated with her Marketing Diploma a year ago. Almost immediately, she found a job as a salesperson for a technology company. Although her take-home pay of $2700 per month seemed reasonable, she was still having trouble gaining control of her personal finances.

In contrast, Brittany's best friend, Manny Martinez, had a reputation for being more careful with his expenses. Brittany would often comment on how Manny would always bring lunch to college from home, whereas Brittany purchased food at the cafeteria almost every day.

Manny was able to show Brittany that she would save a lot of money if she changed her daily spending habits. Brittany made a commitment to herself to reduce her expenses by bringing lunch to work three days a week. For the most part, she kept her promise for the rest of the year.

However, Brittany still feels her spending habits are out of control; once again she is looking to her frugal friend to help her out.

QUESTIONS:

1. What should Manny say to Brittany when he tries to explain to her that she should establish a budget? What information would she need to establish a budget?
2. What alternative budgeting strategies could Brittany use if she is unable to stick to a budget?
3. What information does Brittany need to create a personal balance sheet? Why is a personal balance sheet important?

L.0.1

PERSONAL CASH FLOW STATEMENT

personal cash flow statement
A financial statement that measures a person's income and expenses.

You may often ask yourself whether you can afford a new television, a new car, another year of education, or a vacation. You can answer these questions by determining your financial position. Specifically, you use what you know about your income and your spending habits to estimate how much cash you will have at the end of this week, or quarter, or year. Once you obtain an estimate, you can decide whether you could either increase your income or reduce your spending to achieve a higher level of cash. As mentioned in Chapter 1, budgeting is the process of forecasting future income, future expenses, and savings. When budgeting, the first step is to create a **personal cash flow statement**, which measures your income and expenses. Comparing your income and expenses allows you to see where your money is going. This is necessary so you can then monitor your spending and determine the amount of cash that you can allocate toward an emergency fund, investments, and other purposes.

Income

The main source of income for working people is their salary, but there can also be other important sources of income. Deposits in various types of savings accounts and other forms of debt investments can generate income in the form of interest income. Some stocks also generate income in the form of dividends, and maybe capital gains.

> **myth** or **fact** Students who only work part time do not really benefit from creating a personal cash flow statement.

Expenses

Expenses are both large (for example, monthly rent) and small (for example, dry cleaning costs). It is not necessary to document every expenditure, but you should track how most of your money is spent. Monitoring your expenses is much easier if you use your debit card to pay bills. If you use online banking, you will be able to see clearly any expenses that are paid using your debit card. In contrast, if you pay for most of your expenses using cash, you will have to keep a record of all receipts to effectively monitor your spending. Using a credit card for your purchases provides an online and written record of your transactions. Many people use software programs such as Quicken (www.quicken.com/canada) to record and monitor their expenses.

Creating a Personal Cash Flow Statement

You can create a personal cash flow statement by recording how you received income over a given period and how you used cash for expenses.

EXAMPLE   Rhea Kennedy tried to limit her spending in college but never established a personal cash flow statement. Now that she has begun her career and is earning a salary, she wants to monitor her spending on a monthly basis. She decides to create a personal cash flow statement for the previous month.

Rhea's Monthly Income. Rhea's present salary is about $1460 biweekly ($37 960 annually) before taxes and payroll deductions. For budgeting purposes, she is interested in the income she receives from her employer after taxes.

About $238 of her biweekly salary goes to pay income taxes. In addition, she pays approximately $66 toward Canada Pension Plan (CPP) and $26 toward Employment Insurance (EI) at each pay period. CPP and EI are discussed in Chapter 4. Rhea's **disposable (after-tax) income** is:

disposable (after-tax) income
Your income minus applicable income taxes and other payroll deductions, such as CPP and EI contributions.

Biweekly Salary		$1460
Biweekly Income Taxes	$(238)	
CPP Contribution	(66)	
EI Contribution	(26)	
Total Payroll Deductions		(330)
Biweekly Disposable (After Tax) Income		$1130
Monthly Disposable (After-Tax) Income ($1130 × 2)		$2260

Rhea calculates her monthly income by multiplying her take-home pay by two. Then she considers other potential sources of income. She does not receive any dividend income from stock, and she does not have any money deposited in an account that pays interest. Thus, her entire monthly income comes from her paycheque. She inserts the monthly income of $2260 at the top of her personal cash flow statement.

Rhea's Monthly Expenses. Rhea logs into her online bank account to see how she spent her money last month. Her household payments for the month were as follows:

- $600 for rent
- $50 for cable TV
- $60 for electricity and water
- $60 for telephone expenses
- $200 for groceries
- $60 for a disability insurance policy

Next, Rhea reviews several credit card bills to estimate her other typical monthly expenses:

- About $100 for clothing
- About $200 for car expenses (insurance, maintenance, and gas)
- About $600 for recreation (including restaurants and a health club membership)

Rhea uses this expense information to complete her personal cash flow statement, as shown in Exhibit 3.1. Her total expenses were $1930 last month.

Rhea's Net Cash Flows. Monthly income and expenses can be compared by estimating **net cash flows**, which is equal to disposable (after-tax) income minus expenses. Rhea estimates her net cash flows to determine how easily she covers her expenses and how much excess cash she can allocate to an emergency fund, investments, or other purposes. Her net cash flows during the last month were:

net cash flows
Disposable (after-tax) income minus expenses.

Net Cash Flows = Income − Expenses

= $2260 − $1930

= $330

Rhea enters this information at the bottom of her personal cash flow statement.

EXHIBIT 3.1   Personal Cash Flow Statement for Rhea Kennedy

Income	Last Month
Disposable (after-tax) income	$2260
Interest on deposits	0
Dividend payments	0
Total Income	**$2260**

Expenses	Last Month
Rent	$ 600
Cable TV	50
Electricity and water	60
Telephone	60
Groceries	200
Disability insurance	60
Clothing	100
Car expenses (insurance, maintenance, and gas)	200
Recreation	600
Total Expenses	**$1930**
Net Cash Flows	**+$ 330**

L.O.2

FACTORS THAT AFFECT CASH FLOWS

To enhance your wealth, you want to maximize your (or your household's) income and minimize expenses. Your income and expenses depend on various factors, as will be described next.

Factors Affecting Income

The key factors that affect your income level are the stage of your career path, your job skills, and the number of income earners in your household.

Stage in Your Career Path. Income is low to moderate for people who are in post-secondary education or just starting a career. Income tends to increase as you gain job experience and progress within your chosen career. The relationship between income and job experience is reinforced by the life stage chart discussed in Chapter 1 (refer back to Exhibit 1.2). Younger people in the early career life stage tend to have lower income than older people who are in their prime earning years. This is because older people tend to have more work experience and are farther along in their career paths.

There are many exceptions to this tendency, however. Some older people switch careers and therefore may be set back on their career path. Other individuals who switch careers from a low-demand industry to a high-demand industry may earn higher income. Many individuals put their careers on hold for several years to raise children and then resume their professional lives.

During the retirement life stage, income from a salary may be discontinued. After retirement, individuals rely on their RRSPs and other retirement benefits, as well as interest or dividend income earned on investments for most of their income. Consequently, retired individuals' income tends to be smaller than it was when they were working. Your retirement income will come from your investments and your retirement plan. The manner in which age commonly affects income is summarized in Exhibit 3.2. Notice that there are three distinct phases.

Type of Job. Income also varies by job type. Jobs that require specialized skills tend to pay much higher salaries than those that require skills that can be obtained very quickly

EXHIBIT 3.2 How Your Income Is Related to Your Age

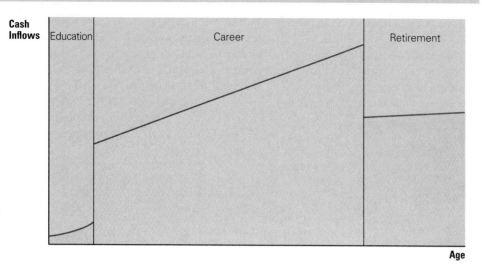

and easily. The income level associated with specific skills is also affected by the demand for those skills. The demand for people with a nursing license has been very high in recent years, so hospitals have been forced to pay higher salaries to attract employees.

Number of Income Earners in Your Household. If you are the sole income earner, your household's income will typically be less than if there is a second income earner. Many households now have two income earners, a trend that has substantially increased the net cash flows to these households.

Factors Affecting Expenses

The key factors that affect expenses are a person's family status, age, and personal consumption behaviour.

Size of Family. A person who is supporting a family will normally incur more expenses than a single person without dependants. The more family members there are, the greater the expenses for food, clothing, daycare, and school tuition.

Age. As people get older, they tend to spend more money on houses, cars, and vacations. This adjustment in spending may result from the increase in their income over time as they progress along their career path. At the end of their career—that is, during their retirement and post-retirement years—people tend to spend less money as they adjust to a decrease in their income and required living expenses.

> **myth** or **fact** The best way to improve your net cash flows is to increase your income.

Personal Consumption Behaviour. People's consumption behaviour varies substantially. At one extreme are people who spend their entire paycheque within a few days of receiving it, regardless of its size. Although this behaviour is understandable for people who have low incomes, it is also a common practice for some people who have very high incomes, perhaps because they do not understand the importance of saving for the future. At the other extreme are "big savers" who minimize their spending and focus on saving for the future. Most people's consumption behaviour is affected by their income. For example, a two-income household tends to spend more money when both income earners are working full time.

CREATING A BUDGET

budget
A cash flow statement that is based on forecasted cash flows (income and expenses) for a future time period.

The next step in the budgeting process is an extension of the personal cash flow statement. You can forecast net cash flows by forecasting the income and expenses for each item on the personal cash flow statement. We refer to a cash flow statement that is based on forecasted cash flows for a future time period as a **budget**. For example, you may develop a budget to determine whether your income will be sufficient to cover your expenses. If you expect your income to exceed your expenses, you can also use the budget to determine the amount of excess cash that you will have available to build an emergency fund, to invest in additional assets, or to make extra payments to reduce your personal debt.

EXAMPLE

Rhea Kennedy wants to determine whether she will have sufficient income this month. She uses the personal cash flow statement she developed last month to forecast this month's cash flows. However, she adjusts that statement for the following additional anticipated expenses:

- Car maintenance expenses will be an additional $600 this month because Rhea has made an appointment to have her brakes replaced.

Rhea revises her personal cash flow statement from last month to reflect the expected changes this month, as shown in Exhibit 3.3. The numbers in boldface show the revised cash flows as a result of the unusual circumstances for this month.

The main effects of the unusual circumstances regarding Rhea's expected cash flows for this month are summarized in Exhibit 3.4. Notice that the expected expenses for this month are $2530, or $600 higher than the expenses in a typical month. In this month, the expected net cash flows are:

$$\text{Expected Net Cash Flows} = \text{Expected Income} - \text{Expected Expenses}$$
$$= \$2260 - \$2530$$
$$= -\$270$$

The budgeting process has alerted Rhea to this $270 cash shortage.

EXHIBIT 3.3 Rhea Kennedy's Revised Personal Cash Flow Statement

Income	Actual Amounts Last Month	Expected Amounts This Month
Disposable (after-tax) income	$2260	$2260
Interest on deposits	0	0
Dividend payments	0	0
Total Income	**$2260**	**$2260**

Expenses	Actual Amounts Last Month	Expected Amounts This Month
Rent	$ 600	$ 600
Cable TV	50	50
Electricity and water	60	60
Telephone	60	60
Groceries	200	200
Disability insurance	60	60
Clothing	100	100
Car expenses (insurance, maintenance, and gas)	200	**800**
Recreation	600	600
Total Expenses	**$1930**	**$2530**
Net Cash Flows	**+$ 330**	**–$ 270**

EXHIBIT 3.4   Summary of Rhea Kennedy's Revised Cash Flows

	Last Month's Cash Flow Situation	Unusual Cash Flows Expected This Month	This Month's Cash Flow Situation
Income	$2260	$ 0	$2260
Expenses	1930	600	2530
Net Cash Flows	$ 330	–$600	–$ 270

FREE APPS for Personal Finance

Managing Your Budget in Real Time

Application:

Use Mint:Personal Finance & Money by Mint Software Inc. to update your budget by entering purchase transactions you just made. Alternatively, you can enter purchases that you are considering in order to assess how those purchases would affect your net cash flows. This allows you to determine whether you have an adequate balance in your account to cover the planned purchases.

Anticipating Cash Shortages

In the example above, Rhea was able to anticipate the expense of having her car's brakes replaced. If she had been able to save her net cash flows of $330 (calculated in Exhibit 3.1) in an emergency fund for a few months prior to having her brakes replaced, Rhea could have covered her cash shortage. If she did not have sufficient money in her emergency fund, she could have temporarily used a line of credit to meet her cash needs. The money management and credit management discussions in Chapters 5 and 6, respectively, will provide you with a better understanding of how to meet short-term liquidity needs. If used consistently over time, the budgeting process can warn you of cash shortages far enough in advance that you can determine how to cover the deficiency. Setting aside funds in a savings account that can serve as an emergency fund in the event of a cash shortage should be a top priority for Rhea.

Assessing the Accuracy of the Budget

Periodically compare your actual income and expenses over a recent period (such as the previous month) to the forecasted income and expenses in your budget to determine whether your forecasts are on target. Many individuals tend to be overly optimistic in their forecasts. They overestimate their income and underestimate their expenses; as a result, their net cash flows are lower than expected. By detecting such forecasting errors, you can take steps to improve your budgeting. You may decide to limit your spending to stay within your budgeted expenses, or you may choose not to adjust your spending habits but to increase your forecast of expenses to reflect reality. By budgeting accurately, you are more likely to detect any future cash flow shortages and therefore can prepare in advance for any deficiencies.

EXAMPLE

Recall that Rhea Kennedy forecasted income and expenses to create a budget for the coming month. Now it is the end of the month, so she can assess whether her forecasts were accurate. Her forecasted income and expenses are shown in the second column of Exhibit 3.5. She compares the actual income and expenses (third column) to her forecast and calculates the difference between them (shown in the fourth column). The difference between columns two and

(continued)

three is referred to as the forecasting error; a positive difference means that the actual income or expense level was less than forecasted, while a negative difference means that the actual income or expense level exceeded the forecast.

While reviewing the fourth column of Exhibit 3.5, Rhea notices that total expenses were $100 more than expected. Her net cash flows were –$370 (a deficiency of $370), which is worse than the expected level of –$270. Rhea assesses the individual expenses to determine where she underestimated. Although grocery expenses were slightly lower than expected, her clothing and recreation expenses were higher than anticipated. She decides that the expenses were abnormally high in this month only, so she believes that her budgeted expenses should be reasonably accurate in most months.

Forecasting Net Cash Flows over Several Months

To forecast your net cash flows for several months, you can follow the same process as for forecasting one month ahead. Whenever particular types of income or expenses are expected to be normal, they can be forecasted from previous months when the levels were normal. You can make adjustments to account for any income or expense amounts that you expect to be unusual in a specific month in the future. (For example, around the winter holidays you can expect to spend more on gifts and recreation.)

Expenses such as prescription drugs, car repairs, and household repairs often occur unexpectedly. Although such expenses are not always predictable, you should budget for them periodically. You should assume that you will likely incur some unexpected expenses for repairs on a car or on household items over the course of several months.

EXHIBIT 3.5   Comparison of Rhea Kennedy's Budgeted and Actual Cash Flows for This Month

Income	Expected Amounts (forecasted at the beginning of the month)	Actual Amounts (determined at the end of the month)	Forecasting Error
Disposable (after-tax) income	$2260	$2260	$ 0
Interest on deposits	0	0	0
Dividend payments	0	0	0
Total Income	**$2260**	**$2260**	**$ 0**

Expenses	Expected Amounts	Actual Amounts	Forecasting Error
Rent	$ 600	$ 600	$ 0
Cable TV	50	50	0
Electricity and water	60	60	0
Telephone	60	60	0
Groceries	200	180	+20
Disability insurance	60	60	0
Clothing	100	170	–70
Car expenses (insurance, maintenance, and gas)	800	800	0
Recreation	600	650	–50
Total Expenses	**$2530**	**$2630**	**–$100**
Net Cash Flows	**–$ 270**	**–$ 370**	**–$100**

Thus, your budget may not be perfectly accurate in any specific month, but it will be reasonably accurate over time. If you do not account for such possible expenses over time, you will likely experience lower net cash flows than expected.

Budgeting with a Biweekly Pay Period

Recall that Rhea is paid biweekly. A biweekly pay period means that she is paid every two weeks. Another way of looking at this is that Rhea will have 26 pay periods during the year. The exhibits above only include 24 pay periods—that is, two pay periods per month for 12 months. Rhea's budgeting method points out an interesting fact about biweekly pay periods. In order to allow for the additional two pay periods under a biweekly structure, an individual will receive an additional paycheque twice a year. During a calendar year, there will be two months during which Rhea will be paid three times. Exhibit 3.6 provides an example of a biweekly pay period schedule for a calendar year (Friday pay dates are in red). This exhibit assumes that the first pay period continues from the end of the previous year until the first pay date of January. As you will notice, May and October contain three pay periods. These extra pay periods provide an ideal opportunity for Rhea to boost her emergency fund or long-term savings plan.

EXHIBIT 3.6 Example of a Bi weekly Pay Period Schedule

January

S	M	T	W	T	F	S
			1	2	3	4
5	6	7	8	9	**10**	11
12	13	14	15	16	17	18
19	20	21	22	23	**24**	25
26	27	28	29	30	31	

February

S	M	T	W	T	F	S
						1
2	3	4	5	6	**7**	8
9	10	11	12	13	14	15
16	17	18	19	20	**21**	22
23	24	25	26	27	28	

March

S	M	T	W	T	F	S
						1
2	3	4	5	6	**7**	8
9	10	11	12	13	14	15
16	17	18	19	20	**21**	22
23	24	25	26	27	28	29
30	31					

April

S	M	T	W	T	F	S
		1	2	3	**4**	5
6	7	8	9	10	11	12
13	14	15	16	17	**18**	19
20	21	22	23	24	25	26
27	28	29	30			

May

S	M	T	W	T	F	S
				1	**2**	3
4	5	6	7	8	9	10
11	12	13	14	15	**16**	17
18	19	20	21	22	23	24
25	26	27	28	29	**30**	31

June

S	M	T	W	T	F	S
1	2	3	4	5	6	7
8	9	10	11	12	**13**	14
15	16	17	18	19	20	21
22	23	24	25	26	**27**	28
29	30					

July

S	M	T	W	T	F	S
		1	2	3	4	5
6	7	8	9	10	**11**	12
13	14	15	16	17	18	19
20	21	22	23	24	**25**	26
27	28	29	30	31		

August

S	M	T	W	T	F	S
					1	2
3	4	5	6	7	**8**	9
10	11	12	13	14	15	16
17	18	19	20	21	**22**	23
24	25	26	27	28	29	30
31						

September

S	M	T	W	T	F	S
	1	2	3	4	**5**	6
7	8	9	10	11	12	13
14	15	16	17	18	**19**	20
21	22	23	24	25	26	27
28	29	30				

October

S	M	T	W	T	F	S
			1	2	**3**	4
5	6	7	8	9	10	11
12	13	14	15	16	**17**	18
19	20	21	22	23	24	25
26	27	28	29	30	**31**	

November

S	M	T	W	T	F	S
						1
2	3	4	5	6	7	8
9	10	11	12	13	**14**	15
16	17	18	19	20	21	22
23	24	25	26	27	**28**	29
30						

December

S	M	T	W	T	F	S
	1	2	3	4	5	6
7	8	9	10	11	**12**	13
14	15	16	17	18	19	20
21	22	23	24	25	**26**	27
28	29	30	31			

Creating an Annual Budget

If you are curious about how much money you may be able to save in the next year, you can extend your budget for longer periods. You should first create an annual budget and then adjust it to reflect anticipated large changes in your cash flows. A large change in cash flows could be due to a change in income and/or expenses. The biweekly bonus discussed above is an example of a change in income. If you pay your car insurance on an annual basis, your car insurance payment is an example of a change in expense.

EXAMPLE

Rhea Kennedy believes that her budget for the previous month (except for the unusual car expense) is typical for her. She wants to extend it to forecast the amount of money she might be able to save over the next year. Her disposable income is predictable because she already knows her salary for the year. Some of the monthly expenses (such as rent and the cable bill) in her monthly budget are also constant from one month to the next. To forecast these types of expenses, she simply multiplies the monthly amount by 12 to derive an estimate of the annual expenses, as shown in the third column of Exhibit 3.7.

Some other items vary from month to month, but last month's budgeted amount seems to be a reasonable estimate for the next 12 months. Over the next 12 months, Rhea expects net cash flows of $3960. As well, Rhea realizes that she will receive an additional $2260 from the two bonus pay periods throughout the year. Therefore, she sets a goal of saving $3960, or $330 per month in an emergency fund, while the $2260 will be put into long-term investments.

EXHIBIT 3.7 Annual Budget for Rhea Kennedy

Income	Typical Month	This Year's Cash Flows (equal to the typical monthly cash flows x 12)
Disposable (after-tax) income	$2260	$27 120
Interest on deposits	0	0
Dividend payments	0	0
Total Income	**$2260**	**$27 120**

Expenses	Typical Month	This Year's Cash Flows
Rent	$ 600	$ 7200
Cable TV	50	600
Electricity and water	60	720
Telephone	60	720
Groceries	200	2400
Disability insurance	60	720
Clothing	100	1200
Car expenses (insurance, maintenance, and gas)	200	2400
Recreation	600	7200
Total Expenses	**1930**	**23 160**
Net Cash Flows	**+$ 330**	**+$ 3960** (difference between income and expenses)

Improving the Budget

As time passes, you should review your budget to determine whether you are progressing toward the financial goals you established. To increase your savings or pay down more debt so that you can more easily achieve your financial goals, you should identify the components within the budget that you can change to improve your financial position over time.

myth or **fact** Personal budgeting is too time-consuming.

EXAMPLE

Recall that Rhea Kennedy expects to spend about $1930 per month and invest her net cash flows in assets (such as a savings account or stocks). She would like to save a substantial amount of money so that she can purchase a new car and a home someday, so she considers how she might increase her net cash flows.

Rhea assesses her personal income statement to determine whether she can increase her income or reduce her expenses. She would like to generate more income than $2260, but she is already paid well, given her skills and experience. She considers pursuing a part-time job on weekends, but does not want to use her limited free time to work. Therefore, she realizes that given her present situation and preferences, she will not be able to increase her monthly income. She decides to reduce her monthly expenses so that she can save more than her current level of net cash flows.

Rhea reviews the summary of expenses on her budget to determine how she can reduce spending. Of the $1930 that she spends per month, about $1330 is spent on what she considers to be necessities (such as her rent and utilities). The remainder of the expenses (about $600) is spent on recreation. Rhea realizes that any major reduction in spending will have to be as a result of a decrease in recreation expenses.

Most of her recreational spending is on her health club membership and eating at restaurants. She recognizes that she can scale back her spending while still enjoying these activities. Specifically, she observes that her health club is overpriced. She can save about $60 per month by joining a different health club that offers essentially the same services. She also decides to reduce her spending at restaurants by about $40 per month. By revising her spending behaviour in these ways, she can reduce her expenses by $100 per month, as summarized here:

	Previous Cash Flow Situation	Planned Cash Flow Situation
Monthly income	$2260	$2260
Monthly expenses	$1930	$1830
Monthly net cash flows	$ 330	$ 430
Yearly net cash flows	$3960 + $2260 = $6220	$5160 + $2260 = $7420

This reduction in spending will increase Rhea's net cash flows. Over the course of a year, her net cash flows will now be $7420. Although Rhea had hoped to find a solution that would improve her personal cash flow statement more substantially, she believes this is a good start. More importantly, her budget is realistic.

Alternative Budgeting Strategies

As mentioned earlier, many individuals tend to be overly optimistic in their budget forecasts. If you find that you have good intentions, but are still unable to anticipate cash shortages or are unable to consistently apply the budget method highlighted above, you might want to try other budgeting methods.

Envelope Method. A common method known as the envelope method forces you to stick to a cash-only budget for some of your expense categories. The expense categories that

Go to
www.themoneybelt.gc.ca/
thecity-lazone/eng/mod2/
mod2-2-eng.aspx

This website provides
a Lifestyle Reality Check to help you see if you can afford the choices you want to make.

you should target for the envelope method are the ones that are the hardest to control, or the ones for which you are able to pay in cash. For Rhea, these might include groceries, clothing, and recreation. For other individuals, the expense categories that are the most difficult to control may be dining out, entertainment, or small day-to-day expenses such as a caramel macchiato at Starbucks. Once you have identified the categories, place the budgeted amount of cash in an envelope. With respect to Exhibit 3.1, Rhea would place $100 in an envelope labelled "Clothing" since this is the amount that she has budgeted for the month for this expense. It is important to create a separate envelope for each category so that you are able to identify spending patterns. During the month, you can spend only the money in the envelope for that particular expense category. If you have any money left over, you can carry forward that balance to the next month. The key to this method is to avoid the temptation to use your debit or credit card for any purchases.

Pay Yourself First Method. The envelope method tries to control the amount of money going out of your bank account after your paycheque comes in. Another popular budgeting method relies on taking money out of your bank account before you have a chance to spend any of it. This is known as the pay yourself first method. Using this method, you would arrange to have an automatic transfer of money from your chequing account to your savings account for the amount that you wish to save. For example, Rhea realizes that she is able to save $330 per month based on her budget. To stop herself from spending this money, she could open a savings account at her bank and set up an automatic transfer for $330 from her chequing to her savings account. The transfer would coincide with when she receives her paycheque. The pay yourself first method differs from the envelope method because it removes net cash flows from your account at the beginning of the budget period. These budgeting strategies can also be used together to further control your net cash flows.

Summary of the Budgeting Steps. The preceding sections described a number of actions that you can undertake to create and improve your budget so that you may realize your goals. The steps below provide a summary of the major concepts that were discussed in the Creating a Budget section.

1. Forecast the income and expenses for each item on the personal cash flow statement. That is, create a budget.

2. Set aside positive net cash flows in an emergency fund and/or maintain a line of credit in order to cover anticipated cash shortages.

3. Assess the accuracy of your budget by comparing your actual income and expenses to your forecasted income and expenses.

4. Forecast your income and expenses for several months into the future.

5. Use any additional income that you may receive—such as when you receive a third biweekly paycheque in a single month—to boost your emergency fund, invest in additional assets, or make extra payments to reduce your personal debt.

6. Create an annual budget to determine how much money you could save in one year.

7. Improve your budget by adjusting any forecasted income and expense categories to reflect reality.

8. Consider ways in which you might increase your net cash flows so that you can save for longer-term goals, such as saving for a car or a home.

9. Consider using a cash-only budgeting method, such as the envelope method, if you are having difficulty anticipating cash shortages or are unable to consistently apply the budget method.

10. Consider taking net cash flows out of your bank account before you have a chance to spend any of it— the pay yourself first method— to remove net cash flows from your account at the beginning of the budgeting period.

FOCUS ON ETHICS: Excessive Financial Dependence

Have you ever been faced with a large unexpected expense that forced you to ask for financial assistance from your family or friends? Perhaps your car broke down and needed some expensive repairs. Or perhaps you saw something that you really wanted to buy, but you knew you could not afford it. If you have not planned for such a large expenditure, you may not have money to pay for it. Faced with a looming debt, it may seem easy to fall back on your family or friends for support. Beware of relying too much on such support, however. When you fail to control your own budget, your reliance on others over long periods of time can create tension and ultimately destroy relationships.

You must become self-reliant. Create a budget and stay within it. Build and maintain an emergency fund so that you do not need to rely on others in times of financial crisis. Before you seek help from family members or friends, ask yourself if you have done all you can on your own. Is your financial crisis an unforeseen emergency or did you spend the money earlier instead of saving it for this expense? Careful budgeting and controlled spending lead to self-reliance and a feeling of financial freedom. You are in control.

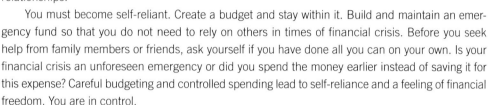

Updating Your Visual Budget

Application:

The Visual Budget app allows you to easily classify your transactions into cash inflows and outflows so that you can have a continually updated balance. It also monitors how you spend your money over time.

PERSONAL BALANCE SHEET

L.O.4

The next step in the budgeting process is to create a personal balance sheet. A budget tracks your cash flows over a given period of time, whereas a personal balance sheet provides an overall snapshot of your wealth at a specific point in time. The **personal balance sheet** summarizes your assets (what you own), your liabilities (what you owe), and your net worth (assets minus liabilities).

Assets

The assets on a balance sheet can be classified as liquid assets, household assets, and investments.

Liquid Assets. **Liquid assets** are financial assets that can be easily converted into cash without a loss in value. They are especially useful for covering upcoming expenses. Some of the more common liquid assets are cash, chequing accounts, and savings accounts. Cash is handy to cover small purchases, while a chequing account is convenient for larger purchases. Savings accounts are desirable because they pay interest on the money that is deposited. For example, if your savings account offers an interest rate of 2 percent, you earn annual interest of $2 for every $100 deposited in your account. The amount of interest you earn will be based on the lowest balance in your account during the month. For example, if you have $500 in an account for 21 days, withdraw $400 for one day and replace it the next day, interest earned for that month will be calculated based on the minimum balance of $100. The management of liquid assets to cover day-to-day transactions is discussed in Part 2.

Go to
www.ic.gc.ca/app/scr/oca-bc/ssc/expense.html?lang=eng

This website provides an estimate of the savings you can accumulate over time if you can reduce your spending on daily or weekly expenses such as a cup of coffee or lunch.

personal balance sheet
A summary of your assets (what you own), your liabilities (what you owe), and your net worth (assets minus liabilities).

liquid assets
Financial assets that can be easily converted into cash without a loss in value.

household assets
Items normally owned by a household, such as a car and furniture.

Household Assets. Household assets include items normally owned by a household, such as a car and furniture. The financial planning involved in purchasing large household assets is also discussed in Part 2. Over time, these items tend to make up a larger proportion of your total assets than do liquid assets.

When creating a personal balance sheet, you need to assess the value of your household assets. The market value of an asset is the amount you would receive if you sold the asset today. For example, if you purchased a car last year for $20 000, the car might have a market value of $14 000 today, meaning that you could sell it to someone else for $14 000. Although establishing the precise market value of some assets may be difficult, you can use recent listing prices of other similar items nearby to obtain a reasonable estimate.

Investments. Some of the more common investments are in stocks, bonds, mutual funds, and rental property.

stocks
Certificates representing partial ownership of a firm.

Stocks are certificates representing partial ownership of a firm. Firms issue stocks to obtain funding for various purposes, such as purchasing new machinery or building new facilities. Many firms have millions of stockholders who own part of the firm.

The investors who purchase stocks are referred to as stockholders or shareholders. You may consider purchasing stocks if you have excess funds. You can sell some of your stock holdings when you need funds. The terms *share* and *shareholder* mean the same as *stock* and *stockholder*, respectively. Another word you may come across is *equity*. If you own shares in a company, you have equity in that company.

The market value of stocks changes daily. You can find the current market value of a stock at many websites, including ca.finance.yahoo.com. Stock investors can earn a return on their investment if the stock's value increases. They can also earn a return if the firm pays dividends to its shareholders.

Investments such as stocks normally are not liquid assets because you will incur a loss if you have to sell your investment at less than you paid for it. Stocks are commonly viewed as a long-term investment and therefore are not used to cover day-to-day expenses. (Stocks will be discussed in detail in Chapter 11.)

bonds
Long-term debt securities issued by government agencies or corporations that are collateralized by assets

Bonds are certificates issued by borrowers (typically, firms and government agencies) to raise funds. When you purchase a $1000 bond that was just issued, you provide a $1000 loan to the issuer of the bond. You earn interest while you hold the bond for a specified period. (Bonds are the subject of Chapter 12.)

mutual funds
Investment companies that sell shares to individuals and invest the proceeds in an overall portfolio of investment instruments such as bonds or stocks.

Mutual funds are investment companies that sell shares to individuals and invest the proceeds in an overall portfolio of investment instruments such as bonds or stocks. They are managed by portfolio managers who decide what securities to purchase so that individual investors do not have to make these investment decisions themselves. The minimum investment varies depending on the particular fund, but it is usually between $500 and $5000. The value of the units of any mutual fund can be found in publications such as *The Globe and Mail* or on various websites. (We'll examine mutual funds in detail in Chapter 13.)

real estate
Principal residence, rental property, and land.

rental property
Housing or commercial property that is rented out to others.

Real estate includes your principal residence and holdings in rental property and land. **Rental property** is housing or commercial property that is rented out to others. Some individuals purchase a second home and rent it out to generate additional income every year. Others purchase apartment complexes for the same reason. Some individuals purchase land as an investment, with an eye to future development.

Liabilities

Liabilities represent personal debts (what you owe) and can be segmented into current liabilities and long-term liabilities.

current liabilities
Personal debts that will be paid in the near future (within a year).

Current Liabilities. **Current liabilities** represent personal debts that will be paid in the near future (within a year). The most common example of a current liability is a credit card balance. Credit card companies send the cardholder a monthly bill that itemizes all purchases made in the previous month. If you pay your balance in full upon receipt of the bill, no interest is charged on the balance. The liability is then eliminated until you receive the next monthly bill. Credit cards deserve special attention when discussing the personal budget.

While they are a convenient source of funds, they also create serious credit problems for many people. Some people use credit cards to purchase products or services that they do not need and cannot afford. There are two psychological forces that cause this behaviour. First, some people make unnecessary purchases with credit cards that they cannot afford to achieve immediate satisfaction and to keep up with their peers. Second, some people are especially willing to spend excessively when using a credit card to make purchases because a credit card avoids the use of cash. That is, they would rather create a current liability (debt) rather than use an asset (cash) to make their purchases. They would feel more pain from using their cash and are more disciplined about how to spend the cash they have. They know that taking $50 out of their wallet to make a purchase will leave $50 less for other cash purchases. Yet when they use a credit card and keep their cash, they feel like they are able to obtain products or services for free. Since the focus of their purchases is on achieving immediate satisfaction by making purchases they cannot afford, they ignore the fact that they will have to pay off the credit card in the future. This type of behaviour tends to result in a large accumulation of current liabilities, which can result in credit problems.

Long-Term Liabilities. Long-term liabilities are debts that will be paid over a period longer than one year. A common long-term liability is a student loan, which reflects debt that a student must pay to a lender over time after graduation. This liability requires you to pay an interest expense periodically. Once you pay off this loan, you eliminate this liability and do not have to pay any more interest expenses. In general, you should limit your liabilities so that you can limit the amount of interest owed.

long-term liabilities
Debt that will be paid over a period longer than one year.

Other common examples of long-term liabilities are car loans and mortgage (housing) loans. Car loans typically have a maturity of between 3 and 5 years, while mortgages typically have a maturity of 15 to 25 years. Both types of loans can be paid off before their maturity.

Net Worth

Your net worth is the difference between what you own and what you owe.

$$\text{Net Worth} = \text{Value of Total Assets} - \text{Value of Total Liabilities}$$

In other words, if you sold enough of your assets to pay off all of your liabilities, your net worth would be the amount of assets you have remaining. Your net worth is a measure of your wealth because it represents what you own after deducting any money that you owe. If your liabilities exceed your assets, your net worth is negative; from another perspective, if you sold all of your assets, you could not cover all of your liabilities. Individuals in this situation may be forced to declare bankruptcy. Students or those in the early career life stage may have a negative net worth. As long as the amounts are reasonable, this may be acceptable. However, those in the latter stages of the life cycle with a negative net worth would have serious financial concerns.

Creating a Personal Balance Sheet

You should create a personal balance sheet to determine your net worth. Update it periodically to monitor how your wealth changes over time.

Rhea Kennedy wants to determine her net worth by creating a personal balance sheet that identifies her assets and liabilities.

EXAMPLE

Rhea's Assets. Rhea owns:

- $500 in cash
- $3500 in her chequing account
- Furniture in her apartment that is worth about $1000
- A car that is worth about $1000
- 100 shares of stock, which does not pay dividends, which she just purchased for $3000 ($30 per share)

(continued)

Rhea uses this information to complete the top of her personal balance sheet, shown in Exhibit 3.8. She classifies each item that she owns as a liquid asset, a household asset, or an investment asset.

Rhea's Liabilities. Rhea owes $2000 on her credit card. She does not have any other liabilities at this time, so she lists the one liability on her personal balance sheet under "Current Liabilities" because she will pay off the debt soon. Since she has no long-term liabilities at this time, her total liabilities are $2000.

Rhea's Net Worth. Rhea determines her net worth as the difference between her total assets and total liabilities. Notice from her personal balance sheet that her total assets are valued at $9000, while her total liabilities are valued at $2000. Thus, her net worth is:

Net Worth = Total Assets − Total Liabilities

$$= \$9000 - \$2000$$

$$= \$7000$$

EXHIBIT 3.8   Rhea Kennedy's Personal Balance Sheet

Assets	
Liquid Assets	
Cash	$ 500
Chequing account	3500
Savings account	0
Total liquid assets	4000
Household Assets	
Home	0
Car	1000
Furniture	1000
Total household assets	2000
Investment assets	
Stocks	3000
Total investment assets	3000
Total Assets	**$9000**
Liabilities and Net Worth	
Current Liabilities	
Credit card balance	$2000
Total current liabilities	2000
Long-Term Liabilities	
Mortgage	0
Car Loan	0
Total long-term liabilities	0
Total Liabilities	**$2000**
Net Worth	**$7000**

Changes in the Personal Balance Sheet

If you earn new income this month but spend it all on products or services that are not personal assets (such as rent, food, and concert tickets), you will not increase your net worth. As you invest in assets, your personal balance sheet will change. In some cases, such as when you purchase a home, your assets increase at the same time that your liabilities increase by taking on a mortgage. In any case, your net worth will not grow unless the increase in the value of your assets exceeds the increase in the value of your liabilities.

Rhea Kennedy is considering purchasing a new car for $20 000. To make the purchase, she would:

■ Trade in her existing car, which has a market value of about $1000.

■ Write a cheque for $3000 as a down payment on the car.

■ Obtain a five-year loan for $16 000 to cover the remaining amount owed to the car dealer.

Her personal balance sheet would be affected as shown in Exhibit 3.9 and explained next.

Change in Rhea's Assets. Rhea's assets would change as follows:

■ Her car would now have a market value of $20 000 instead of $1000.

■ Her chequing account balance would be reduced from $3500 to $500.

Thus, her total assets would increase by $16 000 (her new car would be valued at $19 000 more than her old one, but her chequing account would be reduced by $3000).

Change in Rhea's Liabilities. Rhea's liabilities would also change:

■ She would now have a long-term liability of $16 000 as a result of the car loan.

Therefore, her total liabilities would increase by $16 000 if she purchases the car.

Change in Rhea's Net Worth. If Rhea purchases the car, her net worth would be:

$$\text{Net Worth} = \text{Total Assets} - \text{Total Liabilities}$$
$$= \$25\ 000 - \$18\ 000$$
$$= \$7000$$

Rhea's net worth would remain unchanged as a result of buying the car because her total assets and total liabilities would increase by the same amount.

Rhea's Decision. Because the purchase of a new car will not increase her net worth, she decides not to purchase the car at this time. Still, she is concerned that her old car will require a lot of maintenance in the future, so she will likely buy a car in a few months once she improves her financial position.

EXHIBIT 3.9   Rhea's Personal Balance Sheet if She Buys a New Car

Assets	Present Situation	If She Purchases a New Car
Liquid Assets		
Cash	$ 500	$ 500
Chequing account	3500	500
Savings account	0	0
Total liquid assets	4000	1000
Household Assets		
Home	0	0
Car	1000	20 000
Furniture	1000	1000
Total household assets	2000	21 000
Investment assets		
Stocks	3000	3000
Total investment assets	3000	3000
Total Assets	**$9000**	**$25 000**
Liabilities and Net Worth		
Current Liabilities		
Credit card balance	$2000	$ 2000
Total current liabilities	2000	2000
Long-Term Liabilities		
Mortgage	0	0
Car Loan	0	16 000
Total long-term liabilities	0	16 000
Total Liabilities	**$2000**	**$18 000**
Net Worth	**$7000**	**$ 7000**

EXHIBIT 3.10   How Net Cash Flows Can Be Used to Increase Net Worth

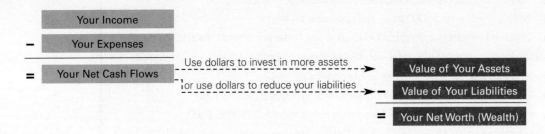

How Cash Flows Affect the Personal Balance Sheet

The relationship between the personal cash flow statement and the personal balance sheet is shown in Exhibit 3.10. This relationship explains how you build wealth (net worth) over time. If you use net cash flows to invest in more assets, you increase the value of your assets without increasing your liabilities. Therefore, you increase your net worth. You can also increase your net worth by using net cash flows to reduce your liabilities. So, the more income that you allocate to savings and investing in assets or to reducing your debt, the more wealth you will build.

Your net worth can change even if your net cash flows are zero. For example, if the market value of your car declines over time, the value of this asset is reduced and your net worth will decline. Conversely, if the value of an investment that you own increases, the value of your assets will rise, and your net worth will increase. This can happen when you purchase stock for $3000 and its market value increases to $4000.

L.O.5

FINANCIAL RATIO CALCULATIONS

The budgeting process helps you to monitor your income and expenses and evaluate your net worth. Financial ratios allow you to analyze your balance sheet and income statement so that you can compare them with a present target or your own previous financial performance. Generally, your purpose in using ratios is to gain a better understanding of how you are managing your financial resources. Financial ratios help you monitor your level of liquidity, your amount of debt, and your ability to save.

Liquidity

Recall that liquidity represents your access to funds to cover any short-term cash deficiencies. You need to monitor your liquidity over time to ensure that you have sufficient funds when they are needed. The current ratio and the liquidity ratio are two ratios that can be used to measure your liquidity. The current ratio is calculated as:

$$\text{Current Ratio} = \text{Liquid Assets/Current Liabilities}$$

A high current ratio indicates a higher degree of liquidity. For example, a current ratio of 3.0 implies that for every dollar of liabilities you will need to pay off in the near future, you have $3 in liquid assets. Thus, you could easily cover your short-term liabilities.

A current ratio of less than 1.0 means that you do not have sufficient liquid assets to cover your upcoming payments. In this case, you might need to borrow funds. In order to cover your short-term liabilities, a current ratio of 2 would be considered adequate. More important than the level of the current ratio is its trend. In other words, is the ratio going up or is it going down? If it is going down, you have to try to find the cause. To do this you have to see what changes have caused the ratio to decrease. One problem with the current ratio is that people generally have a number of monthly expenses that are not considered current liabilities. For example, long-term debt payments such as mortgage payments, car loan payments, and so forth may not be considered current liabilities but still must be paid monthly. Therefore, it is also helpful to calculate the ratio of liquid assets to monthly living expenses. This ratio is called the liquidity ratio, and is calculated as:

$$\text{Liquidity Ratio} = \text{Liquid Assets/Monthly Living Expenses}$$

This ratio tells you how many months of living expenses you can cover with your present level of liquid assets. This ratio is particularly important if you have an emergency, such as a loss of income due to a short-term disability. In general, the liquidity ratio should be between 3.0 and 6.0.

EXAMPLE

Based on the information in her personal cash flow statement, Exhibit 3.1, and her personal balance sheet, Exhibit 3.8, Rhea measures her liquidity:

Current Ratio = Liquid Assets / Current Liabilities

= $4000 / $2000

= 2.0

Liquidity Ratio = Liquid Assets / Monthly Living Expenses

= $4000 / $1930

= 2.1

Rhea's current ratio of 2.0 means that for every dollar of current liabilities, she has $2 of liquid assets. On the other hand, her liquidity ratio of 2.1 means that she can only cover her monthly living expenses for approximately two months if she only relies on her liquid assets. This means that although she has more than enough funds available to cover her current liabilities, she should try to increase the level of her liquid assets and/or decrease her monthly living expenses so that she has an adequate level of liquidity.

Debt Level

You also need to monitor your debt level to ensure that it does not become so high that you are unable to cover your debt payments. A debt level of $20 000 would not be a serious problem for a person with assets of $100 000, but it could be quite serious for someone with hardly any assets. Thus, your debt level should be measured relative to your assets, as shown here:

$$\text{Debt-to-Asset Ratio} = \text{Total Liabilities / Total Assets}$$

A high debt-to-asset ratio indicates an excessive amount of debt. This debt should be reduced over time to avoid any debt repayment problems. An individual's debt-to-asset ratio should be directly related to the financial planning life stages outlined in

Exhibit 1.2 on page 6. The education, early career, and family/mid-career life stages are often characterized by a relatively high debt-to-asset ratio. During those life stages, you may not have adequate resources to own a car without a car loan or purchase a home without a mortgage. As a result of these potential debts, your debt-to-asset ratio will likely be higher than that of someone in the prime earning life stage. Ideally, you should have no debt when you reach the early retirement life stage. A successful financial plan should result in a debt-to-asset ratio that decreases as you pass through the various life stages outlined in Exhibit 1.2. In other words, your level of debt will decrease as you pay off any loans or mortgage debt that you have, and your level of assets should increase as your home and other appreciating assets increase in value. If you feel your debt-to-asset ratio is high, you should review your cash flows to maximize income and minimize expenses.

EXAMPLE

Based on her personal balance sheet, Rhea calculates her debt-to-asset ratio as:

Debt-to-Asset Ratio = Total Liabilities / Total Assets

$$= \$2000 / \$9000$$

$$= 22.22\%$$

This 22.22 percent debt level is not overwhelming. Even if Rhea lost her job, she could still pay off her debt.

Savings Ratio

To determine the proportion of disposable income that you save, you can measure your savings over a particular period in comparison to your disposable income (income after taxes are taken out) using the following formula:

Savings Ratio = Savings during the Period / Disposable Income during the Period

EXAMPLE

Based on her cash flow statement, Rhea earns $2260 in a particular month and expects to have net cash flows of $330 for savings or investments. She calculates her typical savings ratio per month as:

Savings Ratio = Savings during the Period / Disposable Income during the Period

$$= \$330 / \$2260$$

$$= 14.60\%$$

Thus, Rhea saves 14.60 percent of her monthly disposable income. In addition, Rhea will save a total lump sum of $2260 during the months in which there is an extra pay period.

myth or **fact** Everything else being equal, it is better to have a high liquidity ratio than a low debt-to-asset ratio.

EXHIBIT 3.11   Storing Financial Files Checklist

☑ **Tax Records (may be discarded after seven years under normal conditions)**
Tax returns
Paycheques
T4 forms
T4A forms
T5 forms
Charitable contributions
Alimony payments
Medical bills
Property taxes
Any other documentation or tax forms

☑ **Investment Records**
Listing of bank accounts
Bank records and non-tax-related cheques less than a year old
Safety deposit box information
Guaranteed investment certificates
Stock and bond certificates
Collectibles
Stock, bond, and mutual fund transactions
Brokerage statements
Dividends records
Any additional investment documentation

☑ **Retirement and Estate Planning**
Copy of will
Company pension plan documentation
RRSP documentation
Canada Pension Plan information
Any additional retirement documentation

☑ **Personal Planning**
Deed for home if owned
Rental agreement if renting a dwelling
Mortgage
Title insurance policy
Personal balance sheet
Personal income statement
Personal budget
Insurance policies and documentation
Warranties
Receipts for major purchases
Credit card information (account numbers and telephone numbers)
Birth certificates
Powers of attorney
Other personal papers (death certificate(s), alimony, adoption/custody, divorce, military, immigration, etc.)
Any additional personal planning documentation

☑ **Throw Out**
Non-tax-related cheques over a year old
Records from cars and boats you no longer own
Expired insurance policies on which there will be no future claims
Expired warranties
Non-tax-related credit card slips over a year old

Note: Many people keep a copy of their will in a safety deposit box. However, lawyers say that it is better to keep a signed copy with your lawyer.

MyLab Finance   Visit MyLab Finance for additional study and practice tools. Select Financial Planning Problems are available in the Study Plan. Create your own study plan, generate personal cash flow statements and balance sheets, and set personal financial goals.

SUMMARY

L.O.1   Explain how to create your personal cash flow statement

The personal cash flow statement measures your income, your expenses, and their difference (net cash flows) over a specific period. Income results from your salary or from income generated by your investments. Expenses result from your spending.

Your income is primarily affected by the stage in your career path and your type of job. Your expenses are influenced by your family status, age, and personal consumption behaviour. If you develop specialized skills, you

may be able to obtain a job position that increases your income. If you limit your personal consumption, you can limit your spending and therefore reduce your expenses. Either of these actions will increase net cash flows and thus allow you to increase your wealth.

L.O.2   Identify the factors that affect your cash flows

You can forecast net cash flows (and therefore anticipate cash deficiencies) by creating a budget that is based on forecasted income and expenses for an upcoming period.

L.O.3   Explain how to create a budget based on your forecasted cash flows

The budgeting process allows you to control spending. Comparing your forecasted and actual income and expenses will show whether you were able to stay within the budget. By examining the difference between your forecasted and the actual income and expenses you incur, you can determine areas of your budget that may need further control or areas that required less in expenditures than you predicted. This analysis will help you modify your spending in the future or perhaps adjust your future budgets.

L.O.4   Describe how to create your personal balance sheet

The personal balance sheet measures the value of your assets, your liabilities, and your net worth. The assets can be categorized as liquid assets, household assets, and investments. Liabilities can be categorized as current or long-term liabilities. The difference between total assets and total liabilities is net worth, which is a measure of your wealth. The net cash flows on the personal cash flow statement are related to the net worth on the personal balance sheet. When you have positive net cash flows over a period, you can invest that amount in additional assets, which results in an increase in your net worth (or your wealth). Alternatively, you may use the net cash flows to pay off liabilities, which also increases your wealth.

L.O.5   Calculate financial ratios used to analyze personal financial statements

Financial ratios give you a better understanding of how you are managing your financial resources. Your level of liquidity may be monitored by calculating the current ratio and liquidity ratio. Furthermore, your debt level and ability to save may be monitored by calculating your debt-to-assets ratio and savings ratio.

REVIEW QUESTIONS

1. What is a personal cash flow statement? Why is it important?

2. Define income and expenses and identify some sources of each.

3. How are net cash flows determined?

4. What are the factors that affect income?

5. Describe how the stages of your career path affect your net income.

6. What are the factors that affect expenses?

7. What is a budget? What is the purpose of a budget? How can a budget help when you are anticipating cash shortages or cash surpluses?

8. How do you assess the accuracy of your budget? How can finding forecasting errors improve your budget?

9. How should unexpected expenses be handled in your budget? How might these expenses affect your budget for a specific month? Over time?

10. What is the benefit of budgeting with a biweekly pay period?

11. Describe the process of creating an annual budget.

12. Suppose you want to change your budget to increase your savings. What could you do?

13. How do you think people who do not create a budget deal with cash deficiencies? How can this affect their personal relationships?

14. Describe the envelope method. Describe the pay yourself first method. What is the difference between the two?

15. What is a personal balance sheet? What does it provide?

16. Define and describe the three asset categories on the personal balance sheet. Provide an example of each.

17. What are stocks? What are some of the features of a stock?

18. What are bonds? What are some of the features of a bond?

19. What are mutual funds? What are some of the features of a mutual fund?

20. Describe two ways that real estate might provide a return on an investment.

21. Define and describe the two liability categories on the personal balance sheet. Provide an example of each.

22. Describe how the use of credit cards may lead to a large accumulation of current liabilities.

23. What is net worth? How is it a measure of wealth?

24. When does your net worth increase? Will the purchase of additional assets always increase your net worth? Why or why not?

25. What is the current ratio? Is it better to have a high or low current ratio? Explain.

26. What is the liquidity ratio? Is it better to have a high or low liquidity ratio? Explain.

27. What ratio do you use to monitor your debt level? Is it better to have a high or low debt-to-assets ratio? Explain.

28. How do you calculate the savings ratio? What does it indicate?

29. Describe how wealth is built over time. How do your personal cash flow statement and your personal balance sheet assist in building wealth?

FINANCIAL PLANNING PROBLEMS

MyLab Finance Financial Planning Problems marked with a 🌐 can be found in MyLab Finance.

🌐 **1.** Angela earns $2170 per month before taxes in her full-time job and $900 per month before taxes in her part-time job. About $650 per month is needed to pay taxes and other payroll deductions. What is Angela's monthly disposable income?

🌐 **2.** Angela (from Problem 1) inspects her chequebook and credit card bills and determines that she has the following monthly expenses:

Rent	$500
Cable TV	30
Electricity	100
Water	25
Telephone	40
Groceries	400
Car expenses	350
Disability insurance	100
Critical Illness insurance	100
Clothing and personal items	175
Recreation	300

What is Angela's net cash flows?

🌐 **3.** Angela (from problem 1 and 2) makes a budget based on her personal cash flow statement. In two months, she must pay $900 for insurance on her car. How will this payment affect her net cash flows for that month? Suggest ways in which Angela might handle this situation.

🌐 **4.** From the information provided in Problems 1 through 3, how much can Angela expect to save in the next 12 months?

🌐 **5.** Angela analyzes her personal budget and decides that she can reduce her recreational spending by $50 per month. How much will that increase her annual savings? What will her annual savings be now?

🌐 **6.** If Angela is saving $350 per month, what is her savings ratio?

🌐 **7.** A recent car accident has Ali and Nazra Khan concerned about their ability to meet financial emergencies. Help them calculate their current ratio given the following assets and liabilities:

Chequing account	$2000
Savings account	4000
Short-term investments	8000
Utility bills	500
Credit card bills	1000
Auto loan (1 year remaining)	2600

🌐 **8.** Paul is a student. All of Paul's disposable income is used to pay for his post-secondary education expenses. While he has no liabilities (he is on a scholarship), he does have a credit card that he typically uses for emergencies. He and a friend went on a shopping spree in Toronto costing $2000, which Paul charged to his credit card. Paul has $20 in his wallet, but his bank accounts are empty. What is Paul's current ratio? What does this ratio indicate about his financial position?

🌐 **9.** Paul (from Problem 8) has an old TV worth about $100. His other assets total about $150. What is Paul's debt-to-asset ratio? What does this indicate about his financial position?

10. Santos and Cecilia have the following assets:

	Fair Market Value
Condo	$104 000
Car	22 000
Furniture	14 000
Stocks	10 000
Savings account	5 000
Chequing account	1 200
Bonds	15 000
Cash	150
Mutual funds	7 000

What is the value of their liquid assets? What is the value of their household assets? What is the value of their investments?

11. Santos and Cecilia (from problem 10) have the following liabilities:

	Fair Market Value
Mortgage	$81 000
Car loan	2 750
Credit card balance	165
Student loans	15 000
Furniture loan (6 months)	1 200

What are their current liabilities? What are their long-term liabilities? What is their net worth?

🌐 **12.** Based on the information in problems 10 and 11, what is Santos and Cecilia's current ratio? What is their liquidity ratio? What is their debt-to-asset ratio? Comment on each ratio. Assume that the couple incurs monthly living expenses in the amount of $2000 per month.

13. Yasmeen has been saving for the past five years for a European vacation. Her vacation account currently has $5000, and she is ready to book her trip. If she takes the vacation, what impact will it have on her net worth? Should she take the trip?

CHALLENGE QUESTIONS

1. Bill and Ann have the following assets:

Fair Market Value	
Home	$85 000
Cars	22 000
Furniture	14 000
Stocks	10 000
Savings account	5 000
Chequing account	1 200
Bonds	15 000
Cash	150
Mutual funds	7 000
Land	19 000

What is the value of their liquid assets? What is the value of their household assets? What is the value of their investments?

2. Bill and Ann have the following liabilities:

Mortgage	$43 500
Car loan	2 750
Credit card balance	165
Student loans	15 000
Furniture loan (6 months)	1 200

a. What are their current liabilities? What are their long-term liabilities? What is their net worth?

b. Bill and Ann would like to trade in one of their cars, which has a fair market value of $7000, for a new one with a fair market value of $21 500. The dealer will take their car and provide a $14 500 loan for the new car. If they make this deal, what will be the effect on their net worth?

c. What is Bill and Ann's current ratio? What is their debt-to-asset ratio? Comment on each ratio.

ETHICAL DILEMMA

1. Dennis and Nancy are in their early twenties and have been married for three years. They are eager to purchase their first house, but they do not have sufficient money for a down payment. Nancy's Uncle Charley has agreed to lend them the money to purchase a small house. Uncle Charley requests a personal balance sheet and a cash flow statement as well as tax returns for the previous two years to verify their income and their ability to make monthly payments.

For the past two years, Dennis has been working substantial overtime, which has increased his income by more than 25 percent. The cash flow statements for the last two years show that Nancy and Dennis will have no difficulty making the payments Uncle Charley requires. However, Dennis' company has informed its employees that the overtime will not continue in the coming year. Nancy and

Dennis are concerned that if they prepare their personal cash flow statement based on Dennis' base salary, Uncle Charley will not lend them the money because it will show the loan payments can only be made with very strict cost-cutting and financial discipline. Therefore, they elect to present just what Uncle Charley requested, which was the previous two years' personal cash flow statements and tax returns. They decide not to provide any additional information unless he asks for it.

a. Comment on Nancy and Dennis's decision not to provide the information underlying their cash flow statement. What potential problems could result from this decision?

b. Discuss the disadvantages of borrowing money from relatives in general.

FINANCIAL PLANNING ONLINE EXERCISES

1. Go to www.debt101.ca/calculators/the-money-finder-guide and click on "Money-Finder Calculator".

Use the Daily Spending Calculator to identify what weekly total you could save from your present spending habits. You can also customize the list of spending habits to fit your situation. Once you have determined your weekly savings, return to the weblink at the beginning of this question and click on "The Student Loan Whacker". You can complete The Student Loan

Whacker using your personal student loan information. Alternatively, you can use the information provided in the next paragraph. In either case, multiply your weekly savings, that you calculated earlier, by four and enter this number into the "Additional Monthly Payment" box.

Bella Pagtakhan has an outstanding $5000 balance on her student loan. Her annual rate of interest is 5 percent and she is currently making monthly payments of $200. After using the daily spending calculator, she has identified an additional $50 in weekly savings, or $200 per month, that she could apply toward her student loan. If she makes an additional monthly payment of $200, how much interest will she save? How much faster will she pay off this student loan?

2. Go to https://www.rbcroyalbank.com/student/budget-calculator/. Use this calculator to analyze your budget as a full-time student. This calculator is specifically designed to help students understand their expenses and income while attending a university, college, or other full-time educational institution. This calculator allows you to input your expenses and income for the period of time during which you attend school.

a. After school expenses, what are the top three areas of your budget that result in the highest amount of expense?

b. Compare your answers with those of three of your classmates. Is your experience with respect to your expenses similar or different? If different, what could you or your peers learn from how you currently manage your money?

PSYCHOLOGY OF PERSONAL FINANCE: Your Cash Outflows

1. Review your largest cash outflows over the last year and identify your largest expenses (for example, rent, a car loan, and tuition). Were any of your major purchases influenced by psychological forces such as peer pressure? If you could redo last year, would you change any of your major purchases to improve your personal financial situation?

2. Classify all of your spending into categories such as car, rent, school expenses, clothing, and entertainment. Determine the proportion of your cash outflows that are allocated toward each of these categories. Describe the results and explain whether you have any plans to change your consumption pattern.

MINI-CASE 1: Personal Financial Statement Analysis

Hasan Fareed, a 24-year-old college graduate, never took a personal finance class. He pays his bills on time, has managed to save a little in an investment account, and with the help of an inheritance managed to buy a condominium. Hasan worries about his financial situation. Given the following information, prepare a personal cash flow statement and personal balance sheet for Hasan. Also, calculate the current ratio, liquidity ratio, debt-to-assets ratio, and savings ratio associated with Hasan's personal financial statements. Interpret these financial statements and ratios for Hasan. In addition to the list of monthly expenses, assets, and liabilities below, Hasan offers this information:

■ All utility bills for the month are unpaid, and therefore appear as a current liability (phone, cable, electricity, natural gas, water/sewer).

■ Auto and mortgage payments have been paid for the month; note that he lists "mortgage outstanding" and "auto loan outstanding" to indicate the outstanding amount remaining to pay off each loan.

■ "Other expenses, monthly" represents cash spent without a record to verify where.

■ Hasan charges everything on his credit cards and pays the balances off monthly. Credit card bills represent his average monthly balance.

■ Semi-annual auto insurance premium payment is due this month.

List of monthly expenses, assets, and liabilities:

Visa bill	$1355	Water and sewer bill	$ 50
Stocks	5500	Savings account	3100
MasterCard bill	645	Chequing account	1825
Monthly paycheque, net	4700	Auto insurance, semi-annual	450
Mortgage payment, monthly	1030	Residence	265 000
Phone bill	85	Food, monthly	425
Cable bill	42	Auto	9000
Investment account (bank)	1800	Furnishings	5500
RRSP	4500	Mortgage outstanding	202 000
Car payment, monthly	435	Auto loan outstanding	4225
Electricity bill	60	Other personal property	1800
Natural gas bill	70	Other expenses, monthly	350

Study Guide

Circle the correct answer and then check the answers in the back of the book to chart your progress.

Multiple Choice

1. The _____, _____, and _____ are three personal financial statements that provide an overall snapshot of your wealth at a specific point in time, allow you to compare your income and expenses, and provide a forecast of future cash flows, respectively.
   a. personal balance sheet, the personal income statement, a budget
   b. personal balance sheet, the personal cash flow statement, a budget
   c. personal balance sheet, the personal income statement, a net worth report
   d. personal balance sheet, the personal cash flow statement, a net worth report

2. Which of the following transaction methods can be used effectively to monitor your expenses?
   a. Debit card, credit card, chequebook, cash
   b. Debit card, credit card, chequebook
   c. Debit card, credit card, chequebook, receipts
   d. Debit card and credit card

3. Ben's salary is $3000 per month, taxes are $500, fixed expenses are $1500, and savings are $500. His disposable income is:
   a. $1500
   b. $3000

   c. $2500
   d. $500

4. Estimated net cash flows =
   a. Monthly income (after payroll deductions) − Estimated monthly expenses.
   b. Monthly income (before payroll deductions) − Monthly expenses.
   c. Monthly income (after payroll deductions) − Monthly expenses.
   d. Monthly income (after payroll deductions) − Realized monthly expenses.

5. This month Jill received $1000 income from her job and $200 in stock dividends. Her expenses were rent and utilities of $300, $300 on groceries, and $200 on clothing. Which of the following is true?
   a. Jill has a net cash flow of $400.
   b. Jill has net expenses of $400.
   c. Jill has a net cash flow of $200.
   d. Jill has net income of $400.

6. Which of the following situations appears to be the most likely?
   a. A two-income household tends to spend more money when at least one income earner is working part time.

b. A two-income household tends to spend more money when both income earners are working part time.

c. A two-income household tends to spend more money, per capita, than a one-income household.

d. A two-income household tends to spend more money when both income earners are working full time.

7. A budget is a cash flow statement that is based on forecasted cash flows for a future time period. Which of the following may be reasons for developing a budget?
a. To determine whether your income will be sufficient to cover your expenses
b. To determine the amount of excess cash that you will have available to invest in additional assets
c. To determine the amount of extra payments you can make to reduce your personal debt
d. All of the above

8. Which of the following is required in creating a cash flow statement?
a. The values of all assets
b. Value of all liabilities
c. Amounts used for expenses
d. The ideal emergency fund amount

9. Bahni had expected to spend $100 on clothing and $300 on groceries during the month of May. She actually spent $150 on clothing and $275 on groceries. Her forecasting error for clothing was _____; her forecasting error for groceries was _____.
a. +$50, −$25
b. +$50, +$25
c. −$50, −$25
d. −$50, +$25

10. If your budget forecasts a shortfall in cash flow, the best way to use your budget is to:
a. Eliminate all entertainment expenses for that period.
b. Build an emergency fund to prepare for the shortfall.
c. Increase cash flows from all sources not previously recorded.
d. Obtain credit in advance of the predicted shortfall.

11. The assets on a balance sheet can be classified as _____, _____, and _____.
a. current assets, short-term investments, long-term investments
b. current assets, household assets, investments
c. liquid assets, household assets, investments
d. liquid assets, short-term investments, long-term investments

12. Current liabilities include all of the following except:
a. This year's monthly car payments on a three-year loan.
b. The total mortgage on a home.
c. The amount due on a credit card.
d. Next month's payment on a student loan.

13. Which of the following debts would be considered long-term liabilities?
a. Student loans
b. Car loans
c. Mortgages
d. All of the above

14. By analyzing some financial characteristics within your personal balance sheet and cash flow statement, you can monitor your financial health. All else being equal, a _____liquidity ratio combined with a _____debt ratio and a _____savings ratio indicate good financial health.
a. high, low, high
b. low, low, high
c. low, low, low
d. high, high, high

15. Should Shane be concerned about his liquidity ratio of 80 percent?
a. No, he is in good position regarding liquidity.
b. No, this indicates a healthy cash flow.
c. Yes, he may have problems covering upcoming payments.
d. Yes, he may decrease his net worth with too many investments.

True/False

1. True or False? It is important to document every expenditure that you make.

2. True or False? The key factors that influence your level of income are your career path and your job skills.

3. True or False? Most people's consumption behaviour is affected by their income.

4. True or False? The budgeting process will make it more difficult for you to discover any cash shortage you may have in a typical month.

5. True or False? Many individuals tend to be overly pessimistic about their cash flow forecasts.

6. True or False? Your budget may not be perfectly accurate in any specific month, but it will be perfectly accurate over time.

7. True or False? Being paid biweekly means that you will receive 28 paycheques during the year instead of the 24 you would receive if you were paid semi-monthly.

8. True or False? Liquid assets are financial assets that can be converted easily to cash without a loss in value.

9. True or False? Your principal residence is an example of a household asset.

10. True or False? Credit card debt is a type of current liability.

11. True or False? Mortgages typically have a maturity of three to five years.

12. True or False? Your net worth is calculated as the difference between you current assets and current liabilities.

13. True or False? Your net worth can change even if your net cash flows are zero.

14. True or False? The liquidity ratio should be between 3.0 and 6.0.

15. True or False? Ideally, you should have no debt when you reach the late retirement life stage.

Using Tax Concepts for Planning

Rafal Olechowski/Shutterstock

Sam Sharma scrolled down on his smart phone to his tuition fee assessment for the fall semester. Post-secondary education was much more expensive than he thought it would be. Although Sam's parents had put some money away in an RESP, Sam knew that it was not enough to cover the cost of his entire program. Sam realized that he had to be smart with his money and understanding how taxes worked was part of the solution to his problem.

Sam Sharma has been working since he was 16 years old. Now, two years later, he realizes that the time he spent completing an income tax return for the past two years was well worth it. He understood the steps to completing an income tax return. Although he was not sure how they applied to him as a student, he knew that there was a system of deductions and tax credits that would help him reduce the amount of tax he would have to pay on his income. After all, the less he paid in taxes, the more money he would have for tuition fees and books. Sam decided that he would review the income tax and benefit guide published by the Canada Revenue Agency. He wanted to learn about the types of tax deductions and tax credits that would be useful to him while he was in school and once he was finished his program. He also wanted to figure out how he should cover the shortfall in his tuition once his RESP money runs out.

This chapter explains the basics of individual taxation. Knowledge of tax laws can help you to conserve your income, enhance your investments, and protect the transfer of wealth when you die. Whether you are a student or a full-time employee, understanding the taxation of income and wealth is crucial to sound financial planning.

THE LEARNING OBJECTIVES OF THIS CHAPTER ARE TO:

1. Explain the importance of taxes for personal financial planning
2. Explain when you have to file a tax return
3. Outline the steps involved in completing a tax return
4. Describe the major deductions available to a taxpayer
5. Show how tax credits can be used to lower tax payable
6. Describe the difference among tax planning, tax evasion, and tax avoidance
7. Describe tax planning strategies that can be used to reduce tax payable

L.0.1

BACKGROUND ON TAXES

Taxes are an integral part of our economy. They are paid on earned income, consumer purchases, capital assets, and property. Billions of dollars are paid in taxes each year in Canada. These taxes are a significant source of funding for governments and government agencies and are used to pay for a wide variety of government services and programs, including national defence, Canada Health Transfer (CHT) benefits, Canada Social Transfer (CST) benefits, support for the elderly, Employment Insurance (EI), Old Age Security (OAS) benefits, fire and police protection, government employees, road construction and maintenance, and our education systems.

Individuals pay tax at the federal, provincial, and municipal levels. The federal tax system is administered by the Canada Revenue Agency (CRA). While the federal government drafts and revises the *Income Tax Act*, the CRA administers the Act and distributes and collects the forms and publications that taxpayers use to calculate their income tax. The CRA collects taxes on behalf of all provinces and territories with the exception of Quebec, which collects its own provincial taxes. Municipal taxes are collected at the local level. These taxes help to pay for services, such as electricity, water and sewage, garbage collection, public transit, road maintenance, libraries, and police and fire protection.

Taxes Paid on Earned Income

personal income taxes
Taxes imposed on income earned.

Your income is subject to **personal income taxes**, which are taxes imposed on income you earn. Personal income taxes are generally paid as income is earned during the year in a process called withholding. In other words, taxes are withheld (from each paycheque) as income is earned throughout the year. Employees file a form, called a TD1, with their employer, which helps the employer calculate the amount of taxes to withhold. You will complete this form when you start your first job. The TD1 form allows you to specify the personal tax credits for which you qualify. Individuals who qualify for more personal tax credits will have less income tax deducted from their paycheques by their employer. If you are already working, you will have completed this form. It is important to update this form whenever your personal circumstances change, such as when you get married or have a baby. Otherwise, your employer may deduct too little or too much income tax from your paycheque. Individuals can opt to withhold more than the minimum amount from each paycheque, but are not allowed to reduce the amount of withholding below the amount specified by the CRA. Tax money that is withheld is forwarded by your employer to the federal government and held in an account that is credited to you. Self-employed individuals must estimate the amount of taxes payable based on projected earnings, and pay estimated tax instalments quarterly.

For any year that you earn income, you must file a tax return that consists of a completed T1 General Income Tax and Benefit Return (T1 General), plus supporting documents. Your tax return will show whether a sufficient amount of taxes was already withheld from your paycheque, whether you still owe taxes, or whether the government owes you a refund. If you still owe taxes, you should include a cheque for the taxes owed along with your completed T1 General. You could also pay your taxes owing online or through your bank. Tax forms can be downloaded from the CRA website. An example of a completed T1 General is provided in Appendix 4A.

Taxes Paid on Consumer Purchases

Many taxes, such as the goods and services tax (GST), are paid at the time of a transaction. The GST is a sales tax imposed by the federal government in all of the provinces on most goods and services. In contrast, a provincial sales tax (PST) is imposed at the provincial level in most provinces. Some provinces have combined their PST with the GST, thereby introducing a single consumer tax referred to as a harmonized sales tax (HST). The provinces and the rates they levy with respect to the GST, PST, and HST are displayed in Exhibit 4.1. Special taxes, called **excise taxes**, are levied on certain consumer products such as cigarettes, alcohol, and gasoline. Some consider taxes paid on consumer purchases to be extremely fair, as one only pays tax when one consumes. The higher one's income, the higher one's consumption on average will be.

Taxes Paid on Capital Assets

A **capital asset** is any asset that is acquired and held for the purpose of generating income. For example, a winemaker would treat his or her vineyard as a capital asset since the vines are used to produce grapes, which are then processed into wine, which is then sold to generate business income. Generally, tax is paid on these assets when they are sold, gifted, transferred, or inherited. A capital gain arises if the asset is sold at a value greater than its original or adjusted cost. In some cases, the transfer of property may not be immediately subject to a capital gains tax. This often happens in situations where capital assets are

Go to
www.cra-arc.gc.ca/ menu-e.html

This website provides
information about tax rates, guidelines, and deadlines.

excise taxes
Special taxes levied on certain consumer products such as cigarettes, alcohol, and gasoline.

capital asset
Any asset that is acquired and held for the purpose of generating income.

EXHIBIT 4.1   2016 Sales Taxes and Rates in Canadian Provinces and Territories

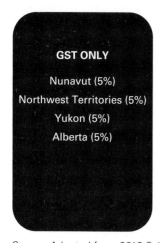

GST ONLY

Nunavut (5%)

Northwest Territories (5%)

Yukon (5%)

Alberta (5%)

GST and PST

British Columbia
(5% and 7%)

Saskatchewan
(5% and 5%)

Manitoba
(5% and 8%)

Quebec
(5% and 9.975%)

HST ONLY

Ontario (13%)

New Brunswick (15%)

Nova Scotia (15%)

Prince Edward Island (15%)

Newfoundland and
Labrador (15%)

Source: Adapted from 2016 Sales Tax Rates in Canadian Provinces and Territories - http://www.taxtips.ca/salestaxes/sales-tax-rates-2016.htm (accessed January 29, 2017).

being transferred to a spouse. If a capital asset has decreased in value, it will generate a capital loss. The concept of capital gains and losses is covered later in this chapter.

> **myth** or **fact** If I do not keep records of my income and investment earnings, the Canada Revenue Agency will be unable to tax me.

Taxes Paid on Property

Homeowners pay property tax on the value of their property. This form of taxation is the major source of revenue for municipal governments. Property taxes are determined based on the assessed value of your property. In order to allocate taxes fairly, a municipality will multiply your assessed property value by a tax rate, also known as a mill rate. The mill rate reflects the amount of taxes that should be paid on property for every $1000 of assessed property value.

FREE APPS for Personal Finance

Sales Tax

Application:

Use the Sales Tax CANADA Calculator by monkeyLabs inc. to calculate Canadian sales taxes for any province or territory in Canada.

L.O.2

DO YOU HAVE TO FILE A RETURN?

It is important to understand the circumstances under which you must file a tax return. You must file a return for a calendar year if any of the following situations apply:

- You have to pay tax for a calendar year
- The CRA sent you a request to file a return
- You and your spouse or common-law partner elected to split pension income for the calendar year
- You received Working Income Tax Benefit (WITB) advance payments in the calendar year
- You disposed of capital property in a calendar year or you realized a taxable capital gain
- You have to repay any of your OAS or EI benefits
- You have not repaid all of the amounts you withdrew from your registered retirement savings plan (RRSP), Home Buyers' Plan (HBP), or Lifelong Learning Plan (LLP)
- You have to contribute to the Canada Pension Plan (CPP)
- You are paying employment insurance premiums on self employment and other eligible earnings.

The WITB is a refundable tax credit intended to provide tax relief for eligible working low-income individuals. OAS is discussed in Chapter 14. **Employment Insurance (EI)** benefits are government benefits that are payable for periods of time when you are away from work due to specific situations. Some examples of situations where EI benefits are payable include a parental leave of absence and a leave of absence as a result of injury, illness, or layoff. The HBP, LLP, and CPP are discussed in Chapter 14.

Generally, you should keep a copy of your tax returns and all supporting documents indefinitely. While many recommend keeping documents for seven years, the government may request earlier documents during audits.

Employment Insurance (EI) Government benefits that are payable for periods of time when you are away from work due to specific situations.

Why Students Should File Tax Returns

Students should file tax returns for a number of reasons. First, you may be eligible for a refundable GST/HST credit. The GST/HST credit is a quarterly tax-free payment made to low- and modest-income earners. Many students would qualify as low- to modest-income earners and would therefore be eligible for the GST/HST credit. You do not have to apply for the GST/HST credit. The CRA will automatically determine your eligibility when you file your next income tax return. To be eligible for this benefit you must meet one of the following criteria:

- You are 19 years of age or older
- You have, or previously had, a spouse or common-law partner
- You are, or previously were, a parent and live, or previously lived, with your child

myth or **fact** Previous years' tax returns can be adjusted for up to seven years.

When filing your return, make sure that you complete the box regarding your marital status (if applicable) located on page 1 of the T1 General. If you have a spouse or common-law partner, only one of you can apply for the credit. Your eligibility will also be affected if you have children who have registered to receive the Canada Child Tax Benefit.

Second, as a student, you likely have eligible tuition tax credits that you can use to reduce your tax payable. If you do not have any tax payable, tax credits earned during that taxation year can be transferred to another taxpayer (a parent or grandparent) or they can be carried forward so that you can claim them in years when you do have tax payable. Filing a return makes the CRA aware that you have these tax credits.

Third, consider that your RRSP contribution room is based on every dollar of income you earn minus pension plan adjustments. By filing a return and declaring income, you will have more room to contribute to your RRSP in the future. Your RRSP is your personal pension plan and it may be in your best interest to maximize your future contributions to it. If you have earned income, filing a tax return increases the amount that you can contribute to an RRSP now or in the future.

Filing Your Return

The tax year for federal income taxes ends on December 31. Individual income tax returns must be filed and taxes must be paid by April 30 of the following year. Self-employed individuals have until June 15 to file their income tax returns, although any taxes owing must be paid by April 30. If a taxpayer does not file his or her tax return on time, interest charges and a late-filing penalty will be assessed based on any amounts owing. If you do not file a tax return and you do not owe any additional taxes, no interest or late-filing penalty is charged. Interest is compounded daily and is calculated based on a prescribed interest rate determined by the CRA. The late-filing penalty amount is 5 percent of the amount owing plus 1 percent for each additional full month that your return is late, to a maximum of 12 months. Late-filing penalties for the current year may be increased if individuals have a history of being assessed a late-filing penalty in previous years.

The CRA allows taxpayers to file tax returns in several ways. First, you can mail hard copies with receipts attached prior to the April 30 deadline (the postmark must be made before midnight). Second, you can file your return by email (NETFILE), in which case you do not have to mail the CRA receipts supporting your deductions and tax credits. The CRA has made it easier for you to find reliable tax preparation software online by listing certified software providers at www.netfile.gc.ca/menu-eng.html. Through this website, you can access income tax preparation software programs that are compatible with the CRA's NETFILE program. Many of these software providers will allow you to use their software at no charge if your income is below a certain amount. Third, you can use EFILE. EFILE is a secure service that lets authorized service providers complete and file your return electronically. Finally, you can auto-fill your return. Auto-fill is a secure CRA service that lets you or your authorized service provider automatically fill in certain parts of your current year return. In order to use this option, you must set up an account with CRA and use a certified software product that offers the auto-fill option. Additional information on sending a tax return can be found at http://www.cra-arc.gc.ca/tx/ndvdls/tpcs/ncm-tx/rtrn/sndng/menu-eng.html.

Once the CRA has processed your return, you will receive a Notice of Assessment from the government. This notice will either confirm your calculations or provide corrections that may result in either additional taxes owing or a larger tax refund. If you are eligible for a refund, a cheque will be attached or the refund will be directly deposited to your bank account. The notice also includes a box outlining your RRSP contribution limits for the following tax year. With respect to maintaining your personal records, you should attach your Notice of Assessment to the copy of your tax return for the same year.

L.O.3

OVERVIEW: COMPLETING AN INCOME TAX RETURN

As shown in Exhibit 4.2, the calculation of income tax requires the completion of eight steps. Step 1 requires you to calculate your total income. Step 2 requires you to determine whether you have any deductions that you can use to reduce your total income. Step 3

EXHIBIT 4.2   Steps to Completing a T1 General Income Tax and Benefit Return

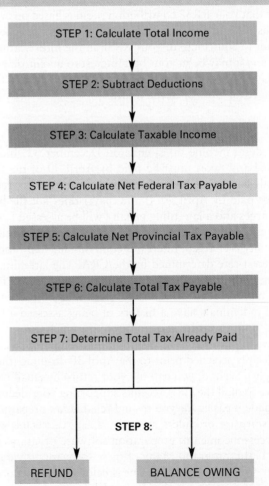

STEP 1: Calculate Total Income

STEP 2: Subtract Deductions

STEP 3: Calculate Taxable Income

STEP 4: Calculate Net Federal Tax Payable

STEP 5: Calculate Net Provincial Tax Payable

STEP 6: Calculate Total Tax Payable

STEP 7: Determine Total Tax Already Paid

STEP 8:

REFUND   BALANCE OWING

requires you to calculate your taxable income after you have taken into account any deductions you have. Your taxable income is then used to determine your federal and provincial tax payable.

In order to calculate your tax payable amounts, you will need to refer to the many supporting documents that the CRA has created. These documents are called Schedules or Forms. Schedule 1 is used to determine your net federal income tax payable. Step 4 requires you to use Schedule 1 to determine the amount of federal tax you owe and to apply any federal non-refundable tax credits for which you are eligible. In Step 5, Form 428 is used to determine your net provincial income tax payable. This form is different for every province.

Step 6 requires you to combine your federal and provincial tax payable. Next, you need to determine the total income tax that has been deducted from your income. Your total income tax deducted can be found on your T4 slip and any other information slips you have received. A **T4 slip** is a document provided to you by your employer that displays your salary and all deductions associated with your employment with that specific employer for the previous year. Exhibit 4.3 provides an example of a T4 slip. Some of the boxes on the T4 slip are discussed throughout the remainder of this chapter. Refer to Exhibit 4.3 whenever necessary. Step 7 requires you to enter the total income tax deducted on your tax return. Your total tax payable, Step 6, minus your tax already paid, Step 7, will determine your refund or balance owing. Determining your refund or balance owing represents Step 8 in completing your T1 General Income Tax and Benefit Return. In order to help you put each of these steps in context, a comprehensive tax example is provided in Appendix 4A.

T4 slip
A document provided to you by your employer that shows your salary and all deductions associated with your employment with that specific employer for the previous year. Your employer is required to provide you with a T4 slip by February 28 each year.

EXHIBIT 4.3   T4 Slip

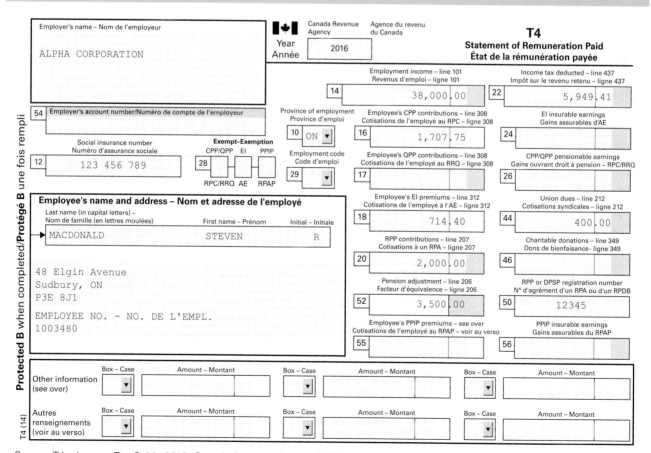

Source: T4 – Income Tax Guide 2016, Canada Revenue Agency (CRA). Retreived from http://www.cra-arc.gc.ca/E/pbg/tf/t4/t4flat-14b.pdf. Reproduced with permission of the Minister of Public Works and Government Services Canada, 2017.

STEP 1: CALCULATE TOTAL INCOME

total income
All reportable income from any source, including salary, wages, commissions, business income, government benefits, pension income, interest income, dividend income, and taxable capital gains received during the tax year. Income received from sources outside Canada is also subject to Canadian income tax.

To calculate your federal income tax, you must first determine your total income. **Total income** consists of all reportable income from any source. Some of the items included in total income are your salary, wages, commissions, some government benefits, pension income, interest income, dividend income, and taxable capital gains received during the tax year. It also includes income from your own business, as well as from tips, prizes and awards, rental property, and various taxable benefits. Examples of taxable benefits include the use of a company automobile, employer-paid education and life insurance, and employer RRSP contributions. Some types of income are not taxed, including GST credits, Canada Child Tax Benefit payments, lottery winnings, most gifts and inheritances, and most life insurance death benefits.

Wages and Salaries

If you work full-time, your main source of total income is probably your salary. Wages and salaries, along with any bonuses, are subject to federal income taxes. The calculation of the federal income tax payable on your salary is discussed later in this chapter. Some benefits are taxable. These will be included on your T4 slip.

myth or **fact** Most students can complete their own tax returns because they have little income and very few deductions.

Self-Employment Income

Self-employment income consists of income from a business, a profession, commissions, farming, or fishing. The issue of whether you are self-employed is not always clear. In general, individuals are considered self-employed if (1) they have control over the work they do, (2) they have taken on the financial risk and reward that comes with being self-employed, (3) their job duties are independent of any employer, and (4) they provide and maintain their own tools and equipment.

interest income
Interest earned from investments in various types of savings accounts at financial institutions; from investments in debt securities such as term deposits, GICs, and CSBs; and from loans to other individuals, companies, and governments.

T5 Statement of Investment Income (slip)
A document provided to you when you receive income other than salary income.

Interest Income

Individuals can earn **interest income** from investments in various types of savings accounts at financial institutions. They can also earn interest income by investing in debt securities such as term deposits, guaranteed investment certificates (GICs), and through loans to other individuals, companies, and governments. You will receive a T5 Statement of Investment Income (slip) from institutions that pay you interest. A **T5 Statement of Investment Income (slip)** is a document provided to you when you receive investment income, including interest income and eligible and non-eligible dividend income. The slip is created by the individual or organization that pays you these other forms of income. Another point to remember is that tax is due on interest income in the year it is earned, not in the year it is received.

EXAMPLE

Shawn Douglas has invested $10 000 in GICs. Shawn's GICs are designed such that any interest he earns is reinvested. By doing this, Shawn hopes to increase his savings more quickly. On average, he will earn 2 percent per year for the next three years on this investment. The table below shows the annual amount of interest Shawn will earn and the total value of his investment at the end of each year. Even though he does not directly receive the interest payments until the end of year 3, Shawn must pay the tax due on the annual interest earned on his investment. For example, at the end of year 1, Shawn will have earned, but not yet received, $200 in interest. He must declare this amount on his income tax return.

Year	Original Investment	Annual Interest Earned	Ending Balance
1	$10 000.00	$200.00	$10 200.00
2	10 200.00	204.00	10 404.00
3	10 404.00	208.08	10 612.08

Dividend Income

Dividend income represents income received from corporations in the form of dividends paid on stock or on mutual funds that hold stock. Dividends are paid to shareholders from the corporation's after-tax earnings. Since the firm has paid corporate income tax prior to the dividend distribution, the federal government has created a dividend adjustment calculation that will reduce the income tax payable by shareholders who receive the dividends. The dividend adjustment, which consists of a dividend gross-up and dividend tax credit, was created to recognize that the federal government has already collected some tax from the corporation and that it would be unfair to collect a regular amount of tax from the taxpayer, as this would constitute double taxation. In general, corporate income taxes in Canada are higher for large public corporations than for Canadian-controlled private corporations (CCPCs). This is because CCPCs are eligible for a small business deduction on their active business income. Dividends paid by large corporations are referred to as eligible dividends whereas dividends paid by CCPCs are referred to as non-eligible dividends.

The distinction between eligible and non-eligible dividends is important. Since large public corporations generally pay more tax than CCPCs, a large corporate shareholder receives an enhanced dividend tax credit. An enhanced dividend tax credit will result in a larger dividend gross-up and dividend tax credit for the shareholder. The dividend gross-up and dividend tax credit applied to non-eligible dividends from a CCPC are lower. This text will focus on eligible dividend income since most investors who receive dividend income will receive it from large corporations. The calculation for eligible dividends is illustrated later in this chapter.

dividend income
Income received from corporations in the form of dividends paid on stock or on mutual funds that hold stock. Dividend income represents the profit due to part owners of the company.

Capital Gains and Losses

As discussed earlier, the sale of a capital asset usually will generate a capital gain or loss. Some financial assets, such as stocks and bonds, are purchased for the purpose of generating dividend or interest income, respectively. You can also invest in other income-producing assets such as rental properties. When you sell these types of assets at a higher price than you paid for them, you earn a **capital gain**. A taxable capital gain represents the portion of a capital gain that is included in total income and, therefore, subject to income tax. A taxable capital gain is currently equal to 50 percent of the capital gain. If you sell a capital asset for a lower price than you paid for it, you sustain a **capital loss**. An allowable capital loss represents the portion of a capital loss that you can deduct from taxable capital gains. An allowable capital loss is currently equal to 50 percent of the capital loss.

capital gain
Money earned when you sell an asset at a higher price than you paid for it.

capital loss
Money lost when you sell an asset at a lower price than you paid for it.

> In 2010, Fatima Hussain sold her shares in TD Bank for a $20 000 capital gain. Her taxable capital gain was equal to $10 000 ($20 000 × 50%). To reduce the amount of capital gain subject to personal income tax, Fatima sold her shares in Bombardier for a $10 000 capital loss. The allowable capital loss of $5000 ($10 000 × 50%) could be used to offset the $10 000 taxable capital gain. As a result, Fatima was able to record a taxable capital gain of $5000 on her T1 General.

EXAMPLE

STEP 2: SUBTRACT DEDUCTIONS

L.O.4

You may be able to claim deductions and exemptions, which reduce the amount of your total income subject to taxation. The discussion below focuses on the more common deductions you will encounter. You can research other potential deductions on the CRA website (www.cra-arc.gc.ca).

Deductions

deduction
An item that can be deducted from total income to determine taxable income.

A **deduction** represents an item that can be deducted from total income to determine taxable income. In general, deductions are allowed for costs you incur that allow you to perform your job duties and/or carry on a business. The more deductions you have, the less tax you will pay. The most common deductions include contributions to a registered pension plan (RPP), contributions to an RRSP, union/professional dues, child care expenses, support payments, carrying charges, moving expenses, and employment expenses.

Registered Pension Plan (RPP). Generally, you can deduct the total of all amounts shown in Box 20 of your T4 slips, in Box 32 of your T4A slips, and on your union or RPP receipts.

Registered Retirement Savings Plan (RRSP). RRSP contributions made by you and/or your employer are deductible in the calculation of net income. The RRSP deduction limit is subject to change every year. Assuming that you or your employer do not contribute to an RPP, the deduction limit for 2017 is the lesser of 18 percent of your 2016 earned income or $26 010.

Union/Professional Dues. The amount of union dues shown in Box 44 of your T4 slip is deductible in the calculation of net income. Professional dues refer to amounts that are paid by you to maintain your status within your area of employment. For example, the professional dues paid by a Certified Financial Planner to maintain his or her CFP designation are deductible, as long as that person is working in the financial planning field.

Child Care Expenses. Child care expenses are deductible if the child was under 16 or had a mental or physical infirmity during the year of your tax return. Generally, only the spouse or common-law partner with the lower net income can claim these expenses. The amount deductible will depend on the income of the lower-income spouse, the age of the child, the reason for the expenses being incurred, and the dollar amount of child care expenses being claimed.

Support Payments. Spousal support payments are deductible in the calculation of net income. Child support payments are deductible if the payments are being made with respect to a court order or written agreement established before May 1, 1997. Child support payments are not deductible if the payments are being made with respect to a court order or written agreement established on or after May 1, 1997.

Carrying Charges. The general rule is that an expenditure paid by a taxpayer to earn income from business or property is deductible from that income. The types of expenses included here are fees for certain investment advice, safety deposit box fees, and interest paid on money borrowed for investment purposes.

Moving Expenses. Moving expenses paid by the taxpayer for the purpose of starting a new job or to attend university, college, or other post-secondary education are deductible. The rule is that the taxpayer must be moving at least 40 kilometres closer to their job or educational institution.

Employment Expenses. You can deduct certain expenses (including any GST/HST) you paid to earn employment income. You can claim the expenses only if your employment contract requires you to pay those expenses and if you did not receive an allowance for the expenses or if the allowance you received is included in your income.

Net Income

net income
The amount remaining after subtracting deductions from your total income.

Taxpayers total their deductions to determine their net income. **Net income** represents the amount remaining after subtracting deductions from your total income. Your net income is used by the federal government to calculate amounts such as the GST/HST credit, whether you have to pay back any of your social benefits, and certain non-refundable tax credits. Social benefits include OAS, Guaranteed Income Supplement (GIS), and EI.

Brenda McDougal reviews the T4 slip that her employer provided to determine what deductions she can take against her total income. Box 20 of her T4 indicates that she has $2000 in RPP contributions. In addition, Box 44 indicates that she has paid $400 in union dues. Brenda has also received a slip from her bank indicating that she has contributed $2000 to her RRSP. Finally, Brenda reviews her bank statement and finds that she has paid $100 for the year to maintain a safety deposit box at her bank. In addition to these deductions, Brenda finds that her employment income, displayed in Box 14 of her T4 slip, is $47 000. Brenda calculates her net income as follows:

Total Income	$47 000
Deductions	
RPP Contributions	2000
RRSP Contributions	2000
Union Dues	400
Safety Deposit Box Fees	100
Total Deductions	$4500
Net Income	$42 500

STEP 3: CALCULATE TAXABLE INCOME

Before calculating the taxes you owe, you need to determine your taxable income. Taxable income is equal to your net income minus some additional deductions. These deductions are more specific than the ones discussed above and often will not apply to the average taxpayer. As a result, they will not be covered in this text. For our purposes, your taxable income will be the same as your net income. You may wonder why the federal government does not simply allow taxpayers to total all of their deductions and determine taxable income without first having to calculate net income. As already discussed, net income serves a different purpose. Net income is used by the government to make adjustments to certain benefits, whereas the calculation of net federal and provincial income tax is based on your taxable income. This system is in place to ensure that all taxpayers are treated fairly with regard to the receipt of social benefits and the calculation of taxes payable.

STEP 4: CALCULATE NET FEDERAL TAX PAYABLE

Once you know your taxable income, you can use the federal tax rates and non-refundable tax credits to determine your federal tax payable. Exhibit 4.4 provides a table that displays the five federal tax brackets. Notice that the income tax system in Canada is progressive. That is, the higher an individual's income, the higher the percentage of income paid in taxes. The federal tax rates displayed in Exhibit 4.4 are known as marginal tax rates. A **marginal tax rate** represents the percentage of tax you pay on your next dollar of taxable income. For example, if you have taxable income of $81 995, you pay 20.5 percent federal tax on the next dollar of taxable income you earn, up to and including $90 563. In contrast, your **average tax rate** represents the amount of tax you pay as a percentage of your total taxable income. To determine this rate, you would divide your tax payable by your taxable income.

marginal tax rate
The percentage of tax you pay on your next dollar of taxable income.

average tax rate
The amount of tax you pay as a percentage of your total taxable income.

EXHIBIT 4.4 Federal 2017 Personal Marginal Income Tax Brackets and Rates

2017 Taxable Income	Tax Rate
First $45 282	15.0%
Over $45 282 up to $90 563	20.5%
Over $90 563 up to $140 388	26.0%
Over $140 388 up to $200 000	29.0%
Over $200 000	33.0%

Source: Federal 2017 Personal Marginal Income Tax Rates - http://www.taxtips.ca/taxrates/canada.htm (accessed January 29, 2017).

L.O.5

TAX CREDITS

tax credits
Specific amounts used directly to reduce tax liability.

refundable tax credit
The portion of the credit that is not needed to reduce your tax liability (because it is already zero) may be paid to you.

non-refundable tax credit
The portion of the credit that is not needed to reduce your tax liability will not be paid to you and cannot be carried forward to reduce your tax liability in the future.

You may be able to reduce your tax liability if you are eligible for tax credits. **Tax credits** are specific amounts used directly to reduce tax liability. Tax credits may be characterized as refundable or non-refundable. With respect to a **refundable tax credit**, the portion of the credit that is not needed to reduce your tax liability (because it is already zero) may be paid to you. The GST/HST credit for low-income individuals, the WITB, and the Ontario Property Tax Credit are examples of refundable tax credits. Overpayments of EI and CPP premiums are also refundable. With a **non-refundable tax credit**, the portion of the credit that is not needed to reduce your tax liability will not be paid to you and cannot be carried forward to reduce your tax liability in the future. Most tax credits are considered non-refundable because they can be used only to reduce your taxes. If the amount of taxes you owe is zero, your tax credits generally will be of no use to you. Non-refundable tax credits that are transferable are covered later in this chapter. Exhibit 4.5 lists the 2017 federal base amounts for the most commonly used non-refundable tax credits. Generally, the base amount is multiplied by the lowest marginal federal tax bracket (15 percent for 2017) to determine the amount of the non-refundable tax credit. For example, the base amount for the basic personal amount tax credit is $11 635 for 2017. The amount of the federal non-refundable tax credit associated with this base amount is $11 635 × 15% = $1745.25. The effect of this tax credit is to reduce your federal taxes payable by $1745.25. The dollar values of the base amounts change every tax year.

It is important to realize that the lowest federal marginal tax bracket is used to calculate the dollar value of the tax credit. By contrast, a tax deduction reduces your tax owing based on your highest marginal tax bracket. Exhibit 4.4 above clearly shows that tax deductions will reduce tax more effectively for taxpayers who have taxable income greater than $45 282 in 2017. For example, if you have taxable income of $46 000, a $1 deduction will result in a tax savings of 20.5 percent on that $1. The higher your marginal tax bracket, the greater the savings you will receive from a tax deduction relative to a tax credit. In general, it is better to have a tax deduction than a tax credit.

Basic Personal Amount. For 2017, the basic personal amount of $11 635 may be claimed by all taxpayers. Essentially, the first $11 635 of taxable income earned by a taxpayer in Canada is tax-free with respect to the federal tax payable.

Spouse or Common-Law Partner Amount. This non-refundable tax credit is available to a taxpayer who supported a spouse or common-law partner in the 2017 tax year. This tax credit is subject to a clawback based on income. A **clawback** is used to reduce (that is, to claw back) a particular government benefit provided to taxpayers who have income that exceeds a certain threshold amount. The idea is that as your income increases, you do not need the full financial assistance that results from tax credits and other government

clawback
Used to reduce (that is, claw back) a particular government benefit provided to taxpayers who have income that exceeds a certain threshold amount.

EXHIBIT 4.5   2017 Federal Base Amounts

Non-Refundable Tax Credit	Federal Base Amount, 2017
Basic personal amount	$11 635
Spousal/common law partner amount	11 635
- Eliminated when spousal/dependent income exceed	11 635
Age amount (65+ years of age)	7225
- Eliminated when income exceeds	84 597
Disability amount	8113
Disability amount supplement for taxpayers under 18 years of age	4732
- Eliminated when child/attendant	7504
Canada caregiver credit - infirm adult dependent relative	6883
- Eliminated when relative's income exceeds	23 046
Pension income amount	2000
Canada employment amount	1177
CPP contributions (employee)	2564.10
EI premiums (excluding Quebec)	836.19
Interest paid on eligible student loans	Amount paid
Tuition amount	Amount paid
Medical expenses amount	Amount paid in excess of 3% of net income of $2268, whichever is less

Source: 2017 Non-Refundable Personal Tax Credits – Base Amounts, excerpts to demonstrate Tax Credit Type. http://www.taxtips.ca/nrcredits/tax-credits-2017-base.htm (accessed November 5, 2017).

benefit programs. In this case, $1 of income reduces the amount by $1. This is referred to as a dollar-for-dollar clawback. The benefit is eliminated once the spouse or common-law partner's income exceeds $11 635.

Age Amount. The age amount may be claimed by a taxpayer who was 65 or older on December 31 of the tax year in question. This tax credit is subject to a clawback based on income. With respect to the age amount, you lose 15 percent of the age amount credit for every dollar of income greater than a certain amount ($36 430 in 2017).

EXAMPLE

Helene Turcotte turned 65 on October 8, 2017. Her taxable income for 2017 was $42 000. Although Helene qualifies for the age amount credit, it will be reduced because her income is above the threshold amount of $36 430. The maximum age amount for 2017 is $7225. Helene qualifies for a reduced age amount calculated as:

$$\$7225 - [(\$42\ 000 - \$36\ 430) \times 0.15]$$
$$= \$7225 - (5570 \times 0.15)$$
$$= \$7225 - \$835.50$$
$$= \$6389.50$$

As a result, Helen will record an age amount of $6389.50 on her Schedule 1 form.

Disability Amount. To claim this amount, you must have had a severe and prolonged impairment in physical or mental functions during the tax year. The current maximum amount you can claim is $8113.

Disability Amount Supplement. If you qualify for the disability amount and you were under 18 at the end of the tax year, you may be able to claim up to an additional $4732 (2017 rate).

Canada Caregiver Amount. You may be eligible to claim a Canada caregiver amount if you provided in-home care to infirm adult dependent relatives. If you qualify, you may be able to claim this credit for more than one dependant. The current maximum amount you can claim is $6883.

Pension Income Amount. You can claim a credit on the first $2000 of eligible pension or annuity income reported on your T1 General.

Canada Employment Amount. Employees are eligible to claim this non-refundable tax credit on their first $1177 of employment income for 2017.

CPP/QPP Contributions. Claim the amount shown in boxes 16 and 17 of your T4 slips. Do not enter more than the maximum amount you can claim for the tax year, which is currently $2564.10 for 2017. This amount is subject to change from time to time.

EI Premiums. Claim the amount shown in Box 18 of your T4 slips. Do not enter more than the maximum amount you can claim for the tax year, which is currently $836.19 for 2017. This amount is subject to change from time to time.

Interest Paid on Your Student Loans. You can claim the amount of interest you paid on a student loan if the loan was made to you under the *Canada Student Loans Act*, the *Canada Student Financial Assistance Act*, or similar provincial or territorial government laws for post-secondary education. You cannot claim interest paid on a student loan that was: 1) taken from a personal loan or line of credit, 2) combined with another kind of loan, or 3) received from another country.

Tuition Amount. You can claim the amount you paid for eligible tuition fees. Beginning in 2017, the federal government eliminated the tax credits associated with education and textbook amounts, both of which used to be a part of the tuition amount tax credit. The elimination of these two credits was not applied equally across all provinces. As such, you will have to refer to the legislation in your province to see how these changes will affect you starting in 2017. As discussed below, amounts claimed for tuition, education, and textbook amounts prior to 2017 may still be carried forward.

Medical Expenses Amount. To qualify for the medical expenses amount, your total medical expenses must be greater than either 3 percent of your net income or $2268, whichever is less.

The non-refundable tax credits discussed above are totalled and entered on Schedule 1. This amount is then multiplied by the lowest federal marginal tax bracket (15 percent in 2017), giving you your total non-refundable tax credits. In general, your net federal tax will be the difference between your tax payable and your non-refundable tax credits. Once you have determined your net federal tax using Schedule 1, you enter this amount on your T1 General.

Transferable Tax Credits

As discussed earlier, most tax credits are non-refundable. That is, if you have reduced your taxes to zero and have not used all of your tax credits, you will not be able to carry forward most tax credits to the following year. However, the tuition amount; the pension income amount; the age amount; and the disability amount can be transferred to other individuals. In the case of the tuition amount, there is a limit as to the maximum amount

Go to
www.cra-arc.gc.ca/E/
pub/tg/p105/README.
html

This website provides detailed tax information for students, such as taxation of the common types of income they earn and the deductions and credits they can use to reduce their taxes payable.

that can be transferred in any year. The age and pension amounts can be transferred only to the taxpayer's spouse. The list of eligible transferees with respect to the other two credits is extensive and generally includes your immediate relatives (parents, grandparents, brothers, sisters, etc.).

Tax Credits Eligible for Carry Forward

Certain tax credits may be carried forward by the taxpayer. These include the medical expenses amount; the tuition amount, and the former tuition, education, and textbook amount, if applicable; and the charitable contribution amount. The charitable contribution amount can be carried forward for a maximum of five years. Tax credits that are carried forward may be used to reduce tax payable in future tax years. It is interesting to note that the tuition amount may be used to reduce tax payable immediately by the taxpayer or a relative of the taxpayer, or it may be used by the taxpayer in future tax years.

John Morris has $3200 in taxes payable for the most recent year. As a student, he is eligible for a number of tax credits, including the basic personal amount, CPP/QPP contributions, EI premiums, and the tuition amount. By using his non-refundable tax credits, John is able to reduce his taxes payable to zero. However, he is not able to use $1500 of the tuition amount that he has available to him. John has two options: he can carry forward the $1500 and apply it against his taxes payable in subsequent years or he can transfer this credit to an eligible transferee, who can then use it to reduce his or her taxable income. Note that because the tax credit was non-refundable, John cannot simply collect the $1500 directly from the CRA.

EXAMPLE

STEP 5: CALCULATE NET PROVINCIAL TAX PAYABLE

Provinces calculate their marginal tax rates as a percentage of net income. This calculation is often referred to as the TONI (tax on net income) system. Under this system, each province has its own set of marginal tax brackets and rates, which are based on the federal tax brackets and rates. Exhibit 4.6 displays the provincial 2014 personal income tax brackets and combined federal and provincial tax rates. As can be seen in the exhibit, the calculation of provincial personal income tax will vary widely from province to province. As discussed earlier, you need Form 428 to determine your net provincial tax payable. The process of completing Form 428 is similar to that used to complete Schedule 1. In fact, the tax credits discussed earlier and listed in Exhibit 4.6 are available in most provinces. For the purposes of this course, a discussion of the tax differences among provinces is not required.

EXHIBIT 4.6 Provincial 2017 Personal Income Tax Brackets and Combined Rates

2017 Taxable Income	Tax Rate
Nunavut	
First $43 780	19.00%
Over $43 780 up to $45 916	22.00%
Over $45 916 up to $87 560	27.50%
Over $87 560 up to $91 831	29.50%
Over $91 831 up to $142 353	35.00%

(continued)

EXHIBIT 4.6   continued

Over $142 353 up to $202 800	40.50%
Over $202 800	44.50%
Northwest Territories	
First $41 585	20.90%
Over $41 585 up to $45 916	23.60%
Over $45 916 up to $83 172	29.10%
Over $83 172 up to $91 831	32.70%
Over $91 831 up to $135 219	38.20%
Over $135 219 up to $142 353	40.05%
Over $142 353 up to $202 800	43.05%
Over $202 800	47.05%
Yukon	
First $45 916	21.40%
Over $45 916 up to $91 831	29.50%
Over $91 831 up to $142 353	36.90%
Over $142 353 up to $202 800	41.80%
Over $202 800 up to $500 000	45.80%
Over $500 000	48.00%
British Columbia	
First $38 898	20.06%
Over $38 898 up to $45 916	22.70%
Over $45 916 up to $77 797	28.20%
Over $77 797 up to $89 320	31.00%
Over $89 320 up to $91 831	32.79%
Over $91 831 up to $108 460	38.29%
Over $108 460 up to $142 353	40.70%
Over $142 353 up to $202 800	43.70%
Over $202 800	47.70%
Alberta	
First $45 916	25.00%
Over $45 916 up to $91 831	30.50%
Over $91 831 up to $126 625	36.00%
Over $126 625 up to $142 353	38.00%
Over $142 353 up to $151 950	41.00%
Over $151 950 up to $202 600	42.00%
Over $202 600 up to $202 800	43.00%
Over $202 800 up to $303 900	47.00%
Over $303 900	48.00%
Saskatchewan	
First $45 225	26.00%
Over $45 225 up to $45 916	28.00%
Over $45 916 up to $91 831	33.50%
Over $91 831 up to $129 214	39.00%
Over $129 214 up to $142 353	41.00%
Over $142 353 up to $202 800	44.00%
Over $202 800	48.00%
Manitoba	
First $31 465	25.80%
Over $31 465 up to $45 916	27.75%

EXHIBIT 4.6   continued

Over $45 916 up to $68 005	33.25%
Over $68 005 up to $91 831	37.90%
Over $91 831 up to $142 353	43.40%
Over $142 353 up to $202 800	46.40%
Over $202,800	50.40%
Ontario	
First $42 201	20.05%
Over $42 201 up to $45 916	24.15%
Over $45 916 up to $74 313	29.65%
Over $74 313 up to $84 404	31.48%
Over $84 404 up to $87 559	33.89%
Over $87 559 up to $91 831	37.91%
Over $91 831 up to $142 353	43.41%
Over $142 353 up to $150 000	46.41%
Over $150 000 up to $202 800	47.97%
Over $202 800 up to $220 000	51.97%
Over $220 000	53.53%
Quebec	
First $42 705	28.53%
Over $42 705 up to $45 916	32.53%
Over $45 916 up to $85 405	37.12%
Over $85 405 up to $91 831	41.12%
Over $91 831 up to $103 915	45.71%
Over $103 915 up to $142 353	47.46%
Over $142 353 up to $202 800	49.97%
Over $202 800	53.31%
New Brunswick	
First $41 059	24.68%
Over $41 059 up to $45 916	29.82%
Over $45 916 up to $82 119	35.32%
Over $82 119 up to $91 831	37.02%
Over $91 831 up to $133 507	42.52%
Over $133 507 up to $142 353	43.84%
Over $142 353 up to $152 100	46.84%
Over $152 100 up to $202 800	49.30%
Over $202 800	53.30%
Nova Scotia	
First $29 590	23.79%
Over $29 590 up to $45 916	29.95%
Over $45 916 up to $59 180	35.45%
Over $59 180 up to $91 831	37.17%
Over $91 831 up to $93 000	42.67%
Over $93 000 up to $142 353	43.50%
Over $142 353 up to $150 000	46.50%
Over $150 000 up to $202 800	50.00%
Over $202 800	54.00%
Prince Edward Island	
First $31 984	24.80%
Over $31 984 up to $45 916	28.80%

(continued)

EXHIBIT 4.6   continued

Over $45 916 up to $63 969	34.30%
Over $63 969 up to $91 831	37.20%
Over $91 831 up to $98 316	42.70%
Over $98 316 up to $142 353	44.37%
Over $142 353 up to $202 800	47.37%
Over $202 800	51.37%
Newfoundland & Labrador	
First $35 851	23.70%
Over $35 851 up to $45 916	29.50%
Over $45 916 up to $71 701	35.00%
Over $71 701 up to $91 831	36.30%
Over $91 831 up to $128 010	41.80%
Over $128 010 up to $142 353	43.30%
Over $142 353 up to $179 214	46.30%
Over $179 214 up to $202 800	47.30%
Over $202 800	51.30%

Source: 2017 Personal Income Tax Rates for Canada and Provinces/Territories for 2017 http://www.taxtips.ca/marginaltaxrates.htm (accessed January 29, 2017).

STEP 6: CALCULATE TOTAL TAX PAYABLE

Calculating total tax payable involves adding together the amount recorded for net federal tax and the amount recorded for provincial or territorial tax.

STEP 7: DETERMINE TOTAL TAX ALREADY PAID

tax planning
Involves activities and transactions that reduce or eliminate tax.

tax avoidance
Occurs when taxpayers legally apply tax law to reduce or eliminate taxes payable in ways that the CRA considers potentially abusive of the spirit of the *Income Tax Act*.

L.O.6

If you are employed by the same company throughout the year and you do not own any other investment assets, the tax you paid in the course of the year can be determined by looking at the amount recorded in Box 22 of your T4 slip. If you are self-employed during the year, any quarterly instalment payments that you made during the year would be the amount of tax you paid. These amounts are entered on your T1 General and then subtracted from your total tax payable.

STEP 8: REFUND OR BALANCE OWING

You will receive a tax refund if the amount of total tax payable is less than the amount of total tax already paid. You will have tax owing if the amount of total tax payable is greater than the amount of total tax already paid.

FOCUS ON ETHICS: Reducing Your Taxes

Do you know anyone who likes to pay taxes? The odds are you do not. Most people dislike paying taxes and put a lot of effort into reducing their tax liability. It is important to distinguish tax planning from tax avoidance and tax evasion. **Tax planning** involves activities and transactions that reduce or eliminate tax. Using deductions and credits for their intended purpose is a legal approach to tax planning. **Tax avoidance** occurs when taxpayers legally apply tax law to reduce or eliminate taxes payable in ways that the CRA considers potentially abusive of the spirit of the *Income Tax Act*. The CRA may challenge any attempt to "bend the rules" in a way that was not intended. **Tax evasion** occurs when taxpayers attempt to deceive the CRA by knowingly reporting less tax payable than what the law obligates them to pay. It can be tempting to report a lower salary than you earned when filing your tax return. Self-employed individuals, for example, may consider doing this. The CRA monitors tax returns to detect underestimated returns, so there is a strong likelihood that it will uncover any illegal behaviour. Attempts to reduce your taxes illegally can subject you to both criminal and civil prosecution.

tax evasion
Occurs when taxpayers attempt to deceive the CRA by knowingly reporting less tax payable than what the law obligates them to pay.

Fortunately, there are many legal ways to reduce your taxes. Organize your records for things such as charitable donations, medical expenses, and rent in a tax planning folder so that you will not overlook potential tax credits and deductions. Prepare your return early in the year, so that you will not make a careless mistake in the rush to meet the April 30 deadline. Make sure that you have included all tax exemptions and deductions you qualify for on your return and that you have not made any miscalculations. You may even seek the advice of an accountant to ensure that you did not overlook any deductible expenses. It is important to save your receipts during the year, as you will need these when you complete your return.

TAX PLANNING STRATEGIES

L.O.7

If you are about to file your taxes, it is generally too late to take steps to lower your tax payable other than to ensure that you include all deductions and credits for which you are eligible. Tax planning is more effective when done in advance of the tax year-end, throughout the tax year. From a student perspective, the key tax planning questions in building your financial plan are:

- What deductions and/or tax credits are currently available to you?
- Are there any sources of income that you can access that will minimize your tax payable?
- What records should you keep?

Because individuals who earn a high level of income can be exposed to higher tax rates, they should consider ways to reduce their tax liability. Strategies that could be used to reduce tax payable include:

- selecting non-registered investments that generate tax advantaged dividend income and capital gain income;
- using registered accounts, such as RESPs, RDSPs, and TFSAs, that generate amounts that will be received tax-free;
- maximizing your RRSP contributions; and
- using tax credits to reduce your taxes payable.

Types of Income

Earlier in this chapter, we differentiated among interest income, dividend income, and capital gains and losses. Recall that interest income is earned on investments such as savings accounts, term deposits, GICs, and CSBs. Dividend income represents income received from corporations in the form of dividends. As has been explained earlier, dividends are classified as eligible or non-eligible. With respect to eligible dividends paid from a large corporation, a dividend adjustment calculation exists so that the amount of income tax payable by eligible dividend-receiving shareholders is reduced to take into account the tax that has already been collected at the corporate level. This dividend adjustment consists of an enhanced dividend gross-up and dividend tax credit. Finally, capital gains or losses are generated from the sale of capital assets. The sale of a capital asset, such as a stock, generates a capital gain if the sale proceeds are greater than the original, or adjusted, cost. Fifty percent of the capital gain is taxable.

EXHIBIT 4.7   2017 Enhanced Dividend Tax Credit Rates as a Percentage of Actual Dividends

Province/Territory	Rate (%)
Nunavut	7.60
Northwest Territories	15.87
Yukon	20.70
British Columbia	13.80
Alberta	13.80
Saskatchewan	15.18
Manitoba	11.04
Ontario	13.80
Quebec	16.42
New Brunswick	16.56
Nova Scotia	12.21
Prince Edward Island	14.49
Newfoundland and Labrador	7.45

Source: 2017 Provincial/Territorial Enhanced Dividend Tax credit Rates. http://www.taxtips.ca/dtc/enhanceddtc/enhanceddtcrates.htm (accessed January 29, 2017).

myth or **fact** Tax preparers are regulated by the Canada Revenue Agency.

In addition to the enhanced federal dividend gross-up and dividend tax credit, there is a parallel system of provincial enhanced dividend tax credits. Exhibit 4.7 outlines the enhanced dividend tax credit, by province, as a percentage of actual dividends paid.

EXAMPLE

Michelle Orobia is a financial planner in Saskatchewan. In order to help show her clients the difference in after-tax income generated by the three types of income, she builds the table below. The table shows the impact on tax payable of $1000 of interest income, eligible dividend income, and capital gain income. With respect to eligible dividends, the enhanced gross-up is 38 percent of the actual dividends paid; the federal and Saskatchewan enhanced dividend tax credits are 20.73 percent and 15.18 percent, respectively, of the actual dividends paid. Assume that Michelle has built the example for an individual who earns $85 000. According to Exhibit 4.6, the combined federal and provincial tax rate in Saskatchewan is 33.5 percent for an individual who earns $85 000. This is composed of 20.5 percent federal tax payable and 13 percent provincial tax payable.

	Interest	Eligible Dividends	Capital Gains
(A) Income Earned	$1000	$1000	$1000
(B) Enhanced Dividend Gross-up (38% of A)	–	380	–
(C) Taxable Portion of Capital Gains (50% of A)	–	–	500
(D) Taxable Income (A + B + C)	1000	1380	500
(E) Federal Tax Payable (20.5% of D)	205	282.90	102.50
(F) Less: Enhanced Dividend Tax Credit (20.73% of A)	–	207.30	–
(G) Total Federal Tax Payable (E − F)	205	75.60	102.50
(H) Provincial Tax Payable (13% of D)	130	179.40	65
(I) Less: Enhanced Dividend Tax Credit (15.18% of A)	–	151.80	–
(J) Total Provincial Tax Payable (H − I)	130	27.60	65
(K) Total Tax Payable (G + J)	335	103.20	167.50
After-Tax Income (A − K)	$ 665	$ 896.80	$ 832.50

Michelle will be able to show her Saskatchewan clients that, for the 2017 taxation year, there is a distinct tax advantage for eligible dividend-earning investments. Before-tax eligible dividends of $1000 will result in an after-tax income of $896.80. In this example, the average tax rate for dividends is 10.32 percent, calculated as [($1000 – $896.80) ÷ $1000] $\times$ 100. In contrast, the average tax rate for $1000 of interest income is 33.5 percent, and the average tax rate for capital gains is 16.75 percent.

Sources of Income

Students can use non-refundable tax credits to reduce the amount of tax they pay on their taxable income. An even better way to eliminate tax payable is to have income that is not subject to tax. Since 2006, students who receive scholarship, bursary, and fellowship income will not have to include these amounts as taxable income. In order to have these amounts exempt from tax, students must first qualify for the education amount tax credit. Furthermore, certain amounts received from a registered education savings plan (RESP) account or a registered disability savings plan (RDSP), and amounts received from a tax-free savings account (TFSA), will be received tax-free.

Registered Education Savings Plan (RESP). Generally, anyone can contribute money to an RESP. Contributors, also known as subscribers, do not receive a tax deduction for the contributions they make. However, the first $2500 of annual RESP contributions will be matched by a 20 percent Canada Education Savings Grant (CESG), to a maximum of $500, from Employment and Social Development Canada (ESDC). If you skip a year of RESP contributions, the CESG can be carried forward one year in any given year. As a result, the maximum CESG may be up to $1000. If your net family income is below a certain amount, you may be eligible for an additional CESG of up to $100 per year; however, the lifetime maximum CESG is $7200 per child. In addition, modest-income families entitled to the National Child Benefit Supplement (NCBS) may be eligible for the Canada Learning Bond (CLB). The CLB provides an initial $500 to children born on or after January 1, 2004, and pays an additional $100 per year, for up to 15 years, for each year families are entitled to the NCBS. There is no annual limit on RESP contributions. The lifetime RESP contribution limit is $50 000.

The taxable amount paid to a beneficiary from an RESP is referred to as an **educational assistance payment (EAP)**. EAPs consist of the CESG, the CLB, and any investment earnings. These amounts are treated as taxable income to the beneficiary — the student. The beneficiary may also receive a refund of contributions. These amounts are tax-free since the subscriber did not receive a tax deduction when they made their contributions. Although EAPs are taxable, students are likely to pay very little in income tax on these amounts once you take into account their non-refundable tax credits and relatively lower incomes. In order to receive EAPs, a student must be enrolled in a qualifying or specified educational program. If a student does not enrol in a qualifying or specified educational program, the CESG and CLB amounts are repaid to HRSDC; and **accumulated income payments (AIPs)** are made to the subscriber. AIPs represent the taxable amount paid to a subscriber from an RESP. AIPs consists of the investment earnings of the RESP. These amounts are subject to regular income tax and an additional tax of 20 percent (12 percent for residents of Quebec). In situations where the beneficiary does not enrol in a qualifying or specified educational program, a refund of contributions may be made to the subscriber or to the beneficiary. An RESP may also provide for payments to be made to a Canadian designated educational institution at any time. For more information on RESPs, go to www.cra-arc.gc.ca/tx/ndvdls/tpcs/resp-reee/menu-eng.html.

educational assistance payment (EAP)
The taxable amount paid to a beneficiary from an RESP.

accumulated income payment (AIP)
The taxable amount paid to a subscriber from an RESP.

Registered Disability Savings Plan (RDSP). A **registered disability savings plan (RDSP)** is a savings plan to help parents and others save for the long-term financial security of a person who is eligible for the disability tax credit. Contributions to an RDSP are not tax

registered disability savings plan (RDSP)
A savings plan to help parents and others save for the long-term financial security of a person who is eligible for the disability tax credit.

deductible. There is no annual maximum contribution limit; however, the lifetime limit is $200 000. Contributions can be made until the end of the year in which the beneficiary turns 59. A Canada disability savings grant and a Canada disability savings bond are payable depending on the beneficiary's family income. Payments received by the beneficiary, or the beneficiary's legal representative, are referred to as disability assistance payments (DAPs). These payments must begin by the end of the year in which the beneficiary turns age 60. The grants, bonds, and investment income earned in the RDSP are taxable; whereas the contributions made are received tax-free.

Tax-Free Savings Account (TFSA). Since 2009, a Canadian resident aged 18 and older can contribute up to $5000 per year in a tax-free savings account. A **tax-free savings account (TFSA)** is a registered investment account that allows you to purchase investments with after-tax dollars, without attracting any tax payable on your investment growth. These contributions are not tax deductible. Students who have extra cash can put money into a TFSA. You do not need to have earned income to contribute to a TFSA. When needed, the contributions and any growth can be withdrawn tax-free. If a student is not able to make the maximum annual contribution of $5500, the contribution room is carried forward. Another big advantage of this savings vehicle is that any money you withdraw will be added back to your contribution room for the following year, thereby allowing you to maintain your average annual contribution limit. The annual TFSA limit is indexed to inflation and rounded to the nearest $500. The TFSA dollar limit from 2009 to 2012, inclusive, was $5000. The limit was increased to $5500 for 2013 and 2014. In 2015, the limit was increased to $10 000, but was subsequently reduced back to $5500 for 2016 and 2017. Students can use the proceeds of a TFSA for whatever purpose they need.

tax-free savings account (TFSA)
A registered investment account that allows you to purchase investments, with after-tax dollars, without attracting any tax payable on your investment growth.

EXAMPLE

Maansi turned 18 in 2008. In August 2009, she opened a TFSA account at her local bank. Maansi had a great summer earning income as a student painter. She decided to put $5000 in her TFSA since she didn't need this money immediately for tuition or living expenses. The TFSA account offered by Maansi's bank paid interest at an annual rate of 2 percent. Over the next year, Maansi would earn $100 in tax-free interest, calculated as $5000 × 2%.

Over the next few years, Maansi's original investment continued to grow at a rate of 2 percent compounded annually. As of February 2017, her investment was only worth $5800 since she had not made any further contributions to her account. Now that she is working full-time and has saved some money, Maansi creates the table below and determines that she can deposit an additional $47 000 in 2017, $41 500 carried forward from 2010 to 2016 and $5500 for 2017.

Year	2010	2011	2012	2013	2014	2015	2016	2017
Limit	$5,000	$5,000	$5,000	$5,500	$5,500	$10,000	$5,500	$5,500
Carry Forward	$5,000	$10,000	$15,000	$20,500	$26,000	$36,000	$41,500	

RRSP Contributions

Of all of the tax deductions discussed earlier in this chapter, the one that most taxpayers will eventually use is RRSP contributions. Recall that a tax deduction reduces your tax owing based on your highest marginal tax bracket. For example, suppose that you live in Manitoba and have an earned income of $39 000. Assume that for the 2017 taxation year, you will make an RRSP contribution of $5000. The effect of this contribution is that it will reduce your income by the amount of your contribution. As a result, your taxable income will decrease from $39 000 to $34 000. As a Manitoban, you are in a 27.75 percent combined provincial/federal tax bracket for the 2017 tax year (see Exhibit 4.6).

By reducing your taxable income, you have saved $1387.50 in tax payable, calculated as $5000 × 27.75%.

Deductions and Tax Credits

As mentioned earlier, moving expenses incurred for the purpose of attending university, college, or another post-secondary educational institution are deductible. For students, these expenses can also be claimed when you are moving back home at the end of an academic year. For example, if you have decided to return home for the summer to work and earn income, you may be eligible to claim your moving expenses. In order to claim this deduction, you must be moving at least 40 kilometres in each direction to and from an educational institution.

Students who have earned enough income will have a tax payable amount on their T1 General. In order to reduce this tax payable, students should try to maximize their non-refundable tax credits. The most likely non-refundable tax credits that will be claimed by a student are the personal amount, the Canada employment amount, the interest paid on eligible student loans, and the tuition amount. Of the credits mentioned here, the tuition amount can be carried forward or transferred, with a maximum limit, to a parent or grandparent who has tax payable for the current taxation year. In addition, you can estimate the amount of your tuition amount tax credit on your TD1 form. This will reduce the amount of tax that your employer deducts from your paycheque. It is important to review the rules regarding tax credits so that you are able to reduce your taxes as much as possible.

Record Keeping

Some actions you can take now will make tax filing easier in the future. For example, if you buy stock within the year but expect to retain it for several years, you should maintain a record of the purchase transaction so that you will be able to calculate the capital gain, or capital loss, when you eventually sell the stock. For students, it is important to note the three non-refundable tax credits that can be carried forward: the medical expenses amount; the tuition amount; and the charitable contribution amount. Medical expenses can be claimed for any 12-month period ending in the taxation year for which you are filing a tax return. As mentioned earlier, charitable contributions can be carried forward for five years. It is important to keep a record of all original receipts related to any of these credits so that you can claim them in later tax filing years and have proof if you are ever audited by the CRA.

While many tax preparers suggest that you retain copies of your completed tax forms along with receipts for a period of seven years, it is advisable to keep completed forms indefinitely. If you are audited by the CRA and an error is found, the government does have the right to review previous years' returns. Keep the files—they will not take up much room.

FREE APPS for Personal Finance

Estimating Your Tax

Application:

Use TurboTax SnapTax by Intuit Inc. to estimate your taxes, and estimate the tax refund that you may be due based on the input (your income, etc.) you provide.

MyLab Finance   Visit MyLab Finance for additional study and practice tools. Select Financial Planning Problems are available in the Study Plan. Create your own study plan, generate personal cash flow statements and balance sheets, and set personal financial goals.

SUMMARY

L.O.1 Explain the importance of taxes for personal financial planning

Taxes are an integral part of our economy in that they are used to pay for a variety of government services and programs. Taxes are paid on earned income, consumer purchases, capital assets, and property. An understanding of the different types of taxes will help you to reduce your tax bill so you can address other financial priorities. Students should file a return to take advantage of various tax credits and to create a record of their income so they can use carry forward credits in the future and/or build contribution room for an RRSP.

L.O.2 Explain when you have to file a tax return

There are several reasons for you to file a tax return, including the possibility that you have outstanding tax to pay and that the CRA asks you to file. Individual income taxes must be filed and paid by April 30 of the year following the tax year.

L.O.3 Outline the steps involved in completing an income tax return

There are eight major steps involved in completing your income tax return. Step 1 is to determine your total income. This information can be found on your T4 slip and other information slips. Total income consists primarily of your salary, commissions, government benefits, pension income, investment income, and various taxable benefits. The remaining steps, in order, are (2) to subtract deductions; to calculate (3) taxable income, (4) net federal tax payable, (5) net provincial tax payable, and (6) total tax payable; (7) to determine total tax already paid; and (8) to calculate the refund or balance owing.

L.O.4 Describe the major deductions available to a taxpayer

The most common deductions include contributions to an RPP, contributions to an RRSP, union/professional dues, child care expenses, support payments, carrying charges, moving expenses, and employment expenses.

L.O.5 Show how tax credits can be used to lower tax payable

After determining your federal tax payable on Schedule 1, you may be eligible to claim certain non-refundable tax credits that can be used to reduce your tax liability. For students, the most common tax credits are the basic personal amount, Canada employment amount, interest paid on student loans, and tuition amount. Certain non-refundable tax credits can be transferred to another individual, while others may be carried forward to future tax years.

L.O.6 Describe the difference among tax planning, tax evasion, and tax avoidance

Tax planning involves activities and transactions that reduce or eliminate tax. Tax evasion is illegal and describes attempts by a taxpayer to deceive the CRA. Tax avoidance refers to situations where taxpayers legally apply tax rules to reduce or eliminate tax payable.

L.O.7 Describe tax planning strategies that can be used to reduce tax payable

Effective tax planning begins by maximizing your tax deductions and using available tax credits. For students, RESPs and TFSAs can be used to minimize the effect of taxes. It is also important to maintain any necessary receipts, forms, and files so that you can take advantage of credits you may not have used while you were in school. Finally, choosing investments that are less exposed to tax and making contributions to your RRSP are effective tax planning tools.

REVIEW QUESTIONS

1. Why do we pay taxes?

2. With respect to taxation, what is the role of the federal government? What is the role of the CRA?

3. Define personal income tax.

4. What is the purpose of the TD1 form? Why is it important?

5. What types of taxes are paid on consumer purchases? Provide some examples of an excise tax.

6. What is a capital asset? Under what circumstances would you incur a capital gain on a capital asset?

7. Which level of government collects property taxes?

8. Under what circumstances do you have to file a tax return?

9. Provide four reasons why students should file a tax return.

10. When does the tax year end? By what date do taxpayers have to file their income tax returns?

11. What is the penalty if you do not pay taxes owing by the due date?

12. Describe the different ways in which a taxpayer may file their tax return.

13. What is the purpose of a Notice of Assessment?

14. What are the eight steps to completing a T1 General?

15. What is a T4 slip?

16. What is total income? List some types of income that are included in total income. What are some types of payments that you might receive that would not be included in total income?

17. In general, under what circumstance is someone considered self-employed?

18. What is interest income? What is the purpose of a T5 slip?

19. What is dividend income? What is the purpose of the dividend adjustment?

20. Describe the distinction between eligible and non-eligible dividends.

21. What is the difference between a capital gain and a capital loss?

22. What are deductions? Describe the most common types of deductions.

23. What is net income? Differentiate between net income and taxable income.

24. What is meant by a progressive tax system? What is the difference between marginal and average tax rates?

25. What is a tax credit? What is the difference between a refundable and non-refundable tax credit?

26. What is the difference between a tax deduction and a tax credit? With respect to reducing the amount of tax paid, which one is more valuable from the taxpayer's perspective?

27. List some examples of refundable and non-refundable tax credits.

28. Under what circumstances can you claim the interest paid on your student loans as a tax credit?

29. Describe the Tuition Amount tax credit.

30. List the non-refundable tax credits that are transferable. List the non-refundable tax credits that may be carried forward.

31. Compare the calculation for net provincial tax payable with the calculation for net federal tax payable.

32. What is the difference between tax avoidance and tax evasion?

33. Explain how different types of income received will make a difference in the amount of tax you pay.

34. What is a registered education savings plan (RESP)? Explain how the Canada Education Savings Grant (CESG) works.

35. What are the differences between an educational assistance payment (EAP) and an accumulated income payment (AIP)?

36. What is the purpose of a registered disability savings plan (RDSP)?

37. What is a tax-free savings account (TFSA)? How can it help to reduce tax payable?

38. What are the major deductions and tax credits that can be used by students to minimize their tax payable?

FINANCIAL PLANNING PROBLEMS

MyLab Finance Financial Planning Problems marked with a 🌐 can be found in MyLab Finance.

1. Harvir purchased a new mountain bike for $429.99 at Canadian Tire. What would be his total purchase price, including GST, if he had made this purchase in Alberta? What would be his total purchase, including GST and PST, if he had made this purchase in Manitoba?

🌐 2. Linda neglected to complete her T1 General in time for the filing deadline of April 30, 2017. This would not be a problem if she did not owe any tax. However, after completing her tax return, she realized that the amount of tax withheld by her employer was not enough to cover the amount of taxes she owed. In fact, Linda owed an additional $2000 of income tax. Linda completed her tax return late and submitted it to the CRA by November 1, 2017. Calculate Linda's income tax penalty. How much will she have to pay in total?

🌐 3. Larry is in the 32 percent combined marginal tax bracket. Last year, he sold stock he had held for nine months for a gain of $1900. How much tax must he pay on this capital gain?

🌐 4. Stuart is in the 35 percent combined tax bracket. Recently, he sold stock for a loss of $20 000. What is Stuart's allowable capital loss?

🌐 5. Jim sold two stocks during the year. The capital gain on the sale of Alpha Corp. stock was $10 000. The capital loss on the sale of Gamma Inc. stock was $8000. What is the taxable capital gain Jim will record for the year?

🌐 6. Freda incurred a $20 000 capital gain during the year. She would like to reduce her capital gain by selling one of two stocks that are currently sitting at a capital loss. She purchased 10 000 shares in Sesame Inc. for $28 each. The shares are currently trading at $21. She also purchased 5000 shares in the Electric Co. for $33 each. These shares are currently trading at $25. Which shares should she sell? How many shares would she need to sell to reduce her taxable capital gain to zero?

 7. Mohammed had total income for the year of $55 000. During the year, he contributed $5000 to an RRSP, $345 toward union dues, $4000 toward child support based on a written agreement established in 2005, and $180 toward a safety deposit box. Calculate his taxable income for the year.

 8. Use the information in Exhibit 4.4 (see page 96) to determine the amount of federal tax payable for each of the following individuals. Non-refundable tax credits are not applicable.

a. Brenda, who has taxable income of $28 000.

b. Earl, who has taxable income of $70 000.

c. Indira, who has taxable income of $200 000.

9. What is the average tax rate for each of the individuals in Problem 8?

10. Daniel has a marginal tax rate of 26%. He suddenly realizes that he neglected to include a $1000 tax deduction. If he now includes this $1000 tax deduction on his tax return, how will this affect his taxes?

11. If Daniel (from problem 11) had forgotten a $1000 tax credit, instead of a $1000 tax deduction, how would his taxes be affected if he were to now include this tax credit on his tax return?

12. Edna qualifies for the age amount; however, she had an earned income of $44 000 in 2017. As a result, her age amount is subject to a clawback of 15 percent for every dollar that her income is greater than the threshold of $36 430. Calculate Edna's age amount credit for 2017.

CHALLENGE QUESTIONS

1. Arene has earned income of $74 000 for the year. In addition, she has capital gain income of $6000 from the sale of some stock and $4500 of eligible dividend income that she received from another corporation in which she is a shareholder. Arene lives in Manitoba. Using the information provided in this chapter, calculate her tax payable for the year. Assume that Arene has no other tax deductions or tax credits for the year.

2. Francisco opened a tax-free savings account (TFSA) in 2015. He contributed $3000 to the account in that year. In January 2016, Francisco withdrew $1500. At the end of 2016, he contributed another $3000 to his TFSA account. What is Francisco's unused TFSA contribution room at the beginning of 2017? Francisco turned 18 in 2012.

ETHICAL DILEMMA

Kristal and Joe have been very active participants in their local real estate market. Two years ago, they completed a real estate deal with their neighbour, Kevin. As a result of the deal, the couple earned a capital gain of $10 000. When the real estate transaction was completed, Kevin had assured the couple that they would receive their money very soon. Unfortunately, two months have passed and Kristal and Joe, who have yet to receive their money, need to complete their tax return. Since they are confident that they will receive their investment gain soon, they decide that the safe thing to do is pay income tax on the $10 000 by reporting it on their tax return.

It is now two years later and the couple has yet to receive their $10 000 capital gain. Kevin has moved to another city. Joe is angry that he paid tax on money he never received.

This year, the couple has earned another $10 000 in capital gains from selling real estate. They decide that in order to make up for what happened two years earlier, they will not report this capital gain on their tax return. If the CRA questions them about this in the future, they feel that they can justify their actions by explaining what happened with Kevin two years ago.

a. Discuss whether you think Kristal and Joe are being ethical in not reporting the $10 000 they received this year.

b. Did the couple do the right thing by reporting the first $10 000 in capital gains on their income tax return two years ago? Explain.

c. Is there anything else the couple could do to clear up their tax mess?

FINANCIAL PLANNING ONLINE EXERCISES

1. Go to http://www.ey.com/ca/en/services/tax/tax-calculators-2017-personal-tax

   a. Using the Personal Tax Calculator for the current year, select your province of residence. Enter a taxable income amount of $50 000. What are the taxes payable? What is the average tax rate?

   b. Compare your province with the amount of taxes payable in other provinces on a taxable income of $50 000. Which province(s) display the lowest taxes payable? Which province(s) display the highest taxes payable?

2. Go to www.knowledgebureau.com/index.php/tools-resources/income-tax-estimator and input the following information:

   Province: Ontario

   Children: None

   Taxpayer/Spouse Age: 18 to 65

   Employment income: $50 000

   Capital gains: $5000

   RRSP deduction: $9000

   a. What is the taxable income? What is the net federal tax? What is the net provincial tax? What is the balance owing?

   b. The federal basic personal amount is $11 635 for 2017. How does this compare to your province? (Change the province at the top of the page to see the impact on the basic personal amount.) Which province(s) display the lowest basic personal amount? Which province(s) display the highest basic personal amount?

   c. Compare the deductions and tax credits on this website with those discussed in the chapter. Are there any differences? How would you incorporate any missing deductions and tax credits into the Income Tax Estimator on this website?

PSYCHOLOGY OF PERSONAL FINANCE: Your Taxes

1. This chapter explains how a portion of your income is withheld throughout the year by your employer, as required by the CRA. You may have some flexibility on how much income can be withheld. A psychological advantage of this so-called "withholding tax" is that the funds are pulled from your income before you receive your paycheque. It is as if that portion of your income was never yours anyway. It may be more painful to receive all the income and then have to pay a portion of the income in taxes later. If you have a choice, would you prefer to have a higher or lower amount of income withheld? Explain your opinion.

2. Read one practical article of how psychology affects behaviour when paying taxes. You can easily retrieve possible articles by doing an online search using the terms "psychology" and "paying taxes". Summarize the main points of the article.

MINI-CASE: Tax Deductions and Tax Credits

Your investment client, Ted Burns, is a 55-year-old service manager for a car dealership. Ted has asked you for advice on preparing his 2017 tax return. Since you do not regularly prepare tax returns, you have referred Ted to a good accountant. However, you will work closely with the accountant on Ted's tax situation. Ted tells you that he received a lump-sum bonus of $15 000 from his employer at the end of 2017. In addition, Ted owns some Canada Savings Bonds on which

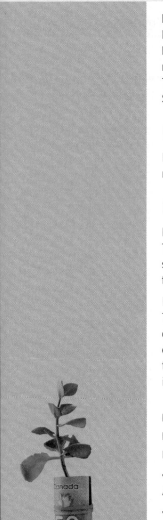

he earned, but did not receive, interest income of $2000 during the 2017 taxation year. Ted has been divorced since 2012. The divorce agreement, which was also reached in 2012, requires him to make annual child and spousal support payments in the amounts of $6000 and $3000, respectively. In addition, Ted pays tuition for his oldest child, who is in her first year of college. Ted's children live with his ex-spouse. Ted rents a safety deposit box at his bank which costs him $120 per year. Ted also made a $5000 RRSP contribution in 2017.

PART A

Indicate whether each of the six items above would increase, decrease, or have no effect on Ted's net income. What would be the total value of this increase or decrease?

PART B

Based on the information provided in the case and in the chapter reading, indicate whether or not Ted likely qualifies for each of the following six non-refundable tax credits: basic personal amount, spousal or common-law partner amount, age amount, CPP contributions, EI premiums, and the tuition amount?

In addition, Ted provided you with a list of unclaimed eligible medical expenses for 2016 and 2017. Ted would like you to help him figure out how to determine which medical expenses he can claim on his 2017 tax return. NOTE: Ted can claim eligible medical expenses in any 12-month period ending in 2017 and not claimed for 2017. As shown in Exhibit 4.5, the amount of the claim is the amount paid in excess of 3 percent of net income or $2268, whichever is less. Ted had a net income of $75 000 in 2017.

Date	Item	Amount
February 2016	Laser eye surgery (one eye)	$1600
March 2016	Dental services (cleaning & x-rays)	250
July 2016	Dental services (fillings)	1200
August 2016	Hearing aid	750
January 2017	Prescription drugs	175
March 2017	Laser eye surgery (one eye)	1600
April 2017	Out-of-country medical services	1400
June 2017	Chiropractic services	800
October 2017	Prescription drugs	450

Study Guide

Circle the correct answer and then check the answers in the back of the book to chart your progress.

Multiple Choice

1. With respect to the federal tax system, the responsibilities of the CRA are:
   a. To draft and revise the *Income Tax Act*.
   b. To administer the *Income Tax Act*, whereas the provincial governments are responsible for distributing and collecting the forms and publications that taxpayers use to calculate their income taxes.
   c. To administer the *Income Tax Act* and distribute and collect the forms and publications that taxpayers use to calculate their income taxes.
   d. To distribute and collect the forms and publications that taxpayers use to calculate their income taxes, whereas the federal government is responsible for the administration of the *Income Tax Act*.

2. Individual income taxes must be filed and paid by ___ of the year following the tax year. Self-employed

individuals have until ___to file their income tax returns and must pay any taxes payable by ___.
   a. April 30, June 15, June 15
   b. April 30, April 30, June 15
   c. April 30, June 15, April 30
   d. June 15, June 15, April 30

3. Canada's taxation rules are called "progressive." This means:
   a. Taxes are deducted from your income and withheld at the source.
   b. Canada's tax system supports progressive social programs.
   c. The higher your income, the higher your tax rate.
   d. Government benefits are clawed back when someone's income exceeds a certain threshold.

4. To be eligible for the GST/HST credit, you must meet which of the following criteria?
   a. You are 19 years of age or older.
   b. You have, or previously had, a spouse or common-law partner.
   c. You are or previously were a parent and live or previously lived with your child.
   d. Any of the above.

5. Even if you have no tax to pay, it is beneficial to file a tax return because:
   a. You can carry forward non-refundable tax credits to future years.
   b. You can get a tax refund for your RSP contributions.
   c. You may be eligible for a tax-free refundable GST/HST credit.
   d. It is required by law, if you are over 18.

6. Which of the following income is taxed at the lowest rate?
   a. Salary
   b. Interest
   c. Capital gains
   d. Tips

7. The list of the most common deductions does NOT include:
   a. Spousal support payments made with respect to a court order made on or after May 1, 1997.
   b. Child support payments made with respect to a court order made on or after May 1, 1997.
   c. Carrying charges.
   d. Contributions to an RPP or RRSP.

8. Which of the following is **not** a legitimate deduction in Canada?
   a. Mortgage interest on your principal residence
   b. Union dues
   c. RRSP contributions
   d. The cost of investment advice

9. For people in the highest marginal tax bracket, which of the following contributions would give them the largest immediate financial benefit?
   a. A $10 000 RRSP contribution
   b. A $10 000 RESP contribution.
   c. A $10 000 TFSA contribution.
   d. These would all be the same.

10. Meg makes RRSP contributions resulting in a tax rebate of $1200 each year. She is in a 30 percent marginal tax bracket. What was the amount of her contribution?
   a. $3000
   b. $4000
   c. $22 222
   d. Unknown

11. Tax credits are used to reduce tax:
   a. When calculating total income.
   b. After taxes payable are calculated.
   c. Before you subtract all deductions.
   d. By deducting them from total income.

12. Alison had a taxable income of $52 000 for the 2017 tax year. Using the information provided in Exhibit 4.4 (see page 96), calculate her federal tax liability and determine her marginal tax rate. (All numbers below have been rounded to the nearest whole number.)
   a. $10 660; 20.5 percent
   b. $7800; 15 percent
   c. $8169; 20.5 percent
   d. $8169; 15 percent

13. With respect to a TFSA, which of the following is true?
   a. Investment growth is taxable.
   b. Withdrawals are added back to your contribution room immediately.
   c. Contributions are tax deductible.
   d. Maximum annual contribution is $5500 in 2017.

14. Which of the following tax credits cannot be carried forward?
   a. Charitable contribution amount.
   b. Tuition amount.
   c. Medical expenses amount.
   d. None of the above; all of these tax credits can be carried forward.

15. For qualified individuals, a contribution to a registered retirement savings plan (RRSP) will be:
   a. A tax credit.
   b. A deduction from total income.
   c. An employment deduction.
   d. A deduction from federal tax payable.

True/False

1. True or False? Employees file a form, called a T4, with their employer, which helps the employer calculate the amount of taxes to withhold.

2. True or False? Generally, higher income individuals will pay more taxes, in the form of GST, PST, HST, and excise taxes on consumer purchases.

3. True or False? If you do not file a tax return by the deadline and you owe taxes, you will be charged 5 percent plus 1 percent for each additional full month that your return is late, to a maximum of six months.

4. True or False? The T1 General is used to determine your net federal income tax payable.

5. True or False? Generally, you should keep your tax returns and all supporting documents for seven years.

6. True or False? Total income consists of all reportable income from any source, including income from prizes and awards.

7. True or False? Capital gains income is always greater than taxable capital gains income.

8. True or False? Moving expenses incurred for the purpose of starting a new job are deductible if you move to within 40 kilometres of your new job location.

9. True or False? The marginal tax rate represents the amount of tax you pay as a percentage of your total taxable income.

10. True or False? The income tax system in Canada is referred to as a progressive tax system because the higher an individual's income, the higher the percentage of income taxes paid.

11. True or False? You can choose to use a refundable tax credit to either reduce your tax liability to zero or have the amount of the credit paid to you.

12. True or False? In general, it is better to have a tax credit than a tax deduction.

13. True or False? You can claim interest paid on a personal loan or line of credit only if the proceeds are used to pay for tuition fees.

14. True or False? Anyone who opens an RESP is eligible to receive the Canada Learning Bond.

15. True or False? Tax avoidance occurs when taxpayers attempt to deceive the CRA by knowingly reporting less tax payable than what the law obligates them to pay.

APPENDIX 4A
Comprehensive Tax Example

STEVEN'S 2016 FEDERAL INCOME TAX RETURN

It is February 28, 2017, and Steven MacDonald is sitting at his kitchen table to complete his tax return for the 2016 calendar year. Steven is aware that his taxes are not due until April 30, but he would like to get a head start since he has all of his information handy.

Steven's employer, Alpha Corporation, has provided him with a T4 slip detailing his employment income, CPP contributions, EI premiums, pension plan contributions, union dues, and income tax deducted. Exhibit 4.1A outlines the information on Steven's T4 slip.

After reviewing the General Income Tax and Benefit Guide – 2016 (http://www.cra-arc.gc.ca/E/pub/tg/5000-g/5000g-16e.pdf), Steven pulls out the four-page T1 General 2016 – Income Tax and Benefit Return. On page 1, Steven completes the identification section by entering his full name and address. He also provides some personal

---

EXHIBIT 4.1A T4 Slip

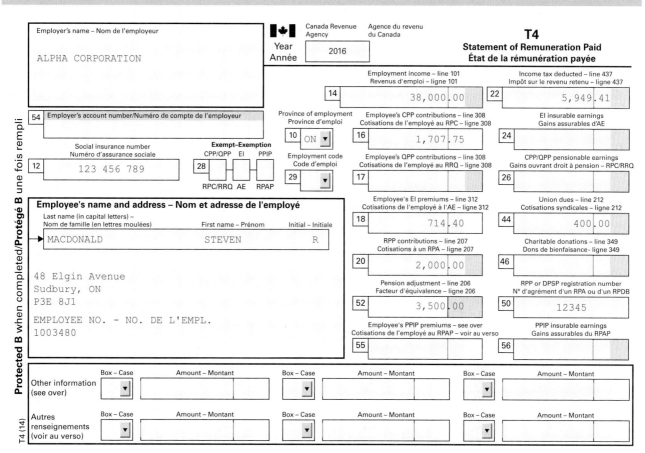

Source: T4 – Income Tax Guide 2016, Canada Revenue Agency (CRA). Retrieved from http://www.cra-arc.gc.ca/E/pbg/tf/t4/t4flat-14b.pdf. Reproduced with permission of the Minister of Public Works and Government Services Canada, 2017.

information in the form of his social insurance number, date of birth, and marital status. Toward the bottom of the page, Steven completes the Elections Canada box and also applies for the GST/HST credit. At the top of page 2, Steven indicates that he does not own or hold foreign property with a total cost of more than $100 000.

With respect to his total income, the only income that Steven earned during the 2016 calendar year was his employment income with Alpha Corporation. This amount is shown in Box 14 of his T4 slip and is recorded on Line 101 of his income tax return.

Steven has a number of deductions available to him. He is able to deduct his RPP contributions, RRSP contributions, union dues, and safety deposit box charges. The RPP contributions and union dues amounts can be found in boxes 20 and 44, respectively of his T4 slip. His bank provided him with an RRSP receipt for his 2013 contribution of $2000. Steven did not make any RRSP contributions in 2016. In addition, Steven was able to determine the amount of his safety deposit box charges by reviewing his bank statements for 2016. He records these amounts on the appropriate lines on page 3 of his return.

As a result of the deductions available to him, Steven was able to reduce his total income by $5000. His taxable income, which he will use to calculate his federal and provincial tax payable, is now $33 000. Exhibit 4.2A displays Steven's completed T1 General Income Tax and Benefit Return.

Calculation of Steven's Federal Tax Payable

Before we move on to discussing the calculation of Steven's tax payable, take a moment to note that it is on page 4 of the T1 General Income Tax and Benefit Return that one records the amount of federal and provincial tax payable. Net federal tax is recorded on Line 420 while provincial tax is recorded on Line 428.

The calculation of federal tax is performed on Schedule 1 – Federal Tax. Steven pulls out the two-page schedule and begins by recording the tax credits he is eligible for on page 1. Exhibit 4.3A displays Steven's completed Schedule 1 – Federal Tax.

Generally, in addition to the basic personal amount, all employees in Canada are eligible to claim a tax credit for CPP contributions, EI premiums, and the Canada employment amount. In addition to these tax credits, Steven is also able to claim a tuition, education, and textbook amount tax credit for a part-time course he took during a four-month period in 2016. Recall that the education and textbook tax credits were not eliminated until after 2016. The course cost him $800 and tuition was not reimbursed by his employer. In order to enter the amount of the credit on Line 323 of page 1 of Schedule 1, Steven must complete Schedule 11 – Tuition, Education, and Textbook Amounts. Exhibit 4.4A displays Steven's completed Schedule 11 – Tuition, Education, and Textbook Amounts. Since Steven completed the course on a part-time basis, he is only eligible to claim the part-time amounts for both education and textbooks. However, the entire $800 cost of the course is covered. Notice that if Steven was not able to use this tax credit to reduce his taxes payable, he would have been eligible to transfer or carry forward the amount of the credit. Once Steven has calculated the amount of this credit on Line 17, this amount is then transferred to Schedule 1, where it is recorded on Line 323.

Steven moves on to page 2 of Schedule 1. On this page, he will calculate the amount of tax payable based on his taxable income and record it on Line 37. The amount of his non-refundable tax credits is recorded on Line 350 and is subtracted from his tax payable. The net result of this calculation is the amount of federal tax that Steven owes. Since Steven has not made any federal political contributions and is not otherwise eligible for any of the other tax credits listed on page 2, the amount of his federal tax will be transferred to Line 420 of his T1 General Income Tax and Benefit Return.

Calculation of Steven's Provincial Tax Payable

As can be seen in Exhibit 4.5A on the following pages, the calculation of provincial tax for a resident of Ontario is fairly similar to the process Steven has just completed for the calculation of federal tax. The provincial tax form is commonly referred to as Form 428.

EXHIBIT 4.2A

Protected **B** when completed

Canada Revenue Agency / Agence du revenu du Canada

T1 GENERAL 2016
Income Tax and Benefit Return

Step 1 – Identification and other information

ON 8

Identification

Print your name and address below.

First name and initial
Steven R

Last name
MacDonald

Mailing address: Apt No – Street No Street name
48 Elgin Avenue

PO Box	RR

City	Prov./Terr.	Postal Code
Sudbury	O N	P 3 E 8 J 1

Email address

I understand that by providing an email address, I am **registering** for online mail. I **have read** and I **accept the terms and conditions** on page 17 of the guide.

Enter an email address:

Information about your residence

Enter your province or territory of residence on **December 31, 2016**:   **Ontario**

Enter the province or territory where you **currently** reside if it is not the same as your mailing address above:

If you were self-employed in 2016, enter the province or territory of self-employment:

If you **became** or **ceased** to be a **resident of Canada** for income tax purposes **in 2016**, enter the date of:

	Month Day		Month Day
entry		or **departure**	

Information about you

Enter your social insurance number (SIN):   1 2 3 4 5 6 7 8 9

	Year	Month	Day
Enter your date of birth:	1 9 8 5	0 6	2 1

Your language of correspondence: English ✓   Français ☐
Votre langue de correspondance :

Is this return for a deceased person?

If this **return** is for a **deceased person**, enter the date of death: Year   Month   Day

Marital status

Tick the box that applies to your marital status on December 31, 2016:

1 ☐ Married   2 ☐ Living common-law   3 ☐ Widowed

4 ☐ Divorced   5 ☐ Separated   6 ✓ Single

Information about your spouse or common-law partner (if you ticked box 1 or 2 above)

Enter his or her SIN:

Enter his or her first name:

Enter his or her net income for 2016 to claim certain credits:

Enter the amount of universal child care benefit (UCCB) from line 117 of his or her return:

Enter the amount of UCCB repayment from line 213 of his or her return:

Tick this box if he or she was self-employed in 2016:   1 ☐

Do not use this area

Elections Canada (For more information, see page 19 in the guide.)

A) Do you have Canadian citizenship? .... Yes ✓ 1   No ☐ 2

Answer the following question **only if you are a Canadian citizenship.**

B) As a Canadian citizen, do you authorize the Canada Revenue Agency to give your name, address, date of birth, and citizenship to Elections Canada to update the National Register of Electors? .... Yes ✓ 1   No ☐ 2

Your authorization is valid until you file your next tax return. Your information will only be used for purposes permitted under the *Canada Elections Act,* which include sharing the information with provincial/territorial election agencies, members of Parliament, and registered political parties, and candidates at election time.

Do not use this area	172				171					

5006-R

(continued)

EXHIBIT 4.2A continued

Protected B when completed **2**

Step 1 – Identification and other information (continued)

Please answer the following question:

Did you own or hold specified foreign property where the total cost amount of all such property,
at any time in 2016, was more than CAN$100,000?
See "Specified foreign property" in the guide for more information . . . . **266** Yes ☐ 1   No ☑ 2

If yes, complete Form T1135 and attach it to your return.

If you had dealings with a non-resident trust or corporation in 2016, see "Other foreign property" in the guide.

Step 2 – Total income

As a resident of Canada, you have to report your income from all sources both inside and outside Canada.
When you come to a line on the return that applies to you, go to the line number in the guide for more information.

Employment income (box 14 of all T4 slips)			**101**	38,000 00
Commissions included on line 101 (box 42 of all T4 slips)	**102**			
Wage loss replacement contributions (see line 101 in the guide)	**103**			
Other employment income			**104** +	
Old age security pension (box 18 of the T4A(OAS) slip)			**113** +	
CPP or QPP benefits (box 20 of the T4A(P) slip)			**114** +	
Disability benefits included on line 114 (box 16 of the T4A(P) slip)	**152**			
Other pensions and superannuation			**115** +	
Elected split-pension amount (**attach** Form T1032)			**116** +	
Universal child care benefit (UCCB)			**117** +	
UCCB amount designated to a dependant	**185**			
Employment insurance and other benefits (box 14 of the T4E slip)			**119** +	
Taxable amount of dividends (eligible **and** other than eligible) from taxable Canadian corporations (**attach** Schedule 4)			**120** +	
Taxable amount of dividends other than eligible dividends, included on line 120, from taxable Canadian corporations	**180**			
Interest and other investment income (**attach** Schedule 4)			**121** +	
Net partnership income: limited or non-active partners only			**122** +	
Registered disability savings plan income			**125** +	
Rental income Gross **160**		Net	**126** +	
Taxable capital gains (**attach** Schedule 3)			**127** +	
Support payments received Total **156**		Taxable amount	**128** +	
RRSP income (from all T4RSP slips)			**129** +	
Other income Specify:			**130** +	
Self-employment income				
Business income Gross **162**		Net	**135** +	
Professional income Gross **164**		Net	**137** +	
Commission income Gross **166**		Net	**139** +	
Farming income Gross **168**		Net	**141** +	
Fishing income Gross **170**		Net	**143** +	
Workers' compensation benefits (box 10 of the T5007 slip)	**144**			
Social assistance payments	**145**			
Net federal supplements (box 21 of the T4A(OAS) slip)	**146** +			
Add lines 144, 145, and 146 (see line 250 in the guide).	=		▶**147** +	
Add lines 101, 104 to 143, and 147. This is your **total income**.	**150** =			38,000 00

EXHIBIT 4.2A continued

Protected B when completed **3**

Attach only the documents (schedules, information slips, forms, or receipts) **requested in the guide** to support any claim or deduction. Keep all other supporting documents.

Step 3 – Net income

Enter your **total income** from line 150.				150		38,000 00
Pension adjustment (box 52 of all T4 slips and box 034 of all T4A slips)	**206**	3,500 00				
Registered pension plan deduction (box 20 of all T4 slips and box 032 of all T4A slips)	**207**	2,000 00				
RRSP/pooled registered pension plan (PRPP) deduction (see Schedule 7 and **attach** receipts)	**208** +	2,000 00				
PRPP **employer** contributions (amount from your PRPP contribution receipts)	**205**					
Deduction for elected split-pension amount (**attach** Form T1032)	**210** +					
Annual union, professional, or like dues (box 44 of all T4 slips, and receipts)	**212** +	400 00				
Universal child care benefit repayment (box 12 of all RC62 slips)	**213** +					
Child care expenses (**attach** Form T778)	**214** +					
Disability supports deduction	**215** +					
Business investment loss Gross **228**	Allowable deduction **217** +					
Moving expenses	**219** +					
Support payments made Total **230**	Allowable deduction **220** +					
Carrying charges and interest expenses (**attach** Schedule 4)	**221** +	600 00				
Deduction for CPP or QPP contributions on self-employment and other earnings (**attach** Schedule 8 or Form RC381, whichever applies)	**222** +					
Exploration and development expenses (**attach** Form T1229)	**224** +					
Other employment expenses	**229** +					
Clergy residence deduction	**231** +					
Other deductions Specify:	**232** +					
Add lines 207, 208, 210 to 224, 229, 231, and 232.	**233** =	5,000 00	▶	–		33,000 00
Line 150 minus line 233 (if negative, enter "0") This is your **net income before adjustments**.	**234** =					
Social benefits repayment (if you reported income on line 113, 119, or 146, see line 235 in the guide). Use the federal worksheet to calculate your repayment.	**235** –					
Line 234 minus line 235 (if negative, enter "0") If you have a spouse or common-law partner, see line 236 in the guide. This is your **net income**.	**236** =					33,000 00

Step 4 – Taxable income

Canadian Forces personnel and police deduction (box 43 of all T4 slips)	**244**	
Employee home relocation loan deduction (box 37 of all T4 slips)	**248** +	
Security options deductions	**249** +	
Other payments deduction (if you reported income on line 147, see line 250 in the guide)	**250** +	
Limited partnership losses of other years	**251** +	
Non-capital losses of other years	**252** +	
Net capital losses of other years	**253** +	
Capital gains deduction	**254** +	
Northern residents deductions (**attach** Form T2222)	**255** +	
Additional deductions Specify:	**256** +	
Add lines 244 to 256.	**257** =	▶ –

Line 236 minus line 257 (if negative, enter "0") This is your **taxable income**.	**260** =	33,000 00

Step 5 – Federal tax and provincial or territorial tax

Use Schedule 1 to calculate your federal tax and Form 428 to calculate your provincial or territorial tax.

5000-R

(continued)

EXHIBIT 4.2A	continued

Step 6 – Refund or balance owing

Protected B when completed **4**

Net federal tax: enter the amount from line 64 of Schedule 1 (**attach** Schedule 1, even if the result is "0")	420		2,487.43
CPP contributions payable on self-employment and other earnings (**attach** Schedule 8 or Form RC381, whichever applies)	421 +		
Employment insurance premiums payable on self-employment and other eligible earnings (**attach** Schedule 13)	430 +		
Social benefits repayment (amount from line 235)	422 +		
Provincial or territorial tax (**attach** Form 428, even if the result is "0")	428 +		1,265.70
Add lines 420, 421, 430, 422, and 428. This is your **total payable**.	435 =		3,753.13 •

Total income tax deducted		437	5,949.41 •		
Refundable Quebec abatement		440 +			
CPP overpayment (enter your excess contributions)		448 +			
Employment insurance overpayment (enter your excess contributions)		450 +			
Refundable medical expense supplement (use the federal worksheet)		452 +			
Working income tax benefit (WITB) (**attach** Schedule 6)		453 +			
Refund of investment tax credit (**attach** Form T2038(IND))		454 +			
Part XII.2 trust tax credit (box 38 of all T3 slips)		456 +			
Employee and partner GST/HST rebate (**attach** Form GST370)		457 +			
Children's fitness tax credit Eligible fees **458**	× 15% =	459 +			
Eligible educator school supply tax credit Supplies expenses **468**	× 15% =	469 +			
Tax **paid** by instalments		476 +			
Provincial or territorial credits (**attach** Form 479 if it applies)		479 +			
Add lines 437 to 479. These are your **total credits**.		482 =	5,949.41 ▶	–	5,949.41
Line 435 minus line 482 This is your **refund** or **balance owing**.				=	

If the result is negative, you have a **refund**. If the result is positive, you have a **balance owing**.

Enter the amount below on whichever line applies.

Generally, we do not charge or refund a difference of $2 or less.

Refund **484**	2,196.28 •	Balance owing **485**	

For more information on how to make your payment, see line 485 in the guide or go to cra.gc.ca/payments. Your payment is due no later than April 30, 2017.

Direct deposit – Enrol or update (see line 484 in the guide)

You do not have to complete this area every year. Do not complete it this year if your direct deposit information has not changed.

To enrol for direct deposit, to update your banking information, or to request that all of your CRA payments you may be receiving or owed be deposited into the same account as your T1 refund, complete lines 460, 461, and 462 below.

By providing my banking information **I authorize** the Receiver General to deposit in the bank account number shown below **any amounts payable** to me by the CRA, until otherwise notified by me. I understand that this authorization will replace all of my previous direct deposit authorizations.

Branch number **460**	Institution number **461**	Account number **462**
(5 digits)	(3 digits)	(maximum 12 digits)

Ontario **Ontario opportunities fund**	Amount from line 484 above		1
You can help reduce Ontario's debt by completing this area to donate some or all of your 2016 refund to the Ontario opportunities fund. Please see the provincial pages for details.	Your donation to the Ontario opportunities fund **465** –		• 2
	Net refund (line 1 minus line 2) **466** =		• 3

I certify that the information given on this return and in any documents attached is correct complete and fully discloses all my income. **Sign here** _____ It is a serious offence to make a false return. Telephone _____ Date _____	**490** **If a fee was charged for preparing this return, complete the following:** Name of preparer: _____ Telephone: _____ EFILE number (if applicable): **489**

Personal information is collected under the *Income Tax Act* to administer tax, benefits, and related programs. It may also be used for any purpose related to the administration or enforcement of the Act such as audit, compliance and the payment of debts owed to the Crown. It may be shared or verified with other federal, provincial/territorial government institutions to the extent authorized by law. Failure to provide this information may result in interest payable, penalties or other actions. Under the *Privacy Act*, individuals have the right to access their personal information and request correction if there are errors or omissions. Refer to Info Source cra.gc.ca/gncy/tp/nfsrc/nfsrc-eng.html, personal information bank CRA PPU 005.

Do not use this area	487	488			•	486	•

5006-R

Source: 5006-R T1 General 2016 – Income Tax and Benefit Return – Version for Ontario (ON) only http://www.cra-arc. gc.ca/E/pbg/tf/5006-r/5006-r-16e.txtc. Reproduced with permission of the Minister of Public Works and Government Services Canada, 2017.

EXHIBIT 4.3A

T1-2016   **Federal Tax**   **Protected B** when completed

Schedule 1

This is **Step 5** in completing your return. Complete this schedule and **attach** a copy to your return. For more information, see the related line in the guide.

Protected B when completed

Step 1 – Federal non-refundable tax credits

Basic personal amount	claim $11,474 **300**	11,474 00	1
Age amount (if you were born in 1951 or earlier) (use the federal worksheet) **(maximum $7,125)** **301** +			2
Spouse or common-law partner amount (**attach** Schedule 5) **303** +			3
Amount for an eligible dependant (**attach** Schedule 5) **305** +			4
Family caregiver amount for infirm children under 18 years of age			
Number of children for whom you **are claiming** the family caregiver amount **352** × $2,121 = **367** +			5
Amount for infirm dependants age 18 or older (**attach** Schedule 5) **306** +			6
CPP or QPP contributions:			
through employment from box 16 and box 17 of all T4 slips (**attach** Schedule 8 or Form RC381, whichever applies) **308** +		1,707 75	• 7
on self-employment and other earnings (**attach** Schedule 8 or Form RC381, whichever applies) **310** +			• 8
Employment insurance premiums:			
through employment from box 18 and box 55 of all T4 slips **(maximum $955.04)** **312** +		714 40	• 9
on self-employment and other eligible earnings (**attach** Schedule 13) **317** +			•10
Volunteer firefighters' amount **362** +			11
Search and rescue volunteers' amount **395**			12
Canada employment amount			
(If you reported employment income on line 101 or line 104, see line 363 in the guide.) **(maximum $1,161)** **363** +		1,161 00	13
Public transit amount **364** +			14
Children's arts amount **370** +			15
Home accessibility expenses (**attach** Schedule 12) **398** +			16
Home buyers' amount **369** +			17
Adoption expenses **313** +			18
Pension income amount (use the federal worksheet) **(maximum $2,000** **314** +			19
Caregiver amount (**attach** Schedule 5) **315** +			20
Disability amount (for self) (claim **$8,001,** or if you were under 18 years of age, use the federal worksheet) **316** +			21
Disability amount transferred from a dependant (use the federal worksheet) **318** +			22
Interest paid on your student loans **319** +			23
Your tuition, education, and textbook amounts (**attach** Schedule 11) **323** +		1,360 00	24
Tuition, education, and textbook amounts transferred from a child **324** +			25
Amounts transferred from your spouse or common-law partner (**attach** Schedule 2) **326** +			26
Medical expenses for **self, spouse or common-law partner, and your dependent children born in 1996 or later** **330**	27		
Enter $2,237 or 3% of line 236 of your return, whichever is less. −	28		
Line 27 minus line 28 (if negative, enter "0") =	29		
Allowable amount of medical expenses for **other dependants** (do the calculation at line 331 in the guide) **331** +	30		
Add lines 29 and 30. =	▶ **332** +		31
Add lines 1 to 26, and line 31. **335** =		16,417 15	32
Federal non-refundable tax credit rate ×		15%	33
Multiply line 32 by line 33. **338** =		2,462 57	34
Donations and gifts (**attach** Schedule 9) **349** +			35
Add lines 34 and 35. Enter this amount on line 48 on the next page. Total federal non-refundable tax credits **350** =		2,462 57	36

Continue on the next page.

5000-S1

EXHIBIT 4.3A   continued

Protected B when completed

Step 2 – Federal tax on taxable income

Enter your **taxable income** from line 260 of your return.   33,000 00   **37**

Complete the appropriate column depending on the amount on line 37.	Line 37 is **$45,282 or less**	Line 37 is more than $45,282 but not more than **$90,563**	Line 37 is more than **$90,563** but not more than **$140,388**	Line 37 is more than **$140,388** but not more than **$200,000**	Line 37 is more than **$200,000**	
Enter the amount from line 37.	33,000 00					**38**
Line 39 minus line 39 (cannot be negative)	− 0 00 = 33,000 00	− 45,282 00 =	− 90,563 00 =	− 140,388 00 =	− 200,000 00 =	**39** **40**
Multiply line 40 by line 41.	× 15% = 4,950 00	× 20.5% =	× 26% =	× 29% =	× 29% =	**41** **42**
	+ 0 00	+ 6,792 00	+ 16,075 00	+ 29,029 00	+ 46,317 00	**43**
Add lines 42 and 43.	= 4,950 00	=	=	=	=	**44**

Step 3 – Net federal tax

Enter the amount from line 44.		4,950 00	**45**
Federal tax on split income (from line 5 of Form T1206)	424 +		•**46**
Add lines 45 and 46.	404 =	▶ 4,950 00	**47**

Enter your total federal non-refundable tax credits from line 36 on the previous page.	350	2,462 57	**48**
Federal dividend tax credit	425 +		•**49**
Minimum tax carryover (**attach** Form T691)	427 +		•**50**
Add lines 48, 49, and 50.	=	▶ − 2,462 57	**51**

Line 47 minus line 51 (if negative, enter "0")   **Basic federal tax** 429 =   2,487 43   **52**

Federal foreign tax credit (**attach** Form T2209)   405 −   **53**

Line 52 minus line 53 (if negative, enter "0")   **Federal tax** 406 =   2,487 43   **54**

Total federal political contributions (**attach** receipts)	409		**55**
Federal political contribution tax credit (use the federal worksheet)	(maximum $650) 410		•**56**
Investment tax credit (**attach** Form T2038(IND))	412 +		•**57**
Labour-sponsored funds tax credit (see lines 413, 414, 411 and 419 in the guide)			
Net cost of shares of a federally registered fund 411	Allowable credit 419 +		•**58**
Net cost of shares of a federally registered fund 413	Allowable credit 414 +		•**59**
Add lines 56 to 60.	416 =	▶ −	**60**

Line 54 minus line 60 (if negative, enter "0")
If you have an amount on line 46 above, see Form T1206.   417 =   2,487 43   **61**

Working income tax benefit advance payments received
(box 10 of the RC210 slip)   415 +   •**62**

Special taxes (see line 418 in the guide)   418 +   **63**

Add lines 61, 62, and 63.
Enter this amount on line 420 of your return.   **Net federal tax** 420 =   2,487 43   **64**

See the privacy notice on your return.

Source: 5000-S1 T1 General 2016 – Schedule 1 – Federal Tax – Common to all EXCEPT for QC and nonresidents. Reproduced with permission of the Minister of Public Works and Government Services Canada, 2017.

EXHIBIT 4.4A

Protected B when completed

T1-2016   **Tuition, Education, and Textbook Amounts**   **Schedule 11**

For more information, see line 323 in the guide.

Only the student must complete this schedule and **attach** it to his or her return. Use it to:

- calculate your federal tuition, education, and textbook amounts;
- determine the federal amount available to transfer to a designated individual; and
- determine the unused federal amount, if any, available for you to carry forward to a future year.

Tuition, education, and textbook amounts claimed by the student for 2016

Unused federal tuition, education, and textbook amounts from your 2015 notice of assessment or notice of reassessment		0.00	1
Eligible tuition fees paid for 2016	**320**	800.00	2

Education and textbook amounts for 2016
Part-time student: use column B of Forms T2202A, TL11A, TL11B, and TL11C.
Do not include any month that is also included in column C.
Only one claim per month (**maximum 12 months**)

Education amount:
Number of months from column **B**   × $120 =   480.00   3

Textbook amount:
Number of months from column **B**   × $20 = +   80.00   4

Add lines 3 and 4.   =   560.00   ▶ **321** +   560.00   5

Full-time student: use column C of Forms T2202A, TL11A, TL11B, and TL11C.
Only one claim per month (**maximum 12 months**)

Education amount:
Number of months from column **C**   × $400 =   6

Textbook amount:
Number of months from column **C**   × $65 = +   7

Add lines 6 and 7.   =   ▶ **322** +   8

Add lines 2, 5, and 8. **Total 2016 tuition, education, and textbook amounts** =	1,360.00	▶ + 1,360.00	9
Add lines 1 and 9. **Total available tuition, education, and textbook amounts**		= 1,360.00	10

Enter the amount of your taxable income from line 260 of your return if it is $45,282 or less. If your taxable income is more than $45,282, enter instead the result of the following calculation: amount from line 45 of your Schedule 1 divided by 15%.   33,000.00   11

Total of lines 1 to 22 of your Schedule 1	− 15,057.15	12
Line 11 minus line 12 (if negative, enter "0")	= 17,942.85	13

Unused tuition, education, and textbook amounts claimed for 2016
Amount from line 1 or line 13, whichever is **less**   −   ▶   0.00   14

Line 13 minus line 14   =   17,942.85   15

2016 tuition, education, and textbook amounts claimed for 2016
Amount from line 9 or line 15, whichever is **less**   +   1,360.00   16

Add lines 14 and 16.   **Total tuition, education, and textbook**
Enter this amount on line 323 of Schedule 1.   **amounts claimed for 2016**   =   1,360.00   17

Transfer or Carryforward of unused amount

Amount from line 10		18
Amount from line 17	−	19
Line 18 minus line 19 **Total unused amount**	=	20

If you are transferring an amount to another individual, continue on line 21.
Otherwise, enter the amount from line 20 on line 25.

Enter the amount from line 9. **(maximum $5,000)**		21
Amount from line 16	−	22
Line 21 minus line 22 (if negative, enter "0") **Maximum transferable**	=	23

You can transfer all or part of the amount on line 23 to your spouse or common-law partner, to his or her parent or grandparent, or to your parent or grandparent. To do this, you have to **designate** the individual and **specify the federal amount** that you are transferring to him or her on your Form T2202A, TL11A, TL11B, or TL11C. Enter the amount on line 24 below.

Note: If your spouse or common-law partner is claiming an amount for you on line 303 or line 326 of his or her Schedule 1, you cannot transfer an amount to your parent or grandparent or to your spouse's or common-law partner's parent or grandparent.

Enter the amount you are transferring (cannot be more than line 23). **Federal amount transferred** **327** −		24
Line 20 minus line 24 **Unused federal amount available to carry forward to a future year** =		25

The person claiming the transfer should not attach this schedule to his or her return.

5000-S11   See the privacy notice on your return.

Source: 5000-S11 T1 General 2016 – Schedule 11 – Tuition, Education, and Textbook Amounts – Common to all EXCEPT for QC and non-residents. Reproduced with permission of the Minister of Public Works and Government Services Canada, 2017.

EXHIBIT 4.5A

	Ontario Tax	**ON428**
Ontario		T1 General – 2016

Complete this form and **attach a copy** to your return. For more information, see the related line in the forms book.

Step 1 – Ontario non-refundable tax credits

		For internal use only	5605			
Basic personal amount		claim $10,011	5804	10,011 00		1
Age amount (if born in 1951 or earlier) (use the *Provincial Worksheet*)		(maximum $4,888)	5808 +			2

Spouse or common-law partner amount

Base amount	9,350.00					
Minus: his or her net income from page 1 of your return	−					
Result: (if negative, enter "0")	=	(maximum $8,500)▶	5812 +			3

Amount for an eligible dependant

Base amount	9,350.00					
Minus: his or her net income from line 236 of his or her return	−					
Result: (if negative, enter "0")	=	(maximum $8,500)▶	5816 +			4
Amount for infirm dependants age 18 or older (use the *Provincial Worksheet*)			5820 +			5

CPP or QPP contributions:

(amount from line 308 of your federal Schedule 1)			5824 +	1,707 75		•6
(amount from line 310 of your federal Schedule 1)			5828 +			•7

Employment insurance premiums:

(amount from line 312 of your federal Schedule 1)			5832 +	714 40		•8
(amount from line 317 of your federal Schedule 1)			5829 +			•9
Adoption expenses		(maximum $12,214)	5833 +			10
Pension income amount		(maximum $1,384)	5836 +			11
Caregiver amount (use the *Provincial Worksheet*)			5840 +			12
Disability amount (for self) (Claim **$8,088**, or if you were under 18 years of age, use the *Provincial Worksheet*.)			5844 +			13
Disability amount transferred from a dependant (use the *Provincial Worksheet*)			5848 +			14
Interest paid on your student loans (amount from line 319 of your federal Schedule 1)			5852 +			15
Your tuition and education amounts (use and **attach** Schedule ON(S11))			5856 +	1,444 00		16
Tuition and education amounts transferred from a child			5860 +			17
Amounts transferred from your spouse or common-law partner (use and **attach** Schedule ON(S2))			5864 +			18

Medical expenses:

(Read line 5868 in the forms book.)	5868		19		
Enter $2,266 **or** 3% of line 236 of your return, whichever is **less**.		−	20		
Line 19 minus line 20 (if negative, enter "0")		=	21		

Allowable amount of medical expenses for other dependants
(use the *Provincial Worksheet*)

	5872 +		22		
Add lines 21 and 22.	5876 =	▶ +			23
Add lines 1 to 18, and line 23.		5880 =	13,877 15		24
Ontario non-refundable tax credit rate		×	5.05%		25
Multiply line 24 by line 25.		5884 =	700 80		26

Donations and gifts:

Amount from line 16 of your federal Schedule 9	× 5.05% =		27		
Amount from line 17 of your federal Schedule 9	× 11.16% =	+	28		
Add lines 27 and 28.	5896 =	▶ +			29
Add lines 26 and 29. Enter this amount on line 42.	Ontario non-refundable tax credits	6150 =	700 80		30

Continue on the next page.

EXHIBIT 4.5A   continued

Step 2 – Ontario tax on taxable income

Enter your **taxable income** from line 260 of your return.
If this amount is more than $20,000, you **must** complete **Step 7 – Ontario health premium**.   33,000.00   **31**

Complete the appropriate column depending on the amount on line 31.	Line 31 is $41,536 or less		Line 31 is more than $41,536 but not more than $83,075		Line 31 is more than $83,075 but not more than $150,000		Line 31 is more than $150,000 but not more than $220,000		Line 31 is more than $220,000	
Enter the amount from line 31	33,000.00									**32**
Line 32 minus line 33 (cannot be negative)	–	0.00	–	41,536.00	–	83,075.00	–	150,000.00	– 220,000.00	**33**
	=	33,000.00	=		=		=		=	**34**
	×	5.05%	×	9.15%	×	11.16%	×	12.16%	× 13.16%	**35**
Multiply line 34 by line 35.	=	1,666.50	=		=		=		=	**36**
Add lines 36 and 37.	+	0.00	+	2,098.00	+	5,898.00	+	13,367.00	+ 21,879.00	**37**
Ontario tax on taxable income	=	1,666.50	=		=		=		=	**38**

Step 3 – Ontario tax

Enter your Ontario tax on taxable income from line 38.	1,666.50	**39**
Enter your Ontario tax on split income from Form T1206. 6151 +		**• 40**
Add lines 39 and 40.	= 1,666.50	**41**
Enter your Ontario non-refundable tax credits from line 30.	– 700.80	**42**
Line 41 minus line 42 (if negative, enter "0")	= 965.70	**43**

Ontario minimum tax carryover:

Enter the amount from line 43.	965.70	**44**
Enter your Ontario dividend tax credit from line 6152 of the *Provincial Worksheet*.	–	**45**
Line 44 minus line 45 (if negative, enter "0").	= 965.70	**46**
Amount from line 427 of your federal Schedule 1 × 33.67% =		**47**

Enter the amount from line 46 or 47, whichever is less. 6154 –	0.00	**• 48**
Line 43 minus line 48 (if negative, enter "0")	= 965.70	**49**

Ontario surtax

Enter the amount from line 49.	965.70	**50**
Enter the amount from line 40.	–	**51**
Line 50 minus line 51 (if negative, enter "0")	= 965.70	**52**

Complete lines 53 to 55 only if the amount at line 52 is **more than $4,484**.
Otherwise, enter "0" on line 55 and continue completing the form.

(Line 52	minus $4,484) × 20% (if negative, enter "0") =		**53**
(Line 52	minus $5,739) × 36% (if negative, enter "0") =	+	**54**
Add lines 53 and 54.	=	▶ +	**55**
Add lines 49 and 55.		= 965.70	**56**

Ontario dividend tax credit:

Enter your Ontario dividend tax credit from line 6152 of the *Provincial Worksheet*. 6152 –		**• 57**
Line 56 minus line 57 (if negative, enter "0")	= 965.70	**58**

Ontario additional tax for minimum tax purposes:

If you entered an amount other than "0" on line 95 of Form T691, enter your Ontario additional tax for minimum tax purposes from line 59 of the *Provincial Worksheet*.	+	**59**
Add lines 58 and 59.	= 965.70	**60**

Continue on the next page.

EXHIBIT 4.5A   continued

Enter the amount from line 60 on the previous page.   =   965 70   **61**

If you are **not** claiming an Ontario tax reduction, there is an amount on line 59, or the amount on line 61 is "0",
enter the amount from line 61 on line 69 and continue completing the form. Otherwise, complete lines 62 to 68
to calculate the Ontario tax reduction.

Step 4 – Ontario tax reduction

Basic reduction   231 00   **62**

If you had a spouse or common-law partner on December 31, 2016, **only** the
individual with the **higher net income** can claim the amounts on lines 63 and 64.

Reduction for dependent children born in 1998 or later
              Number of dependent children **6269**   × $427 =   +   **63**

Reduction for dependants with a mental or physical impairment
              Number of dependents **6097**   × $427 =   +   **64**

Add lines 62, 63 and 64.   =   231 00   **65**

Enter the amount from line 65.   231 00   × 2 =   462 00   **66**
Enter the amount from line 61.   –   965 70   **67**
Line 66 minus line 67 (if negative, enter "0")   **Ontario tax reduction claimed** =   0 00   ▶ –   0 00   **68**
Line 61 minus line 68 (if negative, enter "0")   =   965 70   **69**

Step 5 – Ontario foreign tax credit

Enter the Ontario foreign tax credit from Form T2036.   –   **70**
Line 69 minus line 70 (if negative, enter "0")   =   965 70   **71**

Step 6 – Community food program donation tax credit for farmers

Enter the amount of qualifying donations that have also been
claimed as charitable donations   **6098**   × 25% =   –   **72**
Line 71 minus line 72 (if negative, enter "0")   =   965 70   **73**

Step 7 – Ontario health premium

If your taxable income (from line 31) is not more than $20,000, enter "0".   **Ontario health**
Otherwise, enter the amount calculated in the chart on the next page.   **premium** ▶ +   300 00   **74**

Add lines 73 and 74.
Enter the result on line 428 of your return.   **Ontario tax** =   1,265 70   **75**

Continue on the next page.

EXHIBIT 4.5A   continued

Ontario Health Premium

Enter your **taxable income** from line 31.   33,000|00   1

Go to the line that corresponds to your taxable income.
- If there is an Ontario health premium amount on that line, enter that amount on line 74.
- Otherwise, enter your taxable income in the first box, complete the calculation, and enter the result on line 74.

Taxable income				Ontario health premium
not more than **$20,000**	▶	▶	▶	0
more than **$20,000**, but not more than **$25,000**	[ ] − $20,000 = [ ]	× 6% =		[ ]
more than **$25,000**, but not more than **$36,000**	▶	▶	▶	$300
more than **$36,000**, but not more than **$38,500**	[ ] − $36,000 = [ ]	× 6% = [ ]	+ $300 = [ ]	
more than **$38,500**, but not more than **$48,000**	▶	▶	▶	$450
more than **$48,000**, but not more than **$48,600**	[ ] − $48,000 = [ ]	× 25% = [ ]	+ $450 = [ ]	
more than **$48,600**, but not more than **$72,000**	▶	▶	▶	$600
more than **$72,000**, but not more than **$72,600**	[ ] − $72,000 = [ ]	× 25% = [ ]	+ $600 = [ ]	
more than **$72,600**, but not more than **$200,000**	▶	▶	▶	$750
more than **$200,000**, but not more than **$200,600**	[ ] − $200,000 = [ ]	× 25% = [ ]	+ $750 = [ ]	
more than **$200,600**	▶	▶	▶	$900

See the privacy notice on your return.

5006-C

Source: 5006-C T1 General 2016 – ON428 – Ontario Tax. Reproduced with permission of the Minister of Public Works and Government Services Canada, 2017.

EXHIBIT 4.6A

Protected B when completed

Ontario — Provincial Tuition and Education Amounts

Schedule ON(S11)
T1 General – 2016

Only the student must complete this schedule and attach it to his or her return. Use it to:
- calculate your Ontario tuition and education amounts to claim on line 5856 of your Form ON428;
- determine the provincial amount available to transfer to a designated individual; and
- determine the unused Ontario amount, if any, available for you to carry forward to a future year.

Ontario tuition and education amounts claimed by the student for 2016

Unused Ontario tuition and education amounts from your 2015 notice of assessment or notice of reassessment *		0,00	1

Eligible tuition fees paid for 2016		**5914**	800,00		2

Education amount for 2016: Use columns B and C of forms T2202A, TL11A, TL11B, and TL11C. Only one claim per month (**maximum 12 months**)

Enter the number of months from column **B** (do not include any month that is also included in column C).	4	× $161 = **5916** +	644,00			3
Enter the number of months from column **C**.		× $539 = **5918** +				4
Add lines 2, 3, and 4.	**Total 2016 tuition and education amounts**	=	1,444,00	▶ +	1,444,00	5
Add lines 1 and 5.	**Total available tuition and education amounts**			=	1,444,00	6

Enter the amount of your taxable income from line 260 of your return if it is $41,536 or less. If your taxable income is more than $41,536, enter instead the result of the following calculation: amount from line 39 of your Form ON428 divided by 5.05%.	33,000,00		7
Total of lines 5804 to 5848 of your Form ON428	− 12,433,15		8
Line 7 minus line 8 (if negative, enter "0")	= 20,566,85		9
Unused Ontario tuition and education amounts claimed for 2016: Enter the amount from line 1 or line 9, whichever is **less**.	−	▶	10
Line 9 minus line 10	= 20,566,85		11

2016 tuition and education amounts claimed for 2016: Enter the amount from line 5 or line 11, whichever is **less**.		+	1,444,00	12
Add lines 10 and 12. Enter this amount on line 5856 of your Form ON428.	**Ontario tuition and education amounts claimed by the student for 2016**	=	1,444,00	13

Transfer/Carryforward of unused amount

Amount from line 6			14
Amount from line 13		−	15
Line 14 minus line 15	**Total unused amount**	=	16

If you are transferring an amount to another individual, continue on line 17.
Otherwise, enter the amount from line 16 on line 21.

Enter the amount from line 5.	(maximum $6,922)		17
Amount from line 12		−	18
Line 17 minus line 18 (if negative, enter "0")	**Maximum transferable**	=	19

You can transfer all or part of the amount on line 19 to your spouse or common-law partner, to his or her parent or grandparent, or to your parent or grandparent. To do this, you have to **designate** the individual and **specify the provincial amount** that you are transferring to him or her on Form T2202A, TL11A, TL11B, or TL11C. Enter the amount on line 20 below.

Note: If you have a spouse or common-law partner, special rules may apply. Read line 5856 in the forms book.

Enter the amount you are transferring (cannot be more than line 19).	**Provincial amount transferred 5920**	−	20
Line 16 minus line 20	**Unused provincial amount available to carry forward to a future year**	=	21

The person claiming the transfer should not attach this schedule to his or her return.

* If you resided in another province or territory on December 31, 2015, you must enter on line 1 your unused provincial or territorial tuition and education amounts from your 2015 notice of assessment or notice of reassessment.
If you resided in Quebec on December 31, 2015, enter on line 1 your unused federal tuition, education, and textbook amounts.

See the privacy notice on your return.

5006-S11

Source: 5006-S11 T1 General 2016 – Schedule ON(S11) – Provincial Tuition and Education Amounts - Ontario. Reproduced with permission of the Minister of Public Works and Government Services Canada, 2017.

In Ontario, the form is known as ON428 and a similar convention is followed in the other provinces. For example, in Manitoba, the provincial tax form would be MB428. The 428 refers to the fact that once you have calculated the amount of provincial tax payable, this amount is recorded on Line 428 of page 4 of the T1 General.

Page 1 of Exhibit 4.5A allows Steven to claim the provincial non-refundable tax credits he is eligible to claim in Ontario. In Ontario, the basic personal amount is a little less than what it is on a federal level. Also, you should notice that the amount that Steven is able to claim for his educational expenses is a little higher than what it was on the federal level. In Ontario, the education tax credit is referred to as the Tuition and Education Amount. NOTE: Similar to most other provinces, Ontario's Tuition and Education amount was tied to the changes made to the federal Tuition, Education, and Textbook amount. As such, and in keeping with the federal changes, the Ontario Tuition and Education Amount were both eliminated in 2017. However, for the purposes of this example, the Ontario Tuition and Education Amount tax credits were maintained.

The tuition and education amount is recorded on Line 5856 of Form ON428. Similar to what happens with the federal tax calculation, a Schedule 11 form has to be completed. In Ontario, this form is known as a Schedule ON(S11). Exhibit 4.6A displays the form after Steven has completed it. The Ontario tuition and education amount on Line 13 is transferred to Line 5856 of Form ON428.

Once the non-refundable tax credit amount is totalled at the bottom of page 1 of Exhibit 4.5A, Steven continues to page 2 to calculate the amount of provincial tax payable. Notice on page 2 that residents of Ontario may be charged an Ontario surtax if they have provincial tax payable greater than $4484. There is also an Ontario Tax Reduction plan for individuals who have dependent children and/or disabled or infirm dependants. None of these circumstances apply to Steven. Page 3 of Exhibit 4.5A lists some additional steps that need to be taken into account by residents of Ontario. Steven determines that the Ontario Health Premium also applies to his circumstances. Steven calculates his total Ontario tax on Line 66. This amount is then transferred to page 4 of the T1 General and recorded on Line 428.

Although we have focused on Ontario in this example, it is important to note that each province and territory has its own steps to complete that will take into account the needs of that particular province. As an exercise, it may be beneficial to see how the calculation of provincial tax varies in your province relative to what we have discussed with regard to federal tax. Provincial Form 428 worksheets can be accessed on the CRA website at https://www.canada.ca/en/revenue-agency/services/forms-publications/tax-packages-years/general-income-tax-benefit-package.html.

Calculation of Steven's Refund or Balance Owing

Referring back to Exhibit 4.2A, the total tax payable is determined by totalling Steven's federal and provincial taxes payable. Steven refers back to Box 22 of his T4 slip and records the amount of tax that his employer has withheld and records this amount on Line 437 of the T1 General. The total income tax deducted is then subtracted from the total tax payable. In Steven's case, his total tax payable was $3753.13 and the amount withheld by his employer was $5949.41. Therefore, he will receive a tax refund of $2196.28. Although it is nice to receive such a large tax refund, Steven should investigate why he is receiving such a large refund. Recall that the amount of tax withheld by your employer is determined based on the information you provide on the TD1 form. Perhaps Steven needs to resubmit this form to his employer so that less income tax is deducted from his paycheque.

PART 1: BRAD MacDONALD—A CONTINUING CASE

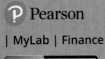

| MyLab | Finance

Your childhood friend Brad MacDonald has asked you to help him gain control of his personal finances. Single and 30 years old, Brad is employed as a salesperson for a technology company. His annual salary is $54 000. After payroll deductions for EI and CPP contributions, and income taxes, his monthly disposable income is $3380. Brad has recently moved from his comfortable two-bedroom apartment with rent of $1200 per month to a condo with rent of $1600 per month. The condo is in a plush property owner's association with two golf courses, a lake, and an activity centre. You review his other monthly expenses and find the following:

Tenant's insurance	$ 20
Car payment (balance on car loan $10 000; market value of car $11 000)	400
Utilities (gas, electric, cable)	100
Smartphone	$210
Food (consumed at home)	200
Clothes	100
Car expenses (gas, insurance, maintenance)	250
Entertainment (dining out, golf, weekend trips)	350
Credit card payment	250

Brad is surprised by how much money he spends on clothes and entertainment. He uses his credit card for these purchases (the balance is $8000 and climbing) and has little trouble making the required minimum monthly payment. He would, however, like to see the balance go down and would eventually like to pay his credit card off completely.

Brad's other goal is to save $4000 a year so that he can retire 20 years from now. He would like to start saving in five years, as he does not think the delay will affect the final amount of retirement savings he will accumulate.

Brad currently has about $4000 in his chequing account and $200 in his savings account. He has furniture valued at $1500 and owns 1000 shares of an internet stock, currently valued at $1300, which he believes has the potential to make him rich.

Case Questions

1. What is Brad's financial planning life stage? With respect to his current financial position what are some of the things Brad should be considering?

2. What are Brad's major goals? Evaluate his goals with respect to how specific, measurable, action-oriented, realistic, and time-bound they are. Are these short-term or long-term goals? What additional goals could you recommend to Brad for the short and long term?

3. Prepare personal financial statements for Brad, including a personal cash flow statement and a personal balance sheet. Based on these statements, make specific recommendations to Brad about what he needs to do to achieve his goals of paying off his credit card balance and saving for retirement.

4. Calculate Brad's current ratio, liquidity ratio, debt-to-assets ratio, and savings ratio. What do these ratios tell you about how Brad is managing his financial resources?

5. Consider Brad's goal to retire in 20 years by saving $4000 per year starting five years from now.

   a. Based on your analysis of Brad's cash flow and your recommendations, is saving $4000 per year a realistic goal? If not, what other goal would you advise?

b. In order for Brad to know what his $4000 per year will accumulate to in 20 years, what additional assumption (or piece of information) must he make (or have)?

c. Assuming that Brad invests $4000 per year for 20 years, starting five years from now and achieves an annual return of 9 percent, compounded monthly, how much will he accumulate in 25 years?

d. Compare the alternative of investing $4000 every year for 25 years beginning today with Brad's plan to invest $4000 every year for 20 years beginning five years from now. How much will Brad have to save each year to accumulate the same amount that he would have in 25 years if he started saving now instead of five years from now? (Again, assume a 9 percent annual return, compounded monthly.)

6. Develop three or four suggestions that could help Brad to reduce his income tax exposure.

Use the worksheets available on MyLab Finance to complete this case.

Managing Your Financial Resources

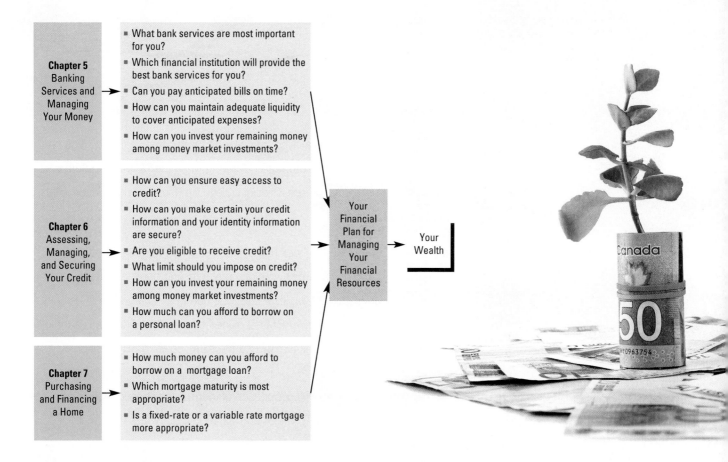

Chapter 5
Banking Services and Managing Your Money

- What bank services are most important for you?
- Which financial institution will provide the best bank services for you?
- Can you pay anticipated bills on time?
- How can you maintain adequate liquidity to cover anticipated expenses?
- How can you invest your remaining money among money market investments?

Chapter 6
Assessing, Managing, and Securing Your Credit

- How can you ensure easy access to credit?
- How can you make certain your credit information and your identity information are secure?
- Are you eligible to receive credit?
- What limit should you impose on credit?
- How can you invest your remaining money among money market investments?
- How much can you afford to borrow on a personal loan?

Chapter 7
Purchasing and Financing a Home

- How much money can you afford to borrow on a mortgage loan?
- Which mortgage maturity is most appropriate?
- Is a fixed-rate or a variable rate mortgage more appropriate?

Your Financial Plan for Managing Your Financial Resources

Your Wealth

The chapters in this part explain the key decisions you can make to ensure adequate financial resources. Chapter 5 explains how to select a financial institution for your banking needs and how you can manage your money to prepare for future expenses. Chapter 6 explains how you can assess, manage, secure, and obtain credit for your credit situation. Chapter 7 describes the process of obtaining a mortgage and the types of decisions that you need to make when considering a mortgage loan. Your selection of a financial institution and your techniques for money management and credit management will affect your cash flows and wealth.

CHAPTER 5

Banking Services and Managing Your Money

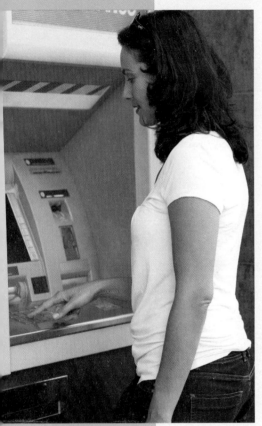

Adam Gregor/Shutterstock

When Shawna arrived on campus for her first year of college she relied on an Automated Banking Machine (ABM) to obtain cash for the many necessities of college life (food, movies, video rentals, and more food).

It was only on a weekend trip back home, when she reviewed her latest bank statement, that Shawna became aware of a problem. Her bank statement showed 34 separate charges for ABM fees. She had been charged $1.00 for each trip to an "out-of-network" ABM not owned by her bank. There was another $1.50 fee charged by the bank that owned the ABM, so each ABM visit created two charges. In addition, Shawna discovered that she had made five balance inquiries on "out-of-network" ABMs and her bank had charged $0.50 for each of them. Altogether, for her 17 visits to an ABM, Shawna had paid $42.50 in ABM fees and $2.50 in inquiry fees for a total of $45. Shocked by this discovery, Shawna decided that she needed to pay more attention to how she used the services offered by her bank. Perhaps she would even need to consider opening an account with a different bank.

QUESTIONS:

1. In addition to automated banking machines, what additional banking services are offered by financial institutions?
2. What steps should Shawna take to reduce her ABM fees?
3. What are some of the things that Shawna should consider when selecting a financial institution?

1. Provide a background on money management
2. Compare the types of financial institutions
3. Describe the banking services offered by financial institutions
4. Explain how to select a financial institution
5. Describe the savings alternatives offered by financial institutions

BACKGROUND ON MONEY MANAGEMENT

L.O.1

Money management describes the decisions you make over a short-term period regarding your income and expenses. It is separate from decisions on investing funds for a long-term period (such as several years) or borrowing funds for a long-term period. Instead, it focuses on maintaining short-term investments to achieve both liquidity and an adequate return on your investments, as explained next.

Liquidity

As discussed in Chapter 1, liquidity refers to your access to ready cash, including savings and credit, to cover short-term and unexpected expenses. Exhibit 5.1 illustrates that the main sources for savings and credit are either: 1) positive net cash flows from the personal cash flow statement, and/or 2) credit cards and/or lines of credit from financial institutions.

Recall from Chapter 3 that the personal cash flow statement determines the amount of net cash flows you have at the end of a period, such as one month from now. If you have positive net cash flows, you should invest these funds in an account that is designed to hold short-term or liquid assets, such as a chequing account or a savings account. Liquidity is necessary because there will be periods when your income is not adequate to cover your expenses. For example, in Chapter 3, Rhea Kennedy incurred a car maintenance expense that left her with a $270 cash shortage. Exhibit 5.1 shows that savings can be used to cover expenses that cannot be paid out of current income.

If Rhea does not have sufficient money in her savings, she could cover the cost of her car maintenance by relying on short-term credit financing from a financial institution. Credit card financing can be inexpensive if you pay the amount owing on your credit card before or on the due date. However, if you do not pay your credit card bills in full and on time, this type of financing can become very expensive because the interest rate on credit cards is usually quite high. A line of credit also provides a source of liquidity when you do not have adequate positive net cash flows. The main advantage of a line of credit versus a credit card is that the interest rate on a line of credit is much lower. Credit cards and lines of credit are discussed further in Chapter 6.

EXHIBIT 5.1   Money Management

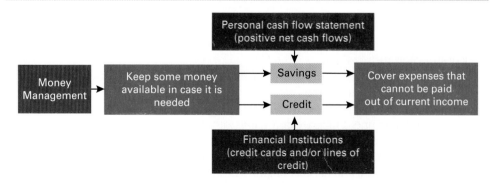

Since the assets you have in savings may need to be accessed on short notice, you should invest your funds in short-term, conservative investments. The rate of return on short-term investments is lower than it would be if you had invested the money in longer-term investments. Therefore, the amount of ready cash you may need access to for unexpected expenses should not be unlimited. The liquidity ratio, from Chapter 3, tells you how many months of living expenses you can cover with your present level of liquid savings. As mentioned in Chapter 3, the liquidity ratio should be between 3.0 and 6.0. In other words, you should have between three and six months' worth of expenses in a savings account, also known as an emergency fund.

▌ **myth** or **fact** I don't make enough money to save.   ▌

EXAMPLE	Sarah Scott's expenses total $1930 per month. She would like to maintain an emergency fund equal to three months' expenses, and calculates that she needs $5790 ($1930 × 3) in the fund. Her disposable income is normally about $2260 per month, leaving her with $330 in net cash flows each month, or $3960 per year. To build up her emergency fund as quickly as possible, Sarah will deposit the entire $330 per month of excess cash into an emergency fund until she reaches her cash value objective. Based on her aggressive savings target, Sarah should be able to reach her goal within 18 months, assuming that she does not need to access the emergency fund during the period she is building it up.

The money allocated to an emergency fund can be invested in a number of different types of investments, including term deposits, guaranteed investment certificates (GICs), money market funds, and Canada Savings Bonds (CSBs). Before determining which investment options you should use to build an emergency fund, it is important to select a financial institution with which you will open an account. Most financial institutions offer many types of accounts where you can invest the net cash flows that you have allocated to short-term savings.

L.0.2

TYPES OF FINANCIAL INSTITUTIONS

Individuals rely on many different financial institutions when they wish to invest or borrow funds. In this section, we'll examine the two major types of financial institutions: depository institutions and non-depository institutions.

depository institutions
Financial institutions that accept deposits from and provide loans to individuals and businesses.

Depository institutions are financial institutions that accept deposits from and provide loans to individuals and businesses. They pay interest on savings deposits and charge interest on loans. The interest rate charged on loans exceeds the interest rate paid on deposits. The institutions use this difference to cover expenses and to generate earnings for their shareholders.

Depository institutions are skilled in assessing the ability of prospective borrowers to repay loans. This is a critical part of their business since the interest collected on loans is a key source of their revenue.

There are three types of depository institutions: chartered banks, trust and loan companies, and credit unions and *caisses populaires*.

non-depository institutions
Financial institutions that do not offer federally insured deposit accounts but provide various other financial services.

Non-depository institutions are financial institutions that do not offer federally insured deposit accounts but provide various other financial services. The main types of non-depository institutions that serve individuals are finance and lease companies, mortgage companies, investment dealers, insurance companies, mutual fund companies, payday loan companies, cheque cashing outlets, and pawnshops.

The main types of depository and non-depository institutions are discussed below.

Depository Institutions

Chartered Banks. **Chartered banks** are financial institutions that accept deposits in chequing and savings accounts and use the funds to provide business and personal loans. The chequing accounts may or may not pay interest. The savings accounts pay interest, while certain other accounts pay interest and can be used to write cheques. These accounts are described in more detail later in this chapter. Eligible deposits at chartered banks are insured up to $100 000 per depositor per insured category by the Canada Deposit Insurance Corporation (CDIC), a federal Crown corporation that ensures the safety of bank deposits.

Eligible deposits include those deposits that are payable in Canada and in Canadian currency. Eligible deposits include chequing accounts, savings accounts, term deposits, guaranteed investment certificates (GICs), money orders, bank drafts, and certified cheques. These deposits are insured separately for each insured category. Some of the more common insured categories include deposits held in one name, deposits held in more than one name, certain registered accounts, and trust accounts.

You can look to a chartered bank to provide a personal loan for the purchase of a car or other big-ticket items. They also offer mortgage loans for purchasing a home. Some chartered banks own other types of financial institutions (such as those described below) that provide additional services to individuals. Chartered banks can be distinguished by their ownership and size.

Schedule I Banks. Schedule I banks are domestic banks that are authorized to accept deposits. There are 23 federally regulated domestic banks in Canada. The six largest banks are the Royal Bank of Canada, TD Bank Financial Group, Scotiabank, BMO Financial Group, CIBC, and National Bank of Canada. These six banks represent over 90 percent of the total assets under administration among Canadian chartered banks.

Schedule II Banks. Schedule II banks are foreign banks that have subsidiaries operating in Canada. There are 18 federally regulated foreign bank subsidiaries in Canada. Schedule II banks are similar to Schedule I banks in that they are authorized to accept deposits. However, Schedule II banks are controlled by a foreign parent corporation while Schedule I banks are controlled domestically. Some of the more visible Schedule II banks are ICICI Bank Canada and HSBC Bank Canada.

Schedule III Banks. Schedule III banks are subsidiaries of foreign banks that are restricted in their authority to accept deposits. Some of the more visible Schedule III banks are Capital One Bank and Citibank N.A.

myth or **fact** Saving 10 percent of my income is plenty to carry me to financial freedom in my retirement.

The largest financial institutions in Canada are referred to more accurately as financial conglomerates. **Financial conglomerates** offer a diverse set of financial services to individuals or firms. The six largest Schedule I banks mentioned earlier are all examples of financial conglomerates. Exhibit 5.2 provides an example of how one of these banks, the Royal Bank of Canada (RBC), is organized into five business segments. The businesses within each of these segments offer a number of services that were previously offered by separate depository institutions.

In addition to accepting deposits and paying interest on savings deposits, RBC Royal Bank is able to offer a range of personal financial services, including student and online banking, mortgages, credit cards, personal loans, investments, and some types of insurance. By offering all types of financial services, a financial conglomerate aims to serve as a one-stop shop where individuals can conduct all of their financial services.

Trust and Loan Companies. **Trust and loan companies** are financial institutions that, in addition to providing services similar to a bank, can provide financial planning services, such as administering estates and acting as trustee in the administration of trust accounts.

chartered banks
Financial institutions that accept deposits in chequing and savings accounts and use the funds to provide business and personal loans. These banks are federally incorporated.

eligible deposits
Include those deposits that are payable in Canada and in Canadian currency.

Go to:
www.cdic.ca

This website provides information on what is, and what is not, covered by deposit insurance and why it is important.

financial conglomerates
Financial institutions that offer a diverse set of financial services to individuals or firms.

trust and loan companies
Financial institutions that, in addition to providing services similar to a bank, can provide financial planning services, such as administering estates and acting as trustee in the administration of trust accounts.

EXHIBIT 5.2 RBC Business Segments

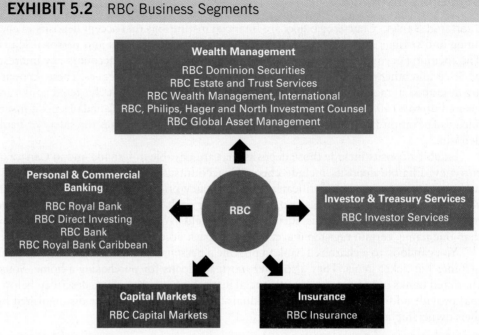

Source: www.rbc.com/aboutus/about2.html (accessed February 11, 2017). Reproduced with permission of Royal Bank of Canada.

Most trust companies are subsidiaries of banks. For example, RBC offers these services through its RBC Estate and Trust Services business segment.

credit unions/*caisses populaires*
Provincially incorporated co-operative financial institutions that are owned and controlled by their members.

Credit Unions and *Caisses populaires*. Credit unions and *caisses populaires* (as they are referred to in francophone regions of Canada) are provincially incorporated co-operative financial institutions that are owned and controlled by their members. Membership in a credit union involves the purchase of at least one share of the credit union. Credit unions were created to serve the financial needs of specific employee groups, such as those in hospitals, universities, and even some corporations. These groups were held together through a common bond that created a social obligation for borrowers, ensuring that loans were paid back promptly. In essence, the loan was extended by other members of the credit union or *caisse populaire*, and default rates were low. Today, this common bond may be residential, religious, employment-related, or cultural. Credit unions, which are not-for-profit financial organizations, offer their members deposit accounts, mortgages, personal loans, and other products similar to those offered by chartered banks and trust and loan companies. In addition, these accounts are eligible for deposit insurance protection through provincial deposit insurance agencies. In Ontario, deposit insurance is provided by the Deposit Insurance Corporation of Ontario (DICO). Credit unions and *caisses populaires* also differ in that they do not operate outside provincial boundaries.

FREE APPS for Personal Finance

Your Banking Services

Application:

The CIBC Mobile Banking app allows customers who have established an account to pay bills and credit cards, transfer money between accounts, and see their cash balance from a mobile device. You can check to see if the financial institutions that you use offer apps like this.

Non-Depository Institutions

Finance and Lease Companies. **Finance and lease companies** specialize in providing personal loans or leases to individuals. These loans may be used for various purposes, such as purchasing a car or other consumer products or making renovations to a home. Many of the major car manufacturers have in-house finance and lease companies. For example, Ford Motor Company of Canada Ltd. allows customers to finance or lease vehicles using the services of Ford Credit. Finance and lease companies tend to charge relatively high rates on loans and leases because they lend to individuals who they perceive to have a higher risk of defaulting on the loans. When the economy weakens, borrowers may have more difficulty repaying loans, causing finance and lease companies to be subject to higher levels of loan defaults.

finance and lease companies
Non-depository institutions that specialize in providing personal loans or leases to individuals.

Mortgage Companies. **Mortgage companies** specialize in providing mortgage loans to individuals. These companies are able to offer their clients competitive mortgage rates from a number of different financial institutions. This type of non-depository institution acts as a financial intermediary between depository institutions and the consumer. Referring to Exhibit 5.2, RBC offers these services through its RBC Royal Bank business segment.

mortgage companies
Non-depository institutions that specialize in providing mortgage loans to individuals.

Investment Dealers. **Investment dealers** facilitate the purchase or sale of various investments, such as stocks or bonds, by firms or individuals by providing investment banking and brokerage services. Investment banking services include assisting corporations and governments in obtaining financing for many activities, such as building projects and expansion plans. This financing advice helps both corporations and governments to price their securities for sale and assists them in finding investors such as individuals, mutual funds, and other organizations willing to invest in their securities. Investment banking services also include advising and evaluating businesses with regard to mergers, acquisitions, and other similar corporate activities.

investment dealers
Non-depository institutions that facilitate the purchase or sale of various investments by firms or individuals by providing investment banking and brokerage services.

In addition to offering investment banking services, investment dealers provide brokerage services, which facilitate the trading of existing securities. That is, the firms execute trades in securities for their customers. One customer may want to sell a specific stock while another may want to buy that stock. Brokerage firms create a market for stocks and bonds by matching willing buyers and sellers. In the case of RBC, these services are offered through its RBC Capital Markets business segment (see Exhibit 5.2).

Insurance Companies. **Insurance companies** sell insurance to protect individuals or firms from risks that can result in financial loss. Specifically, life and health insurance companies provide insurance in the event of a person's death, disability, or critical illness. Property and casualty companies provide insurance against damage to property, including automobiles and homes. Insurance serves a crucial function for individuals because it protects them (or their beneficiaries) from a significant loss of income and/or savings that may occur as a result of injury, illness, or death. Chapters 8 and 9 discuss insurance options in detail. Exhibit 5.2 shows that RBC offers these services through its RBC Insurance business segment.

insurance companies
Non-depository institutions that sell insurance to protect individuals or firms from risks that can incur financial loss.

Mutual Fund Companies. **Mutual fund companies** sell units to individuals and use the proceeds to invest in securities to create mutual funds. The minimum amount an individual can invest in a mutual fund is typically between $500 and $5000. Since the investment company pools the money it receives from individuals and invests it in a portfolio of securities, an individual who invests in a mutual fund is a part owner of that portfolio. Thus, mutual funds provide a means by which investors with a small amount of money can invest in a portfolio of securities. More details on mutual funds are provided in Chapter 13. As shown in Exhibit 5.2, RBC offers these services through its RBC Global Asset Management business segment.

mutual fund companies
Non-depository institutions that sell units to individuals and use the proceeds to invest in securities to create mutual funds.

In addition to offering the services described above, many financial conglomerates are able to offer more specialized services to individuals and firms who have particular needs.

For example, RBC Direct Investing provides online tools, information, and learning resources for individuals who want to manage their own investments. On the other hand, RBC Dominion Securities offers professional wealth management services through a national network of qualified financial advisers. In addition to these national services, many financial conglomerates, such as RBC, offer a range of international services that are of strategic importance to their business model.

Payday Loan Companies. Payday loan companies provide single-payment, short-term loans (usually for between 30 and 50 percent of an individual's biweekly salary) based on personal cheques held for future deposit (often postdated) or on electronic access to personal chequing accounts. Costs (interest and fees) are quite high.

Cheque Cashing Outlets. Cheque cashing outlets cash third-party cheques immediately, as long as you have adequate personal identification, and for a fee (usually a per-cheque fee plus a percentage of the face value of the cheque). Money Mart (www.moneymart.ca) is an example of a non-depository financial institution that offers both payday loans and cheque cashing services.

Pawnshops. Pawnshops provide small, secured loans for a fee and usually require a resaleable item worth more than the loan as a deposit (the security). If the loan is not repaid, the security is forfeited.

Go to:
www.canpayday.ca/
payday-loan-calculator.
aspx

This website provides
a calculator that allows you to determine the interest cost of a payday loan.

> **L.O.3**

BANKING SERVICES OFFERED BY FINANCIAL INSTITUTIONS

Go to:
http://itools-ioutils.fcac-acfc.gc.ca/STCV-OSVC/ccst-oscc-eng.aspx

This website provides
a useful step-by-step guide to selecting a credit card that meets your specific needs.

A depository institution may offer you a wide variety of banking services. While a non-depository institution does not offer banking services, it may own a subsidiary that can. For example, Manulife Securities and Manulife Bank are both wholly owned subsidiaries of Manulife Financial. Manulife Securities is a large Canadian mutual fund company (that is, a non-depository institution), whereas Manulife Bank is a Schedule I, federally chartered bank (that is, a depository institution). A representative of Manulife Financial may be able to offer you services from both subsidiary companies. Exhibit 5.3 provides an illustration of some of the many banking services offered by depository institutions. Some of the more important banking services offered to individuals are described here.

Chequing Services

You use a chequing account to draw on funds by writing cheques against your account. Most individuals maintain a chequing account so that they do not have to carry much cash when making purchases. In reality, as the popularity of electronic banking and the use of debit and credit cards have increased, cheque writing has become obsolete for many types of transactions; however, financial institutions in Canada still process nearly one billion cheques each year. To illustrate how your chequing account works, assume that you pay a phone bill of $60 today with a cheque. The phone company provides the cheque to its bank. The bank electronically increases the phone company's account balance by $60. At the same time, the bank reduces your account balance by $60 if your chequing account is at that same bank, or electronically signals your bank to reduce your balance by $60. This process is referred to as clearing or honouring.

Debit Cards

debit card
A card that not only is used as identification at your bank, but also allows you to make purchases that are charged against an existing chequing account.

You can use a **debit card** to make purchases that are charged against an existing chequing account. If you use a debit card to pay $100 for a car repair, your chequing account balance is reduced by $100. Thus, using a debit card has the same result as writing a cheque. There is no risk of extra charges for insufficient funds with debit transactions because individuals cannot spend more than they have in their chequing accounts.

EXHIBIT 5.3 Banking Services

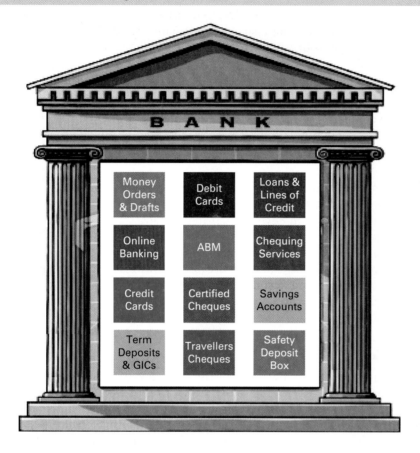

Monitoring Your Account Balance. If you write cheques, you should record them in your chequebook so you can always determine how much money is in your account. The **cheque register** is a booklet in your chequebook where you record the details of each transaction you make, including deposits, cheque writing, withdrawals, and bill payments. Simpler methods for monitoring your account balance include asking your bank to send you a monthly statement or using the online banking services, discussed below, provided by your bank. A bank statement will provide you with a list of the transactions you made using cheques and/or your debit card. By keeping track of your account balance, you can make sure that you do not exceed it. This is very important because you are charged fees when you write a cheque that is not honoured, referred to as an NSF cheque (NSF stands for not sufficient funds). These fees are not small. For example, one Canadian chartered bank charges a $40 fee for NSF cheques. The person or institution to whom you wrote the cheque may charge a fee as well, anywhere from $25 to $40 or more. In addition to the fees charged, you may lose some credibility when writing a bad cheque, even if it is unintentional. If you intentionally write a bad cheque, you are committing fraud. As mentioned earlier, debit cards eliminate the possibility of NSF charges.

cheque register
A booklet in your chequebook where you record the details of each transaction you make, including deposits, cheque writing, withdrawals, and bill payments.

myth or **fact** Canada's banks are the most sound in the world and rank first in the world in terms of financial strength.

Overdraft Protection. Some depository institutions offer **overdraft protection**, which protects customers who exceed their chequing account balances. It is essentially a short-term loan from the depository institution where the chequing account is maintained. For example, if you withdraw $300 but have a chequing account balance of only $100,

overdraft protection
An arrangement that protects customers who write cheques for amounts that exceed their chequing account balances; it is a short-term loan from the depository institution where the chequing account is maintained.

the depository institution will provide overdraft protection by making a loan of $200 to cover the difference. Overdraft protection carries a fee every time you use the service. As well, a high interest rate (as much as 21 percent per year compounded monthly) will be charged on the loan. Some banks also charge a monthly fee simply for having overdraft protection available on your account.

Stop Payment. If you have a regular monthly automatic withdrawal from your account, such as a monthly fitness club membership fee, you may request that the financial institution **stop payment,** which means that the institution will not allow money to be withdrawn from your account to cover the monthly charge. To create a stop payment, you must provide accurate information, such as the date and the amount of the withdrawal and the name of the payee, to the financial institution. Normally, a fee is charged for stop payment service.

No Interest. A disadvantage of keeping funds in a chequing account is that very little interest accrues on these funds. For this reason, you should keep only enough funds in your chequing account to cover anticipated expenses and a small excess amount for unanticipated expenses that may arise. You should not deposit more funds in your chequing account than you think you may need because you can earn interest by putting your money in other investments. Because of this disadvantage, many financial institutions have introduced accounts that both earn interest and provide chequing services. It is important to check what account options are available at your financial institution.

Online Banking

Many financial institutions allow you to verify your chequing account balance by using online banking services. The advantage to this service is that the information you get on your chequing account should be up to date. In addition to real-time reporting, **online banking** services allow you to not only check the balance of bank, credit card, and investment accounts, but also transfer funds, pay bills electronically, and perform a number of administrative tasks. Although managing a chequing account using a cheque register was a prudent practice in the past, using online banking to manage an account is more common in today's fast-paced world.

Interac® e-Transfer

In addition to being able to transfer money among your accounts using online banking, most financial institutions now provide a service, known as Interac® e-Transfer, that allows individuals to send and receive money directly from one bank account to another. In order to use this service, you would first need to access your bank's online banking system and select the Interac® e-Transfer link. Next, you would enter the e-mail address of the individual or business that will be receiving the transfer and you would specify a dollar amount to send. In order to secure the transaction, you would also enter a security question and answer for the recipient to answer in order to complete the transfer. With Interac® e-Transfer, the money comes right out of your account and is transferred immediately to the recipient once they answer the security question. The sender will receive a confirmation e-mail once the transaction is completed. The cost of an Interac® e-Transfer varies among financial institutions from $0 to $1.50 per transaction.

Credit Card Financing

Individuals use credit cards to purchase products and services on credit. At the end of each billing cycle, you receive a bill for the credit you used over that period. Credit cards allow you to finance your purchases through various financial institutions. Therefore, if you are able to pay only the minimum balance on your card, the financial institution

stop payment
A financial institution's notice that it will not honour a regular monthly automatic withdrawal; usually occurs in response to a request by the account owner.

online banking
A service offered by financial institutions that allows a customer to check the balance of bank, credit card, and investment accounts, transfer funds, pay bills electronically, and perform a number of administrative tasks.

will finance the outstanding balance and charge interest for the credit, or loan, that it provides to you.

Safety Deposit Boxes

Many financial institutions offer access to a safety deposit box, in which a customer can store documents, jewellery, and other valuables. Customers are charged an annual fee, which depends on the size of the box, for access to a safety deposit box.

safety deposit box
A box at a financial institution in which a customer can store documents, jewellery, and other valuables. It is secure because it is stored in the bank's vault.

Automated Banking Machines (ABMs)

Bank customers can deposit and withdraw funds at an **automated banking machine** (ABM) by using their ABM or debit card and entering their personal identification number (PIN). Located in numerous convenient locations, these machines allow customers access to their funds 24 hours a day, any day of the year. The major chartered banks have ABMs throughout Canada and in many foreign countries. You can usually use ABMs from financial institutions other than your own, but you may be charged additional fees. Exhibit 5.4 provides an example of how fees can quickly increase when you are using an ABM. When you use an ABM from your own financial institution, you can reduce or eliminate fees by purchasing a service package that covers a certain number of withdrawals per month. If you use an ABM from another financial institution, your own institution may charge you an additional fee to cover the cost of completing the transaction with the other institution. In addition, the other institution may charge you a convenience fee for using their ABM. In addition to ABMs owned by financial institutions, many ABMs are privately owned. These machines are often located in areas where someone may need access to cash. For example, privately owned ABMs can be found in malls, restaurants, pubs, and even at your post-secondary institution. Unfortunately, these ABMs charge convenience fees that may be even greater than the fees you would pay for using an ABM of a financial institution other than your own. As mentioned in Exhibit 5.4, the fee from a privately owned ABM can be 35%, or perhaps higher, for a $20 withdrawal. ABMs are also known as Automated Teller Machines (ATMs).

automated banking machine (ABM)
A machine that individuals can use to deposit and withdraw funds at any time of day.

FREE APPS for Personal Finance

Finding an ATM Nearby

Application:

Use the ATM Hunter app to find a nearby ATM. You can use your current location when searching, or input an address or nearby airport.

Certified Cheques

A **certified cheque** can be cashed immediately by the payee without the payee having to wait for the bank to process and clear it. When a cheque is certified, it means that the cheque writer's bank has already withdrawn the money from the cheque writer's account. Therefore, the bank is able to guarantee that the money will be available to the payee.

certified cheque
A cheque that can be cashed immediately by the payee without the payee having to wait for the bank to process and clear it.

Money Orders and Drafts

Money orders and drafts are products that direct your bank to pay a specified amount to the person named on them. You pay for a money order or draft at the time of purchase. They are similar to certified cheques in that the bank guarantees the amount indicated on the money order or draft. The difference is that money orders and drafts tend to be used for smaller amounts of money.

money orders and drafts
Products that direct your bank to pay a specified amount to the person named on them.

EXHIBIT 5.4   Example of ABM Fee Charges

	ABM Belongs to...		
	Your Financial Institution	**Another Financial Institution**	**A Private ABM Operator**
Service Fee	$1	$1	$1
Network Access Fee		$1	$1
Convenience Fee		$2.50	$5
TOTAL Fees	**$1**	**$4.50**	**$7**

Note: With respect to the example above, fee would be 35% on a withdrawal of $20, calculated as $7 ÷ $20, from a privately operated ABM.

Traveller's Cheques

traveller's cheque
A cheque written on behalf of an individual that will be charged against a large, well-known financial institution or credit card sponsor's account.

A traveller's cheque is a cheque written on behalf of an individual that will be charged against a large, well-known financial institution or credit card sponsor's account. It is similar to a certified cheque, except that no payee is designated on the cheque. Traveller's cheques are accepted around the world. If they are lost or stolen, the issuer usually will replace them without charge. The fee for a traveller's cheque varies among financial institutions. It is considered to be much safer to carry traveller's cheques than cash when out of the country.

L.0.4

SELECTING A FINANCIAL INSTITUTION

Your choice of a financial institution should be based on convenience, deposit rates, deposit insurance, and fees.

Convenience

Go to:
www.canada.ca/en/services/finance/tools.html

Click on
Bank account selector tool

This website provides an online tool to help you find the banking package that fits your needs.

You should be able to deposit and withdraw funds easily, which means that the financial institution should be located close to where you live or work. You also may benefit if it has ABMs in convenient locations. In addition, a financial institution should offer most or all of the services you might need. Many financial institutions offer internet banking, which allows you to keep track of your deposit accounts and even to apply for loans online.

Finally, does the financial institution that you are considering offer convenient in-branch banking hours. For example, is it open late so that you can go there after work if you need to?

Tangerine (www.tangerine.ca/en) is an example of a web-based bank. While web-based banks allow you to keep track of your deposits online, they may not be appropriate for customers who prefer to deposit funds directly at a branch. For customers who prefer to make deposits at a branch but also want easy online access to their account information, the most convenient financial institutions are those with multiple branches and online access. Some web-based banks do not offer chequing accounts per se and so you may be required to maintain a chequing account at another institution.

Deposit Rates and Insurance

The interest rates offered on deposits vary among financial institutions. You should comparison shop by checking the rates on the types of deposits you might make.

Financial institutions also vary on the minimum required balance needed to earn interest. For example, assume that Bank A pays 1 percent interest on a savings account without taking into consideration a minimum required balance. This means that every dollar you deposit earns interest. In contrast, Bank B requires you to have at least $1000 on deposit throughout the entire month in order to earn 1 percent interest. In this case, a lower minimum required balance is preferable because it gives you more flexibility if you do not want to tie up the entire $1000. Make sure that any deposits are insured by the CDIC or the credit union/*caisses populaires* deposit insurance corporation for the province in which you live.

Web-based financial institutions tend to pay a higher interest rate on deposits than institutions with physical branches because they have lower overhead (fewer expenses). Customers must weigh these higher interest rates against the lack of access to branches. Those who prefer to make deposits through the mail may want to capitalize on the higher rates at web-based financial institutions.

Go to:
www.ratehub.ca

Click on
Savings Accounts within the Banking drop down menu

This website provides a comparison of what savings accounts rates you could earn based on your deposit amount and where you live

Fees

Many financial institutions charge fees for various services. The amount of fees you will be charged depends on your banking habits and the number of services you use. If you tend to use the ABM on a daily basis, you will need an account that is suited for people with high ABM withdrawal habits. If you plan to write a number of cheques every month, you will want to look for an account that has cheque-writing privileges. The number of bank accounts and options available to you is truly unlimited. Avoid financial institutions that charge high fees on services you will use frequently, even if they offer relatively high rates on deposits.

SAVINGS ALTERNATIVES OFFERED BY FINANCIAL INSTITUTIONS

L.0.5

Tax-Free Savings Account (TFSA)

Recall from Chapter 4 that a TFSA is not a type of investment. Instead, it is a registered investment account that allows you to purchase investments with after-tax dollars, without attracting any tax payable on your investment growth. Withdrawals from a TFSA are tax-free. The 2017 contribution limit is $5500. If you contribute less than the contribution limit, any remaining contribution room can be carried forward to subsequent years. In addition, any contribution withdrawals may be recontributed in subsequent years. As such, TFSAs are a very flexible savings alternative that can be used as a short-term or long-term savings alternative. The use of TFSAs as a long-term savings alternative is discussed in Chapter 14. The investment alternatives discussed below are some of the investments that qualify to be held inside a TFSA.

Savings Deposits

Traditional savings accounts offered by a depository institution pay interest on deposits. Depositing funds to a savings account is one option for money that is not needed to cover anticipated expenses. Funds can normally be withdrawn from a savings account at any time. A traditional savings account does not provide chequing services. However, a savings account is just as convenient as a chequing account because you can use an ABM to access funds. On the other hand, savings accounts may have fees on basic transactions and/or limit the number of transactions that you can make. Exhibit 5.5 provides a comparison between savings accounts and chequing accounts. The interest rate offered on savings deposits varies among depository institutions. Many institutions quote their rates on their websites.

EXHIBIT 5.5   Comparison between Chequing Accounts and Savings Accounts

Chequing Accounts	Savings Accounts
• Designed for everyday transactions	• Designed for saving money
• Usually no restriction on number of transactions	• May limit number of transactions per month
• Pay little or no interest	• Pay a relatively higher amount of interest, especially if you maintain a large balance
• Debit card or cheques are included	• Debit cards and cheques may not be included
• Basic services are usually offered at no fee	• Basic services may include a fee
• A limited number of transfer of funds between accounts may be free	• Usually all transfer of funds between accounts have a fee
• Transfer of funds is usually not delayed	• Transfer of funds may be delayed

EXAMPLE

Stephanie Spratt wants to determine the amount of interest she would earn over one year if she deposits $1000 in a savings account that pays 2 percent interest annually.

Recall, $I = P \times r \times t$

Interest Earned = Principal × Annual Interest Rate (expressed as a decimal) × Time (in years)

$$= \$1000 \times 0.02 \times 1$$
$$= \$20$$

Although the interest income is attractive, Stephanie cannot write cheques on a savings account. Since she expects to need the funds in her chequing account to pay bills in the near future, she decides not to switch those funds to a savings account at this time.

Term Deposits

Term deposits are offered as short-term or long-term investments. These investments offer slightly lower returns than GICs because they are cashable. They are designed for individuals who do not know when they will need access to their funds, but who would like an interest rate higher than that offered by savings accounts.

Guaranteed Investment Certificates

guaranteed investment certificate (GIC)
An instrument issued by a depository institution that specifies a minimum investment, an interest rate, and a maturity date.

Most depository institutions issue **guaranteed investment certificates (GICs)**, which specify a minimum investment, an interest rate, and a maturity date. For example, a bank may require a $500 minimum investment on all of the GICs it offers. The maturity dates may include one month, three months, six months, one year, and five years. The money invested in a GIC usually cannot be withdrawn until the maturity date, or it will be subject to a penalty for early withdrawal.

The term *guaranteed* here refers to the coverage of the principal investment. Recall that some depository institutions are covered by the CDIC. Their deposits in bank accounts, including GICs, are protected against loss in the event of bankruptcy. Ensure that your investments and deposits are covered by the CDIC. Any deposits not covered should earn a much higher interest rate because of the additional risk.

myth or **fact** A debit card that uses chip technology is more secure than a debit card that uses a magnetic strip.

Return. Depository institutions offer higher interest rates on GICs than on savings deposits and term deposits. This higher return is compensation for being willing to maintain the investment until the maturity date. Interest rates are quoted on an annualized (yearly) basis and vary according to maturity dates. The interest generated by your GIC is based on the annualized interest rate and the amount of time until maturity. For example, an annual interest rate of 6 percent on your deposit means that at the end of one year, you will receive interest equal to 6 percent of the amount you originally deposited.

EXAMPLE

A three-month (90-day) GIC offers an annualized interest rate of 2 percent and requires a $5000 minimum deposit. You want to determine the amount of interest you would earn if you invested $5000 in this GIC. Since the interest rate is annualized, you will receive only a fraction of the 2 percent rate because your investment is for a fraction of the year:

$$\text{Interest Earned} = \text{Principal} \times \text{Annual Interest Rate} \times \text{Time}$$
$$= \$5000 \times 0.02 \times 90/365$$

This calculation can be more easily understood by noting that the interest rate is applied for only 90 days, whereas the annual interest rate reflects 365 days. The interest rate that applies to your 90-day investment is for about one-fourth (90/365) of the year, so the applicable interest rate is:

$$\text{Interest Rate} = 0.02 \times 90/365 = 0.0049 \,(.49\%)$$

The 0.49 percent interest rate represents the actual return on your investment.

Now the interest can be determined by simply applying this return to the principal:

$$\text{Interest Earned} = \text{Principal} \times \text{Interest Rate}$$
$$= \$5000 \times 0.0049$$
$$= \$24.50$$

Liquidity. A penalty is imposed for early withdrawal from GICs, so these deposits are less liquid than funds deposited in a savings account or a term deposit. You should consider a GIC only if you are certain that you will not need the funds until after it matures. You may decide to invest some of your funds in a GIC and other funds in more liquid assets. Many financial institutions have introduced cashable GICs to make this investment more attractive. However, a cashable GIC does not offer the same interest rate as a regular GIC. If you are considering a cashable GIC, consider all of the savings alternatives that are available to you as well.

Choice among GIC Maturities. GICs with longer terms to maturity typically offer higher annualized interest rates. However, these GICs tie up your funds for a longer period of time and are therefore less liquid. Your choice of a maturity date for a GIC may depend on your need for liquidity. For example, if you know that you may need your funds in four months, you could invest in a three-month GIC and then place the funds in a more liquid asset (such as your chequing account or savings account) when the GIC matures. If you do not expect to need the funds for one year, you may consider a one-year GIC.

FOCUS ON ETHICS: Risky Deposits

Consider the case of a financial institution that promises depositors an annual rate of interest that is 4 percent higher than GIC rates offered by local banks.

While this certificate sounds appealing, it is probably much riskier than you think. A firm is not going to offer an interest rate that is 4 percent higher than other interest-bearing investments unless it needs to pay such a high return to compensate for risk. Ask whether the deposit is insured by the CDIC. While you could possibly earn 4 percent more on this investment, you also could lose 100 percent of your money if the financial institution goes bankrupt. There are many investment companies that prey on individuals (especially the elderly) who presume that because an investment sounds like a bank deposit, it is insured and safe. If an investment sounds too good to be true, it probably is.

Canada Savings Bonds (CSBs)

Canada Savings Bonds (CSBs)
Short-term to medium-term, high-quality debt securities issued by the Government of Canada.

Canada Savings Bonds (CSBs) are short-term to medium-term, high-quality debt securities that were issued by the Government of Canada up to November 1, 2017. Another type of bond issued by the Government of Canada under this program, the Canada Premium Bond (CPB), has also been discontinued as of November 1, 2017. CSBs and CPBs were virtually risk-free because they were issued by the federal government. In addition, these bonds were highly liquid because they were cashable at any bank or financial institution. CSBs were a cashable investment whereas Canada Premium Bonds (CPBs) offered a more competitive interest rate and were only cashable once per year. CSBs and CPBs were issued as either a regular or a compound interest bond. A regular interest bond pays out the interest earned every year, while a compound interest bond reinvests the interest earned. However, the interest income earned each year is taxable, even if it is reinvested in the bond.

Money Market Funds (MMFs)

money market funds (MMFs)
Accounts that pool money from individuals and invest in securities that have short-term maturities, such as one year or less.

Money market funds (MMFs) pool money from individuals and invest in securities that have short-term maturities, such as one year or less. In fact, the average term of debt securities held in an MMF is typically less than 90 days. Many MMFs invest in short-term Treasury securities or in wholesale GICs (valued at $100 000 or more). MMFs are not insured, but most invest in very safe investments and have a very low risk of default. Similar to bonds, the interest income earned each year from an MMF is taxable.

Determining the Optimal Allocation of Short-Term Investments

In general, your money management should be guided by the following steps:

1. Anticipate your upcoming bills and ensure that you have sufficient funds in your chequing account to cover all of these expenses.

2. Estimate the additional funds you might need in the near future and consider investing them in an instrument that offers sufficient liquidity (such as an MMF). You may even keep a little extra in reserve for unanticipated expenses.

3. Use the remaining funds in a manner that will earn you a higher return, within your level of risk tolerance.

Your optimal allocation likely will be different than the optimal allocation for another individual. If your future net cash flows will be far short of upcoming expenses, you will need to keep a relatively large proportion of funds in a liquid investment. Another person who has sufficient cash flows to cover expenses will not need much liquidity. This difference is illustrated in Exhibit 5.6. Even though the two individuals have the same level of net cash flows, one person must maintain more liquidity than the other.

Your decision on how to invest your short-term funds (after determining how much money to maintain in your chequing account) should account for your willingness to

EXHIBIT 5.6   How Liquidity Is Affected by Anticipated Expenses

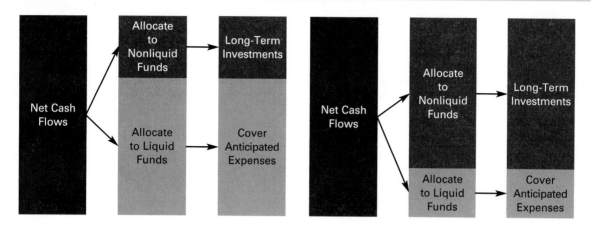

tolerate risk. If you want to minimize all forms of risk, you may consider investing all of your funds in an MMF that focuses on Treasury securities maturing within a month or less. However, you will likely improve the yield if you are willing to accept some degree of risk. For example, if you know that you will not need your funds for at least six months and do not expect interest rates to rise substantially over that period, you might consider investing your funds in a six-month GIC. A compromise would be to invest a portion of your short-term funds in the six-month GIC and the remaining funds in the MMF that focuses on Treasury securities. The GIC offers you a higher expected return (although less liquidity) while the MMF offers you liquidity in case you need funds immediately.

MyLab Finance   Visit MyLab Finance for additional study and practice tools. Select Financial Planning Problems are available in the Study Plan. Create your own study plan, generate personal cash flow statements and balance sheets, and set personal financial goals.

SUMMARY

L.O.1   Provide a background on money management

When applying money management techniques, you should invest any positive net cash flows in an account that is designed to hold short-term or liquid assets, such as a chequing account or a savings account. Liquidity is necessary because there will be periods when your income is not adequate to cover your expenses. A line of credit and/or a credit card are possible sources of short-term financing when short-term investments are insufficient.

L.O.2   Compare the types of financial institutions

Depository institutions (chartered banks, trust and loan companies, and credit unions/*caisses populaires*) accept deposits and provide loans. Financial conglomerates offer a wide variety of these services so that individuals can obtain all of their financial services from a single firm. Non-depository institutions include finance and

lease companies (which provide financing and leasing options for assets, such as a car), mortgage companies (which provide mortgage brokerage services), investment dealers (which provide brokerage and other services), insurance companies (which provide insurance), mutual fund companies (which offer mutual funds), payday loan companies (which provide short-term loans), cheque cashing outlets (which cash cheques for a fee), and pawnshops (which provide small secured loans).

L.O.3   Describe the banking services offered by financial institutions

A depository institution may offer a wide variety of savings alternatives, including chequing services, debit cards, overdraft protection, a stop payment service, online banking, credit card financing, safety deposit boxes, automated banking machines (ABMs), certified cheques, money orders and drafts, and traveller's cheques.

L.O.4   Explain how to select a financial institution

Your choice of financial institution should be based on convenience, deposit rates, deposit insurance, and fees. You should be able to deposit and withdraw funds easily. Deposit rates vary for different types of savings alternatives at different financial institutions. The fees charged by financial institutions vary from one to the next.

L.O.5   Describe the savings alternatives offered by financial institutions

Popular short-term investments considered for money management include savings deposits, term deposits, GICs, Canada Savings Bonds, and money market funds. Savings deposits offer the most liquidity, while GICs and money market funds offer the highest return. In order to avoid tax on growth, a tax-free savings account can be used to hold many types of short-term investments.

REVIEW QUESTIONS

1. Define money management. How does it differ from long-term investment or long-term borrowing decisions?

2. What is liquidity? How is your personal cash flow statement used to help manage your liquidity? Why is liquidity necessary?

3. Name some ways in which an individual might handle a cash flow deficiency. Which would be preferable? Why?

4. What types of investments are appropriate as short-term investment alternatives?

5. What is a depository institution? List the three types of depository institutions.

6. Define and describe a chartered bank. Differentiate among Schedule I, Schedule II, and Schedule III banks.

7. What is a financial conglomerate? List some services that financial conglomerates provide. Give some examples of financial conglomerates.

8. Define and describe a trust and loan company.

9. Define and describe credit unions and *caisses populaires*.

10. List and describe the eight types of non-depository financial institutions.

11. Why do individuals use chequing accounts? What is the disadvantage of having funds in a chequing account?

12. Define and describe a debit card.

13. Why is it important to keep track of your account balance?

14. Explain overdraft protection. With respect to overdraft protection, are all bank fee structures the same? Explain.

15. What is a stop payment? How do you create a stop payment?

16. Define and describe online banking.

17. What is the difference between a debit card and a credit card?

18. Define and describe automated banking machines (ABMs).

19. Differentiate among certified cheques, money orders and drafts, and traveller's cheques.

20. Steve just received his first paycheque and wants to open a chequing account. There are five banks in his home town. What factors should Steve consider when choosing a bank?

21. What features of a tax-free savings account (TFSA) allow it to be considered a very flexible savings alternative?

22. Compare and contrast savings accounts and chequing accounts.

23. What is a GIC? Why are rates on GICs higher than those on savings accounts? What factor would most affect your choice of maturity date on a GIC?

24. What are the two types of Canada Savings Bonds (CSBs)? What is a regular interest bond? What is a compound interest bond?

25. What are money market funds (MMFs)? Describe the features of an MMF.

26. Compare and contrast the return and liquidity characteristics of the various money market investments. Give specific examples.

27. What steps should you take to determine the best allocation of your money market investments? What factors should you consider in determining your allocation?

FINANCIAL PLANNING PROBLEMS

MyLab Finance   Financial Planning Problems marked with a ⊕ can be found in MyLab Finance.

Refer to the chart on the next page when answering Problems 2 through 5.

1. Benjo has a monthly income of $2500. After taking into account taxes and other deductions, his disposable income is $1900. He has $270 in net cash flows each month based on his current level of expenses. Benjo has decided to deposit his monthly net cash flows in a savings account. He would like to establish

an emergency fund equal to six months' worth of expenses. Approximately how many months will it take Benjo to reach his goal?

2. Stuart wants to open a chequing account with a $100 deposit. Stuart believes he will write 15 cheques per month and use other banks' ABMs eight times a month. He will not be able to maintain a minimum balance. Which bank should Stuart choose?

3. Julie wants to open a chequing account with $75. Julie estimates that she will write 20 cheques per month and use her ABM card only at the home bank. She will maintain a $200 balance. Which bank should Julie choose?

4. Veronica plans to open a chequing account with her $1200 tax refund. She believes she can maintain a $500 minimum balance. Also, she estimates that she will write 10 cheques per month and will use other banks' ABMs as much as 15 times per month. Which bank should Veronica choose?

5. Randy, a student, has $500 to deposit in a new chequing account but he knows he will not be able to maintain a minimum balance. He will not use an ABM card, but will write a large number of cheques. Randy is trying to choose between the unlimited cheque writing offered by West Trust and the low per-cheque fee offered by East Coast. How many cheques would Randy have to write each month for the account at West Trust to be the better option?

6. Paul has an account at ICBC Bank. He does not track his chequing account balance in a cheque register. Yesterday evening, he placed two cheques in the mail, for $156.66 and $238.94. Paul accesses his account online and finds that his balance is $568.40 and that all of the cheques he has written except for the two mailed yesterday have cleared. Based on his balance, Paul writes a cheque for a

new stereo for $241. He has no intention of making a deposit in the near future. What are the consequences of his actions?

7. Mary's previous bank statement showed an ending balance of $168.51. This month, she deposited $600 in her account and withdrew a total of $239. Furthermore, she wrote a total of five cheques, two of which have cleared. These two cheques total $143. The three outstanding cheques total $106.09. Mary pays no fees at her bank. What is the balance shown this month on Mary's bank statement?

8. Nancy is depositing $2500 in a six-month term deposit that pays 0.5 percent interest. How much interest will she accrue if she holds the term deposit to maturity?

9. Travis has invested $3000 in a one-year GIC at 1.85 percent. How much will Travis have when the GIC matures?

10. Akida has invested $10 000 in an 18-month GIC that pays 1.95 percent. How much interest will Akida receive at maturity?

11. What rate of interest did Alberto receive over a period of 67 days if he invested $7444 and received interest in the amount of $157?

12. How many days would it take for Shelby's investment of $4300 to accrue $147 in interest if she is able to earn a rate of 1.25 percent?

13. Bart is a college student who has never invested his funds. He has saved $1000 and has decided to invest in an MMF with an expected return of 2 percent, compounded annually. Bart will need these funds in one year. The MMF imposes fees that will cost Bart $20 when he withdraws the funds in one year. How much money will Bart have in one year as a result of this investment?

	Winnipeg Bank	Canadian National	West Trust Bank	East Coast Bank
ABM charges				
Home bank	Free	Free	Free	Free
Other bank	4 free, then $1 per use	$1.25	$1.25	$1.25
Chequing				
Minimum deposit	$100	$25	$1	$1
Minimum balance required to avoid fees	N/A	N/A	$500	N/A
Monthly fees	$6	$7	$11	$2.50
Cheque writing charges	12 free, then $1 per cheque	7 free, then $1 per cheque	Unlimited	50 cents per cheque

CHALLENGE QUESTIONS

1. Hamza has recently received a bonus of $5000 from her employer. She is not sure what she would eventually like to do with this money. For the time being she is considering two GIC investment options:

   a. Invest $5000 in a 2-year GIC that pays interest at 1.65 percent, compounded annually.

   b. Invest $5000 in a 1-year GIC that pays interest at 1.3 percent, compounded annually, and then reinvest the maturity amount for another year at the same rate of return.

   Which option will provide Hamza with the greatest return on her money? By how much?

2. Bart, 19, received $1000 from his grandparents as a birthday present. He wants to use this money to purchase a new $1200 mountain bike. Since he does not have enough money, Bart has decided to invest his $1000 in a TFSA that pays interest at 2.50 percent per annum. How long will Bart have to wait before he has enough money to purchase the mountain bike?

ETHICAL DILEMMA

1. Mike, a recent college graduate, opened a chequing account with a local bank. He asked numerous questions before deciding on this bank, including inquiring about chequing account fees and annual credit card fees. When Mike returns from his first international business trip, he is surprised to see numerous fees on his credit card statement and his bank statement. When he calls the bank, he is informed that it recently added service charges on international transactions involving its chequing and credit card accounts. When Mike protests, the bank points out that his last statement included a flyer detailing these changes. Looking back, Mike realizes that he did, in fact, receive the information but had ignored it because it was included with considerable advertising about car loan rate specials and because the lengthy document was in very small print.

   a. Comment on the ethics of banks and other financial institutions' efforts to notify customers of fee changes. Should a letter specifically dealing with these changes be sent to ensure that customers are aware of the information?

   b. Is there a lesson to be learned from Mike's experience?

2. Ernie is in his mid-fifties and was raised by parents from the Depression era. As a result, he is very risk averse. Ernie recently came into a very large amount of money and he wants to put it where it will be safe but also earn him some return. His banker tells him that he should put the money in a five-year GIC. Ernie asks if there is any way he can lose his money and he is told that the CDIC insures the deposit and the GIC will give him a higher return than a passbook savings account. Ernie purchases the GIC and goes home happy, knowing that his money is safe and available whenever he needs it.

   Four months later, the roof on Ernie's barn collapses. He needs the money in his GIC to make repairs but finds that he can only withdraw it at a substantial penalty.

   a. Comment on the ethics of the banker in not fully discussing all risks associated with GIC investments.

   b. Is Ernie correct in his thinking that he can find a totally risk-free investment?

FINANCIAL PLANNING ONLINE EXERCISES

1. Go to www.atb.com/personal-banking/tools-and-resources/Pages/investment-and-savings-calculators.aspx and click on Savings Planner.

   a. Enter "vacation" as your reason for saving. For how many years are savings being calculated? What is the average tax rate and inflation rate? What is the current cost of the vacation you are saving for? What is the annual rate of return? According to this calculator, how much do you need to save on a monthly basis to reach your goal?

b. Suppose that you have already saved $2000. Enter this amount in the Savings Details section (at Current Savings). Click on Calculate. What is the new amount you need to save on a monthly basis to reach your goal?

2. Go to www.canada.ca/en/financial-consumer-agency/services/rights-responsibilities/rights-banking.html.

   a. Do you have a right to open a personal bank account even if you do not have a job? Do you have to put money in the account right away? If you have been bankrupt in the past, can you still open an account?

   b. What are your rights if you are trying to cash a Government of Canada cheque?

3. Go to www.tangerine.ca/en. How do the services of this web-based bank differ from the services offered by a "regular" bank? What is the savings account interest rate at this online bank? Would you bank at an online financial institution? Why or why not?

4. Go to www.gicdirect.com.

   a. What is today's best three-year GIC rate?

   b. How large is the difference between the one-year and five-year GIC rates?

5. Go to www.ratesupermarket.ca/savings_accounts. Compare the savings account interest rate offered by various financial institutions in a particular province. Select a province, savings amount, and choose "Savings Account" for account type. How do the rates compare? How many financial institutions offer a lower rate than that found in Exercise 3? How many financial institutions offer a higher rate than that found in Exercise 3? Repeat this exercise for other account types.

PSYCHOLOGY OF PERSONAL FINANCE: Paying Your Bills

1. Some people purposely ignore a bill and put it out of their minds in order to avoid the stress associated with it. Other people pay their bills immediately because they worry that they might forget about paying them. What drives your behaviour toward paying bills?

2. Read one practical article on how psychology can affect bill-paying behaviour. You can easily retrieve possible articles by doing an online search using the terms "psychology" and "paying bills." Summarize the main points of the article.

MINI-CASE 1: Money Management

Robert Foster's new job pays $34 500. After taxes and other deductions, his disposable income is $24 000. His monthly expenses total $1600. Robert's most important goal is to save for a new car purchase. However, his older brother, Frank, has urged Robert to start saving from "day one" on the job. Frank has lost a job twice in the past five years through company downsizing and now keeps $35 000 in a money market fund in case it happens again. Frank's annual take home pay is $46 000.

1. Does Robert need an emergency fund? If so, how much emergency savings should he try to set aside? What type of account would you recommend for his emergency fund?

2. Comment on Frank's use of liquid assets.

3. Robert has heard that some local auto dealerships may require a certified cheque for down payments. Why would they require a certified cheque?

MINI-CASE 2: Savings Alternatives

Sandra Chan, 22, has just moved to Winnipeg to begin her first professional job. She is concerned about her finances and, specifically, wants to save for a "rainy day" and a new car purchase in two years. In order to finance her move, Sandra had put aside some money. Now that her move is finished, Sandra has $1000 remaining in her chequing account at the bank. Sandra is unsure if she should put this money aside in a "rainy day" fund, or if she should put this money aside for a new car purchase. Sandra has reduced her savings options to four choices:

a. Leave the $1000 in her chequing account where it will earn 0.25 percent per year.

b. Deposit her $1000 in an online investment savings account where she will earn 1.35 percent per year.

c. Invest her $1000 in a Canada Premium Bond that pays interest of 1.00 percent per year.

d. Invest her $1000 in a 2-year GIC that pays interest of 1.50 percent per year.

1. Which short-term investment is most appropriate for Sandra's situation?

2. Assuming Sandra remains unsure as to what she will do with the $1000, does it really matter if Sandra puts her $1000 in a "rainy day" fund or a "car purchase" fund?

Study Guide

Circle the correct answer and then check the answers in the back of the book to chart your progress.

Multiple Choice

1. Which of the following statements regarding liquidity is incorrect?
   a. Liquidity is necessary because there will be periods when your income is not adequate to cover your expenses.
   b. Alternative sources of liquidity include access to a credit card, a line of credit, or an emergency fund.
   c. Maintaining adequate liquidity is important for situations where your income exceeds your expenses.
   d. A useful rule of thumb is that you should have between three and six months' worth of expenses in an emergency fund.

2. Which of the following financial institutions specialize in making personal loans to people who are perceived to have a higher risk of default?
   a. Finance company
   b. Commercial bank
   c. Trust company
   d. Credit union

3. Which of the following is a type of non-depository institution?
   a. Chartered bank
   b. Trust company
   c. Credit union
   d. Finance company

4. The main types of non-depository institutions that serve individuals include finance and lease companies, pawnshops, investment dealers, and ___.
   a. financial advisers
   b. insurance companies
   c. Schedule III banks
   d. *caisses populaires*

5. All of the following are advantages of online banking, except:
   a. Provides real-time reporting of account information.
   b. Allows you to transfer funds among accounts.
   c. Allows you to close chequing, savings, or other accounts.
   d. Allows you to pay bills electronically.

6. The primary advantage of calling an automated phone service or logging on to your financial institution's website in order to check your account balance is:
   a. You do not have to talk to someone.
   b. The information on your account balance should be up to date.
   c. You can also conveniently check your email and/ or chat with friends if you are already online.

d. You can transfer money from your savings account to your chequing account if you realize that you do not have enough money in your chequing account for upcoming expenses.

7. The advantage of overdraft protection is that it protects a customer who writes a cheque for an amount that exceeds the balance of the chequing account. The cost of this service may include all of the following, except:
   a. A high interest rate charged on the overdraft balance.
   b. A limit to the number of banking services you can have with one financial institution.
   c. A one-time fee every time you need to use the protection.
   d. A monthly fee to your account simply for having the protection available.

8. Which of the following is a disadvantage of using debits cards over credit cards?
   a. You will not have a good record of your transactions.
   b. The interest rates are higher than for credit cards.
   c. You cannot tell if your bank account will become overdrawn.
   d. The fees charged to the cardholder can become significant.

9. Rank the following ABM machines in order of cost to you, from least expensive to most expensive. ABM1 belongs to the bank with which you have a chequing account. ABM2 is owned privately. ABM3 is owned by a financial institution with which you do not have an account.
   a. ABM1, ABM2, ABM3
   b. ABM2, ABM1, ABM3
   c. ABM3, ABM2, ABM1
   d. ABM1, ABM3, ABM2

10. Which of the following banking products can be cashed immediately upon receipt?
    a. Certified cheque
    b. Traveller's cheque
    c. Draft
    d. All of the above

11. Regarding TFSA accounts, which of the following is true?
    a. Using your TFSA for tuition savings makes sense as long as the funds are replaced before the next term.
    b. If your TFSA investment deposit grows from $5000 to $10 000 you can withdraw only the $5000 deposit tax-free.
    c. Using a TFSA account for your everyday banking would be a good way to avoid paying tax on the interest from your bank account.
    d. Using a TFSA account to hold a cashable GIC for an emergency will mean you do not have to pay tax on the interest earned.

12. In planning a money management strategy, which of the following is most important?
    a. Select a combination of investments with varying risk and return.
    b. Select a combination of investments to achieve both adequate liquidity and return.
    c. Ensure all short-term investments are fully liquid.
    d. Shop around to find the institution paying the highest interest rates on GICs.

13. Donald is considering how he should allocate the money he has in his emergency fund. He expects that interest rates will decrease sharply in the next six months. As a result, he is considering investing in a two-year GIC. He feels that when his investment matures, interest rates will have increased back to where they are right now. However, his current net cash flows are less than $100 and he is concerned that if he incurs any unexpected expenses, he will need access to his funds. Which of the following investments would be inappropriate given his circumstances?
    a. Two-year GIC
    b. Money market fund
    c. One-month term deposit
    d. A savings account paying 2 percent on all deposits

14. To get the better rate on an emergency fund investment you should invest in a:
    a. Five-year cashable GIC.
    b. One-year non-cashable GIC.
    c. Money market fund.
    d. One-year Canada Premium Bond.

15. The Canada Deposit Insurance Corporation insures money on deposit at:
    a. Insurance companies.
    b. Brokerage and securities dealers.
    c. Chartered banks.
    d. All of the above.

True/False

1. True or False? Money management focuses on maintaining long-term investments to achieve both liquidity and an adequate return on your investments.

2. True or False? The largest chartered banks operating in Canada, based on total assets, are Canadian-owned Schedule I banks.

3. True or False? Credit unions/*caisses populaires* are provincially incorporated co-operative financial institutions that are owned and controlled by their members.

4. True or False? Investment dealers use money provided by individuals to invest in securities to create mutual funds.

5. True or False? A mutual fund is a type of depository institution that sells units to individuals and uses the proceeds to invest in securities to create mutual funds.

6. True or False? If an organization is making regular monthly automatic withdrawals from your account, you must first ask the organization to stop withdrawing money before you can make a stop payment request at your financial institution.

7. True or False? With respect to a TFSA, if you contribute less than $5500 per year, any remaining contribution room cannot be carried forward to subsequent years.

8. True or False? A debit card differs from a credit card in that it does not provide credit.

9. True or False? The annual fee for a safety deposit box at a branch of ABC Bank is the same for all boxes.

10. True or False? As compared to certified cheques, money orders and drafts tend to be used for smaller amounts of money.

11. True or False? A lower minimum balance required on a savings account is preferable because it gives you more flexibility if you do not want to tie up your funds in a savings account.

12. True or False? Term deposits offer slightly higher returns than GICs because they are cashable.

13. True or False? Web-based financial institutions tend to pay the same interest rates on deposits compared to financial institutions with physical branches.

14. True or False? A savings account is not as convenient as a chequing account because you cannot write cheques on a savings account.

15. True or False? The average maturity date of debt securities held in a money market fund is typically less than 90 days.

Assessing, Managing, and Securing Your Credit

CHAPTER 6

Diego Cervo/Shutterstock

Kim and Tara are sisters who have very different perspectives on the use of credit. Kim avoids using credit. She has paid cash for everything, including her car. When Tara began her first year of college, she was on a tight budget. To cover her spending needs, she decided to apply for a credit card so that she would be able to make emergency purchases. Three years and two additional credit cards later, Tara graduated with $4000 of debt.

Although she has always been financially responsible, Kim was surprised to recently learn that she had a very low credit rating. When she decided to finance part of the cost of a motorcycle purchase, she was surprised to learn that the finance company considered her a high-risk applicant on their credit rating system — simply because she had no history of using credit. In addition to carrying debt, Tara recently had her wallet stolen from her car and received a phone call from her credit card company concerning some transactions that were made at a hardware store on her credit card. Apparently, someone had impersonated Tara and made a number of purchases of high end power tools. Tara didn't recognize any of the transactions.

QUESTIONS:

1. What are some of the things that Kim could have done to establish a positive credit history?
2. What strategies could have helped Tara manage her debt more effectively?
3. Describe some ways in which your identity can be stolen. How can you protect against identity theft?

157

L.O.1

credit
Funds provided by a creditor to a borrower that the borrower will repay with interest or fees in the future.

BACKGROUND ON CREDIT

Credit represents funds provided by a creditor to a borrower that the borrower will repay with interest or fees in the future. The funds borrowed are sometimes referred to as the principal and we segment repayment of credit into principal payments and interest. Credit is frequently extended to borrowers as a loan with set terms, such as the amount of funds provided and the maturity date when the funds will be repaid. For instalment loans, the interest and principal payments are blended, meaning that each payment includes both principal and interest. For other types of loans, interest payments are made monthly and the principal payment is made at the maturity date, when the loan is terminated.

Types of Credit

Credit can be classified as instalment or revolving open-end.

instalment loan
A loan provided for specific purchases, with interest charged on the amount borrowed. It is repaid on a regular basis, generally with blended payments.

Instalment Loan. An **instalment loan** is provided for specific purchases, such as a car. Also referred to as instalment credit, the amount borrowed is repaid on a regular basis over a period of time (usually a few years). The timing and amount of each payment depend on the terms of the loan. In general, loan repayments are made according to a specific repayment schedule with a portion of the payment being applied to the principal and the remainder representing interest paid to the lender.

Some types of instalment loans allow payments to be structured so that the borrower pays interest only until the maturity date, when the balance of the loan is due. The payment made at the maturity of the loan is referred to as a balloon payment.

revolving open-end credit
Credit provided up to a specified maximum amount based on income, debt level, and credit history; interest is charged each month on the outstanding balance.

Revolving Open-End Credit. **Revolving open-end credit**, such as a credit card or a line of credit, allows consumers to borrow up to a specified maximum amount (such as $1000 or $10 000). The credit limit is determined by the borrower's income level, debt level, credit history, and other factors determined by the lender. The consumer can pay the entire amount borrowed at any time, up to and including the payment due date, or pay a portion of the balance and have interest charged on the remainder. Unlike an instalment loan, the borrower can re-borrow the amount that was paid when using revolving open-end credit. Typically, a minimum payment is due each month. The minimum payment on revolving credit is usually 3 percent of the outstanding amount as of the date specified in the terms of the credit agreement.

Revolving open-end credit can also be referred to as a demand loan because the financial institution providing the loan can ask for repayment at any time. However, it would be unusual for a financial institution to demand repayment of a revolving open-end credit facility.

Go to
www.atb.com/personal-banking/tools-and-resources/Pages/loan-calculators.aspx

This website provides
a personal loan payment calculator that will help you determine how much you can borrow (the loan amount), the length of your loan (term in months), or the monthly payment if you already know the interest rate and payment frequency.

Advantages of Using Credit

Access to credit allows you to achieve some of your goals, such as purchasing a home or a car, sooner than you would be able to otherwise. Without credit capacity, individuals and families would have to wait until enough savings have accumulated in order to make such purchases. The appropriate use of credit also helps you to establish a good credit history, which in turn helps you to build a good credit score. Credit is convenient because it eliminates the need for carrying cash. In addition, credit allows you to make purchases where cash may not be an option; for example, when you make a purchase over the internet or on the phone. Many credit cards offer additional benefits to their members. Air miles and travel insurance are two of the more popular benefits available on credit cards. If used correctly, credit can be a source of short-term loans since you do not have to pay the balance outstanding on your credit card until the statement due date. Perhaps the most important benefit of using credit cards is that a record of your past transactions is maintained by the credit card company, which then sends you a history of your past purchases.

Disadvantages of Using Credit

There can be a high cost to using credit. If you borrow too much money and fail to make a budget for your debt payments, you may have difficulty making your payments. It is easier to obtain credit than to pay it back, and having a line of credit can tempt you to make impulse purchases that you simply cannot afford. If you are unable to make the minimum required repayment on the credit you use, you can damage your credit rating. As a result, you may not be able to obtain credit again or will have to pay a very high interest rate to obtain it. The interest cost of using credit increases the amount that you ultimately have to pay for items that you purchase on credit. Your ability to save money will also be reduced if you have large credit payments, as illustrated in Exhibit 6.1. If your spending and credit card payments exceed your net cash flows, you will need to withdraw savings to cover the deficiency. Exhibit 6.2 summarizes the advantages and disadvantages of using credit.

myth or **fact** Creditors prefer that an individual's credit report display relatively more instalment loan credit as opposed to revolving open-end credit.

Credit History

You receive credit when you apply for and are approved to use credit instruments such as credit cards, retail credit cards (for example, a Best Buy card), lines of credit, and personal loans and leases. When you have accounts with companies that offer credit, you develop a credit history that documents how timely you are in paying your bills. You can establish a favourable credit history by paying the monthly payment associated with your

Go to
www.oaccs.com

This website provides information on how to establish, use, and protect credit.

EXHIBIT 6.1   Impact of Credit Payments on Savings

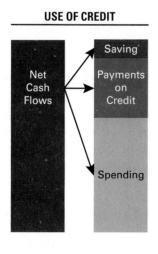
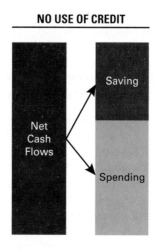

EXHIBIT 6.2   Advantages and Disadvantages of Using Credit

Advantages	Disadvantages
• Allows you to achieve your goals sooner	• You may have difficulty making your payments
• Helps you establish a good credit history and credit score	• You may make impulse purchases that you cannot afford
• Eliminates the need for carrying cash	• You may damage your credit rating
• Allows you to make purchases when cash is not an option	• There is an interest cost to using credit
• Provides additional benefits, such as air miles and travel insurance	• Large credit payments take away from your ability to save
• Provides short-term loans for emergencies	• You may need to access savings to cover net cash flow deficiencies
• Statements help you record and keep track of past transactions	

debt obligations, such as your cell phone, on or before the due date. Doing so indicates to potential creditors that you may also repay other credit in a timely manner. This helps to establish your character for new creditors.

The Credit Application Process

The process of applying for credit from a financial institution usually involves filling out an application form, negotiating the interest rate, and negotiating the loan contract. In the case of revolving open-end credit, such as a credit card, the interest rate is often non-negotiable and the terms of the loan contract are pre-determined.

Application Process. When applying for credit, you need to provide information from your personal balance sheet and personal cash flow statement to document your ability to repay the loan. You may need to provide proof of income using either a recent pay slip or a T4 slip, or both.

- **Personal Balance Sheet.** Recall from Chapter 3 that your financial condition is partially measured by a personal balance sheet. The personal balance sheet indicates your assets, liabilities, and net worth at a specific point in time. The assets are relevant because they indicate the level of capital, i.e., funds in the form of savings and investments that you currently have. In addition, your assets may serve as collateral to back a loan. The liabilities are relevant because they represent your existing debt.

- **Personal Cash Flow Statement.** Your financial condition is also represented by a personal cash flow statement, as discussed in Chapter 3. This statement indicates your income and expenses and therefore suggests how much free cash flow you have on a periodic basis. Lenders use this cash flow information to determine whether you qualify for a loan and, if so, the maximum size of the loan you can afford. An individual with existing loans or credit card debt may have insufficient cash flow to cover the payments on any additional loans.

The key component of most prospective borrowers' personal cash flow statements is their income. Lenders require income documentation, such as a T4 slip, which indicates annual earnings, or pay stubs, which indicate recent salary. Lenders may also require additional information depending on the type and amount of the loan.

Creditors generally prefer that you have a high level of revenues, a low level of expenses, a large amount of capital and collateral, and a good credit history. Nevertheless, they commonly extend credit to individuals who do not have all of these attributes. For example, although creditors recognize that university and college students may not earn much income, they may still provide a limited amount of credit if they believe that the students are likely to repay it. Some creditors may also extend credit at higher interest rates to individuals who have a higher risk of default. The higher interest rates that creditors charge on these types of loans will offset the number of individuals who will not be able to repay their debt. For example, the interest rate charged on a credit card not only is relatively high, but also is calculated on the daily outstanding balance. It is important to pay your credit card bill in full every month to avoid losing money by paying high interest charges.

Credit Check. When you apply for credit, a lender typically conducts a credit check as part of the application review process. The lender can obtain a credit report, discussed later in this chapter, which indicates your creditworthiness. A credit report summarizes credit repayment with banks, retailers, credit card issuers, and other lenders. Credit problems remain on a credit bureau's report for up to 10 years.

Credit Insurance

Because access to credit is essential these days, some consumers attempt to ensure that they will be able to keep making credit payments (and therefore maintain their credit standing) under adverse conditions. They purchase credit insurance, which represents a commitment to cover their credit repayments under various circumstances. For instance, credit accident and sickness insurance ensures that monthly credit payments are made when consumers cannot work due to an accident or illness. Credit unemployment insurance ensures that monthly payments are made for consumers when they are unemployed. It is important to read the fine print with respect to credit insurance because the payment period is usually limited to a short term. In some instances, your payments may only be covered for as little as three months. Credit insurance of this type is not a good substitute for the types of insurance coverage discussed in Chapters 8 and 9.

CREDIT BUREAUS

Credit bureaus provide **credit reports** that document your credit payment history to lenders and others. Your credit report shows every time you have applied for credit, whether you pay your bills on time, whether you maintain balances on your accounts, and whether you pay late fees. It may also contain information about public records such as bankruptcies and court judgments, and identify inquiries made by various companies and potential employers about your credit rating. Canada's two primary credit bureaus are Equifax Canada and TransUnion Canada.

L.0.2

credit reports
Reports provided by credit bureaus that document a person's credit payment history.

FOCUS ON ETHICS: Guarding Your Financial Information

You must give written permission (usually your signature on the application form) to allow firms to access your credit report. This permission is usually granted at the time of your application for credit, insurance, or employment.

While the sharing of financial information may ease your application process, it also allows firms to access more information than you may want to disclose. Financial institutions must provide customers with privacy policies that detail what information they collect and intend to share. For example, a bank that receives a credit card application from you may intend to pass this financial information to an affiliate that can market its financial services to you. Don't overlook these notices, which are often tucked in with your monthly statement or bill. The privacy notices also give you the opportunity to limit some of that sharing by opting out, which typically involves calling a phone number or filling out a form to return to the service provider. No one can access the information in your credit report without your prior consent.

The information provided in a credit report includes:

- Your personal information
- A consumer statement showing the details of any explanation that you have submitted to the credit bureau regarding a particular account
- A summary of your accounts
- Your account history
- Bank information regarding any accounts that were closed for derogatory reasons
- Public information regarding bankruptcies, judgments, and secured loans
- The names of creditors who have made account inquiries
- A list of creditor contacts

Credit Score

A credit score is a rating that indicates a person's creditworthiness. It reflects the likelihood that an individual will be able to make payments for credit in a timely manner.

Lenders commonly assess the credit payment history provided by one or more credit bureaus when deciding whether to extend a personal loan or mortgage. For example, financial institutions may rely on this information when deciding whether to approve your credit card application, provide you with a car loan, or provide you with a home (mortgage) loan. Your credit score can also affect the interest rate quoted on the loan you request. A high credit score could reduce your interest rate substantially, which may translate into savings of thousands of dollars in interest expenses over time.

The credit bureaus rely on a credit scoring model created by the Fair Isaac Corporation (FICO). In Canada, this credit scoring model is referred to as your BEACON score. Exhibit 6.3 provides a chart of the factors that the credit bureaus consider important when calculating your score. The most important factor used in BEACON credit scoring is your credit payment history, which accounts for 35 percent of the score. If you have paid your bills on time over the last seven years, you will receive a high rating on that portion of your credit score.

Credit use, the amount of your available credit that you use each month, accounts for 30 percent of the score. If you continue to rely on most of the credit you were granted, you will receive a lower score. Put another way, if you have a high credit limit but do not rely much on that credit, you will receive a higher score. This second situation suggests that you have access to credit but have enough discipline not to use it.

myth or **fact** Everything else being equal, the more money you make, the higher your credit score.

EXHIBIT 6.3 Credit Score Criteria

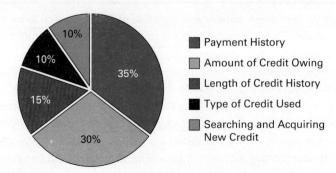

- Payment History
- Amount of Credit Owing
- Length of Credit History
- Type of Credit Used
- Searching and Acquiring New Credit

Source: Reprinted with permission from Alberta's Best Mortgages, www.alberta-mortgages.com/articles/credit-bureau.html (accessed February 20, 2007).

Your score is also affected by the length of the relationship with your creditors. This factor accounts for 15 percent of the score. You will receive a higher score if you maintain longer relationships with creditors. A fourth factor is the type of credit that you use, which accounts for 10 percent of the score. Everything else being equal, someone who uses only credit cards as a source of credit will have a lower score than someone who uses only personal loans as a source of credit.

Finally, your score is affected by recent credit inquiries. A large number of credit inquiries may indicate that you are desperately seeking a creditor that will provide you with a loan. Therefore, you will receive a higher score if the number of inquiries is relatively low. This accounts for 10 percent of the score.

Overall, if you make your credit payments on time, maintain a low level of debt, and have demonstrated your ability to make timely credit payments over many years, you are likely to receive a very high credit score. The credit score is not allowed to reflect your sex, race, religion, national origin, or marital status.

Differing Scores among Bureaus. While the credit bureaus mentioned earlier rely on BEACON to determine your credit score, each bureau may give you a different score. The reason for differing scores is that the information each bureau receives about you is not exactly the same. Assume that Equifax received information from a utility company that you made a payment one month late, while that information was not made available to TransUnion. In this case, your credit score assigned by Equifax would likely be lower than that assigned by TransUnion. A difference in credit scores can easily be sufficient to cause you to be approved for a loan based on the credit bureau that provided the highest credit score, but to not receive approval for a loan based on the credit bureau that provided the lowest credit score. Keep in mind that some financial institutions may use more than one credit bureau for information about an applicant, so if either one of the bureaus assigns a low credit score, the lender may be more cautious in providing credit.

Interpreting Credit Scores. Exhibit 6.4 shows the percentage of the Canadian population that falls into each credit score range. Scores range from 300 to 900. A score of 600 or higher is considered good, and may indicate that you are worthy of credit. Bear in mind, though, that each financial institution sets its own criteria to determine whether to extend credit. Some may require a minimum score of 580, while others require a minimum of 620. Very high credit scores (such as 750 or higher) normally result in easy credit approval. Other creditors may be willing to extend credit if you have a relatively low credit score (such as 570 or lower), but they may charge a higher interest rate.

EXHIBIT 6.4 National Distribution of BEACON Scores

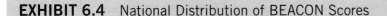

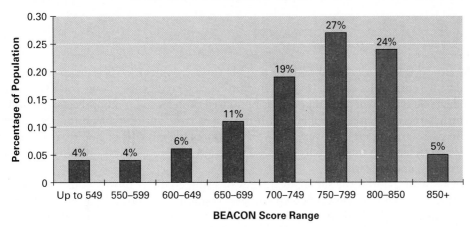

Source: Reprinted with permission from Alberta's Best Mortgages, www.alberta-mortgages.com/articles/credit-bureau.html (accessed February 20, 2007).

The lower your score, the riskier lenders think you are. Risk to a lender can be interpreted to mean a higher rate of default, late payment, or nonpayment.

The acceptable credit score may vary with the type of credit (credit card, car loan, home loan, and so forth) you are seeking. While lenders commonly rely on credit information and a credit score from a credit bureau, they also consider other information not disclosed by credit bureaus, such as your income level. For example, a person with a high credit score may not be approved for a specific loan that would require a very large payment each month. In this example, your income level may be the key factor that prevents a lender from giving you the loan.

A low credit score is normally due to either missed payments or carrying an excessive amount of debt, both of which will be noted on your credit report. A poor credit history will appear on your credit report for three to ten years, depending on the type of information contained in the item reported. Filing for bankruptcy will remain on your credit record for six to seven years, depending on the province you lived in at the time of the bankruptcy.

You can begin to improve your credit score immediately by catching up on late payments, making at least the minimum payments on time, and reducing your debt.

Reviewing Your Credit Report

You should review your credit report from each of the credit bureaus at least once a year. Since each credit bureau has its own process for reporting credit information, you should check the accuracy of the credit report provided by each one. A review of your credit report is beneficial for three reasons. First, you can ensure that the report is accurate. If there are any errors, you can contact each of the credit bureaus to inform them of those errors. Second, a review of the report will show you the types of information that lenders or credit card companies may consider when deciding whether to provide credit. Third, your credit report indicates what kind of information might lower your credit rating, so that you can attempt to eliminate these deficiencies and improve your credit rating prior to applying for additional credit.

Go to
www.equifax.com/ecm/
canada/EFXCreditRe-
portRequestForm.pdf

This website provides
a PDF document that you can
complete and send in order
to obtain a free credit report
from Equifax.

Go to
www.transunion.ca/
resources/transunion-ca/
doc/personal/Consumer_
Disclosure_Request_
Form_en.pdf

This website provides
a PDF document that you can
complete and send in order
to obtain a free credit report
from Transunion.

L.O.3

CONSUMER CREDIT PRODUCTS

There are many credit products available to consumers. They differ on many characteristics, such as their purpose, the length of time they are used, the limit to the amount of credit you can receive, their interest rate and repayment terms, and other features we will outline below. The most common consumer credit products are credit cards, personal loans, home equity lines of credit, car loans, and student loans.

CREDIT CARDS

The easiest way to establish credit is to apply for a credit card. There is no shortage of credit card companies eager to extend credit to you. A credit card allows you to purchase products on credit wherever that card is honoured. You receive a monthly statement that identifies the purchases you made with the credit card during that period. Normally, credit cards are not used for very large expenditures such as cars or homes, but they are very convenient for smaller purchases, such as meals at restaurants, gasoline, clothing, car repairs, and groceries.

Credit cards offer the same advantages of using credit as those discussed earlier in this chapter. That is, credit cards help you to (1) establish a good credit history, (2) create credit capacity, (3) eliminate the need for carrying cash, (4) provide a method for payment when cash is not an option, (5) earn additional benefits, (6) receive free financing until the due date on your credit card statement, and, perhaps most importantly, (7) keep track of all expenses made using a credit card. Credit card companies provide you with a monthly statement that contains a consolidated list of the purchases you made with the credit card. The monthly statement enables you to keep track of your spending. In some cases, you can receive an annual statement as well, detailing expenses by category, which can be useful in preparing your income tax return if you can claim such expenses. You can also check your up-to-date credit card statement online through your bank.

Types of Credit Cards

The most popular credit cards are MasterCard, Visa, and American Express. These three types of cards are especially convenient because they are accepted by most merchants. The merchants honour credit cards because they recognize that many consumers will make purchases only if they can use their cards. A credit card company receives a percentage (commonly between 2 and 4 percent) of the payments made to merchants with its credit card. For example, when you use your MasterCard to pay for a $500 car repair at a Petro-Canada Certigard service centre, Petro-Canada will pay MasterCard a percentage of that amount. In the case of your car repair, Petro-Canada would pay MasterCard 3 percent of $500, or $15.

Many financial institutions issue MasterCard and Visa credit cards to individuals. Each financial institution makes its own arrangements with credit card companies to do the billing and financing when necessary. For example, CIBC has an agreement with Visa that allows CIBC to provide credit cards to its customers under the Visa brand. The institution, CIBC in this case, provides financing for individuals who choose not to pay their balances in full when they receive a statement. The financial institutions benefit by providing financing because they typically earn a high rate of interest on the credit extended. Some universities and charitable organizations also issue MasterCard and Visa credit cards and provide financing if needed.

Prestige Credit Cards. Financial institutions may issue **prestige cards** to individuals who have an exceptional credit standing. These cards, sometimes referred to as gold cards or platinum cards, provide extra benefits to cardholders above and beyond the benefits available from a standard credit card, which was described in the previous section. A prestige card may provide travel insurance, insurance on rental cars, and special warranties on purchases. Prestige cards usually charge an annual fee for the additional benefits they provide. You must carefully assess the usefulness of these benefits versus the cost of any annual fee.

prestige cards
Credit cards, such as gold cards or platinum cards, issued by a financial institution to individuals who have an exceptional credit standing.

Specialized Credit Cards. An alternative to standard or prestige credit cards is specialized credit cards. A **retail (or proprietary) credit card** is a specialized credit card because it is honoured only by a specific retail establishment. For example, many department stores (such as The Bay and Home Depot) and gas stations (such as Petro-Canada and Esso) issue their own credit cards. If you use an Esso credit card to pay for gas at an Esso station, Esso does not have to pay a small percentage of the proceeds to MasterCard or any other credit card company. You can usually obtain an application for a retail card when paying for products or services. The interest rate charged when financing with retail credit cards is normally higher than that charged on standard or prestige cards. One disadvantage of a retail credit card is that it limits your purchases to a single merchant.

retail (or proprietary) credit card
A credit card that is honoured only by a specific retail establishment.

A student credit card can help you to establish a credit rating while you are still in school. By using credit wisely, you create the capacity to access credit when you need to finance large purchases, such as a car or a home. Generally, the application process for student credit cards is simplified since most students do not have a high income or any assets or liabilities. A U.S. dollar credit card is ideal for individuals who travel to the United States since the amount billed on the monthly statement will be shown in U.S. dollars. If you use a credit card other than a U.S. dollar credit card, the credit card company will convert your U.S. dollar purchase into Canadian dollars. A secured credit card is used by individuals who have had credit problems in the past and want to rebuild their credit score. A personal bankruptcy or being new to Canada are two of the circumstances under which this type of credit card is appropriate.

Although there are many types of credit cards you could obtain, having several credit cards also means that you will have several credit card bills to pay each month. Using one card for all purchases allows you to make only one payment each month to cover all of your expenses.

Credit Limit

Credit card companies set a credit limit, which specifies the maximum amount of credit allowed. The credit limit varies among individuals. It may be a relatively small amount (such as $500) for individuals who have a low income. The credit limit usually can be increased for individuals who prove that they are creditworthy by paying their credit card bills on time. Some credit card companies may allow a large limit (such as $10 000 or more) to households that have made their payments consistently and have higher incomes.

Overdraft Protection

Some credit cards provide overdraft protection, which allows you to make purchases beyond your stated credit limit. This is similar to the overdraft protection provided on some chequing accounts at financial institutions. The overdraft protection on credit cards prevents your card being rejected because you are over your credit limit. On the other hand, people can spend beyond their credit limit if they have overdraft protection.

Fees are charged, however, whenever overdraft protection is needed. The fees vary among credit card issuers, but can be as high as $30 or more each time protection is needed. Thus, a person who made five transactions after reaching the credit limit in a particular month may incur overdraft protection fees of $150 (5 transactions × $30 per transaction) in that month.

Annual Fee

Some credit card companies charge an annual fee, such as $50 or $70, for the privilege of using their cards. The fee is sometimes waived for individuals who use their credit cards frequently and pay their credit card bills in a timely manner.

Incentives to Use the Card

Some credit card companies offer a bonus to cardholders. For example, they may award a point toward a free airline ticket for every dollar spent. After accumulating 20 000 points, for example, you will receive a coupon for a free flight anywhere within Canada. Therefore, if you spend $20 000 over the year on purchases and use this particular credit card for all of them, you will accumulate enough points by the end of the year to earn this free flight. Some airlines issue their own credit cards, which provide similar benefits.

Grace Period

Credit cards typically allow a grace period during which you are not charged any interest on your purchases. The grace period is usually about 20 days from the time the credit card statement is "closed" (any purchases after that date are put on the following month's bill) to the time the bill is due. The credit card issuer essentially provides you with free credit from the time you made the purchase until the bill is due, but only if you start the month with a zero balance.

EXAMPLE

On June 3, Ted Jones paid a car repair bill of $1000 with his credit card. The billing period for Ted's credit card starts on the first of every month and ends with the last day of every month. For the month of June, the closing date for Ted's billing statement is June 30. The grace period Ted receives from the credit card company is 20 days. Therefore, his bill is due on July 20. As shown in the timeline below, Ted receives about 47 days of free credit.

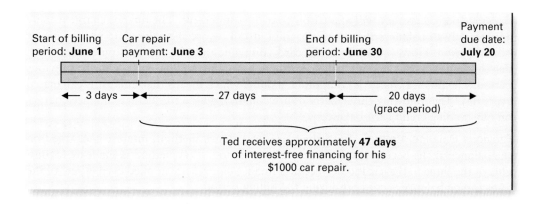

Ted receives approximately **47 days** of interest-free financing for his $1000 car repair.

Cash Advances/Convenience Cheques

Most credit cards allow cash advances at automated banking machines (ABMs). They also may provide cheques, often referred to as convenience cheques, that can be used to make purchases that cannot be made by credit card. Since a cash advance represents credit extended by the sponsoring financial institution, interest is charged on this transaction from the date it is made. Interest is also charged from the date a purchase is made using a convenience cheque. Therefore, the grace period that applies to purchases with a credit card does not apply to cash advances or to purchases made using convenience cheques. Although cash advances and convenience cheques are advantageous they can also be extremely costly. These features of credit cards should be used only as a last resort since they represent an expensive source of funds.

Financing

Some individuals use credit cards as a means of financing their purchases. That is, they pay only a portion of the credit card bill at the end of the month, and the sponsoring financial institution extends credit for the remainder and charges an interest rate on it. This interest rate is commonly between 20 and 30 percent on an annualized basis and does not vary much over time. Although financing is convenient for individuals who are short of funds, it is expensive and should be avoided if possible.

Credit cards can offer a variable rate, a fixed rate, or a tiered rate. A variable rate adjusts in response to a specified market interest rate, such as the prime rate. For example, the credit card interest rate could be based on the prime lending rate plus 6 percent. The bank that provides financing on a credit card can change the fixed interest rate it charges, but it must notify you if it does so.

Some banks offer a tiered interest rate on their credit cards, in which cardholders who make late payments are charged a higher rate. Banks that offer a tiered interest rate are expected to inform their cardholders of this practice.

> **myth** or **fact** In order to prevent credit card fraud, write "Ask for ID" on the back of your credit card instead of signing it.

Many credit cards advertise a very low "teaser" interest rate, which is normally applicable for the first three to six months. Some people transfer their balances from one credit card to another as soon as the period of low interest rates has ended. The issuer of one credit card may charge a fee when transferring the balance to another new credit card with the low teaser rate. Some credit card companies will also negotiate a lower interest rate if you are planning to switch cards.

The **finance charge** represents the interest and fees you must pay as a result of using credit. Normally, the amount that you have to pay at the end of each billing cycle is the greater of $10 or 3 percent of the outstanding balance. Purchases after the statement closing date are not normally considered when determining the finance charge because of

finance charge
The interest and fees you must pay as a result of using credit.

the grace period, as they will appear on your next statement. The finance charge usually applies only to balances that were not paid in full before their due date in the current billing period. However, some credit card companies add in any new purchases when determining the average daily balance if there is an outstanding balance in the previous period. The finance charge is compounded daily, which means that interest is calculated every day. The following three methods are commonly used to calculate finance charges on outstanding credit card balances.

Previous Balance Method. With the previous balance method, interest is charged on the balance at the beginning of the new billing period. This method is the least favourable of the three to the cardholder because finance charges are applied even if part of the outstanding balance is paid off during the billing period.

Average Daily Balance Method. The most frequently used method is the average daily balance method. For each day in the billing period, the credit card company adds together the ending balance of your credit card account. The company then determines the average daily balance for the billing period by dividing the total of the ending balances by the number of days in the billing period. The interest charged to your account is determined by multiplying the average daily balance by the daily interest rate, and then multiplying this result by the number of days in the billing period. This method takes into account your paying any part of the outstanding balance. Thus, if you pay part of the outstanding balance during the billing period, your finance charges will be lower under this method than under the previous balance method. There are variations of this method. It may be adjusted to exclude any new purchases or to compute the average over two billing periods instead of one period.

Adjusted Balance Method. Under the adjusted balance method, interest is charged based on the balance at the end of the new billing period. This method is most favourable because it applies finance charges only to the outstanding balance that was not paid off during the billing period.

The following example illustrates the three methods used to determine finance charges.

EXAMPLE

Assume that as of June 10, you have an outstanding credit card balance of $2700 due to purchases made over the previous month. The new billing period begins on June 11. Assume that your outstanding balance for the first 15 days of this new billing period (from June 11 to June 25) is $2700. Then, on June 25, the financial institution receives a payment of $1200 from you, reducing the balance to $1500. This is the balance for the remaining 15 days of the billing period. The annual interest rate is 21 percent, compounded daily.

- Previous Balance Method. With this method, you will be subject to a finance charge that is calculated by multiplying the $2700 outstanding at the beginning of the new billing period, by the daily interest rate and the number of days in the billing cycle. The daily interest rate is calculated as 21% ÷ 365 = 0.057534247%. Your finance charge is:

$$\$2700 \times 0.057534247\% \times 30 \text{ days} = \$46.60$$

- Average Daily Balance Method. With this method, the daily interest rate is applied to the average daily balance. Since your daily balance was $2700 for the first 15 days and $1500 for the last 15 days, your average daily balance was $2100 for the 30-day billing period. As a result, your finance charge is:

$$\$2100 \times 0.057534247\% \times 30 \text{ days} = \$36.25$$

- Adjusted Balance Method. With this method, you will be subject to a finance charge that is calculated by applying the monthly interest rate to the $1500 outstanding at the end of the new billing period. In this case, your finance charge is:

$$\$1500 \times 0.057534247\% \times 30 \text{ days} = \$25.89$$

Minimum Monthly Payments

In addition to the amount of interest you are charged in each billing cycle, it is also important to understand the negative impact of making only the minimum monthly payment that is required. As mentioned earlier, using your credit card to finance your purchases is a very expensive proposition. You should always strive to pay off your entire credit card balance in full each month.

TVM EXAMPLE

Continuing with the previous example, the credit card company issues a statement indicating that the outstanding balance for the billing period is $1500. The initial minimum monthly payment required is $10 or 3 percent of the balance outstanding as of the statement date. Therefore, the initial minimum monthly payment would be $45, since 3 percent of $1500 is $45, which is greater than $10. If you make no additional purchases, how many months would it take to pay off the $1500 balance if you continue to make monthly payments of $45? How much interest would you pay over this period of time? The annual interest rate is fixed at 21 percent, compounded daily. You can use your TI BA II Plus calculator to determine the number of months it would take to pay off your credit card.

The calculator key strokes are as follows:

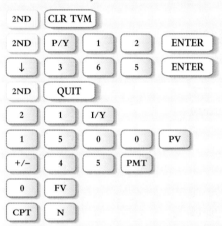

The loan will be paid off in 50.7261 months. Since each monthly payment is $45, the total amount paid to clear the balance on the credit card is $2282.68, calculated as 50.7261 × $45 per payment. Notice that the total interest paid, $782.67 ($2282.68 − $1500), is more than 50 percent of the original balance on the credit card. At the minimum monthly payment amount, it took more than four years to pay off the credit card, and the amount of interest paid was relatively high given the initial statement balance.

Credit Card Statement

Individuals typically receive a credit card statement at the end of their billing cycle. It lists all purchases made with that credit card during that period, as well as any balance carried over from the previous statement.

A credit card statement includes the following information:

- Previous balance: the amount carried over from the previous credit card statement
- Purchases: the amount of credit used this month to make purchases
- Cash advances: the amount of credit used this month by writing cheques against the credit card or by making ABM withdrawals
- Payments: the payments you made to the sponsoring financial institution this billing cycle

- Finance charge: the finance charge applied to any credit that exceeds the grace period or to any cash advances
- New balance: the amount you owe the financial institution as of the statement date
- Minimum payment: the minimum amount you must pay by the due date

The credit card statement details why your new balance differs from the balance shown on your statement for the previous month. The difference between the previous balance and the new balance results from any new purchases, cash advances, or finance charges, which increase your balance, versus any payments, which reduce your balance. The statement also shows the method of calculating finance charges, typically explained in full on the reverse of the statement.

EXAMPLE

Suppose that you have a credit card balance of $700 due to purchases made last month that you did not pay off. During that billing period, you pay $200 of your outstanding balance. You also use the credit card for $100 of new purchases. Since you relied on the sponsoring financial institution to pay $500 of last month's bill, you owe a finance charge. Assuming that the institution imposes a finance charge of 1.5 percent (effective interest) per month and uses the adjusted balance method to determine the finance charge (which results in a finance charge of $7.50), your credit card statement would be as follows:

Previous Balance	$700.00
+ New Purchases	100.00
+ Cash Advances	0
+ Finance Charges	7.50
− Payments	200.00
= New Balance	$607.50

If you had paid the full amount of the previous balance ($700) during the billing period, the statement would have been as follows:

Previous Balance	$700.00
+ New Purchases	100.00
+ Cash Advances	0
+ Finance Charges	0
− Payments	700.00
= New Balance	$100.00

In other words, if you had paid $700 instead of $200, you would not have borrowed from the sponsoring financial institution and would not have incurred a finance charge. The new balance at the end of this billing period would simply be the amount of purchases that occurred over the period.

When you receive your account statement, you should always scrutinize it for errors. There may be a math error, a double charge for a purchase, or an incorrect amount on a purchase. Under consumer protection laws, you have the right to dispute possible errors. To prove that an error exists, you should always keep your credit card receipts and check them against your statement. Once you reconcile your statement, simply staple receipts to the statement for filing.

Comparing Credit Cards

Some individuals have numerous credit cards, which can complicate record keeping and increase the probability of losing one or more cards. You can consolidate your bills by using just one credit card to cover all purchases. If you decide to use only one credit card, the following criteria will help you to determine which card is most desirable.

Acceptance by Merchants. You should ensure that your credit card is accepted by the types of merchants from whom you typically make purchases. MasterCard and Visa are accepted by more merchants than other credit cards.

Annual Fee. Shop around for a credit card that does not charge an annual fee or, if there is a fee, assess whether the card's benefits are worth the additional cost. Will you actually use those benefits?

Interest Rate. Interest rates vary among financial institutions that provide financing on credit cards. Shop around for the lowest rate if you intend to carry a balance.

The interest rate may be a key factor that determines which credit card is appropriate for you if you plan to carry over part of your balance each month. A card with a higher interest rate can result in substantially higher interest expenses.

EXAMPLE

You plan to pursue credit card X because it has no annual fee, while credit card Y has an annual fee of $30. You typically have an outstanding credit balance of $3000 each month. Credit card X charges an annual interest rate of 18 percent on balances carried forward, while credit card Y charges an interest rate of 12 percent on balances carried forward. The difference in the expenses associated with each credit card are shown here.

	Credit Card X	Credit Card Y
Average monthly balance	$3000	$3000
Annual interest rate	18%	12%
Annual interest expenses	18% × $3000 = $540	12% × $3000 = $360
Annual fee	$0	$30
Total annual expenses	$540	$390

The annual interest expenses can be determined by knowing the average monthly balance over the year. The higher the average monthly balance, the higher your interest expenses because you will have to pay interest on the balance.

Notice that credit card X results in $540 in annual interest expenses, which is $180 more than the annual interest expenses from credit card Y. Thus, while credit card X does not charge an annual fee, your interest expenses from using credit card X could be very high. The high interest expenses more than offset the advantage of no annual fee.

If you always pay off your balance in the month that it occurs, you will not have any interest expenses. In this case, the interest rate on the credit card would not be important, and you may prefer credit card X because it does not have an annual fee. That is, you would benefit from no annual fee and would not be adversely affected by the higher interest rate of credit card X.

Go to
www.fcac-acfc.gc.ca/
Eng/resources/
toolsCalculators/Pages/
CreditCa-OutilsIn.aspx

This website provides
a credit card selector tool to help you determine which credit card is right for you.

As mentioned earlier, some credit cards offer a low "teaser rate" to entice you to apply for that card. Be aware, however, that this rate is likely to be available only for a short time. After the introductory period elapses, the normal interest rate is charged.

Maximum Limit. Some credit cards allow a higher maximum limit on monthly purchases than do others. A very high maximum limit may not be necessary and may tempt you to spend excessively. Make sure that the maximum limit is high enough to cover any necessary monthly purchases, but not so high that it encourages you to spend more than you can afford.

HOME EQUITY LINE OF CREDIT (HELOC)

home equity line of credit (HELOC)
A loan in which the equity in a home serves as collateral.

equity
The market value of your home less any outstanding mortgage balance and/or debts held by others that are secured against your property.

home equity
The market value of a home minus the debt owed on the home.

A **home equity line of credit** (HELOC) is a loan in which a home serves as collateral. This allows homeowners to borrow, up to a specific credit limit, against the equity in their homes. In this context, **equity** refers to the market value of your home less any outstanding mortgage balance and/or debts and other obligations that are secured against your property.

You pay monthly interest only on the funds that you borrow and then pay the principal at a specified maturity date. You also may be allowed to pay off the principal at any point prior to maturity and still have access to the funds if you need them in the future. The borrowed funds can be used for any purpose, including a vacation, home renovation expenses, or tuition payments.

Home equity is determined by subtracting the amount owed on the home from its market value. For example, if a home has a market value of $300 000 and the homeowner has a mortgage loan (discussed in Chapter 7) with a balance of $160 000, the equity value is $140 000. A home equity line of credit is commonly referred to as a HELOC. The acronym, HELOC, will be used throughout the remainder of this section.

Credit Limit on a HELOC

Financial institutions provide HELOCs of up to 80 percent (or more in some cases) of the market value of your home minus any outstanding mortgage balance. When the market value of a home increases, they are willing to provide more credit than when the market value remains the same.

If you default on a HELOCs, the lender can claim your home, use a portion of the proceeds to pay off the mortgage, and use the remainder to cover your HELOC. If the market price of the home declines, the equity you invested is reduced. For this reason, lenders do not like to lend the full amount of the equity when extending a HELOC.

second mortgage
A secured mortgage loan that is subordinate (or secondary) to another loan.

Since the credit limit calculation for a HELOC usually takes into account an existing mortgage, a HELOC can also be considered a second mortgage. A **second mortgage** is a secured mortgage loan that is subordinate (or secondary) to another loan. In the case of a HELOC, the primary lender is the financial institution that provided the first mortgage. The secondary lender is the financial institution that provided the HELOC, or second mortgage. Although you can get a HELOC from the same institution that provided you with your mortgage, this does not have to be the case. When researching a HELOC, make sure you shop around.

The following example illustrates how to determine the maximum amount of credit that can be provided on a HELOC.

EXAMPLE

Suppose you own a home worth $300 000 that you purchased five years ago. You initially made a down payment of $100 000 and took out a $200 000 mortgage. Over the last five years, your mortgage payments have added $25 000 in equity. Thus, you have invested $125 000 in the home, including your $100 000 down payment. At the same time, your mortgage has decreased to $175 000. Assume that the home's market value has not changed. Also assume that a creditor is willing to provide you with a home equity line of credit of 80 percent based on the current market value of your home minus the outstanding mortgage balance.

Maximum Amount of Credit That Can Be Provided or Extended

= Market Value of Your Home × 0.80 − Mortgage Balance

= $300 000 × 0.80 − $175 000

= $65 000

Interest Rate

A HELOC typically uses a variable interest rate that is tied to a specified interest rate index that changes periodically. The loan contract specifies how the interest rate will be determined. For example, it may be set at the prime rate plus 3 percentage points. The **prime rate** is the interest rate a bank charges its best customers. Because the home serves as collateral for a HELOC, the lender faces less risk than with an unsecured loan, thus the interest rate is lower.

As mentioned earlier, the borrower may have to pay only the interest portion on the amount borrowed with a HELOC. Since the borrower is being charged a variable interest rate, there is always risk that the monthly payment on the loan will increase as interest rates increase. Interest-only payments and variable interest rates may create two problems for the borrower. First, the borrower may never get around to paying down the principal of the loan. Second, interest rates may rise to a point where the borrower is no longer able to afford the minimum interest-only payments. Although HELOCs provide a convenient source of funds for expenses such as vacations, home renovations, and tuition, you should apply for and use this source of credit with caution. Always have a plan for the repayment of the HELOC. Having a HELOC is convenient, as you get to decide how much of the credit to use and how and when to pay off the debt. However, you must consider the borrowing costs. Often, HELOCs have variable or floating interest costs. Rates that are steady or even decreasing work in favour of the borrower. However, sometimes rates rise and they may rise dramatically, increasing the costs of borrowing beyond comfort levels. The borrower should monitor interest rates; if rates are expected to rise, the borrower should consider locking in current rates instead of being at risk.

prime rate
The interest rate a bank charges its best customers.

FREE APPS for Personal Finance

Estimating the Time to Repay Your Debt

Application:

The Debt Payoff Lite app by SVT Software allows you to estimate how long it will take you to pay off your debt based on input you provide about the amount of debt you have, the interest rate, and the amount of funds you will have per period to repay debt.

PERSONAL LOANS

The most common source of financing from a financial institution is a personal loan. Chartered banks, finance companies, and credit unions all provide personal loans. Some finance companies are subsidiaries of automobile manufacturers that finance car purchases. For example, Ford Motor Credit Company is the financial services arm of Ford Motor Company. Chartered banks are the primary lenders to individuals who need mortgage loans, the subject of Chapter 7.

Loan Contract

If the lender approves your loan application, it will work with you to develop a **loan contract**, which specifies the terms of the loan as agreed to by the borrower and the lender. Specifically, the loan contract identifies the amount of the loan, the interest rate, the repayment schedule, the maturity date, the collateral, and the lender's rights if payments are late or the loan is not repaid.

loan contract
A contract that specifies the terms of a loan as agreed to by the borrower and the lender.

- **Amount of the Loan.** The principal amount of the loan is based on how much the lender believes you can pay back in the future. You should borrow only the

EXHIBIT 6.5   Effect of Loan Maturity on Total Interest Paid

	Loan Amount	APR (compounded monthly)	Monthly Payment	Total Interest	Total Repaid
Four-Year Loan	$16 000	4.9%	$367.74	$1651.73	$17 651.73
Five-Year Loan	$16 000	4.9%	$301.21	$2072.44	$18 072.44
		Difference	**$66.53**	**$420.71**	

amount you will need because you will be charged interest on the entire amount you borrow. The lender may have self-interest when determining the amount of the loan, since it will be collecting interest from you.

- **Interest Rate.** The interest rate is critical because it determines the cost incurred on a personal loan. It must be specified in a loan contract. The interest rate specified in the loan contract is the nominal interest rate of the loan. Recall from Chapter 2 that the nominal interest rate is also known as the annual percentage rate (APR). More information about interest rates is provided later in this chapter.

amortize
To repay the principal of a loan (the original amount borrowed) through a series of equal payments. A loan repaid in this manner is said to be amortized.

maturity or term
With respect to a loan, the life or duration of the loan.

- **Loan Repayment Schedule.** Personal loans are usually **amortized**, which means that the principal of a loan is repaid through a series of equal payments. Each loan repayment includes both interest and a portion of the principal. As more of the principal is paid down, the amount of interest is reduced and a larger portion of the payment is used to repay principal.

- **Maturity or Term.** A loan contract specifies the **maturity or term**, the life or duration of the loan. A longer maturity for a loan results in lower monthly payments and therefore makes it easier to cover the payments each month. With a longer maturity loan, however, you are in debt for an additional period of time, and you pay more interest over the life of the loan than you would on a shorter maturity loan. Exhibit 6.5 shows that the monthly payment on a five-year loan for $16 000 is $66.53 less than the monthly payment on a four-year loan for the same amount. With the five-year loan, however, you pay $420.71 more interest over the life of the loan because you are in debt for an additional year. In general, you should select a maturity that is as short as possible, as long as you allow yourself sufficient liquidity. If you find yourself with extra funds during the term of the loan, you should consider paying it off early for two reasons. First, you can reduce the total amount of interest. Second, you will be able to save the money that you would otherwise have used to make the loan payments. If you have a variable interest rate loan, the amount of interest you will pay and, therefore, the amount of money you will save on your loan depends on how interest rates change during the term of the loan. In general, you will reduce the total amount of interest you have to pay if interest rates stay the same or decrease. If interest rates increase during the term of the loan, you may end up paying more in interest—even if you decide to pay off the loan early.

- **Security.** Often, lenders require borrowers to provide them with some kind of assurance that the borrower will pay back the debt. This assurance can take several forms. The first, and most common, is simply a promise to repay the debt as per the loan agreement. This is an important promise and should not be taken lightly. Other forms of security include assets, either cash that is kept on deposit at the financial institution or personal belongings of which ownership is transferred to the lender by way of a chattel mortgage until the debt is repaid. This is referred to as collateral, defined below.

- **Collateral.** A loan agreement also describes the **collateral**, or assets of a borrower (if any) that back or secure a loan in the event that the borrower defaults. When a loan is used to purchase a specific asset, that asset is commonly used as collateral. For example, if your purchase of a boat is partly financed, the boat would serve as collateral. That is, the lender could repossess the boat if you did not make the loan payments.

collateral
Assets of a borrower that back a loan in the event that the borrower defaults. Collateral is a form of security for the lender.

A loan that is backed or secured by collateral is referred to as a **secured loan**; a loan that is not backed or secured by collateral is an **unsecured loan**. In general, you will receive more favourable terms (such as a lower interest rate) on a secured loan because the lender has less to lose in the event that the loan is not repaid. A credit card is one example of unsecured credit, while a car loan or home mortgage represents a secured form of credit.

secured loan
A loan that is backed or secured by collateral.

unsecured loan
A loan that is not backed or secured by collateral.

Some loans are backed by assets other than those purchased with the loan. For example, a boat loan could be backed by investments that you own, such as guaranteed investment certificates (GICs), term deposits, or Canada Savings Bonds (CSBs). Generally, lenders prefer other assets that are less likely to decrease in value. That way, if these assets are repossessed, the lender is much more likely to get its money back.

> **myth** or **fact** You don't need collateral or any other security to get a personal loan.

Some borrowers are only able to obtain a personal loan if someone with a stronger credit history co-signs the loan. The co-signer is responsible for any unpaid balance if the borrower does not repay the loan. If the borrower defaults and the co-signer does not repay the loan, the lender can sue the co-signer or try to seize the co-signer's assets, just as if the co-signer were the borrower. In addition, co-signing on a loan can restrict the amount that the co-signer is able to borrow. Co-signing a loan can have significant financial implications for the co-signer if he or she has to reduce some existing credit limits to satisfy the lender. For example, the lender may require the co-signer to reduce his or her credit card limit. Once the co-signer reduces the amount of credit available, he or she may not be able to get it back, even if the loan is paid off by the borrower. In general, co-signing a loan should be an action of last resort. You should never feel pressured or obligated to co-sign a loan.

A **payday loan** is a short-term loan provided to you if you need funds in advance of receiving your paycheque. To obtain a payday loan, you write a cheque to the lender for the amount of the loan plus interest and fees. You date the cheque for the day when you will receive your paycheque. The payday loan firm will hold the cheque until that time, and will cash it then because your chequing account will have sufficient funds. After you provide this cheque to the payday loan firm, it provides you with a loan in cash or by transmitting funds into your chequing account.

payday loan
A short-term loan provided in advance of receiving a paycheque.

As an example, assume that you need $400 for some immediate purpose but will not have any money until you receive your paycheque one week from today. You provide the payday loan firm with a cheque dated one week from today. Be aware that firms such as Money Mart, Rentcash, and Cash Money, which provide payday loans, may charge a high rate of interest on these short-term loans and/or fees such as administration costs. The payday loan firm may request that your payment be $440, which reflects the loan of $400 and $40 in interest and/or fees. You are paying $40 more than the loan you received, which reflects 10 percent of the loan amount. The cost of financing this payday loan is shown below.

Cost of Financing = 10 percent × (Number of days in a year/Number of days in which you have the loan)

$$= 10\% \times (365/7)$$

$$= 521\%$$

While the federal government has usury laws that place a limit on the maximum interest rate that can be charged, the regulation of payday loan firms is shared between the federal and provincial governments. The result is that the payday loan industry has gone largely unregulated in Canada. Under section 347 of the Criminal Code, the maximum interest rate that can be charged on a consumer loan is 60 percent per annum.

There may be a number of reasons why people are willing to pay annual interest rates in excess of the maximum allowed by law. With respect to the example above, an individual may take into account the $40 cost of the loan without realizing what this works out to on an annual basis. Individuals also may prefer the convenience of obtaining loans at payday loan outlets. Finally, some people who need money quickly may not be creditworthy and therefore have difficulty obtaining funds from other sources.

You should avoid payday loans. By using your next paycheque to cover a loan payment, you may not have sufficient cash available to make normal purchases afterwards. Thus, you may need another loan to cover your purchases in that period, and this can create a continuous cycle in which your paycheque is always needed to repay short-term loans. The simple solution is to avoid borrowing money; wait to make a purchase until you have the funds to spend.

FOCUS ON ETHICS: Predatory Lending

Watch out for dishonest predatory lenders who use illegal practices. Several of the more common predatory lending practices are listed here.

- A lender charges high loan fees, which cause the financing cost to be much higher than the quoted interest rate.
- A lender provides a secured loan with the expectation that the loan will not be repaid because the lender wants to take ownership of the collateral backing the loan.
- A lender stipulates that a loan will be provided only if the borrower purchases insurance or other financial services.
- A lender includes a large balloon payment at the end of a loan that will require additional financing to pay off.
- A loan agreement includes confusing information that does not clearly disclose the borrower's obligations.

Borrowers who accept these kinds of terms often think they have no alternatives, but shopping around for the best loan terms and interest rates is always the best option. You can take several other steps to protect yourself. Be wary of any lenders who pursue you with high-pressure tactics. Short-term offers and up-front application fees also indicate a disreputable lender. Always make sure you understand the loan terms before signing a loan agreement. If you cannot obtain reasonable loan terms, reconsider whether you truly need a loan at this time.

The Real Cost of Borrowing on Personal Loans

To determine the real cost of borrowing on personal loans, the APR must be converted to an effective interest rate, also known as the effective yield. The formula and calculator key strokes for computing effective yield were provided in Chapter 2 on page 49. Although the effective yield shows the actual rate of interest you pay on a loan, the real cost of borrowing must also take into account the payment of additional fees, such as service charges and appraisal fees for any collateral.

You obtain a four-year loan of $15 000 with an APR of 11 percent, compounded monthly. Given this information, you generate a loan repayment schedule shown in Exhibit 6.6. Notice that each monthly payment is $387.68. You can use your TI BA II Plus calculator to determine the monthly payment.

The calculator key strokes are as follows:

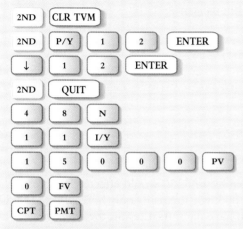

Each monthly payment of $387.68 consists of interest and a portion that pays down the loan principal. At the end of the first month, the interest owed on $15 000 based on an APR of 11 percent, compounded monthly, is $137.50.

Since the total monthly payment is $387.68 and the interest portion is $137.50, the remainder ($250.18) is applied to pay down the principal. The outstanding loan balance after one month is:

Outstanding Loan Balance = Previous Balance − Principal Payment

$$= \$15\ 000 - \$250.18$$

$$= \$14\ 749.82$$

As each month passes, the outstanding loan balance is reduced, so the interest payment in the following month is reduced. Since the total monthly payment remains at $387.68, the principal payment will increase over time.

EXHIBIT 6.6 Example of Loan Repayment Schedule: Four-Year Loan, 11 Percent Nominal Interest Rate

Month	Monthly Payment	Interest Payment	Payment of Principal	Outstanding Loan Balance
1	$387.68	$137.50	$250.18	$14 749.82
2	$387.68	$135.20	$252.48	$14 497.34
3	$387.68	$132.89	$254.79	$14 242.55
...	...	...	...	...
12	$387.68	$111.08	$276.60	$11 841.72
...	...	...	...	...
24	$387.68	$79.07	$308.61	$8317.98
...	...	...	...	...
36	$387.68	$43.36	$344.32	$4386.46
...	...	...	...	...
48	$387.68	$3.52	$384.16	0

As mentioned at the beginning of this section, the real cost of borrowing on personal loans must also take into account the additional fees and/or charges you incur. If the $15 000 loan in the example above required you to pay a $100 service charge and a $250 charge for the appraisal of an asset that you used as collateral, your real cost of borrowing would be greater than an APR of 11 percent, compounded monthly. To determine your real cost of borrowing, you must convert your nominal interest rate to an effective yield. Using the formula from Chapter 2 on page 49, we get:

$$EY = \left(1 + \frac{i}{n}\right)^n - 1$$

$$EY = \left(1 + \frac{0.11}{12}\right)^{12} - 1$$

$$EY = (1.00917)^{12} - 1$$

$$EY = 0.1157 \text{ or } 11.57\%$$

The service charge of $100 and appraisal fee of $250 would effectively increase the cost of your loan. Instead of borrowing $15 000, you are really only borrowing $14 650, once you take into account the fees that you have paid. As a result, the effective yield of 11.57 percent would increase to 11.85 percent (calculated as 11.57 ÷ 14 650 × 15 000).

CAR LOANS

A common type of personal loan is a car loan. When you decide to buy a car, you must select the car, negotiate the price, and determine whether to finance the purchase of the car or lease it.

Selecting the Car

Before making any car-buying decisions, you should take into account the following criteria.

Personal Preference. First, determine the type of car you need. Keep in mind that the car you want may be different than the car you need. Reduce the list of available cars by deciding on the type and size of the car you need. Do you want an SUV, pickup truck, convertible, or some other type of car? Do you want a small car that is easy to park and gets good gas mileage? You can always narrow the cars on your list further by deciding on the size of the engine. Do you want a car with a large engine that has fast acceleration or a car with a small engine that is less expensive?

Price. Stay within your budget. Avoid purchasing a car that will require you to obtain a second job or establish an unrealistic monthly budget to afford the car payments. You should also consider the cost of insurance, maintenance, and gas.

Condition. When buying a used car, be sure to assess its condition, beginning with the exterior. Has some of the paint worn off? Is there rust? Are the tires in good shape? Are the tires worn on one side (which may indicate that a wheel alignment is needed)? Next, check the interior. Are the seats worn? Do the electric devices work? Now look under the hood. Is there any sign of leaks? If you are still seriously considering the vehicle, ask the car owner for repair and maintenance records. Has the car been properly maintained and serviced over time? Has the oil been changed periodically?

All of these checks can help you to assess a car's condition, but none replaces the expertise of a qualified mechanic. The cost of having a mechanic evaluate the car is worthwhile, because it may enable you to avoid buying a car that will ultimately need expensive repairs.

myth or **fact** The best time to buy a car is at the end of the month.

Insurance. Some cars are subject to significantly higher insurance costs because they are more difficult to repair after accidents, are more expensive, or are common targets of theft. Obtain insurance estimates on any car before making a purchase.

Resale Value. Some cars have a much higher resale value than others. For example, you can expect an Acura to have a higher resale value than a Hyundai. Although you cannot predict the future resale value of a car, you can look at today's resale value of similar cars that were sold years ago. Numerous sites on the internet, such as www.usedcarscanada.com, provide information on the current selling price of different makes and models of used cars across Canada. You can use this information to estimate the resale value as a proportion of the original sales price.

Repair Expenses. Some cars are subject to much higher repair bills than others. To compare potential repair expenses, review *Consumer Reports* magazine, which frequently estimates the typical repair expenses for various cars.

Financing Rate. If you plan to finance your car purchase through the car dealer, you should compare financing rates among dealers. One dealer may charge a lower price for the car but higher financing costs for the loan. Other dealers may offer an unusually low financing rate, but charge a higher price on the car. If you obtain financing from a financial institution rather than the dealer, you can easily compare financing rates of various financial institutions on the internet.

In some cases, you may wish to determine how much you can borrow before you decide which car to purchase. You can use auto loan websites to estimate the maximum amount you can borrow, based on financial information you provide.

Go to
www.bankrate.com/
finance/auto/current-
interest-rates.aspx

This website provides
car loan interest rate quotations
from various lenders based on
the term of the loan and the
loan amount.

FREE APPS for Personal Finance

Searching for Cars in Your Location

Application:

The Auto Trader app (by autoTRADER.ca) allows you to search for new and used cars that are for sale near you. Listing of used cars for sale near your location includes the price, the number of kilometres, a photo, and seller contact information for each car.

Negotiating the Price

When shopping for a car, you will generally find that the majority of dealers will negotiate the price of a car. Any dealer that negotiates will purposely price its cars well above the amount for which it is willing to sell the car. For example, the dealer initially may quote the manufacturer's suggested retail price (MSRP). This is also referred to as the sticker price. Another price, known as the invoice price, is the amount that the dealer may have paid the manufacturer for the car. However, the invoice price is not necessarily what the dealer paid to the manufacturer. A manufacturer may offer dealers sales incentives to push certain models that are selling poorly or that are overstocked. The dealer may, or may not, pass these sales incentives on to the customer by reducing the price of the car. In addition, a manufacturer may provide the dealer with a percentage refund of the MSRP, known as a holdback, in order to compensate the dealer for the cost of holding cars in inventory. Sales incentives and holdbacks allow the dealer to make a sizeable profit on a car even when it's sold below the invoice price.

Salespeople are trained to act as if they are almost giving the car away to the customer by reducing the price by 5% to 20% below the MSRP. During the negotiations, they will say that they must discuss the price you offer with the sales manager. They already know the price at which they can sell the car to you, but this creates the appearance that they are pleading with the sales manager. During the negotiations, the dealer may offer you "free" rustproofing, an entertainment system, leather seats or other features. These features are usually priced very high to make you believe that you are getting a good deal.

If you are in the market for a car, do your homework. Thoroughly research the car you are looking for using the internet. There are a number of consumer websites available to help you, such as edmunds.com and carhelpcanada.com. Determine, the colour, trim level, and price that you are willing to pay before negotiating the price with the seller. When you are ready to negotiate, always negotiate based on the price and never based on what you are able to pay in monthly payments.

Negotiating by Phone. When purchasing a new car, it may be beneficial to negotiate by phone. After deciding on the type of car you want, call a dealer and describe the car and options you desire. Explain that you plan to call other local car dealers and that you will select the dealer that offers the lowest price. To meet monthly sales quotas, dealers may be more willing to give you a deal toward the end of a month. You may also want to emphasize that you will only call each dealer once.

Trade-in Tactics. If you are trading in a car, some dealers will pay a relatively high price for your trade-in, but also charge a high price for the new car. For example, they may pay you $500 more than your used car is worth, but then charge you at least $500 more than they would have charged for the new car if you did not have a trade-in. Attempt to negotiate the price on the new car first, before mentioning that you have a car to trade in.

The Value of Information. Some car dealers attempt to make a higher profit from customers who are not well informed about the price they should pay for a car. To avoid being taken advantage of when purchasing a car, you should become informed. Shop around and make sure that you know the typical sales price for your car. You can obtain this information from *Consumer Reports* and other consumer magazines. Some websites will provide you with a quote based on the car model and features you want. You can do all of your research through your computer.

Purchasing a Car Online. You can buy a car online directly from some car manufacturers or from car referral services such as AutoNet or Driving.ca. Car referral services forward your price request to specific dealerships, which then respond by sending you a quote. In other words, the referral service acts as the intermediary between you and the dealership. If a customer agrees to a price, the car-buying service informs the dealership to deliver the car. Reviews of online buying sites can be found at www.thecanadianwheels.ca/blog/top-5-canadian-sites-selling-used-cars/.

Financing Decisions

If you consider purchasing a new car and plan to finance the purchase, you should estimate the amount of the monthly payments. By evaluating your typical monthly income and expenses, you can determine whether you can afford to make the required payments to finance the car. You should conduct this estimate before shopping for a car so that you know how much you can afford. The more money needed to cover the car payments, the less you can add to your savings or other investments.

EXAMPLE

Go to
www.allstate.com

Click on
Search, and type in "Auto Loans Calculator"

Dawn Swanson wants to compare her monthly car payments if she borrows $15 000 versus $17 000 to buy a car. She must also decide whether to repay the loan over three, four, or five years. The larger the down payment she makes, the less she will need to borrow. However, she wants to retain some of her savings to maintain liquidity and to use for a future down payment on a house.

Dawn goes to a bank website where she is asked to input the approximate amount she will borrow. The website then provides the available interest rate and shows the payments for each loan amount and repayment period, as shown in Exhibit 6.7. The interest rate of 7.6 percent compounded monthly at the top of the exhibit is a fixed rate that Dawn can lock in for the loan period. The possible loan amounts are shown at the top of the columns and each row shows a different repayment period.

Notice that the payments decrease if Dawn extends the loan period. If she borrows $17 000, her monthly payment would be $530 for a three-year loan, $412 for a four-year loan, or $341 for a five-year loan. Alternatively, she can lower her monthly payments by reducing her loan amount from $17 000 to $15 000. Notice that if she takes out a four-year loan for $15 000, her monthly payment is less than if she borrows $17 000.

Dawn selects the $17 000 loan with a four-year term and a $412 monthly payment. The four-year term is preferable because the monthly payment for a three-year term is higher than she wants to pay. Since the purchase price of the car is $18 000, she will use the proceeds from selling her old car to cover the $1000 down payment.

This website provides a comparison of what your car loan payments would be depending on the term of the loan.

Purchase versus Lease Decision

A popular alternative to buying a car is leasing one. An advantage of leasing is that you do not need a substantial down payment. In addition, you return the car to the dealer at the end of the lease period, so you do not need to worry about finding a buyer for the car. Leasing will also result in lower monthly car payments since you only have to pay for the portion of the car that you use over the term of the lease.

Leasing a car also has disadvantages. Since you do not own the car, you have no equity investment in it, even though the car still has value. You are also responsible for maintenance costs while leasing it. Keep in mind that you will be charged for any damage to the car over the lease period. Damage may include customizing the car with aftermarket car accessories. Remember, you have no equity investment in the car, and therefore you do not own it.

Some dealers impose additional charges beyond the monthly lease payments. You will be charged if you drive more than the maximum number of kilometres specified in the lease agreement. You may be assessed a fee if you end the lease before the period specified in the contract. You also may have to purchase more car insurance than you already have. Be aware that some of these charges may be hidden within the lease agreement. Hundreds of customers have filed legal claims, alleging that they were not informed of all possible charges before they leased a car. If you ever seriously consider leasing, make sure you read and understand the entire lease agreement.

myth or **fact** Buying a car is always cheaper than leasing it.

EXHIBIT 6.7   Dawn's Possible Monthly Loan Payments (7.6 Percent Interest Rate)

	Loan Amount	
Loan Maturity	**$15 000**	**$17 000**
36 months (3 years)	$467	$530
48 months (4 years)	363	412
60 months (5 years)	301	341

EXAMPLE

Jiu Wa Ling wonders whether she should lease the car she selected, rather than purchasing it for $18 000. If she purchases the car, she can invest $1000 as a down payment, and the remaining $17 000 will be financed by a car loan. She will pay $412 per month over four years to cover the financing. She expects that the car will be worth $10 000 at the end of four years. By purchasing instead of leasing, she forgoes interest that she could have earned by investing the $1000 down payment over the next four years. If she invests the funds in a bank, she would earn 4 percent annually after considering taxes paid on the interest income.

Alternatively, she could lease the same car for $300 per month over the four-year period. The lease would require an $800 security deposit, which would be refunded at the end of the four-year period. She would forgo interest she could have earned if she had invested the $800 instead. At the end of the lease, she would have no equity and no car.

Jiu's comparison of the cost of purchasing versus leasing is shown in Exhibit 6.8. She estimates the total cost of purchasing the car to be $10 936 (after resale is accounted for) while the total cost of leasing is $14 528. Therefore, she decides to purchase the car.

EXHIBIT 6.8   Jiu's Comparison of the Cost of Purchasing versus Leasing

Cost of Purchasing the Car

	Cost
1. Down payment	$1 000
2. Down payment of $1000 results in forgone interest income:	
Forgone Interest	
Income per Year = Down Payment $\times$ Annual Interest Rate	
= $1000 $\times$ 0.04	
= $40	
Forgone Interest over Four Years = $40 $\times$ 4	
= $160	160
3. Total monthly payments are:	
Total Monthly Payments = Monthly Payment $\times$ Number of Months	
= $412 $\times$ 48	
= $19 776	19 776
Total	$20 936
Minus: Expected amount to be received when car is sold in four years	− 10 000
Total cost	$10 936

Cost of Leasing the Car for Four Years

	Cost
1. Security deposit of $800 results in forgone interest income (although she will receive her deposit back in four years):	
Forgone Interest	
Income per Year = Down Payment $\times$ Annual Interest Rate	
= $800 $\times$ 0.04	
= $32	
Forgone Interest over Four Years = $32 $\times$ 4	
= $128	$128
2. Total monthly payments are:	
Total Monthly Payments = Monthly Payment $\times$ Number of Months	
= $300 $\times$ 48	
= $14 400	14 400
Total cost	$14 528

The decision to purchase versus lease a car depends greatly on the estimated market value of the car at the end of the lease period. If the expected value of the car in the previous example had been $6000 instead of $10 000 after four years, the total cost of purchasing the car would have been $4000 more. Substitute $6000 for $10 000 in Exhibit 6.8 and recalculate the cost of purchasing to verify this. With an expected market value of $6000, the total cost of purchasing the car would have been higher than the total cost of leasing, so leasing would have been preferable. Remember that some dealers may impose additional charges for leasing, such as a fee for driving more than the maximum kilometres allowed. Include any of these charges in your estimate of the leasing expenses.

Go to
www.ic.gc.ca/app/scr/oca-bc/ssc/vehicle.html

This website provides a comparison of the cost of leasing versus purchasing a car.

FREE APPS for Personal Finance

Your Decision to Purchase or Lease a Car

Application:

Car Finance Tools can help you easily simulate auto loans and leases. Its results include detailed estimates, loan/lease breakdowns, and full amortization schedules to help you gain a thorough understanding of any car loan or lease scenario.

STUDENT LOANS

Another popular type of personal loan is a **student loan**, which is a loan provided to finance a portion of a student's expenses while pursuing a post-secondary education. One of the best sources of information about student loans is the Canada Student Loans website at www.canada.ca/en/employment-social-development/services/student-financial-aid/student-loan/student-loans.html.

The lender may be the federal government or one of many financial institutions that participate in student loan programs. There are set limits on how much a student can borrow each year, based on the student's assessed need. Provincial programs can be used to cover the difference between the cost of education and what is provided through the federal Canada Student Loans Program. Loan limits are lower for students who are dependants. The repayment schedule is deferred, so full-time students do not begin repaying the loans until they have completed their education and entered the workforce. Part-time students must make interest payments while studying. You can claim a deduction for the interest paid on your student loans if you received the loan under the Canada Student Loans Act, the Canada Student Financial Assistance Act, the Apprentice Loans Act, or under similar provincial or territorial government laws.

student loan
A loan provided to finance a portion of a student's expenses while pursuing post-secondary education.

myth or **fact** A government student loan (1) does not require a guarantor, (2) does not charge interest while you are in school, (3) does not require repayment until six months after you leave school, and (4) provides repayment assistance for those who need it.

Even if you do not complete your education, you still have to pay back your student loans. Failure to do so will damage your credit history. In the event that you declare bankruptcy *within* seven years of ceasing to be a student, you must still pay back your student loan. In other words, if you finished your post-secondary education on May 31, 2017, any bankruptcies that you declare after May 31, 2024, will result in your Canada Student Loan being discharged. If you declare bankruptcy before May 31, 2024, you are still responsible for your Canada Student Loan.

L.0.4

DEBT MANAGEMENT

Finance charges not only reduce your financial freedom and flexibility, but also can have a negative impact on your credit score and future efforts to obtain credit if you are unable to make your minimum monthly payments. A low credit score is normally due either to missed payments or to carrying an excessive amount of debt, both of which will be noted on your credit report. Unfortunately, past missteps will stay with you for a while since a poor credit history will appear on your credit report for three to ten years, depending on the type of information contained in the item reported. In addition, filing for bankruptcy will remain on your credit record for six to seven years, depending on the province you lived in at the time of the bankruptcy.

You can begin to improve your score immediately by catching up on late payments, making at least the minimum payments on time, and reducing your debt. Your debt management strategy should also consider how you use your credit cards, since you are likely to have one or more credit cards during your lifetime.

Review Your Personal Financial Statements

If you are having difficulty controlling your debts, it is important to re-establish control over your financial statements. This process begins by analyzing your budget, your personal balance sheet, and your personal cash flow statement. Use your budget to establish a self-imposed credit limit. The difference between your expected income and your expenses is the maximum amount of credit you can use and still ensure that you make the minimum payments on your debts.

Next, review your personal balance sheet to see if you have any financial assets that can be used to pay down your debts immediately. As shown in the example below, the likely return that you might earn from your short-term investments is less than the financing rate you will be charged when you delay paying your bills in full.

Some individuals use their money to purchase risky investments (such as stocks) rather than pay off their credit card bills. They apparently believe that their return from the investments will be higher than the cost of financing. Although some investments have generated large returns in specific years, it is difficult to earn returns that consistently exceed the high costs of financing with credit cards. If the thrill of a good return on your investment makes you consider delaying your credit card payment, consider the following. When you use money to pay your credit card bill immediately, you are preventing a charge of about 20 percent interest on an annual basis. Therefore, you have effectively increased your savings by 20 percent by using these funds to pay off the credit card debt.

EXAMPLE

Maya Cecilia just received a credit card bill for $700. The sponsoring financial institution charges a 20 percent effective annual interest rate on the outstanding balance. Maya has sufficient funds in her chequing account to pay the credit card bill, but she is considering financing her payment. If she pays $100 toward the credit card bill and finances the remaining $600 for one year, she will incur interest expenses of:

$$\text{Interest} = \text{Loan Amount} \times \text{Interest Rate}$$
$$= \$600 \times 0.20$$
$$= \$120$$

She could use the $600 to invest in savings rather than pay off her credit card bill. After one year, the $600 in a savings account will accumulate to $618 based on a 3 percent annual interest rate, as shown here:

$$\text{Interest Earned on Deposit} = \text{Initial Deposit} \times \text{Interest Rate}$$
$$= \$600 \times 0.03$$
$$= \$18 \text{ (before tax)}$$

Her interest owed on the credit card loan ($120) exceeds the interest earned on the deposit ($18) in one year by $102. Maya decides that she would be better off using her cash to pay off the credit card bill immediately. By using her money to cover the credit card bill, she gives up the opportunity to earn 3 percent on that money, but she also avoids the 20 percent interest rate that would be charged on the credit card loan. Her wealth is $102 higher as a result of using funds to pay off the credit card bill rather than investing in a bank deposit. Although she could have used the funds to invest in a high-risk investment that might achieve a greater return, paying off the credit card guarantees that she can avoid a 20 percent financing rate.

Finally, reassess your personal cash flow statement to determine where you need to cut back on expenses in order to increase your net cash flow. If you find yourself with a debt balance that doesn't allow you to make the minimum monthly payments, there are several steps you can take. First, spend as little as possible. This could include reducing your entertainment and recreation expenses and/or choosing to take public transit instead of paying for fuel and insurance for your car. Second, consider how you can obtain funds to meet your monthly payments or to pay off your balance. Get a job if you don't have one, or work more hours at your current job. However, for students, additional work hours could disrupt their school schedule. Third, obtain a debt consolidation loan from a financial institution. The structured schedule for paying off the loan within a set time period will instill more discipline than meeting low minimum monthly payments on a credit card. However, self-discipline is critical. A debt consolidation loan gives the temporary appearance that you have re-established control over your finances because the monthly finance charge is typically lower. While consolidation costs less each month, you can wind up paying more over the long term since all you have really done is extended your payback period.

Consumer Proposal

A last resort before filing for bankruptcy is to make a **consumer proposal**, which is an offer made by a debtor to his or her creditors to modify his or her payments. When a consumer files a proposal with a Licensed Insolvency Trustee (LIT), creditors have up to 45 days to object; otherwise, the proposal is deemed to be accepted by the creditors. The term of a consumer proposal cannot exceed five years. Under current legislation, a consumer proposal can be made as long as your debts are less than $250 000. A consumer proposal will be removed from your credit bureau report once its terms have been met. Often, the entire debt is not completely paid off by the end of the proposal's term.

consumer proposal
An offer made by a debtor to his or her creditors to modify his or her payments.

> **myth** or **fact** A well-trained, highly qualified credit counsellor will help someone to avoid bankruptcy.

Bankruptcy

If all else fails, you may need to file for personal bankruptcy. Individuals can file for bankruptcy when they become **insolvent**. They may be deemed to be insolvent if they owe at least $1000 and are unable to pay their debts as they come due. When you declare bankruptcy, your property is given to a **Licensed Insolvency Trustee**, a person licensed to administer consumer proposals and bankruptcies and manage assets held in trust. Your unsecured creditors will not be able to take legal steps, such as seizing property or garnishing wages, to recover their debts from you. However, the trustee in bankruptcy will sell your assets and distribute the money obtained to your creditors on a pro rata basis. Certain assets are exempt from your bankruptcy (the amount and types of assets exempt differs among provinces). To determine the amount that is exempt from bankruptcy in the province in which you live, visit https://debtsolutions.bdo.ca/bankruptcy/can-i-keep-my-assets.

insolvent
A person who owes at least $1000 and is unable to pay his or her debts as they come due.

Licensed Insolvency Trustee
A person licensed to administer consumer proposals and bankrupticies and manage assets held in trust.

Go to
www.bankruptcycanada
.com

This website provides
useful bankruptcy tools,
including video presentations,
a bankruptcy predictor, and a
bankruptcy trustee locator for
the province in which you live.

It is important to note that your spouse or common-law partner is not affected by your personal bankruptcy as long as he or she is not responsible for your debt. Bankruptcy should be considered only if there is no other option to deal with overwhelming debt.

Avoid Credit Repair Services

Companies that offer credit repair services claim to be able to solve your credit problems. For example, they may help you to fix a mistake on your credit report. However, you can do this yourself, without paying for the service. If you have made late credit payments or have defaulted on a loan, a credit repair service does not have the power to remove such information from your credit report.

L.O.5

IDENTITY THEFT: A THREAT TO YOUR CREDIT

identity theft
Occurs when an individual
uses personal, identifying
information unique to you,
such as your social insurance
number, without your
permission for their personal
gain.

Identity theft occurs when an individual uses personal, identifying information unique to you, such as your social insurance number, driver's licence number, credit card account numbers, bank account numbers, or simply your name and date of birth, without your permission for their personal gain. Criminals use this stolen personal information to open accounts in your name. If you are a victim of identity theft, any purchases charged to the accounts appear under your name. When these accounts go unpaid, they appear on your credit report. Meanwhile, you are not even aware that these accounts exist. Your credit score may be reduced to the point that you no longer have access to credit. As well, you may be held responsible for the repayment of these fraudulent accounts. After all, these are your debts.

In some instances of identity theft, the criminal is not attempting to acquire money, goods, or services. Instead, the object is to obtain documents such as a driver's licence, birth certificate, social insurance number, passport, visa, or other official government documents. These documents can then be used to establish a new identity unknown to the authorities to facilitate various criminal activities. Although these actions do not result in financial loss to the victim, embarrassing situations can occur. For example, the victim may be arrested or detained by customs or immigration authorities as a result of the identity thief's actions.

The Scope of Identity Theft

The scope of identity theft may prove surprising to many people. The Canadian Anti-Fraud Centre (CAFC) creates an annual statistical report that highlights mass marketing fraud and identity theft activities in Canada. The report is available upon request by contacting the CAFC at www.antifraudcentre-centreantifraude.ca/reports-rapports/index-eng.htm. You will discover that identity theft is a profitable business that affects Canadians in every province.

The Cost of Identity Theft

Go to
www.competitionbureau
.gc.ca/eic/site/cb-bc.
nsf/vwapj/Little-Black-
Book-Scams-e.pdf

This website provides
a pdf link to The Little Black
Book of Scams, which highlights the many types of
frauds targeting Canadians.

The personal cost of identity theft is difficult to measure but easy to imagine, beginning with the victim's feeling of being violated and the resulting insecurity. Identity theft victims have been turned down for employment because of incorrect information found in background checks. They have been hounded for back taxes on income they did not earn or receive, and they have been referred to collection agencies for nonpayment of mortgages and student loans obtained by identity thieves. They have been refused loans for which they would normally have qualified, have had their driver's licences revoked for violations they did not commit, and have been enrolled for welfare benefits they did not receive. One identity theft victim is even listed on a birth certificate as the mother of a child she didn't bear.

Calculating the financial costs of identity theft is an easier task. According to the U.S. Federal Trade Commission, the average individual loss due to identity theft is $1868.

Financial losses are not the only costs incurred by an identity theft victim. Time is lost as well. Recent estimates suggest that the average victim spends 600 hours dealing with damage control necessitated by identity theft. The cost of the actual losses incurred and the additional expenses of repairing the damage are substantial in terms of both time and money to both individuals and businesses and, ultimately, to our economy.

IDENTITY THEFT TACTICS

The identity thief has a wide variety of tactics at hand that can be used to obtain your personal data.

Shoulder Surfing

Shoulder surfing occurs in public places where you can be readily seen or heard by someone standing close by. An example of shoulder surfing is someone standing close to you in a hotel or other business establishment and reading the number of your credit card. Shoulder surfing may also occur if you make a telephone call and someone is close enough to observe you entering your calling card number and personal identification number (PIN).

shoulder surfing
Occurs in public places where you can be readily seen or heard by someone standing close by.

Dumpster Diving

As the name implies, **dumpster diving** occurs when an identity thief goes through your trash. The thief is looking for discarded items that reveal personal information that can be used for fraudulent purposes. Targets include information that might contain your social insurance number, bank account numbers, or credit card numbers. As one example, if the thief finds something that contains your credit card number, he or she can contact the credit card company to report a change of address and then obtain a card in your name.

The thief also may retrieve similar personal information from the dumpsters of places where you do business. Let us say that you complete a credit card application at a local store. If this credit card application, which contains substantial personal and financial information, is disposed of in the company's dumpster, it can be used by an identity thief. Other business dumpsters that could provide usable information are those of your health care providers, your broker, your accountant, and even your bank.

dumpster diving
Occurs when an identity thief goes through your trash looking for discarded items that reveal personal information that can be used for fraudulent purposes.

Skimming

Skimming occurs when identity thieves steal your credit card or debit card number by copying the information contained in the magnetic strip on the card. Often, skimmers are the employees of stores and restaurants you patronize. When you are not looking, they swipe your card through a reader that captures and stores your data. Skimmers also attach card readers to ABMs that allow them to collect your information when you swipe your card for access. They then use the data to create fake debit cards and credit cards.

skimming
Occurs when identity thieves steal your credit card or debit card number by copying the information contained in the magnetic strip on the card.

Pretexting, Phishing, and Pharming

Another method of obtaining personal information is **pretexting**, which occurs when individuals access personal information under false pretenses. The pretexter may use information obtained from dumpster diving to identify the companies with which you do business. The pretexter then may pose as a survey taker or an employee of a financial institution, insurance company, or other firm with which you do business. You may be asked for information such as your social insurance number, driver's licence number, or bank, brokerage, or credit card numbers. The pretexter will sound as if soliciting the information is part of routine business such as updating your file. Pretexters may use the information to steal your identity or they may sell it to others for illegal use.

When pretexting happens online, it is called **phishing**. A phisher sends an email message falsely claiming to be from a legitimate source that directs the recipient to a website where he or she is asked to update account information such as passwords, credit card numbers, bank account numbers, and social insurance numbers. The website, in reality, is a fake.

A practice similar to phishing, but that reaches many more targets with a single effort, is known as **pharming**. By manipulating email viruses and host files, pharmers redirect users, without their knowledge, from the legitimate commercial websites they thought they were visiting to bogus ones that look like the genuine sites. When users enter their login names and passwords, the pharmers collect the data.

pretexting
Occurs when individuals access personal information under false pretenses.

phishing
Occurs when pretexting happens online.

pharming
Similar to phishing, but targeted at larger audiences, it directs users to bogus websites to collect their personal information.

Abusing Legitimate Access to Records

Employees at places where you work, bank, go to the doctor, and shop can steal your data. In many cases, these people have easy and legitimate access to personal information that can be used to steal your identity.

As well, anyone who has gone through a divorce has most, if not all, of their personal financial information, including social insurance number, included in the court records. In most provinces, this information is considered part of the public record, making it easier to steal.

Crime Rings

In some cases, identity thieves may be part of a well-organized crime ring that has systematically infiltrated corporations and financial institutions for the sole purpose of obtaining information to facilitate large-scale identity thefts.

Violating Your Mailbox

A last source of information worth mentioning is your mailbox. Both incoming and outgoing mail may provide the necessary information to allow your identity to be stolen. Outgoing mail may provide credit card and bank information if you leave letters in your mailbox for the postal carrier to pick up. Incoming mail can also provide your credit card account numbers, bank information, driver's licence number, and social insurance number.

FREE APPS for Personal Finance

Identifying Permissions You Allowed in the Past

Application:

In a few minutes, the MyPermissions app can identify all the permissions you have allowed due to your use of social media websites over time. These permissions can possibly expose your account to identity theft. You may find that you granted some permissions for creating accounts that you no longer use, so you could eliminate these accounts to avoid exposure.

L.O.7

PROTECTING AGAINST IDENTITY THEFT

There are many ways to safeguard your personal information and make it harder for an identity thief to prey on you. Most of these safeguards are relatively easy and inexpensive. Below is a list of some of the more common ways in which you can protect yourself against identity theft.

- Never give out personal information, such as your PIN numbers and social insurance number, over the internet, over the phone, or through the mail. Only give out personal information if you have initiated the call and you know with whom you are dealing with – your bank, a credit card company, a charity, etc. . .
- Minimize the amount of cards and documents that you carry around in your wallet or purse. It is normally unnecessary to carry your social insurance number, your birth certificate, rarely used credit cards, or information regarding your PIN numbers and passwords with you. Instead, maintain these items in a safe, secure place, such as a locked fireproof safe.
- Do not leave your wallet or purse unattended when you are out in public.
- Shred or destroy items that contain personal information, including credit card receipts and offers, expired ID cards, and other documents containing personal or account information.

- Empty your mailbox on a daily basis and become familiar with when you normally receive credit card statements and other financial documents. If you are not receiving these documents on time, contact your financial institution to investigate the delay.

- Be aware of your surroundings. Shield your PIN number when using an ATM or a PIN pad. Use ATMs that are located in well lighted areas that you are familiar with. Whenever possible, maintain site of your card when you have to hand it over to complete a transaction.

- Actively manage your bank account and credit card statements. Check the accuracy of your statements and report any discrepancies, even small ones, to your bank or credit card company. Also, check your credit report periodically to ensure that there are no errors with respect to your accounts.

- Avoid signing up for too many company loyalty and/or reward programs. In particular, be aware of the information that you are sharing with companies and what their policy is concerning sharing that information with other companies. You can find information about a company's privacy policy by finding a link to the company's privacy statement when you visit its website.

- When shopping online, verify the security of the website you are using by identifying the closed-lock or unbroken-key symbol on the website. When these symbols appear in the locked position, it indicates that you are sending information securely over the internet. You can also check the security of a website by identifying that the URL begins with "https".

- Don't post sensitive information to social media sites that can be used to verify your identity or check your passwords. Posting information such as your date of birth, your mother's middle name, the name of your first pet, and the colour of your first car are examples of information that could be used to verify your identity on websites that require answers to security questions.

- Before you get rid of your computer, tablet, or phone, have the hard drive wiped clean or destroyed.

- Be suspicious of any information you received thorough your email or social media accounts that arouse your curiosity. Many illegitimate claims to rewards, prizes, and exclusive offers are designed to get you to visit websites where you are then solicited to provide personal information. Never click on a link unless you are sure as to its legitimacy.

- Install and regularly update anti-virus, anti-phishing, and malware software. Also, do not ignore regular updates that are provided for your computer programs, such as Microsoft Office. These updates are an important part of ensuring that your data is safe and does not become corrupted.

myth or **fact** It is safe to give your personal information over the phone, but only if your caller ID confirms the identity of the organization to which you are talking.

RESPONSE TO IDENTITY THEFT

L.O.8

If you are a victim of identity theft, you must take action immediately to clean up your credit report. The Office of the Privacy Commissioner of Canada (www.priv.gc.ca/en) has suggested a number of actions to take if you suspect that you are a victim of identity theft. The discussion below highlights the main features of its fact sheet on identity theft.

Go to
www.antifraudcentre-centreantifraude.ca

This website provides information on identity theft and tools to report identity theft.

- Report the crime to the police immediately.
- Report the incident to the Canadian Anti-Fraud Centre if the matter involved a scam or fraud.

- Take steps to undo the damage. Avoid credit repair companies, as there is usually nothing they can do.
- Document the steps you take and the expenses you incur to clear your name and re-establish your credit.
- Cancel your credit cards and have new ones issued immediately.
- Have your credit report annotated to reflect the identity theft.
- Close your bank accounts and open new ones immediately.
- Obtain new ABM cards and telephone calling cards, with new passwords or PINs.
- In the case of passport theft, advise Passport Canada immediately.
- Contact Canada Post if you suspect that someone is diverting your mail.
- Advise your telephone, cable, and utilities providers that someone using your name could try to open new accounts fraudulently.
- Obtain a new driver's licence.

Notify the major credit reporting companies. Request that a fraud alert be placed in your file. An initial fraud alert will stay on your report for up to 90 days. An extended alert will remain on your credit report for seven years if you provide the credit bureau with an identity theft report. This report consists of a copy of the report filed with the police and any documentation beyond that verifying your identity to the satisfaction of the credit bureau. This alert will enable the bureau to contact you if there is any attempt

---

EXHIBIT 6.9   Contacts If You Are Subjected to Identity Theft

Major National Credit Bureaus

Equifax Canada
P.O. Box 190, Station Jean-Talon
Montreal, QC H1S 2Z2
Tel. (toll-free): 1-800-465-7166
Fax: (514) 355-8502
On-line: www.consumer.equifax.ca

TransUnion Canada
All provinces except Quebec:
Attention: Consumer Relations
P.O. Box 338, LCD1
Hamilton, ON L8L 7W2
Tel. (toll-free): 1-800-663-9980
Fax: (905) 527-0401
On-line: www.transunion.ca

Quebec residents:
TransUnion
Centre de relations au consommateur
CP 1433 Succ. St-Martin
Laval, QC H7V 3P7
Tel. (toll-free): 1-877-713-3393
Fax: (905) 527-0401

Governmental Agencies

Office of the Privacy Commissioner of Canada
Notification Officer
30 Victoria Street
Gatineau, Quebec K1A 1H3
Tel. (toll-free): 1-800-282-1376
Email: notification@priv.gc.ca;
On-line: www.priv.gc.ca

Competition Bureau
50 Victoria Street
Gatineau, Quebec K1A 0C9
Tel. (toll-free): 1-800-348-5358
Fax: 1-819-997-0324
On-line: www.competitionbureau.gc.ca/
eic/site/cb-bc.nsf/eng/home

Canadian Anti-Fraud Centre
Tel. (toll-free): 1-888-495-8501
Fax. (toll-free): 1-888-654-9426
Email: info@antifraudcentre.ca
On-line: www.antifraudcentre-centreantifraude.ca

Financial Consumer Agency of Canada
427 Laurier Avenue West, 6th Floor
Ottawa ON K1R 1B9
For services in English:
Tel. (toll-free): 1-866-461-3222
For services in French:
Tel. (toll-free): 1-866-461-2232
Fax: 1-866-814-2224
On-line: www.fcac-acfc.gc.ca/
Pages/Welcome-Bienvenue.aspx

to establish credit in your name. Also, request a credit report for your review to determine whether the identity theft has already affected your score.

Contact all of your creditors and any creditors with whom unauthorized accounts have been opened in your name. Many may request a copy of the police report. While contacting your credit card companies and financial institutions, take the opportunity to change all of your passwords. Do not use your mother's maiden name, the last three digits of your social insurance number, your birthday, street address, wedding anniversary, or any other readily available information that the identity thief may have obtained.

If the identity thief has gained access to your bank accounts or created accounts in your name, you should also contact cheque verification companies. These companies maintain a database of individuals who have written bad cheques and of accounts in which there have been excessive or unusual transactions.

If you believe that the identity thief has obtained your data or illegally used your personal information involving Canada Post in any way, you should contact your local post office. If the identity thief has compromised your social insurance number, contact the authorities immediately. Exhibit 6.9 provides a list of contacts you can use if you are subjected to identity theft.

MyLab Finance   Visit MyLab Finance for additional study and practice tools. Select Financial Planning Problems are available in the Study Plan. Create your own study plan, generate personal cash flow statements and balance sheets, and set personal financial goals.

SUMMARY

L.O.1   Provide a background on credit

Credit represents funds provided to a borrower that will be repaid in the future. An instalment loan is provided for specific purchases and the borrower has a longer time (such as a few years) to repay the amount borrowed. Revolving open-end credit is used for credit cards. Consumers can repay the entire balance at the end of the month or repay a portion of the balance and have interest charged on the remainder. The consumer may spend up to the credit limit at any time.

Credit helps you to establish a good credit history and credit capacity. Another advantage is the convenience that credit provides in making day-to-day purchases without carrying large amounts of cash. A disadvantage is that, if not used properly, credit can result in bankruptcy or cause a significant reduction in the money you can save.

Good credit is easy to create by paying utility bills promptly and limiting the use of credit cards. A complete history of your credit transactions is maintained by credit bureaus that rate your credit score and report this information to interested parties.

When making a credit application, you need to disclose your personal balance sheet and cash flow statement so that the lender can evaluate your ability to repay a loan. A high level of revenues, a low level of expenses, a large amount of capital and collateral, and a good credit history are preferred.

L.O.2   Describe the role of credit bureaus

Lenders commonly access the credit payment history provided by one or more credit bureaus when deciding whether to extend a personal loan. You can obtain a credit report from either of the two credit bureaus to ensure that the report is accurate. The credit report contains potentially negative information from public records, such as bankruptcy filings. It also offers information on late payments, accounts in good standing, inquiries made about your credit history, and personal information. You should review your credit report at least once a year.

L.O.3   Explain the key characteristics of consumer credit products

The advantages of using credit cards include helping you to (1) establish a good credit history, (2) create credit capacity, (3) eliminate the need for carrying cash, (4) provide a method for payment when cash is not an option, (5) earn additional benefits, (6) receive free temporary financing, and (7) keep track of your past transactions. A disadvantage of credit is that it is easier to obtain it than to pay it back. Some individuals use too much credit and are unable to make their payments, which may prevent them from obtaining credit in the future. When individuals apply for credit, they provide information about their cash inflows (income), cash outflows (spending habits), and collateral. Creditors also evaluate your credit report, which contains information on your credit history collected by a credit bureau.

Credit cards are distinguished by whether the sponsor is Visa, MasterCard, or American Express, and whether the card is a standard, gold, or platinum card. Specialized credit cards include cards offered by retail establishments such as the Hudson's Bay Company and cards created for specific groups, such as students, travellers to the United States, and individuals with credit problems. Credit cards are also distinguished by credit limit, overdraft protection, annual fee, incentives, the grace period, whether they provide cash advances, and the method used in determining the interest rate charged on balances not paid by the due date.

A home equity line of credit (HELOC) has a relatively low interest rate because of the collateral (the home) that backs the loan. In general, a home equity line of credit requires interest-only payments based on a variable rate of interest. However, the lender should plan to repay the principal at some point.

The most common source of financing from a financial institution is a personal loan. A loan contract specifies the amount of the loan, interest rate, maturity date, and collateral.

The real cost of borrowing on personal loans can be determined by first converting the annual percentage rate to an effective yield and then taking into account the additional fees that are paid on personal loans. A financial calculator can be used to determine the payment amount for a loan.

Your decision to purchase a car may require financing. You can reduce your monthly payments on the car loan if you make a higher down payment, but doing this may reduce your liquidity. Alternatively, you can reduce your monthly payments by extending the loan period.

The decision either to purchase a car with a car loan or to lease a car requires you to estimate the total cost of each alternative. The total cost of purchasing a car consists of the down payment, the forgone interest income on the down payment, and the total monthly loan payments. The total cost of leasing consists of the forgone interest income from the security deposit and the total monthly lease payments.

Provincial programs can be used to cover the difference between the cost of education and what is provided through the federal Canada Student Loan Program. Dependant students have lower loan limits. All full-time students do not have to begin paying back their loan until they have completed their education. Part-time students must make interest payments. You have to pay back your student loans even if you declare bankruptcy, unless seven years have elapsed since you ceased being a student.

L.O.4   Explain how to manage debt

Credit cards should be used with discipline. You should catch up on late payments, make the minimum payments on time, and reduce your debt. In addition, it is important to review your personal financial statements so that you can re-establish control over your finances. You should impose your own credit limits rather than spend to the limit granted by the card issuer. You should attempt to avoid financing costs, either by using income to cover the amount owing or by withdrawing money from savings, if necessary, to ensure that the balance is paid in full each month.

If you are not able to re-establish control over your finances, you may have to make a consumer proposal or file for bankruptcy.

L.O.5   Provide a background on identity theft

Not all threats to your credit score are the result of your actions. Identity theft, which involves the use of your personal, identifying information without your permission, is one of the fastest-growing crimes in Canada. An identity thief may use your personal information to obtain goods, services, and money, or to create a new identity. All of these actions can have a negative effect on your credit history.

L.O.6   Describe identity theft tactics

The identity thief has a wide variety of tactics at hand that can be used to obtain your personal data, including shoulder surfing, dumpster diving, skimming, pretexting, phishing, and pharming. Ultimately, protecting yourself from an identity thief is your responsibility.

L.O.7   Explain how to avoid identity theft

One of the things you can do to avoid identity theft is to not give out personal information on the phone, through the mail, or over the internet unless you have initiated contact. Pay attention to when your bills arrive in the mail and install and maintain a firewall on your personal computer.

L.O.8   Discuss how to respond to identity theft

Should your identity be stolen, notify the police and request a copy of the police report. Notify credit bureaus, credit card companies, financial institutions, and, when appropriate, the Canadian Security Intelligence Service (CSIS), and the Royal Canadian Mounted Police (RCMP).

REVIEW QUESTIONS

1. Define and describe credit.

2. Define and describe the two types of credit. Under what conditions might a consumer find each type useful?

3. What are the advantages and disadvantages of using credit?

4. Explain credit history.

5. What does the personal loan process involve?

6. Name the two major credit bureaus. What information do credit reports provide?

7. What eight major areas of information may be included on your credit report?

8. What is a credit score? What five factors are used to determine your credit score? Describe the importance of each factor.

9. Will both bureaus always produce the same credit score? What is the impact of differing credit scores between the two bureaus?

10. What is the credit score range? What is a good score? If you have good credit, will you automatically be approved for a loan?

11. What is the main cause of a poor credit score? How long will a poor credit score appear on your credit report? How do you improve a poor credit score?

12. Why is it important to review your credit score on a regular basis?

13. What are seven advantages of using a credit card? What are the disadvantages?

14. How do credit card companies, such as MasterCard and Visa, generate revenue?

15. Define and describe a prestige card.

16. Define and describe a retail credit card.

17. What is the main purpose of student, U.S. dollar, and secured credit cards?

18. What is a credit limit? How can you increase your credit limit?

19. What are the advantages and disadvantages of overdraft protection on credit cards?

20. How might you eliminate the annual fees charged by some credit cards?

21. Discuss how credit card companies offer incentives to use their cards. How else might credit card companies reward cardholders with excellent credit ratings?

22. What is a grace period? Describe how you can use it to your advantage.

23. What is a cash advance? How is it commonly obtained? Discuss interest rates and grace periods with respect to cash advances.

24. When is a finance charge applied to credit purchases? What are teaser rates? What is the common range of interest rates on credit cards?

25. What are the three methods used by financial institutions to calculate finance charges on outstanding credit card balances? Briefly describe how interest is computed under each method.

26. List some items that appear on the credit card statement. What accounts for the difference between your previous balance and your new balance?

27. If you find an error on your credit card statement, how do you prove that an error was made?

28. What should you consider when comparing credit cards?

29. What is a loan contract? What information is included in a loan contract?

30. Define and describe collateral. When obtaining a loan, what is the benefit of providing collateral?

31. Define and describe a payday loan. What is the maximum interest rate that can be charged on a consumer loan?

32. What are your responsibilities if you co-sign a loan? What are the potential consequences of failing to live up to your responsibilities as a co-signer?

33. How do you determine the real cost of borrowing on personal loans?

34. Differentiate between a home equity line of credit (HELOC) and home equity. Describe how a HELOC works.

35. What is the credit limit for a home equity line of credit (HELOC)?

36. How are interest rates calculated for home equity lines of credit? Why may borrowers prefer home equity lines of credit to other loans?

37. What is a second mortgage?

38. What are the potentially negative impacts a borrower may experience because of the interest-only payments and variable interest rates associated with a HELOC?

39. List the steps in buying a car. What financial criteria should be considered? Discuss each briefly.

40. Describe some techniques that car salespeople might use in negotiating the price of the car.

41. What should be the first step in financing a car purchase? Aside from the interest rate, what two factors will have the largest impact on the size of your monthly payment?

42. What are the advantages and disadvantages of leasing? How does the estimated market value of the car affect the purchase versus lease decision?

43. What are the characteristics of student loans? If you declare personal bankruptcy, will your student loans be discharged?

44. What are the first few steps you should take to manage your debt? What is the purpose behind reviewing each of your personal financial statements with respect to the debt management process?

45. What is a consumer proposal? When should you use a consumer proposal?

46. You may be deemed insolvent under what circumstances? What amount is exempt from bankruptcy in your province? How is your spouse affected by your personal bankruptcy?

47. What is identity theft?

48. Is identity theft only perpetrated to acquire money, goods, or services?

49. Aside from the financial losses, what other negative impacts might a victim of identity theft encounter?

50. Define and describe shoulder surfing.

51. Define and describe dumpster diving.

52. Define and describe skimming, pretexting, phishing, and pharming.

53. Can identity theft occur through legitimate access to your personal information? Explain.

54. Discuss the steps you can take to safeguard your personal information, both while you are offline and on the internet.

55. What steps should you take if you become a victim of identity theft?

FINANCIAL PLANNING PROBLEMS

| **MyLab Finance** Financial Planning Problems marked with a 🌐 can be found in MyLab Finance.

1. Sue obtains a one-year loan of $3000 based on an interest rate of 12 percent compounded annually. What would be the monthly payment to pay it off in one year?

🌐 2. Jack needs to borrow $1000 for the upcoming year. West Coast Bank will give him a loan at 9 percent. East Coast Bank will give him a loan at 7 percent with a $50 loan origination fee. First Canadian will give him a loan at 6 percent with a $25 loan origination fee. Assume that the interest rate on each loan is compounded monthly. Determine the total interest and fees Jack will be charged in each case. Which loan should he choose?

🌐 3. Jarrod has narrowed his choice to two credit cards that may meet his needs. Card A has an interest rate of 21 percent. Card B has an interest rate of 14 percent, but also charges a $50 annual fee. Jarrod will not pay off his balance each month, but will carry forward a balance of about $400 each month. Assume that interest is compounded daily. Which credit card should he choose?

🌐 4. Beth has just borrowed $5000 on a four-year loan at 8 percent, compounded monthly. She will be making monthly payments on her loan. Complete the amortization table below for the first five months of the loan.

Payment Number	Beginning Balance	Payment Amount	Applied to Interest	Applied to Principal	New Balance
1	$5000.00	$122	$33.33	$88.73	$4911.27
2	a	122	32.74	b	4821.95
3	4821.95	c	d	89.92	4732.03
4	4732.03	122	e	90.52	f
5	4641.51	122	30.94	g	h

🌐 5. The end of the billing period on Paul's credit card is the thirtieth of the month. He has a grace period of 21 days. If Paul purchases a stereo for $2300 on June 12, how many interest-free days will he have? When will he have to pay for the stereo in full in order to avoid finance charges?

🌐 6. Chrissy currently has a credit card that charges 15 percent interest. She usually carries a balance of

about $500. Chrissy has received an offer for a new credit card with a teaser rate of 3 percent for the first three months; after that, the rate increases to 19.5 percent. Assume that interest is compounded daily. What will her total annual interest be with her current card? What will her interest be the first year after she switches? Should she switch?

7. Tracy is borrowing $8000 on a six-year loan that has an APR of 11 percent, compounded monthly. What is her real cost of borrowing? What will her monthly payments be?

8. Margie has had a tough month. First, she had dental work that cost $2700. Then, she had major car repairs, which cost $2400. She put both of these unexpected expenses on her credit card. If she does not pay her balance when due, she will be charged 15 percent interest, compounded daily. Margie has $15 000 in a money market account that pays 5 percent interest, compounded monthly. How much interest would she pay (annualized) if she does not pay off her credit card balance? How much interest will she lose if she transfers the money from her money market account? Should she transfer the money from her money market account?

9. Harry purchased his condo for $330 000 and now the appraised value is $360 000. His outstanding mortgage is $228 000. What is the maximum home equity line of credit Harry would qualify for?

10. A house was purchased for $300 000 and has a market value of $325 000 and a mortgage of $213 000. What is the equity in this house?

11. Sharon is considering the purchase of a car. After making the down payment, she will finance $15 500. She is offered three maturities. On a four-year loan, Sharon will pay $371.17 per month. On a five-year loan, her monthly payments will be $306.99. On a six-year loan, they will be $264.26. Sharon rejects the four-year loan, as it is not within her budget. How much interest will Sharon pay over the life of the loan on the five-year

loan? On the six-year loan? Which should she choose if she bases her decision solely on total interest paid?

12. Bob bought a new car for $28 000 with a loan that will be amortized over five years. The best interest rate he got from his bank for the loan was 1.99 percent compounded annually. What is Bob's monthly car payment? How much interest was paid in the first car payment? How much interest will be paid over the entire life of the car loan?

13. Troy has a credit card that charges 18 percent, compounded daily, on outstanding balances and on cash advances. The closing date on the credit card is the first of each month. Last month Troy left a balance of $200 on his credit card. This month he took out a cash advance of $150 on the fifteenth of the month and made $325 in purchases throughout the month. He also made a payment of $220 on the day before the closing date on his credit card. What will be Troy's new balance on his next credit card statement, taking into account finance charges?

14. Eileen is a college student who consistently uses her credit card as a source of funds. She has maxed out her card at its $6000 limit. She does not plan to increase her credit card balance any further, but has already been declined for a car loan on a badly needed vehicle due to her existing debt. Her credit card charges 20 percent, compounded daily, on outstanding balances. If Eileen does not reduce her debt, how much will she pay annually to her credit card company? If she makes only the minimum monthly payment, how much interest will she pay before her credit card balance is cleared? Assume that Eileen will make a constant minimum monthly payment calculated as the amount due in the first month.

CHALLENGE QUESTIONS

1. Cory and Tisha found a used car that costs $12 000. They can finance through their bank at an interest rate of 8 percent interest for a maximum of 48 months. The rate for new car financing is 7.50 percent for 60 months or 7.35 percent for 48 months. All interest rates are compounded monthly. Would they save any money in interest charges if they could find a comparably priced new vehicle, and if they finance the new vehicle for 48 months or 60 months?

2. Ibrahim wants a new big-screen TV and Dolby digital stereo. He figures the system will cost $3000. The store will finance up to $2500 for 2 years at a 10.5 percent interest rate, compounded monthly. Assuming Ibrahim accepted the store's financing, how much would he have saved in total interest if he had increased his down payment to $1000?

ETHICAL DILEMMA

Chen recently graduated from college and accepted a job in a new city. Furnishing his apartment has proved more costly than he anticipated. To assist him in making purchases, he applied for and received a credit card with a $5000 limit. Chen planned to pay off the balance over six months.

Six months later, Chen finds that other expenses incurred in starting his career have restricted him to making only minimum payments on his credit card. As well, he has borrowed to the full extent of its credit limit. Upon returning from work

today, Chen finds a letter from the credit card company offering to increase his limit to $10 000 because he has been a good customer and has not missed a payment.

a. Discuss the ethics of credit card companies that offer to increase credit limits for individuals who make only minimum payments and who have maxed out their cards.

b. Should Chen accept the credit card company's offer?

FINANCIAL PLANNING ONLINE EXERCISES

1. Go to www.themint.org/kids/debt-calculator.html.

   a. Complete the debt calculator for each of the four items. Compare the interest charge based on the minimum monthly payment and the interest charge given what you are informed that you can afford to pay.

   b. For all four items, calculate the total extra cost from paying as much as you can afford versus making only the minimum monthly payment. Next, calculate the total interest saved. Comment on how much interest is saved by paying up to your maximum allowable level of affordability.

2. Go to www.themint.org/kids/what-is-your-credit-card-iq.html. Complete the quiz and determine your Credit Card IQ.

3. Go to www.themint.org/kids/take-the-spending-challenge.html.

   a. Complete the spending challenge by purchasing as many items as possible. How much debt do you have at the end? What is your take-home pay?

   b. Do you think this spending is a fair representation of what someone would spend over the course of 16 weeks? Explain.

4. Go to www.autos.ca/helpful-tools.

   a. Click on Loan Calculator. In the fields provided, input 30 000 for Purchase price, 2500 for Down payment, 0 for Trade in, 36 months for Loan term, 6.0 for Interest rate (%), and Manitoba for Province. Click on CALCULATE. What is the monthly loan payment? What is the total interest paid?

   b. Return to the link above. Click on Lease Calculator. In the fields provided, input 30 000 for Final negotiated price, 36 months for Total number of months leased, Manitoba for Province, 0 for Security deposit, 2500 for Capitalized cost of reduction, 15 000 for Residual value of car at lease end, and 6.0 for Interest rate. Click on CALCULATE. What is the monthly lease payment? Is the monthly lease payment lower than the monthly loan payment? By how much?

   c. What happens to the monthly lease payment if the residual value is decreased? Increased? At the end of a lease, what does the residual value represent? Based on the information you have gathered, is it better to have a relatively high or a relatively low residual value?

5. Go to https://www.mastercard.ca/en-ca.html. Click on "Frequently Asked Questions" and then click on "Chip Card".

   a. What is chip technology?

   b. What are its benefits?

   c. Go to www.aarp.org/money/scams-fraud/info-09-2011/is-it-scam-or-real-quiz.html.
      Complete the Is It a Scam or Is It Real? quiz.

PSYCHOLOGY OF PERSONAL FINANCE: Your Credit Cards and Car Loans

1. For many people, there is less pain associated with using a credit card to make purchases than to use cash, even if the amount of the payment is exactly the same. The use of the credit card almost feels like there is no payment, but the use of cash means that there is less cash available for other purchases. Therefore, spending decisions are made more carefully when using cash. Describe your opinion on this topic. Do you feel less pain when using a credit card? Are your spending decisions made more carefully when you use cash as opposed to credit cards?

2. Read one practical article or review a video of how psychology affects decisions when using a credit card. You can easily retrieve possible articles by doing an online search using the terms "psychology" and "pain of paying." Summarize the main points of the article.

3. People are tempted to spend much more money on a car than they need to because credit is so easily available. Some students make decisions based on whether they can cover the monthly payment rather than what they need. Describe your own behaviour toward financing the purchase of a car.

MINI-CASE 1: Credit Card Use

Garnett was amazed to hear that his friend Lindsey always pays off her credit card at the end of each month. Garnett just assumed that everyone used credit cards the same way — buy now, pay later. Garnett buys almost everything he needs or wants, including clothes, food, and entertainment, with his credit card. When Lindsey asked him about the APR for his credit card, Garnett did not have a clue. He also did not know the length of the grace period or how his minimum monthly payment was calculated. When Lindsey asked about this, Garnett replied that it did not really matter because he never paid off his balance like she did. Garnett reasoned that his credit card made purchases easier by allowing him to buy expensive items that he could otherwise not afford; thereby allowing him to only have to make minimum monthly payments. Overall, Garnett thinks that he is a responsible credit card user, but he admits that over the past two or three years he has been late making a few monthly payments and, once or twice, has gone over his limit. He also uses his card regularly to obtain cash advances. After hearing all of this, Lindsey is worried about her friend. She has come to you for help in answering the following questions. How long will it take Garnett to pay off the outstanding $5000 balance on his credit card if he makes the minimum monthly payment of $150? His APR is 19 percent compounded daily. What is the total amount of his payments? How much interest will he have paid? Is Garnett correct in thinking that one advantage of using credit is that it allows him to purchase expensive things today and pay for them tomorrow? If you agree, what is the opposite side of the argument?

MINI-CASE 2: Car Ownership

After about 10 months of saving $500 a month, Naresh and Shareen Walia have achieved their goal of saving $5000 for a down payment on a new car. Shareen's new car is priced at $25 000 plus 12 percent HST. She will receive a $1000 trade-in credit on her existing car and will make a $5000 down payment on the new car. The Walias would like to allocate a maximum of $500 per month to the loan payments on Shareen's new car. The annual interest rate on a car loan is currently 7 percent compounded monthly. They would prefer to have a relatively short loan maturity, but cannot afford a monthly payment higher than $500. The couple is considering monthly loan maturity options of 36 months, 48 months, and 60 months. The couple have asked you to help them figure out the total cost of financing the loan under each loan maturity option. What would be their monthly car loan payment under each option? How much are their total payments? How much interest would they pay? Based on your analysis, advise the Walias on the best loan maturity for their needs.

Study Guide

Circle the correct answer and then check the answers in the back of the book to chart your progress.

Multiple Choice

1. Which of the following most likely would not be considered an advantage of using credit?
   a. Credit helps you build a good credit score.
   b. Credit is inexpensive to use.
   c. Credit is convenient to use.
   d. Credit sometimes offers added benefits, such as Air Miles and/or travel insurance.

2. A poor credit history will appear on your credit report for:
   a. 3 to 5 years.
   b. 3 to 10 years.
   c. 5 to 7 years.
   d. 7 to 10 years.

3. You should avoid payday loans for all of the following reasons, except:
   a. You may end up creating a continuous cycle in which your paycheque is always needed to repay short-term loans.
   b. If you shop around, you may find more affordable borrowing rates.
   c. You shouldn't spend money unless you have the money to spend.
   d. You may be able to obtain a temporary loan by using your credit card.

4. The most important factor used in BEACON credit scoring is:
   a. Your credit payment history.
   b. The amount of credit owing.

   c. The length of time that credit has been established.
   d. The types of credit you have established.

5. The president of Warehouse Distributors Inc. is considering the introduction of a retail credit card for use by its customers. Which of the following factors would not be considered an advantage when evaluating whether a retail credit card should be considered?
   a. Warehouse Distributors does not have to pay a small percentage of the proceeds of retail credit card sales to another credit card company.
   b. Customers are able to make larger purchases because they only have to pay a small portion of the balance owed each month.
   c. Customers will be restricted to making purchases at Warehouse Distributors, which restricts their use of credit.
   d. Customers will save on interest costs because the interest rate charged when financing with a retail credit card is normally lower than that charged on non-proprietary cards.

6. Which of the following is a predatory lending practice?
   a. A loan agreement includes confusing information that does not clearly disclose the borrower's obligations.
   b. A lender stipulates that a loan will be provided only if the borrower purchases life insurance on the loan.
   c. A lender provides a home equity line of credit with the expectation that the loan may not be

repaid immediately. The borrower may decide to make interest payments only.

    d. A lender charges a loan fee that is higher than the competition.

7. To determine the real cost of borrowing on personal loans, the APR must be converted to an _____ interest rate.
    a. effective
    b. simple
    c. complex
    d. compound

8. Which of the following is a disadvantage to leasing versus buying a car?
    a. You are not responsible for maintenance costs while you are leasing a car.
    b. You need a substantial down payment when you lease a car.
    c. You have no equity value in a leased car.
    d. You may need to find a buyer for the car once the lease term is up.

9. Doug Bishop, CFP, is a financial adviser who specializes in helping clients get out of credit card debt. Most of his clients have large savings and investment portfolios. Which of the following tips does Doug most likely not provide to this particular client base?
    a. Pay credit card bills before investing money.
    b. Use savings if necessary to pay credit card bills on time.
    c. If you cannot avoid credit card debt, pay it off before other debt.
    d. Use the services of a credit repair company.

10. Two years ago, Kristal and Joe purchased a home for $300 000. It has increased in value over the past two years and is currently worth $400 000. Their current mortgage balance is $150 000. Calculate the credit limit they would receive on a home equity line of credit. Assume that the financial institution they deal with will provide home equity lines of credit of up to 80 percent of the market value of the home, less outstanding mortgages.
    a. $170 000
    b. $75 000
    c. $300 000
    d. $225 000

11. Using email messages from a legitimate source to obtain account information for the purpose of identity theft is referred to as:
    a. Pharming.
    b. Phishing.
    c. Pretexting.
    d. Skimming.

12. A large number of recent credit inquiries suggests:
    a. You have a high BEACON score.
    b. You are having trouble getting credit.
    c. You have a good rating with many financial institutions.
    d. You are very diligent in tracking your credit information.

13. Errors on credit reports can occur. If there is an error on your report:
    a. It is your responsibility to review it once a year for accuracy and inform of any errors.
    b. It can result in the credit agency being charged under the Fair Credit Reporting Act.
    c. The creditor reporting to the agency must correct it at your request.
    d. You must inform the Better Business Bureau to take your case to the authorities.

14. A proposal to creditors is made by an insolvent debtor having difficulty meeting payments. Which of the following is true?
    a. The proposal must be rejected by creditors within 45 days or it will be deemed to be accepted.
    b. The history will remain on the credit bureau report for three years after terms have been met.
    c. The proposal must be for an amount over $50 000.
    d. The proposal must require at least 50 percent of the total debt to be repaid.

15. Which of the following is a true statement about student loans?
    a. All student loans are provided directly to students.
    b. All student loans are provided to parents of students.
    c. The repayment schedule is deferred.
    d. Students who declare bankruptcy within seven years of graduation may have their loans forgiven.

True/False

1. True or False? Instalment credit allows consumers to borrow up to a specified maximum amount, such as $10 000.

2. True or False? All else being equal, a loan with a longer maturity will have lower monthly payments than a loan with a shorter maturity.

3. True or False? The primary credit bureaus in Canada will provide a different BEACON score for the same individual.

4. True or False? In order to protect your credit rating, you must pay off your full credit card balance each month.

5. True or False? You should review your credit report from one of the major credit bureaus at least once a year.

6. True or False? The lender has the right to seize the assets of someone who has co-signed a loan. However, if the borrower has a spouse, the lender must first try to seize the assets of the spouse before attempting to seize the assets of the co-signer.

7. True or False? The interest rate charged on a cash advance is applied at the time of the cash advance.

8. True or False? Dealers may impose additional charges when you lease versus making a purchase.

9. True or False? Treat a credit card as a means of convenience, not a source of funds.

10. True or False? When you lease a car, you will be charged if you drive more than the maximum number of kilometres specified in the lease agreement.

11. True or False? The grace period makes it possible for you to obtain free credit for a period of time.

12. True or False? Phishing occurs when individuals access personal information online from a large audience under false pretenses.

13. True or False? Full-time students do not begin repaying their student loans until they have completed their education.

14. True or False? In the event that you declare bankruptcy within 10 years of ceasing to be a student, you do not have to repay your student loans.

15. True or False? If you receive a phone call that seeks to verify or update personal information, you should ask several questions of the solicitor to verify his or her authenticity.

Purchasing and Financing a Home

Two years ago, Brian Menke purchased a small home that he could easily afford near the firm where he works. His co-worker, Tim Remington, also bought a home. Unlike Brian, Tim would need most of his paycheque to cover the mortgage and expenses of his home, but he thought the purchase would make a good investment.

jehsomwang/Shutterstock

Because his mortgage payment was relatively low, Brian was able to save money during the first year after buying his home. Since he was so close to work, Brian was also able to get back home from work at a reasonable time, which gave him an opportunity to take his kids to all their after school activities, which were also close to home. Tim, however, was unable to save any money and had large credit card bills on which he was paying only the minimum amount. In addition, Tim did not consider some of the additional costs of owning a home, such as property taxes and maintenance expenses. Although Tim and his wife had a beautiful older home, their busy work schedules made it difficult to maintain the large yard. In addition, their kids attended a private school which was some distance from their home. With the lack of time and financial resources, Tim suddenly realized he could not afford his home.

QUESTIONS:

1. How does a financial institution determine how much home you can afford?
2. What criteria should you use in order to determine the home you should purchase?
3. What are some of the costs associated with buying a home?

THE LEARNING OBJECTIVES OF THIS CHAPTER ARE TO:

1. Explain how to select a home to purchase
2. Describe the transaction costs of purchasing a home
3. Describe the characteristics of various mortgage options
4. Describe the characteristics of a fixed-rate mortgage
5. Describe the characteristics of a variable-rate mortgage
6. Show how to compare the costs of purchasing versus renting a home
7. Explain the mortgage refinancing decision

L.O.1

Go to:
www.atb.com/personal-banking/tools-and-resources/Pages/mortgage-calculators.aspx

Click on:
Rent vs. Own Calculator

This website provides access to a calculator that will help you to determine whether it is in your best interest to rent or own a particular property.

SELECTING A HOME

Buying a home may be the single biggest investment you will ever make, so you should take the decision very seriously and carefully consider several factors. Evaluate the homes for sale in your target area to determine the typical price range and features. Once you decide on a realistic price range, identify a specific home that you desire. You can compare the cost of buying that home to the cost of renting. That way, you can weigh the extra costs against the benefits of home ownership.

> **myth** or **fact** You should look at some houses to see what you like before you get a pre-approval certificate.

When many people consider purchasing a home, they are usually referring to a single-family detached home. This type of home is a free-standing home that is situated on its own lot. Typically, this type of home is occupied by one family. There are many other types of homes that you can choose from. A semi-detached home is a home that has a common wall with another home. This type of home is less expensive to maintain than a single-family detached home but it offers many of the same benefits, such as a private yard. A semi-detached home is sometimes incorrectly referred to as a duplex. A duplex, however, consists of one house that contains two distinct family homes—one on top of the other. A townhouse consists of many single-family homes with each attached to the next by a common wall. A carriage home consists of houses that are joined by garages or carports. All of the types of homes mentioned so far are built on the lot on which they are situated. In contrast, a manufactured or mobile home is built in a factory and then placed on a lot. A condominium arrangement is best suited for situations where the common areas cannot be easily separated among the owners. An apartment complex is an example of a property that is well suited for the condominium form of ownership.

The benefits of a condominium are somewhat different from those of a house. Whereas a house is generally detached, units in a condominium are typically attached, so there is less privacy. Condominium expenses are shared among unit owners, while the owners of a house pay for expenses on their own. Nevertheless, the factors to be considered when selecting or financing a house are also relevant when purchasing a condominium.

How Much Can You Afford?

When selecting a home, you should first determine how much you can afford to pay per month for a mortgage based on your budget. Once you remove homes that are too expensive from consideration, you should use various criteria to evaluate those you are still considering.

Most individuals pay for a home with a down payment (between 5 and 20 percent of the purchase price) and obtain a mortgage loan to finance the remaining cost. You then pay regular mortgage payments over the term of the loan. Mortgage lenders determine how much they will lend you based on your financial situation and credit history. Various websites can estimate the maximum mortgage you can afford based on your financial situation (such as your income and your net worth). Most financial institutions will issue a **pre-approval certificate**, which provides you with a guideline on how large a mortgage you can afford and an estimate of your mortgage payment based on your financial situation. This certificate also provides you with a mortgage interest rate guarantee that is valid for 60 to 120 days, depending on the financial institution. This guarantee is useful if interest rates increase while you are home shopping since the lender will apply the interest rate on the pre-approval certificate when calculating the mortgage payment during the mortgage approval process. However, the pre-approval certificate does not guarantee that you will be approved for a mortgage. That is another process.

When you select a home and make an offer, you will usually put a financing condition on your offer to purchase. This tells the seller that you are interested in purchasing the home, but you must first get sufficient financing from a financial institution before you can actually buy it. Again, it is important to remember that the pre-approval certificate does not mean that you have a pre-approved mortgage; you must still apply for a mortgage when you have found the home you would like to purchase.

In most cases, financial institutions will provide you with a mortgage loan only if your gross debt service (GDS) ratio is no more than 32 percent. Your **gross debt service (GDS) ratio** is your monthly mortgage-related debt payments—including mortgage loan repayments, heating costs, property taxes, and half of any condominium fees—divided by your total monthly gross household income. The mortgage loan repayments must be calculated using the greater of the mortgage interest rate agreed to in the mortgage contract and the current Bank of Canada five-year fixed mortgage interest rate, which is an average of the five-year fixed mortgage interest rates of the big six banks. In most cases, the current five-year fixed mortgage interest rate will be higher than the contracted mortgage interest rate.

In addition, financial institutions will normally require that your total debt service (TDS) ratio be no more than 40 percent. Your **total debt service (TDS) ratio** is your mortgage-related debt payments plus all other consumer debt payments divided by your total monthly gross household income. These generalizations do not apply to everyone, as other financial information and spending habits of the homeowners should also be considered. In addition, financial institutions base the mortgage on the property as well. Since the home serves as security for the mortgage loan, the value of the home must be greater than the value of the mortgage.

pre-approval certificate
Provides you with a guideline on how large a mortgage you can afford and an estimate of your mortgage payment based on your financial situation.

gross debt service (GDS) ratio
Your monthly mortgage-related debt payments—including mortgage loan repayments, heating costs, property taxes, and half of any condominium fees—divided by your total monthly gross household income.

total debt service (TDS) ratio
Your mortgage-related debt payments plus all other consumer debt payments divided by your total monthly gross household income.

EXAMPLE

Blake and Donna Braithwaite have asked their bank to help them determine whether they qualify for a mortgage on a $375 000 home on which they would like to make an offer. The couple will make a down payment of $75 000 and the mortgage will be amortized over 25 years. As part of its initial assessment, the bank has to calculate the couple's GDS and TDS ratios. The current five-year fixed mortgage interest rate is 6 percent, compounded semi-annually. Based on its discussion with the couple, the bank gathers the following additional information:

Blake's monthly gross income = $3500

Donna's monthly gross income = $3500

Monthly mortgage payment = $1919*

Monthly heating costs = $120

Monthly property taxes = $250

Monthly consumer debt payment = $500

*The required information and calculator steps for the monthly mortgage payment will be discussed later in this chapter.

GDS = ($1919 + $120 + $250) ÷ $7000 = 0.3270 × 100 = 32.70%

TDS = ($1919 + $120 + $250 + $500) ÷ $7000 = 0.3984 × 100 = 39.84%

The GDS ratio actually exceeds the previously stated max (though by only 0.7%). Based on this initial assessment, it appears that they are eligible for a mortgage. The Braithwaites have qualified for their mortgage based on the current five-year fixed mortgage interest rate. If they are able to negotiate a lower rate than this, their financial position will be even better since their monthly mortgage payment will be less than the $1919 they were required to use as part of their GDS and TDS ratio calculations.

Affordable Down Payment

You can determine your maximum down payment by estimating the market value of the assets you are willing to convert to cash for a down payment and for transaction costs (such as closing costs) incurred when obtaining a mortgage. Be sure to maintain some funds for liquidity purposes to cover unanticipated bills and closing costs.

Saving for the down payment on your first home is a daunting task. It takes planning and discipline. Currently, a federal program can help first-time home buyers reach their goals more quickly. The Home Buyers' Plan (HBP) allows you to "borrow" up to $25 000 from your registered retirement savings plan (RRSP), interest-free. If you buy the home together with your spouse, partner, or other individuals, each of you can withdraw up to $25 000. You then have 15 years, beginning with the second year after the year of the withdrawal, to pay back this "loan" to your respective RRSPs. The advantage of using your RRSP to fund part of your down payment is the RRSP's tax-deferral feature.

This program will be discussed further in Chapter 14.

Affordable Monthly Mortgage Payments

Go to:
www.cmhc-schl.gc.ca/
en/co/buho/buho_005.
cfm

This website provides
an estimate of how much
you could borrow to finance
a home, based on your
income and other financial
information.

How large a monthly mortgage payment can you afford? Refer to your cash flow statement to determine how much net cash flow you have available to make a mortgage payment. If you purchase a home, you will no longer have a rent payment, so that money can be used as part of the mortgage payment. You should also be aware, however, that owning a home entails periodic expenses (such as property taxes, homeowner's insurance, and home maintenance repairs). You should not plan to purchase a home that will absorb all of your current excess income. The larger your mortgage payments, the less you can add to your savings or other investments.

Once some home buyers determine the maximum that they can afford, they tend to use the maximum amount as their budget with the plan to spend it all. By spending the maximum, they may have no funds available for unanticipated expenses that could occur.

In fact, another behavioural characteristic of home buyers is that they tend to buy a home for more money than they originally planned to spend. This occurs because as they start looking at homes for sale, they commonly notice a home that offers some nice features that is priced beyond the amount they had planned to spend. They may justify a purchase beyond what they had intended to spend with the following reasoning:

- The more expensive house may not require any additional down payment if they just obtain a larger mortgage.

- They can possibly obtain a second job to afford the higher mortgage payment.

- They will benefit from buying a more expensive home because if prices rise over time, the more expensive homes will likely rise in value by a greater degree.

Each of their reasons is questionable. First, they may be able to obtain a larger mortgage, but that means more debt, and they will need to make larger monthly mortgage payments. Second, obtaining an extra job just to afford a more expensive home might reduce the enjoyment of that home because you may be too busy working in order to make mortgage payments. Third, home values might rise over time, but they could decline over time, and if the values drop, the more expensive homes will likely suffer a larger decline in value.

Like many purchasing decisions, buying a home provides immediate satisfaction and the pain of paying for it is not felt until later. Therefore, home buyers can find many reasons to spend more money on a home than what they can afford. By the time home buyers feel the pain from paying off the debt that was needed to make the initial purchase, it is too late to reverse their decision. Normally, home buyers cannot easily sell a home that they just purchased, and even if they could, the transactions costs (discussed later in this chapter) are substantial. Therefore, home buyers should carefully assess how much they can afford to spend on a home, and should use that amount as a maximum when reviewing homes for sale.

Criteria Used to Select a Home

The most important factors to consider when selecting a home are identified here.

- *Price.* Stay within your budget. Avoid purchasing a home you cannot afford. Although your favourite home may have ample space and a large yard, it may not be worth the stress of struggling to make the monthly mortgage payments. A pre-approval certificate is particularly useful in controlling the price you pay for a house. If you know in advance how large a mortgage the bank is willing to provide, you can limit your search to homes within your price range. Be sure, though, to use the bank's information only as a starting point. Lenders have a vested interest in maximizing loan amounts. Therefore, the mortgage amount they suggest may end up cramping your lifestyle.

- *Convenient location.* Focus on homes in a convenient area so that you can minimize commuting time to work or travel time to other activities. You may save 10 or more hours of travel time a week through a convenient location. Remember, as well, that you must take into account additional commuting costs if you buy a home some distance from work.

- *Maintenance.* Newer homes tend to need fewer and less costly repairs than older homes. For example, replacing the hot water tank, a major appliance, or the shingles on the roof must be considered when buying an older home. This should not be as much of a concern with a newer home. A home with a large yard may require more maintenance depending on how you landscape the yard. Recall that in condominium buildings, residents share common areas, such as a swimming pool or tennis court. They normally pay a fixed monthly fee to cover the costs of maintaining these common areas. In addition, they may be assessed an extra cost to maintain the structure of the building, which can include a new roof or other repairs. These extras may be very costly or may result in an increase to your condo fee.

- *School system.* If you have children, the reputation of the local school system is very important. Even if you do not have children, the resale value of your house benefits from a good school system.

- *Insurance.* When you own a home, you need to purchase homeowner's insurance, which covers burglary, damage, or fire. The cost of insurance varies among homes. It is higher for more expensive homes and homes in high-risk areas (such as flood zones) because the replacement value of an expensive home is higher and homes in high-risk areas are exposed to a higher probability of claims.

- *Taxes.* Property taxes are imposed on homes to pay for local services, such as the local school system, the local park system, and garbage collection. The amount of property taxes that you pay is determined by the mill rate. Each jurisdiction that has taxing authority, for example a municipality, will calculate its mill rate based on a number of factors. The mill rate is then multiplied by the assessed property value and divided by 1000. For example, the property taxes on a $300 000 property in a municipality that has a mill rate of 7.2 would be $2160, calculated as ($300 000 $\times$ 7.2) $\div$ 1000. Taxes vary substantially among locations.

myth or **fact** You can borrow the down payment for the home you wish to purchase.

- *Resale value.* The resale value of a home depends greatly on its location. Most homes with similar features within a specific subdivision or neighbourhood are in the same range. Although home prices in a given subdivision tend to move in the same direction, price movements can vary substantially among homes. For example, homes in a subdivision that are within walking distance of a school may be worth more than comparable homes several kilometres from the school.

You cannot accurately predict the future resale value of a home, but you can evaluate today's resale value of similar homes that were sold years ago in the same location. Information about home prices is provided on numerous websites. Be aware, however, that the rate of increase in home prices in previous years does not necessarily serve as a good predictor of the future. The rate of increase in home prices is difficult to predict because of the number of factors involved in determining resale value. Home prices are very dependent on economic and market conditions; in particular, positive economic growth is associated with an increase in real gross domestic product (GDP). First and foremost, you should select a home according to the criteria mentioned above. Although resale value is important, it should not be the primary reason for selecting the home in which you live.

- *Personal preferences.* In addition to the general criteria described above, you will have your own personal preferences regarding features such as the number of bedrooms, size of the kitchen, and size of the yard.

FREE APPS for Personal Finance

Searching for a Home

Application:

The REALTOR.ca real estate app allows you to search for homes and property across Canada and connect with realtors for more detailed information. The app will even connect you with a realtor to view, buy, or sell a property.

Relying on a Realtor

Advice from a real estate broker can assist you when assessing homes, deciding whether to buy a home, or determining which home to purchase. Keep in mind that when you use a realtor to sell a home (as most people do), you will pay the realtor a commission. The home seller is responsible for paying the commission to the realtor. Traditionally, real estate commissions have been a scaled percentage of the selling price for the home; for example, 7 percent of the selling price on the first $100 000 and 3 percent on the remaining price. Thus, if you resell your home for $400 000, you will probably pay a commission of about $7000 on the first $100 000 and $9000 on the next $300 000. The commission payment will reduce the amount that the seller will receive from the sale of their home. Many realtors have moved to a flat fee structure that may be a fixed percentage (e.g., 2 percent) or a fixed dollar amount (e.g., $2500). It is important to consider a realtor's input, but make decisions that meet your needs and preferences. A good real estate agent will ask you about your preferences and suggest appropriate homes.

Using Online Realtor Services

Increasingly, online services are being used to facilitate home purchases. Websites such as www.realtor.ca allow realtors to present detailed information about the homes they have available for sale in a database that is made accessible to other realtors. **Multiple Listing Service (MLS)** is an information database of homes available for sale through realtors who are members of the service. Essentially, MLS is a marketing service that allows you and your realtor to shop online for homes. By using this service, you can narrow down the homes you wish to view in person. The local real estate board administers and operates the local MLS system. The process of buying and selling a home is otherwise unchanged. You would still use the services of a realtor to complete the transaction.

Other online services, such as ComFree (comfree.com), allow sellers to list their homes in a database without providing real estate-related services through a realtor. Instead, the

Multiple Listing Service (MLS)
An information database of homes available for sale through realtors who are members of the service.

transaction would have to be completed by the buyer and seller without the help of a realtor. The advantage of this type of service is that it charges lower or no commissions. Usually, a flat one-time fee will give you a professional online listing, advertising exposure in a newsstand magazine, and access to professional services such as property appraisers, inspectors, and lawyers.

FOCUS ON ETHICS: Disclosing Defects

For both the buyer and the seller, the sale of a home is stressful due to the large amount of money involved. Concerns about unethical behaviour only add to the tension. For example, there are many cases of sellers who did not disclose problems (such as a leaky roof or cracked foundation) with their homes.

As a seller, the law requires that you fully disclose any defect that may affect the value of the home. In addition to being the legal thing to do, disclosure is the moral thing to do. You would hope that a seller would be completely honest with you, so you should treat a potential buyer in the manner that you would wish to be treated. As well, if any problem arises shortly after you sell a house, the buyer can sue you for any misrepresentations.

Negotiating a Price

Once you find a home that meets most or all of your criteria, you need to negotiate a price with the seller by making an offer. Some homes are initially priced above the amount the seller will accept. As with any investment, you want to make sure that you do not pay more than you have to for a home.

You may consider the advice of your real estate broker on the offer you should make. Most sellers are willing to accept less than their original asking price, depending on local market conditions. Once you decide on an offering price, you can submit an offer in the form of a contract to buy the home, which must be approved by the seller. Your real estate broker takes the contract to the seller and serves as the intermediary between you and the seller during the negotiation process.

The seller may accept your offer, reject it, or suggest that you revise it. If the asking price is $425 000 and you offer $390 000, the seller may reject that offer but indicate a willingness to accept an offer of, say, $410 000. Then the decision reverts to you. You can agree, reject that offer, or revise the contract again. For example, you may counter by offering $400 000. The contract can go back and forth until the buyer and seller either come to an agreement or decide that it is no longer worthwhile to pursue an agreement. The contract stipulates not only the price, but also other conditions requested by the buyer, such as the completion of a home inspection, the date on which the buyer will be able to move into the home (known as the possession date), and the approval of a mortgage by the bank.

TRANSACTION COSTS OF PURCHASING A HOME
L.O.2

Once you start the offer process, you should apply for a mortgage from a financial institution. As discussed earlier, this process is different than the pre-approval certificate process in that it requires the completion of a detailed loan application. The loan application process requires that you summarize your financial condition, including your income, assets, and liabilities. You will need to provide proof of income, such as a T4 slip, an employment letter, or a recent paycheque. The lender will sometimes check your financial condition by contacting your employer to verify both your employment and your present salary. The lender will request a credit report as well.

In addition to applying for a mortgage, you need to plan to cover the transaction costs of purchasing the home. These include the down payment and closing costs.

Down Payment

When you purchase a home, you use your money to make a down payment and pay the remaining amount with financing. Your down payment represents your equity investment in the home.

conventional mortgage
A mortgage where the down payment is at least 20 percent of the home's appraised value.

A **conventional mortgage** refers to a mortgage where the down payment is at least 20 percent of the home's appraised value. The lender expects you to cover a portion of the purchase price with your own money because the home serves as collateral to back the loan. The lending institution bears the risk that you may default on the loan. If you are unable to make your mortgage payments, the lender can repossess the home by applying for foreclosure through the legal system. Foreclosure allows the lender to take possession and sell the home with the permission of the courts.

If the home's value declines over time, however, a creditor may not obtain all of the funds it initially loaned. Your down payment provides a cushion in case the value of the home declines. With a conventional mortgage, the lender is more likely to be able to still recover the full amount of the mortgage loan even when they sell the home for less than the original purchase price. If you are unable to make a down payment of at least 20 percent, the lender will still give you a mortgage. However, this type of mortgage is referred to as a high ratio mortgage. A **high ratio mortgage** refers to a mortgage where the down payment is less than 20 percent of the home's appraised value.

high ratio mortgage
A mortgage where the down payment is less than 20 percent of the home's appraised value.

Since the cushion provided by the down payment is much smaller with a high ratio mortgage, the lender will require that your mortgage be insured. Mortgage default insurance can be purchased from insurers, such as the Canada Mortgage and Housing Corporation (CMHC), www.cmhc-schl.gc.ca, or Genworth Canada, genworth.ca. With insured mortgages, a traditional lender extends the loan, but the mortgage insurer insures it in the event of default, thereby protecting the lender's investment. The mortgage insurer will charge the lender a mortgage loan insurance premium. The lender will pass on the cost of the insurance to the borrower. The borrower will have the option of paying the mortgage loan insurance immediately or having the lender add this premium to the cost of the mortgage. In Ontario and Quebec, provincial sales tax is added to the premium. Exhibit 7.1 displays the premium charged by CMHC based on the amount of financing required. In most cases, a traditional down payment refers to a down payment made using your own savings, an RRSP, HBP withdrawal, non-repayable gifts from an immediate relative such as a parent, and/or money received from the sale of another property. A non-traditional down payment refers to a down payment made using borrowed money, gifts, and/or lender cashback incentives, which are explained later in this chapter. It is important to note that the extended amortization surcharges displayed in Exhibit 7.1 are not available for high ratio mortgages. In this case, homebuyers are restricted to a maximum amortization period of 25 years.

EXHIBIT 7.1   CMHC Mortgage Loan Insurance Costs

Loan-to-Value Ratio	Standard Premium
Up to and including 65%	0.60%
Up to and including 75%	1.70%
Up to and including 80%	2.40%
Up to and including 85%	2.80%
Up to and including 90%	3.10%
Up to and including 95%	4.00%
90.01% to 95% - Non-Traditional Down Payment	4.50%

Source: Based on Canada Mortgage and Housing Corporation. https://www.cmhc-schl.gc.ca/en/co/moloin/moloin_005.cfm

Paul Ezako makes a $20 000 down payment on a $350 000 home. Since the mortgage is a high ratio mortgage, the lender will need to purchase mortgage loan insurance. Paul decides that he would like the lender to add the mortgage loan insurance premium to his mortgage. Paul's mortgage payments will be calculated based on the adjusted mortgage balance.

Mortgage required = Value of home − Down payment = $350 000 − $20 000 = $330 000

Mortgage size as a percentage of lending value = $330 000 ÷ $350 000
$$= 0.9429 \times 100 = 94.29\%$$

Paul has used his personal savings to make the $20 000 down payment. Since he has made a traditional down payment, the mortgage loan insurance premium is calculated using a rate of 4.00 percent.

Mortgage loan insurance premium = Mortgage required × Mortgage loan insurance
rate = $330 000 × 4.00% = $13 200

Adjusted mortgage balance = $330 000 + $13 200 = $343 200

In rare situations, the lender may require mortgage insurance even though the down payment is greater than 20 percent. For example, the lender may determine that there is a high probability that the borrower may default on the mortgage based on his or her financial history.

FREE APPS for Personal Finance

Ready Set Home

Application:

The Ready Set Home app helps homebuyers, especially first-time homebuyers, make informed choices when buying a home. The app offers tools to guide you to figure out how much you can comfortably afford to spend as well as keep track of all the details during your home-buying process.

Vendor Take-Back Mortgage. An alternative to a high ratio mortgage is a vendor take-back mortgage. A **vendor take-back mortgage** is a mortgage where the lender is the seller of the property. In this case, the buyer will take out a second mortgage equal to the difference between the value of the home and the existing mortgage that the seller has on the property, less any down payment. As mentioned in Chapter 6, a second mortgage is a secured mortgage loan that is subordinate to another loan. In this case, the seller's loan from the lender would be paid before the buyer's loan from the seller. The buyer will make mortgage payments directly to the seller. The title of the property transfers to the buyer. If the buyer defaults on the mortgage payments, the property transfers back to the seller.

A vendor take-back mortgage may be better for the buyer than a high ratio mortgage because total interest costs may be lower than those associated with a high ratio mortgage. In addition, the seller will likely require less documentation than a bank would require. The incentive for the seller to set up a vendor take-back mortgage is that the interest earned by providing a second mortgage to the buyer is usually higher than what the seller could earn from other investments. A vendor take-back mortgage can be complicated. It is important for the buyer and seller to seek legal advice so that the rights and responsibilities of both parties are clearly understood.

vendor take-back mortgage
A mortgage where the lender is the seller of the property.

EXAMPLE

Meredith and Jason Crane own a $450 000 home that has a remaining mortgage balance of $220 000. Bernard and Maria Santos would like to purchase the home. The couples have agreed that a vendor take-back mortgage would best meet their respective needs. The Santoses have a $50 000 down payment. A second mortgage for the amount of $180 000 would be arranged between the couples.

Second mortgage required = ($450 000 − $220 000) − $50 000 = $180 000

The Santoses' monthly mortgage payments will cover the existing mortgage payment currently paid by the Cranes plus the payments associated with the second mortgage. The Cranes will continue to make mortgage payments to their lending institution, and the payment they receive on the second mortgage will provide them with a regular source of income.

Closing Costs

A buyer incurs various fees when purchasing a home. These fees are often referred to as closing costs. The most important fees are identified here.

home inspection
A report on the condition of the home.

Home Inspection Fee. A **home inspection** is a report on the condition of the home. It should be a condition in your offer to purchase whenever you are not the original owner of the home. Home inspectors will evaluate the structure and systems of the home on which you have made an offer and provide a written report. If the home requires any major repairs, you can re-evaluate your decision to purchase. Any conditions in your offer to purchase that are not met to your satisfaction will allow you to take back your offer and have your deposit refunded. A home inspection commonly costs around $350 to $600.

Appraisal Fee. An appraisal is used to estimate the value of the home and thus protects the financial institution's interests. Recall that if you are unable to make your monthly mortgage payments, the financial institution can sell the home to recoup the loan it provided. The appraisal fee commonly ranges between $300 and $500. The appraised value is used to calculate the mortgage size and should be no less than the purchase price, if not more.

Real Property Report. A real property report, also known as a land survey, is a legal document that clearly illustrates the location of significant visible improvements relative to property boundaries. You should ask for a real property report to ensure that any improvements, such as a deck, are in conformance with municipal property improvement guidelines. Normally, the seller should have paid for an up-to-date real property report as they made improvements to their property. However, this may not be the case and the buyer may end up paying for an up-to-date real property report during the home purchase negotiation. A real property report commonly ranges between $1000 and $2000.

Land Transfer Tax. Some provinces charge a land transfer tax that must be paid by the purchaser. This tax is levied when property is sold. For example, in Ontario the land transfer tax for a $300 000 home is $5700. In addition to the tax, a registration fee may be applied. Land transfer tax is also charged in British Columbia, Manitoba, Nova Scotia, and Quebec.

Legal Fees and Disbursements. The purchase of a home should be completed using the services of lawyer. If you are obtaining a mortgage on a property, the bank will require that the mortgage loan be disbursed in accordance with the mortgage loan agreement. In addition, a lawyer will ensure that a property is registered correctly with your local land titles office. Exhibit 7.2 provides an example of the estimated statement of funds required worksheet that a legal office would prepare. This document provides an illustration of any outstanding amounts and/or other documents that are needed to complete the sale of the home. It is composed of four major sections: the sale price less the initial deposit and mortgage amount, other charges, disbursements, and GST/HST payable. In Exhibit 7.2, the total amount required represents the total of these individual sections. In addition to a final payment, the statement may also include notes at the bottom indicating that proof of home insurance is required. In some provinces, property can be transferred without

EXHIBIT 7.2 Estimated Statement of Funds Required

SALE PRICE		$413 130.38
DEPOSIT PAID (5% of sale price)	$ 20 656.52	
NET MORTGAGE (20% down payment)	330 504.30	
		351 160.82
Difference		**61 969.56**
Plus ABC Law Group Fees		**1000.00**
Re: Purchase and Mortgage		
Other Charges		
Printing Fee	15.00	
Photocopying	42.50	
Postage	4.93	
Fax Transmissions	42.00	
TOTAL OTHER CHARGES	104.43	**104.43**
Disbursements		
Transfer of Land registration	106.00	
Land Titles Agent	20.00	
Courier Charges	39.00	
Certified Copies of Title & Fax Fee	4.00	
Document Copy	7.00	
Land Titles Searches	7.00	
Tax Search and Certificate	31.75	
Mortgage Registration	86.00	
TOTAL DISBURSEMENTS	300.75	**300.75**
GST OF 5% ON FEES, CHARGES & DISBURSEMENTS		57.42
TOTAL AMOUNT REQUIRED		$ 63 432.16

the services of a lawyer if no mortgage is involved. This type of property transfer is not recommended since property transactions require a good understanding of real estate law. Legal fees and disbursements commonly range between $500 and $1000.

GST/HST. You are normally required to pay GST/HST on the purchase of a brand new home.

Title Insurance. Title insurance protects the insured against loss resulting from title defects and defects that would have been revealed by an up-to-date survey/real property report or building location certificate. Sometimes the real property report might be outdated or non-existent. Title insurance protects you if it is later determined that the real property report is inaccurate. If the seller does not provide you with a current real property report, you should purchase title insurance. Title insurance commonly ranges between $300 and $400.

Interest Adjustment. An **interest adjustment** occurs when there is a difference between the date you take possession of your home and the date from which your lender calculates your first mortgage payment. For example, Surj and Pam have purchased a home and received a mortgage from their bank in the amount of $200 000. They will take possession of their new home on April 15. On the possession date, the bank will advance the mortgage proceeds to the couple's lawyer. Surj and Pam will be charged interest starting on April 15. The mortgage documents indicate that the couple will make monthly mortgage payments on the first of each month. As a result, the bank will calculate the first mortgage payment starting on May 1. The interest adjustment will be calculated as the amount of interest that accumulates between April 15 and May 1. The bank will withdraw the accumulated interest for this period from the bank account that Surj and

interest adjustment
Occurs when there is a difference between the date you take possession of your home and the date from which your lender calculates your first mortgage payment.

Pam specified when they took out the mortgage. As per the mortgage documents, regular mortgage payments will begin on the first of each month, starting with May 1.

Prepaid Property Tax and Utility Adjustments. If the seller has prepaid some bills before the closing date, you must reimburse the seller for the payments made. For example, if the seller has prepaid property tax for the entire calendar year on a home the buyer takes possession of on July 1, the buyer must reimburse the seller for six months' worth of taxes paid. In contrast, the buyer may end up in a position where the taxes and/or utility bills are in default. In this case, the buyer may be forced to cover these taxes and/or bills. The end result is that the adjustment for property tax and utilities may be higher than the buyer expected. Any unexpected bills may result in immediate financial difficulties for the buyer; therefore, it is important to be aware of the status of bills that should have been paid before finalizing the purchase of a home.

myth or **fact** Mortgage insurance protects you and/or the lender against losses in the event that you default on your mortgage payments.

Homeowner's Insurance. Homeowner's insurance protects you against financial loss that may result from damage to your home or its contents. It is discussed in more detail in Chapter 8. The cost of homeowner's insurance primarily depends on the size of the home and commonly ranges between $700 and $1000 per year. The lender will require you to purchase property or homeowner's insurance before the mortgage proceeds are advanced to your lawyer. As part of the mortgage process, the lender will request proof that you have purchased this insurance.

Loan Protection Life and Disability Insurance. Loan protection life and disability insurance protects the lender against financial loss as a result of injury, illness, or death to you, the borrower. It is commonly referred to as creditor insurance. Creditor insurance is discussed in more detail in Chapter 9. The cost of this type of insurance varies based on the age of the applicant(s) and the size of the mortgage.

Some closing costs are paid as a part of legal fees and disbursements—that is, the lawyer's office makes the payment on your behalf. These payments would be reflected on the estimated statement of funds required, which was illustrated in Exhibit 7.2. Other closing costs will be paid directly by the buyer. Exhibit 7.3 displays examples of closing

EXHIBIT 7.3 Examples of Closing Costs and their Approximate Cost

Cost	Who Takes Care of It?	Approximate Cost
Home inspection fee	Buyer	$350–$600
Appraisal fee	Buyer	$300–$500
Real property report/land survey	Lawyer	$1000–$2000
Legal fees and disbursements	Lawyer	$500–$1000
GST/HST	Lawyer	5%–15%
Title insurance	Lawyer	$300–$400
Interest adjustment	Lawyer	$100–$1000
Prepaid property tax and utility adjustments	Lawyer	$300–$500
Homeowner's insurance	Buyer	$700–$1000
Loan protection life and disability insurance	Buyer	Costs vary based on age of applicant(s)

costs, whether they are paid directly by the buyer or by the lawyer, and their approximate cost. Both the closing costs and the down payment are due after the offer for the home has been accepted at the time of the closing. During the closing, the title for the home is transferred to the buyer, the seller is paid in full, and the buyer takes possession of the home.

MORTGAGE OPTIONS

L.O.3

The amount of your monthly mortgage payment and how quickly you will be able to pay off your mortgage loan depends on the mortgage options you choose.

Amortization Period

You will have to decide over what period of time you would like to amortize your mortgage loan. This is known as **amortization**, which is the expected number of years it will take a borrower to pay off the entire mortgage loan balance. Amortization is usually expressed in number of years. For example, if you choose an amortization period of 20 years, your monthly mortgage payment will be calculated based on your mortgage being paid off during the next 240 months. The maximum amortization period is different among financial institutions, but generally will be no more than 25 years, or 300 months. A longer amortization period results in lower monthly mortgage payments and a higher amount of mortgage interest payable over the life of the mortgage.

amortization
The expected number of years it will take a borrower to pay off the entire mortgage loan balance.

Mortgage Term

You will also need to determine the mortgage term you need. The **mortgage term** represents the period of time over which the mortgage interest rate and other terms of the mortgage contract will not change. Typical mortgage terms include six months and one, two, three, four, five, and ten years. Since the mortgage term will always be less than or equal to the amortization period, you will likely renew or renegotiate your mortgage a number of times before it is paid off. At the time your mortgage is renewed or renegotiated, the interest rate may be higher than or lower than the rate you had during your previous mortgage term.

mortgage term
The period of time over which the mortgage interest rate and other terms of the mortgage contract will not change.

Payment Frequency

The **payment frequency** on a mortgage refers to the frequency with which you make a mortgage payment. Almost all financial institutions provide a number of payment frequencies. Exhibit 7.4 provides a list of the mortgage payment frequencies that are

payment frequency
The frequency with which you make a mortgage payment.

EXHIBIT 7.4   Mortgage Payment Option Calculations

Mortgage Payment Frequency	Number of Payments per Year	Calculation
Monthly	12	
Semi-monthly (twice per month)	24	Monthly payment ÷ 2
Biweekly (every two weeks)	26	(Monthly payment × 12) ÷ 26
Accelerated biweekly	26	Monthly payment ÷ 2
Weekly (every week)	52	(Monthly payment × 12) ÷ 52
Accelerated weekly	52	Monthly payment ÷ 4

EXHIBIT 7.5   Time and Interest Savings for a $250 000 Mortgage, Amortized over 25 Years at an Interest Rate of 6% Compounded Semi-Annually

Mortgage Payment Frequency	Periodic Payment Amount	Number of Months to Pay Down Mortgage	Interest Paid	Interest Saved
Monthly	$1600	300	$229 855	$ 0
Semi-monthly	800	299	228 505	1350
Biweekly	738	299	228 401	1454
Accelerated biweekly	800	252	187 315	42 540
Weekly	369	299	227 781	2074
Accelerated weekly	400	252	186 822	43 033

commonly available. In general, the more payments you make in a year, the quicker you pay off your mortgage and the less interest you pay.

The most significant savings are achieved by using the accelerated mortgage payment frequency methods. The accelerated mortgage payment frequency options allow you to make the equivalent of one extra monthly payment per year. The mortgage example in Exhibit 7.5 shows that with either the accelerated biweekly or the accelerated weekly mortgage payment frequencies, the mortgage is paid down 48 months sooner and the amount of interest saved is more than $40 000.

Mortgage Type

There are two basic types of mortgages: closed and open. A **closed mortgage** restricts your ability to pay off the mortgage balance during the mortgage term unless you are willing to pay a prepayment penalty, also known as a prepayment charge. An **open mortgage** allows you to pay off the mortgage balance at any time during the mortgage term. Closed mortgages are more popular than open mortgages because interest rates on closed mortgages are lower. The lower interest rate offered by a closed mortgage needs to be weighed against the ability to prepay, without penalty, the entire balance of an open mortgage at any time.

Financial institutions have made closed mortgages more attractive by offering prepayment privileges. **Prepayment privileges** are features that allow borrowers to increase their monthly mortgage payment and to pay off a lump sum of the original mortgage balance during the course of each mortgage year. For example, many financial institutions will allow you to increase your monthly mortgage payment once per year by 20 percent of the original mortgage payment amount. A limitation of this increase is that the borrower will normally be required to maintain this increased mortgage payment for a period of time. In addition, many financial institutions will allow the borrower to make lump sum payments once per year of up to 20 percent of the original mortgage amount. These accelerated payment features will be different among financial institutions, so it is in your best interest to shop around.

closed mortgage
Restricts your ability to pay off the mortgage balance during the mortgage term unless you are willing to pay a financial penalty.

open mortgage
Allows you to pay off the mortgage balance at any time during the mortgage term.

prepayment privileges
Features that allow borrowers to increase their monthly mortgage payment and to pay off a lump sum of the original mortgage balance during the course of each mortgage year.

Go to:
www.ratehub.ca

This website provides national closed mortgage rates offered by financial institutions.

Recall our earlier example of Blake and Donna Braithwaite. The couple has decided to purchase the $375 000 home they were considering. They will be taking out a conventional mortgage since their down payment of $75 000 represents 20 percent of the value of the home. The couple obtains a $300 000 closed mortgage with a five-year mortgage term that is amortized over 25 years at an interest rate of 6 percent, compounded semi-annually. Their monthly mortgage payment will be $1919.42.

The calculator key strokes are as follows:

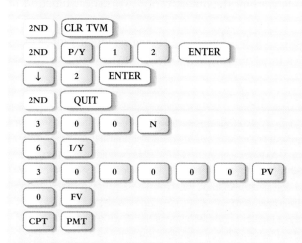

The Braithwaites will not be able to pay off the balance of the mortgage during the mortgage term since it is a closed mortgage. However, the bank will allow them to increase their mortgage payments by up to 20 percent of the regular monthly amount. In addition, the couple can pay off up to 20 percent of the original mortgage balance at any time during each year of the mortgage term.

Although closed mortgages are not as flexible as open mortgages, the accelerated payment features are usually sufficient to meet the needs of most borrowers. At the end of a mortgage term you are able to pay off a closed or open mortgage without any financial penalty. You can also renegotiate new mortgage terms for an additional period of time. The borrower should read the terms of the mortgage contract to fully understand the options and penalties the lender is offering.

CHARACTERISTICS OF A FIXED-RATE MORTGAGE

A mortgage loan is most likely the biggest loan you will ever obtain in your lifetime. In addition to the mortgage options discussed above, you will need to decide whether to obtain a fixed-rate or variable-rate mortgage. A **fixed-rate mortgage** specifies a fixed interest rate for the term of the mortgage. When homeowners expect that interest rates will rise, they tend to prefer fixed-rate mortgages because their mortgage payments will be sheltered from rising interest rates during the term of the mortgage. You can access various websites to obtain a general summary of prevailing mortgage rates. Although posted rates are similar among financial institutions, rates will vary based on your ability to negotiate with different lenders. It pays to shop around, as the mortgage industry is very competitive. Lenders are usually willing to decrease their posted rates if they know you are considering several institutions to get the best mortgage rate possible. If you sell a home before the mortgage is paid off, you can use a portion of the proceeds to pay off the mortgage. Alternatively, it may be possible for the buyer to assume your mortgage under some conditions.

fixed-rate mortgage
A mortgage in which a fixed interest rate is specified for the term of the mortgage.

| **myth** or **fact** It's better to have a shorter amortization. This will result in higher mortgage payments, which will allow you to pay off the mortgage faster.

Amortization Schedule

Your monthly mortgage payments for a fixed-rate mortgage are based on an amortization schedule. This schedule discloses the monthly payments you will make based on a specific mortgage amount, a fixed interest rate level, and an amortization period. An amortization schedule can be generated using the amortization worksheet function of your TI BA II Plus calculator.

Allocation of the Mortgage Payment. Each monthly mortgage payment represents a partial equity payment that includes a portion of the principal of the loan and an interest payment.

EXAMPLE

Continuing with the Blake and Donna Braithwaite example, once you have entered all of the information and calculated the monthly payment of $1919, you can immediately generate an amortization schedule by pressing 2ND | AMORT | on your TI BA II Plus calculator. Next, in order to determine how the first $1919 monthly mortgage payment is split between principal and interest, you must set P1 and P2 equal to 1. On your calculator, you can set P1 equal to 1 by pressing 1 | ENTER | . To set P2, press the down arrow, | ↓ | . You can now set P2 equal to 1 by pressing 1 | ENTER | . Once these steps are complete, press the down arrow, | ↓ | . The calculator will display the balance of the mortgage remaining after the first payment, $299 562. If you press the down arrow again, the calculator will display how much of the $1919 monthly mortgage payment was allocated to principal, $438. If you press the down arrow again, the calculator will display how much of the monthly mortgage payment was allocated to interest, $1481.

These amounts are recorded in Exhibit 7.6. This process is repeated for each monthly mortgage payment. For example, for the second mortgage payment, you would set P1 and P2 equal to 2. For the second monthly mortgage payment, you will find that $440 is applied to the principal and $1479 is used to pay the interest expense. Since the Braithwaites' mortgage is amortized for 25 years, there will be a total of $25 \times 12 = 300$ monthly mortgage payments. Initially, when the amount of principal is large, most of each payment is needed to cover the interest owed. As time passes, the proportion of the payment allocated to equity increases. Notice in Exhibit 7.6 that by month 300, $1910 of the monthly mortgage payment is applied to principal and only $9 to interest.

Notice also that the Braithwaites' balance after 100 months is $243 559. This means that over the first eight years of the mortgage amortization period, the Braithwaites have paid off less than $57 000 of the loan outstanding on their home—in other words, less than 20 percent of the original mortgage amount. After 150 months (half of the life of the mortgage), their mortgage balance would be about $203 031, which means they would have paid off about one-third of the original $300 000 mortgage.

The amount of Blake and Donna's annual mortgage payment that would be allocated to paying off the principal is shown in Exhibit 7.7. In the first year, they would pay off only $5399 of the principal, while the rest of their mortgage payment, $17 634, would be used to pay interest. This information is very surprising to the Braithwaites, so they review the mortgage situation further to determine whether it is possible to build equity—that is, pay off their mortgage—more quickly.

Go to:
www.ratehub.ca/
variable-or-fixed-
mortgage

This website provides
valuable information regarding variable-rate and fixed-rate mortgages that may be useful when deciding whether to finance your home with a variable-rate or fixed-rate mortgage.

Go to:
www.fcac-acfc.gc.ca/
Eng/resources/tools-
Calculators/Pages/
Mortgage-Calculat.
aspx

This website provides
a mortgage calculator to determine the monthly payments on a mortgage based on the mortgage amount, mortgage term, interest rate, payment frequency, and amortization period.

Impact of the Mortgage Amount, Interest Rate, and Amortization Period on Monthly Payments

The larger the mortgage amount, the larger your monthly payments will be for a given interest rate and maturity. Given the large amount of funds you may borrow to finance

EXHIBIT 7.6 Amortization Schedule for a Fixed-Rate, $300,000 Mortgage Amortized over 25 Years at an Interest Rate of 6 Percent, Compounded Semi-Annually

Month	Payment	Principal	Interest	Balance
1	$1919	$438	$1481	$299 562
2	1919	440	1479	299 122
...				
10	1919	458	1461	295 523
...				
25	1919	493	1426	288 380
...				
49	1919	554	1365	275 795
...				
100	1919	713	1206	243 559
...				
150	1919	912	1007	203 031
...				
300	1919	1910	9	0

a home, you should make every effort to obtain a mortgage loan that has a low interest rate. The lower the interest rate is, the smaller the monthly mortgage payments will be.

Over the last decade, mortgage rates have been decreasing steadily. This has been to the advantage of borrowers who selected a variable-rate mortgage. If you expect interest rates to continue to decrease, a variable-rate mortgage may be in your best interest. Homeowners seek a fixed-rate mortgage when they believe that interest rates will rise in the future. When negotiating the mortgage rate with your lender, you should be aware of economic conditions. In some circumstances, lenders are very aggressive and will negotiate better interest rates to get your business. You should be able to take advantage of market conditions to improve your interest rate. However, sometimes market conditions are such that negotiation is impossible.

EXHIBIT 7.7 Allocation of Principal versus Interest Paid per Year on a $300 000 Mortgage

Year	Principal Paid in That Year	Interest Paid in That Year
1	$ 5399	$17 634
2	5728	17 305
3	6077	16 956
4	6447	16 586
...	...	...
10	9192	13 841
...	...	...
15	12 353	10 680
...	...	...
20	16 601	6432
...	...	...
25	22 310	723

The amortization period of the mortgage indicates how long you will take to complete your financing payments and pay off the mortgage in full. As discussed earlier, a longer amortization period will result in lower monthly mortgage payments and a higher amount of mortgage interest payable over the life of the mortgage. If you increase your monthly payments by decreasing your amortization, you will pay your mortgage off at a faster pace and reduce the total amount of interest paid over the life of the mortgage. For example, you will have paid off your mortgage after 20 years if your amortization period is 20 years and interest rates do not change, whereas a 25-year amortization period will require mortgage payments for an additional 5 years.

You may be able to accelerate your mortgage payments according to your mortgage contract. This means that you may be able to double up your monthly mortgage payments. These additional payments go directly to pay off principal and can reduce your overall amortization period by years.

L.O.5

CHARACTERISTICS OF A VARIABLE-RATE MORTGAGE

variable-rate mortgage (VRM)
A mortgage where the interest charged on the loan changes in response to movements in a specific market-determined interest rate. The rate used is usually referred to as prime. Lenders will add a percentage to prime for the total mortgage rate.

An alternative to a fixed-rate mortgage is a **variable-rate mortgage** (VRM), in which the interest charged on the loan changes in response to movements in a specific market-determined interest rate. The rate used is usually referred to as prime. Lenders will add a percentage to prime for the total mortgage rate. A VRM is sometimes referred to as an adjustable-rate mortgage. VRMs definitely should be considered along with fixed-rate mortgages. Like a fixed-rate mortgage, a VRM can be obtained for various amortization periods, such as a 20-year or a 25-year maturity. VRMs have various characteristics that must be stated in the mortgage contract.

myth or **fact** Pay off your mortgage as soon as possible.

Initial Rate

A VRM may be open or closed. Although your mortgage payment is not likely to increase during the term of the mortgage, the allocation of your mortgage payment to principal and interest will change if the VRM mortgage rate changes. If the mortgage rate decreases, more of each mortgage payment will go toward principal and less will go toward interest. In contrast, if the mortgage rate increases, more of each mortgage payment will go toward interest and less will go toward principal. If the mortgage interest rate increases too much, the bank may require you to increase your mortgage payment because your current mortgage payment no longer covers the interest portion of the mortgage. For this reason, many people prefer a fixed-rate mortgage because they know exactly how much of each mortgage payment goes toward principal and interest. The change in the initial mortgage rate is usually determined by a change in the relevant interest rate index. The relevant interest rate index, known as the prime rate, is discussed below.

convertible mortgage
Allows you to renew your mortgage before the end of the current mortgage term without paying a penalty.

To provide additional flexibility to individuals who are concerned about increasing mortgage interest rates, many banks offer convertible mortgages. A **convertible mortgage** allows you to renew your mortgage before the end of the current mortgage term without paying a penalty. This type of mortgage is useful for individuals who feel that mortgage rates are about to increase and would like to "lock in" the current mortgage interest rate for a longer mortgage term than what they have remaining on their existing mortgage. If available, the convertibility feature is provided on VRMs or on closed fixed-rate mortgages that have very short terms to maturity, such as one to two years.

Interest Rate Index

The initial mortgage rate will be adjusted to stay in line with the prime rate of interest. If the prime rate of interest does not change, the interest rate on your VRM usually will not change. Many VRMs use this rate because it is tied to the average cost of deposits of financial institutions. For example, the interest rate charged on a VRM might be set at 3 percentage points above the prime rate. Thus, if the benchmark is 4 percent in a given year, the VRM will apply an interest rate of 7 percent (computed as 4 percent plus 3 percent). If the interest rate index has risen to 5 percent by the time of the next mortgage rate adjustment, the new mortgage rate will be 8 percent (computed as 5 percent plus 3 percent).

DECISION TO OWN VERSUS RENT A HOME

When considering the purchase (and therefore ownership) of a home, you should compare the costs of purchasing and renting. People attribute different advantages and disadvantages to owning a home versus renting because preferences are subjective. Some individuals value the privacy of a home, while others value the flexibility of an apartment, which allows them to move without much cost or difficulty. The financial assessment of owning a home versus renting can be performed objectively. Once the financial assessment is conducted, personal preferences can also be considered.

Estimating the Total Cost of Renting and Owning

The main cost of renting a home is the monthly rent payments. There is also an opportunity cost of tying up funds in a security deposit. Those funds could have been invested if they were not needed for the security deposit. Another possible cost of renting is the purchase of renter's insurance.

The primary costs of purchasing a home are the down payment and the monthly mortgage payments. The down payment has an opportunity cost because the funds could have been invested if they were not tied up in the purchase of the home. As well, closing costs are incurred at the time the home is purchased. Owning a home also involves some additional costs, such as maintenance and repair. Property taxes are assessed annually as a percentage of the home's value. Homeowner's insurance is paid monthly or annually and is based primarily on the value of the home and its contents.

EXAMPLE

Maya Benson has found a home she desires and has researched the financing she needs. Before making a final decision, she wants to compare the cost of the home to the cost of remaining in her apartment. Although she would prefer a home, she wants to determine how much more expensive the home is compared to the apartment. If she purchases the home, she expects to live in it for at least three years. Therefore, she decides to compare the cost of owning a home to the cost of renting for the next three years. First, Maya calculates the cost of renting:

- Cost of Rent. Her estimated cost of renting is shown in the top panel of Exhibit 7.8. Her rent is currently $750 per month, so her annual rent is $9000 (computed as $750 × 12). She does not expect a rent increase over the next three years and therefore estimates her cost of renting over this period to be $9000 × 3 = $27 000. (If she had expected a rent increase, she simply would have added the extra cost to the estimated rent over the next three years.)

- Cost of Tenant's Insurance. She does not have tenant's insurance at this time, as the value of her household assets is low.

- Opportunity Cost of Security Deposit. She provided a security deposit of $750 to the apartment complex. While she expects to be refunded this deposit when she stops renting, there is an opportunity cost associated with it. She could have invested those funds in a money market fund earning 2.8 percent after tax annually, which would have generated annual interest of $21, assuming a tax rate of 30 percent (computed as ($750 × 0.04) × (1 − 0.3). The opportunity cost over three years is three times the annual cost, or $63.

- Total Cost of Renting. Maya estimates the total cost of renting as $9021 per year and $27 063 over the next three years, as shown in Exhibit 7.8.

(continued)

EXHIBIT 7.8   Comparing the Total Cost of Renting versus Buying a Home over a Three-Year Period

Cost of Renting

	Amount per Year	Total over Next Three Years
Rent ($750 per month)	$9000	$27 000
Tenant's insurance	0	0
Opportunity cost of security deposit	21	63
Total cost of renting	$9021	$27 063

Cost of Purchasing

	Amount per Year	Total over Next Three Years
Mortgage payment ($867 per month)	$10 404	$31 212
Down payment	41 250	41 250 (first year only)
Opportunity cost of down payment	1155	3465
Property taxes	2500	7500
Home insurance	600	1800
Closing costs	3865	3865 (first year only)
Maintenance costs	1000	3000
Total costs		**$92 092**
Value of equity		**$63 938**
Cost of purchasing home over three years		**$28 154**

Maya determines the total cost of purchasing a home by adding up expenses and subtracting the value of the equity:

- Mortgage Payment. The primary cost of buying a home is the mortgage payment, which she expects to be $867 per month, or $10 404 per year (not including payments for property taxes or home insurance).

- Down Payment. Maya would make a down payment of $41 250 to buy the home.

- Opportunity Cost of the Down Payment. If Maya did not buy a house, she could have invested the $41 250 in an investment and earned 2.8 percent per year, after tax. Therefore, the annual opportunity cost (what she could have earned if she had invested the funds) is $1155, assuming a tax rate of 30 percent (computed as ($41 250 $\times$ 0.04) $\times$ (1 $-$ 0.3).

- Property Taxes. Maya assumes that the annual property tax will be $2500 based on last year's property tax paid by the current owner of the home.

- Home Insurance. Insurance on this home will cost $600 per year (this estimate is based on the insurance premium paid by the current owner of the home).

- Closing Costs. Closing costs (transaction costs) associated with buying a home must be included, although those costs are incurred only in the first year. The closing costs are estimated to be $3865.

- Maintenance Costs. Maya expects maintenance costs on the home to be $1000 per year.

- Utilities. She will pay for utilities such as water and electricity and will incur a cable TV bill if she buys the home. She already incurs those costs while renting an apartment, so she does not need to include them in her analysis.

- Value of the Equity Investment. Another advantage of owning a home is that Maya will have an equity investment in it. Her down payment will be $41 250, and she will pay about $6188 in principal on her mortgage over the three-year period.

- The value of this equity investment could be higher in three years if the market value of the home increases. As a conservative estimate, Maya expects the home to increase

10 percent in value over the next three years. Based on this assumption, the increase in the value of the home will be $16 500 ($165 000 × 0.10). The value of the equity investment will be $63 938 (computed as $41 250 + $16 500 + $6188).

■ Total Cost of Purchasing a Home. The total cost of purchasing a home is determined by adding all expenses, and then subtracting the equity investment. As shown in Exhibit 7.8, Maya estimates that the total cost of purchasing the home over the three-year period will be $28 154.

The total cost of purchasing a home over three years is about $1091 more than the cost of renting. Maya decides that she wants to buy the home. Aside from the fact that she would rather live in a home than an apartment, Maya realizes that building equity in a home will put her further ahead, in the long term, than renting.

Now that Maya has decided that she wants to purchase a home and can afford it, she submits her offer of $165 000, which is accepted by the seller.

MORTGAGE REFINANCING

L.O.7

Mortgage refinancing involves paying off an existing mortgage with a new mortgage that has a lower interest rate. You may use mortgage refinancing to obtain a new mortgage if market interest rates (and therefore mortgage rates) decline. Mortgage refinancing is not the same as having a convertibility feature in your mortgage. With mortgage refinancing, you will incur closing costs again. In addition, you will be charged prepayment penalties if you have a closed mortgage and choose to refinance your mortgage before the end of the term. Nevertheless, it may still be advantageous to refinance because the savings on your monthly mortgage payments may exceed the new closing costs and any prepayment penalties. Mortgage refinancing is more likely to be worthwhile when the prevailing mortgage interest rate is substantially below the rate on your existing mortgage. It is also more likely to be worthwhile when you expect to be living in the home for a long time because you will reap greater benefits from the lower monthly mortgage payments that result from refinancing.

mortgage refinancing
Paying off an existing mortgage with a new mortgage that has a lower interest rate.

Rate Modification

When interest rates decline, some mortgage lenders may be willing to allow a "rate modification" to existing mortgage holders who have fixed-rate mortgages. This option is often referred to as a "blend-and-extend" option. The mortgage lender may charge a one-time fee for this, which is typically between $500 and $1500. Your fixed-rate mortgage may be revised to reflect the prevailing mortgage rate. You can benefit from receiving the lower interest rate and you would not need to go through the process of mortgage refinancing or incur costs associated with a new mortgage application. Some mortgage lenders are willing to allow rate modifications because they realize that if they do not provide you with an opportunity to pay the lower interest rate, you will likely obtain a new mortgage from another lender and will pay off your existing mortgage. In this case, you would no longer make payments at the high interest rate and your existing mortgage lender would lose you as a customer. By allowing a rate modification, your existing mortgage lender retains you as a customer by offering you a mortgage that is similar to what it is presently offering to new customers. The lender also earns a one-time fee from you for modifying the mortgage rate you are charged.

EXAMPLE

Marni and Patrick have an outstanding mortgage balance of $250 000. They have 15 months remaining on their five-year mortgage term at an annual interest rate of 5 percent compounded semi-annually. The current five-year fixed rate of interest for a mortgage is 3 percent compounded semi-annually. The couple would like to "blend-and-extend" their existing mortgage for another five-year, or 60-month, term.

Their mortgage broker explains to them that the old rate and new rate will be blended together by taking into consideration the remaining 15 month term on their existing mortgage at the old rate and the additional 45 months that they would like to add at the new rate. The calculation is as follows:

$$\left(\frac{15}{60} \times 5\%\right)\left(\frac{45}{60} \times 3\%\right) = 1.25\% + 2.25\% = 3.5\%$$

The "blend-and-extend" option allows the couple to obtain a five-year mortgage term at a blended rate of 3.5% compounded semi-annually.

Go to:
www.ratehub.ca/
mortgage-refinance-
calculator

This website provides
a mortgage refinancing calculator to help you determine whether refinancing is a better option than remaining in your existing mortgage.

Refinancing Analysis

To determine whether you should refinance, you can compare the advantage of monthly savings of interest expenses to the cost of refinancing. If the benefits from reducing your interest expenses exceed the prepayment penalties incurred from refinancing, the refinancing is feasible.

The advantages of refinancing (lower interest payments) occur each year, while the disadvantage (prepayment penalties) occurs only at the time of refinancing. Therefore, refinancing tends to be more beneficial when a homeowner plans to own the home for a longer period. The savings from a lower interest payment can accumulate over each additional year the mortgage exists.

MyLab Finance   Visit MyLab Finance for additional study and practice tools. Select Financial Planning Problems are available in the Study Plan. Create your own study plan, generate personal cash flow statements and balance sheets, and set personal financial goals.

SUMMARY

L.O.1   Explain how to select a home to purchase

When considering the purchase of a home, you should evaluate your financial situation to determine how much you can afford. Some of the key criteria used in the selection process are price, convenience of the location, condition of the home (taking into account maintenance and potential repairs), the school system, and the potential resale value.

You can conduct a valuation of a home with a market analysis. Homes in the same area that were recently sold can be used to determine the average price per square foot. This price per square foot can then be applied to the square footage of the home you wish to value.

L.O.2   Describe the transaction costs of purchasing a home

The transaction costs of purchasing a home include the down payment and closing costs. Some of the important

closing costs include the home inspection fee, the appraisal fee, legal fees, and title insurance.

L.O.3   Describe the characteristics of various mortgage options

The amount of your monthly mortgage payment and how quickly you will be able to pay off your mortgage loan depend on the mortgage options you choose. These mortgage option choices include the length of the amortization period and mortgage term, the frequency with which you choose to make mortgage payments, and the type of mortgage, closed or open, you choose.

L.O.4   Describe the characteristics of a fixed-rate mortgage

A fixed-rate mortgage specifies a fixed interest rate to be paid over the term of the mortgage. Since most of the monthly mortgage payments on a mortgage amortized over 30 years are allocated to cover the interest expense in the early years, a relatively small amount of principal is paid off in those years. A shorter amortization period, such as 25 years, should be considered to reduce the time it takes to pay off the mortgage. It requires a larger monthly payment, but a larger proportion of the payment is allocated to principal in the early years.

L.O.5 **Describe the characteristics of a variable-rate mortgage**

A variable-rate mortgage (VRM) ties the interest rate to the prime rate, so the mortgage interest rate changes over time with the change in this prime rate. Homeowners who expect interest rates to decline in the future are especially likely to choose VRMs.

L.O.6 **Show how to compare the costs of purchasing versus renting a home**

Before making a final decision to buy a home, you can compare the total cost of owning a home versus renting over a particular period to determine which choice will enhance your financial position. The total cost of owning a home is estimated by adding up the expenses associated with the home and subtracting the expected value of the equity of the home at the end of the period.

L.O.7 **Explain the mortgage refinancing decision**

You may consider mortgage refinancing when quoted interest rates on new mortgages decline. When refinancing, you will incur closing costs. Thus, you should consider refinancing only if the benefits (expected reduction in interest expenses over time) exceed the closing costs.

REVIEW QUESTIONS

1. List and describe the various types of homes that someone can choose from.

2. Define and describe a pre-approval certificate.

3. What is the gross debt service (GDS) ratio? What is the total debt service (TDS) ratio? How do financial institutions use these ratios?

4. How do you determine your maximum down payment? Describe the Home Buyer's Plan (HBP).

5. What are the factors that you need to consider when determining how large a monthly mortgage payment you can afford?

6. Describe how behavioural characteristics of home buyers affect their decisions concerning their monthly mortgage payment.

7. List the criteria you should use when selecting a home.

8. How do price, convenience of the location, and maintenance affect your home-buying decisions?

9. Why is the reputation of the school system in the area of the home you are buying important?

10. Why do insurance costs and taxes vary among homes?

11. What is the main factor in determining a home's resale value? How can you predict a home's resale value?

12. What other factors are home prices dependent on?

13. How can a real estate broker help you? Who pays commissions when a home is sold?

14. How can online services be used to help you purchase a home?

15. What should you consider when determining the offer price you should make on a home that you are considering? What normally happens after you make an offer for a home?

16. Define and describe a conventional mortgage.

17. What is the difference between a conventional mortgage and a high ratio mortgage?

18. Describe mortgage default insurance.

19. Define and describe a vendor take-back mortgage. With respect to a vendor take-back mortgage, what are the incentives for the buyer and the seller?

20. What is a home inspection? Why is it important to get a home inspection completed when you purchase a home?

21. What is the purpose of an appraisal fee?

22. What is a real property report? Why is it important?

23. Which provinces charge a land transfer tax?

24. Why is it important to use the services of a lawyer when completing the purchase and sale of a home?

25. When do you pay GST/HST on a home purchase?

26. Define and describe an interest adjustment?

27. What is the effect of prepaid property taxes and/or utility payments?

28. Describe homeowner's insurance, and loan protection life and disability insurance.

29. What is the difference between the amortization period and the mortgage term?

30. Describe the various types of mortgage payment frequencies that are available. Which mortgage payment frequencies allow you to pay off your mortgage quickly?

31. Define and differentiate between a closed mortgage and an open mortgage.

32. What are prepayment privileges? Why are they important?

33. Describe the characteristics of a fixed-rate mortgage. Why do certain homeowners prefer a fixed-rate mortgage to a variable-rate mortgage?

34. Define and describe an amortization schedule.

35. Describe how the mortgage amount, the interest rate, and the amortization period affect the amount of the monthly mortgage payment.

36. Describe the characteristics of a variable-rate mortgage. What influences your choice between a fixed-rate and variable-rate mortgage?

37. What is a convertible mortgage?

38. Describe and differentiate between the costs associated with renting or buying a home.

39. What is mortgage refinancing? Describe when it would be advantageous to refinance your mortgage.

40. What is a rate modification? Differentiate between a rate modification and mortgage refinancing.

41. How do you determine whether you should refinance? Under what circumstance is mortgage refinancing most beneficial?

FINANCIAL PLANNING PROBLEMS

MyLab Finance   Financial Planning Problems marked with a ⊕ can be found in MyLab Finance.

⊕ **1.** Isabella and Raphael are interested in buying a home. They have completed the initial steps in the home-buying process, including contacting a realtor and obtaining a pre-approval certificate from their bank. During the process of determining an affordable down payment, they have asked you to determine whether their GDS and TDS ratios are within the guidelines set by their bank. They have provided you with the following information. Isabella earns $35 000 per year, while Raphael earns $30 000 per year. They believe that they could afford a mortgage payment of about $1000 per month. The annual property taxes in the area where they would like to purchase a home average about $1600. Heating costs should be about $125 per month. The couple has an outstanding balance on their line of credit of $15 000. In addition, Raphael has an outstanding balance on his student loan of $10 000. Currently, the couple is making a monthly payment of $450 on their line of credit and $300 on the student loan. Their bank requires that the GDS ratio be no more than 32 percent and the TDS ratio be no more than 40 percent. Do Isabella and Raphael meet these requirements?

2. Jose and Rosa are looking for a condo. Their combined gross annual income is $72 000. The best mortgage rate offered by their bank is 3.02 percent five-year fixed rate compounded semi-annually with a 20-year amortization. The annual property taxes are estimated at $1460, and the annual heating costs are $1440. Their personal debt consumption is $700 per month. Condo fees are estimated at $500 per month. The bank's guideline for TDS is 40 percent. Based on this information, what is the maximum monthly mortgage payment they could afford?

⊕ **3.** Dorothy and Matt are ready to purchase their first home. Their current monthly income is $4900, and their current monthly expenses are $3650. Their rent makes up $650 of their cash flow. They would like to put 10 percent of their income in savings every month and leave another $200 per month in their chequing account for emergencies. How much of a mortgage payment, including taxes and utilities, can they manage under these conditions?

⊕ **4.** Larry and Laurie have found a home and made a $325 000 offer that has been accepted. They make a down payment of 10 percent. The CMHC mortgage loan insurance premium is 3.10 percent of the mortgage amount required. Larry and Laurie have decided to pay this fee at the time of closing instead of having it added to the mortgage. Other fees include a $175 loan application fee, a $250 appraisal fee, a $300 home inspection fee, $540 in legal fees, and $350 for title search and insurance. How much cash will Larry and Laurie need at closing?

5. The bank has determined that, based on a TDS ratio of 40 percent and other factors, the maximum monthly mortgage payment that Ianna qualifies to make is $2214. The five-year fixed rate of interest is 4 percent compounded semi-annually and the mortgage is to be amortized over 25 years. What is the maximum value of the mortgage that Ianna may obtain from the bank?

6. A $120 000 mortgage is amortized over 25 years. If interest on the mortgage is 4.5 percent compounded semi-annually, calculate the size of monthly payments made at the end of each month.

7. Referring to question 6, calculate the number of years to pay off the mortgage if payments are made on an accelerated biweekly basis, instead of monthly.

 8. Lloyd and Jean are considering purchasing a home requiring a $275 000 mortgage. The monthly payment on a mortgage amortized over 25 years at a fixed rate of 7 percent, compounded semi-annually, for this amount is $1926.14. The monthly payment on a mortgage amortized over 15 years at the same fixed rate is $2456.44. What is the difference in the total interest paid between the two different maturities?

9. The Taylors agreed to make monthly payments on a mortgage of $136 000 amortized over 15 years. Interest for the first three years was 8.5 percent compounded semi-annually. Determine the mortgage balance at the end of the three-year term.

10. Teresa rents her apartment for $850 per month, utilities not included. When she moved in, she paid a $700 security deposit using money from her savings account that was paying 3 percent interest, after tax. Her tenant's insurance costs her $60 per year. What are Teresa's total annual costs of renting?

11. Matt has found a condominium in an area where he would enjoy living. He would need a $10 000 down payment from his savings and would have to pay closing costs of $2500 to purchase the condo. His monthly mortgage payments would be $850, including property taxes and insurance. The condominium's board of directors charges maintenance fees of $400 per month. Calculate the cost of Matt's condo during the first year if he currently has the $10 000 down payment invested in an account earning 5 percent interest, compounded annually, after tax.

12. Paul really wants to purchase his own condo. He currently lives in an apartment and his rent is being paid by his parents. Paul's parents have informed him that they would not pay his mortgage payments. Paul has no savings but can save $700 per month. The condo he desires costs $120 000 and his real estate broker informs him that a down payment of 10 percent would be required. If Paul can earn 6 percent, compounded annually, on his savings, after tax, how long will it take him to accumulate the required down payment?

13. For this problem, assume that the CMHC mortgage loan insurance premium of 3.10 percent will be added to the mortgage. Paul (from Problem 7) will be able to save $700 per month (which can be used for mortgage payments) for the indefinite future. If Paul finances the remaining cost of the home (after making the $12 000 down payment) at a rate of 5 percent, compounded semi-annually, over a 25-year amortization period, what are his resulting monthly mortgage payments? Can he afford the mortgage? If not, over what period of time must the mortgage be amortized to make the mortgage payment affordable for Paul?

CHALLENGE QUESTIONS

1. Boris and Mihaela want to purchase a new home. Their combined income is $118 000, and they have saved enough for a down payment of $200 000 The couple's debt payments include a car loan payment of $450 and a student loan payment of $173. The couple believes that they will live in their new home for a number of years and, as a result, would like to consider a five-year fixed term mortgage at 5.14 percent, compounded semi-annually, over a 25-year amortization. The couple has estimated annual property taxes, heating costs, and home insurance premiums to be $3125, $1700, and $625, respectively. Use the formula for the total debt service (TDS) ratio to determine the maximum mortgage that the couple would qualify for assuming that their TDS cannot be higher than 40 percent. Taking into consideration their down payment, what is the maximum value of the home for which they would qualify?

2. Frank and Vanessa purchase a home with a $200 000 mortgage amortized over 20 years. They decide on a five-year mortgage term at an interest rate of 4.87 percent. During their first mortgage term, interest rates rise sharply. When it comes time to renew their mortgage at the end of the five-year term, they decide on a three-year term at an interest rate of 6.39 percent, compounded semi-annually.

   a. What is their outstanding mortgage balance at the end of the original five-year term?

   b. What will be the impact on how long it will take the couple to pay off their mortgage if they do not change their monthly mortgage payment and interest rates remain at the three-year mortgage term interest rate? HINT: Determine how many monthly payments the couple would now need to make in order to pay off their mortgage after interest rates have increased.

ETHICAL DILEMMA

Sarah and Joe own a small home that they would like to sell in order to build their dream home. Their current home has a mortgage and needs extensive repairs to make it marketable. A local loan company is offering home equity loans equal to 125 percent of a home's value. Since Sarah and Joe have good jobs and can make the additional home equity loan payments, they easily qualify for the 125 percent home equity loan. The entire home equity loan is required to complete the repairs and upgrades to their home.

To their shock, they find that, even after the upgrades, they are unable to sell the home for enough to repay the mortgage and the home equity loan. In other words, they have negative equity in the home.

a. Comment on the finance company's ethics in making loans in excess of a home's appraised value.

b. What are Sarah and Joe's options in their current situation? Is there a way they can proceed with building their dream home?

FINANCIAL PLANNING ONLINE EXERCISES

1. Go to www.fcac-acfc.gc.ca/Eng/resources/toolsCalculators/Pages/Mortgage-Calculat.aspx and select the Mortgage Qualifier Tool.

   a. Input a $150 000 estimated property value. Enter a down payment of 5 percent. What is the dollar value of the CMHC premium?

   b. Enter an anticipated annual interest rate of 4.5 percent, compounded semi-annually, and an amortization period of 25 years. What are the monthly mortgage payments?

   c. Enter $40 000 per year as your gross income. Heating costs and property taxes are $80 and $100, respectively. What is the GDS ratio?

   d. You are considering leasing a car. The lease would result in a $400 car payment. If you take on this car payment, will your TDS ratio remain below 40 percent? You have no other debt. What is the maximum car payment you can afford such that your TDS ratio remains below 40 percent?

2. Go to www.cmhc-schl.gc.ca/en/co/buho/buho_005.cfm Click on Mortgage Affordability Calculator and then input:

   $5000 for Gross Monthly Household Income

   $25 000 for Down Payment

   7 percent for Mortgage Interest Rate

   30 years for Amortization

   $200 for Monthly Property Taxes

   $110 for Monthly Heating Costs

   $0 for Monthly Condominium Fees

   $200 for Monthly Debt Payments

   What is the estimate for the maximum affordable home price? What are the estimated monthly mortgage payments?

3. Go to www.canadamortgage.com/RatesShow/ShowRates.php.

   a. What is the most common closed-term rate over six months? One year? Two years? Three years? Four years? Five years?

   b. What is the best 10-year closed-term rate? Do all banks offer 10-year mortgage rates? Why do you think this is the case?

   c. What is the maximum open-term rate? Why do you think this is the case?

PSYCHOLOGY OF PERSONAL FINANCE: Your Cash Outflows

1. Home buyers tend to buy a home for more money than they originally planned to spend. This occurs because as they start looking at homes for sale, they commonly notice a home that is priced beyond the amount they had planned to spend that offers some desirable features. Describe your behaviour if you were going to buy a home. Does the behaviour described in this question reflect your behaviour, or would you be more disciplined?

2. Read one practical article of how psychology affects decisions when buying a home. You can easily retrieve possible articles by doing an online search using the terms "psychology" and "buying home." Summarize the main points of the article.

MINI-CASE 1: Home Ownership

With a raise from his employer, an investment firm, Seyed Abdullah, 31, is inspired to look for a new home. He has come to you for help.

Financially he is fairly secure, but he is also very averse to risk. His salary is $93 000 a year, but he does not know how much he should spend on housing. His current housing expenditures include rent for his apartment of $1600 per month and tenant's insurance premiums totalling $300 per year. Although he has been paying his rent on a monthly basis, Seyed would like to convert the payment frequency of any monthly mortgage payment he takes on to accelerated biweekly. His monthly bills include a $500 per month lease payment for his 2012 Acura MDX and a $300 per month student loan payment.

Seyed has researched the recurring costs of home ownership. He has found that property taxes and home insurance premiums for the average home in the city in which he lives are about $2400 and $450 per year, respectively. He is unsure of the maintenance and heating costs but estimates them at $1000 and $1300 per year, respectively. Given how busy he is at work, Seyed thinks that a high-end condo might best suit his lifestyle. The condo fees associated with such a property would be approximately $400 per month.

Seyed likes the idea of owning his own home because as the real estate values increase, the value of his home will increase. Local property values have been increasing at 5 percent per year over the past seven years. One concern about buying a home is the immediate cost of down payment and closing costs. These closing costs, he has found, come to about $5000. He also knows that he would want to make a 20 percent downpayment.

Seyed's bank will use a maximum TDS ratio of 40 percent to qualify him for a mortgage. In addition, the posted five-year mortgage rate is 5.35 percent, compounded semi-annually. List and describe four types of housing that Seyed should consider. Using the information provided in the case, determine the maximum mortgage payment that Seyed would qualify for. What would be the accelerated biweekly payment on his mortgage? At an amortization period of 25 years, what is the maximum mortgage amount that Seyed would qualify for? If Seyed would like to make a 20-percent down payment, what is the maximum value of the home that he would qualify for? Including maintenance, closing costs, and his required down payment, how much money does Seyed need to set aside?

MINI-CASE 2: Mortgage Planning

Olani and Harriet are trying to determine which one of two mortgage scenarios would help them save the most money with respect to interest charges on their mortgage. The couple need a mortgage in the amount of $200 000. They are interested in a closed mortgage with a mortgage term of five years. The current interest rate for a five-year mortgage term is 5.14 percent, compounded semi-annually. The couple have also decided that a mortgage amortized over 20 years will best suit their financial planning needs.

Under scenario one, the couple will make regular monthly mortgage payments for the five-year mortgage term. At the end of the term, Harriet expects to receive a $10 000 inheritance that was gifted to her in her aunt's will. The couple are considering applying the $10 000 amount to the mortgage at the end of the mortgage term. Not only will this option reduce the outstanding balance on their mortgage, it will also reduce their mortgage interest charges and the number of years it will take for them to pay off their mortgage.

Although scenario one will help the couple achieve their goal of saving money with respect to their mortgage interest charges, they would also like to consider the option of applying the $10 000 toward a vehicle purchase, since their current vehicle is already nine years old. Under this scenario, the couple would not apply the $10 000 inheritance to the mortgage, but would instead change their mortgage payment frequency to accelerated biweekly. Although an accelerated biweekly payment schedule will also allow the couple to save on their mortgage interest charges, they are not sure if the amount that they would save would be more than what they would save in mortgage interest charges under scenario one.

The couple have asked you to determine their mortgage payment for both scenarios.

How many years would they save off their mortgage, and how much mortgage interest would they save? Use this information to recommend which scenario the couple should pursue. As part of your analysis, complete the table below. Assume that the mortgage interest rate will not change for the duration of the mortgage amortization period.

	Mortgage Payment	Total # of Years to Pay Off Mortgage	Mortgage Interest Savings
Scenario 1 (monthly payments with $10 000 lump sum deposit at end of mortgage term)			
Scenario 2 (accelerated biweekly payments)			

PART 2: BRAD MACDONALD—A CONTINUING CASE

| MyLab | Finance

Brad MacDonald is pleased with your assistance in preparing his personal financial statements and your suggestions for improving his personal financial situation. He has called on you for additional guidance.

Second, he wants to know what factors he should consider when selecting a financial institution. He is mostly interested in financial institutions that will assist him in making investment and money management decisions. He finds savings accounts boring and has no desire to have one because the interest rate is so low.

Second, he has decided that it is time to upgrade his car and housing situations; however, he is concerned about his liquidity. His credit card, with a $65 annual fee and 21 percent annual interest rate, compounded daily, is nearing its credit limit of $10 000. He is reluctant to sell his stock to get cash to pay off part of the credit balance. Recall that Brad thinks his stock has the potential to make him rich.

Brad is questioning whether to pay off his credit card. He can easily afford the required minimum monthly payment and sees no reason to pay off the balance.

In order to address his liquidity concerns, Brad has more closely monitored the cost of his smartphone and his entertainment expenses, reducing them by $50 per month and $150 per month, respectively. As a result, his monthly income now exceeds his expenses. However, now Brad has the urge to upgrade his car and housing situations.

Brad is interested in purchasing an SUV for $25 000, which includes all fees and taxes. He still owes $10 000 on his three-year-old sedan, which has 87 000 kilometres on it, and has found a buyer who will pay him $15 000 cash. This would enable him to pay off his current car loan and still have $5000 for a down payment on the SUV. He would finance the remainder of the purchase price for four years at 8 percent, compounded monthly. Anticipating your objections to purchasing the SUV, Brad has an alternate plan to lease the SUV for three years. The terms of the lease are $400 per month, a $0.35 charge per kilometre over 24 000 kilometres annually, and $1200 due upon signing for the first month's lease payment and security deposit.

Brad would also like to purchase his condo. He can make the purchase with 10 percent down. The total purchase price is $140 000. A mortgage with a five-year term and a 25-year amortization period is available with an annual interest rate of 6 percent, compounded semi-annually. The CMHC insurance premium does not need to be added to the mortgage because Brad will pay for it separately. Closing costs due at signing will total $3100. The property taxes on his condo will be $1800 per year, his condo fee is $70 per month, and his household insurance will increase by $240 a year if he buys the condo. Heating costs should be about $125 per month.

Case Questions

1. What factors should Brad consider in selecting a financial institution?

2. If Brad's stock doubles in value over the next five years, what annual return, compounded monthly, would he realize? Based on his projected annualized return, would it be advisable to sell the stock to pay off his credit card? Should Brad consider shopping for a new credit card? If so, how should he go about doing this?

3. Address Brad's reluctance to pay off his credit card balance. Show him what he could earn in five years if he paid the credit card balance off and invested the required minimum monthly payment saved at 6 percent, compounded monthly. Note: The required minimum monthly payment is 3 percent of the outstanding balance of $8000.

4. Assume that Brad has managed to pay off his credit card and no longer has a required minimum monthly payment of $250. All other expenses remain the same. Refer to Brad's personal cash flow statement that you developed in Part 1. Recompute his expenses to determine whether Brad can afford to:

   a. Purchase the new car

   b. Lease the new car

   c. Purchase the condo

   d. Purchase the car and the condo

   e. Lease the car and purchase the condo

5. Based on the information you provided, Brad decides not to buy the condo at this time. How can he save the necessary funds to purchase a condo or house in the future? Be specific in your recommendations.

6. In talking to Brad, you mentioned the increasing threat of identity theft. Brad seems concerned, and after asking him several questions, you determine the following:

   a. Brad has several credit cards in his wallet but uses only one regularly. He also carries his social insurance card, as he can never remember the number.

   b. Brad recycles, including old invoices, credit card statements, and bank statements after retaining them for the appropriate legal time period.

   c. Brad uses his smartphone for virtually all his telephone calls, including ordering merchandise and paying by credit card.

Comment on each of these points in terms of the risk of identity theft, and make recommendations to Brad for appropriate changes that will reduce his risk of exposure to identity theft.

Use the worksheets available on MyLab Finance to complete this case.

Study Guide

Circle the correct answer and then check the answers in the back of the book to chart your progress.

Multiple Choice

1. What is the purpose of getting a pre-approval certificate from a financial institution?
   a. To guarantee you a mortgage interest rate valid for 30 days
   b. To provide you with a guideline on how large a mortgage you can afford
   c. To guarantee funding so you can make an offer on a house
   d. To guarantee you will be approved for a mortgage

2. When selecting a home, you should first determine how much money you can afford to pay per month for a mortgage based on your budget. Which of the following is an appropriate method you could use to help you determine how much of a monthly mortgage payment you can afford?
   a. Compare your financial situation to that of your friends/colleagues, and purchase a house that is similar in value to friends/colleagues who have the same income level as you do.
   b. Obtain a pre-approval certificate from your financial institution.
   c. Look at your cash flow statement and determine what you think you can afford based on the net cash flow you have available.
   d. All of the above.

3. Financial institutions normally will require that your total debt service (TDS) ratio is no more than _____ percent.
   a. 40
   b. 32

   c. 38
   d. 36

4. What would be the gross debt service (GDS) ratio based on the following information?

   Current monthly gross income = $4000

   Current monthly after-tax income = $2800

   Monthly mortgage payment = $950

   Monthly heating cost = $90

   Monthly garbage/recycling pickup cost = $20

   Monthly property taxes = $100

   Monthly credit card payment = $200
   a. 28.50 percent
   b. 40.71 percent
   c. 34.00 percent
   d. 48.57 percent

5. Which of the following is the least important factor to consider when selecting a home?
   a. If you are concerned about excessive maintenance costs, you should consider newer homes or renovated older homes that have received upgrades to costly items, such as a new hot water tank, furnace, or roof.
   b. You should consider the school system in the area where you are looking. A good school system near your home will increase its resale value and provide your children with a good school nearby.
   c. You should consider the cost of insurance. Insurance is more expensive for larger homes and/or homes in and around high-risk areas, such as an area prone to flooding.

d. You should consider who your neighbours will be. It is important to walk around the area and talk to those who would live near you. The sooner you can identify "troublemakers," the sooner you can move on in your search for a home.

6. A duplex is
   a. a free-standing home that is situated on its own lot.
   b. a home that has a common wall with another home.
   c. a home that contains two distinct family homes, one on top of the other.
   d. a home that is joined to another home by a garage or carport.

7. Which of the following costs associated with home ownership is hardest to budget for?
   a. Insurance
   b. Taxes
   c. Repairs
   d. Mortgage payments

8. What is the most important factor in determining the offer price of a home?
   a. An estimate of the future value of the home for resale
   b. The market analysis to find the per-foot price of other homes nearby
   c. The highest price you are willing to pay that the seller will accept
   d. The quality of the structure and materials

9. Title insurance
   a. Protects the insured against financial loss that may result from damage to the home or its contents.
   b. Protects the insured in situations where someone else has claimed title to the home.
   c. Protects the lender if the homeowner defaults on the mortgage payments by guaranteeing that title will pass back to the lender.
   d. Protects the insured against loss resulting from defects that would otherwise have been detected by an up-to-date real property report or land survey.

10. Which one of the following provinces does not charge a land transfer tax?
    a. Manitoba
    b. British Columbia
    c. Alberta
    d. Ontario

11. Which of the following is true regarding conventional mortgages?

a. They require a down payment of at least twenty-five percent.
b. They require a down payment of at least twenty percent.
c. They receive more favourable interest rates for the buyer.
d. They are a form of closed mortgage.

12. Lenders require Canada Mortgage and Housing Corporation insurance on high ratio mortgages. What is the primary purpose of this insurance?
    a. Life insurance for the borrowers to make sure they can pay off the house if one of them dies
    b. Disability insurance for the borrowers to make sure they can pay off the house if one of them can no longer work
    c. Insurance for the borrower in the event of foreclosure to compensate them for the full price they paid for the home
    d. Insurance for the lender to protect their collateral in case the borrower defaults and the home has declined in value

13. Mohammed and Riza are recently married and neither of them has ever owned a home. They wish to use the Home Buyers' Plan (HBP) to make their down payment on their first home. If they each have $75 000 in their RRSPs, how much can they access for their down payment through the HBP?
    a. $100 000
    b. $40 000
    c. $25 000
    d. $50 000

14. A longer amortization period will result in ___monthly mortgage payments and a ___amount of mortgage interest payable over the life of the mortgage.
    a. Lower; higher
    b. Lower; lower
    c. Higher; lower
    d. Higher; higher

15. When is refinancing a home worthwhile?
    a. When interest rates have dropped more than 2 percent
    b. When you can decrease your monthly payment significantly
    c. When the penalty cost is less than the financial benefit
    d. When interest rates have dropped significantly

True/False

1. True or False? Multiple Listing Service (MLS) is a marketing service that allows you and your realtor to shop online for homes.

2. True or False? Your gross debt service (GDS) ratio is the ratio of your mortgage-related debt payments plus all other consumer debt payments divided by your total monthly gross household income.

3. True or False? Once you have determined your net cash flows, you should go ahead and purchase a home that will absorb all of your current excess cash flows.

4. True or False? When it comes to resale value, the rate of increase in home prices in previous years does not necessarily serve as a good predictor of the future.

5. True or False? Most sellers are willing to accept less than their original asking price.

6. True or False? The home buyer is responsible for paying the commission to the realtor.

7. True or False? When a borrower takes out a high-ratio mortgage, they must pay the cost of the mortgage loan insurance immediately.

8. True or False? Title insurance protects you if it turns out that the real property report was inaccurate.

9. True or False? The amortization period will be greater than or the same as the mortgage term.

10. True or False? A conventional mortgage is a mortgage where the down payment is less than 20 percent of the home's selling price.

11. True or False? In the case of a vendor take-back mortgage, the buyer will make mortgage payments directly to the seller, and the seller will maintain ownership of the property until the buyer has paid off the mortgage.

12. True or False? If property taxes have been prepaid for the entire calendar year and possession of the home is transferred to the buyer on July 1, the seller will have to reimburse the buyer for six months' worth of taxes paid.

13. True or False? Prepayment privileges include the option to increase your mortgage payment and to make lump sum payments.

14. True or False? With a variable rate mortgage (VRM), your mortgage payments will increase if interest rates go up at all during your mortgage term.

15. True or False? Individuals will normally refinance their mortgages if market interest rates have decreased.

PART 3

Protecting Your Wealth

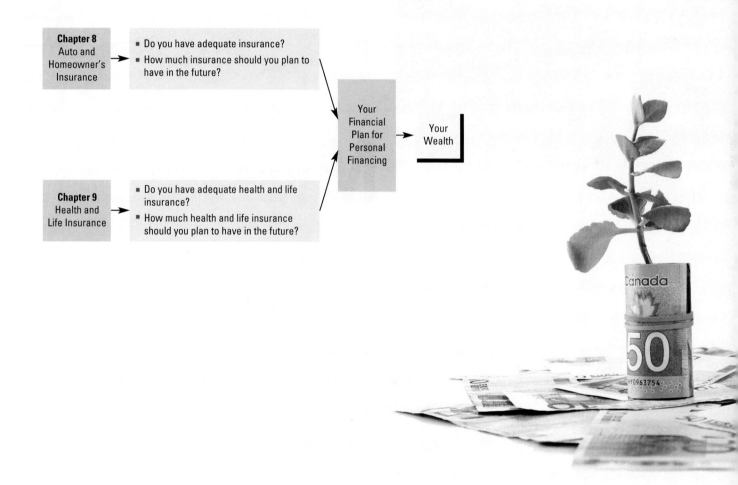

Chapter 8
Auto and Homeowner's Insurance

- Do you have adequate insurance?
- How much insurance should you plan to have in the future?

Your Financial Plan for Personal Financing

Your Wealth

Chapter 9
Health and Life Insurance

- Do you have adequate health and life insurance?
- How much health and life insurance should you plan to have in the future?

The chapters in this part focus on insurance, which is critical to protect you and your personal assets against damages and liability. Chapter 8 focuses on decisions about auto and homeowner's insurance. Chapter 9 presents key considerations regarding health, disability, critical illness, long-term care, and life insurance.

Auto and Homeowner's Insurance

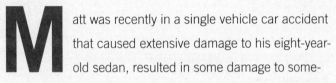

Robert Crum/Shutterstock

Matt was recently in a single vehicle car accident that caused extensive damage to his eight-year-old sedan, resulted in some damage to someone's fence, and caused Matt to suffer a serious neck injury. The accident was not Matt's fault since he swerved to avoid a pedestrian who had suddenly run out on to the road.

When the insurance company asked Matt to get an estimate of the costs of repairs, he took it to a well-respected repair shop. They quoted a total repair bill of $5240. Matt's car is only worth $3250. The damage to the fence was significant and the home owner received a quote that it would cost $1500 to repair his fence. Finally, Matt's neck injury required him to get some physiotherapy and take 10 days off work for treatment. Before his injury, Matt lived in a province where he had a pure no-fault auto insurance policy provided by a government agency. In his current province of residence, he has private auto insurance coverage and he is concerned about how this may impact his benefits.

QUESTIONS:

1. Will the insurance company pay for Matt's car repair?
2. Under what sections of an auto insurance policy will the insurance company cover, if they are covered, the damage to the fence, Matt's neck injury, and Matt's loss of income?
3. What are the main features of a private auto insurance system? Will this have a significant impact on how much medical and financial support Matt will receive for his injuries and lost employment?

THE LEARNING OBJECTIVES OF THIS CHAPTER ARE TO:

1. Explain the role of risk management
2. Outline typical provisions of auto insurance
3. Describe financial coverage provided by homeowner's insurance

BACKGROUND ON INSURANCE

Property insurance ensures that any damages to your auto and home are covered, and that your personal assets are protected from any liability. In the context of insurance, the term *liability* is used to mean that you may be required to pay someone for damages you caused. Health insurance can ensure that most of your health care needs, such as physician, dental, and vision care, will be covered. Disability insurance can ensure that your monthly income will continue in the event that you are unable to work as a result of an injury or illness. Critical illness insurance can ensure that you have access to lump sum benefits in the event that you suffer a critical illness, such as a heart attack, stroke, or life-threatening cancer. Long-term care insurance can ensure that you have access to benefits that will help to cover added living costs, such as in-home nursing care, when you are unable to take care of yourself as a result of an injury or illness. Life insurance can ensure financial support for your dependants, other individuals, or charities when you die.

The primary function of insurance is to maintain your existing level of wealth by protecting you against potential financial losses or liability as a result of unexpected events. It can ensure that your income continues if an accident or illness prevents you from working, or it can prevent others from taking away your personal assets.

You benefit from having insurance even when you do not receive any payments from the insurance company because you have the peace of mind of knowing that your assets are protected should you suffer a loss. Insurance may seem costly, but it is well worth the cost to ensure that your wealth will not be taken away from you.

MANAGING RISK

L.O.1

As described in Chapter 1, risk management represents decisions about whether and how to protect against risk. The first step in risk management is to recognize the risks to which you are exposed. Then you must decide whether to protect against those risks. Once you decide whether to obtain a particular type of insurance, you must decide on the amount of coverage you need and the policy provisions you require. When deciding whether to protect against risk, your alternatives include avoiding, reducing, accepting, and sharing risk.

Avoid Risk

One method of managing risk is simply to avoid it. Consider actions that expose you to a financial loss. Owners are exposed to a financial loss if their property is improperly maintained. You can avoid the risk of property damage if you do not own any property. However, you cannot completely avoid risk by avoiding ownership of property. If you lease a car, you are still exposed to liability and financial loss if the car is in an accident. Other types of risk are unrelated to property. For example, you are exposed to a financial loss if you require medical attention or become disabled.

Reduce Risk

Another method of managing risk is to reduce your exposure to financial loss. For example, you can purchase a small home rather than a large one to reduce the maximum possible financial loss due to property damage. You can purchase an inexpensive car to limit the possible financial loss due to property damage. You may be able to reduce your exposure to an illness or a disability by getting periodic health checkups.

Yet these steps do not fully block your exposure to financial loss. If you drive a car, you are subject not only to property damage, but also to liability. Your financial loss could be large even if the car you drive has little value.

Accept Risk

A third alternative when managing risk is to accept risk by not seeking to limit your exposure to a financial loss. This alternative may be feasible when the likelihood of an event that could cause a financial loss is very low and the potential financial loss due to the event is small. For example, if you seldom drive your car and live in a town with little traffic, you are relatively unlikely to get into an accident. You are also more likely to accept risk when the possible financial loss resulting from the event is limited. For example, if you drive an inexpensive and old car, you may be willing to accept your exposure to financial loss due to property damage by removing collision coverage from your auto insurance policy. However, you are still subject to liability, which could put all of your personal assets in jeopardy.

PSYCHOLOGY of Personal Finance

Psychology behind Accepting Risk. Many people opt to accept risk rather than pay for insurance because they do not feel much satisfaction from buying insurance. They make a payment and might feel like they receive nothing in return. Buying insurance is different from buying many other products or services in which the benefits are enjoyed immediately. In fact, some people might argue that the only benefit from insurance is if an unfortunate event occurs that causes them to need it. Otherwise, they may perceive insurance as a waste of money. They should, however, consider their potential liability if an adverse event happens and they do not have insurance. In many cases, people do not make an informed decision to accept risk, but simply defer the decision to buy insurance because they do not want to spend the money. Or they may have a mindset that they will be careful and will therefore avoid any undesirable event that would require insurance.

However, people do not have complete control to avoid adverse events. Careful drivers can have a major car accident. Prudent homeowners can be subject to major house damage due to weather. People with healthy diets can suffer from a major illness. The cost of an adverse event could completely wipe out one's savings.

Share Risk

A final alternative is to share risk. If you cannot avoid a specific type of risk, and you cannot reduce that risk, and you do not wish to be exposed to financial loss as a result of the risk, you should consider insurance. The concept of risk sharing is covered later in this chapter.

insurance premium
The cost of obtaining insurance.

The decision to obtain insurance is determined by weighing its costs and benefits. The cost of obtaining insurance is the **insurance premium** that is paid for a policy each year. The benefit of obtaining insurance is that it can protect your assets or income from events that otherwise might cause financial loss. Consequently, you protect your existing net worth and also increase the likelihood that you will be able to increase your net worth in the future. Without insurance, you could lose all of your assets if you are involved in an accident that causes major damages and/or liability as a result of an injury to others.

You cannot insure against all types of risk, as some types of insurance are either unavailable or too expensive. Your risk management strategy will determine which types of risk you wish to insure against. When there is a high likelihood that an event will cause a financial loss and the potential financial loss from that event is large, insurance should be considered. You may choose to accept the types of risk that might result in only small financial losses. In this and the following chapter, you will learn the key provisions of auto, homeowner's, health, disability, critical illness, long-term care, and life insurance. With this background, you can create your own risk management plan.

Your risk management decisions are also affected by your degree of risk tolerance. For example, you and your neighbour could be in the same financial position and have the same exposure to various types of risk. Yet you may obtain more insurance than your neighbour because you are more concerned about exposure to financial loss. While you incur annual insurance expenses from insurance premiums, you are protected from financial losses resulting from covered **perils** (hazards or risks you face). A covered peril would include an unexpected or accidental event, such as vandalism or flooding. On the other hand, perils like regular wear and tear of the shingles on your roof are not covered

peril
A hazard or risk you face.

ROLE OF INSURANCE COMPANIES

Insurance companies offer insurance policies that can protect you against financial loss. Since there are many different types of risk that could cause financial losses, there are many different types of insurance policies that can protect you from those risks. Exhibit 8.1 describes some common events that can cause major financial loss and the related types of insurance that can protect you from these events. The most popular forms of insurance for individuals are property and casualty insurance, life insurance, and health insurance.

Property and casualty insurance is used to insure property and therefore consists of auto insurance and home insurance. Some insurance companies specialize in a particular type of insurance, while others offer all types of insurance for individuals. Companies that offer the same type of insurance vary in terms of the specific policies they offer.

In recent years, chartered banks and other types of financial institutions have established insurance businesses. Some financial institutions have an insurance centre within their branches. This enables customers to take care of their insurance needs where they receive other financial services.

myth or **fact** Filing an insurance claim will automatically increase your insurance premium.

EXHIBIT 8.1 Common Events That Could Cause a Financial Loss

Event	Financial loss	Protection
You have a car accident and damage your car	Car repairs	Auto insurance (collision)
You have a car accident in which another person in your car is injured	Medical bills and liability	Auto insurance (accident benefits)
You have a car accident in which another person in the other driver's car is injured	Medical bills and liability	Auto insurance (liability)
Your home is damaged by a fire	Home repairs	Homeowner's insurance
Your neighbour is injured while in your home	Medical bills and liability	Homeowner's insurance (liability)
You become ill and need medical attention	Prescription drugs	Health insurance
You develop an illness that requires long-term care	Nursing care	Long-term care insurance
You become disabled	Loss of income	Disability insurance
You die while family members rely on your income	Loss of income	Life insurance

Insurance Company Operations

When an insurance company sells an insurance policy to you, it is obliged to cover claims as described in the insurance policy. For example, if your car is insured by a policy, the insurance company is obligated to protect you from financial loss due to an accident up to the policy limits. If you are in a car accident while driving that car, the insurance company provides payments (subject to limits specified in the contract) to cover any liability to passengers and others and to repair property damage resulting from the accident.

As mentioned earlier, one method of protecting against risk is to share it with others. Insurance companies help policy owners share risk by pooling together a number of insurance policies based on the type of insurance purchased and the characteristics of a group of policy owners. The insurance company is able to generate a profit because it knows that the majority of policy owners will not need to file claims during the coverage period. Consider a policy owner who pays $1000 in auto insurance for the year. Assume that he is in an accident and that the insurance company has to pay $20 000 to cover liability and repair the car. The payout by the insurance company is 20 times the premium received. In other words, it would take 20 auto insurance policy premiums to generate enough revenue to cover the cost of this one claim. To generate sufficient revenue, the insurance company will sell a number of auto insurance policies. Based on historical claims information, it can estimate the number of policies it must sell and the price at which to sell these policies to ensure a profit for the company. In general, insurance companies generate their revenue by receiving payments for policies and by earning a return from investing the proceeds until the funds are needed to cover claims. They incur costs by making payments to cover policy owner claims. When an insurance company makes payments on a claim, these payments are commonly less than the total annual premium received by the group of policy owners. The difference between the amount of premiums collected from all policy owners plus the investment income earned by investing these premiums and the total value of claims and other business expenses represents the amount of profit the insurance company generates.

$$\text{Profit} = (\text{Premiums} + \text{Investment Earnings}) - (\text{Claims} + \text{Business Expenses})$$

When you buy insurance, you are relying on the insurance company to provide you with adequate coverage over a future period. However, if the insurance company mismanages its operations, it could experience large losses and not be able to cover your claim. In addition, you would probably lose the premium that you had already paid. Thus, it is important that you select an insurance company that is financially strong. There are several services that rate insurance companies, including A.M.Best (www.ambest.com), Moody's Investor Services (www.moodys.com), and Standard & Poor's Corporation (www.standardandpoors.com).

Relationship between Insurance Company Claims and Premiums. Since insurance companies rely mostly on their premiums to cover claims, they price their insurance policies to reflect the probability of a claim and the size of that claim. For an event that is very unlikely and could cause minor damage, the premium would be relatively low. For an event that is more likely and could cause major damage, the insurance premium would be relatively high. In a sense, a high insurance premium indicates that there is a greater probability that you may use the insurance coverage provided.

Insurance Underwriters. An insurance company relies on **underwriters**, who calculate the risk of specific insurance policies and decide what policies to offer and what premiums to charge. Underwriters recognize that their insurance company must generate revenue that is greater than its expenses to be profitable, so they set premiums that are aligned with anticipated claims.

Role of Insurance Agents and Brokers

When contacting an insurance company, you will probably communicate with an insurance agent or broker. An **insurance agent** represents one or more insurance companies and recommends insurance policies that fit customers' needs. **Captive (or exclusive) insurance agents** work for one particular insurance company, whereas **independent insurance agents**

Go to
http://www.ambest.com/ratings/index.html

Used with permission from A.M. Best Company, Inc.

This website provides information on how insurance companies are rated.

underwriters
Employees of an insurance company who calculate the risk of specific insurance policies and decide what policies to offer and what premiums to charge.

insurance agent
Represents one or more insurance companies and recommends insurance policies that fit customers' needs.

captive (or exclusive) insurance agent
Works for one particular insurance company.

independent insurance agent
Represents many different insurance companies.

(also called insurance brokers) represent many different insurance companies. These independent agents are linked to various insurance companies online and therefore can quickly obtain quotations for different policies from different vendors. In addition to helping customers with various types of insurance, insurance agents may offer financial planning services, such as retirement planning and estate planning. Some insurance agents are also licensed to serve as sales representatives for mutual funds or other financial products. The best insurance companies provide quick and thorough claims service. Sources of information on level of service by insurance companies include the Better Business Bureau and *Consumer Reports* magazine.

AUTO INSURANCE

L.0.2

Auto insurance insures against the legal liability that may arise from causing death or injury to others; the expense associated with providing medical care to you, your passengers, and other persons outside your vehicle; and the costs associated with damage to your automobile. In this way, it limits your potential liabilities (expenses due to an accident) and also protects one of your main assets (your car). If you own or drive a car, you are required to have a minimum level of auto insurance. Auto insurance is provided by a government agency in British Columbia, Saskatchewan, and Manitoba. In Quebec, the expense associated with providing medical care to you, your passengers, and pedestrians is covered through a government agency. All other auto insurance coverages in Quebec are purchased through private property and casualty (P&C) insurance companies. In all other provinces and territories, auto insurance is purchased through private P&C insurance companies. Your policy specifies the amount of coverage you have if you are legally liable for bodily injury, if you and your passengers incur medical bills, or if your car is damaged as the result of an accident or some other event (such as a tree falling on it).

The estimated average automobile insurance premium by province, in 2011, is shown in Exhibit 8.2. Premiums vary among provinces. Recent reforms in the way private

EXHIBIT 8.2 Estimated Average Net Automobile Insurance Premium, 2011, by Province

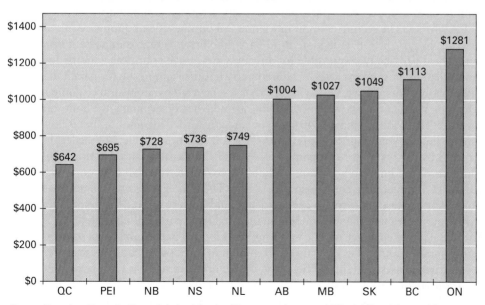

Source: Based on Fraser institute digital publication, The personal cost and Affordability of Automobile insurance in Canada (2011 edition), October 2011.

insurers are able to charge premiums have resulted in a significant decrease in the cost of auto insurance. As a result, Exhibit 8.2 shows that three of the four most expensive average net automobile insurance premiums in 2011 were in provinces that provide auto insurance through a government agency.

myth or **fact** The colour of your car has an impact on your auto insurance premiums.

Auto Insurance Policy Provisions

insurance policy
Contract between an insurance company and the policy owner.

An **insurance policy** is a contract between an insurance company and the policy owner. An **auto insurance policy** specifies the coverage (including dollar limits) provided by an insurance company for a particular individual and vehicle. The contract identifies the policy owner and family members who are also insured if they use the vehicle. You should have insurance information such as your policy number and the name of a contact person at the insurance company with you when you drive. If you are in an accident, exchange your insurance information with that of the other driver and also fill out a police report if damages to any property exceed $1000 or if there are injuries to passengers and/or pedestrians.

auto insurance policy
Specifies the coverage provided by an insurance company for a particular individual and vehicle.

Every auto insurance policy explains what is covered in detail. Generally, auto insurance policies contain three sections: third party liability coverage, accident benefits, and loss or damage to the insured automobile. If you have a policy, review your own auto insurance policy as you read on, so that you understand your coverage.

Section A: Third Party Liability Coverage

third party liability
A legal term that describes the person(s) who have experienced loss because of the insured.

Third party liability is a legal term that describes the person(s) who have experienced loss because of the insured. Third party liability coverage, which is also known as civil liability coverage in Quebec, consists of two key components: bodily injury liability and property damage liability. **Bodily injury liability coverage** protects you against liability associated with injuries you (or family members listed on the policy) cause to others. This section of the policy also covers you or your family members if you cause injuries to others while driving someone else's car with their permission. Bodily injury expenses include medical bills, pain and suffering, and economic loss as a result of an accident you cause. The coverage is designed to protect you if you cause an accident and the driver of the other car sues you.

bodily injury liability coverage
Protects you against liability associated with injuries you cause to others.

Every province and territory recognizes that it is critical for drivers to have adequate liability coverage. As such, third party liability coverage is mandatory in all provinces and territories. The second column in Exhibit 8.3 outlines the minimum required liability coverage by jurisdiction. Adequate third party liability coverage is important because you can be held personally responsible for any amounts above your policy limits. Exhibit 8.3 shows that, in most provinces, the injured party has the right to sue for pain and suffering and economic loss. However, any legal expenses incurred by an insurance company while defending you against a lawsuit are not considered when determining the limits on liability coverage. For example, if a person sues you and is awarded an amount that is less than the liability limit in your contract, it is covered by your policy regardless of the legal expenses incurred by the insurance company. However, if the award granted in a lawsuit against you exceeds the limit on your policy's liability coverage, you will be required to pay the difference and therefore could lose your assets. The financial loss to you and your family from a lawsuit resulting from a car accident could be devastating. Therefore, you should always purchase more than the minimum required third party liability listed in Exhibit 8.3. You should have coverage of at least $1 million for third party liability. In some provinces, auto insurance companies offer up to $5 million of third party liability coverage. As your net worth increases, you should review your liability coverage with an eye to increasing it.

property damage liability coverage
Protects against losses that result when the policy owner damages another person's property with his or her car.

Property damage liability coverage protects against losses that result when the policy owner damages another person's property with his or her car. Examples include damage to a car, fence, lamppost, or building. Note that property damage liability does not cover your own car or other property that you own. The minimum third party liability amounts

EXHIBIT 8.3   Minimum Required Auto Insurance Coverage Amounts by Province/Territory

Province/Territory	Compulsory Minimum Third Party Liability	Accident Benefits (Per Person)*	Right to Sue for Pain and Suffering?	Right to Sue for Economic Loss in Excess of No-Fault Benefits?	Administration
Alberta	$200 000	$50 000	Yes, with conditions	Yes	Private
British Columbia	$200 000	$150 000	Yes	Yes	Government
Manitoba	$200 000	No time or amount limit	No	No	Government
New Brunswick	$200 000	$50 000	Yes, with conditions	Yes	Private
Newfoundland & Labrador	$200 000	$25 000 (optional)	Yes, with conditions	Yes	Private
Northwest Territories	$200 000	$25 000	Yes	Yes	Private
Nova Scotia	$500 000	$50 000	Yes, with conditions	Yes	Private
Nunavut	$200 000	$25 000	Yes	Yes	Private
Ontario	$200 000	$3500 – minor injury $65 000 – non-minor injury; non-catastrophic injury $1 000 000 – catastrophic injury	Yes, with conditions	Yes, with conditions	Private
Prince Edward Island	$200 000	$50 000	Yes, with conditions	Yes	Private
Quebec	$50 000	No time or amount limit	No	No	**Bodily injury:** Government **Property damage:** Private
Saskatchewan	$200 000	**No-fault option:** $6 719 606	**No-fault option:** No	**No-fault option:** Yes	**No-fault option:** Government
		Tort option: Up to $26 273 for non-catastrophic injury, up to $197 056 for catastrophic injury	**Tort option:** Yes, subject to deductible of $5,000	**Tort option:** Yes	**Tort option:** Government
Yukon	$200 000	$10 000	Yes	Yes	Private

*In most cases, amount includes coverage for rehabilitation and excludes coverage from health insurance and other medical plans. Time limit for payments and other conditions may apply.

Source: Based on Insurance Bureau of Canada, http://www.ibc.ca/

listed in Exhibit 8.3 also apply to property damage liability. However, check with your insurance agent on the impact that total claims in excess of the provincial minimum will have on your property damage coverage. In most provinces, there is a cap on the amount of property damage coverage if a total claim against you exceeds the provincial minimum. You should always purchase additional property damage liability coverage.

Section B: Accident Benefits

Accident benefits coverage insures against the cost of medical care for you and other passengers in your car. In addition to coverage for medical payments, such as the cost of rehabilitation, accident benefits generally include coverage for funeral benefits, loss of

accident benefits coverage
Insures against the cost of medical care for you and other passengers in your car.

income as a result of death or total disability, and uninsured motorist coverage. Accident benefits coverage is mandatory in all provinces except Newfoundland and Labrador. Exhibit 8.3 displays the per person coverage limits for the medical payment amounts that are available in the accident benefits section of an auto insurance policy. Notice that the limits are highest in provinces that have some level of government administration when it comes to auto insurance. The medical coverage applies only to the passengers, including the driver of the insured car. If you were driving someone else's car at the time of the accident, the owner of that car would be responsible for the medical coverage for passengers.

myth or **fact** In general, private auto insurance, such as that offered in Alberta, is more expensive than public auto insurance offered in provinces such as Manitoba.

uninsured motorist coverage
Insures against the cost of bodily injury when an accident is caused by another driver who is not insured.

Uninsured motorist coverage insures against the cost of bodily injury when an accident is caused by another driver who is not insured. The coverage also applies if you are in an accident caused by a hit-and-run driver or by a driver who is at fault but whose insurance company goes bankrupt. The payments for uninsured motorist coverage are made from a provincially administered Motor Vehicle Accident Claims Fund. Like the third party liability insurance, there are policy limits. This coverage applies to bodily injury when you are not at fault, while the third party liability coverage from Section A applies to bodily injury when you are at fault.

Section C: Loss of or Damage to Insured Automobile

collision insurance
Insures against costs of damage to your car resulting from an accident in which the driver of your car is at fault.

comprehensive coverage
Insures you against damage to your car that results from something other than a collision, such as floods, theft, fire, hail, explosions, riots, vandalism, and various other perils.

Collision insurance and comprehensive coverage insure against damage to your car. Both types of coverage are optional in all provinces. If you drive an old car that is not worth very much, you may decide not to carry this type of insurance. **Collision insurance** insures against costs of damage to your car resulting from an accident in which the driver of your car is at fault. **Comprehensive coverage** insures you against damage to your car that results from something other than a collision, such as floods, theft, fire, hail, explosions, riots, vandalism, and various other perils.

Although collision insurance and comprehensive coverage are optional, car loan providers may require the borrower to maintain insurance that will cover any property damage to the car to protect the lender in the event that the car owner has an accident and stops making loan payments. The car that serves as collateral on the loan may be worthless if it is damaged in an accident. In this event, the insurance company may pay the lender up to the book value of the car.

Collision insurance and comprehensive coverage are especially valuable if you have a new car that you would likely repair if it were damaged. Some insurance companies offer a new-car rider or standard endorsement form (S.E.F.), known as a Limited Waiver of Depreciation (S.E.F. 43), which can protect you from the loss, as a result of depreciation, that occurs when you drive a new or leased car "off the lot." With a Limited Waiver of Depreciation on your insurance policy, the insurance company will not charge you for depreciation on your car when it is calculating how much to reimburse you for damages that are beyond repair. Instead of paying you the actual cash value, you will be paid an amount based on the actual purchase price or the manufacturer's suggested retail price. This endorsement only applies if you are the original owner/lessee of the car and the loss occurred within a set period, usually 24 to 30 months, from when the vehicle was purchased.

Collision coverage can be valuable even if you do not believe you were at fault in an accident. If the other driver claims that you were at fault, you and your insurance company may need to take the matter to court. Meanwhile, you can use the collision coverage to have the car repaired. If your insurance company wins the lawsuit, the other driver's insurance company will be required to pay the expenses associated with repairing your car.

Collision coverage is normally limited to the car itself and not to items that were damaged while in the car. For example, if you were transporting a new computer at the time of an accident, the damage to the computer would not be protected by comprehensive coverage. The computer may be covered by your homeowner's insurance, which is discussed later in this chapter.

Deductible. The **deductible** is a set dollar amount that you are responsible for paying before any coverage is provided by your insurer. For example, a deductible of $500 means that you must pay the first $500 in damages due to an accident. The insurance company pays any additional expenses beyond the deductible, which is normally between $250 and $1000. This deductible should be an amount you can easily afford (part of your emergency fund or liquidity needs). However, the higher the deductible, the lower the insurance premium.

deductible
A set dollar amount that you are responsible for paying before any coverage is provided by your insurer.

Facility Association

Facility Association is a not-for-profit organization made up of all auto insurance providers operating in every province and territory except British Columbia, Manitoba, Saskatchewan, and Quebec. **Facility Association** ensures that drivers unable to obtain insurance with an individual company are able to obtain the coverage they need to operate their vehicles legally. Higher-risk drivers may have difficulty obtaining insurance for many reasons: a poor driving record or claims history, the type of vehicle, and location or area of residence. Additional information on Facility Association coverage can be found at www.facilityassociation.com.

Facility Association
Ensures that drivers unable to obtain insurance with an individual company are able to obtain the coverage they need to operate their vehicles legally.

No-Fault Auto Insurance

The benefits provided under the accident benefits section of an auto insurance policy are provided under what is known as a "no-fault" system. No-fault auto insurance does not mean that nobody is at fault when an accident occurs. However, determining who is at fault may take some time. To ensure that all insured individuals receive immediate medical treatment for their injuries, **no-fault auto insurance** allows policy owners in all provinces to receive immediate medical payments through their own insurance policy, regardless of who is at fault for causing the accident. The rationale is that the sooner you receive treatment, the sooner you will get better. The driver who is ultimately found to be at fault will likely see his or her premiums increase and may have to face other penalties for violating traffic laws.

no-fault auto insurance
Allows policy owners in all provinces to receive immediate medical payments through their own insurance policy, regardless of who is at fault for causing the accident.

The government agencies in Saskatchewan, Manitoba, and Quebec operate pure no-fault auto insurance systems. Under a pure no-fault system, you are unable to sue the at-fault driver for pain and suffering and economic loss. Exhibit 8.3 shows that the accident benefits in Manitoba and Quebec are unlimited with respect to how long you can receive benefits and the total dollar amount you can receive. In Saskatchewan, you can choose a no-fault option (cannot sue for damages) or a tort option (can sue for damages). The dollar value of the accident benefits available under the no-fault option is much higher. As shown in Exhibit 8.3, in all other provinces, the dollar amount that you receive for accident benefits is capped at some level, and there is usually a time limit of two to four years during which you can receive these benefits. The trade-off occurs because, in these other provinces, you can sue the at-fault driver for amounts above and beyond your provincial or territorial limits.

Other Endorsement Forms

You can elect to have coverage for expenses not included in the standard policy. There are a number of these optional coverages, referred to as insurance endorsements. For example, a policy can cover the cost of a rental car, known as loss of use (S.E.F. 20), while your car is being repaired after an accident. You can also elect to have coverage for emergency service expenses (S.E.F. 35), like towing, even if the problems are not the result of an accident. Your premium will increase slightly for these endorsements.

You can also include an endorsement on your auto insurance policy to cover any car you rent. This endorsement is referred to as legal liability for damage to non-owned automobiles (S.E.F. 27). If you do not have such an endorsement, the rental car agency typically will offer to sell you collision damage coverage, liability insurance, medical coverage, and even coverage for theft of personal belongings from the car. If rental car insurance is not covered by your policy, some credit cards provide you with collision and comprehensive insurance benefits when you use that card to pay for the rental services.

Another endorsement that can be very important is family protection coverage (S.E.F. 44). This endorsement covers you and your family to the same limits as your third party liability coverage if you are involved in an accident with an underinsured, or hit-and-run driver. **Underinsured motorist coverage** insures against the additional cost of bodily injury when an accident is caused by a driver who has insufficient coverage. Suppose that you suffer bodily injury as a result of an accident caused by an at-fault driver who has purchased only the minimum $200 000 of third party liability coverage. The total amount of your bodily injury damages is $600 000. The at-fault driver is underinsured relative to the bodily injury damages you have suffered. However, when you purchased your auto insurance, you purchased $1 million of third party liability coverage and added the family protection coverage provision as an option. As a result of your claim for bodily injury, you will receive $200 000 from the at-fault driver's insurance company and $400 000 from your insurance company.

An auto insurance policy also specifies **exclusions** (items or circumstances that are specifically excluded from insurance coverage) and limitations of the coverage. For example, coverage may not apply if you intentionally damage a car, if you drive a car that is not yours without the permission of the owner, or if you drive a car that you own but that is not listed on your insurance policy. It also explains how you should comply with procedures if you are in an accident.

Summary of Auto Insurance Provisions

The most important types of coverage identified above are included in a standard insurance policy. They are summarized in Exhibit 8.4. Notice that the exhibit classifies the potential financial damages as being related to:

- Your car in an accident
- The other car or other property in an accident
- Your car when not in an accident

underinsured motorist coverage
Insures against the additional cost of bodily injury when an accident is caused by a driver who has insufficient coverage.

exclusions
A term appearing in insurance contracts or policies that describes items or circumstances that are specifically excluded from insurance coverage.

EXHIBIT 8.4   Summary of Auto Insurance Provisions

Financial Damages Related to Your Car in an Accident	Auto Insurance Provision
Liability due to passengers in your car when you are at fault	Bodily injury liability
Liability due to passengers in your car when you are not at fault but driver of other car is uninsured or underinsured	Uninsured/underinsured motorist coverage
Damage to your own car	Collision
Treatment of injuries to driver and passengers of your car	Accident benefits

Financial Damages Related to the Other Car or Other Property in an Accident	
Liability due to passengers in the other car	Bodily injury liability
Liability due to damage to the other car	Property damage liability
Liability due to damage to the other property	Property damage liability

Financial Damages Related to Your Car When Not in an Accident	
Damage to your car as a result of theft, fire, vandalism, or other non-accident events	Comprehensive

FACTORS THAT AFFECT YOUR AUTO INSURANCE PREMIUMS

Your insurance premium is influenced by the likelihood that you will submit claims to the insurance company and the estimated cost to the insurance company for covering those claims. As explained earlier, your auto insurance premium will be higher for a policy that specifies a greater amount of liability coverage and a lower deductible. In provinces where insurance is provided by a government agency (British Columbia, Saskatchewan, and Manitoba), personal characteristics such as your age are not considered when determining auto insurance rates. Factors that are common to all provinces include the following.

How You Use Your Vehicle. People who use their cars to go to and from work are more likely to be involved in auto accidents than those who drive their cars only on weekends. Commuting distance is also considered.

Value of Car. Insurance premiums are high when the potential financial loss is high. Collision and comprehensive insurance premiums are higher for new cars. In addition, the premium is normally higher for an expensive car than an inexpensive car of the same age. For example, the insurance on a new Mercedes is higher than that on a new Mazda.

Repair Record of Your Car. Some car models require more repair work for the same type of damage. For example, replacing a door on a Ford may be easier than on some other cars, which reduces the repair bill. When a car can be repaired easily and inexpensively, its insurance premium is lower.

Your Location. Auto insurance is more expensive in large cities, where the probability of being involved in an accident is higher. In contrast, auto insurance is less expensive in rural areas, where the probability of being involved in an accident is lower because there will be fewer cars on the road. In Saskatchewan, your location is not taken into consideration when determining auto insurance premiums.

Your Driver Training. Insurance companies recognize that driver training can improve driver performance and therefore can reduce the likelihood of accidents in the future. They encourage drivers to enrol in driver training programs. If you have completed a driver training program, you may qualify for a discount.

Your Driving Record. If you have an excellent driving record, including no accidents and no moving violations for a year or longer, you may be charged a lower premium than other drivers. For example, drivers in Manitoba receive merit discounts depending on the number of years that they do not have any at-fault claims. No one purposely creates a bad driving record, but some drivers do not realize how much their insurance premium will increase if their record is poor. In provinces with private auto insurance, these drivers cannot comparison shop effectively. In many cases, they will have to rely on Facility Association coverage to have any auto insurance at all. Once drivers are labelled as high risk, it takes several years of safe driving to prove that they have improved their driving habits. As a result, they will pay very expensive insurance premiums for several years. After all, all drivers in the Facility Association are high risk and claims will be higher and greater in number.

In addition to the factors listed above, provinces that offer auto insurance through private property and casualty insurers may take into consideration the following factors.

Your Age and Sex. Insurance companies often base their premiums on personal profiles, and age is one of the most important characteristics. Younger drivers are more likely to get into accidents, and therefore they pay higher insurance premiums. In particular, drivers between the ages of 16 and 25 are considered to be high risk. Insurance companies incur higher expenses from covering their claims and offset these higher expenses by charging higher premiums. Another important characteristic is sex, as male drivers tend to get into more serious or expensive accidents than female drivers. For these reasons, male teenagers are charged higher auto insurance premiums.

Your Driving Distance. You are more likely to get into an accident the more kilometres you drive. Thus, your premium will be higher if you drive more kilometres. Many insurance companies classify drivers into two or more driving distance groups. For example, if you drive fewer than 16 000 kilometres per year, you may qualify for the low driving distance group, which entitles you to a lower premium.

Comparing Premiums among Insurance Companies

One final factor that affects your auto insurance premium is the insurance company you select. Premiums can vary substantially among insurance companies, so always obtain several quotes before you select a company. The opportunity to shop around for auto insurance is only available in provinces where auto insurance is offered through private P&C insurers. Several websites, such as www.kanetix.ca/auto-insurance, provide auto insurance quotes online.

If you have specific questions about the coverage offered and want to speak to an insurance salesperson, you can call some insurance companies directly. A comparison of quotes online might at least help you to determine which companies to call for more information. Alternatively, you can call an independent insurance agent, who can help you to purchase insurance from one of several companies.

When comparing premiums, recognize that the premium may vary with the type of policy desired. For example, an insurance company may have relatively low premiums compared to its competitors for a policy involving substantial coverage for bodily injury liability, but relatively high premiums for a policy involving collision coverage. Therefore, you should not select a company based on advice you receive from friends or family members. If their policies are different from the one you desire, another company may offer better coverage. In addition, companies change their premiums over time, so they may charge relatively low premiums in one period but relatively high premiums in the following period for the same policy because of their claims experience (the number and monetary values of claims the company has paid out over a recent period).

Comparing Prices at the Time of Renewal. Once an auto insurance policy has been in effect for 60 days, an insurance company can cancel your policy only if you provided fraudulent information on your application, if your driver's licence is suspended, or if you do not pay your premiums. However, it may decide not to renew your policy when it expires if you had a poor driving record over the recent policy period. For example, it is unlikely you will be able to renew your policy if you caused an accident as a result of drunk driving.

If an insurance company is willing to renew your policy, it may raise the premium in the renewal period even if your driving record has been good. You can switch to a different insurance company when the policy expires if you are not satisfied with your present one or think that the premium is too high. You should compare auto insurance prices among companies before renewing your policy. However, recognize that your driving record will follow you. If you recently caused one or more accidents, you will likely be charged a higher premium whether you continue with your existing company or switch to a new one. Some insurance companies also offer teaser rates. Soon after you switch, premiums are raised. Switching policies frequently can also raise your premiums.

FREE APPS for Personal Finance

Estimating the Cost of Car Insurance

Application:

The Kanetix Car Insurance Quick Quote app makes car buying easier than ever because knowing how much it could cost to insure in advance of buying could sway your decision and save you hundreds of dollars in the process.

IF YOU ARE IN AN AUTO ACCIDENT

If you are in an auto accident, contact the police immediately if any of the following apply:

- Someone has sustained an injury
- You think the other driver may be guilty of a Criminal Code offence, such as drunk driving
- There is significant property damage

If it is safe to move your car, try to move it out of traffic. If you are unable to move your vehicle, use your hazard lights and any other warning devices you may have, such as flares. Exhibit 8.5 provides a checklist of information that you want to gather before you leave the scene of the accident. Note the date, time, and location of the accident. In many cases, road conditions and the time of day can have an impact on the determination of fault. Request information from the other drivers in the accident, including their names, licence numbers, home addresses, phone numbers, insurance information, the make and model of the vehicles they were driving, and the plate numbers of those vehicles. Record the damage that you see to the other vehicles. You should also sketch the accident scene, including the position and direction of all vehicles involved in the accident. You should keep some paper and a pen or pencil in your glove compartment for such occasions. Try to determine if there were any passengers in the other vehicles. Take pictures of any evidence that may prove you were not at fault. While they are fresh in your mind, write down the details of how the accident happened, including your estimate of the speed of all cars and road and weather conditions. You may also obtain contact information (including licence plate numbers) from witnesses, in case they leave before the police arrive. Make sure that you can validate whatever information other drivers provide. Some drivers who believe that they are at fault and are without insurance may attempt to give you false names and leave before police arrive. Finally, make sure you ask for a copy of the police report once the accident is reported.

> **myth** or **fact** If you have home insurance, valuables such as jewellery, furs, and electronics will be covered if stolen from your home.

File a claim with your insurance company immediately. It will review the police report and may contact witnesses. It will also verify that your insurance policy is still

---

EXHIBIT 8.5   Information Checklist

- Date, Time, and Location of Accident
- Driver's Name
- Driver's Licence Number
- Home Address
- Phone Number (home, cell, business)
- Insurance Information (company, policy no., expiry)
- Make and Model of Vehicle
- Plate Number (province where issued)
- Is There Damage to Other Vehicle? (provide details)
- How Many Passengers Were in Other Vehicle?
- Description of What Happened
- Were There Any Independent Witnesses?
- Is There a Police Report? (If so, get a copy.)

in effect and determine whether repairs and medical treatment will be covered based on your policy's provisions. The insurance policy may specify guidelines for having your car repaired, such as obtaining at least two estimates before you have repairs done. A claims adjuster employed by the insurance company may investigate the accident details and attempt to determine how much you should be paid.

Once you incur expenses, such as car repairs or medical expenses, send this information along with receipts to the insurance company. It will respond by reimbursing you for a portion of the expenses based on your policy. It may provide full or partial reimbursement. Alternatively, it may state that some or all of your expenses are not covered by your policy. Keep copies of all correspondence and receipts sent to your insurance company.

If your insurance company believes that the other driver is at fault, it should seek damages from the other driver's insurance company. If the other driver is not insured, your insurance company will pay your claim up to the per person accident benefits limit shown in Exhibit 8.3. For any amounts above this, you will receive benefits for bodily injury and economic loss from the Motor Vehicle Accident Claims Fund in your province. As mentioned earlier, if you purchased the family protection coverage provision, you may be entitled to additional benefits for bodily injury and economic loss above and beyond the limits of the provincial fund. If your claim is denied by your insurance company and you still believe that the other driver is at fault, you may need to file a claim against the other driver or the other driver's insurance company. This is also the case when an injured party seeks damages greater than those offered by his or her policy. You must pay your deductible while you await the results of your claim against the other driver. If your claim is successful, you can request that your deductible be refunded by the other driver's insurance company.

HOMEOWNER'S INSURANCE

L.O.3

homeowner's insurance
Provides insurance in the event of property damage, theft, or personal and third party liability relating to home ownership.

Homeowner's insurance provides insurance in the event of property damage, theft, or personal and third party liability relating to home ownership. It not only protects many individuals' most valuable asset, but also limits their potential liabilities (expenses) associated with the home. Premiums on homeowner's insurance are commonly paid either monthly or yearly.

Types of Perils Covered by Homeowner's Insurance

As discussed earlier, risk can be defined as exposure to events (or perils) that can cause a financial loss. Financial loss due to the ownership of a home could occur as a result of a wide variety of adverse events, such as flood, theft, burglary, fire, earthquake, or tornado. Homeowner's insurance can be structured to cover a few or all of these and similar perils. **All perils coverage** protects the home and any other structures on the property against all events except those that are specifically excluded by the policy. **Named perils coverage** protects the home and any other structures on the property against only those events named in the policy. To reduce premiums, a homeowner can apply coverage differently to the home and to the contents of the home.

all perils coverage
Protects the home and any other structures on the property against all events except those that are specifically excluded by the policy.

named perils coverage
Protects the home and any other structures on the property against only those events named in the policy.

HOMEOWNER'S INSURANCE POLICY PROVISIONS

A homeowner's insurance policy typically provides coverage for the building, its contents, and the liability of the homeowner. As shown in Exhibit 8.6, the specific details regarding coverage vary among policies. Comprehensive coverage provides full coverage for all causes of financial loss. At the other end, basic coverage only covers losses for named perils. Although the premium for a basic policy will be lower than for a comprehensive policy, the potential to lose your home to an uncovered peril should not be ignored. Broad coverage will allow the homeowner to save on the cost of homeowner's insurance

EXHIBIT 8.6 Types of Perils Protected by Various Types of Homeowner's Insurance Policies

	Level of Coverage	
Policy Type	Building	Contents
Comprehensive Coverage	all perils	all perils
Basic Coverage	named perils	named perils
Broad Coverage	all perils	named perils

while maintaining full coverage for all causes of financial loss related to the house. Most homeowner's insurance policies focus on the following types of coverage.

Building (Property Damage)

The homeowner's policy covers damage to the home. The specific provisions of the policy explain the degree of coverage. A standard homeowner's insurance policy provides coverage based on the actual cash value of the building and its contents. An **actual cash value policy** pays you the value of the damaged property after considering its depreciation (wear and tear). A **replacement cost policy** pays you the cost of replacing the damaged property with an item of a similar brand and quality. A replacement cost policy is preferable because the cost of replacing damaged property is normally higher than the depreciated or assessed value of property. For example, assume that a home is completely destroyed and was valued at $400 000 just before that happened. An actual cash value policy would provide insurance coverage of $400 000, even though the cost of rebuilding (replacing) the home could be $440 000 or more. In contrast, the replacement cost policy would insure the home for its replacement cost, and therefore would cover the entire cost of repairing the damage up to a limit specified in the homeowner's policy. In most cases, the replacement cost value provision should be added to the standard homeowner's insurance policy. A homeowner's policy typically specifies a deductible, or an amount that you must pay for damage before the insurance coverage is applied.

actual cash value policy
Pays you the value of the damaged property after considering its depreciation.

replacement cost policy
Pays you the cost of replacing the damaged property with an item of a similar brand and quality.

▌ **myth** or **fact** You do not need insurance if you do not own a home. ▌

Minimum Limit. Many insurers require that your homeowner's insurance policy cover at least 80 percent of the full replacement cost. The financial institution that provides your mortgage loan likely will require homeowner's insurance that would cover at least your mortgage. In most cases, you want more insurance than is required by the mortgage lender. You should have sufficient insurance not only to cover the mortgage loan balance, but also to replace the property and all personal assets that are damaged.

EXAMPLE

Haim owns a house with a current replacement cost of $375 000. When he purchased the home 10 years ago, it was valued at $210 000 and he had purchased a homeowner's insurance policy for $210 000 at that time. He has not updated his coverage amount since. A fire that began in the second floor laundry room of his house resulted in $150 000 worth of damage. Although he owns a replacement cost policy, Haim is not fully covered for the damage to his house since he did not maintain the 80% minimum coverage amount. Haim should have maintained coverage of $300 000, calculated as $375 000 × 80%, but he only has coverage of $210 000, which represents 70% of the required amount. As a result, the insurance company will only pay for damages in proportion to the amount of insurance Haim has, relative to what he should have had. In this instance, the insurance company will cover 70% of the damages, or $105 000, calculated as $150 000 × 70%. Haim will have to pay the remaining $45 000 out of his own pocket.

Other Structures on Property

The homeowner's insurance policy also specifies whether separate structures such as a garage, shed, or swimming pool are covered and the maximum amount of coverage for these structures. Trees and shrubs are usually included, with a specified maximum amount of coverage. A deductible may be applied to these other structures.

Contents (Personal Property)

A policy normally covers personal assets such as furniture, computers, or clothing up to a specified maximum amount. For example, a policy may specify that all personal assets such as furniture and clothing are covered up to $40 000. Standard homeowner's insurance policies limit the coverage of personal property to no more than half of the coverage on the dwelling. A deductible may be applied to the personal property.

home inventory
Contains detailed information about your personal property that can be used when filing a claim.

A **home inventory** contains detailed information about your personal property that can be used when filing a claim. Create a list of all of your personal assets and estimate the market value of each item. Use a video camera to film your personal assets in your home for proof of their existence. Keep the list and the video in a safe place outside of your home, so that you have access to them if your home is destroyed.

Policy Limits and Exclusions

The policy you purchase is not open ended, meaning that the insurance company will reimburse you only up to a certain maximum amount as stated in the policy. Exclusions are things or perils that are not specifically covered by the policy.

Personal Property Replacement Cost Coverage. As mentioned earlier, many homeowner's insurance policies cover personal property for their actual cash value. Just as the dwelling can be insured at replacement cost rather than cash value, so can personal assets. This provision will increase your premium slightly, but it may be worthwhile if you have personal assets that have high replacement costs.

personal property floater
An extension of the homeowner's insurance policy that allows you to itemize your valuables.

Personal Property Floater. Some personal assets are very valuable and are not fully covered by your homeowner's policy. You may need to obtain a **personal property floater** (also called supplementary insurance), which is an extension of the homeowner's insurance policy that allows you to itemize your valuables. For example, if you have very expensive computer equipment or jewellery in your home, you may purchase this additional insurance to protect those specific assets. An alternative to the scheduled personal property floater described above is an unscheduled personal property floater, which provides blanket protection for all of your personal property without having you itemize your valuables.

Home Office Provision. Assets in a home office, such as a personal computer, are not covered in many standard homeowner's policies. You can request a home office provision, which will require a higher premium. Alternatively, you could purchase a separate policy to cover the home office.

Liability

A homeowner's policy specifies coverage in the event that you are sued as the result of something that occurs in your home or on your property. Normally, you are responsible for an injury to another person while they are on your property. For example, if a neighbour falls down the steps of your home and sues you, your policy would likely cover you. In most cases, liability coverage purchased through your homeowner's insurance policy also extends to events that occur away from your home. For example, if you are skiing at Mont Tremblant and you run over someone on the slopes and cause injury, your homeowner's insurance liability coverage will protect you.

Your exposure to liability is not tied to the value of your home. Even if you have a small home of modest value, you need to protect against liability. Some insurance companies provide minimum coverage of $100 000 against liability. However, a higher level of coverage, such as $300 000, is commonly recommended. If you have uncommon risks, such as certain breeds of dogs or a pool, you may want to consider a much higher liability amount. Coverage includes court costs and any awards granted as a result of lawsuits against you due to injuries on your property.

Medical payments and voluntary property damage are also covered under the liability portion of homeowner's insurance. The medical payments provision covers the costs of medical care if someone is accidentally injured on your property. The voluntary damage provision provides coverage to you in the event that you accidentally damage the property of others (for example, if your child inadvertently throws a ball through your neighbour's window while playing catch). This event would be covered under the voluntary property damage provision of your liability coverage. Medical payments and voluntary property damage are designed to cover costs that are incurred before a lawsuit occurs.

Other Types of Expenses

Many other possible provisions could be included in a policy to cover a wide variety of circumstances. For example, if an event such as a fire forces you to live away from home, you will incur additional living expenses. A loss-of-use provision specifies whether your policy covers these expenses and the maximum amount of coverage.

Expenses Incurred by Homeowner's Insurance Companies

The allocation of expenses incurred by homeowner's insurance companies is shown in Exhibit 8.7. Overall, claims paid represent 62 percent of total expenses. The cost of settling claims represents 11 percent of total expenses.

EXHIBIT 8.7   Expense Allocation for Homeowner's Insurance Companies

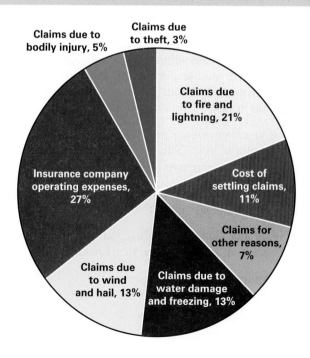

HOMEOWNER'S INSURANCE PREMIUMS

The annual cost of insuring a home can be substantial over time. This section describes the factors that influence the premium charged and explains how you can reduce your premium. Your homeowner's insurance premium is influenced by the likelihood that you will submit claims to the insurance company and by the cost to the insurance company of covering those claims.

Factors That Affect Homeowner's Insurance Premiums

The premium you pay for homeowner's insurance primarily depends on the following factors.

- **Value of Insured Home.** Insurance premiums reflect the value of the insured home and therefore are higher for more expensive homes.
- **Deductible.** A higher deductible reduces the amount of coverage provided by the homeowner's insurance and therefore results in a lower insurance premium.
- **Location.** The potential for damage is greater in some areas, and therefore the premiums are higher. For example, homes in Atlantic Canada are more likely to be damaged by severe weather than homes in Saskatchewan. Home insurance rates are therefore much higher along the coast. Similarly, premiums will be higher for homes in locations prone to tornadoes, floods, or earthquakes.
- **Degree of Protection.** If you want protection against an earthquake on a home in Vancouver, you must pay a higher premium. If you want protection against a flood, you may need to buy an additional insurance policy.
- **Discounts.** You may obtain discounts on your insurance by maintaining an alarm system or a household fire extinguisher in your home, paying for your insurance in one lump sum, or purchasing multiple types of insurance (such as auto, health, and life) from the same insurer.

Reducing Your Homeowner's Insurance Premium

Consider the following actions you can take to reduce your homeowner's insurance premium.

Increase Your Deductible. If you are willing to pay a higher deductible, you can reduce your premium. For example, if you use a deductible of $1000 instead of $100, you may be able to reduce your premium by about 20 percent or more. Keep in mind that you must have access to $1000 in cash in the event of a claim.

Improve Protection. If you improve the protection of your home, your insurance premium will decline. For example, you could install storm shutters to protect against bad weather or a monitored security system to protect against robbery.

Use One Insurer for All Types of Insurance. Some insurance companies offer lower premiums to customers who purchase more than one type of insurance from them.

Stay with the Same Insurance Company. When you stay with the same insurance company, you may be rewarded with a lower insurance premium in future years.

Shop Around. As with auto insurance, you may be able to reduce your premium by obtaining quotations from various insurance companies. Premiums can vary substantially among insurers. Remember to compare policies and coverage, not just premiums.

Go to
www.kanetix.ca/home-insurance

This website provides answers to many important questions concerning homeowner's insurance.

FREE APPS for Personal Finance

Documenting Home Inventory

Application:

The SureSafe app allows you to document the inventory of your home or apartment by taking photos of the inventory with your phone and storing the photos.

FILING A CLAIM

If your property is damaged, you should contact your insurance company immediately. A claims adjuster will come to your home to estimate the damage. Present your home inventory to the adjuster. The adjuster's estimate will include the cost of repairing the damage done to your home and compensation for damaged property. The insurance company may be willing to issue a cheque so that you can hire someone to make repairs. You should consider obtaining an independent estimate of the repairs to ensure that the amount the insurance company offers you is sufficient. If the insurance company's estimate is too low, you can appeal it.

TENANT'S INSURANCE

Tenant's insurance protects your possessions within a house, condominium, or apartment that you are renting. It does not insure the structure itself because the insurance is for the tenant only, not for the owner of the property. It covers personal assets such as furniture, a television, computer equipment, and stereo equipment. The insurance protects against damage due to weather or the loss of personal assets due to burglary. It can cover living expenses while the rental property is being repaired. It also covers liability in the event that a friend or neighbour is injured while on the rental property.

Tenants whose personal assets have a high market value need tenant's insurance to protect those assets. Even tenants without valuable personal assets may desire tenant's insurance to protect against liability.

tenant's insurance
An insurance policy that protects your possessions within a house, condominium, or apartment that you are renting.

Tenant's Insurance Policy Provisions

Tenant's insurance specifies the maximum amount of coverage for your personal assets. It may also specify maximum coverage for specific items such as jewellery. The premium depends on the amount of coverage you desire. Your tenant's insurance may also cover liability resulting from injury to a person while on your premises. For example, if your pet injures a neighbour in your yard, your tenant's insurance may cover your liability up to a limit. Because tenant's insurance policies vary, you should closely review any policy to ensure that the insurance coverage is appropriate for you.

UMBRELLA PERSONAL LIABILITY POLICY

You can supplement your auto and homeowner's insurance with an **umbrella personal liability policy**, which provides additional personal liability coverage. This type of policy is intended to provide additional insurance, not to replace those other policies. In fact, the insurance will not be provided unless you show proof of existing coverage. Umbrella policies are especially useful when you have personal assets beyond a car and home that you wish to protect from liability. You may be able to purchase an umbrella policy for about $200 per year for coverage of $1 million.

umbrella personal liability policy
A supplement to auto and homeowner's insurance that provides additional personal liability coverage.

MyLab Finance Visit MyLab Finance for additional study and practice tools. Select Financial Planning Problems are available in the Study Plan. Create your own study plan, generate personal cash flow statements and balance sheets, and set personal financial goals.

SUMMARY

L.O.1 Explain the role of risk management

Your risk management decisions determine whether and how to protect against risk. Your alternatives are to avoid, reduce, accept, or share risk. Some types of risk are difficult to avoid and dangerous to accept. For these types of risk, insurance is needed. Once you decide whether to obtain a particular type of insurance, you must decide on the amount of coverage and on where to purchase the insurance.

L.O.2 Outline typical provisions of auto insurance

Automobile insurance insures against the legal liability that may arise if your property (car) causes death or injury to others, as well as the expense associated with

providing medical care to you, your passengers, and pedestrians, and the costs associated with damage to your automobile. The premium paid for auto insurance depends on how you use the vehicle, the vehicle's value and repair record, where you live, your driving record, your age and sex, and the features of the policy you choose, including the insurance deductible.

L.O.3 Describe financial coverage provided by homeowner's insurance

Homeowner's insurance provides insurance in the event of property damage or personal liability. The premium paid for homeowner's insurance depends on the home's value, the deductible, and the likelihood of damage to the home.

REVIEW QUESTIONS

1. What is the purpose of property, health, disability, critical illness, long-term care, and life insurance? What is meant by the term *liability*?

2. What is the primary function of insurance? How can individuals benefit from insurance?

3. What is risk management? Describe the four risk management alternatives.

4. Explain the psychology behind accepting risk.

5. Describe the costs and benefits of obtaining insurance.

6. What is the responsibility of the insurance company that sells you a policy? How do insurance companies determine their profits?

7. What is the relationship between insurance company claims and premiums paid by policy owners?

8. What is the role of insurance underwriters?

9. How do insurance company credit ratings and service levels help you to find the right insurance company?

10. What is the role of insurance agents? Define the two different types of insurance agents.

11. What does auto insurance insure against?

12. In which provinces is auto insurance provided by a government agency?

13. Define and describe an auto insurance policy.

14. What is third party liability? Define and describe the two components of third party liability coverage.

15. Explain why it is important to have adequate bodily injury liability coverage.

16. Define and describe accident benefits coverage. What is uninsured motorist coverage? How does it work?

17. Define and describe collision insurance and comprehensive coverage. Is this type of coverage required by most provinces? Who may require this type of coverage?

18. What is a deductible?

19. What is the purpose of Facility Association? Is it available in all provinces? Why or why not?

20. What is no-fault auto insurance? What is the rationale for no-fault auto insurance?

21. What is the difference between a no-fault system and a pure no-fault system?

22. Describe four other options, or endorsements, that can be added to an auto insurance policy.

23. List and briefly discuss factors that will affect your auto insurance premium. Which factors may not apply in provinces where auto insurance is provided by a provincial government agency?

24. What factors should you compare when you are shopping among insurance companies to purchase auto insurance?

25. If you are in an auto accident, under what circumstances should you contact the police immediately? What information should you gather before you leave the site of an accident?

26. When should you file a claim with your insurance company? Describe what happens after you file a claim with your insurance company.

27. What is homeowner's insurance? How are the premiums normally paid?

28. What is the difference between all perils coverage and named perils coverage?

29. Differentiate among comprehensive, basic, and broad coverage policy types.

30. What is the difference between an actual cash value homeowner's policy and a replacement cost homeowner's policy?

31. Is personal property typically insured under a homeowner's insurance policy? If so, are there limits to the coverage of personal property? What is a home inventory?

32. What is a personal property floater? What is the difference between scheduled and unscheduled floaters?

33. How does homeowner's liability coverage work? What does the medical payments provision cover? What does the voluntary property damage provision cover?

34. List and briefly describe some of the factors that affect homeowner's insurance premiums.

35. What are some steps you could take to reduce your homeowner's insurance premium?

36. Describe the steps you would take to file a claim on your homeowner's insurance.

37. How is tenant's insurance different from homeowner's insurance? Who should consider purchasing tenant's insurance? Briefly describe some of the provisions of a tenant's insurance policy.

38. What is the purpose of an umbrella personal liability policy? Who might need one?

 ETHICAL DILEMMA

You teach Personal Finance at a local community college. The province in which you teach requires proof of auto insurance to renew your licence plates.

During the discussion of this topic in class, several students admit that they obtain auto insurance policies just prior to the renewal of their licence plates and then cancel them immediately thereafter. They do this because they know that the province has no system for following up on the cancellation of the auto insurance policies once the licence plates are issued.

These students, who are out of work as a result of a local plant shutdown, indicate that they cannot afford to maintain their insurance but must have access to cars for transportation.

a. Discuss whether you consider the conduct of the students to be unethical.

b. How does the conduct of these students potentially affect other members of the class who maintain auto insurance on their vehicles?

 FINANCIAL PLANNING ONLINE EXERCISES

1. Go to www.kanetix.ca/auto-insurance.

a. Enter your postal code, click on Go, and then enter the requested information. Click on Next Step and enter the requested vehicle details. Click on Next Step and select "No" for discounts. Click on Get Quotes. The screen will display quotes for coverage from various auto insurance companies.

b. On the right side of the quote page, select a $500 deductible for both comprehensive and collision coverage. What is loss of use? What is legal liability for damage to non-owned automobiles? How much liability coverage can you purchase? What is comprehensive coverage limited glass? What is limited waiver of depreciation?

c. Click on the Features button for each insurance company. Do any of the insurance companies offer any discounts? If so, what types of discounts do they offer? What are the credit ratings for the various insurance companies? Which company has the highest credit rating?

PSYCHOLOGY OF PERSONAL FINANCE: Your Auto Insurance

1. Consumers commonly focus on the price when buying auto insurance. They feel less pain from buying auto insurance by paying as little as possible. However, this strategy can backfire, because the insurance they receive may reflect the low price they paid. Describe your own behaviour when purchasing auto insurance. Do you request specific insurance coverage or pursue the cheapest policy possible?

2. Read one practical article of how psychology affects decisions when buying auto insurance. You can easily retrieve possible articles by doing an online search using the terms "psychology" and "buying auto insurance." Summarize the main points of the article.

MINI-CASE 1: Auto Insurance

Nikita Stewart recently graduated from college with a degree in forestry management. She has a promising career ahead of her. Already her employer has offered to pay for graduate school, and in the past two years she has been promoted three times. Two years ago she purchased a townhouse for $130 000; today her townhouse is valued at more than $160 000. Last year, Nikita purchased a new Toyota Rav4. She loves the feeling of quality that she associates with the vehicle. She also loves the creature comforts offered by such a reasonably priced vehicle when she makes her 45-kilometre round trip commute. Overall, Nikita feels economically secure. When she last checked, she had more than $35 000 in savings and a growing retirement plan. On her drive home from work last night she heard a report on the radio of a person who lost everything when he caused an auto collision and found out that he was underinsured. Nikita certainly does not want this to happen to her. Help her think through the following questions and issues. After reviewing her personal automobile policy Nikita noted that she had $200 000 in third party liability coverage, $50 000 in accident benefits, and collision and comprehensive coverage. Is Nikita adequately insured?

Explain your answer. What would you recommend as a minimum amount of coverage for third party liability coverage? Should Nikita maintain her section C coverage? When should she consider reducing or cancelling this part of her policy?

MINI-CASE 2: Homeowner's Insurance

Grant and Brenda Unger are planning to buy a $385 000 home. The home is located three kilometres from a river that occasionally overflows its banks after a heavy rain. They estimate that their personal property is worth $75 000 but they really are not sure. This includes the office and computer equipment that Brenda uses as a freelance writer and a $5000 coin collection inherited from Grant's father. The Ungers' net worth, including their current $220 000 home, is $500 000. The Ungers asked their insurance agent to find them the best coverage possible, taking advantage of all possible cost-savings measures. They do not want a lot of out-of-pocket expenses if their home or personal property is destroyed and they want insurance to keep pace with increasing building costs. What type of homeowner's insurance policy is best for the Ungers? Explain. Should the Ungers buy flood insurance? How do they go about purchasing it? Should the couple buy an umbrella personal liability policy? Explain.

Study Guide

Circle the correct answer and then check the answers in the back of the book to chart your progress.

Multiple Choice

1. Critical illness insurance can ensure that you have access to ___ in the event that you suffer a critical illness, such as a heart attack, stroke, or life-threatening cancer.
   a. a cure
   b. monthly income
   c. lump-sum benefits
   d. in-home nursing care

2. The alternatives available to you if you decide to protect against risk include all of the following, except:
   a. Avoiding risk.
   b. Reducing risk.
   c. Sharing risk.
   d. Accepting risk.

3. Getting the flu vaccine is an example of:
   a. Avoiding risk.
   b. Reducing risk.
   c. Accepting risk.
   d. Transferring risk.

4. Consider a policy owner who pays $1000 in auto insurance premiums for the year. Assume that he is in an accident and the insurance company has to pay $25 000 to cover liability and repair the car. The insurance company expects to pay a total of $500 000 in claims for the year with respect to the group of policy owners of which this individual is a member. Business expenses for the year are $50 000. Investment earnings on premiums received are $25 000. How many insurance policies must the insurance company sell to break even (that is, to earn $0 in profit)? Assume that all policies are sold for a $1000 premium.
   a. 500
   b. 525
   c. 550
   d. 575

5. Insurance agents who work for one particular company are called:
   a. Company agents.
   b. Captive agents.
   c. Independent agents.
   d. Insurance brokers.

6. Generally, auto insurance policies contain the following three sections:
   a. Third party liability coverage, accident benefits, and loss or damage to insured automobile.
   b. Third party liability coverage, accident and sickness benefits, and loss or damage to insured automobile.
   c. Third party liability coverage, accident benefits, and loss or damage to insured/uninsured automobile.
   d. Third party liability coverage, accident and sickness benefits, and loss or damage to insured/uninsured automobile.

7. Which of the following is not normally included as a covered expense in the accident benefits section of an auto insurance policy?
   a. Funeral benefits
   b. Loss of income as a result of total disability
   c. Uninsured motorist coverage
   d. Liability arising from injuries you have caused

8. No-fault accident benefits allow policy owners in all provinces to receive immediate medical payments through:
   a. The insurance policy of the at-fault driver.
   b. Their own insurance policy.
   c. Their provincial government plan.
   d. The federal government auto insurance reserve fund program.

9. Facility Association ensures that drivers unable to obtain insurance with an individual company are able to obtain the coverage they need to operate their vehicles legally. In which of the following provinces would this coverage be valuable?
   a. Manitoba
   b. Ontario
   c. British Columbia
   d. Quebec

10. Which of the following will reduce your insurance rate?
    a. Decreasing your deductible.
    b. Paying all speeding tickets promptly.
    c. Driving antique classic cars.
    d. Increasing your deductible.

11. You are in an accident which causes $3000 in damages to your car, and your policy has a $500 deductible for collision and $300 for comprehensive. If the other driver is at fault, which is correct?
    a. You pay $500 deductible and claim it from the other driver's insurance company.
    b. You pay $300 deductible and claim it from the other driver's insurance company.

c. Your insurance company covers the deductible.

d. You have to pay the deductible and can claim it back if you have an umbrella policy.

12. Which of the following factors that affect your auto insurance premiums is not considered in provinces in which auto insurance is offered through a government agency?

a. Your age

b. The repair record of your car

c. Your location

d. Your driving record

13. You have actual cash value coverage for your personal property on your homeowner's policy. Your camera cost $300 eight years ago and had a life expectancy of 10 years. The camera was stolen, and a new one will cost $100. How much will the insurance company pay?

a. $60

b. $100

c. $200

d. $300

14. With respect to a homeowner's insurance policy, a personal property floater would be useful if you wish to insure which of the following assets?

a. Your personal clothing

b. Furniture

c. Jewellery that you keep in your home

d. All of the above

15. Which of the following actions would not be considered an effective method to help you reduce your homeowner's insurance premium?

a. Increase your deductible.

b. Install storm shutters.

c. Purchase all of your insurance from one company.

d. Purchase a larger fire extinguisher than the one you currently have.

True/False

1. True or False? The primary function of insurance is to maintain your existing level of wealth by protecting you against potential financial losses or liability as a result of unexpected events.

2. True or False? Assuming that you have enough money, you should be able to insure against all types of risks.

3. True or False? Many people do not feel much satisfaction from buying insurance, so they decide to share the risk of something happening to them.

4. True or False? A high insurance premium may indicate that there is a greater probability you may use the insurance coverage provided.

5. True or False? An increase in investment earnings will decrease the premium that an insurance company requires from its policy owners.

6. True or False? Insurance brokers work for one particular insurance company.

7. True or False? Third party liability protects you against liability associated with injuries that you cause and losses that result when you damage another person's property.

8. True or False? Accident benefits are mandatory in all provinces.

9. True or False? Collision coverage is especially valuable because it provides coverage not only for the car, but also for items that were damaged in the car during the accident.

10. True or False? Under a no-fault system, you are unable to sue the at-fault driver for pain and suffering and economic loss.

11. True or False? Personal characteristics, such as your age, are considered in all provinces when determining auto insurance rates.

12. True or False? If the other driver is not insured, you will only be entitled to receive benefits for bodily injury and economic loss up to the limit of your policy.

13. True or False? All perils coverage protects the home and any other structures on the property against all events except those that are specifically excluded by the homeowner's policy.

14. True or False? When purchasing a homeowner's insurance policy, you should consider an actual cash value policy because the actual cash value of replacing damaged property is normally higher than the assessed value of property.

15. True or False? Tenant's insurance covers personal assets such as furniture, a television, computer equipment, and stereo equipment. It does not insure the structure itself.

Health and Life Insurance

emilie zhang/Shutterstock

Greg couldn't wait to embark on his new career. As the former Director of Technology Development for a major technology firm, Greg felt that he had the right skill set to become a self-employed consultant to the industry. Before starting out on his own, Greg decided to consult his insurance broker to see what type of coverage, if any, he would need now that he was planning on being self-employed.

Through work Greg had a comprehensive group insurance benefits package, which included dental care, vision care, prescription drugs, and life and disability insurance. Greg wanted to find out which of these benefits he could keep. He also thought it would be a good opportunity to check to see if he had sufficient coverage since he was married and had three children.

QUESTIONS:

1. Will Greg be able to keep his group benefits when he leaves his employer? If not, what should Greg do before he decides to become a self-employed consultant?
2. Greg lives in Canada and, as a result, has universal health care benefits. What is covered under Canada's health care system? Is this adequate to cover the needs of Greg and his family?
3. What information does Greg's insurance broker need to have in order to determine Greg's life insurance needs? Does Greg need disability insurance? Explain.

L.0.1

BACKGROUND ON HEALTH AND LIFE INSURANCE

health insurance
A group of insurance benefits provided to a living individual as a result of sickness or injury.

life insurance
Insurance that provides a payment to a specified beneficiary when the insured dies.

face amount
The amount stated on the face of the policy that will be paid on the death of the insured.

beneficiary
A person specified in a will to receive part of an estate (also known as an heir); also, the named individual who receives life insurance payments upon the death of the insured.

life insured
The individual who is covered in the life insurance policy.

policy owner
The individual who owns all rights and obligations to the policy.

Health insurance refers to a group of insurance benefits provided to a living individual as a result of sickness or injury. Health insurance is unique because the benefit is payable to the insured or to a health care professional who is working with the insured. Health insurance includes medicare, private health care, disability, critical illness, and long-term care insurance. In contrast, **life insurance** provides a payment to a specified beneficiary when the insured dies. The payment is usually referred to as the **face amount**, which is the amount stated on the face of the policy that will be paid on the death of the insured. The **beneficiary** is the named individual who receives life insurance payments upon the death of the insured. The amount received by the beneficiary is not usually taxed. The **life insured** is the individual who is covered in the life insurance policy. Life insurance contracts represent an agreement between a life and health insurance company and the **policy owner**, the individual who owns all rights and obligations to the policy. Although there can be situations in which the policy owner and the life insured are two different parties, we will assume throughout this chapter that they are the same person. Without health and life insurance, the high expenses of returning to good health and/or the significant loss of income as a result of sickness, injury, or death could quickly eliminate most of your wealth. Health and life insurance are critical components of your financial planning.

Recall from Chapter 8 that the primary function of insurance is to maintain your existing level of wealth by protecting you against potential financial losses or liability as a result of unexpected events. It can ensure that your income continues if an accident or illness prevents you from working, or it can prevent others from taking away your personal assets. Insurance is important because your personal financial assets are needed to meet your financial goals.

Health insurance provides coverage for the financial goals you have set for yourself. For example, private health care may provide you with chiropractic services that help you to maintain your quality of life so that you are able to work toward your financial goals. The most common financial goal related to life insurance is to maintain financial support for your dependants. For example, life insurance provides the family with financial support to cover burial expenses or medical expenses not covered by health insurance. In addition, it can maintain the family's future lifestyle even without the breadwinner's income.

As time passes, rethink your health and life insurance decisions. Even if you decide not to purchase health insurance now because you have group insurance benefits at work, you may require it in the future since most group benefits are not transferable to you if you leave your employer. If you already have a life insurance policy, you may need to increase the coverage or add a beneficiary at a future point in time.

| **myth** or **fact**   Medicare provides access to all needed services to every Canadian.

As of 2016, there were 156 life and health insurance companies operating in Canada. More than 22 million Canadians owned life insurance, and the total amount of coverage was more than $4.3 trillion. In addition, health insurance plans provided 12 million people with disability insurance, 24 million people with extended health care, and 21 million people with accidental death and dismemberment, long-term care, and critical illness coverage. There were 148 600 Canadians working in the life and health insurance industry in Canada, and Canadians received $84.2 billion in payments from life and health insurance companies in 2015. This chapter will first look at the types of health insurance coverage, such as medicare, private health care, disability, critical illness, and long-term care insurance that are available. A discussion of the major types of life insurance will follow.

CANADA'S HEALTH CARE SYSTEM

Canada's health care system, known as medicare, is not a single national health insurance plan. Instead, the system is designed such that the federal, provincial, and territorial governments assume roles and responsibilities that ensure a standard of coverage that is consistent across the country. As such, **medicare** is an interlocking system of 10 provincial and 3 territorial health insurance plans provided by the governments, including the federal government. In Canada, our health care system is predominantly publicly financed. Public sector funding represents about 70 percent of total health care expenditures. The remaining 30 percent is financed privately through private health care plans, such as supplementary insurance and employer-sponsored benefits, or directly out-of-pocket. Health insurance has received much attention in recent years because it has become so expensive. The need for health care is greater for individuals who are older, and the average age of the population has increased in recent years. Since older individuals require more health care, the cost of providing it is rising. People are living longer, partly due to effective health care, and therefore require medical attention for a longer period of time.

Role of the Federal Government

With respect to the delivery of health care, the fundamental role of the federal government is to ensure that universal coverage for medically necessary services is provided to eligible residents on the basis of individual need, rather than on the ability of the individual to pay.

The *Canada Health Act* is Canada's federal health insurance legislation. It establishes the criteria and conditions related to insured health care services that provinces and territories must meet to receive money from the federal government for health care. **Insured health care services** are medically necessary hospital, physician, and surgical-dental services provided to insured persons. An **insured person** is an eligible resident of a province, but this does not include someone who may be covered by other federal or provincial legislation.

Principles of the *Canada Health Act*. The provinces and territories must meet five principles to qualify for the full **Canada Health Transfer (CHT)**. The CHT is the largest federal transfer of money to the provinces and territories and provides them with cash payments on an equal per capita basis in support of health care. Provinces and territories that violate the five principles of the *Canada Health Act* may be subject to a reduction in the amount of CHT they receive. The five principles are:

Public Administration. Plans must be administered and operated on a non-profit basis by a public authority accountable to the provincial or territorial government.

Comprehensiveness. Plans must insure all medically necessary services provided by hospitals, medical practitioners, and dentists working within a hospital setting.

L.O.2

medicare
An interlocking system of 10 provincial and 3 territorial health insurance plans provided by the governments, including the federal government.

Canada Health Act
Establishes the criteria and conditions related to insured health care services that provinces and territories must meet to receive money from the federal government for health care.

insured health care services
Medically necessary hospital, physician, and surgical-dental services provided to insured persons.

insured person
An eligible resident of a province.

Canada Health Transfer (CHT)
The largest federal transfer of money to the provinces and territories, providing them with cash payments and tax transfers in support of health care.

Universality. Plans must entitle all insured persons to health insurance coverage on uniform terms and conditions.

Portability. In order to give insured persons time to get health insurance within their new province of residence, existing plans must cover all insured persons for three months when they move to another province or territory within Canada. Insured persons are covered when they travel abroad. However, the provinces and territories have some limits on coverage for services provided outside Canada and may require prior approval for non-emergency services delivered outside their jurisdiction.

Accessibility. Plans must provide all insured persons with reasonable access to medically necessary hospital and physician services without financial or other barriers.

Role of the Provincial and Territorial Governments

Although the federal government sets and administers national standards for the national health care system through the *Canada Health Act*, the provincial and territorial governments are constitutionally responsible for the administration and delivery of insured health care services. That is, they decide where their hospitals will be located, how many physicians they will need, and how much money they will spend on their health care systems.

However, insured health care services provided by the *Canada Health Act* cover only basic medical needs, such as a trip to your doctor or in-patient/outpatient hospital care. As a result, most provincial and territorial governments offer and fund supplementary benefits for certain groups (for example, seniors, children, and social assistance recipients). These supplementary benefits include coverage for drugs prescribed outside hospitals, ambulance costs, hearing aids, vision care, medical equipment and appliances (prostheses, wheelchairs), home care and nursing, and the services of other health professionals, such as podiatrists and chiropractors. To view a summary of the main types of benefits provided by each province, go to www.canada-health-insurance.com/governmentcoverage.html. It is important to emphasize that the level of coverage for these supplementary benefits varies across the country. Medical expenses that are not covered by the provincial plan either must be paid in full by the individual or can be partially paid by a supplemental health insurance plan. This is the main reason why supplemental health insurance is necessary: to cover the health care needs that provincial and territorial plans do not.

Health care is a significant expense for the provinces and territories. For example, in Alberta, health care spending is estimated to be 40% of the provincial government's operational spending in 2016/17. Many people feel that the rising cost of health care will be the greatest challenge facing Canadians in the next 50 years.

Role of Private Health Insurance

Private health insurance companies provide additional medical coverage through either group or individual supplemental health insurance plans. If you are not part of a group plan with your work or if the company you work for does not offer sufficient coverage, you should consider an individual plan. It may be wise to purchase private health insurance if the coverage offered through the *Canada Health Act* and the supplemental coverage offered through your province or territory is not sufficient.

Group Health Insurance. Because employees are the most essential part of any business, many business owners offer group health insurance to their employees. Grouping individuals together under a policy generates savings for everyone when compared to individual coverage. The coverage in a group benefit plan will vary significantly among private health insurers. Coverage may include, but would not be limited to, dental care, vision care, medical care, life and disability insurance, and travel insurance for employees and/or their families. Offering a group plan to employees has a number of benefits. From the employee's perspective, group plans provide added protection beyond what is available from government plans. In addition, the employee may save money on provincial premiums or the cost of having to purchase individual insurance. Some employees may be uninsurable on an individual basis, but they may be able to get coverage as part of a group. From the employer's perspective, group plans:

- Provide owners with the opportunity to write off premiums as business expenses
- Encourage loyalty and trust among employees
- Enable better staff retention because employees feel secure
- Help keep the workforce healthy and productive

To determine what is covered under your group plan, ask your human resources department what, if any, group health insurance plans the company provides.

Exhibit 9.1 provides a general overview of the items covered in many basic supplemental group health insurance plans. This is not a reflection of all plans offering health insurance, as details may vary for individual companies. Depending on your annual contribution, your basic supplemental health insurance plan will cover anywhere from 40 to 80 percent of the health care benefits shown in Exhibit 9.1.

Individual Health Insurance. A family with health care needs beyond those covered by an employer's group plan might wish to buy additional supplemental health insurance. To obtain individual health insurance, you can contact an insurance agent. In exchange for paying a premium to an insurance company, you will be provided with specific health insurance coverage for an agreed-upon period. Individual health insurance plans provide coverage for drug, dental, and paramedical costs for you and your family if you do not have coverage through a group plan. Disability insurance provides an income benefit to replace a portion of your earnings if you become ill or are injured and cannot work.

EXHIBIT 9.1   Benefits Commonly Covered by Group Health Insurance Plans

Benefit	Description
Dental Care	• Coverage: 90% of basic services and 50% of major services • Basic services: examinations, scaling and polishing, X-rays, cleanings, major services: inlays, crowns, bridges • Maximum: $2000 per year (all coverage types)
Vision Care	• Optometrist fees: maximum $50 per visit per year • Prescription lenses and frames: maximum $250 per year
Prescription Drugs	• 80% coverage for any and all prescribed medications • Maximum: $5000 per year
Life Insurance	• Minimum employer-paid coverage: 1 times salary • Optional coverages: 2 to 5 times salary; spousal life insurance
Disability Insurance	• General illness: coverage for 100% of income for the first 10 consecutive days of missed employment due to illness or injury • Short-term and long-term disability insurance: 70 per cent of your income up to two years, and coverage beyond two years to age 65 or death, respectively • Definition of disability: general illness and short-term – regular occupation; long-term – any occupation
Employee Assistance Program (EAP)	• A counselling and referral service for personal and/or job stress, relationship issues, eldercare and childcare, addictions and related issues

Source: Based on Canada Health Insurance website, www.canada-health-insurance.com/basicplans.html (accessed April 24, 2014).

Critical illness insurance provides a lump-sum benefit if you are diagnosed with a covered illness such as cancer, heart attack, or stroke. Long-term care insurance provides an income if you lose the ability to care for yourself as a result of illness or injury. Unlike disability insurance, this final benefit is not linked to employment.

L.O.3

DISABILITY INSURANCE

When people consider the value of their assets, many think of their automobile or home as their most valuable asset. This statement could not be further from the truth. Your most valuable asset is your ability to earn an income. For example, if Jeff earns $40 000 per year from ages 30 to 60 with no increase in pay, he will earn $1.2 million during the course of his career. Jeff's lifetime earned income would be even higher if you consider increases in pay due to inflation and promotions.

myth or **fact** Disability insurance is more important than life, critical illness, or long-term care insurance.

disability income insurance
A monthly insurance benefit paid to you in the event that you are unable to work as a result of an injury or an illness.

In the event of an injury or illness, most people recognize that it is important to have adequate disability insurance to provide income for their family. **Disability income insurance** is a monthly insurance benefit paid to you in the event that you are unable to work as a result of an injury or an illness. Although you receive the benefit, the ultimate purpose of this income stream is to ensure that you are able to provide for your family adequately, even though you are unable to work. What is the possibility of this happening? Exhibit 9.2 displays the probability of becoming disabled for three months or longer before age 65. Exhibit 9.3 displays the average duration of a disability lasting more than three months.

Exhibits 9.2 and 9.3 show that disabilities are relatively probable and can become relatively long. For example, a 35-year-old has a 50 percent probability of being disabled

EXHIBIT 9.2   Probability of Becoming Disabled for Three Months or Longer before Age 65

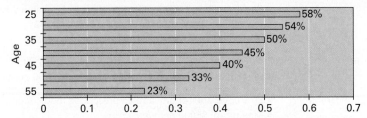

Source: Data derived from the 1985 Commissioner's Disability Table, Society of Actuaries. Reprinted with permission of Society of Actuaries.

EXHIBIT 9.3   The Average Duration of a Disability Lasting More Than Three Months

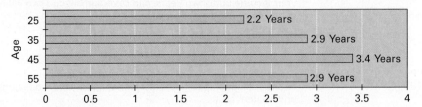

Source: Data derived from the 1985 Commissioner's Disability Table, Society of Actuaries. Reprinted with permission of Society of Actuaries.

for three months or longer, and the average length of a disability lasting more than three months for someone this age is 2.9 years. If you are disabled for 2.9 years, where will the money come from? Potential sources of income include your spouse's income, emergency savings, investments, registered retirement savings plans (RRSPs), borrowing against your home equity, or borrowing against a life insurance policy. If you review your personal circumstances, you will probably find that none of these options would be adequate for 2.9 years. If your personal resources are inadequate, what are your other options? Exhibit 9.4 outlines potential sources of income in the event of an injury or illness and the problems associated with each.

Exhibit 9.4 shows that, although benefits are available from many sources, those benefits may be unavailable to you or may be difficult to qualify for. Workers' compensation benefits are payable only for injuries and illnesses that occur while you are at work. This is like having auto insurance that provides coverage only between 8 a.m. and 4 p.m. What about injuries and illnesses that occur when you are not at work? Most disabilities result from illnesses that cannot be linked to employment circumstances. Workers' compensation benefits do not provide comprehensive coverage and should be viewed as supplemental to other types of disability income benefits.

Canada Pension Plan (CPP) disability benefits are payable if you are totally disabled and your disability is severe and prolonged in nature. Severe means that a person is incapable of regularly pursuing any substantially gainful occupation. Prolonged means that the disability will prevent the individual from returning to work in the next 12 months or is likely to result in death. Relative to other types of disability insurance, CPP disability benefits are difficult to qualify for. However, individuals who make CPP contributions must apply for CPP disability benefits, even if they believe they will not qualify.

Employment Insurance (EI) benefits provide sickness-related benefits for a 15-week period. As a result, this benefit does not provide adequate coverage for a long-term disability.

EXHIBIT 9.4   Sources of Disability Income

Benefit Source	What to Watch For
Workers' Compensation	You may not be covered since workers' compensation may not be provided at your place of work. This benefit is only available for work-related injuries or illnesses. What if you are injured or become ill while away from work? In general, the benefit amount, within a prescribed maximum, is up to 90% of your net income, which is your gross income less your income tax payable, and less your CPP and EI contributions.
Group Insurance	In addition to health insurance, many group plans provide benefits for long-term disability. Although most plans will cover your full after-tax income, the most important issue you should consider is the definition of disability in your group plan. In general, the benefit amount is 60% to 70% of your gross salary.
Canada Pension Plan	The definition of disability requires that you must be totally disabled, and that your disability must be severe and prolonged in nature. Severe means that a person is incapable of regularly pursuing any substantially gainful occupation. Prolonged means that the disability will prevent the individual from going back to work in the next 12 months, or is likely to result in death. For 2017, the maximum disability benefit amount is $1,313.66 per month.
Employment Insurance (EI)	The disability benefit under EI is only payable for 15 weeks. As of January 2017, the benefit amount is 55% of your average insurable weekly earnings up to a maximum weekly benefit of $543.

Source: Based on Disability benefits, Financial Consumer Agency of Canada, www.canada.ca/en/services/benefits.html.

Individual disability insurance may provide the best source of protection. The policy owner is able to select the definition of disability; most choose a "regular occupation to age 65" definition or an "own occupation" definition. In addition, benefits may be payable in the event of a total or partial disability. Individual disability insurance policies may contain provisions that allow benefits to be paid for the insured's lifetime. Finally, these types of policies are portable. This means that you will have the insurance regardless of where you are working at the time of the disability.

Disability Insurance Provisions

The specific characteristics of disability insurance vary among insurance companies, as explained here.

Definition of Disability. With respect to group disability insurance, the most important provision is the definition of disability. Benefits are paid to you only if you meet the definition of disability as defined by your policy. The most liberal definition of disability is the "own occupation" definition. It means that the policy will provide benefits if you are unable to do the duties required of your own occupation, and it will also allow you to find employment elsewhere without a reduction in benefits. This definition of disability is particularly important to people, such as surgeons or accountants, who work in a professional occupation. Surgeons may be unable to perform surgery if they develop arthritis in their hands; however, they would still be able to teach surgery to others. Similarly, accountants may be unable to sit for prolonged periods of time because they have back problems, but they may be able to work in other jobs where they are able to stand more often. The "own occupation" definition is attractive to these professionals because they are able to use their knowledge elsewhere without losing their benefits. Since "own occupation" provides additional flexibility to disabled policy owners, this definition is also the most expensive to purchase.

A more basic definition of disability is the "regular occupation" definition. It means that the policy will provide benefits if you are unable to perform the duties required by your occupation. However, your benefits will be reduced if you find employment elsewhere. This may be advantageous for people who would like to return to the workforce in another job at some later date. Although it seems as if a disabled individual is being penalized for working after a disability, it is important to remember that insurance is based on the principle of indemnification. **Indemnification** refers to the concept of putting an insured individual back into the same position he or she was in prior to the event that resulted in insurance benefits being paid. Payment of insurance benefits normally should not result in an improvement in your lifestyle.

A more restrictive definition of disability is the "any occupation" definition. This means that the policy will provide benefits only if you cannot perform the duties of any job that fits your education and experience. Since the coverage provided by this type of policy is more restrictive, it has a lower premium than "own occupation" and "regular occupation" policies. Definitions of disability may be combined within a policy. For example, group insurance policies offer coverage if you are unable to do your job in your regular occupation for an initial period, such as two years. After that point, they generally offer coverage only if you are unable to perform the duties of any job that fits your education and experience.

Amount of Coverage. The disability insurance policy specifies the amount of income that will be provided if you become disabled. This amount may be specified as a maximum dollar amount or as a percentage of the income you were earning before becoming disabled. The higher your coverage, the more you will pay for disability insurance.

You should have enough coverage to maintain your lifestyle and continue to support your dependants if you become disabled. You can determine the disposable (after-tax) income you would normally need to support your lifestyle and your dependants.

Waiting Period. The disability insurance contract should specify whether there is a **waiting period** (such as three or six months) from when you become disabled until you begin to receive disability income benefits. Ideally, your emergency fund should have

indemnification
The concept of putting an insured individual back into the same position he or she was in prior to the event that resulted in insurance benefits being paid.

waiting period
The period from the time you become disabled until you begin to receive disability income benefits.

enough funds for all household expenses for the duration of the waiting period. Chapter 3 discussed how to create a cash flow statement to identify net cash flows that may be used for short-term or long-term savings. A successful short-term savings plan will allow you to cover your expenses during any waiting period. For example, if you become disabled today and your policy specifies a three-month waiting period, you will receive benefits only if your disability lasts beyond that three-month period. Waiting periods eliminate many claims that would occur if people could receive benefits if they were disabled for just a few days or weeks because of a sore neck or back. The premiums for disability insurance would be higher if there was no waiting period or a very short waiting period.

Benefit Period. Disability benefits may be limited to a few years or may last for the policy owner's lifetime. The longer the period over which your policy provides disability income, the more you will pay for disability insurance. The most common length of time is to age 65.

Non-cancellable Provision. A non-cancellable provision gives you the right to renew the policy each year at the same premium, with no change in the benefits. In exchange, you pay a higher premium now to ensure that it will not be increased in the future.

Guaranteed Renewable Provision. A renewable provision gives you the right to renew the policy with the same benefits. The insurance company can increase your premium if it is increasing the premium for all of its insured customers with the same profile.

CRITICAL ILLNESS INSURANCE

L.0.4

Critical illness insurance provides a lump-sum benefit in the event that you suffer a life-altering illness listed in the policy. The amount of the benefit usually is between $25 000 and $1 million. There are two main differences between critical illness insurance and disability insurance. First, critical illness insurance benefits are paid in one lump sum whereas disability insurance is a monthly benefit that may be paid for a long period of time. Second, critical illness insurance provides coverage for insured conditions. If your life-altering illness is not listed in the insurance policy as an insured illness, you are not covered for it. In contrast, disability insurance provides coverage for any injury or illness that prevents you from working. Many people consider critical illness insurance to be living life insurance since it generally pays a benefit only if you are able to survive a covered life-altering illness for at least 30 days.

Most group plans will not provide a lump-sum benefit for a critical illness. Although you will be covered for many of the treatments required when you suffer a critical illness, such as a stroke, the coverage may be limited or restricted to your province of residence. Critical illness insurance benefits may be valuable if you would like to obtain a second medical opinion or would like to receive treatment outside of Canada. The lump-sum benefit you receive from a critical illness policy can be used in whatever manner you choose.

Critical illness insurance is purchased from health and life insurance companies. The three major critical illnesses are stroke, life-threatening cancer, and heart disease. With advances in medicine and treatments, more people than ever are surviving these illnesses. For example, the Heart and Stroke Foundation of Canada estimates that more than 80 percent of people who have a stroke survive the initial event. Unfortunately, more than 50 percent of individuals who survive a stroke are left with moderate to severe impairment or are severely disabled. Critical illness benefits can be used to cover the costs that stroke victims incur while having to live with their impairment or disability. Critical illness insurance provides protection by allowing you to choose how you will meet your health care needs while preserving your savings or investments. It can be considered as both health insurance and a component of an overall financial plan.

The number of life-altering illnesses covered by critical illness insurance policies is not restricted to the three major illnesses listed above and will vary among health and life insurance companies. In addition, a similar life-altering illness will be defined differently among companies. Some companies will offer additional features not offered by their competitors. As a result, it is important to shop around if you are considering this type of coverage.

L.O.5

LONG-TERM CARE INSURANCE

Many people who are elderly or who have long-term illnesses need some assistance with everyday tasks such as bathing, eating, dressing, toileting, continence, or transferring positions. Others need around-the-clock medical assistance. Seven percent of Canadians age 65 and over reside in health care institutions. An additional 28 percent receive care due to a long-term health problem, although they do not live in health care institutions. Long-term care can be very expensive. The cost of having an aide provide basic care, such as feeding or dressing, at home each day can easily exceed $1000 per week. The cost of care by a nurse is higher. The cost of a nursing home is about $55 000 per year on average.

long-term care insurance
Covers expenses associated with long-term health conditions that cause individuals to need help with everyday tasks.

Long-term care insurance covers expenses associated with long-term health conditions that cause individuals to need help with everyday tasks. It is provided by many private insurance companies and typically covers nursing care, rehabilitation and therapy, personal care, homemaking services, and supervision by another person. However, given the high costs associated with long-term care, the premiums for this type of insurance can be very high.

Long-term Care Insurance Provisions

Like other insurance policies, you can design a long-term care policy that fits your needs. Some of the more common provisions are listed here.

Eligibility to Receive Benefits. Policies include the range of benefits for which policy owners can file claims. For example, a policy may specify that the long-term care be restricted to medical health care services, while a more flexible policy also may allow other care such as feeding or dressing.

Types of Services. Policies specify the types of medical care services that are covered. A policy that covers nursing home care or assisted living will have higher premiums than a policy that covers only nursing home care. For individuals who prefer a more flexible long-term care policy that covers the cost of home health aides, premiums will be higher.

Amount of Coverage. Policies also specify the maximum amount of coverage provided per day. If you want the maximum amount of coverage a company will provide, you will pay a high premium. If you are willing to accept a lower maximum amount of daily coverage, your premium can be reduced. A policy with less coverage may not completely cover the daily costs you could incur. In that case, you would need to cover a portion of your expenses.

A policy can contain a co-insurance provision that requires the policy owner to incur a portion of the health care expense. For example, a policy owner can select a policy in which the insurance company pays 80 percent of the specified health care expenses, while the policy owner pays the remaining 20 percent. Since the potential expense to the insurance company is lower as a result of the co-insurance provision, the premium will be lower.

Elimination Period to Receive Benefits. A policy may specify an elimination (or waiting) period before policy owners are eligible to have their long-term care costs covered. An elimination period of between 60 and 90 days is common. The policy owner is responsible for covering expenses until the elimination period is completed. If the health care is needed over a period shorter than the elimination period, it will not be covered by the long-term care insurance.

Maximum Period to Receive Benefits. You can choose to receive insurance benefits for the entire period in which you need long-term care, even if the period is 30 years or longer.

If you choose to receive insurance benefits for a limited period, you will be charged a lower premium. For example, your long-term care could be covered for up to three years.

Continued Coverage. A policy may contain a waiver of policy premium provision that allows you to stop paying premiums once you need long-term care. Some alternative provisions may also allow a limited amount of coverage after you have a policy for a specified number of years, without having to pay any more premiums. In general, any provision that provides additional benefits in the future will require higher premiums today.

Inflation Adjustment. Some policies allow for the coverage to increase in line with inflation over time. Therefore, the maximum benefits will rise each year with the increase in an inflation index. You will pay a higher premium for a long-term health care policy that contains this provision.

Other Factors That Affect Long-term Care Insurance Premiums

The premium charged for long-term care insurance is influenced by the likelihood that the insurance company will have to cover claims and the size of those claims. Since the long-term care policy provisions described above affect the likelihood and size of claims, they affect the premiums on long-term care insurance. In addition to the provisions of the policy, the following characteristics of the policy owner also affect the premiums on long-term care insurance.

Age. Individuals who are older are more likely to need long-term care insurance, so they are charged higher premiums. Policy premiums are especially high for individuals who are 60 years of age or older.

Health Condition. Individuals who have an existing long-term illness are more likely to file a claim, so they are charged higher premiums.

Reducing Your Cost for Long-term Care Insurance

When comparing long-term care insurance offered by insurance companies, recognize that a higher premium will be charged for various provisions that offer more comprehensive coverage. You can save money by selecting a policy that is flexible only on the provisions that are most important to you. For example, if you can tolerate a longer elimination period before the policy goes into effect, you can reduce your premium. If you think that the continued coverage or the inflation-adjustment provisions are not very beneficial to you, select a policy that does not contain these provisions.

Insurance companies charge varying premiums for long-term care insurance policies, so you should shop around. Internet quotes are one option when researching policies. Also, review how insurance premiums have changed over time, since this may serve as an indication of future premiums.

Determining the Amount of Coverage

To determine whether you need long-term care insurance, consider your family's health history. If there is a history of long-term illnesses, you are more likely to need coverage. In addition, consider your financial situation. If you can afford substantial coverage for long-term care insurance, it may be worthwhile. Individuals who are under age 60 and have no serious illnesses can obtain long-term care insurance at reasonable rates.

LIFE INSURANCE

L.O.6

While the need for life insurance is straightforward, there are many options available. Policies belong to one of two main categories: Term insurance is a common form of temporary or short-term insurance, while whole life and universal life insurance are common forms of permanent insurance.

Term Insurance

Term insurance is life insurance that is provided over a specified time period, typically from 10 to 20 years. Term insurance is intended strictly to provide insurance to a beneficiary in the event of death. If the insured person remains alive over the term, the policy expires at the end of the term. If your term insurance policy has a renewability option (discussed later), the policy can be renewed for an additional term at the option of the policy owner. Renewability is no longer an option when the policy owner reaches a certain age.

myth or **fact** When you consider all of your expenses, such as your mortgage payment, taxes, food, clothing, shelter, and other personal expenses, life insurance is just not affordable for many individuals.

Premiums on Term Insurance. Insurance companies may require that the premiums on term insurance be paid monthly, quarterly, semi-annually, or annually. If the premium is not paid by the due date, the policy owner is given a **grace period**, usually 30 days, before the policy will lapse due to nonpayment. If the premium is not paid during the grace period, the policy will be terminated.

Reviewing Premiums on Term Insurance Using the Internet. Some websites such as Kanetix (www.kanetix.ca) and Term4Sale (www.term4sale.ca) provide quotes from various life insurance companies based on your specific needs, and may link you directly to those companies. They first request some information as described above, then list various quotes on term insurance by different companies. This allows you to select the company you believe would best accommodate your needs. Once you have screened the list of possible insurance companies, you can speak to an insurance agent before selecting a company. Of course, you should also assess the financial soundness of the company you select.

Why Premiums for Term Insurance Vary. The annual insurance premiums for term insurance vary for several reasons. First, the longer the term of the policy, the higher the annual premiums since the insurance company must provide coverage for a longer period of time. Second, the older the policy owner, the higher the premiums since older people have a higher probability of dying during a given term. Third, the greater the insurance coverage (benefits upon death), the higher the premiums since the potential benefits to be paid are higher. Fourth, the annual premiums are higher for a male than for a female of the same age because the probability of a male dying during a specified term is higher than that of a female of the same age. Fifth, the annual premiums are substantially larger for smokers than for non-smokers. In fact, the annual premiums for smokers are more than twice that of non-smokers, which reflects the decreased life expectancy that results from smoking. Sixth, annual premiums may be much larger for policy owners whose family members have a history of medical problems.

Finally, a better understanding of the causes of the number of deaths in a population or in a subgroup of the population, referred to as the **mortality rate**, has allowed the life insurance industry to develop preferred underwriting criteria. **Underwriting** is the process all life insurance companies undertake to evaluate an insurance application based on the applicant's age, sex, smoking status, driving record, and other health and lifestyle considerations and then issue insurance policies based on the responses. If you were to apply for a life insurance policy, the insurance company may request that you take a medical exam. Your physician or a physician of the company's choice would be asked to evaluate your blood pressure, your cholesterol level, your weight-to-height ratio, whether you have a history of alcohol or drug abuse, or whether you participate in any dangerous sports. A high weight-to-height ratio may be indicative of a greater likelihood of developing diseases such as heart disease and adult-onset diabetes.

All life insurance companies implement underwriting criteria based on an applicant's health and lifestyle considerations. Some companies go even further by offering multiple premium categories to address these diverse considerations. It is important to look for a policy that best suits your lifestyle and the premium you are willing to pay.

EXAMPLE

Identical twin brothers Kenyon and James Burris, both 32-year-old non-smokers, have each applied for a $100 000 life insurance policy with Lighthouse Life Insurance Company. Lighthouse Life offers three different premium levels to male non-smokers: gold, silver, and bronze. The policy type that both brothers have applied for contains the same features and benefits. Based on the criteria of age, sex, smoking status, and family medical history alone, both men expect to qualify for the silver premium level, which represents the average premium charged to a 32-year-old male non-smoker. However, Lighthouse Life has determined that Kenyon and James do not fall into the silver level.

The company received Kenyon's driving record from his car insurance company, which indicated that he has received two speeding tickets in the last year. In addition, Kenyon is a licensed scuba diver who likes to dive at the Broken Group Islands off the coast of Pacific Rim National Park in British Columbia at least twice a year. Based on these lifestyle considerations, Kenyon would have to pay a higher-than-average premium at the bronze level.

The company received the results of James's physical and has determined that his blood pressure, cholesterol levels, and weight-to-height ratio are better than average for a 32-year-old male non-smoker. Furthermore, his clean driving record, combined with no history of alcohol or drug abuse and no participation in any hazardous sports, means that James would pay a lower-than-average premium at the gold level.

FOCUS ON ETHICS: Applying for Life Insurance

When applying for life insurance, you fill out a detailed form on which you provide information about your medical history and lifestyle that is used to determine your eligibility and premium. If you suffer from a chronic illness such as diabetes or heart disease or are a smoker, your premium will be higher. You may be tempted to omit some information in the hopes that you can pay a lower premium. As part of the application process, however, you will most likely undergo a medical exam. Between the exam results and information available from the Medical Information Bureau, a clearinghouse of medical information that insurers share, the insurance company will most likely uncover any inaccuracies in your application.

If your application does slip through with inaccuracies, your insurance benefits could be eliminated at a later date if the company discovers them. The policy is a legal contract between you and the insurance company, so you must be truthful. It is not worth jeopardizing the peace of mind that life insurance provides by trying to save a relatively small amount on premiums.

Creditor Insurance. Creditor **insurance** is a type of term life insurance where the beneficiary of the policy is a creditor. A **creditor** is an individual or company to whom you owe money. For example, a common type of creditor insurance, referred to as mortgage life insurance, pays off a policy owner's mortgage in the event of his or her death. In this case, the beneficiary is the financial institution with whom the policy owner set up his or her mortgage life insurance. People purchase mortgage life insurance to ensure that their families can afford to continue living in the home in the event of the death of one or more income earners.

creditor insurance
Term life insurance where the beneficiary of the policy is a creditor.

creditor
An individual or company to whom you owe money.

Creditor Insurance versus Personally Owned Term Insurance. Generally, an applicant chooses creditor insurance over personally owned term insurance because of the convenience of the purchase. For example, when you are approved for a mortgage, the bank representative will offer you the opportunity to buy mortgage life insurance, which is a type of creditor insurance. If you do not already have personally owned term insurance, it makes sense to purchase mortgage life insurance. A first-time home buyer is often a first-time life insurance buyer. Before making such an important financial decision, it is

EXHIBIT 9.5   Comparison of Creditor Insurance and Personally Owned Term Insurance

Creditor Insurance	Personally Owned Term Insurance
The policy is owned and controlled by a creditor, for example, a bank, trust company, or credit union.	The policy owner owns the policy.
In the event of the death of the life insured, benefits are payable directly to the creditor.	In the event of the death of the life insured, the policy owner determines who will be the beneficiary.
Benefits are used to pay off the remaining credit balance, for example, the mortgage balance.	Beneficiaries determine if they wish to pay off the mortgage balance or if they would like to use the benefits for another purpose.
As the credit balance decreases, the insurance coverage decreases. However, premiums do not decrease.	The policy owner determines if insurance coverage should be decreased. If coverage is reduced, premiums may decrease.
If the credit balance is paid off, life insurance coverage will terminate. If credit is reapplied for with another creditor, life insurance will have to be reapplied for, possibly resulting in increased premiums.	The life insurance policy exists independent of any credit facility. Therefore, the policy is cancelled only if the policy owner (you) decides to cancel it.

important to understand the difference between mortgage life insurance and personally owned term insurance. The discussion below and the comparison shown in Exhibit 9.5 will help you to assess the difference between mortgage life insurance and personally owned term insurance.

Before deciding to purchase mortgage life insurance, an applicant should consider the advantages of personally owned term insurance over creditor insurance. As discussed in Chapter 7, your mortgage balance decreases each time you make a mortgage payment. The face amount under mortgage life insurance decreases to match the balance outstanding on your mortgage. This is why mortgage life insurance is also known as decreasing term insurance. **Decreasing term insurance** is a type of creditor insurance where the life insurance face amount decreases each time a regular payment is made on debt that is amortized over a period of time. Although the face amount decreases over time, the premium you are paying on the mortgage life insurance policy does not.

With personally owned term insurance, the face amount does not decrease. As a result, if you purchase personally owned term insurance instead of mortgage life insurance, there will be money left over if you die and the remaining mortgage balance is paid off using the life insurance benefit. After paying off the mortgage balance, the remaining life insurance benefit can be used for other purposes.

As discussed in Chapter 8, you may decide to switch your mortgage to another lender at the end of your mortgage term because the new lender offers a better interest rate or provides better services. Since the bank is not the beneficiary of a personally owned term insurance policy, you can switch your mortgage and still maintain your insurance policy. However, if you applied for mortgage life insurance when you were first approved for the mortgage, you would now have to reapply for mortgage life insurance at the new financial institution. Your premiums would be higher, based on your age, and you also run the risk of not being insurable depending on your health and lifestyle at the time of reapplication.

Since personally owned term insurance offers some advantages to the policy owner relative to creditor insurance, you should expect it to be a little more expensive. This may or may not be the case depending on the financial institutions from which you are

decreasing term insurance
A type of creditor insurance, such as mortgage life insurance, where the life insurance face amount decreases each time a regular payment is made on debt that is amortized over a period of time.

obtaining quotes. As a home buyer, it is in your best interest to understand the benefits and costs of each type of policy so that you can make an informed decision when the time comes. It is important to note that you cannot be denied a loan based on the fact that you have decided not to purchase creditor insurance from the financial institution. Therefore, you should know that it is within your rights to shop around for the coverage that is appropriate for you and your family.

myth or **fact** My spouse/partner doesn't work so he or she doesn't need to purchase life insurance.

Group Term Insurance. **Group term insurance** is term insurance provided to a designated group of people with a common bond, such as the same employer. Group term premiums are usually lower than the typical premiums an individual would pay because the policy owner receives a group discount. Some companies that have a group plan may provide term insurance to its employees as a benefit.

group term insurance
Term insurance provided to a designated group of people with a common bond that generally has lower-than-typical premiums.

Permanent Insurance

Permanent insurance is life insurance that continues to provide insurance for as long as premiums are paid. A unique feature of the premium you pay for a permanent life insurance policy is that part of it may be used to create a savings account, known as the cash value of the policy. For most permanent insurance policies, life insurance companies divide premium payments into two portions. The **cost of insurance** represents the insurance-related expenses incurred by a life insurance company to provide the actual death benefit. The **cash value** is the portion of the premium in excess of insurance-related and company expenses that is invested by the insurance company on your behalf. The **death benefit** is the total amount paid tax-free to the beneficiary on the death of the policy owner. The death benefit may include the cash value of the policy if the policy owner has set up the policy to include it.

The cash value is available to the policy owner prior to his or her death. For example, the policy owner may decide to use the cash value for some specific purpose, such as paying for a child's tuition or purchasing a car. It is important to note that if you withdraw a cash amount, the amount by which the cash value exceeds the premiums that were paid is subject to tax. We will discuss three forms of permanent insurance: whole life, universal life, and term to 100.

permanent insurance
Life insurance that continues to provide insurance for as long as premiums are paid.

cost of insurance
The insurance-related expenses incurred by a life insurance company to provide the actual death benefit, sometimes referred to as the pure cost of dying.

cash value
The portion of the premium in excess of insurance-related and company expenses that is invested by the insurance company on behalf of the policy owner.

death benefit
The total amount paid tax-free to the beneficiary on the death of the policy owner.

Whole Life Insurance. **Whole life insurance** is a form of permanent life insurance that builds cash value based on a fixed premium that is payable for the life of the insured. The long-term growth rate of the cash value in the savings account depends on the types of investments the life insurance company selects. Exhibit 9.6 displays how premiums are allocated between the cost-of-insurance portion and the cash value portion of a whole life insurance policy.

As shown in Exhibit 9.6, the premium on whole life insurance is constant for the duration of the policy. In the earlier years of the policy, the portion of the premium dedicated to paying for the cost of insurance, including company expenses and sales commissions, is relatively low. At the same time, the remaining premium is invested by the insurance company in the savings account, which creates a cash value. The portion of the premium dedicated to savings is high in the earlier years, when the life insured is young, because the portion of the premium needed to insure against the possibility of death is relatively low. In the later years of the policy, the opposite is true: The cost of insurance increases as the policy owner ages. As a result, the portion of the premium required to insure against possible death is relatively high. At some point, the cost of insurance will exceed the insurance premium. Thus, a portion of the policy's cash value is used to supplement the premium paid in these later years. The main purpose of the cash value in a whole life policy is to pay for the cost of insurance in the later years.

whole life insurance
A form of permanent life insurance that builds cash value based on a fixed premium that is payable for the life of the insured.

EXHIBIT 9.6   Allocation of Whole Life Insurance Premiums

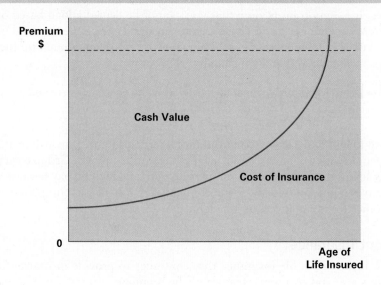

Universal Life Insurance. **Universal life insurance** is a form of permanent life insurance for which you do not pay a fixed premium and in which you can decide to invest the cash value portion in a variety of investments.

universal life insurance
A form of permanent life insurance for which you do not pay a fixed premium and in which you can decide to invest the cash value portion in a variety of investments.

The flexible premium for a universal life insurance policy results from the cost of insurance, company expenses, and other pricing factors being unbundled and reported separately. In a universal life policy, the policy owner is able to choose their cost of insurance and investments.

With a universal life insurance policy, the policy owner can choose between two cost-of-insurance options: level term and yearly renewable term (YRT). Exhibit 9.7 shows the impact of these two different options on the cash value and cost of insurance. If the policy owner selects the level term option, the amount withdrawn from the savings account

EXHIBIT 9.7   Level Term versus Yearly Renewable Term (YRT) Cost of Insurance (COI) Options

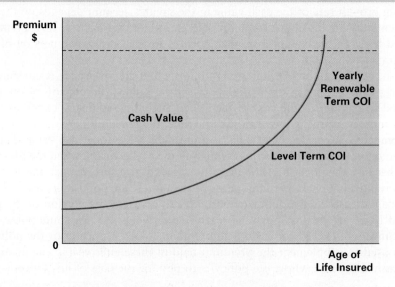

to cover the cost of insurance is the same every year. However, the cash value does not increase as quickly. If the policy owner selects the YRT option, the cash value will grow more quickly since the cost of insurance is relatively low in the early years of the policy. A policy owner focused on increasing the cash value of the policy would choose the YRT option for the early years of the policy. During the later years of the policy, the policy owner can switch to the level term option so that the cost of insurance will remain the same every year for future years.

Similarities and Differences between Whole Life and Universal Life. Whole life and universal life are both permanent insurance policies that provide an opportunity to build cash value inside a savings account. In addition, the accumulated growth of savings inside these types of policies is tax-sheltered until it is withdrawn. As such, whole life and universal life insurance can be useful tools for tax, retirement, and estate planning.

There are key differences between these two forms of insurance. First, the premium you pay for a whole life insurance policy is fixed for the life of the policy. Many people consider whole life insurance as a form of forced savings. In a universal life insurance policy, the premium is flexible between a minimum and a maximum range. Second, in a whole life policy, the insurance company selects the investments for the cash value. In a universal life policy, the policy owner controls the investment choices. The cash value generated in the investment account is determined by how successfully the policy owner chooses investments. The investment choices offered in a universal life insurance policy will differ among companies, but common options include term deposits, guaranteed investment certificates (GICs), and segregated funds that invest in index-linked accounts, equities, and fixed-income securities. Segregated funds are discussed in more detail in Chapter 13.

Non-forfeiture Options. In the event that the policy owner decides to cancel a policy that has accumulated cash value, the life insurance company will provide four non-forfeiture options with respect to the cash value. **Non-forfeiture options** represent the options available to a policy owner who would like to discontinue or cancel a policy that has cash value. The four non-forfeiture options are to: 1) cancel the policy and keep the cash value; 2) use the cash value to pay the policy premium until the cash value runs out and the policy subsequently terminates; 3) use the cash value as a one-time premium payment to purchase as much term insurance as the cash value will purchase; or 4) use the cash value as a one-time premium payment to purchase as much permanent insurance as the cash value will purchase.

non-forfeiture options
The options available to a policy owner who would like to discontinue or cancel a policy that has cash value.

Term to 100 Insurance. **Term to 100 insurance** is a form of permanent life insurance that does not build cash value. This form of insurance is more expensive than term insurance. As a result, you pay quite a bit more in the early years of the policy compared to other types of term life insurance. On the other hand, it is less expensive than whole life or universal life insurance since the premium does not include a savings component. In most cases, the policy owner does not need to pay premiums if he or she lives beyond the age of 100. Exhibit 9.8 provides an overview of the types of life insurance that have been discussed to this point.

term to 100 insurance
A form of permanent life insurance that does not build cash value.

participating policy
A life insurance policy that is eligible to receive policy dividends.

Classifying Life Insurance. Life insurance policies can be classified as either participating or non-participating. A **participating policy** is a life insurance policy that is eligible to receive policy dividends, whereas a **non-participating policy** is a life insurance policy that is not eligible to receive policy dividends. All life insurance policies, with the exception of whole life insurance, are non-participating. A participating whole life insurance policy is eligible to receive policy dividends. A **policy dividend** is a refund of premiums that occurs when the long-term assumptions that the insurance company made with respect to the cost of insurance, company expenses, and investment returns have changed. Specifically, for a policy dividend to be paid, one of three things must occur: the cost of insurance was lower than expected, the insurance company's investment earnings with respect to the cash value in the savings account were higher than expected, or company expenses

non-participating policy
A life insurance policy that is not eligible to receive policy dividends.

policy dividend
A refund of premiums that occurs when the long-term assumptions the insurance company made with respect to the cost of insurance, company expenses, and investment returns have changed.

EXHIBIT 9.8   Types of Life Insurance

Policy Type	Term	Whole Life	Universal Life	Term to 100
Period of coverage	Depends on term in contract. Often renewable for additional terms but usually not past age 70 or 75.	Life	Life	To age 100 or life, depending on contract.
Premiums	Guaranteed in contract	Guaranteed. Usually remain level.	Flexible. Can be increased or decreased by policyholder within certain limits.	Guaranteed. Usually remain level.
Death benefits	Guaranteed in contract	Guaranteed in contract Remain level. Dividends may be used to enhance death benefits in participating policies.	Flexible. May increase or decrease according to fluctuations in cash value fund.	Guaranteed in contract. Remain level.
Cash values	Usually none. (Some long-term policies have a small cash value or other non-forfeiture value.)	Guaranteed in contract.	Flexible. May increase or decrease according to investment returns and level of policyholder deposits.	Usually none. (Some policies have a small cash value or other non-forfeiture value after a long period, say, 20 years.)
Other non-forfeiture Options	See above.	Guaranteed in contract.	Guaranteed in contract.	See above.
Dividends	Most policies do not pay dividends.	Payable on "participating" policies; not guaranteed.	Most policies do not pay dividends.	Most policies do not pay dividends.
Advantages	■ Suitable for short-term insurance needs or specific liabilities like a mortgage. ■ Provides more immediate protection because, initially, it is less expensive than permanent insurance. ■ Can be converted to permanent insurance without medical evidence (if it has a convertibility option), often up to ages 65 or 70.	■ Provides protection for your entire lifetime, if kept in force. ■ Premium cost usually stays level, regardless of age or health problems. ■ Has cash values that can be borrowed, used to continue protection if premiums are missed, or withdrawn if the policy is no longer required. ■ Other non-forfeiture options allow the policyholder various possibilities of continuing coverage if premiums are missed or discontinued. ■ If the policy is participating, it receives dividends that can be taken in cash, left to accumulate as interest or used to purchase additional insurance.		■ Provides protection to age 100, if kept in force. ■ Premium cost usually stays level, regardless of age or health problems. ■ Premium cost is lower relative to traditional permanent policies.
Disadvantages	■ If renewed, premium increase with age and at some point higher premium costs may make it difficult or impossible to continue coverage. ■ Renewability of coverage will terminate at some point, commonly age 65 or age 75. ■ If premium is not paid, the policy terminates after 30 days and may not be reinstated if health is poor. ■ Usually no cash values and no non-forfeiture options.	■ Initial cost may be too high for a sufficient amount of protection for your current needs. ■ May not be efficient means of covering short-term needs.	■ Cash values tend to be small in the early years. You have to hold the policy for a long time, say over 10 years, before the cash values become sizeable.	■ Usually no cash values and no or limited non-forfeiture values.

Source: Reprinted by permission from Canadian Life and Health Insurance Association Inc., A Guide to Buying Life Insurance, 1996.

were lower than expected. A policy dividend should not be confused with the dividend a company pays to its shareholders when it makes a net profit at the end of its fiscal year.

Comparison of Life Insurance Premiums. With respect to term insurance policies, the length of the term determines the premium to be paid for the insurance. Exhibit 9.9 illustrates the relative cost of the types of life insurance. Term insurance is the least

EXHIBIT 9.9   Relative Cost of Types of Life Insurance (35-Year-Old Male Non-Smoker Purchasing $250 000 of Life Insurance)

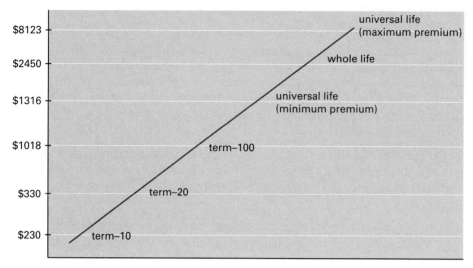

Source: Based on The Canada Life Assurance Company, Zoom Illustration System, Version 7.1, 1999–2004.

expensive form for two reasons: It will expire earlier than permanent insurance policies and it does not build cash value. In Exhibit 9.9, the policy with a shorter term (Term10) is less expensive than the policy with a longer term (Term20). With respect to permanent insurance policies, the amount of the premiums deposited to the savings account portion of the policy determines the premium to be paid. Term to 100 is the least expensive form of permanent insurance because the policy owner is not contributing toward a cash value portion of the policy. The cost of insurance for whole life and universal life policies is similar to that for term to 100. The difference in premiums among types of permanent insurance is mainly a result of the amount you choose to deposit to the savings or investment account portion of each policy. A minimum premium payment universal life insurance policy is less expensive than whole life insurance because the minimum premium amount is generally lower than most whole life policy premiums. A maximum premium payment universal life insurance policy provides the greatest opportunity for tax-deferred growth.

DETERMINING THE AMOUNT OF LIFE INSURANCE NEEDED

L.O.7

Once you identify the type of policy that best suits your needs, your next decision is the policy amount. You can determine the amount of life insurance you need by applying the income method or the budget method.

Income Method

The **income method** is a general formula that determines how much life insurance is needed based on your annual income. This method normally specifies the life insurance amount as a multiple of your annual income, such as 10 times your income. For example, if you have an annual income of $40 000, this formula suggests that you need $400 000 in life insurance. This method is very easy to use. The disadvantage is that it does not consider your age or household situation (including annual household expenses). Therefore, it does not differentiate between a household with no children and one with children, which will likely need more life insurance because its expenses are higher.

income method
A general formula that determines how much life insurance is needed based on the policyholder's annual income.

| EXAMPLE | The Trent household earns $50 000 per year. The Carlin household also earns $50 000 per year. Both households seek the advice of a neighbour who sells insurance and are told that they should have coverage of 10 times their annual income. However, the Trent household's financial situation is completely different from that of the Carlin household. |

The Trents are in their early thirties and have two very young children. Darren Trent is the sole breadwinner, and Rita Trent plans to stay at home for several more years. They have even discussed having more children. They have large credit card balances, two car loans, and a mortgage loan. Their $50 000 annual income barely covers their existing expenses, and they have very little savings. They tend to overspend on their children and will likely continue to do so. They want to send their children to college or university, and they would like to purchase a bigger home in the future.

The Carlins do not have any children. They are in their late fifties, and both work part time. They have established a very large amount of savings and a substantial retirement account, so they could retire now if they had to. They have completely paid off their mortgage and do not have any other debt.

Given the distinct differences in financial conditions, insurance coverage should not be the same for both households. The Trents should apply a higher multiple of their annual income, while the Carlins should apply a lower multiple. Some insurance agents would likely suggest that the Trents use a multiple of 20, so that their life insurance would be 20 × $50 000 = $1 million. The Carlins may use a much smaller multiple, such as 6, so that their life insurance coverage would be 6 × $50 000 = $300 000.

The difference in the appropriate amount of coverage in the example above is due to the difference in future funds needed in the event of death. However, the adjustments here are arbitrary and may not provide proper coverage. Thus, the income method is limited, even if it allows for some adjustments to account for differences in financial situations.

Budget Method

budget method (or needs method)
A method that determines how much life insurance is needed based on the household's future expected expenses and current financial situation.

An alternative method is the **budget method** (also referred to as the **needs method**), which determines how much life insurance is needed based on your future expected expenses and current financial situation. This method requires a little more effort than the income method, but it provides a better estimate of necessary coverage. The main reason for having life insurance is to ensure that a household's needs are covered in the event of death, not simply to replace lost income. The budget method estimates the amount of future funds that will be needed, so that the insurance coverage will be adequate. Some important factors that should be considered when determining household needs are:

- **Annual living expenses.** You should have sufficient insurance so that your family can live comfortably without your income. Your family's future expenses will be higher if you have children, and younger children will need financial support for a longer period of time.
- **Special future expenses.** If you want to ensure college or university educations for your children, you need adequate life insurance to cover the existing or future expenses.
- **Debt.** If your family relies on your income to cover debt, you may want to ensure that your life insurance can pay off credit card bills and even a mortgage.
- **Job marketability of spouse.** If your spouse has very limited job marketability, you may need more life insurance so that he or she can receive job training.

- **Value of existing savings.** If you have accumulated a large amount of savings, your family may draw interest or dividends from these savings to cover a portion of their periodic expenses. The more savings your household has accumulated, the less life insurance you need.

myth or **fact** Life insurance is a bit of a rip-off because the odds are you will not die, so you wind up paying a premium and get nothing in return.

EXAMPLE

You wish to purchase a life insurance policy that generates a pre-tax income of at least $30 000 per year at the beginning of each year for the next 20 years to cover living expenses (excluding the mortgage payment) for your spouse and two children in the event that you die. You have just enough savings to cover burial expenses, and you anticipate no unusual expenses for the household in the future.

To determine your insurance needs, you must estimate the amount of insurance today that will cover your household's living expenses in the future. You can use the time value of money concepts in Chapter 2 to determine the amount of funds that can provide an annuity equal to $30 000 over each of the next 20 years. First, assume that your spouse will be able to earn at least three percent annually by investing the money received from the life insurance policy. Next, estimate the present value of an annuity that can provide your household with a $30 000 annuity over 20 years if it generates an annual return of 3 percent:

Amount of Insurance Needed = Annuity Amount $\times$ PVIFA ($i = 3\%$, $n = 20$)

$$= \$30\ 000 \times 14.878$$

$$= \$446\ 340$$

Since payments are required at the beginning of the year, the amount of insurance calculated above needs to be multiplied by 1.06. Therefore, the amount of insurance needed from the beginning of the year is $364 746. Based on the following additional information about your household, you then adjust the amount of insurance needed.

- *Special future expense.* You also want to allocate an extra $50 000 in life insurance to pay for your two children's college or university expenses. Although these expenses will rise in the future, the money set aside will accumulate interest over time and therefore should be sufficient.

- *Job training.* You want to have additional insurance of $20 000 to ensure that your spouse can pay for job training in the event of your death.

- *Debt.* You have a $250 000 mortgage and no other loans or credit card debt. You decide to increase the life insurance amount so that the mortgage can be paid off in the event of your death. Therefore, you specify an extra $250 000 in life insurance.

By summing your preferences, you determine that you need a total of $779 730 in life insurance. You round off the number and obtain quotes for a policy with coverage of $800 000.

Go to
www.cpp.ca/insurance-needs-calculator

This website provides
a life insurance needs calculator that uses the budget method.

FREE APPS for Personal Finance

Estimating the Amount of Life Insurance Needed

Application:

The LIFE Foundation Needs Calculator app provides you with recommendations regarding how much life insurance you need based on your situation.

L.O.8

CONTENTS OF A LIFE INSURANCE POLICY

A basic life insurance policy contains a number of standard features. Some of the more common policy contents include the beneficiary, grace period, reinstatement, living benefits, premium schedule, loans, suicide clause, incontestability date, and misstatement of age or sex. Although most of these features are common to both term life insurance and permanent insurance, a premium schedule is usually found in a term life policy, while living benefits and a loan clause are found in a permanent insurance policy.

Beneficiary

When naming a beneficiary on your life insurance policy, keep the following points in mind. You can name multiple beneficiaries and specify how you want the death benefits to be divided. You can also name a contingent beneficiary who would receive the benefits in the event that your primary beneficiary is no longer living at the time of your death. You can change the beneficiary any time you wish, but until you do, the existing contract will be enforced. If you name a person rather than your estate as beneficiary, the benefits can be paid to the person directly and avoid probate and related expenses.

Grace Period

The insurance policy specifies the grace period allowed beyond the date when payment is due. As mentioned earlier, the typical grace period is 30 days. During this period, benefits are payable even though the premium amount is due. A policy is said to be in lapse status after this 30-day period.

Reinstatement

reinstatement
The process of completing a reinstatement application to restore a policy that is in lapse status.

After a policy has gone into lapse status, it may be reinstated within two years. **Reinstatement** is the process of completing a reinstatement application to restore a policy that is in lapse status. In addition to completing a reinstatement application, the policy owner must provide evidence of insurability (good health) and make all overdue payments. The advantage of reinstatement is that it allows the policy owner to maintain the premiums determined when the original policy was issued. This premium figure is likely to be lower than any new premium that would be calculated (due to the policy owner now being older).

Living Benefits

living benefits (accelerated death benefits)
Benefits that allow the policyholder to receive a portion of the death benefits prior to death.

Some whole life insurance policies allow **living benefits** (also referred to as **accelerated death benefits**), in which policyholders can receive a portion of the death benefits prior to death. Certain special circumstances must exist, such as terminal illness or long-term care needs of the insured.

Premium Schedule

A term life insurance policy includes a schedule of premiums that indicates what the new annual premium will be when the policy is renewed. For example, a Term10 policy will contain a premium schedule that indicates the new annual premium every 10 years. The premiums in the schedule are guaranteed. Therefore, the policy owner can shop around at the renewal date to see whether he or she could buy life insurance at a lower cost from another company. However, care should be taken when switching policies since some benefits may be lost. If you are considering a switch, consult an insurance agent.

Loans

You can borrow cash from your policy only if it can accumulate cash value. For example, a whole life policy accumulates cash value. The loan rates may be lower than those offered on personal loans, and interest is paid back into the cash value of the policy.

Suicide Clause

Life insurance benefits are not payable if the policy owner commits suicide within two years of the policy's effective date. After two years, benefits are payable in the event of a suicide. Some life insurance companies offer a suicide clause in which the restriction on benefit payments is only one year.

Incontestability Date

Policies specify a date, usually two years from the effective date, after which the policy provisions are incontestable. Until that date, an insurance company can cancel a policy if it determines that some of the information provided by the policy owner is misstated. The policy can be cancelled even if the information was misstated accidentally. Once the policy has passed the incontestability date, it cannot be cancelled because of an accidental misstatement of information. The misstatement must be proven to be intentional (fraudulent) for the life insurance company to cancel the policy. Misstating your age or sex is the one exception to this provision.

Misstatement of Age or Sex

If you misstate your age or sex on your application form and the life insurance company discovers this discrepancy, it will adjust your benefits to reflect what you are entitled to based on the existing premium you are paying. For example, if you indicated that you are 32 years old but you are really 34 years old, the benefit amount would be decreased. It is your responsibility to ensure that the correct age and sex is entered on your application form. If the insurance agent enters your age or sex incorrectly, you will still be held responsible for this error. Always review your entire application before signing it.

Renewability and Conversion Options

A **renewability option** allows you to renew your policy for another term (up to an age limit specified in the policy) once the existing term expires. The premium for the next term will be higher than for the current term, since you will be older. In addition, the premium charged in the next term may increase to reflect changes in your health.

A **conversion option** allows you to convert your term insurance policy into a whole life policy that will be in effect for the rest of your life. A policy with a conversion option specifies the period during which the conversion can occur. At the time of this conversion, the premium will be increased, but it will then stay constant for the rest of your life.

The renewability and conversion options apply only to term life insurance. If you are considering term life insurance, it is very important to ensure that these options are available in your policy. The two major drawbacks of term life insurance are that the policy will expire at the end of the term and that it will not be available beyond a certain age. The advantage of the renewability option is that your renewal is guaranteed at the end of each term, up to a specified age limit. Without this option, you may not be able to renew your insurance if your health has deteriorated. If you decide that a permanent life insurance policy better suits your needs, the conversion option will allow you to convert your term insurance to permanent insurance.

If you are covered by group life insurance, it may be possible to convert this type of insurance into a personally owned policy. If you leave your employer and still require insurance, this conversion privilege can be useful.

renewability option
Allows you to renew your policy for another term once the existing term expires.

conversion option
Allows you to convert your term insurance policy into a whole life policy that will be in effect for the rest of your life.

Riders

Riders are options that allow you to customize a life insurance policy to your specific needs. Riders are available on both term and permanent life insurance policies at an additional cost to you. Some of the more common riders and their specific features are discussed below.

riders
Options that allow you to customize a life insurance policy to your specific needs.

Waiver of Premium. The waiver of premium rider provides a benefit in the case of the policy owner becoming totally disabled. Total disability often leads to a decrease in income, which may force the policy owner to stop making premium payments on the life insurance. This rider waives the obligation of premium payments by the policy owner for the period during which they are totally disabled. If the disability is permanent, the coverage will continue for the duration of the policy.

Guaranteed Insurability. The guaranteed insurability rider allows you to purchase additional life insurance without having to resubmit evidence of medical insurability, which you would otherwise need to do. If you no longer qualify for additional insurance because your health has deteriorated, this rider guarantees that you can purchase additional life insurance nonetheless. You may decide to purchase additional life insurance for two reasons: You did not purchase adequate insurance at the time of initial application, or you anticipate that you will require additional insurance in the future but are unsure of the amount. You may not have purchased an adequate amount of insurance because you could not afford the premium at the time of the application. The need for additional insurance also arises when your financial responsibilities increase. For example, the birth of a child or the purchase of a cottage with a mortgage will increase your financial responsibilities.

Accidental Death. In the event of accidental death of the policy owner, this rider increases the death benefit payout of the policy. The death benefit is usually doubled if accidental death occurs. For example, if you purchase $250 000 of term life insurance and add the accidental death rider as an option, the death benefit will increase to $500 000 if you die as a result of an accident.

Child Term Coverage. The child term rider provides cash benefits in the event that a child of the policy owner dies. The benefit is usually limited to between $5000 and $25 000. The policy continues even if this benefit is paid.

Term Insurance Coverage. You can purchase term insurance coverage as a rider on permanent life insurance policies to help finance temporary needs. This rider is ideal for individuals who wish to purchase permanent insurance but also require affordable protection for temporary needs.

EXAMPLE

The Cheungs determine that they need $500 000 of life insurance. They would prefer to purchase whole life insurance so that they will be able to build cash value inside their policy. However, the premium for $500 000 of whole life insurance is more than they can afford to pay. To meet their budget, the Cheungs decide to purchase $150 000 of whole life insurance with a $350 000 Term10 rider. This alternative meets both their budget and their life insurance needs. After 10 years, the Cheungs can renew their Term10 rider or let it expire.

Riders provide benefits that may be of value to you. However, you should first determine the amount of coverage you need and the type of policy that will provide this level of coverage within your budget. In the example above, assume that the Cheungs cannot afford a $150 000 whole life insurance policy with a $350 000 Term10 rider. Although they would prefer to purchase whole life insurance, their need for $500 000 of affordable insurance is more important. They should look at options that meet this need. Riders should be considered only once the insurance goal is accomplished and if you have money left in your budget.

MyLab Finance Visit MyLab Finance for additional study and practice tools. Select Financial Planning Problems are available in the Study Plan. Create your own study plan, generate personal cash flow statements and balance sheets, and set personal financial goals.

SUMMARY

L.O.1 Provide a background on health and life insurance

Health insurance, which includes medicare, private health care, disability, critical illness, and long-term care insurance, provides benefits to living individuals as a result of sickness or injury. Life insurance provides benefits to a beneficiary when the life insured dies. Whereas health insurance allows you to maintain your quality of life as you work toward your financial goals, life insurance allows your dependants to receive financial support after you have passed away.

L.O.2 Outline Canada's health care system

The backbone of Canada's health care system is the *Canada Health Act*, which ensures adequate medically necessary coverage for all Canadians. The medicare program provides health insurance to individuals who are residents of Canada. There are also provincial government health plans. These health care plans supplement the coverage provided for medically necessary health issues. Provincial health care plans provide coverage for things such as drugs prescribed outside hospitals and vision care on a very limited, selected basis only. Group health insurance covers health care expenses incurred by policy owners. These health care plans can be classified as private plans that provide additional coverage and flexibility in the choice of the health care provisions you want for you and your family.

L.O.3 Explain the benefits of disability insurance

Disability insurance provides income to you if you become disabled. It can replace a portion of the income you would have received had you been able to continue working. This type of insurance is available from a number of federal, provincial, and private sources. In general, private disability insurance is the most comprehensive and the most expensive form of coverage.

L.O.4 Describe critical illness insurance

Critical illness insurance provides a lump-sum benefit that will allow you to cover additional living expenses after a critical illness. You also may use the money to seek additional medical advice.

L.O.5 Describe long-term care insurance

Long-term care insurance covers expenses associated with long-term illnesses, including care in a nursing home, in an assisted living facility, or at home. The premium for long-term care insurance is very high but can be reduced by accepting a longer elimination period.

L.O.6 Describe the types of life insurance that are available

Life insurance provides payments to specified beneficiaries if the policy owner dies. Term insurance is strictly intended to provide insurance in the event of the death of the insured, while whole life insurance and universal life insurance use a portion of the premium to build a cash value. The premiums for whole life and universal life insurance are higher to account for the portion distributed into a savings plan and for the administrative fees.

L.O.7 Examine the decision of how much life insurance to purchase

The amount of life insurance you need can be measured by the income method, in which you attempt to replace the income that would be discontinued due to death. However, this amount can be more precisely measured by the budget method, which considers factors such as your household's future expected expenses and existing debt.

L.O.8 Describe the contents of a life insurance policy

Although the basic contents of a life insurance policy are similar across the industry, a number of riders can be used to customize the policy to the needs of the individual. These riders provide additional benefits, but should be considered only once the insurance goal is accomplished and if you still have money left in your budget.

REVIEW QUESTIONS

1. What is health insurance? What does health insurance include?

2. What is the purpose of life insurance? Define the terms *face amount*, *beneficiary*, *life insured*, and *policy owner*.

3. Do you think that everyone needs health and/or life insurance? Explain.

4. With respect to financial goals, what is the difference between health and life insurance?

5. What is medicare? How is the health care system in Canada financed?

6. What is the role of the federal government in the provision of health care?

7. Describe the features and principles of the *Canada Health Act.*

8. What is the role of the provincial and territorial governments in the provision of health care?

9. What is private health insurance? What are the differences between group health insurance and individual health insurance?

10. What is the purpose of disability income insurance? Why might younger individuals consider purchasing it?

11. Under what circumstances are workers' compensation disability benefits payable? What is the benefit amount?

12. What is the most important issue to consider when evaluating disability insurance provided through a group insurance benefit plan?

13. Describe the definition of disability under the Canada Pension Plan.

14. How long, and in what amount, is the disability insurance benefit payable under Employment Insurance?

15. What are the benefits of individual disability insurance relative to the disability insurance benefits provided under workers' compensation, group insurance, Canada Pension Plan, and Employment Insurance?

16. What are the differences among the "own occupation," "regular occupation," and "any occupation" definitions of disability?

17. Describe the concept of indemnification.

18. How do you determine the amount of disability coverage you should have?

19. Define and describe the waiting period and the benefit period.

20. What is the difference between the non-cancellable provision and the guaranteed renewable provision?

21. What is critical illness insurance? What is the difference between critical illness insurance and disability insurance?

22. What are the three major life-altering illnesses covered by critical illness insurance policies?

23. What is long-term care insurance? What everyday tasks are considered when determining your eligibility for long-term care insurance benefits?

24. What are some of the common provisions of a long-term care insurance policy?

25. In addition to the policy provisions, what other factors influence the decision as to what premium to charge on a long-term care insurance policy?

26. What is term insurance?

27. Define and describe the grace period.

28. What seven factors determine the premium for term insurance?

29. Define underwriting and describe the underwriting process.

30. What is creditor insurance? Provide an example of a common type of creditor insurance.

31. What are the differences between creditor insurance and personally owned term insurance?

32. What is mortgage life insurance? What is another name for it? Is mortgage life insurance a good buy? Why or why not?

33. Define and describe group term insurance.

34. What is permanent insurance? Define the terms *cost of insurance* and *cash value.*

35. What are the benefits of building cash value inside a permanent life insurance policy?

36. What is whole life insurance? What is the main purpose of cash value inside a whole life policy?

37. What is universal life insurance?

38. Differentiate between the two cost of insurance options in a universal life insurance policy.

39. Describe the similarities and differences between whole life insurance and universal life insurance.

40. What are non-forfeiture options? What are the non-forfeiture options within a permanent insurance policy?

41. What is term to 100 insurance?

42. Differentiate between the two classifications of life insurance policies?

43. What is a policy dividend? Under what circumstances is it paid?

44. Compare and contrast life insurance policy premiums.

45. Describe the income method of determining the amount of life insurance needed. What is the disadvantage of this method?

46. Describe the budget method of determining the amount of life insurance needed. What elements must be considered in making this calculation?

47. List the more common life insurance policy contents.

48. What should you keep in mind when naming beneficiaries?

49. Explain the benefit of the grace period.

50. What is reinstatement? How does it work?

51. What are living benefits?

52. What type of life insurance policies have a premium schedule?

53. Provide one reason as to why you may want to borrow from the cash value of your permanent insurance policy.

54. Describe the suicide clause.

55. What is the incontestability date?

56. Explain what happens if you misstate your age or sex.

57. What is the benefit of the renewability option? What is the benefit of the conversion option?

58. What is a rider?

59. Describe the features of the waiver of premium, guaranteed insurability, accidental death, child term, and term insurance riders.

FINANCIAL PLANNING PROBLEMS

MyLab Finance Financial Planning Problems marked with a 🌐 can be found in MyLab Finance.

🌐 **1.** Pete's group insurance policy specifies that he pays 30 percent of expenses associated with orthodontic treatment for his children. If Pete incurs expenses of $5000, how much would he owe?

🌐 **2.** Christine's monthly expenses typically amount to $1800. About $50 of these expenses are work-related. Christine's employer provides disability insurance coverage of $500 per month. How much individual disability insurance should Christine purchase?

🌐 **3.** Ingrid is a widow with two teenage children. Her total income is $3000 per month, and taxes take about 30 percent of this income. Using the income method, Ingrid calculates she will need to purchase about eight times her after-tax income in life insurance to meet her needs. How much insurance should she purchase?

🌐 **4.** Ingrid's employer provides her with two times her annual gross salary in life insurance. How much additional insurance should she purchase based on the information provided in problem 3?

🌐 **5.** Roberto is married and has two children. He wants to be sure that he has sufficient life insurance to take care of his family if he dies. Roberto's wife is a homemaker but attends college part-time, pursuing a finance diploma. It will cost approximately $40 000 for her to finish her education. Since their children are teenagers, Roberto feels that he will need to provide the family with income for only the next 10 years. He further calculates that the household expenses run approximately $35 000 per year. The balance on the home mortgage is $30 000. Roberto set up an education fund for his children when they were babies and it currently contains a sufficient amount for them to attend college

or university. Assuming that Roberto's wife can invest the insurance payments at eight percent, calculate the amount of insurance Roberto needs to purchase.

6. Mahood and Murtaz have jobs and contribute to the household expenses according to their income. Mahood contributes 75 percent of the expenses, and Murtaz contributes 25 percent. Currently, their household expenses are $30 000 annually. Mahood and Murtaz have three children. The youngest child is 12, so they would like to ensure that they could maintain their current standard of living for at least the next eight years. They feel that the insurance proceeds could be invested at four percent. In addition to covering the annual expenses, they would like to make sure that each of their children has $25 000 available for college. If Mahood was to die, Murtaz would go back to school part time to upgrade her training as a nurse. This would cost $20 000. They have a mortgage on their home with a balance of $105 000. How much life insurance should they purchase for Mahood?

7. Considering the information in problem 7, how much life insurance should they purchase for Murtaz?

🌐 **8.** Bart is a college student. He plans to get a job immediately after graduation and determines that he will need about $250 000 in life insurance to provide for his future wife (he is not yet married) and children (he does not yet have any children). Bart has obtained a quote over the internet that would require him to pay $200 in life insurance premiums annually. As a student, this is a significant expense, and Bart would likely need to borrow money to pay for the insurance premiums. Advise Bart on the timing of his life insurance purchase.

CHALLENGE QUESTIONS

1. Lei purchased a life insurance policy three years ago and mistakenly checked a box on her application that said she did not have high blood pressure. She does. Yesterday, she died of a heart attack. Will her beneficiary receive the face value of the policy or only the premiums paid to date?

2. The Balderson family has a basic health insurance plan that pays 80 percent of supplementary medical expenses after a deductible of $250 per person. If three family members have prescription drug and other insured expenses of $980, $1340, and $220, respectively, how much will the Baldersons and the insurance company each pay?

 ## ETHICAL DILEMMA

Abdel is a self-employed convenience store owner. An insurance agent has approached him about his need for critical illness insurance. Abdel is very interested and would like to purchase as much protection as he can. Unfortunately, his family health history is very poor. His father had a heart attack at age 40 and his mother had a stroke in her mid-30s. Abdel understands that he may have difficulty qualifying for coverage based on his family health history. While filling out the application for critical illness insurance, Abdel tells the insurance agent that he was adopted and does not have any information on his biological parents that would indicate any family health concerns.

a. Assuming that Abdel is otherwise healthy, do you think that the insurance company would issue a policy? Why or why not?

b. If Abdel makes a claim, what are the potential problems he has created for himself?

c. If you were the insurance agent, what could you do to minimize the risk that someone may provide you with fraudulent information?

 ## FINANCIAL PLANNING ONLINE EXERCISES

1. Go to www.sunnet.sunlife.com/Buyonline/phi/quoteinfo.asp.

   a. Obtain a personal health insurance estimate for yourself from Sun Life Financial. What features are available in the basic plan? How are the standard and enhanced plans different from the basic plan? What, if any, options are available?

   b. Select the standard plan. What is the monthly premium quoted? Complete this step for the basic and enhanced plans. What is the difference in premiums? Which plan do you find most attractive? Why?

2. Go to www.rbcinsurance.com/healthinsurance/index-disability.html.

   a. Click on Compare Disability Insurance Plans. This tool allows you to compare two different types of disability insurance policies. In the first column, click on The Foundation Series Policy. In the second column, click on Bridge Series Policy. What are the differences between these two types of disability insurance? Based on your career goals, which type of policy would be appropriate for you?

   b. Now compare The Professional Series Policy to the policy you selected in step a. What are the differences between these two types of disability insurance? Would you change your mind as to the type of insurance that is appropriate for you based on this new information? Why or why not?

3. Go to www.kanetix.ca/life_cov_calc.

   a. Determine the amount of life insurance you need by entering the following information:

Cost of your funeral arrangements	$ 10 000
Total amount owing on your mortgage	$150 000
Total amount of your outstanding debts	$ 20 000
Estimate the total of your children's future education	$ 30 000
How much income would your family need every month if you passed away?	$ 3000
How many years would your family need to rely on this monthly insurance income?	15

   Click on Submit. How much life insurance will you need?

   b. How will the answer in part a change if you have other investments and/or life insurance policies?

   c. Increase the Estimated inflation rate to 3.0 and click on Submit. What happens to the amount of life insurance required? Why does this happen? Reset the Estimated inflation rate to 2.0 and click on Submit. This will bring you back to your original answer in part a. Now, increase After-tax investment yield to 5.0 and click on Submit. What happens to the amount of life insurance required? Why does this happen?

4. Go to www.term4sale.ca. Using the answer obtained in part a of Exercise 1, complete a term life insurance comparison. Set your health as Regular (Average), and premiums to be paid as Monthly. Click on Compare Now to see your results.

   a. What is the range of premiums for the 10-Year Guaranteed Term option? What is the range of premiums for the 20-Year Guaranteed Term option?

   b. Click on Health Analyzer. What factors are being considered in this health questionnaire? Complete the questionnaire. What is the impact on the premium comparison for the 10-Year Guaranteed Term and 20-Year Guaranteed Term options after completing the questionnaire?

   c. Return to the first webpage. Change the initial level term option to Guaranteed Whole Life. All other information should be entered as in part a. Click on Compare Now. What is the monthly premium? What is the difference among the monthly premiums for Guaranteed Whole Life, 10-Year Guaranteed Term, and 20-Year Guaranteed Term?

PSYCHOLOGY OF PERSONAL FINANCE: Your Life Insurance

1. People tend to put off the decision to purchase life insurance. They might argue that they cannot afford it. They do not want to sacrifice any other type of spending so that they could afford to pay for life insurance. Describe your own behaviour when purchasing life insurance. If you do not have life insurance, why not?

2. Read one practical article of how psychology affects decisions when buying life insurance. You can easily retrieve possible articles by doing an online search using the terms "psychology" and "buying life insurance." Summarize the main points of the article.

MINI-CASE 1: Group Insurance

Adam and Heidi Larrsson were delighted when Adam landed a new job with a promotion and an increased salary, but disappointed to learn that he would not be eligible for group benefits for the first 90 days of his employment. As they approach the 90-day deadline, they are not sure if there will be enough time to handle all the decisions that they need to make regarding the group benefit options they have. The company offers a comprehensive package of supplementary medical insurance, life insurance (1.5 times salary at no premium charge), and disability insurance. An employee can choose how to spend the employer-provided premium dollars to purchase supplementary medical or disability insurance or additional life insurance. Fortunately, Heidi has supplementary group medical insurance through her work. In the mix of premiums to be spent, how should Adam and Heidi rank Adam's insurance needs? What factors would be important to consider? Name two to three factors of importance when purchasing disability insurance.

MINI-CASE 2: Life Insurance

Wendy and Frank Cotroni, ages 30 and 35, plan to purchase life insurance. Wendy does not have any coverage, while Frank has a $150 000 policy at work. The Cotronis have two children, ages three and five. Wendy earns $28 000 from a home-based business. Frank's annual salary is $55 000. They save $7500 annually. The children will be financially dependent for another 15 years.

In preparation for a visit with their insurance agent, the Cotronis have estimated the following expenses if Frank were to die:

- immediate needs at death: $25 000
- outstanding debt (including mortgage repayment): $90 000
- transitional funds for Wendy to expand her business: $35 000
- post-secondary expenses for their two children $50 000

Wendy projects her annual income to be $40 000 after her business expansion. Once the children are self-supporting, she estimates her pre-retirement income needs at $55 000 per year, from age 45 to 65. She would also like to replace 50 percent of her income in retirement, from age 65 to age 85. She anticipates receiving a 6 percent return, compounded annually, on her investments. To date, the Cotronis have accumulated a total of $107 000 of assets. This includes $10 000 considered as an emergency fund, $32 000 for Wendy's retirement, $35 000 in joint non-registered investments, and $30 000 for Frank's retirement. Using the budget method, estimate the amount of additional life insurance, if any, that the Cotronis should purchase to protect Wendy and the kids if Frank should die. Wendy would like you to determine this amount on a pre-tax basis and does not need to adjust the income benefit for annual inflation. What type of life insurance policy would you recommend that Frank purchase? Should Wendy purchase a life insurance policy? Why or why not? If so, what type of policy would you recommend for Wendy?

Study Guide

Circle the correct answer and then check the answers in the back of the book to chart your progress.

Multiple Choice

1. Which of the following would not qualify as an insured health care service?
   a. Jackson has been diagnosed with appendicitis and will require an appendectomy.
   b. Tarlochan has been wearing glasses since he was nine years old. Now that he is in his early twenties, he has decided to have laser surgery on his eyes so that he will no longer have to wear glasses.
   c. Johanna has a fever. She visited her family physician, who diagnosed her with a cold and prescribed two days of bed rest before she returns to work.
   d. Tanya needs to have medically necessary dental surgery. The surgery can only be completed in a hospital.

2. Which of the following is not one of the five principles of the *Canada Health Act*?
   a. Public administration
   b. Comprehensiveness
   c. Accountability
   d. Universality

3. Most provincial and territorial governments offer and fund supplementary benefits for certain groups because:
   a. Plans must ensure that all medically necessary services are available to all residents of the province.
   b. Insured health care services provided by the *Canada Health Act* cover only basic medical needs.
   c. Plans cannot create situations in which there would be financial or other barriers.
   d. They will not be re-elected if they do not meet the needs of the groups that have voting power.

4. Which of the following is not one of the features of the "own occupation" definition of disability?
   a. This definition of disability is particularly important to people who would like to return to the workforce in another job at some later date.
   b. The policy will provide benefits if you are unable to perform the duties required of your occupation.
   c. The policy will allow you to find employment elsewhere without a reduction in benefits.
   d. This definition of disability is particularly important to people who work in a professional occupation.

5. Which of the following statements is true regarding disability insurance?
   a. Disability benefits are paid in one lump sum.
   b. The principle of indemnification will limit the amount of coverage you can get.
   c. If you are self-employed, you are not eligible for disability insurance.
   d. Disability insurance from an employee group plan is the best source of coverage.

6. Employee group health insurance policies do not commonly offer:
   a. Critical illness insurance.
   b. Employee assistance programs.
   c. Health insurance coverage for family members.
   d. Life insurance.

7. Which of the following long-term care insurance provisions is likely to increase the premium charged?
   a. Coverage of medical health care services only
   b. A benefit period of one year instead of three years
   c. The minimum amount of coverage that an insurance company will provide
   d. An elimination period of 90 days instead of 60 days

8. Which of the following is not one of the reasons why premiums for term insurance vary?
   a. The annual premium is higher for a male than for a female of the same age because males tend to live longer than females.
   b. The annual premium is higher for policies of a longer term.
   c. The older the policy owner, the higher the premium.
   d. Some policy owners may have a family history of medical problems, resulting in higher premiums.

9. In comparing term insurance with mortgage life insurance, which of the following is true?
   a. The premiums decrease with mortgage insurance but not with term insurance.
   b. Mortgage insurance is less expensive because of the group discount.
   c. The owner has more control with term insurance.
   d. Mortgage insurance is guaranteed renewable.

10. Which of the following factors is most important in determining your life insurance premium rate?
    a. Your profession
    b. Your health

c. Your net worth
d. The amount of coverage

11. Which of the following statements does not apply when discussing universal life insurance?
    a. The long-term growth rate of the cash value in the investment account depends on the types of investments the life insurance company selects.
    b. It is a form of permanent life insurance for which you do not pay a fixed premium.
    c. Premium payments are deposited directly into the savings account portion of the policy.
    d. The cash value under the YRT option grows more quickly because the money the insurance company withdraws to cover the cost of insurance is lower relative to the premium cost of the level term option.

12. _____ is a form of permanent life insurance for which you do not pay a fixed premium and in which you can decide to invest the cash value portion in a variety of investments.
    a. Universal life insurance
    b. Whole life insurance
    c. Term to 100 insurance
    d. Variable term life insurance

13. The budget method for determining the amount of life insurance needed is based on:
    a. Your investments and cash flow.
    b. Your debt history.
    c. Your current situation and your company pension.
    d. Your current situation and expected future needs.

14. If Bart has an annual income of $100 000, debt of $400 000, net worth of $200 000, and a multiple (or factor) of 8, how much insurance should he buy using the income method?
    a. $200 000
    b. $400 000
    c. $800 000
    d. None, because of his net worth.

15. The term *grace period* is very important to an insurance policy because:
    a. It refers to living benefits that can be paid for a grace period prior to death in special circumstances.
    b. It refers to the period when a policy can no longer be contested by an insurance company.
    c. It refers to the period when the policy has lapsed and can be reinstated.
    d. It refers to the period when benefits are still payable while premiums are in arrears.

True/False

1. True or False? Insurance is important because your personal financial assets are needed to meet your financial goals.

2. True or False? Medicare refers to that portion of Canada's health care system that is privately funded.

3. True or False? With respect to portability, the provinces and territories may require prior approval for emergency services delivered outside their jurisdiction.

4. True or False? One advantage of group health insurance is that some employees may be uninsurable on an individual basis, but may be able to get coverage as part of a group.

5. True or False? Critical illness insurance provides an income benefit to replace a portion of your earnings if you become ill or are injured and cannot work.

6. True or False? Your most valuable asset is your ability to earn an income.

7. True or False? The regular occupation definition of disability means that the policy will provide benefits only if you cannot perform the duties of any regular job that fits your education and experience.

8. True or False? With respect to long-term care insurance, everyday tasks include bathing, eating, dressing, toileting, continence, or transferring.

9. True or False? A term life insurance policy can be renewed as often as necessary during the lifetime of the life insured.

10. True or False? The mortality rate refers to the number of deaths in a population or in a subgroup of the population in one year.

11. True or False? One of the main advantages of creditor insurance is the ability to name a minor as a beneficiary of the policy.

12. True or False? Mortgage life insurance is a type of creditor insurance.

13. True or False? The three forms of permanent insurance include whole life, universal life, and term to 100.

14. True or False? For a household composed of two adult income earners and three children, the budget method of determining the amount of life insurance needed is probably most appropriate.

15. True or False? The guaranteed insurability rider allows you to purchase additional life insurance without having to resubmit evidence of financial insurability.

PART 3: BRAD MACDONALD—A CONTINUING CASE

Brad tells you about his plans to upgrade his auto insurance. Specifically, he would like to add several types of coverage to his policy, such as family protection coverage and rental car coverage. Recall that Brad is 30 years old. Brad also has a driving record that contains several speeding tickets and two accidents (one of which was his fault). He realizes that adding coverage will increase the cost of his insurance. Therefore, he is thinking about switching insurance companies to a more inexpensive carrier. When you ask Brad whether he has tenant's insurance, it is obvious that Brad does not know what tenant's insurance is.

Brad mentions that he is generally happy with the group insurance benefits that are available to him through his employer. With respect to these benefits, Brad's greatest concern is making sure that he has adequate coverage in the event of a long-term disability. Luckily, Brad's coverage at work provides him with 90 percent replacement of his after-tax income. When you ask Brad about the definition of disability under his group plan, he has no idea what it might be.

Brad's group life insurance covers only one year of his salary, or $48 000. He is not sure if this is enough insurance and is trying to decide between additional term life insurance and permanent life insurance. Brad likes permanent life insurance, as he believes that the loan feature on that policy will give him an option to meet his liquidity needs.

Case Questions

1. Regarding Brad's auto insurance decision, comment on:
   a. His plan to add different types of coverage to his auto insurance policy.
   b. The associated costs of adding different types of coverage to his auto insurance policy.
   c. Any resulting negative consequences of switching to a more inexpensive auto insurance company.
   d. Any other factors Brad should consider before switching insurance companies.

2. Describe tenant's insurance to Brad. What determines whether tenant's insurance is appropriate for Brad?

3. Describe to Brad how he could benefit from an evaluation of the definition of disability in his group disability insurance policy. Is it likely that Brad has coverage for critical illness through his employer? What are the advantages of purchasing critical illness insurance that Brad should consider?

4. Concerning Brad's life insurance decision, comment on:
   a. His need for life insurance.
   b. Whether permanent life insurance is his best choice, if you think he needs life insurance.
   c. His plan to use the whole life policy's loan feature as a means of maintaining liquidity.

Use the worksheets available on MyLab Finance to complete this case.

Personal Investing

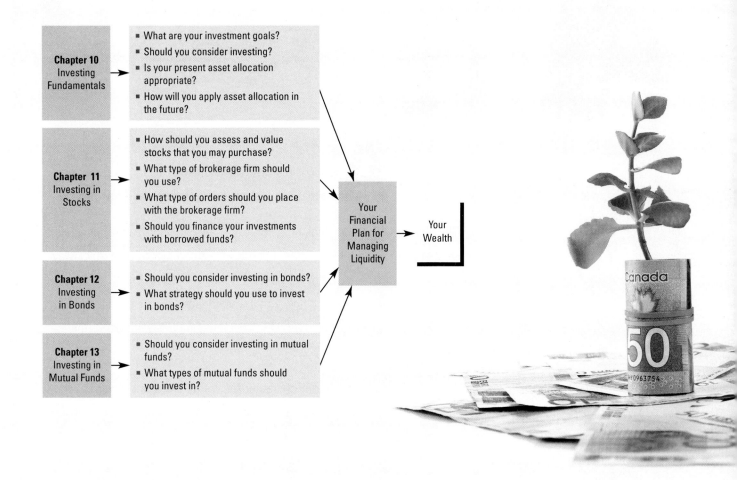

Chapter 10
Investing
Fundamentals

- What are your investment goals?
- Should you consider investing?
- Is your present asset allocation appropriate?
- How will you apply asset allocation in the future?

Chapter 11
Investing in
Stocks

- How should you assess and value stocks that you may purchase?
- What type of brokerage firm should you use?
- What type of orders should you place with the brokerage firm?
- Should you finance your investments with borrowed funds?

Chapter 12
Investing
in Bonds

- Should you consider investing in bonds?
- What strategy should you use to invest in bonds?

Chapter 13
Investing in
Mutual Funds

- Should you consider investing in mutual funds?
- What types of mutual funds should you invest in?

Your
Financial
Plan for
Managing
Liquidity

Your
Wealth

The chapters in this part explain the various types of investments that are available, how to value investments, and how to determine which investments to select. Chapter 10 provides a background on investing. Chapter 11 explains how to decide which stocks to buy, Chapter 12 focuses on investing in bonds, and Chapter 13 explains the advantages and disadvantages of investing in a portfolio of securities, such as mutual funds, rather than individual stocks and bonds. Your decisions regarding whether to invest, how much to invest, and what to invest in will affect your cash flows and wealth.

Investing Fundamentals

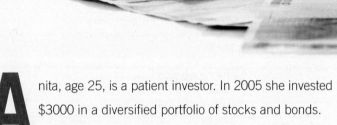

Cheryl Savan/Shutterstock

Anita, age 25, is a patient investor. In 2005 she invested $3000 in a diversified portfolio of stocks and bonds. By 2013, her original investment was worth $8000.

In 2005, Lisa, age 25, invested $1500 in stock of Zyko Co. because the company suggested its technology would change the world. Lisa hoped that this investment would be a quick way to wealth. When the stock dropped in value by 20 percent during the next six months, Lisa felt that it was a good idea to buy additional stock now that it was cheaper, so she invested another $1500. Unfortunately, Zyko's technology failed, and in 2013 the company went bankrupt. Consequently, Lisa's stock was worthless.

Lisa did not understand that the risk and return characteristics of different stocks varies widely. In addition, and as Lisa should now understand, an investment portfolio that contains only one investment has the potential to lose as much money as an investor expects to gain. By holding a portfolio of diversified stocks and bonds, Anita's portfolio perhaps offers a better opportunity for growth, since no one investment may drag down the entire portfolio.

QUESTIONS:

1. What was Anita's total return on her investment from 2005 to 2013? If Anita, now age 33, added $5 per day to her $8000 portfolio, how much money would she have when she reaches her planned retirement age of 65? Assume Anita will earn an annual return of 7 percent compounded monthly.

2. What is the relationship between the return that an investment can earn and the risk of the investment?

3. What is meant by the term "diversifying your portfolio"? What are the benefits of portfolio diversification?

THE LEARNING OBJECTIVES OF THIS CHAPTER ARE TO:

1. Describe the common types of investments
2. Explain how to measure the return on investments
3. Identify the risks of investments
4. Explain the trade-off between the return and risk of investments
5. Explain how diversification among asset classes can reduce risk
6. Describe strategies that can be used to diversify among stocks
7. Explain asset allocation strategies
8. Identify factors that affect your asset allocation decisions
9. Describe common investment mistakes that can be avoided

TYPES OF INVESTMENTS

L.0.1

Before considering how to invest money, review your personal balance sheet. If you have any existing loans, you should consider paying off those loans before investing any money. Some individuals receive a much larger psychological boost from using money to make investments rather than to pay off existing loans. However, such behaviour can backfire as illustrated here.

> **EXAMPLE**
>
> Mandeep just received an expected bonus of $10 000 from her job. She has a an existing car loan of $10 000 on which she is paying an interest rate of eight percent. If she pays off the existing loan, she will no longer have to make monthly payments on this loan. However, Mandeep wants to generate a much larger return on her money than just paying off the loan. She decides to invest the entire $10 000 in a very risky investment that could rise substantially over the next year under ideal conditions, but which could also become worthless under less favourable conditions. Over the next several months, adverse conditions occurred, which caused the investment to become worthless. Consequently, Mandeep not only lost her entire investment, but she still has a $10 000 loan outstanding that she could have paid off. Mandeep feels like a victim because her investment failed, but in truth her investment was a gamble: She had chosen to ignore information that suggested the investment could fail, because she decided that luck was on her side.

Money Market Securities

Recall from Chapter 5 that there are several different savings alternatives available, including term deposits, guaranteed investment certificates (GICs), Canada Savings Bonds (CSBs), and money market funds. Most money market securities provide interest income. Even if your liquidity needs are covered, you may invest in these securities to maintain a low level of risk. Yet, you can also consider some alternative securities that typically provide a higher rate of return but are riskier.

Stocks

As defined in Chapter 3, stocks are certificates that represent partial ownership of a firm. Firms issue shares to obtain funds to expand their business operations. Investors buy shares when they believe that they may earn a higher return than those offered on alternative investments. Since shares are a popular type of investment, they are the focus of Chapter 11.

Primary and Secondary Stock Markets. Shares can be traded in a primary or a secondary market. The **primary market** is a market in which newly issued securities are traded. Firms can raise funds by issuing new shares in the primary market. The first offering of

primary market
A market in which newly issued securities are traded.

initial public offering (IPO)
The first offering of a firm's shares to the public.

secondary market
A market which facilitates the trading of existing securities.

a firm's shares to the public is referred to as an **initial public offering (IPO)**. A **secondary market** facilitates the trading of existing securities, which allows investors the opportunity to sell their shares to other investors at any time. These shares are purchased by other investors who wish to invest in that company. Thus, even if a firm is not issuing new shares, investors can easily obtain that firm's shares by purchasing them in the secondary market. On a typical day, more than one million shares of any large firm are traded in the secondary market. The price of the shares changes each day in response to fluctuations in supply and demand.

Types of Stock Investors. Stock investors can be classified as institutional investors or individual investors. **Institutional investors** are professionals employed by a financial institution who are responsible for managing large pools of money on behalf of their clients. A pension fund, such as the Ontario Teachers' Pension Plan, is an example of a pool of money managed on behalf of clients. Institutional investors, also known as portfolio managers, attempt to select stocks or other securities that will provide a reasonable return on investment. More than half of all trading in financial markets is attributable to institutional investors.

This website provides
Canadian IPO search capabilities by underwriters, offering size, stock exchange, industry, and other parameters.

institutional investors
Professionals responsible for managing large pools of money, such as pension funds, on behalf of their clients.

individual investors
Individuals who invest funds in securities.

day traders
Investors who buy stocks and then sell them on the same day.

Individual investors commonly invest a portion of their income in stocks. Like institutional investors, they invest in stocks to earn a potentially better or higher return on their investment. In this way, their money can grow by the time they want to use it. The number of individual investors has increased substantially in the last 20 years.

Many individual investors hold their stocks for periods beyond one year. In contrast, some individual investors called **day traders** buy stocks and then sell them on the same day. They hope to capitalize on very short-term movements in security prices. In many cases, their investments may last for only a few minutes. Many day traders conduct their investing as a career, relying on their returns as their main source of income. This type of investing is very risky and requires skill, nerves, and capital. Day trading is not recommended for most investors.

myth or **fact** Always hold stocks long-term in order to reduce taxes and/or improve opportunities for capital gains.

Return from Investing in Stocks. Stocks can offer a return on investment through dividends and/or stock price appreciation. Some firms distribute quarterly income to their shareholders in the form of dividends rather than reinvest the earnings in their operations. They tend to keep the dollar amount of the dividends per share fixed from one quarter to the next, but may periodically increase the amount. They rarely reduce the dividend amount unless they experience relatively weak performance and cannot afford to make their dividend payments. The amount of dividends paid out per year is usually between 1 and 3 percent of the stock's price.

growth stocks
Shares of firms with substantial growth opportunities.

Go to:
http://investcom.com/ipo/index.htm

This website provides
Canadian IPO search capabilities by underwriters, offering size, stock exchange, industry, and other parameters.

value stocks
Stocks of firms that are currently undervalued by the market for reasons other than the performance of the businesses themselves.

A firm's decision to distribute earnings as dividends may depend on the opportunities available to it. In general, firms that pay high dividends tend to be older, established firms that have less chance of substantial growth. Conversely, firms that pay low dividends tend to be younger firms that have more growth opportunities. The shares of firms with substantial growth opportunities are often referred to as **growth stocks**. An investment in these younger firms offers the prospect of a very large capital gain because they have not yet reached their full potential. At the same time, investment in these firms is exposed to much higher uncertainty because young firms are more likely than mature firms to fail or experience very weak performance.

Value stocks are another type of stock investment that offers the prospect of a substantial return. However, the returns on these stocks may not be based on the growth opportunities available to the firm. Instead, **value stocks** represent the stocks of firms that are currently undervalued by the market for reasons other than the performance of the businesses themselves. Value stocks are usually not newsworthy because they are often not associated with up-and-coming younger firms. As a result, the assets of value stocks are often underappreciated, and undervalued by the market. A knowledgeable investor will recognize the hidden value in these stocks and purchase shares in the hope that the stock will eventually be recognized for its true potential by other investors.

The higher the dividend paid by a firm, the lower its potential stock price appreciation. When a firm distributes a large proportion of its earnings to investors as dividends, it limits its potential growth and the potential degree to which its value (and stock price) may increase. Stocks that provide investors with periodic income in the form of large dividends are referred to as **income stocks**.

income stocks
Stocks that provide investors with periodic income in the form of large dividends.

Shareholders can also earn a return if the price of the stock appreciates (i.e., increases) by the time they sell it. The market value of a firm is based on the number of shares of stock outstanding multiplied by the price of the stock. The price of a share of stock is determined by dividing the market value of the firm by the number of shares of stock outstanding. Therefore, a firm that has a market value of $600 million and 10 million shares of stock outstanding has a value per share of:

$$\text{Value of Stock per Share} = \text{Market Value of Firm} \div \text{Number of Shares Outstanding}$$

$$= \$600\ 000\ 000 \div 10\ 000\ 000$$

$$= \$60$$

The market price of a stock depends on the number of investors willing to purchase the stock (the demand) and the number of investors wanting to sell their stock (the supply). There is no limit to how high a stock's price can rise. The demand for the stock and the supply of stock for sale are influenced by the respective firm's business performance, as measured by its earnings and other characteristics. When the firm performs well, its stock becomes more desirable to investors, who demand more shares. In addition, investors holding shares of this stock are less willing to sell it. The increase in the demand for the shares and the reduction in the number of shares for sale results in a higher stock price.

Conversely, when a firm performs poorly (has low or negative earnings), its market value declines. The demand for shares of its stock also declines. In addition, some investors who had been holding the stock will decide to sell their shares, thereby increasing the supply of stock for sale and resulting in a lower price. The performance of the firm depends on how well it is managed.

Investors benefit when they invest in a well-managed firm because the firm's earnings usually will increase, and so will its stock price. Under these conditions, investors may generate a capital gain, which represents the difference between their selling price and their purchase price. In contrast, a poorly managed firm may have lower earnings than expected, which could cause its stock price to decline.

Common versus Preferred Stocks. Stocks can be classified as common stock or preferred stock. **Common stock** is a certificate issued by a firm to raise funds that represents partial ownership in the firm. Investors who hold common stock normally have the right to vote on key issues such as the sale of the company. They elect the board of directors, which is responsible for ensuring that the firm's managers serve the interests of its shareholders. In general, investors who purchase common stock are seeking a return on their investment from stock price appreciation, rather than dividends. Nevertheless, many companies that issue common stock also pay dividends to investors. **Preferred stock** is a certificate issued by a firm to raise funds that entitles shareholders to first priority (ahead of common stockholders) to receive dividends. Investors who purchase preferred stock are seeking the regular income that comes from dividend payments rather than the potential for stock price appreciation. The price of preferred stock is not as volatile as the price of common stock and does not have as much potential to increase substantially. For this reason, investors who strive for high returns typically invest in common stock, while those interested in income purchase preferred shares. Corporations issue common stock more frequently than preferred stock.

common stock
A certificate issued by a firm to raise funds that represents partial owner-ship in the firm.

preferred stock
A certificate issued by a firm to raise funds that entitles shareholders to first priority to receive dividends.

Bonds

Recall that bonds are long-term debt securities issued by government agencies or corporations. Government bonds are issued by the Bank of Canada on behalf of the federal government and backed by the Canadian government. Corporate bonds are issued by corporations.

Return from Investing in Bonds. Bonds offer a return to investors in the form of fixed interest (coupon) payments and bond price appreciation. Bonds are desirable for investors who want their investments to generate a specific amount of income each year. More details about bonds are provided in Chapter 12.

Mutual Funds

Recall from Chapter 5 that mutual funds sell units to individuals and invest the proceeds in a portfolio of investments that may include money market securities, stocks, bonds, and other investment types. In broader terms, mutual funds are a type of **pooled investment fund**, which is an investment vehicle that pools together money from many investors and invests that money in a variety of stock, bonds, and other investment types. They are managed by experienced portfolio managers and are attractive to investors who have limited funds and want to invest in a diversified portfolio.

pooled investment fund
An investment vehicle that pools together money from many investors and invests that money in a variety of securities.

publicly traded stock indexes
Securities whose values move in tandem with a particular stock index representing a set of stocks.

Publicly Traded Indexes. Another pooled investment fund option for investors who want a diversified portfolio of stocks is to invest in **publicly traded stock indexes**, which are securities whose values move in tandem with a particular stock index representing a set of stocks. These indexes are also known as exchange-traded funds (ETFs) because they trade on the stock exchanges like individual stocks.

Much research has shown that sophisticated investors (such as well-paid portfolio managers of financial institutions) are unable to outperform various stock indexes on average. Thus, by investing in an index, individual investors can ensure that their performance will come close to matching that index.

One of the most popular publicly traded indexes is the iShares Core S&P/TSX Capped Composite ETF, which tracks the S&P/TSX Capped Composite index. This ETF seeks to provide long-term growth by replicating, to the extent possible, the performance of the S&P/TSX Capped Composite. The ETF is able to do this by investing in and holding securities of the stocks that comprise the index. When investors expect that the Canadian stocks represented by the S&P/TSX will experience strong performance, they can capitalize on their expectations by purchasing shares of the iShares Core S&P/TSX Capped Composite ETF.

Investors can also invest in specific sector indexes as well as in market indexes. There are publicly traded indexes that represent a variety of specific sectors, including the internet, energy, technology, and financial sectors. Because an index represents several stocks, you can achieve some degree of diversification by investing in an index.

Return from Investing in Pooled Investment Funds. Since a pooled investment fund represents a portfolio of securities, its value changes over time in response to changes in the values of the various types of investments it is made up of. Investors who own a pooled investment fund may earn a return from interest income, dividends, and/or the price appreciation of the investments in the fund. Mutual funds and similar types of pooled investment funds are discussed in more detail in Chapter 13.

myth or **fact** Investing in real estate is only for wealthy investors.

Real Estate

One way of investing in real estate is to buy a home. For many individuals, the purchase of their first home is the largest real estate investment they will ever make. The value of a home changes over time in response to supply and demand. When the demand for homes in your area increases, home values tend to rise. The return that you earn on your home is difficult to measure because you must take into account the upfront financing costs, the costs associated with selling the home, and carrying costs, such as mortgage interest and property taxes. However, a few generalizations are worth mentioning. For a given amount invested in the home, your return depends on how the value of your home changes over the time you own it. Your return also depends on your original down payment on the home. The return will be lower if you made a smaller down payment when purchasing the home because interest and other costs will be higher. Since the value of a home can also decline over time, there is the risk of a loss (a negative return) on your investment. If you are in a hurry to sell your home, you may have to lower your selling price to attract potential buyers, which will result in a lower return on your investment. You can also invest in real estate by purchasing rental property or land. A rental property may include the purchase of additional homes, apartments, office buildings, or other commercial property. These properties can then be leased out to generate a rental income. If you are looking to sell these properties, they may also generate a capital gain or loss based on the supply and demand of similar properties in the area. Similarly, the price of land is also based on supply and demand. When there is little open land and dense population, as is the case in southern Ontario, land typically sells for a higher price.

Return from Investing in Real Estate. As has been discussed, real estate, such as office buildings and apartments, can be rented to generate income in the form of rent payments. In addition, investors may earn a capital gain if they sell a rental property for a higher price than they paid for it. Alternatively, they may sustain a capital loss if they sell the property for a lower price than they paid for it. With respect to your principal residence, any capital gains are usually exempt from taxation.

The price of land changes over time in response to real estate development. Many individuals may purchase land as an investment, hoping that they will be able to sell it in the future for a higher price.

INVESTMENT RETURN AND RISK

L.O.2

When individuals consider any particular investment, they must attempt to assess two characteristics: the potential return that will be earned on the investment and the risk of the investment.

Measuring the Return on Your Investment

For investments that do not provide any periodic income (such as dividends or interest payments), the return can be measured as the percentage change in the price (P) from the time the investment was purchased (time $t - 1$) until the time at which it is sold (time t):

$$R = \frac{P_t - P_{t-1}}{P_{t-1}}$$

For example, if you pay $1000 to make an investment and receive $1100 when you sell the investment one year later, you earn a return of:

$$R = \frac{\$1100 - \$1000}{\$1000}$$

$$= 0.10, \text{ or } 10\%$$

Incorporating Dividend or Coupon Payments. If you also earned dividend or interest payments over this period, your return would be even higher. For a short-term period such as one year or less, the return on a security that pays dividends or interest can be estimated by adjusting the equation above. Add the dividend or interest amount to the numerator. The return on your investment accounts for any dividends or interest payments you received as well as the change in the investment value over your investment period. For stocks that pay dividends, the return is:

$$R = \frac{(P_t - P_{t-1}) + D}{P_{t-1}}$$

where R is the return, P_{t-1} is the price of the stock at the time of the investment, P_t is the price of the stock at the end of the investment horizon, and D is the dividends earned over the investment horizon.

Here's an example: You purchased 100 shares of Wax Inc. stock for $50 per share one year ago. The firm experienced strong earnings during the year. It paid dividends of $1 per share over the year and you sold the stock for $58 per share at the end of the year. Your return on your investment was:

$$R = \frac{(P_t - P_{t-1}) + D}{P_{t-1}}$$

$$= \frac{(\$58 - \$50) + \$1}{\$50}$$

$$= 0.18, \text{ or } 18\%$$

TVM EXAMPLE

In the example above, the 18 percent return on your investment is an annual rate of return since the holding period for the investment was one year. What would be the annual return on your investment if the holding period had been five years? In this case, you can use your TI BA II Plus calculator to solve for [1/Y]. Assume that the $1 dividend per share is paid at the end of year 5, when you sell the stock.

The calculator key strokes are as follows:

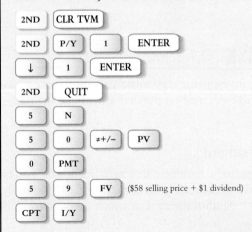

The annualized return on your investment would be 3.37 percent.

Differing Tax Rates on Returns. Recall from Chapter 4 that incomes received from interest payments, dividend payments, and capital gains are treated differently for tax purposes. An investor who receives $1000 of capital gains or dividend income will pay less tax than an investor who receives $1000 of interest income. Individuals who are in the highest marginal tax bracket will pay the most amount of taxes on capital gains. At lower marginal tax brackets, eligible dividend payments from large corporations that qualify for the enhanced dividend tax credit will result in the least amount of tax payable.

How Wealth Is Influenced by Your Return on Investment

When an investment provides income to you, any portion of that income that you save will increase the value of your assets. For example, if you receive a coupon payment of $100 this month as a result of holding a bond and deposit the proceeds in your savings account, your assets will increase by $100. If the value of your investments increases and your liabilities do not increase, your wealth increases.

The degree to which you can accumulate wealth partially depends on your investment decisions. You can estimate the amount by which your wealth will increase from an investment based on some assumed rate of return. The following example shows how your investment decisions and the performance of your investments can affect your future wealth.

EXAMPLE

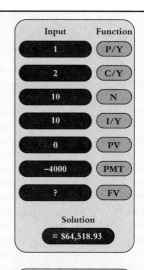

Input	Function
1	P/Y
2	C/Y
10	N
10	I/Y
0	PV
−4000	PMT
?	FV

Solution
= $64,518.93

Ha Lu believes that she can save $4000 to invest in stocks at the end of each year for the next 10 years. If she expects the investment value to increase by 10 percent, compounded semi-annually, she will accumulate $64 518.93. The input for the financial calculator is shown here.

Input	Function
1	P/Y
2	C/Y
10	N
12	I/Y
0	PV
−4000	PMT
?	FV

Solution
= $71,428.33

What if Ha's investment value increases by 12 percent per year, compounded semi-annually? Under this scenario, she will accumulate $71 428.33. The input for the financial calculator is shown here.

Notice how the increase in Ha's wealth is sensitive to the rate of return earned on her annual investment. An annual increase in investment value of 12 percent would allow her to accumulate $6909.40 more than if the annual increase is 10 percent.

L.O.3

Risk of Investing

The risk of an investment comes from the uncertainty surrounding its return. The return you will earn on a specific stock is uncertain because its future dividend payments are not guaranteed and its future price (when you sell the stock) is uncertain. The return you will earn on a bond is uncertain because its coupon payments are not guaranteed and its future price (when you sell the bond) is uncertain when you sell the bond before it matures. The return you will earn from investing in real estate is uncertain because rental income may not be paid and its value when you sell it is uncertain. Chapters 11, 12, and 13 discuss specific risks that stock, bond, and mutual fund investments are subject to.

unsystematic risk
Risk that is specific to a company, an industry, or a country.

systematic risk
Risk that affects all companies, industries, and countries.

Unsystematic and Systematic Risk. The specific risks of various types of investments are commonly referred to as unsystematic risks. An **unsystematic risk** is a risk that is specific to a company, an industry, or a country. For example, a poorly managed company may suffer a decrease in its stock price. This is an example of business management risk. Diversification and asset allocation can be used to eliminate, or at least minimize, unsystematic risk. **Systematic risk** is risk that affects all companies, industries, and countries. It is a category of risk that cannot be avoided. For example, many firms suffered a significant decrease in their stock price when Lehman Brothers went bankrupt during the 2008–2009 credit crisis. Many stocks of large, well-known companies experienced price declines of 40 percent or more during the credit crisis. The impact of systematic risk is usually even greater on small company stocks since their earnings are more volatile. Although some firms are more stable than others and are therefore less likely to experience a major decline in their market value, some investors prefer investments that have a higher growth potential, and they tolerate the higher level of risk. Before you select an investment, you should assess the risk of the investment and weigh this risk against your own risk tolerance. By diversifying your portfolio and allocating your assets across a number of different types of investment, you can reduce some of the risk in your portfolio of investments.

Measuring an Investment's Risk. Investors measure the risk of investments to determine the degree of uncertainty surrounding their future returns. Three common measures of an investment's risk are its range of returns, the standard deviation of its returns, and its beta. These measures can be applied to investments whose prices are frequently quoted over time.

range of returns
Returns of a specific investment over a given period.

Range of Returns. By reviewing the monthly returns of a specific investment over a given period, you can determine the **range of returns**, from the smallest (most negative) to the largest return. Compare an investment that has a range of monthly returns from 0.2 percent to 1.4 percent over the last year with an investment that has a range of 23.0 percent to 4.3 percent. The first investment is less risky because its range of returns is smaller and therefore it is more stable. Investments with a wide range have more risk because they have a higher probability of experiencing a large decline in price.

standard deviation
The degree of volatility in an investment's returns over time.

Standard Deviation of Returns. A second measure of risk is the **standard deviation** of an investment's monthly returns, which measures the degree of volatility in the investment's returns over time. A large standard deviation means that the returns deviate substantially from the mean over time. The more volatile the returns, the greater the chance that the stock could deviate far from its mean in a given period. Thus, an investment with a high standard deviation is more likely to experience a large gain or loss in a given period. The investment's return is subject to greater uncertainty, and for this reason it is perceived as riskier.

beta
Measures the systematic risk of an investment relative to a benchmark index.

Beta. A third measure of an investment's risk is its **beta**, which measures the systematic risk of an investment relative to a benchmark index. An investment with a beta of 1 suggests that the volatility of the investment and its performance will be similar to that of its benchmark. An investment with a beta of less than 1 suggests that the volatility of the investment and its performance will be less than that that of its benchmark An investment with a beta of greater than 1 suggests that the volatility of the investment and its performance will be greater than that of its benchmark.

Although these three measures differ, they tend to rank the risk levels of investments rather consistently. That is, a very risky investment will normally have a relatively wide range of returns, a high standard deviation of returns, and a beta much greater than one.

Subjective Measures of Risk. The use of the range of returns, standard deviation of returns, and beta is limited because these measures of risk are not always accurate predictors of the future changes in an investment's price. For example, an investment that had stable returns in the past could experience a substantial decline in price in the future in response to poor economic conditions or poor management. Because of this limitation, the risk of some investments is commonly measured subjectively. For example, the risk of a bond may be measured by a subjective assessment of the issuing firm's ability to repay its debt. The assessment may include an estimate of the firm's future monthly revenue to determine whether it will have sufficient funds to cover its interest and other expenses. Investors may rely on experts to offer their risk assessment of a particular type of investment. Bond rating agencies offer risk assessments of various bonds, as explained in Chapter 12.

TRADE-OFF BETWEEN RETURN AND RISK

L.O.4

Every individual investor would like investments that offer a very high return and have no risk. However, such investments do not exist. Investors must weigh the trade-off between the potential return of an investment and the risk. If you want an investment that may generate a higher return, you have to tolerate the higher degree of uncertainty (risk) associated with that investment.

Investors expect a higher return for taking on additional risk. As a result, any investment that is not risk-free contains a **risk premium**, which is the extra yield required, or additional return earned, by investors to compensate for default risk. The higher the potential risk of an investment, the higher the risk premium you should expect.

risk premium
The extra yield required by investors to compensate for default risk; an additional return beyond the risk-free rate you could earn from an investment.

If a particular risky deposit is supposed to offer a specific return (R) over a period and you know the risk-free rate (R_f) offered on a deposit backed by the government, you can determine the risk premium (RP) offered on the risky deposit:

$$RP = R - R_f$$

EXAMPLE

Daya Rai has $10 000 that she could invest for the next three months in a three-month Government of Canada T-bill or in a stock. The T-bill offers a return of two percent over the three-month period. Alternatively, she thinks that the price of the stock will rise by five percent over the next three months. However, since the future price of the stock is uncertain, her return from investing in this stock is also uncertain. The return could be less than five percent and might even be negative. Daya decides to invest in the T-bill rather than the stock because the three percent risk premium offered by the stock is not enough to entice her to take on the additional risk.

The example above illustrates the trade-off between a risk-free investment and a risky investment. There are also trade-offs between assets with varying degrees of risk, as explained below for each type of investment.

Return–Risk Trade-off among Stocks

Some firms have the potential to achieve a much higher performance level than others. But to do so, they take on more risk than other firms. That is, they may try to operate with less funding and pursue riskier opportunities. Investors who invest in one of these firms may earn very high returns if the firm's strategies are successful. However, they could lose most or all of their investment if the firm's strategies fail.

In general, smaller firms have more potential for faster growth and their stocks have the potential to increase in value to a greater degree. However, their stocks are risky because many small firms never reach their potential. The more mature firms that have already achieved high growth have less potential for future growth. However, these firms tend to be less risky because their businesses are more stable.

Initial public offerings (IPOs) are another stock investment option. You may have heard that IPO returns may exceed 20 percent over the first day. However, there is much risk with this type of investment. Individual investors rarely have access to these IPOs at the initial price. Institutional investors (such as mutual funds or insurance companies with large amounts of money to invest) normally have the opportunity or chance to purchase shares of an IPO. Most individual investors can invest (if there are any shares left) after the institutional investors' needs have been satisfied. By the time individual investors are able to invest in a newly issued stock, the price will have already risen. For example, Twitter's IPO price was $26 per share. By the end of its first trading day, Wednesday, November 6, 2013, the stock closed at $44.90, an increase of 73 percent! A significant portion of this increase would have gone to institutional investors, who would have had the opportunity to buy the stock before individual investors. Individual investors commonly obtain the shares only after the price has reached its peak and then incur large losses as the stock price declines over the next several months.

Many IPOs have performed poorly. On average, the long-term return on IPOs is weak compared to typical returns of other stocks in aggregate. Many firms that engage in IPOs (such as pets.com) fail within a few years, causing investors to lose all of their capital investment.

Return–Risk Trade-off among Bonds

You may invest in a bond issued by a firm to earn the high interest payment. The risk of your investment is that the firm may be unable to make this payment if its financial condition deteriorates. If you purchase a bond of a large, well-known, and successful firm, there is minimal risk that the firm will default on its payments. If you purchase a bond issued by a firm that is struggling financially, there is more risk that this firm will default on its payments. If this firm defaults on the bond, your loss may be total.

High-risk bonds tend to offer higher interest payments. Therefore, you must weigh the trade-off between the potential return and the risk. If you are willing to tolerate the higher risk, you may consider investing in a bond issued by a weak firm. Alternatively, if you prefer less risk, you can purchase a bond issued by a successful and established firm, as long as you are willing to accept a lower return on your investment.

Return–Risk Trade-off among Mutual Funds

When you invest in a mutual fund composed of stocks, you earn a return from the dividend payments and the increase in the prices of the stocks held by the mutual fund. The risk of a stock mutual fund is that the prices of the stocks can decline in any particular period. Since the mutual fund is composed of numerous stocks, the adverse impact caused by any single stock is reduced. However, when economic conditions weaken, most stocks tend to perform poorly. Just as the shares of smaller companies (in terms of capital) tend to be riskier than those of companies with larger capitalization, mutual funds that hold mostly small capitalization (small-cap) companies will be riskier than those that hold the larger capitalization companies. Yet, some investors still prefer mutual funds that contain small stocks because they expect a higher return from these stocks.

When you invest in a mutual fund composed of bonds, your primary risk is that the bonds held by the mutual fund could **default**, which occurs when a company borrows money through the issuance of debt securities and does not pay either the interest or the principal. Since a bond mutual fund contains numerous bonds, the adverse effect of a single bond default within a mutual fund is reduced. However, when economic conditions deteriorate, many firms that issued bonds could experience financial problems and have

default
Occurs when a company borrows money through the issuance of debt securities and does not pay either the interest or the principal.

difficulty making their interest payments. Some bond mutual funds are not highly exposed to risk because they invest only in corporate bonds issued by the most creditworthy corporations. Others are highly exposed because they invest in bonds issued by relatively weak corporations that pay higher interest rates. Investors who prefer risky bond mutual funds because of their potential to offer a high return must tolerate the higher level of risk. There is another risk with debt securities: interest-rate risk. This will be discussed in Chapter 12.

Return–Risk Trade-off among Real Estate Investments

When you invest in real estate, your risk depends on your particular investment. If you buy rental property, it may not generate your anticipated periodic income if you cannot find renters or if your renters default on their rent payments. In addition, there is a risk that the property's value will decline over time. The degree of risk varies with the type of real estate investment. If you purchase an office building that is fully occupied, the risk is relatively low. Conversely, if you purchase a piece of open land in Saskatchewan because you hope you will someday discover oil on the land, the risk in your investment is high.

Comparing Different Types of Investments

As a prudent investor, you must choose investments that suit your personal objectives. If you want to achieve a fixed return over a short-term period with little risk, you should consider investing in a term deposit. The disadvantage of this type of investment is that it offers a relatively low return. If you want to achieve a stable return over a long-term period, you should consider a GIC or mutual funds that contain GICs. At the other extreme, if you desire a very high return, you could consider investing in land or in high-growth stocks.

Many investors fall in between these two extremes. They prefer a higher return than is offered by term deposits or GICs but want to limit their risk. There is no formula that can determine your ideal investment because the choice depends on how much risk you want to take and on your financial situation.

To illustrate, consider the situations and possible solutions shown in Exhibit 10.1. In general, you are in a better position to take some risk when you know that you will not need to sell the investment in the near future. Even if the value of the investment declines, you have the flexibility to hold on to the investment until the value increases. Conversely, individuals investing for the short term should play it safe. Since the prices of risky investments fluctuate substantially, it is dangerous to invest in a risky investment when you know that you will be selling that investment in the near future. You could be forced to sell it when the investment has a low value. Investors who decide to pursue higher potential returns must be willing to accept the high risk associated with these investments.

EXHIBIT 10.1   How Investment Decisions Vary with Your Situation

Situation	Decision
You have $1000 to invest but will need the funds in one month to pay bills.	You need liquidity. You should only consider money market securities.
You have $3000 to invest but will need the funds in a year to make a tuition payment.	You should consider safe money market securities such as a one-year GIC.
You have $5000 to invest and will likely use the funds in about 3 years when you buy a home.	Consider a three-year GIC or stocks of relatively stable firms that have relatively low risk.
You have $10 000 to invest and have no funds set aside for retirement in 20 years.	Consider investing in a diversified stock mutual fund.
You have $5000 to invest. You expect that you will be laid off from your job within the next year.	You should probably invest the funds in money market securities so that you will have easy access to the funds if you lose your job.

By having a variety of investments, you can find a tolerable risk level. You can diversify your investments among many different investments, thereby reducing your exposure to any particular investment. If you divide your money equally among five investments and one investment performs poorly, your exposure is limited.

Even if you diversify your portfolio among various investments, you are still exposed to general economic conditions since the values of most types of investments can decline during periods in which economic conditions are weak. For this reason, you should consider diversifying among various types of investments that are not equally sensitive to economic conditions. The strategy of diversification, also known as asset allocation, is crucial for investors.

L.O.5

HOW DIVERSIFICATION REDUCES RISK

If you knew which investment would provide the highest return for a specific period, investment decisions would be easy: you would invest all of your money in that particular investment. In the real world, there is a trade-off between risk and return when investing. Although the return on some investments (such as GIC) is known for a specific investment period, these investments offer a relatively low rate of return. Many investments such as stocks, some types of bonds, and real estate offer the prospect of higher rates of return.

Benefits of Portfolio Diversification

asset allocation
The process of allocating money across financial assets (such as mutual funds, stocks, and bonds) with the objective of achieving a desired return while maintaining risk at a tolerable level.

portfolio
A set of multiple investments in different assets.

insider information
Non-public information known by employees and other professionals that is not known by outsiders. It is illegal to use insider information.

Because the returns from many types of investments are uncertain, it is wise to allocate your money across various types of investments so that you are not completely dependent on any one type. **Asset allocation** is the process of allocating money across financial assets (such as mutual funds, stocks, and bonds) with the objective of achieving a desired return while maintaining risk at a tolerable level.

Building a Portfolio. You can reduce your risk by investing in a **portfolio,** which is a set of multiple investments in different assets. For example, your portfolio may consist of various stocks, bonds, and real estate investments. By constructing a portfolio, you diversify across several investments rather than focus on a single investment. Investors who had all of their funds invested in Nortel Networks stock saw their investments fall from more than $124 per share in March 2000 to less than $1 per share by September 2002. As of June 26, 2009, Nortel Networks stock was removed from the Toronto Stock Exchange at a final price of $0.185 per share. Given the difficulty in anticipating when an investment might experience a major decline, you can at least reduce your exposure to any one stock by spreading your investments across several firms' stocks and bonds. A portfolio can reduce risk when its investments do not move in perfect tandem. Then, even if one investment experiences very poor performance, the other investments may perform well.

FOCUS ON ETHICS: The Risk of Insider Trading

It can be tempting to seek **insider information** (non-public information known by employees and other professionals that is not known by outsiders) when deciding how to invest your funds. For example, you might casually ask friends for tips about the firms that employ them, hoping that you can buy a company's stock before any significant news is released that will cause the stock price to rise. Investors are legally bound to use only information that is publicly available. When insider trading occurs, investors who play by the rules are at a disadvantage.

You can minimize your risk by using proper asset allocation. For example, if your assets are widely diversified among different types of mutual funds and other investments, you minimize your exposure to any one investment (such as a stock) that could experience a substantial decline in value once any negative news is released.

Determining Portfolio Benefits

To determine a portfolio's diversification benefits, you compare the return on the individual investments it consists of to the overall portfolio.

You are considering investing in a portfolio consisting of investments A and B. Exhibit 10.2 illustrates the portfolio diversification effect of using these two stocks. It shows the return per year for investments A and B, as well as for a portfolio with 50 percent of the investment allocated to A and 50 percent to B. The portfolio return in each year is simply the average return of A and B. Notice that the portfolio's range of returns is smaller than the range of returns of either stock. Also notice that the portfolio's returns are less volatile over time than the returns of the individual stocks. Since the portfolio return is an average of A and B, it has a smoother trend than either individual investment. The smoother trend demonstrates that investing in the portfolio is less risky than investing in either individual investment. You decide to create a partially diversified portfolio of both investments to reduce your risk.

As the previous example illustrates, the main benefit of diversification is that it reduces the exposure of your investments to the adverse effects of any individual investment. In Exhibit 10.2, notice that when investment A experienced a return of –20 percent in Year 2, the portfolio return was –5 percent. The adverse effect on the portfolio was limited because B's return was 10 percent during that year. Investment A's poor performance still affected the portfolio's performance, but less than if it had been the only investment. When B experienced a weak return (such as –15 percent in Year 5), its poor performance was partially offset because A's performance was 5 percent in that year.

EXHIBIT 10.2   Example of Portfolio Diversification Effects

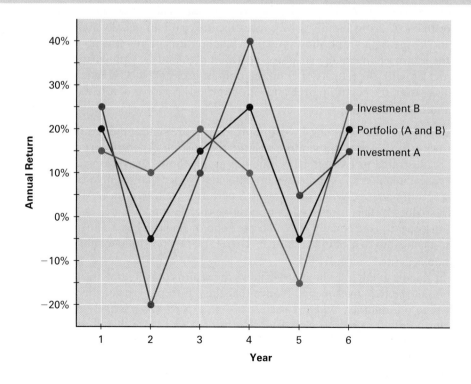

EXHIBIT 10.3   Impact of an Investment's Volatility on Portfolio Diversification Effects

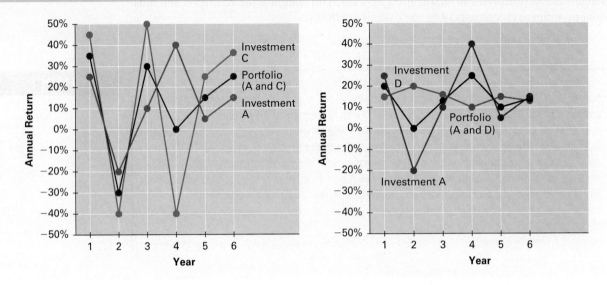

Factors That Influence Diversification Benefits

A portfolio's risk is often measured by its degree of volatility because the more volatile the returns, the more uncertain the future return on the portfolio. By recognizing the factors that reduce a portfolio's risk, you can ensure that your portfolio exhibits these characteristics. The volatility of a portfolio's returns is influenced by the volatility of returns on each individual investment within the portfolio and by the **correlation** (a mathematical measure that describes how two securities' prices move in relation to one another) of the returns among investments.

correlation
A mathematical measure that describes how two securities' prices move in relation to one another.

Volatility of Each Individual Investment. As Exhibit 10.3 illustrates, the more volatile the returns of individual investments in a portfolio, the more volatile the portfolio's returns are over time (holding other factors constant). The left graph shows the returns of investment A (as in Exhibit 10.2), investment C, and an equally weighted portfolio of A and C; the right graph shows the individual returns of investments A and D, along with the return of an equally weighted portfolio of A and D. Comparing the returns of C on the left with the returns of D on the right, it is clear that C is much more volatile. For this reason, the portfolio of A and C (on the left) is more volatile than the portfolio of A and D (on the right).

Impact of Correlations among Investments. The more similar the returns of individual investments in a portfolio, the more volatile the portfolio's returns are over time. This point is illustrated in Exhibit 10.4. The left graph shows the returns of A, E, and an equally weighted portfolio of the two investments. Notice that the investments have very similar return patterns. When investment A performs well, so does E. When A performs poorly, so does E. This is referred to as positive correlation.

Consequently, the equally weighted portfolio of A and E has a return pattern that is almost identical to that of either A or E. Therefore, this portfolio exhibits limited diversification benefits.

The middle graph in Exhibit 10.4 shows the returns of A, F, and an equally weighted portfolio of the two investments. Notice that the return patterns of the investments are opposite to one another. When A performs well, F performs relatively poorly. When A performs poorly, F performs well. The returns of A and F are therefore negatively correlated. Consequently, the equally weighted portfolio of A and F has a very stable return pattern because the returns of the stocks moved in opposite directions. Due to the negative correlation of returns, this portfolio offers substantial diversification benefits.

EXHIBIT 10.4 Impact of Correlations on Portfolio Diversification

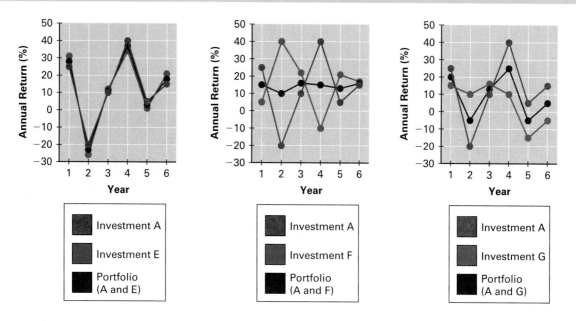

The right graph in Exhibit 10.4 shows the returns of A, G, and an equally weighted portfolio of the two investments. Notice that the return patterns of the two stocks are independent of each other. That is, A's performance is not related to G's performance. The return pattern of the equally weighted portfolio of A and G is more volatile than the returns of the portfolio of A and F (middle graph), but less volatile than the returns of the portfolio of A and E (left graph). Thus, the portfolio of investments A and G exhibits more diversification benefits than a portfolio of two investments that are positively related, but fewer diversification benefits than a portfolio of negatively correlated investments.

This discussion suggests that when you compile a portfolio you should avoid including investments that exhibit a high positive correlation. Although finding investments that are as negatively correlated as A and F may be difficult, you should at least consider investments whose values are not influenced by the same conditions. In reality, many investments are similarly influenced by economic conditions. If economic conditions deteriorate, most investments perform poorly. Nevertheless, some are influenced to a higher degree than others.

Go to:
http://finance.yahoo.com

Click on:
Basic Chart after inserting a stock symbol. Then enter the symbol for another stock in the box labelled Compare and perform your own comparison.

This website provides
a graph that shows the returns on two stocks so that you can compare their performance over time and determine their degree of correlation.

STRATEGIES FOR DIVERSIFYING

L.O.6

There are many different strategies for diversifying among investments. Some of the more popular strategies related to stocks are described here.

Diversification of Stocks across Industries

When you diversify your investments among stocks in different industries, you reduce your exposure to one particular industry. In other words, you reduce your exposure to unsystematic risk. For example, you may invest in the stock of a firm in the publishing and music industry, the stock of a firm in the banking industry, the stock of a firm in the health care industry, and so on. When demand for books declines, conditions may still be favourable in the health care industry. Therefore, a portfolio of stocks diversified across industries is less risky than a portfolio of stocks that are all from the same industry.

EXHIBIT 10.5   Benefits of Portfolio Diversification

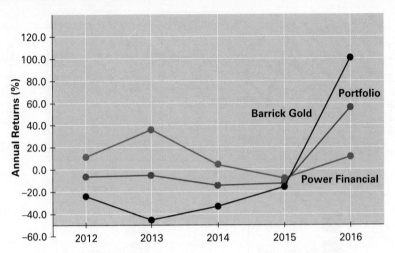

Source: Data from Yahoo! Canada, Historical Prices for S&P/TSX Composite Index, https://ca.finance.yahoo.com, accessed March 10, 2017.

| **myth** or **fact** Diversification reduces the risk of a portfolio, and consequently it usually will reduce the returns of the portfolio.

The graph in Exhibit 10.5 illustrates the diversification benefits of a portfolio consisting of two equally weighted stocks: Barrick Gold Corporation and Power Financial Corporation. Each of these firms is in a different industry and therefore is subjected to different industry conditions. Annual stock returns are shown for a recent period in which stock market conditions were mixed. Diversification is especially valuable during poor conditions. Notice that Power Financial experienced relatively strong stock price performance in 2012 and 2013 as compared to Barrick Gold. Overall, the relatively strong performance of one stock in specific periods was partially offset by the relatively weak performance of the other stock within the portfolio. Notice how the returns of the two-stock portfolio are less volatile than those of either individual stock. When adding more stocks to the portfolio, the diversification benefits are even greater because the proportional investment in any stock is smaller.

Limitations of Industry Diversification. Although diversification among stocks in different industries is more effective than diversification within an industry, the portfolio can still be very susceptible to general economic conditions. Stocks exhibit market risk, or susceptibility to poor performance because of weak stock market conditions. A stock portfolio composed of stocks of Canadian firms based in different industries may perform poorly when economic conditions in Canada are weak. Thus, diversification will not necessarily prevent losses when economic conditions are poor, but it can limit the losses.

Diversification of Stocks across Countries

Because economic conditions (and therefore stock market conditions) vary among countries, you may achieve more favourable returns by diversifying your stock investments across countries. For example, you may wish to invest in a variety of Canadian stocks across different industries, American stocks, European stocks, and Asian stocks. Many investment advisers recommend that you invest about 20 to 30 percent of your money in Canadian stocks and allocate 70 to 80 percent to foreign countries.

Diversifying among stocks based in different countries makes you less vulnerable to economic conditions in any one country. Economic conditions in countries can be interrelated, however. In some periods, all countries may simultaneously experience weak economic conditions, causing stocks in all countries to perform poorly at the same time. When investing in stocks outside Canada, recognize that they are typically even more volatile than Canadian-based stocks, as they are subject to more volatile economic conditions. Therefore, you should diversify among stocks within each foreign country rather than rely on a single stock in any foreign country. Also, keep in mind that the returns in stock markets of small developing countries may be very volatile, so an international portfolio may be less risky if it is focused on developed countries that have well-established stock markets with very active trading.

FREE APPS for Personal Finance

Diversification

Application:

The iDiversify app by John Hancock Funds, LLC is a practical, user-friendly app that can help you explore and analyze the annual performance of equity, fixed-income, and alternative asset classes. The interactive format allows for a quick, side-by-side comparison of performance from 2003–2012 and lets you compare how a diversified portfolio would have done over the same time period.

ASSET ALLOCATION STRATEGIES

L.O.7

When investors make asset allocation decisions, they should not restrict their choices to stocks. All stocks can be affected by general stock market conditions, so diversification benefits are limited. Greater diversification benefits can be achieved by including other financial assets, such as money market funds, bonds, mutual funds, income trusts, and real estate. Your portfolio size and knowledge level will help to determine the financial assets you should include in your portfolio.

Including Bonds in Your Portfolio

The returns from investing in stocks and from investing in bonds are not highly correlated. Stock prices are influenced by each firm's expected future performance and general stock market conditions. Bond prices are inversely related to interest rates and are not directly influenced by stock market conditions. Therefore, including bonds in your portfolio can reduce your susceptibility to stock market conditions. The expected return on bonds is usually less than the return on stocks, however, since bonds are often perceived as having less risk.

As you allocate more of your investment portfolio to bonds, you reduce your exposure to stock market risk but increase your exposure to interest-rate risk. Your portfolio is more susceptible to a decline in value when interest rates rise because the market values of your bonds will decline. As will be discussed in Chapter 13, you can limit your exposure to interest-rate risk by investing in bonds with relatively short maturities because the prices of those bonds are less affected by interest-rate movements than the prices of long-term bonds.

In general, the larger the proportion of your portfolio that is allocated to bonds, the lower your portfolio's overall risk (as measured by the volatility of returns). The portfolio's value will be more stable over time, and it is less likely to generate a loss in any given period. Investors who are close to retirement and are more concerned about periodic income from their investments commonly allocate much of their portfolio to income-producing investments, such as bonds. Conversely, investors who are 30 to 50 years old and are more concerned about growth tend to focus their allocation on stocks. Although stocks fluctuate in value, investors in their earlier life stages have time to recover their investment if stocks decrease significantly in value.

Including Income Trust Investments in Your Portfolio

income trust
A flow-through investment vehicle that generates income and capital gains for investors.

An **income trust** is a flow-through investment vehicle that generates income and capital gains for investors. It is similar to a mutual fund in that many investors purchase units of the trust. This money is used by the trust to invest in income-producing assets.

In theory, one of the main benefits of an income trust is that almost 100 percent of the income generated by the trust assets is "flowed through" to the investors who have purchased units in the trust. Many investors have misinterpreted this steady cash flow as a reliable substitute for bonds and dividend-paying stocks. Although many income trusts have bond-like features, such as the regular distribution of income, an income trust is similar to a stock investment. A stock's price will decrease if a company cannot generate adequate earnings from its assets. Similarly, the unit price of an income trust will decrease if the assets in the trust are unable to generate adequate income. Income trust investors may earn income from the trust but lose part of their capital if the value of the units decreases.

real estate investment trusts (REIT)
An income trust that pools funds from individuals and uses that money to invest in real estate.

There are three major categories of income trusts: royalty income trusts, business investment trusts, and real estate investment trusts (REITs). Some REITs continue to benefit from the tax advantages available to income trusts. A **real estate investment trust (REIT)** is an income trust that pools funds from individuals and uses that money to invest in real estate. REITs commonly invest in commercial real estate such as office buildings and shopping centres.

REIT shares are traded on stock exchanges. REITs are popular among individual investors because the shares can be purchased with a small amount of money. For example, an investor could purchase 100 shares of a REIT priced at $30 per share for a total of $3000 (computed as $30 × 100 shares). Another desirable characteristic of REITs is that they are managed by skilled real estate professionals who decide what properties to purchase and who will maintain the properties.

How Asset Allocation Affects Risk

Some asset allocation strategies reduce risk to a greater degree than others. To maintain a very low level of risk, an asset allocation may emphasize GICs, Canadian government bonds, and the stocks of large, established Canadian, American, and international firms. These types of investments tend to have low risk, but also offer a relatively low rate of return. To strive for a higher return, the asset allocation should include more real estate and stocks of developing countries. Exhibit 10.6 compares different asset allocation strategies in terms of risk and potential return. In 2008, stocks, real estate, and low-rated corporate bonds experienced losses. Therefore, an asset allocation strategy that diversified among these types of assets would have resulted in a large loss. Subsequently, almost all major asset types experienced a bounce-back year in 2009. Even the most conservative asset allocation strategy shown here could result in a loss over a given period because some of the investments included in the portfolio are subject to losses.

myth or **fact** Asset allocation explains more than 90 percent of the investment returns of an investment portfolio.

An Affordable Way to Conduct Asset Allocation

When allocating money across a set of financial assets, you are subject to transaction fees on each investment you make. As a result, it can be costly to invest in a wide variety of investments. You can reduce your diversification costs by investing in mutual funds. Since a typical stock mutual fund contains more than 50 stocks, you can broadly diversify by investing in a few stock mutual funds.

EXHIBIT 10.6   Comparison of Asset Allocation Strategies

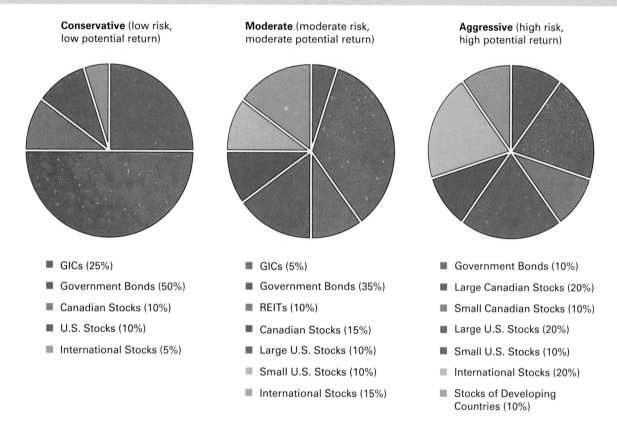

Conservative (low risk, low potential return)

- GICs (25%)
- Government Bonds (50%)
- Canadian Stocks (10%)
- U.S. Stocks (10%)
- International Stocks (5%)

Moderate (moderate risk, moderate potential return)

- GICs (5%)
- Government Bonds (35%)
- REITs (10%)
- Canadian Stocks (15%)
- Large U.S. Stocks (10%)
- Small U.S. Stocks (10%)
- International Stocks (15%)

Aggressive (high risk, high potential return)

- Government Bonds (10%)
- Large Canadian Stocks (20%)
- Small Canadian Stocks (10%)
- Large U.S. Stocks (20%)
- Small U.S. Stocks (10%)
- International Stocks (20%)
- Stocks of Developing Countries (10%)

FACTORS THAT AFFECT YOUR ASSET ALLOCATION DECISION

L.O.8

Your ideal asset allocation may not be appropriate for someone else because of differences in your personal characteristics and investment goals. The asset allocation decision hinges on several factors, including your stage in life and your risk tolerance.

Your Stage in Life

Investors in the early life stages need easy access to funds, so they should invest in relatively safe and liquid securities such as money market investments. If they do not expect to need the invested funds in the near future, they may want to consider investing in a diversified portfolio of individual stocks, individual bonds, stock mutual funds, and bond mutual funds. Investors who expect to be working for many more years may invest in stocks of smaller firms and growth stock mutual funds, which have high growth potential.

Conversely, investors nearing retirement age may allocate a larger proportion of money toward investments that will generate a fixed income, such as individual bonds, stock mutual funds containing high-dividend stocks, bond mutual funds, and some types of REITs. In any case, you must have enough money saved to invest wisely.

Although no single asset allocation formula is suitable for everyone, the common trends in asset allocation over a lifetime are shown in Exhibit 10.7. Notice the heavy emphasis on stocks at an early stage of life, as individuals take some risk in the hope that they can increase their wealth. Over time, they gradually shift toward bonds or to stocks of stable firms that pay high dividends. The portfolio becomes less risky as investments become more heavily weighted in bonds and stocks of stable firms. This portfolio is less likely to generate large returns, but it will provide periodic income upon retirement.

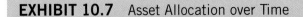

EXHIBIT 10.7   Asset Allocation over Time

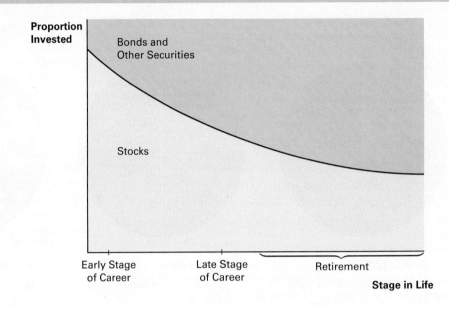

Go to:
www.vanguardcanada.ca

Click on:
Individual investors

This website provides
a personalized recommended
asset allocation once you
input some basic information
about your preferences and
degree of risk tolerance.

For almost all individuals, your stage in life is closely associated with your age. In this case, a useful rule of thumb that you can use to determine what percentage of your portfolio should be in stocks at any given time is 100 minus your age. Therefore, a 30 year-old should have approximately 70 percent of his or her portfolio invested in stocks.

Your Degree of Risk Tolerance

Investors also vary in their degree of risk tolerance. If you are unwilling to take much risk, you should focus on safe investments. For example, you could invest in government bonds with relatively short maturities. If you are willing to accept a moderate level of risk, you may consider a stock mutual fund that represents the S&P/TSX Composite Index (an index of the stock prices of the largest companies on the Toronto Stock Exchange) and/or large-cap stock mutual funds that invest in stocks of very large and stable firms. These investments offer more potential return than an investment in bonds, but they also may result in losses in some periods.

If you are willing to tolerate a higher degree of risk in order to strive for higher returns, you may consider individual stocks. Smaller stocks that are focused on technology tend to have potential for high returns, but they are also very risky. Even if you can tolerate a high level of risk, you should still diversify your investments. You might consider various mutual funds that have the potential to achieve a high return but contain a diversified set of stocks, so you are not overexposed to a single stock. Chapter 13 discusses some of the types of funds you could choose from, including various growth funds, capital appreciation funds, and even funds focused on sectors such as health care or financial firms. You may also consider bond mutual funds that invest in corporate bonds. You can increase your potential return (and therefore your risk) by focusing on high-yield (junk) bond mutual funds with long terms to maturity.

Some investors use an unrealistic perception of the investment environment to justify their investment behaviour. They are unwilling to recognize how much risk they are taking, and make investments that tend to generate a very strong return when economic conditions are favourable but a very weak return when economic conditions are unfavourable. When economic conditions are favourable, these investors are very pleased and believe that they have very good investment skills. However, when economic conditions are unfavourable, these types of investments perform poorly.

Some investors simply are unwilling to accept that unfavourable economic conditions might occur. They always have a very optimistic outlook on the economy, but they should be realistic rather than overly optimistic. That is, as they make risky investments, they should recognize that they could easily incur large losses if the economy weakens. If they are not in a position in which they can afford to incur large losses, they should seriously consider safer types of investments. Safer investments, however, are not as exciting because they do not offer the potential for high returns. Thus, some investors end up gambling their money in risky investments, and therefore possibly risk major losses that they cannot afford.

Your Expectations about Economic Conditions

Your expectations about economic conditions also influence your asset allocation. If you expect strong stock market conditions, you may shift a larger proportion of your money into your stock mutual funds. Conversely, if you expect a temporary weakness in the stock market, you may shift a larger proportion of your money to your bond mutual funds. If you expect interest rates to decrease, you may consider shifting money from a bond mutual fund containing bonds with short maturities to one containing bonds with long maturities.

If you anticipate favourable real estate conditions, you may allocate some of your money to REITs. As time passes, your expectations may change, causing some types of financial assets to become more desirable than others. You should change the composition of your investment portfolio in response to changes in your market expectations, investment goals, and life circumstances. While a review can take place when you conduct your overall financial plan review, investments typically need more attention. Despite the fact that mutual funds are considered to be long-term investments (with the exception of money market mutual funds), investors should review portfolio performance and composition on a regular basis. If investors are investing in individual stocks and bonds, reviews must be done a great deal more frequently.

Because it is nearly impossible to predict economic conditions, it is difficult to determine which types of investments will perform best in a given period. Consequently, you may be better off basing your asset allocation decisions completely on your stage in life and degree of risk tolerance. Then, once you establish a diversified portfolio of investments, you will need to revise the portfolio only when you enter a different stage in life or change your degree of risk tolerance.

LEARNING FROM INVESTMENT MISTAKES

L.O.9

Many individual investors learn from their own mistakes or from the mistakes of others. Consider the following investment mistakes so that you can avoid them.

Making Decisions Based on Unrealistic Goals

One of the most common mistakes is letting unrealistic goals dictate your investment decisions. These goals may force you to take more risk than you should and can result in major losses.

EXAMPLE

Laurie Chen has $4000, which should cover her school expenses next year. She is considering investing the money in a one-year GIC that would earn about four percent, or about $160, in interest before next year. However, she would like to earn a higher return within the next year so that she can buy a used car. She decides to invest in a small stock that earned a return of 50 percent last year. If the stock's value increases by 50 percent again over the next year, her investment would generate a gain of $2000, which would allow her to buy a used car.

(continued)

Unfortunately, the stock's value declines by 30 percent over the year. At the end of the year, her investment is worth $2800, a $1200 loss. She does not have sufficient funds to cover her school expenses or to buy the car. She did not view her investment as a gamble, as the money was invested in the stock of a firm. However, her investment in one small stock was just as risky as gambling, especially since she had no information to support her decision except that the stock performed well in the previous year.

Borrowing to Invest

Another common mistake is to invest money that could have been used to pay off an existing loan. The potential to earn a high return on an investment can tempt individuals to take on more risk than they should.

EXAMPLE   François Tremblay recently took out a $5000 loan to cover this year's college expenses. His parents then gave him $5000 so that he could pay off the loan. Rather than doing that, François invested the $5000 in one stock. He had hoped that he could earn a large return on the $5000, so that he could sell the investment at the end of the year, pay off the loan, and have enough funds left over to travel through Europe during the summer. During the year, he had to make interest payments on the existing loan. The stock that he purchased declined in value by 90 percent, leaving him with just $500 at the end of the year. He now has insufficient funds to pay off the loan or to take a vacation.

Taking Risks to Recover Losses from Previous Investments

Another common mistake is to take excessive risks to recover your losses. This can lead to additional losses and may even push individuals toward bankruptcy.

EXAMPLE   Sarah Richards lost 10 percent of her investment over the last year in a diversified mutual fund. She needs the money before next winter to purchase a new furnace for her home. She wants to make up for her loss, so has shifted her money into a risky mutual fund that will likely generate a higher return if economic conditions are favourable but will perform poorly if economic conditions are unfavourable. She experiences a 20 percent loss on this investment because economic conditions weakened. She no longer has a sufficient amount of funds to pay for the furnace.

During the late 1990s, many investors bid up the prices of stocks because of their unrealistic expectations about how well these stocks would perform in the future. The media hype added to the investors' irrational exuberance. These actions created a so-called speculative bubble, meaning that once the prices are blown up to a certain level, the bubble will burst, and stock prices will decline to more realistic levels. One reason for the generally poor stock performance in 2000 to 2002 was that the speculative bubble burst. In addition, economic conditions weakened.

While there may someday be another period in which stocks or other investments earn abnormally high returns, you should be realistic when making investment decisions. An investment that has the potential to rise substantially in value also has the potential to decline substantially in value. If you cannot afford the possible loss, you should not make that investment.

FOCUS ON ETHICS: Falling Prey to Online Investment Fraud

The internet is a remarkably easy and inexpensive means of obtaining investment advice and researching investment opportunities. Hundreds of online newsletters recommend investments, such as specific stocks or bonds. Investors can use online bulletin boards to share information. Advice is also distributed in the form of spam, or junk email.

With all of these sources at hand, it can be difficult to tell the difference between legitimate and fraudulent opportunities. The recommendations could be provided by unqualified individuals or by people paid by the companies to recommend their stocks or bonds. In some cases, individuals send out millions of emails and set up websites to promote a particular firm's stock. Others push specific investments that they already own, hoping to create more demand to drive the price higher. For some small stocks that have less than 1000 shares traded per day, orders instigated by internet rumours could easily push the stock price higher, at least temporarily.

To protect against this type of fraud, avoid making any investment decisions until you have the facts at hand. Obtain the annual report of the firm to review general background information. Check credible news sources such as *The Globe and Mail*. If you would rather not wait a day to read a financial newspaper, use trustworthy online services such as the Business News Network (www.bnn.ca). However, be careful how you interpret news about a rumour. The news source may repeat a rumour, but will not necessarily confirm that the rumour is true. Another option is to check with a trusted financial adviser. As a general rule, be wary of promises of quick profits, "guaranteed" or limited-time opportunities, or investments that are in foreign countries.

MyLab Finance   Visit MyLab Finance for additional study and practice tools. Select Financial Planning Problems are available in the Study Plan. Create your own study plan, generate personal cash flow statements and balance sheets, and set personal financial goals.

SUMMARY

L.O.1   Describe the common types of investments

Common types of investments include money market securities, stocks, bonds, mutual funds, and income trusts. Each type of investment is unique in terms of how it provides a return to its investors.

L.O.2   Explain how to measure the return on investments

The return on an investment is determined by the income the investment generates and the capital gain of the investment over the investment period. Some stocks offer periodic income in the form of dividends, while bonds offer periodic income in the form of interest payments.

L.O.3   Identify the risks of investments

The risk from making an investment varies among types of investments. In particular, money market securities tend to have low risk, while many stock and income trust investments have high risk. However, the risk also varies within a particular type of investment. Some money market securities have more risk than others. Some stocks have more risk than others.

L.O.4   Explain the trade-off between the return and risk of investments

Investors weigh the trade-off between risk and return when making investments decisions. When they select investments that have the potential to offer high returns, they must accept a higher degree of risk. Alternatively, they can select investments that have lower risk, but they must accept a relatively low return. The proper choice depends on the investor's willingness to accept risk, which is influenced by the investor's financial position and psychological attitude to loss of capital. Some investors are not in a financial position in which they can afford to take much risk, and should therefore select investments that have little or no risk. Some investors cannot abide loss of capital, regardless of potential return. Again, low-risk securities would be the best choice.

L.O.5   Explain how diversification among asset classes can reduce risk

Asset allocation uses diversification to reduce your risk from investing. In general, a portfolio achieves more benefits when it is diversified among assets whose returns are less volatile and are not highly correlated with each other over time.

L.O.6   Describe strategies that can be used to diversify among stocks

Common stock diversification strategies include diversifying among stocks across industries and among stocks across countries. You should consider using these two types of diversification so that you limit the exposure of your stock investments to any external forces that could affect their value.

L.O.7   Explain asset allocation strategies

Your asset allocation decision should not be restricted to stocks. Because bond returns are primarily influenced by interest-rate movements rather than stock market conditions, they are not highly correlated with stock returns over time. Therefore, bonds can help reduce the risk of an investment portfolio. Real estate investment trusts (REITs) are primarily influenced by real estate conditions and can also be useful for diversifying an investment portfolio.

L.O.8   Identify factors that affect your asset allocation decisions

Your asset allocation decision should take into account your stage in life, your degree of risk tolerance, and your expectations of economic conditions. If you are young, you may be more willing to invest in riskier securities to build wealth. If you are near retirement, you should consider investing more of your money in investments that can provide you with a stable income (dividends and interest payments) over time. If you are more willing to tolerate risk, you would invest in riskier stocks and bonds. Your asset allocation is also influenced by your expectations about future economic conditions. These expectations affect the expected performance of stocks, bonds, and REITs and therefore should shape your decision of how to allocate your money across these financial assets.

L.O.9   Describe common investment mistakes that can be avoided

You can learn from investment mistakes made by others. In particular, do not make investments that are driven by unrealistic goals. Do not invest when the funds could be more properly used to pay off existing debt. Do not attempt high-risk investments as a means of recovering recent losses. Finally, recognize the risk of investing when the market is inflated because of a speculative bubble.

REVIEW QUESTIONS

1. What should you do before investing any money? Explain.

2. Describe money market securities.

3. What is the primary market? What is an initial public offering (IPO)?

4. Define and describe a secondary market.

5. Define and describe an institutional investor.

6. Define and describe an individual investor.

7. What is the difference between a day trader and other individual investors?

8. What are the two ways in which you earn a return on a stock investment?

9. Describe the features of a dividend distribution.

10. Define and describe a growth stock.

11. Define and describe a value stock.

12. Define and describe an income stock.

13. How do you calculate the price of a share of stock?

14. What are the circumstances that determine the market price of a stock?

15. Define and differentiate between common stock and preferred stock.

16. What are bonds? What are the two ways in which you earn a return on a bond investment?

17. What is a mutual fund? What are the two ways in which you earn a return on a mutual fund investment?

18. What are the two ways in which you earn a return on a real estate investment? Why is it difficult to measure the return that you earn on your home?

19. How do you calculate the return on your investment? How does the calculation change when you also earn dividend income and/or interest income?

20. Explain how differing tax rates affect your return from different types of income.

21. How is your wealth influenced by your return on investment?

22. Define and differentiate between unsystematic risk and systematic risk.

23. Define and describe range of returns.

24. Define and describe standard deviation.

25. Define and describe beta.

26. Why do we use subjective measures of risk in addition to range of returns, standard deviation, and beta?

27. Describe the return–risk trade-off? What is a risk premium? How do you calculate the risk premium?

28. Describe the return–risk trade-off among stocks.

29. Describe the return–risk trade-off among bonds.

30. Describe the return–risk trade-off among mutual funds composed of stocks.

31. What is a bond default? How do mutual fund investments help address the issues caused by a bond default?

32. Describe the return–risk trade-off among real estate investments.

33. Describe how investment decisions may vary with your personal situation.

34. What is asset allocation? Why is it important to allocate your assets across many different types of investments?

35. What is a portfolio? How can a portfolio help you to reduce risk?

36. How does the volatility of each individual investment impact the volatility of the overall portfolio?

37. What is correlation? How do the correlations among investments impact the volatility of the overall portfolio?

38. Describe the concept of diversifying stocks across industries. What are the limitations of industry diversification?

39. Describe the concept of diversifying stocks across countries.

40. How can allocating some of your assets to bonds reduce the level of risk in your portfolio?

41. What is an income trust? What are the major categories of income trusts? What are real estate investment trusts (REITs)? What are some attractive characteristics of REITs?

42. Do all asset allocation strategies reduce risk to the same degree? Explain.

43. Discuss the role that your stage in life plays in the asset allocation decision.

44. How does your degree of risk tolerance affect the asset allocation decision?

45. How might your expectations of economic conditions influence your asset allocation? What is the problem with relying on your expectations of economic conditions to determine your asset allocation strategy?

46. Describe common investment mistakes made by individuals.

FINANCIAL PLANNING PROBLEMS

MyLab Finance Financial Planning Problems marked with a ⊕ can be found in MyLab Finance.

1. Olafanu owns shares in a stock where the market value of the firm is $500 million and the number of shares outstanding is 90 000. What is value of the stock on a per share basis?

2. Joel purchased 100 shares of stock for $20 per share. During the year, he received dividend cheques amounting to $150. After three years, Joel sold the stock for $32 per share. What was his holding period return? What was Joel's annualized return on the stock? What is the dollar amount of Joel's return?

3. Emma bought 100 shares of stock a year ago for $53 per share. She received no dividends on the stock and sold the stock today for $38 per share. What is Emma's annualized return on the stock?

4. Tammy has $3500 that she wants to invest in stock. She believes that she can earn a 12 percent return, compounded semi-annually. What will the value of Tammy's investment be in 10 years if she is able to achieve her goal?

5. Dawn decides to invest $2000 per year in stock at the beginning of each of the next five years. She believes that she can earn a nine percent return, compounded annually, over that time period. How much will Dawn's investment be worth at the end of five years?

6. Bob purchased a dot-com stock, which was heavily advertised on the internet, for $40 per share shortly after the stock's IPO. Over the next three years, the stock price declined at a compound annual rate of 15 percent each year. What is the company's stock price after three years?

7. Morris will start investing $1500 at the end of each year in stocks. He believes that he can average a 12 percent return, compounded monthly. If he follows this plan, how much will he accumulate in five years? In 10 years?

8. Thomas purchased 400 shares of stock A for $23 per share and sold them more than a year later for $20 per share. He purchased 500 shares of stock B for $40 per share and sold them for $53 per share after holding them for the same time period. If Thomas is in a 25 percent tax bracket, what will his taxable capital gains be for the year?

 9. Floyd wants to invest the $15 000 he received from his grandfather's estate. He wants to use the money to finance his education when he pursues his doctorate in five years. What amount will he have in five years if he earns a nine percent return? If he receives

a 10 percent return? A 12 percent return? All rates of return are compounded monthly.

10. Odell pays $8500 for a bond that pays an annual dividend of $300. The bond has a par value of $10 000. If Odell holds the bond until it matures in exactly three years' time, what will be his return on investment? What will be the annualized return on his investment?

CHALLENGE QUESTIONS

1. Outline the typical investment goals associated with each of the following financial planning life stages. Provide a recommended asset allocation for each life stage. Refer back to Exhibit 1.2 for a brief overview of each life stage.

a. Early career

b. Family and mid-career

c. Prime earning

d. Early retirement

2. Charles just sold 500 shares of stock A for $12 000. He then sold 600 shares of stock A for $6000. Charles paid $20 per share for all of his shares of stock A. What amount of allowable capital loss will he have?

 ETHICS ## ETHICAL DILEMMA

Mike has decided that it is time he put his money to work. He has accumulated a substantial nest egg in a savings account at a local bank but he realizes that, earning less than three percent interest, he will never reach his financial goals. After doing some research, he withdraws the money, opens an account at a local brokerage firm, and buys 500 shares of a large manufacturing company and 600 shares of a well-known retail store. From the beginning, his broker emphasizes that his portfolio is not sufficiently diversified with just two stocks. Over time, the broker convinces Mike to sell these two stocks to purchase stock in other companies. Two years later, Mike owns stock in 14 different companies and views his portfolio as well diversified. His cousin Ed, who has recently graduated from business school, looks at his portfolio and comments, "You are not very well diversified, as 10 of the stocks you own are considered technology stocks." Mike

tells Ed that he followed his broker's recommendations and sold his original stocks to purchase the new stocks in order to attain a diversified portfolio. Ed comments that Mike's brokerage firm is noted as a specialist in technology stocks. Mike is disappointed because he thought he was getting good advice about building a well-diversified portfolio. After all, Mike followed his broker's advice to the letter, and why would his broker give him bad advice?

a. Comment on the broker's ethics in recommending the sale of the original stocks to purchase a portfolio weighted so heavily toward technology stocks. Include in your discussion reasons why the broker may have followed the course of action that he did.

b. To achieve diversification, what other course of action could Mike have taken that would not have involved buying individual stocks in a variety of companies?

FINANCIAL PLANNING ONLINE EXERCISES

1. Go to www.mackenziefinancial.com/en/pub/tools/calculators/index.shtml*. Locate the Advantage of Early Investing calculator under the Investment and Saving heading. This calculator will help you to understand the importance of early investing as a part of wealth accumulation.

a. Once you are in the calculator, enter Start Ages of 25, 35, and 45 for Scenarios 1, 2, and 3, respectively. For each scenario, enter an End Age of 65, and an Initial Deposit Amount of $1000. The Periodic Deposit Amounts should be $1000, $2000, and $3000 for Scenarios 1, 2, and 3, respectively. Finally, maintain a Deposit Frequency of "Annually"

*Used with permission from Mackenzie Investments.

and enter 6.00 percent as your Annual Rate of Return. Click on Next. Which scenario provides the greatest accumulated value?

b. Click on Back. Based on the data you entered, what was the most important variable in increasing the accumulated value under each scenario? Explain.

c. Increase the annual rate of return under Scenarios 2 and 3 by one percent. Click on Next. What is the impact of the change in the annual rate of return on accumulated value? Is the accumulated value under either scenario higher than the accumulated value under Scenario 1?

d. Increase the annual rate of return under Scenario 2 such that the accumulated value of Scenario 2 is equal to that of Scenario 1. What is the required annual rate of return for Scenario 2? Complete this procedure for Scenario 3. What is the required annual rate of return for Scenario 3? With respect to Scenario 3, what other options may be available to increase the accumulated value if the annual rate of return is the same as that calculated for Scenario 2?

2. Go to www.atb.com/personal-banking/resources/Pages/mutual-funds.aspx.

a. This website describes a variety of asset allocation portfolios. Under Compass Portfolio Series, click on Maximum Growth Portfolio. What is the asset allocation range for each of the types of investments in this portfolio?

b. Create a table that will display the asset allocation range for each of the different types of Compass portfolios. Comment on the differences in the asset allocation ranges among the various portfolios. Why is there a difference?

PSYCHOLOGY OF PERSONAL FINANCE: Your Investments

1. Some investors get a bigger thrill from gambling with money than paying off a loan. Thus, they invest in stocks hoping to make a larger return than whatever interest rate they are paying on their loan. Describe your behaviour of investing. Do you use money to invest that could have been used to pay off a credit card loan? If so, why? Do you think there is any risk associated with such a strategy?

2. Read one practical article of how psychology affects decisions when investing in stocks. You can easily retrieve possible articles by doing an online search using the terms "psychology" and "investing stocks." Summarize the main points of the article.

MINI-CASE 1: Investment Planning

Marcel, age 28, and Teresa, age 27, have just had their first child, Hanna. They have a combined income of $75 000 and rent a two-bedroom apartment. For the past several years Marcel and Teresa have taken financial responsibilities one day at a time, but it has finally dawned on them that they now must start thinking about their financial future. For several months Marcel has seen the stock market move higher, and he is convinced that they should be investing in stocks. Teresa is more interested in investing in collectibles such sports memorabilia because she has been reading online reports of baseball trading card speculators making huge profits. When asked what their goals are, Marcel replies that he would like to save for retirement, and Teresa mentions her top priority as saving for Hanna's post-secondary school expenses. They both agree that they would like to buy a house and pay off their credit card bills, which amount to $4000. When asked to list their investments, all they could come up with was a savings account worth $650. What should be Marcel and Teresa's first priority before investing or making any investment plans? Suppose that Marcel and Teresa asked you to prioritize their goals. Where would you rank their investment objectives? Should Marcel and Teresa invest all their money in one investment strategy? Explain your answer in terms of diversification and the asset allocation process.

MINI-CASE 2: Diversification

Last year, Joban graduated from high school and received several thousand dollars from an uncle as a graduation gift. Joban is now in his first year of college. He just heard of a guy in his dorm who invested in a software company and made a huge profit in a few months. Joban likes the idea of making some money fast and is considering investing his graduation gift money in the a company that has its business based on servicing the internet. Joban's roommate, Shawn, just finished a personal finance course and is concerned that Joban has run up a large credit card bill and has trouble balancing his monthly budget. Money that Joban receives from his job he tends to spend. In addition, Joban really does not know much about investing or how people actually make money by investing. Shawn has asked you to help him by giving him some advice so that he can talk to Joban about his investment plans. With respect to the trade-off between return and risk, what should Shawn explain to Joban? Shawn will urge Joban to invest for the long-term using a diversified approach. However, Joban will probably react with some scepticism. Explain to Shawn why he is correct. How should Joban allocate his assets given his life stage?

Study Guide

Circle the correct answer and then check the answers in the back of the book to chart your progress.

Multiple Choice

1. In the secondary market, stock prices are:
   a. Determined by supply and demand.
   b. Often undervalued.
   c. Easy to predict.
   d. Less expensive than on the primary market.

2. Which of the following statements is correct?
   a. Institutional investors are semi-professionals employed by a financial institution who are responsible for managing money on behalf of the clients they serve.
   b. Day traders are professionals who work on a day-to-day basis.
   c. Portfolio managers are the employees of financial institutions who make investment decisions.
   d. Institutional investors commonly invest a portion of the money earned from their jobs.

3. Investing in growth stocks usually refers to:
   a. Younger companies paying large dividends.
   b. Large companies paying large dividends.
   c. Younger companies with potential for large capital gains.
   d. Any company with a market expansion strategy.

4. The difference between common and preferred stock is that preferred stock:
   a. May or may not receive dividends.
   b. Has predictable income and more safety.

   c. Has greater potential for capital appreciation.
   d. Is issued more frequently than common stock.

5. If you wish to have a direct voice in the running of a company, you should purchase:
   a. Directorships.
   b. Debentures.
   c. Common stock.
   d. Preferred stock.

6. Fernando purchased 1500 shares of Johnson Enterprises Inc. for $23 per share in 2006. During 2007, Johnson Enterprises paid a dividend of $1 per share. Fernando sold his shares in Johnson Enterprises for $26 per share at the end of 2007. What was his investment return during the holding period? Round your answer to one decimal place.
   a. 13.0 percent
   b. 11.5 percent
   c. 14.8 percent
   d. 17.4 percent

7. Investment risk refers to:
   a. The risk premium in the markets.
   b. Beta.
   c. The risk of investments dropping in value.
   d. Volatility in investment returns.

8. Which of the following statements regarding the trade-off between risk and return is incorrect?
   a. Since the prices of risky investments fluctuate substantially, it is dangerous to invest in a risky

investment when you know that you will be selling that investment in the near future.

b. A risk premium is an additional return beyond the risk-free rate you could earn from an investment.

c. By the time individual investors are able to invest in a newly issued stock, the price has already risen.

d. The risk of your investment is that the firm may be unable to make its dividend payment if its financial condition deteriorates.

9. You can reduce your investment risk most effectively through:
a. Asset allocation.
b. Limiting the time horizon.
c. Diversifying stocks.
d. Maximizing the beta.

10. With respect to investment return, the benefits of portfolio diversification include:
a. A portfolio of investments will result in a smoother trend of returns since returns are averaged among the investments in the portfolio.
b. On average, the range of returns of a portfolio of investments is less than the range of returns of any individual investment.
c. An equally weighted portfolio of two stocks will have a rate of return that is equal to the average return of the two stocks combined.
d. All of the above.

11. When investment A performs well, investment E does poorly. When A performs poorly, E does well. This is referred to as:
a. Positive correlation.
b. Negative correlation.
c. Insignificant correlation.
d. Rapid correlation.

12. To diversify your portfolio against weak economic conditions in Canada, it is important to diversify your stocks across:
a. The Atlantic Ocean.
b. Industries.
c. Countries.
d. Sectors.

13. Lee Ann would like to diversify her individual stock portfolio with other investments. Currently, she owns a portfolio of five stocks. Which of the following investments would you be least likely to recommend to Lee Ann in order to help her achieve her goal?
a. A bond
b. Real estate

c. An income trust
d. A stock-based mutual fund

14. Your current investment portfolio is equally diversified across stocks, bonds, and real estate. You have decided to reposition your portfolio based on your expectations about economic conditions. For the upcoming year, you expect stock market conditions to be weak, interest rates to decrease, and real estate conditions to be unfavourable. Which of the following investments would you most likely add to your portfolio?
a. A bond mutual fund containing bonds with short maturities
b. A stock mutual fund
c. A bond mutual fund containing bonds with long maturities
d. A real estate investment trust (REIT) fund

15. Which of the following is not a common investment mistake?
a. Making decisions based on realistic goals.
b. Borrowing to invest.
c. Taking risks to recover losses from previous investments.
d. None of the above. All of these choices represent common investment mistakes.

True/False

1. True or False? Common stock refers to a certificate issued by a firm to raise funds that entitles shareholders to first priority to receive dividends.

2. True or False? The secondary market facilitates the trading of existing securities by enabling investors to sell their shares at any time.

3. True or False? Value stocks represent the stocks of firms with substantial growth opportunities.

4. True or False? The price of preferred stock is not as volatile as the price of common stock.

5. True or False? Real estate can be rented to generate income in the form of rent payments. In addition, investors may earn a capital gain if they sell the property for a higher price than they paid for it.

6. True or False? A poorly managed company that suffers a decrease in its stock price is an example of systematic risk.

7. True or False? An investment with a high standard deviation is more likely to experience a large gain or a small loss in a given period.

8. True or False? Investors expect a higher return for taking on additional risk.

9. True or False? Portfolio construction involves the selection of investments that exhibit positive correlation.

10. True or False? The returns on stocks and the returns on bonds are highly correlated.

11. True or False? To reduce your exposure to stock market risk, you could invest in either long-term debt securities or money market securities.

12. True or False? If you have aversion to risk, you should invest in small-cap mutual funds.

13. True or False? An investment that has the potential to rise substantially in value also has the potential to decline substantially in value.

14. True or False? When economic conditions weaken, most stocks tend to perform poorly.

15. True or False? If your portfolio is performing poorly, you should increase the risk of your portfolio in order to recover your losses as quickly as possible.

Investing in Stocks

Blake thought he had a good strategy for investing. For any company in which he was interested, he carefully read the summary provided by the chief executive officer (CEO) in the company's annual report. He also read research reports about those companies, which were provided by investment companies. His confidence in investing grew because each company in which he was interested also had a very optimistic outlook in its annual report. In addition, the research reports that were provided about these companies were always very positive.

Blake was so confident, he purchased 500 shares of a particular stock at $40 per share. His research seemed to be paying off, as the price rose steadily over the course of several months to more than $48 per share. Blake felt that this stock had reached the upper limit of its price increase. He decided to implement a sell strategy that would take the uncertainty out of the sales transaction.

QUESTIONS:

1. What type of stock order would allow Blake to automatically sell the stock if it reaches a price of $50 per share?
2. If Blake was concerned that the stock price may decrease, what type of stock order should he place to automatically sell the stock as it goes down?
3. In addition to comments made by the CEO in the annual report and research reports published by investment companies, what other information and methods should Blake use to determine the value of a stock?

L.O.1

STOCK EXCHANGES

stock exchanges
Facilities that allow investors to purchase or sell existing stocks.

By understanding some very basic methods of evaluating stocks, you can start to make stock investments. **Stock exchanges** are facilities that allow investors to purchase or sell existing stocks. They facilitate trading in the secondary market so that investors can sell stocks that they previously purchased. An organized securities exchange occupies a physical or virtual location where trading occurs. A stock must be listed on a stock exchange to be traded there, meaning that it must fulfill specific requirements of the exchange. Canadian stocks are traded on two markets: the Toronto Stock Exchange (TSX) and the TSX Venture Exchange. The TSX is where senior equities are traded while the TSX Venture Exchange serves the public venture capital market. **Venture capital** refers to investors' funds destined for risky, generally new businesses with tremendous growth potential. Both markets are owned and operated by a for-profit organization, the TMX Group. There are 3278 companies listed on the TSX and the TSX Venture Exchange.

venture capital
Refers to investors' funds destined for risky, generally new businesses with tremendous growth potential.

Canada's other exchange, the Montreal Exchange, is a derivatives exchange. Investors interested in trading options and futures would use the services of the Montreal Exchange to meet their trading needs. The Montreal Exchange is part of TMX Group.

To be listed on the TSX, a firm must meet minimum listing requirements in areas such as revenue, cash flow, net tangible assets, working capital, and cash. The exchange's requirements ensure that there will be an active market for stocks in which shares are commonly traded.

Electronic Trading. The major exchanges in Canada offer trading services electronically. This has eliminated the open-outcry system, where floor traders would complete trades on behalf of their brokerage houses' customers. For example, on the TSX and TSX Venture Exchange, an integrated system of several order routing and terminal vendors allows electronic access to the exchange. This integrated system continually receives and processes buy and sell orders from investors. The price at which a buyer would like to purchase stock is referred to as the **bid price**. The price at which a seller would like to sell a stock is referred to as the **ask price**. A high-quality stock exchange is characterized by a small difference between the bid price and the ask price (known as the bid–ask spread), a large volume of shares being offered for purchase or sale with each trade request, which supports market liquidity, and a large volume of traders making these requests, which creates market depth.

bid price
The price at which a buyer would like to purchase a stock.

ask price
The price at which a seller would like to sell a stock.

market makers
Securities dealers who are required to trade actively in the market so that liquidity is maintained when natural market forces cannot provide sufficient liquidity.

Liquidity of an electronic trading system is enhanced by using market makers. **Market makers** are securities dealers who are required to trade actively in the market so that liquidity is maintained when natural market forces cannot provide sufficient liquidity. A market maker earns money by maintaining a spread, referred to as a bid–ask spread, on each stock they cover. For example, suppose a market maker executed an order where they offered to purchase shares from a seller for $20.00 per share (the ask price) and then immediately sold those shares to a buyer for $20.12 per share (the bid price). The bid–ask spread of $0.12 per share went to the market maker. In this example, a trade of 1000 shares allowed the market maker to earn $120 because of the bid–ask spread.

New York Stock Exchange. The most popular organized exchange in the United States is the New York Stock Exchange (NYSE), which handles transactions for approximately

2800 stocks. In 2007, the NYSE merged with Euronext (which represented various European exchanges) to form NYSE Euronext, the first global exchange. In 2013, NYSE Euronext was acquired by Intercontinental Exchange (ICE). Today, the NYSE and Euronext operate as divisions of ICE. The transactions on the NYSE are conducted by the traders who have been authorized to trade stocks listed on the exchange for themselves or others.

The rapid consolidation that is occurring in global capital markets has been fuelled by the demutualization of stock exchanges. **Demutualization** refers to the transformation of a firm from a member-owned organization to a publicly owned, for-profit organization.

demutualization
Refers to the transformation of a firm from a member-owned organization to a publicly owned, for-profit organization.

| **myth** or **fact** The stock market sometimes crashes and can take decades to recover. |

Over-the-Counter (OTC) Market

The **over-the-counter (OTC) market** is an electronic communications network that allows investors to buy or sell securities. It is not a transparent facility like the organized exchanges. Stock exchanges are considered to be transparent because you can see the trading taking place, even if only online, and you have access to the trade information as it occurs. The debt marketplace, however, is less transparent, as trade information is compiled at the end of the day rather than as it occurs. Some OTC markets are similar to the debt marketplace.

over-the-counter (OTC) market
An electronic communications network that allows investors to buy or sell securities.

The OTC market is less hindered by rules and regulations and can be driven more by supply and demand than organized stock exchanges. OTC markets are also characterized by trading methods. In an OTC market, you are transacting business with one person, principal to principal, at their price and their price alone. In contrast, an organized exchange market is an auction market and the price paid for a security is the best price at that time.

The Canadian OTC market was designed for companies that do not meet the listing requirements of the TSX or the TSX Venture Exchange. OTC stocks can be accessed using the NEX board on the TSX Venture Exchange. OTC markets also exist in other countries where companies do not meet the listing requirements of the exchanges in that particular country.

STOCK QUOTATIONS

L.O.2

If you are considering investing in stocks, you will need to learn how to obtain and interpret stock price quotations. Fortunately, price quotations are readily available for actively traded stocks. The most up-to-date quotes can be obtained online. Price information is available from stockbrokers and is widely published by the news media. Popular sources of stock quotations are financial newspapers (such as the *National Post* and *The Globe and Mail*), business sections of many local newspapers, financial news television networks (such as BNN), and financial websites.

Stock quotations provide information about the price of each stock over the previous day or a recent period. An example of a stock quotation for Canadian National Railway created using data obtained from the *Financial Post* website is shown in Exhibit 11.1. The first column contains the name of the stock. To the right is the ticker symbol (Ticker) associated with the stock. The next column shows the closing price (Close), which is the price at which the final trade for the stock occurred on that particular day. The fourth column discloses the net change (Net ch) in the price of the stock, which is measured as the change in the closing price from the previous day. Investors review this column to determine how stock prices changed from one day to the next.

The fifth column shows the net change in the price of the stock as a percentage (% ch). The sixth column shows the volume of trading (in 000s). For some widely traded stocks, a million shares may trade per day, while 20 000 or fewer shares may trade per day for other stocks. The next two columns display the daily high (Day high) and the daily

EXHIBIT 11.1 Example of a Stock Quotation

Stock	Ticker	Close	Net ch	% ch	Vol 000s	Day high	Day low	% Yield	P/E	52 wk high	low
CN Rail	CNI	$72.16	($0.05)	(0.07)	1293	$72.87	$72.14	1.74	20.80	$73.28	$55.73

Source: Data from (CNI) Canadian NTL Rail PR, Markets, Financial Post. http://www.financialpost.com/markets/company/profile/index.html?symbol=CNI&id=31970, retrieved March 19, 2017

low (Day low) at which the stock was traded. The dividend yield (annual dividends as a percentage of the stock price) is shown in the ninth column. This represents the annual return you would receive solely from dividends if you purchased the stock today and if the dividend payments remain unchanged for the entire year. In the tenth column is the price–earnings (P/E) ratio, which represents the stock price divided by the firm's earnings per share. Some investors closely monitor the P/E ratio when attempting to value stocks, as discussed in more detail later in this chapter.

The last two columns display the high (52 wk high) and low (52 wk low) price of the stock during the last year. Stocks that are subject to much more uncertainty tend to have a wider range in prices over time. Some investors use this range as a simple measure of the firm's risk.

Review the stock quotations of CN Rail in Exhibit 11.1. The ticker symbol for this stock is CNI. The last price at which this stock traded during the day was $72.16. The net change in the price was down $0.05 per share from the day before. This translates into a percent change of 0.07. CN Rail's volume of trading for the day was 1 293 000 shares. For the day, the stock price traded between $72.87 and $72.14. The annual dividend yield of 1.74 percent means that investors purchasing the stock at the time of this quotation would earn an annual dividend equal to 1.74 percent on their investment if the annual dividend remains unchanged. The price–earnings ratio is 20.80, which means that the prevailing stock price of CN Rail is approximately 21 times its annual earnings per share. Its stock price has traded between $73.28 and $55.73 per share over the last year.

Go to:
www.financialpost.com

This website provides stock quotations for the stocks you specify. It also provides a summary of financial market conditions and links to information about investments.

FREE APPS for Personal Finance

Obtaining Real-Time Stock Quotes

Application:

The Real-Time Stocks app provides quotes that are in real time for investors who wish to access up-to-the-minute stock prices.

L.O.3

PURCHASING OR SELLING STOCKS

When trading stocks, you need to begin by selecting a brokerage firm and placing an order. These functions are discussed next.

Selecting a Broker

When selecting a broker, consider the following characteristics.

Analyst Recommendations. A full-service broker can provide you with investment advice. You also have access to stock ratings that are assigned by stock analysts employed by brokerage firms.

Recommendations from brokers and analysts have limitations. Some advisers may suggest that you buy or sell securities frequently, rather than holding on to your investment portfolio over time. Keep in mind that you must pay a commission to that adviser for each transaction.

Many studies have shown that recommendations made by brokers or analysts do not lead to better performance than the stock market in general. Some advisers have very limited experience in analyzing and valuing securities. Even those who are very experienced will not necessarily be able to help you achieve unusually high performance.

FOCUS ON ETHICS: Relying on Analyst Recommendations

Brokers and analysts tend to be overly optimistic about stocks. They are generally unwilling to recommend that investors sell stocks because they do not want to offend any firms with which their own investment firm might do business in the future. In 1999, the firm First Call tracked 27 000 recommendations of stocks by analysts, and only 35 of these recommendations were to sell a specific stock. In other words, analysts made about 1 "sell" recommendation for every 770 "buy" recommendations.

In response to much criticism, some analysts recently have been more willing to offer "sell" recommendations on some stocks. However, there is still a tendency for them to be generally optimistic about most stocks, and there may be some conflicts of interest. For example, analysts may own the stock they are recommending, so it is in their best interest to create a demand for the stock so that its price will rise. However, analysts must disclose ownership of stocks they recommend.

Individual Broker Skills. Brokers within a brokerage firm have unique skills and personalities. Your preference for a specific firm might be heavily influenced by the individual broker who serves you. You can obtain information about individual brokers on the internet.

Brokerage Commissions. You can choose a discount or full-service brokerage firm. A **discount brokerage firm** executes transactions but does not offer investment advice. A **full-service brokerage firm** offers investment advice and executes transactions. Full-service brokerage firms tend to charge higher fees for their services than discount brokers. For example, a full-service firm may charge a commission of $100 for a transaction, whereas a discount firm will likely charge you between $8 and $30 for the same transaction.

discount brokerage firm
A brokerage firm that executes transactions but does not offer investment advice.

full-service brokerage firm
A brokerage firm that offers investment advice and executes transactions.

Placing an Order

Whenever you place an order to buy or sell a stock, you must specify the following:

- Name and class of the stock
- Buy or sell
- Number of shares
- Market order or limit order

Name and Class of the Stock. It is important to know the ticker symbol for your stock. The **ticker symbol** is the abbreviated term used to identify a stock for trading purposes. For example, WestJet Airlines's symbol is WJA and Suncor's symbol is SU. A symbol is shorter and simpler than the formal name of a firm and easily distinguishes between different firms with similar names. As well, the class of that stock is also included, reducing the risk of error when choosing different equities offered by the same firm.

ticker symbol
The abbreviated term used to identify a stock for trading purposes.

Buy or Sell. Brokerage firms execute both buy and sell transactions. Therefore, it is necessary to specify whether you are buying or selling a security when you place an order. Once you place your order and it is executed, you are bound by the instructions you gave. You must indicate when selling whether you own the stock now or are selling borrowed stock.

board lot
Shares bought or sold in multiples of typically 100 shares. The size of the board lot depends on the price of the security.

odd lot
Less than a board lot of that particular stock.

market order
An order to buy or sell a stock at its prevailing market price.

Number of Shares. Shares are typically sold in multiples of 100, referred to as a **board-lot** transaction. An order to buy or sell fewer than 100 shares is referred to as an **odd-lot** transaction. Lower-priced stocks may sell in board lots of 1000 shares while higher-priced stocks may sell in board lots of 10.

Market Order or Limit Order. You can buy or sell a stock by placing a **market order**, which is an order to buy or sell a stock at its prevailing market price. The advantage of a market order is that you are assured that your order will be executed quickly. A disadvantage is that the stock price could change abruptly just before you place your order. Prevailing market prices are just that, and the market can change more rapidly than you expect.

> **EXAMPLE**
>
> You want to buy 100 shares of Trendy stock, which had a closing price of $40. You assume that you will pay about $40 per share when the market opens this morning, or $4000 ($40 × 100 shares) for the order ignoring the commission. However, your order is executed at $43, which means that you pay $4300 ($43 × 100 shares). Unfortunately, many other investors wanted to buy Trendy stock this morning, creating increased demand. The strong demand relative to the small number of shares available for sale caused the stock price to increase to $43 before your broker could find a willing seller of Trendy stock.

limit order
An order to buy or sell a stock only if the price is within limits that you specify.

Alternatively, you can buy or sell stock by placing a **limit order**, which is an order to buy or sell a stock only if the price is within limits that you specify. A limit order sets a maximum price at which the stock can be purchased and can be for one day only or valid until cancelled (normally cancelled in six months if a transaction has not been executed by then). The limit order will specify whether you are willing to accept a portion of the shares desired (normally in board lots of 100); alternatively, you can specify that you want the full number of shares to be traded or none at all.

> **EXAMPLE**
>
> Using the information provided in the previous example, you place a limit order on Trendy stock, with a maximum price of $41, good for the day. When the stock opens at $43 this morning, your order is not executed because the market price exceeds your limit price. Later in the day, the stock price declines to $41, at which time your order is executed.

The example above illustrates the advantage of a limit order. However, the disadvantage is that you may miss out on a transaction you desire. If the price of Trendy stock had continued to rise throughout the day after opening at $43, your order would not have been executed at all.

Limit orders can also be used to sell stocks. In this case, a limit order specifies a minimum price at which the stock should be sold.

myth or **fact** Stocks that go up must come down and those that go down must come up.

> **EXAMPLE**
>
> You own 100 shares of Zina stock, which is currently worth $18 per share. You do not have time to monitor the market price but would be willing to sell the stock at $20 per share. You place a limit order to sell 100 shares of Zina stock at a minimum price of $20, good until cancelled. A few months later, Zina's stock price rises to $20 per share. You soon receive confirmation from your brokerage firm that the transaction has been executed.

Stop Orders. An **on-stop order** is a special form of limit order; it is an order to execute a transaction when the stock price reaches a specified level. A **buy-stop order** is an order to buy a stock when the price rises to a specified level. Conversely, a **sell-stop order** is an order to sell a stock when the price falls to a specified level. However, if the stock price changes rapidly, an on-stop order may not be filled at the specified price level, since an on-stop order becomes a market order once the specified price level is reached. Since there is no guarantee as to the price at which the order will be filled, an on-stop order is usually less expensive to execute than a limit order. These are specialized types of orders that should be used only by experienced trader-investors who fully understand their implications.

on-stop order
An order to execute a transaction when the stock price reaches a specified level; a special form of limit order.

buy-stop order
An order to buy a stock when the price rises to a specified level.

sell-stop order
An order to sell a stock when the price falls to a specified level.

Placing an Order Online

Individuals who wish to buy or sell stocks are increasingly using online brokerage services such as Qtrade Investor. One advantage of placing orders online is that the commission charged per transaction is very low, such as $8 or $20, regardless of the size of the transaction (up to a specified maximum level). A second advantage is convenience. In addition to accepting orders, online brokers provide real-time stock quotes and financial information. To establish an account with an online brokerage service, go to its website and follow the instructions to set up an account. Then send the online broker a cheque. Once the cheque has cleared, your account will show that you have funds you can use to invest online.

Many online brokerage firms have a money market fund where your cash is deposited until it is used to make transactions. Consequently, you can earn some interest on your funds until you use them to purchase securities. Once you place an order, the online brokerage firm will use the money in your fund to pay for the transaction. You may even receive blank cheques so that you can write cheques against your money market account.

Because many investors have shifted to online brokerage services, financial conglomerates such as RBC offer online brokerage services in addition to traditional brokerage firm services. You can place a market order from your computer in less than a minute and it usually will be executed within a minute. Timely execution depends on the liquidity of the security as well as the type of order entered.

Go to:
www.qtrade.ca/investor

This website provides information that you can use when making investment decisions. It also illustrates how you can trade stocks online through their services, which typically reduces your transaction costs.

Buying Stock on Margin

Some investors choose to purchase stock **on margin**, meaning that a portion of their purchase is funded with money borrowed from their brokerage firm. Buying a stock on margin enables you to purchase stocks without having the full amount of cash necessary. Interest rates are sufficiently high so that brokerage firms earn a decent return on their loans.

The Investment Industry Regulatory Organization of Canada (IIROC) limits the maximum amount that can be borrowed for a TSX list stock to 70 percent for stocks that trade for more than $5 per share. For example, you decide to purchase 500 shares of a stock that is currently trading at $20. The margin requirement is calculated as:

$$500 \text{ shares} \times \$20 \text{ per share} \times 30\% \text{ margin rate} = \$3000$$

This is the amount of money you are required to have in order to purchase this stock. The brokerage firm is lending you the other 70 percent of the purchase price, or $7000. This amount is called the maximum loan value. If the value of investments purchased on margin declines, you will receive a **margin call** from your brokerage firm, a request to increase the cash in your account in order to return the margin to the minimum level.

In the case of stocks that are listed at less than $5 per share and/or trade on the TSX Venture Exchange, the margin requirement is higher. In this case, the maximum loan value received from the broker will be relatively less.

When you buy a stock on margin, the gain on your investment is magnified, because you are able to create a larger investment with the borrowed funds. However, if the stock experiences a decline in price, your loss will be magnified. For example, if you invest

on margin
Purchasing a stock with a small amount of personal funds and the remainder of the funds borrowed from a brokerage firm.

margin call
A request from a brokerage firm for the investor to increase the cash in their account in order to return the margin to the minimum level.

$1000 of your own money but do not borrow any funds, your maximum loss is $1000. Conversely, if you invest $1000 of your own money and borrow an additional $1000 to invest, your maximum loss is now $2000. You still need to repay the funds you borrowed, regardless of the performance of your investment.

Some investors achieve high returns from buying stocks on margin. However, they commonly use the proceeds to make more investments in stocks. With their confidence boosted from their recent investment performance, they make riskier investments. Ultimately, some of these investors end up losing much of the money they invested because of taking excessive risk.

L.O.4

ANALYZING STOCKS

The price of a stock is based on the demand for that stock versus the supply of stock for sale. The demand for shares is determined by the number of investors who wish to purchase shares of the stock. The supply of stock for sale is determined by the number of investors who decide to sell their shares.

The valuation process involves identifying a firm that you think may perform well in the future and determining whether its price is overvalued, undervalued, or on target. You buy a stock when you think that it is undervalued and that you can therefore achieve a high return from investing in it. Yet your purchase of the stock means that some other investor was willing to sell it. So, although you believe the stock is undervalued, others apparently think it is overvalued. This difference in opinion is what causes a high volume of trading. When valuing stocks, investors may use technical analysis or fundamental analysis. **Technical analysis** is the valuation of stocks based on historical price patterns. For example, you might purchase a stock whenever its price rises for three consecutive days because you expect that a trend in prices indicates future price movements. Alternatively, you may decide to sell a stock if its price declines for several consecutive days because you expect that the trend will continue.

Fundamental analysis is the valuation of stocks based on an examination of fundamental characteristics such as revenues or earnings. There are many different ways to apply fundamental analysis, as explained later.

technical analysis
The valuation of stocks based on historical price patterns.

fundamental analysis
The valuation of stocks based on an examination of fundamental characteristics such as revenue or earnings, or the sensitivity of the firm's performance to economic conditions.

Analyzing a Firm's Financial Condition

One firm can outperform another in the same industry because its managers make better decisions about how to finance its business, market its products, and manage its employees. By conducting an analysis of a firm, you can assess its future performance. Firms that are publicly traded create an annual report that contains standardized financial information. Among other things, the report includes a corporate profile, a message from the firm's chief executive officer (CEO), and a section summarizing recent performance and expected future performance. It also contains financial statements measuring the firm's financial condition that you can examine in the same manner that you evaluate your personal financial statements to determine your financial condition. Many annual reports can be downloaded online. Prospective investors typically focus on the balance sheet and the income statement.

balance sheet
A financial statement that indicates a firm's sources of funds and how it has invested those funds as of a particular point in time.

Balance Sheet. The firm's **balance sheet** indicates its sources of funds and how it has invested those funds as of a particular point in time. The balance sheet is segmented into two parts: (1) assets and (2) liabilities and shareholder's equity. These two parts must balance.

The firm's assets indicate how it has invested its funds and what it owns. Assets are often classified as short-term and long-term assets. Short-term assets include cash, securities purchased by the firm, accounts receivable (money owed to the firm for previous sales), and inventories (materials used to produce products and finished products waiting to be sold).

Long-term assets (sometimes called fixed assets) include machinery and buildings purchased by the firm.

The liabilities and shareholder's equity indicate how the firm has obtained its funds. Liabilities represent the amount owed to creditors or suppliers and are classified as short term or long term. Shareholder's equity is the net worth of the firm. It represents the investment in the firm by investors.

Income Statement. The firm's **income statement** measures its revenues, expenses, and earnings over a particular period of time. Investors use it to determine how much income (earnings) the firm generated over a particular period and what expenses the firm incurred. An annual report may include an income statement for the year of concern and for the four quarters within that year.

income statement
A financial statement that measures a firm's revenues, expenses, and earnings over a particular period of time.

The income statement starts with revenues generated by the firm over the period of concern. Then the cost of goods sold (which includes the cost of materials used in production) is subtracted to derive gross profit. Operating expenses (such as salaries) are subtracted from the gross profit to determine earnings before interest and taxes (also referred to as operating profit). Finally, interest payments and taxes are subtracted to determine the earnings after taxes (also referred to as net profit).

The impact of the firm's financial condition on its value and stock price (for firms that have publicly traded stock) is summarized in Exhibit 11.2. When a firm's sales and profits are strong, investors have confidence that the firm will perform well in the future, and they are willing to invest in the firm's stock. However, there are few investors willing to sell the stock of this firm because they may also believe the stock will perform well. When the demand for the stock is much larger than the supply of stock for sale by investors, the price at which sellers can sell the stock rises.

When a firm's sales and profits are weak, the opposite effects occur. Investors become concerned that the firm will perform poorly in the future and might even go bankrupt. They are not willing to invest in the firm's stock, because the stock might become worthless if the firm fails. When there are few investors who want to buy a stock being sold by investors, and many investors who want to sell that stock because of its recent poor performance, the price at which sellers can sell the stock falls. In other words, sellers must be willing to accept a very low price in order to entice another investor to buy their stock.

EXHIBIT 11.2   Impact of a Firm's Performance on Its Stock Price

Impact of Strong Firm Performance on Stock Price of Firm

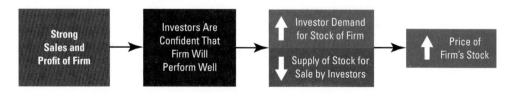

Impact of Weak Firm Performance on Stock Price of Firm

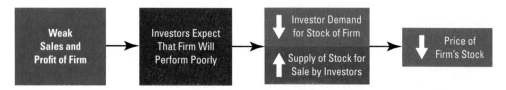

Firm-Specific Characteristics

Investors use a firm's balance sheet and Comprehensive Statement of Income to analyze the following characteristics:

- Liquidity
- Financial leverage
- Efficiency
- Profitability

Each of these characteristics is described below. Some popular ratios used to measure these characteristics are summarized in Exhibit 11.3.

Liquidity. A firm's assets and liabilities can be assessed to determine its liquidity, or its ability to cover expenses. A firm has a high degree of liquidity if it has a large amount of assets that can be easily converted to cash and has a relatively small amount of short-term liabilities. You can assess a firm's liquidity by computing its **current ratio**, which is the ratio of its short-term assets to its short-term liabilities. In general, a current ratio of 2.0 or higher is considered a reasonable level of liquidity for most industries.

Financial Leverage. Investors assess a firm's balance sheet to determine its ability to make debt payments. A firm obtains funds by borrowing from suppliers or creditors or by selling shares of its stock (equity) to investors. Many firms prefer to borrow funds rather than issue stock. An excessive amount of stock may spread the shareholder

current ratio
The ratio of a firm's short-term assets to its short-term liabilities.

EXHIBIT 11.3   Some Useful Ratios for Financial Analysis

Measures of Liquidity

$$\text{Current ratio} = \frac{\text{current assets}}{\text{current liabilities}} \qquad \text{Current ratio} = \frac{\$1000}{\$300} = 3.33$$

Measures of Financial Leverage

$$\text{Debt ratio} = \frac{\text{total long-term debt}}{\text{total assets}} \qquad \text{Debt ratio} = \frac{\$200}{\$1300} = 0.15$$

$$\text{Times interest earned ratio} = \frac{\text{earnings before interest and taxes}}{\text{interest payments}} \qquad \text{Times interest earned ratio} = \frac{\$470}{\$20} = 23.5$$

Measures of Efficiency

$$\text{Inventory turnover} = \frac{\text{cost of goods sold}}{\text{average daily inventory}} \qquad \text{Inventory turnover} = \frac{\$1400}{\$500^*} = 2.8 \text{ times}$$

$$\text{Average collection period} = \frac{\text{average receivables}}{\text{average daily sales}} \qquad \text{Average collection period} = \frac{\$400}{(\$3000/365)} = 48.67 \text{ days}$$

$$\text{Asset turnover ratio} = \frac{\text{sales}}{\text{average total assets}} \qquad \text{Asset turnover ratio} = \frac{\$3000}{\$1300^\dagger} = 2.31$$

Profitability Ratios

$$\text{Net profit margin} = \frac{\text{earnings}}{\text{sales}} \qquad \text{Net profit margin} = \frac{\$300}{\$3000} = 10\%$$

$$\text{Return on assets} = \frac{\text{earnings}}{\text{assets}} \qquad \text{Return on assets} = \frac{\$300}{\$1300} = 23\%$$

$$\text{Return on equity} = \frac{\text{earnings}}{\text{equity}} \qquad \text{Return on equity} = \frac{\$300}{\$800} = 37.5\%$$

*This assumes that the inventory level represents the average level during the year.
†This assumes that the prevailing asset level represents the average level.

ownership of the firm too thin, placing downward pressure on the stock price. If a firm borrows too much money, however, it may have difficulty making its interest payments on loans. A firm's **financial leverage** indicates its reliance on debt to support its operations.

A firm's financial leverage can be measured by its **debt ratio**, which calculates the proportion of total assets financed with debt. A firm with a high debt ratio relative to the similar companies in its industry has a high degree of financial leverage and therefore may have a relatively high risk of default on its future debt payments. Some firms with a relatively high degree of financial leverage can easily cover their debt payments if they generate stable cash inflows over time. The debt ratio focuses just on the firm's level of debt and does not account for its cash flows. Thus, a more appropriate measure of a firm's ability to repay its debt is the **times interest earned ratio**, which indicates the ratio of the firm's earnings before interest and taxes to its total interest payments. A high times interest earned ratio means that the firm should be more capable of covering its debt payments. The earnings figure is before taxes, as all debt interest costs are paid before taxable income is calculated. Interest costs are thus categorized as a business expense.

Efficiency. The composition of assets can indicate how efficiently a firm uses its funds. If it generates a relatively low level of sales and earnings with a large amount of assets, it is not using its assets efficiently. A firm that invests in assets must obtain funds to support those assets. The fewer assets it uses to generate its sales, the fewer funds it needs to borrow or obtain by issuing stock.

You can use **inventory turnover** to measure how efficiently a firm manages its inventory. It is calculated as the cost of goods sold divided by average daily inventory. A higher number relative to similar companies in the same industry represents relatively high turnover, which is more efficient.

You can use a firm's **average collection period** to determine the average age of accounts receivable. It is measured as accounts receivable divided by average daily sales. A higher number relative to similar companies in the same industry means a longer collection period, which is less efficient.

You can use the **asset turnover ratio** to assess how efficiently a firm uses its assets. This ratio is measured as sales divided by average total assets. A higher number relative to similar companies in the same industry reflects higher efficiency.

Profitability. You can also use the income statement and the balance sheet to assess a firm's profitability. The **operating profit margin** is the operating profit divided by sales, and the **net profit margin** measures net profit as a percentage of sales. The **return on assets** is the net profit divided by total assets. The **return on equity** is measured as net profit divided by the owners' investment in the firm (or shareholders' equity). The higher the profitability ratios relative to similar companies in the same industry, the higher the firm's profitability.

financial leverage
A firm's reliance on debt to support its operations.

debt ratio
A measure of financial leverage that calculates the proportion of total assets financed with debt.

times interest earned ratio
A measure of financial leverage that indicates the ratio of the firm's earnings before interest and taxes to its total interest payments.

inventory turnover
A measure of efficiency; computed as the cost of goods sold divided by average daily inventory.

average collection period
A measure of efficiency, computed as accounts receivable divided by average daily sales.

asset turnover ratio
A measure of efficiency, computed as sales divided by average total assets.

operating profit margin
A firm's operating profit divided by sales.

net profit margin
A measure of profitability that measures net profit as a percentage of sales.

return on assets
A measure of profitability, computed as net profit divided by total assets.

return on equity
A measure of profitability, computed as net profit divided by the owners' investment in the firm (shareholders' equity).

FOCUS ON ETHICS: Accounting Fraud

Motivation for Fraud. The top managers of a firm are commonly evaluated according to how the firm's value (as measured by stock price) changes over time. These managers may receive shares of the firm's stock as part of their compensation. Their goal is to increase the value of the firm so that they can sell their shares at a high price and earn a high level of compensation.

Consequently, they may seek an accounting method that will either inflate the firm's level of revenue or deflate the reported level of expenses, so that it can boost its reported earnings. Investors who use those reported earnings to derive the stock value will buy the stock when they believe that the firm's earnings have risen. Their actions push the value of the stock higher.

(continued)

Go to:
www.globeinvestor.
com/v5/content/filters

Used with permission from
Globe and Mail.

This website provides
information on various industry groups and allows you to
obtain financial information on
firms you specify in any industry. By reviewing financial
information for various firms
within an industry, you can
measure the industry norm.

Some accounting methods may only inflate revenue or deflate expenses for a short-term period, which means that the managers cannot boost the firm's reported earnings indefinitely. At some point, investors will recognize that the estimates are misleading, and they will sell their holdings in the firm's stock.

Revenue-Inflating Techniques. The accounting methods used to measure revenue can vary substantially, which makes it difficult for investors to compare various financial ratios among firms. Several examples of accounting methods used to inflate revenue are listed here:

- A service firm may have a five-year contract with a client, in which the client can cancel the agreement after the first year. The firm records the expected revenue over the next five years in the first year of the contract, even though it only received payment for the first year.
- A publisher of a magazine receives three-year subscriptions, in which payment is made annually. It reports all of these sales as revenue even when the cash has not been received. The cash flow attributed to the sales will occur either in a future period or not at all.
- A firm uses a lenient policy that allows customers to cancel their orders. The firm counts all orders as revenue even though it is likely that many of these orders will be cancelled.

Go to:
www.oecd.org/Canada

This website provides
information about economic
conditions that can affect the
value of investments.

Preventing Future Accounting Fraud. Publicly traded firms are required to have their financial statements audited by an independent auditor to ensure that the statements are accurate. Yet, auditors did not prevent Enron, Nortel Networks, or many other firms from issuing inaccurate financial statements. One reason for this type of negligence may be that the auditors want to retain these clients. They may worry that if they force a firm to report more accurate earnings, it will hire a different auditor in the future. Arthur Andersen was the accounting firm responsible for auditing Enron. In 2000, it received $25 million in auditing fees and $27 million in consulting fees from Enron. If it did not sign off on Enron's books, it would have risked losing annual fees of this scale in future years. Investors learned from the Enron scandal that they cannot necessarily trust that a firm or its auditor will provide reliable information about earnings.

As a result of scandals such as the one that occurred at Enron, the Sarbanes-Oxley Act was introduced in the United States. The Act was created in order to restore investor confidence in the markets and to prevent further occurrences of corporate fraud. Shortly afterwards, similar legislation, which takes into account the differences in Canadian financial markets, was adopted in Canada.

Economic Analysis of Stocks

A firm's future revenue and earnings are influenced by demand for its products, which is typically influenced by economic and industry conditions. In addition, firm-specific conditions (such as managerial expertise) can influence the firm's revenue or earnings.

An economic analysis involves assessing any economic conditions that can affect a firm's stock price, including economic growth, interest rates, and inflation. Each of these conditions is discussed in turn.

economic growth
The growth in a country's
economy over a particular
period.

**gross domestic product
(GDP)**
The total market value of all
products and services produced in a country.

fiscal policy
How the government imposes
taxes on individuals and corporations and how it spends
tax revenues.

Economic Growth. **Economic growth** is the growth in a country's economy over a particular period. It is commonly measured by the amount of production in a country, or the **gross domestic product (GDP)**, which reflects the total market value of all products and services produced in the country. The production level of products and services is closely related to the aggregate (overall) demand for products and services. When consumers have more money to spend, there is additional aggregate demand for products and services. The firms that provide products and services experience higher sales (revenue) and earnings, and their stock prices may rise. When economic conditions are weak, the aggregate demand for products and services declines. Firms experience lower level of sales and earnings, and their stock prices may decline as a result.

Given the potential impact of economic growth on stock prices, Canadian investors also monitor the federal government's **fiscal policy**, or how the government imposes taxes on individuals and corporations and how it spends tax revenues. When corporate tax rates are increased, after-tax earnings of corporations are reduced, which means that there is less money for shareholders. When individual tax rates are increased, individuals have less money to spend and therefore consume fewer products. Either one, or both, of these types of tax increases can have a negative impact on economic growth. The demand for products and services may decline and firms' earnings may be reduced. On the other hand, as economic growth continues, taxpayers/consumers typically demand more government services, such as health care. As a result, taxes may have to be increased. Fiscal policy is closely linked to the need to grow an economy, create jobs, and provide services.

Interest Rates. Interest rates can also affect economic growth and therefore have an indirect impact on stock prices. In general, stocks perform better when interest rates are low because firms can obtain financing at relatively low rates. Firms tend to be more willing to expand when interest rates are low, and their expansions stimulate the economy. When interest rates are low, investors also tend to shift more of their funds into stock because the interest earned on fixed-income securities is relatively low. The general shift into stocks increases the demand for stocks, which places upward pressure on stock prices.

Lower interest rates may enable more consumers to afford cars or homes. Car manufacturers and home builders then experience higher earnings, and their stock prices tend to increase as well.

| **myth** or **fact** Fundamental analysis includes economic analysis, industry analysis, and company analysis.

Financial publications often refer to the Bank of Canada when discussing interest rates because it uses **monetary policy** (techniques used to affect the economy of a country) to influence interest rates. Through its interest-rate policies, the Bank of Canada affects the amount of spending by consumers with borrowed funds and therefore influences economic growth.

In addition to influencing interest rates, the Bank of Canada can use other techniques to affect the economy, including managing the money supply (how much currency is available) and trading currency on the international markets.

Inflation. Stock prices are also affected by **inflation**, which is the increase in the general level of prices of products and services over a specified period. One of the most common measures of inflation is the **consumer price index (CPI)**, which represents the increase in the prices of consumer products such as groceries, household products, housing, and gasoline over time. Inflation can cause an increase in the prices that firms pay for materials or equipment. These firms may then pass on these price increases to the consumer in the form of higher selling prices for their products. Thus, inflation, in the form of increased prices of inputs such as materials or equipment, may lead to more inflation, in the form of increased prices of outputs such as products available for sale to consumers. In this situation, the Bank of Canada may use monetary policy to control inflation so that its effect on stock prices and the general economy is not too negative. The main publications providing information about inflation and other economic conditions are listed in Exhibit 11.4. These publications commonly provide historical data for inflation, economic growth, interest rates, and many other economic indicators.

Industry Analysis of Stocks

A firm's stock price is also susceptible to industry conditions. The demand for products or services within an industry changes over time. For example, the popularity of the internet increased the demand for computers, disks, printers, and internet guides in the 1990s. Producers of these products initially benefited from the increased demand. However, as other firms notice increased demand in a particular industry, they will often enter that industry and cause increased competition. Competition is another industry factor that frequently affects sales and earnings, and therefore the stock price of a firm. Competition has intensified for many industries as a result of the internet, which has reduced the costs of marketing and delivering products for some firms.

monetary policy
Techniques used by the Bank of Canada (central bank) to affect the economy of the country.

inflation
The increase in the general level of prices of products and services over a specified period.

consumer price index (CPI)
A measure of inflation that represents the increase in the prices of consumer products such as groceries, household products, housing, and gasoline over time.

EXHIBIT 11.4   Sources of Economic Information

Published Sources

- **Bank of Canada Weekly Financial Statistics:** provides key banking and money market statistics.

- **The Daily:** issues news releases on current social and economic conditions and announces new products. It provides a comprehensive one-stop overview of new information available from Statistics Canada.

- **Bank of Canada Monetary Policy Report and Update:** provides a detailed summary of the Bank's policies and strategies, and of the economic climate and its implications for inflation.

Online Sources

- **Bank of Canada (www.bankofcanada.ca/):** provides reports on interest rates, other economic conditions, and news announcements about various economic indicators.

- **Statistics Canada (www.statcan.gc.ca):** provides information and news about economic conditions by subject area.

- **Department of Finance Canada (www.fin.gc.ca/fin-eng.asp):** provides detailed information on economic and fiscal conditions.

Industry Indicators

Investors can obtain information about firms and their corresponding industry from various sources, as summarized in Exhibit 11.5. Numerous financial websites also provide information on specific industries. Another indicator of industry performance is the industry stock index, which measures how the market value of the firms within the industry has changed over a specific period. The prevailing sector stock index for a particular industry indicates the general expectations of investors about that industry.

EXHIBIT 11.5   Sources of Industry Information

Published Sources

Although some government publications offer industry information, the most popular sources are provided by the private sector.

- **Value Line Industry Survey:** provides an industry outlook, performance levels of various industries, and financial statistics for firms in each industry over time.

- **Report on Canada's Industrial Performance:** provides a semi-annual analysis of the current economic and financial performance of Canadian industries.

- **Standard & Poor's Analysts Handbook:** provides financial statistics for various industries over time.

Online Sources

- **Investcom (www.investcom.com):** identifies the performance of various industry sectors on a daily basis.

- **Report on Business (www.theglobeandmail.com, then click on "Business"):** contains news articles related to specific industries.

- **Yahoo! Canada (http://ca.yahoo.com):** provides financial news and statistics for each industry.

- **TMX Group (www.tmx.com):** provides equity and bond market indices for various industry sectors.

EXHIBIT 11.6   Factors that Increase and Decrease a Stock's Price

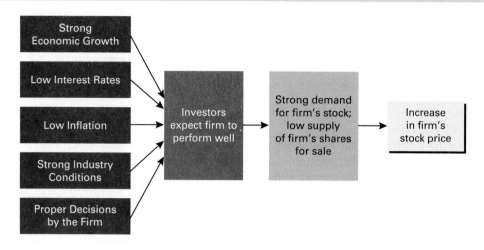

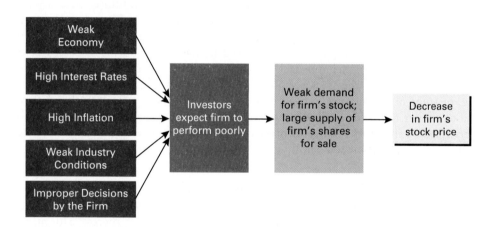

Integrating Your Analyses

By conducting an analysis of the firm itself, the economy, and the industry, you can assess a firm's possible future performance. This process enables you to determine whether to purchase the firm's stock. Exhibit 11.6 summarizes the potential impact of economic, industry, and firm-specific conditions on a firm's stock price.

FREE APPS for Personal Finance

Fundamentals

Application:

The Nutshel Stocks – Fundamental Analysis for Investors app provides access to comprehensive fundamental analysis data, including revenues, profitability, and valuation ratios.

L.O.5

STOCK VALUATION

Go to:
www.globeinvestor.
com/v5/content/filters

This website provides a list of stocks that meet criteria that you specify for performance over the last year, such as specific price–earnings (P/E) ratios and other characteristics.

intrinsic valuation model
A model that attempts to find the value of an investment by focusing on the amount of future cash flows generated by the investment, the timing of these cash flows, and the rate of return required on the investment.

relative valuation model
A model that attempts to find the value of an investment by comparing it to other similar investments.

dividend discount model (DDM)
A method of valuing stocks in which a firm's future dividend payments are discounted at an appropriate rate of interest.

Some stocks of high-performing firms are priced high and therefore may not be good investments for the future. Before investing in a stock, you should estimate its market value just as you would estimate the market value of a car or a home. A stock is different from a car or a home, however, in that it does not serve a physical function such as transportation or housing. A stock is simply intended to generate a return on the money invested.

Recall from our previous discussion that fundamental analysis is the valuation of stocks based on an examination of fundamental characteristics such as revenue, earnings, and/or the sensitivity of the firm's performance to economic conditions. The previous section discussed the financial, economic, and industry conditions that impact the price of a stock. You can apply your understanding of these conditions to valuing stocks by using either intrinsic or relative valuation models of stock valuation. An **intrinsic valuation model** attempts to find the value of an investment by focusing on the amount of future cash flows generated by the investment, the timing of these cash flows, and the rate of return required on the investment. A **relative valuation model** attempts to find the value of an investment by comparing it to other similar investments.

The underlying premise of the intrinsic valuation model is that the value of an investment equals the present, or discounted, value of all of its expected future cash flows. For non-dividend paying stocks, the expected future cash flows are those cash flows that are available to common stock holders. For dividend-paying stocks, the expected future cash flows are the dividend payments. The dividend discount model is discussed below. In a relative valuation model approach, it is common practice to determine the value of a stock by first relating the stock's share price to either earnings, cash flow, sales, book value, or some other measure of the firm's profitability. These ratios can then be compared to similar ratios for similar companies to determine whether the stock is over- or undervalued by investors relative to other companies. The price–earnings (P/E) relative valuation method is discussed below.

Dividend Discount Model (DDM) Method

The **dividend discount model (DDM)** is a method of valuing stocks in which a firm's future dividend payments are discounted at an appropriate rate of interest. This method of valuing stocks works best for mature firms that pay a large stable dividend, such as a utility company. As discussed below, there are many limitations to the DDM model; however, in stock valuation, the DDM provides a basic building block from which to describe and implement more robust discounted cash flow models.

Limitations of the DDM Method. Dividend payments may not be stable over time. Therefore, valuation of a stock based on dividends will be unreliable if dividends cannot be accurately predicted for the life of the stock. Also, if dividends are expected to grow over time, when and by how much will they grow? Investors who overestimate the growth in future dividends risk overpaying for a stock.

Even if the forecast of growth in dividends is accurate, dividends may not accurately reflect the cash flows available to shareholders. For example, the amount of dividends paid may be unsustainable given the growth in a company's earnings. Investors who rely on these dividend payments to value a stock risk putting too high a value on the stock, which may result in overpayment. Finally, the DDM model cannot be applied to firms that do not pay dividends.

Price–Earnings (P/E) Method

The price–earnings (P/E) method is used to determine the value of a stock based on the value of the firm's earnings. The higher the earnings, the more funds the firm has to pay dividends to its shareholders or to reinvest for further expansion (which will ultimately generate additional earnings). A high P/E ratio suggests that a firm is either overvalued relative to comparable companies and/or an industry benchmark, or that it has higher growth prospects relative to comparable companies and/or an industry benchmark. In order to use P/E ratios, a firm needs to have positive and predictable earnings. In practice, since no one valuation method is perfect, it is appropriate to calculate and compare many valuation models when valuing stocks.

Limitations of the P/E Method. Forecasting earnings is difficult. Therefore, valuations of a stock that are based on expected earnings may be unreliable. Investors who overestimate future earnings risk overpaying for a stock.

Even if the forecast of earnings is accurate, there is still the question of the proper P/E multiple that should be used to value a stock. The firm that you are valuing may deserve to have a lower P/E ratio than other firms if its future performance is subject to more uncertainty. For example, perhaps the firm is using less advanced technology than its competitors, which could adversely affect its performance in a few years. Consequently, its lower P/E ratio may not necessarily mean that the firm's stock is undervalued by the market.

Another limitation of the P/E method is that results will vary depending on the firms selected to derive a mean industry P/E ratio. Should this ratio be derived from the three closest competitors or from the 10 closest competitors? For firms that conduct several types of business, it is difficult to determine who the closest competitors are. Investors who apply the wrong industry P/E ratio will derive an inaccurate valuation, which may cause them to buy stocks that are not really undervalued.

Stock Market Efficiency

Because investors use different methods to value and analyze stocks, they derive different valuations for a stock. Stock market efficiency is relevant for investors who are attempting to achieve abnormally high returns by analyzing financial information or relying on investment advisers. If stock prices fully reflect information that is available to investors, the stock market is said to be an **efficient stock market**.

efficient stock market
A market in which stock prices fully reflect information that is available to investors.

Conversely, the stock market is referred to as an **inefficient stock market** if stock prices do not reflect all public information that is available to investors. In general, an efficient stock market implies that you and other investors will not be able to identify stocks that are undervalued because stocks are valued properly by the market.

inefficient stock market
A market in which stock prices do not reflect all public information that is available to investors.

▌ **myth** or **fact** When someone makes money in the stock market, someone else loses money. ▐

The argument for efficiency is that demand for shares by investors should drive the equilibrium price of a stock toward its proper value. If a stock was really priced below its estimated value, the large institutional investors who have more access to information about the stock than individual investors would buy substantial amounts of it. The strong demand for shares would force the price of the stock higher, bringing the stock's price close to its estimated value. Thus, institutional investors capitalizing on the discrepancy would push the stock price back to its estimated value.

Reviewing historical stock prices, investors can identify several stocks that experienced very large returns. Some stocks have doubled in price in a single day. Some stocks will experience very large returns in the future. These performances do not mean that the stock market is inefficient, however, unless information that was available to investors should have justified higher valuations of those stocks before their prices increased. It is easy to look back and realize that you would have benefited from purchasing shares of Microsoft or Dell Computer when their stocks were first publicly traded. Yet who really knew that these stocks would perform so well at that time? An investor can achieve high returns from a hunch about a specific stock. The concept of market efficiency acknowledges that when you invest in stocks, some of those stocks may outperform the market in general.

However, it implies that stock selections by an investor will not consistently beat the market.

L.O.6

ASSESSING PERFORMANCE OF STOCK INVESTMENTS

How can you measure the performance of your stock investments? How can you distinguish between performance due to general market conditions and performance of the stock?

Comparing Returns to an Index

A convenient and effective method of measuring performance is to compare the return on your stock (or stock portfolio) to the return on a stock index representing similar types of stocks. Stock index returns are provided in most business periodicals and on numerous websites such as Yahoo! Canada.

EXAMPLE

Stephanie Spratt invested in one stock about one year (or four quarters) ago. The returns on her stock are shown in Column 2 of Exhibit 11.7. Her return was lowest in the first quarter but increased in the following three quarters. Stephanie wants to compare her stock's return to the market in general to get a true assessment of its performance. This comparison will indicate whether her specific selection generated a higher return than she could have earned by simply investing in a stock index. In Exhibit 11.7, the return on a market index over the same period is shown in Column 3. Given the information in Columns 2 and 3, Stephanie determines the excess return on her stock as

$$ER = R - Ri$$

where ER is excess return, R is the return on her stock, and Ri is the return on the stock index.

The excess return of the stock was negative in each of the four quarters. Stephanie is disappointed in its performance and decides to sell it in the near future if its performance does not improve. She intends to review her initial evaluation to ensure that her assumptions were correct when she conducted her analysis.

Go to:
http://ca.finance.
yahoo.com

This website provides
a summary of recent stock market performance and other key indicators.

EXHIBIT 11.7   Stock Performance Evaluation

	Return on Stephanie's Stock	Return on a Canadian Stock Index	Excess Return of Stephanie's Stock (above the market)
Quarter 1	–1%	3%	–4%
Quarter 2	2	3	–1
Quarter 3	2	4	–2
Quarter 4	3	4	–1

FREE APPS for Personal Finance

Investing Game

Application:

The Stock Wars app allows you to simulate investing in a stock portfolio and monitoring the performance of your portfolio over time. You can see how you would have performed from investing without risking any money.

MyLab Finance   Visit MyLab Finance for additional study and practice tools. Select Financial Planning Problems are available in the Study Plan. Create your own study plan, generate personal cash flow statements and balance sheets, and set personal financial goals.

SUMMARY

L.O.1   Identify the functions of stock exchanges

Stocks are listed on stock exchanges, where they can be purchased or sold. Recently, stock exchanges have been demutualized. This has resulted in the consolidation of stock exchanges throughout North America and Europe. Unlisted stocks can be purchased on the over-the-counter (OTC) market. In Canada, this means using the NEX board on the TSX Venture Exchange.

L.O.2   Describe how to interpret stock quotations

Quotations for exchange-traded stocks are provided in daily newspapers and online. These quotations should be considered when deciding whether to purchase a stock.

L.O.3   Explain how to execute the purchase or sale of stocks

Once you have decided which stocks to buy or sell, you contact a brokerage firm. You can also use an online brokerage firm, which may be more convenient and also less costly than a traditional full-service brokerage firm. Upon receiving your order, the brokerage firm sends it to the stock exchange where the trade is executed.

L.O.4   Explain how to analyze a stock

An analysis of a firm involves reviewing the firm's annual report and the financial statements (such as the balance sheet and the Comprehensive Statement of Income), along with other financial reports. This analysis includes an assessment of the firm's liquidity, financial leverage, efficiency, and profitability. Be careful when interpreting financial statements, since accounting guidelines allow firms to use methods that may exaggerate or underestimate their performance.

An economic analysis involves assessing how a stock's price can be affected by economic conditions. The most closely monitored economic factors that can affect stock prices are economic growth, interest rates, and inflation. In general, stocks are favourably affected by economic growth, a decline in interest rates, and a decline in inflation.

An industry analysis involves assessing how a stock's price can be affected by industry conditions. Two closely monitored industry characteristics are consumer preferences within an industry and industry competition. Stocks are favourably affected when the firms recognize and take advantage of shifts in consumer preferences and/or when the firms face a relatively low degree of competition.

L.O.5   Explain how to value stocks

Stocks can be valued using either intrinsic or relative valuation models. The dividend discount model (DDM) method estimates the value of a stock based on the discounted value of the firm's dividends. The price–earnings (P/E) method estimates the stock's value based on the value of the firm's earnings.

Stock market efficiency implies that stock prices reflect all public information. If the stock market is efficient, there may be little or no benefits to trying to use public information to achieve unusually high returns. Many investors, however, believe that the stock market is not efficient and therefore attempt to determine whether a specific stock is undervalued. It is the interpretation of public information that can lead to higher returns.

L.O.6   Explain how to assess your stock portfolio's performance

After you execute a stock transaction, you should monitor the performance of your investment over time. Compare the return on that stock with an index of stocks that represents similar firms or even the general market. Several stock market indexes and sector indexes are available to use as benchmarks when assessing a stock's performance.

REVIEW QUESTIONS

1. What are stock exchanges? How do they facilitate the trading of stocks?

2. What are the two major stock exchanges in Canada? What is the purpose of the Montreal Exchange?

3. Describe electronic trading.

4. What is a bid price? What is an ask price? What are the three characteristics of a high quality stock exchange?

5. Define and describe the role of market makers.

6. Describe the New York Stock Exchange.

7. What is demutualization?

8. What is the over-the-counter (OTC) market? How is the OTC market different from an organized exchange?

9. What information does a stock quotation provide about a stock?

10. Define and differentiate between a discount brokerage firm and a full-service brokerage firm.

11. How reliable are full-service broker and analyst recommendations? Explain.

12. What information must you provide when placing an order to buy or sell stock? What is a ticker symbol and why is it important?

13. What do the terms *board lot* and *odd lot* mean in stock transactions?

14. Define and differentiate between a market order and a limit order.

15. Define an on-stop order, a buy-stop order, and a sell-stop order.

16. Describe the characteristics associated with placing an order online.

17. What does it mean to buy stock on margin?

18. What may happen if the value of the stock bought on margin declines?

19. What are the advantages to investors and brokerage firms when stocks are bought on margin?

20. What two basic factors drive the price of a stock? Explain.

21. What is the first step in the valuation process of a stock? What are you trying to determine through stock valuation? What two methods may be used to value a stock?

22. What is technical analysis? What is fundamental analysis?

23. Why is it necessary to analyze a firm? What is an annual report? What information does it contain to aid in your analysis?

24. How do differences in stock valuation affect the volume of trading?

25. What is a balance sheet? What are the two parts of the balance sheet and what do they indicate about the firm?

26. What is an income statement? Describe its features.

27. Describe the impact of a firm's financial condition on its value and stock price.

28. What is liquidity? What does it mean for a firm to have a high degree of liquidity? How is liquidity measured?

29. What is financial leverage? Why do some firms prefer to borrow funds rather than issue stock?

30. Define and discuss two ways to measure a firm's financial leverage.

31. Describe how the efficiency of a firm can be determined from the composition of its assets.

32. Define inventory turnover, average collection period, and asset turnover ratio. Is it better when these measures are higher or lower in value? Explain.

33. Define operating profit margin, net profit margin, return on assets, and return on equity.

34. Why may the top managers of a firm be tempted to use misleading estimates of revenues and expenses? How might managers to boost the reported earnings of their firm?

35. What is economic growth? How is it measured? How does economic growth affect stock prices?

36. What is fiscal policy? How does fiscal policy potentially impact economic growth?

37. What is monetary policy? What is it used to influence?

38. How does the level of interest rates affect economic growth?

39. What is inflation? How is inflation measured? How does inflation affect stock prices?

40. Why is it important to perform an industry analysis when evaluating a stock?

41. What is an intrinsic valuation model? What is the underlying premise of this model?

42. What is a relative valuation model?

43. What is the dividend discount model (DDM) method? When is it best to use this method? What are the limitations of the DDM method?

44. What is the price–earnings (P/E) method? What does a high P/E ratio suggest about a firm? What are the limitations of using the P/E method?

45. What is an efficient stock market? What is an inefficient stock market?

46. What is the argument for market efficiency?

47. Historically, some stocks that provide very high returns can be identified. Does this mean that the market is inefficient? Why or why not?

48. Describe an effective method of measuring the performance of a stock.

FINANCIAL PLANNING PROBLEMS

 MyLab Finance Financial Planning Problems marked with a can be found in MyLab Finance.

1. Denise has a choice between two stocks. Stock A has a current stock price of $33.50 and earnings per share of $2.23. Stock B has a current stock price of $30.50 and earnings per share of $2.79. Both stocks are in the same industry, and the average P/E ratio for the industry is 13. Using the P/E ratio, which stock is the better choice? Why?

The following information applies to Problems 2 through 5.

Balance Sheet for Polly Corporation (in millions)

Assets

Cash and marketable securities	$ 150
Accounts receivable	320
Inventories	430
Net fixed assets	700
Total assets	$1600

Liabilities and Shareholders' Equity

Accounts payable	$ 350
Short-term debt	100
Long-term debt	300
Shareholders' equity	850
Total liabilities and shareholders' equity	$1600

Income Statement for Polly Corporation (in millions)

Revenue	$4500
Cost of goods sold	2800
Gross profit	1700
Operating expenses	1200
Earnings before interest costs and taxes (EBIT)	500
Interest	50
Earnings before taxes	$ 450
Taxes	200
Earnings after taxes	250

2. What is Polly Corporation's current ratio? If the current ratio averages 2.5 in Polly's industry, is Polly liquid?

3. Compute two measures of financial leverage for Polly Corporation and interpret them.

4. What is Polly Corporation's average collection period? Other firms in the industry collect their receivables in 25 days, on average. How does Polly compare to other firms in the industry?

5. Use ratios to assess Polly Corporation's profitability.

6. A year ago, Rebecca purchased 100 shares of Havad stock for $25 per share. Yesterday, she placed a limit order to sell her stock at a price of $30 per share before the market opened. The stock's price opened at $29 and slowly increased to $32 in the middle of the day, before declining to $28 by the end of the day. The stock did not pay any dividends over the period in which Rebecca held it. What was Rebecca's return on her investment?

7. Explain how the results in Problem 6 would be different if Rebecca had placed a limit order of $33.

8. Trey purchases 200 shares of Turner stock for $40 per share. Trey pays $4000 in cash and borrows $4000 from his broker at 11 percent interest to complete the purchase. One year later, Trey sells the stock for $50 per share. What is Trey's return if the stock paid no dividends during the year?

9. What return would Trey (from Problem 8) receive if he had purchased the stock for cash?

CHALLENGE QUESTIONS

1. The Wildcat Corporation recently announced that its year-end estimated earnings per share next year will be $3.25. Wildcat stock is currently selling for $43 per share.

   a. What is the P/E ratio for the Wildcat Corporation?

   b. Assume prospects for the Wildcat Corporation deteriorate and the company now estimates next year's earnings to be $2 per share. If the P/E ratio remains the same, what would be the new selling price for Wildcat stock?

   c. Since it is so simple to calculate, analysts at Trident Investments Ltd. use only the P/E ratio to determine the value of a stock. Is this an appropriate strategy? Explain.

2. Paula is considering buying stock on margin. She wants to buy $50 000 in stock; she will put 30 percent down and borrow the remaining $35 000 at 12 percent interest.

   a. If Paula's investment goes up 50 percent after one year and she pays off her loan, how much will she make in dollars? What percent rate of return does this represent?

   b. If Paula's investment instead drops by 20 percent, how much will she lose in dollars? In terms of a percentage loss, how much will she lose?

ETHICAL DILEMMA

Nick, a recent college graduate, wishes to begin investing to meet some of his financial goals. His father recommends a stockbroker who he says has always given him good advice. Nick's grandfather has also begun doing business with the same stockbroker as a result of Nick's father's recommendation. Over the next several months, the broker recommends four stocks as a must for Nick's portfolio. Nick buys all four stocks based on this advice. During the family's annual reunion, Nick, his father, and his grandfather compare their experiences with the same broker. Nick is surprised to learn that the broker recommended the same four stocks to both his father and his grandfather. His father defends the broker by saying that if it is a good stock for Nick, why would it not be a good stock for all of them? Besides, his father says, since the broker's company does all of the investment banking for the four stocks he recommended, he undoubtedly knows everything there is to know about these four firms.

a. Discuss the ethical issues of the broker's recommending the same four stocks to Nick, his father, and his grandfather.

b. Why might these four stocks be a good investment for Nick, but not for his father or his grandfather? Why might all four stocks be a good investment for all three of them?

FINANCIAL PLANNING ONLINE EXERCISES

1. In this exercise, you will examine information on the financial condition of a stock. Go to www.stockhouse.com.

a. In the search box, enter the stock symbol IMO and click on Search. From the list, select the stock that trades on the TSX. You will get information on Imperial Oil. Click on Profile. You will be provided with information on this company, including a description of its business, the head office address, a link to the company website, some financial numbers, the status of company shares, related companies, a list of board members, and officers of the company. How is this information useful to investors?

b. Click on Financials. Use the financial ratios provided in the chapter to assess the company's liquidity, financial leverage, efficiency, and profitability characteristics. Do you think Imperial Oil shares are a good investment at the current share price?

c. Now enter the symbol BNS beside Search: Quote and obtain information on Bank of Nova Scotia. Click on Financials. Use the financial ratios provided in the chapter to assess the company's liquidity, financial leverage, efficiency, and profitability characteristics. Do you think Bank of Nova Scotia shares are a good investment at the current price? Why or why not?

d. How do Imperial Oil and Bank of Nova Scotia compare as investments based on the financial information available on this website?

2. Go to www.globeinvestor.com/v5/content/filters.

a. This exercise allows you to identify stocks that satisfy your criteria. For Industry, choose Food Processing; for Security, choose Common; for Country, choose Canada. Click on Get Results and then on View Report. What information is displayed on the screen? Which stocks have a five-star rating? How has this rating changed over the last year? How does the return on the various stocks compare with the return in the industry? Do five-star stocks have higher returns than lower-ranked stocks? Why or why not?

b. You can also use this website to filter stocks based on their performance statistics. Return to www.globeinvestor.com/v5/content/filters. For Security, choose Common. Next, enter a minimum and maximum value for Price/Earnings per Share of 10 and 20, respectively. Enter a minimum and maximum value for the Dividend Yield of 3 and 10, respectively. Finally, enter a minimum and maximum value for the 3 Year % Revenue Growth of 5 and 20, respectively. Click on Get Results and then on View Report. In general, what types of companies have the performance statistics parameters you entered? Are these growth stocks or value stocks? Of the stocks that are from the same industry, which would you select for your portfolio?

3. Go to www.investcom.com. This website provides a sector watch list showing the most recent performance of each of the major sectors of the TSX. In addition, you can access the opinion of various stock analysts with respect to any particular stock.

   a. Click on Gold under Sector Watch and then pick one of the stocks in that sector. Next, click on Research Report next to the stock you have chosen and review the Analyst Research. What is the opinion of the various stock analysts with respect to this stock? Do they all agree?

   b. Compare stock analysts' opinions for four or five stocks from within the same sector. Do all of the analysts agree on each individual stock? In general, are there any stocks within the sector that are receiving a favourable opinion, while other stocks are not in favour?

PSYCHOLOGY OF PERSONAL FINANCE: Your Investments

1. Some investors are naïve and overconfident that the stocks in which they invest will perform well. They know that they might achieve high returns from buying stocks on margin, but they ignore that they could incur large losses. What is your behaviour toward buying stocks on margin? What is the risk associated with this strategy?

2. Read one practical article of how psychology affects decisions when buying stocks on margin. You can easily retrieve possible articles by doing an online search using the terms "psychology" and "buying stocks on margin." Summarize the main points of the article.

MINI-CASE 1: Financial Ratio Calculations and Analysis

You are given the following balance sheet and income statement information for Ultra Corporation:

Balance Sheet for Ultra Corporation
(Numbers are in Millions)

Assets		Liabilities and Shareholders' Equity	
Short-term (current) assets		Short-term liabilities	
Cash and marketable securities	$ 300	Accounts payable	$1300
Accounts receivable	800	Short-term debt	500
Inventories	1000	Total short-term liabilities	$1800
Total short-term assets	**$2100**		
Fixed Assets	$1500	**Long-term debt**	**$ 800**
Less depreciation	−500		
Net fixed assets	**$1000**	**Shareholders' equity**	**$ 500**
Total assets	**$3100**	**Total liabilities and shareholders' equity**	**$3100**

Income Statement for Ultra Corporation
(Numbers are in Millions)

Revenue (sales)	$4000
Cost of goods sold	2900
Gross profit	**$ 1100**
Operating expenses	830
Earnings before interest and taxes	**$ 270**
Interest expense	200
Earnings before taxes	**$ 70**
Taxes	14
Earnings after taxes	**$ 56**

What is the purpose of Ultra Corporation's balance sheet and income statement? Use the information in the financial statements above to calculate the liquidity, financial leverage, efficiency, and profitability ratios for Ultra Corporation. Using these ratios, describe your impressions of Ultra Corporation's firm-specific characteristics. The table below displays the average ratios for similar firms in the industry in which Ultra Corporation operates.

Table 1   Average Industry Ratios

Current ratio	2.2	Inventory turnover	5	Net profit margin	11.3%
Debt ratio	44.3%	Average collection period	44 days	Return on assets	14.7%
Times interest earned ratio	6.7	Asset turnover ratio	3.26	Return on equity	17.1%

MINI-CASE 2: Using Stock Quotes

Use the daily stock quotation below to answer the following questions.

Stock	Ticker	close	Net ch	% ch	Vol 00s	Day high	Day low	% Yield	P/E	52 wk high	low
ABC Ltd.	ABC	$106.30	(0.75)	(.0071)	2785	$108.90	$104.10	?	79	$111.10	$38.20

ABC Ltd. recently paid a dividend of $1.70 per share. What is the current dividend yield for ABC Ltd. (ABC) based on the stock's recent closing price? What is your estimate of ABC's earnings per share for the year based on the recent closing price? Based on the net change listed above, at what price did ABC close yesterday?

Study Guide

Circle the correct answer and then check the answers in the back of the book to chart your progress.

Multiple Choice

1. A high-quality stock exchange is characterized by all of the following, except:
   a. A small difference between the bid price and the ask price.
   b. A large volume of shares being offered for purchase or sale with each trade request.
   c. A large number of venture capitalists acting as market makers.
   d. A large volume of traders making purchase or sale requests.

2. Under which of the following circumstances would a market maker earn money on an executed order?.
   a. When the ask price is greater than the bid price.
   b. When the bid price is greater than the ask price.
   c. When the bid price is the same as the ask price.
   d. When the bid price is less than the ask price.

3. All of the following are pieces of information displayed in a stock quotation, except:
   a. The value of the stock based on the value of discounted dividends.
   b. The price at the end of the day when the stock market closes (Close).
   c. The daily high at which the stock was traded (Day high).
   d. The ticker symbol associated with the stock (Ticker).

4. A firm has a high degree of _____ if it has a large amount of assets that can be easily converted to cash and has a relatively small amount of short-term liabilities.
   a. efficiency
   b. financial leverage
   c. liquidity
   d. profitability

5. Rebecca would like to purchase a stock on margin in her margin account. Currently, the stock she is considering is trading at $18 per share and she would like to purchase 600 shares. What is her margin requirement if the margin rate is 30 percent and her brokerage firm is willing to lend her 70 percent of her purchase price?
   a. $3240
   b. $7560
   c. $10 800
   d. $0

6. Which of the following situations provides an example of how accounting methods can be used to inflate revenue?
   a. A firm uses a lenient policy that allows customers to cancel their orders. The firm does not count cancelled orders as revenue.
   b. A publisher of a magazine receives three-year subscriptions, for which payment is made annually. It reports these sales as revenue in the year in which the magazine is delivered. The cash flow attributed to the sales will occur either in a future period or not at all.
   c. A service firm has a five-year contract with a client, in which the client can cancel the agreement after the first year. The firm records the expected revenue over the next five years in each of the five years of the contract.
   d. None of the above.

7. What is gross domestic product (GDP)?
   a. A measure of the total market value of all products and services produced in Canada by Canadians
   b. A measure of the total market value of all products and services produced by Canadians
   c. A measure of the total market value of all products and services produced in Canada
   d. A measure of the total market value of all products and services produced in Canada by foreigners

8. What is the return on assets for a firm that has a gross profit of $1.2 million, an operating profit of $550 000, a net profit of $200 000, short-term assets of $1 million, and long-term assets of $5 million?
   a. 3.3 percent
   b. 20 percent
   c. 4 percent
   d. 9.2 percent

9. In general, stocks perform better when interest rates are low. This statement is true because low interest rates normally will result in all of the following, except
   a. Firms tend to be more willing to expand.
   b. Investors tend to shift more of their funds into bonds to take advantage of interest rates before they decrease.
   c. Consumers are able to afford cars or homes.
   d. Investors tend to shift more of their funds into stock.

10. Which of the following methods represents an application of the technical analysis method for evaluating stocks?
    a. You will purchase a stock if its price rises for three consecutive days.
    b. You will purchase a stock if its price–earnings (P/E) ratio is 15 or lower.
    c. You will purchase a stock if you are able to determine that its exposure to a weakening of economic condition is below average.
    d. You will purchase a stock if the dividend discount model (DDM) suggests that the stock price should be higher than what it currently is.

11. Which of the following is not a limitation of the P/E method?
    a. Forecasting earnings is difficult.
    b. It is subject to error if it is based on an overestimate of revenues.
    c. It is difficult to determine the proper multiple that should be used to value a stock.
    d. The results will vary depending on the firms that are selected to derive a mean industry ratio.

12. Investors who wish to trade options and futures would place their orders through which of the following exchanges?
    a. Toronto Stock Exchange
    b. Winnipeg Stock Exchange
    c. TSX Venture Exchange
    d. Montreal Exchange

13. Whenever you place an order to buy or sell a stock, you must specify all of the following, except:
    a. The number of shares you wish to purchase.
    b. The name of the firm selling you the stock.
    c. Whether you are buying or selling the stock.
    d. The name of the stock.

14. The advantage of a market order is that:
    a. You are assured that your order will be executed quickly.
    b. You can control the price at which you are willing to purchase the stock.
    c. You can specify that you want the full number of shares to be traded or none at all.
    d. Your order will expire if it is not completed within three hours.

15. The Bank of Canada uses _____ policy to influence interest rates.
    a. public
    b. fiscal
    c. monetary
    d. financial

True/False

1. True or False? Among other things, a firm's annual report includes a message from the chief environmental officer (CEO).

2. True or False? Many firms prefer to borrow funds rather than issue stock to avoid placing upward pressure on the stock price.

3. True or False? The average collection period can be used to determine the average age of accounts payable. A higher number relative to the industry norm means a longer collection period, which is less efficient.

4. True or False? One of the reasons top managers may inflate the revenue of their firm is to be able to sell their shares at a higher price at some point in the future.

5. True or False? High-priced stocks of well-performing firms are a good investment for the future.

6. True or False? An efficient stock market is a market in which stock prices reflect most of the information available to investors.

7. True or False? The OTC market was designed for companies that do not meet the listing requirements of the TSX or the TSX Venture Exchange.

8. True or False? One of the advantages of relying on analyst recommendations is that many studies have shown that these recommendations often lead to better performance than the stock market in general.

9. True or False? An on-stop order, which is a special form of limit order, is an order to execute a transaction when the stock price reaches a specified level.

10. True or False? A convenient and effective method of measuring performance is to compare the return on your stock to the return on that stock in the past.

11. True or False? The rapid and ongoing consolidation in global capital markets has been fuelled by the demutualization of stock exchanges.

12. True or False? Fiscal policy refers to how the government imposes taxes on individuals and corporations and how it spends tax revenues.

13. True or False? A relative valuation model attempts to find the value of an investment by focusing on the amount of future cash flows generated by the investment.

14. True or False? A limitation of intrinsic valuation models is that forecasting future dividends and earnings is too easy.

15. True or False? A firm's possible future performance can only be assessed by conducting an analysis of the firm, the economy, and the industry within which the firm operates.

APPENDIX 11A
Including Stock Options in Your Portfolio

When making your asset allocation decisions, you may want to consider **stock options**, which are options to purchase or sell stocks under specified conditions. Like stocks, stock options are traded on exchanges. Some employers include stock options in compensation packages, so you should be aware of them.

CALL OPTIONS

A **call option** on a stock provides the right to purchase 100 shares of a specified stock at a specified price (called the **exercise price or strike price**) by a specified expiration date. The advantage of a call option is that it locks in the price you have to pay to purchase the stock and also gives you the flexibility to let the option expire if you wish. The price you pay when purchasing a call option is referred to as the **premium of a call option**. The premium of a call option is influenced by the number of investors who wish to buy call options on that particular stock. Investors can purchase call options through their brokerage firm, which charges a commission for executing the transaction.

stock option
An option to purchase or sell stocks under specified conditions.

call option
Provides the right to purchase 100 shares of a specified stock at a specified price by a specified expiration date.

exercise (strike) price
The price at which a call option is exercised.

premium of a call option
The price paid when purchasing a call option.

EXAMPLE

On September 10, you pay a premium of $2 per share, or $200, to purchase a call option on Gamma stock. The stock price is currently $28. The call option gives you the right to buy 100 shares of Gamma stock at the exercise price of $30 at any time up until the end of November. Thus, no matter how much Gamma's stock price rises before the end of November, you can still buy the stock at $30 per share.

For every buyer of a call option, there must be a seller who is willing to sell the call option. The seller of a call option is obligated to sell the shares of the specified stock to the buyer for the exercise price if and when the buyer exercises the option.

Joan Reynolds sold you the call option on Gamma stock. Joan receives the $200 premium that you paid to buy the call option. She is obligated to sell 100 shares of stock to you for $30 per share if and when you exercise the call option.

EXAMPLE

Your net gain or loss from buying a call option can be determined by considering the amount received when you sell the stock, the amount you paid for the stock when exercising the option, and the amount you paid for the premium. Exhibit 11.1A illustrates a payoff diagram for a call option on Gamma stock. A **payoff diagram** is a graph that illustrates the gains or losses generated from an option and can be used to illustrate the value of an option to a buyer or seller. Exhibit 11.1A shows that, at a stock price of $28, the buyer will have a net loss of $2 per share, whereas the seller will have a profit of $2 per share. However, as the stock price rises, the buyer's position will turn toward a profit and the seller's position will turn toward a loss. Furthermore, the buyer's/seller's profits/losses are unlimited.

payoff diagram
A graph that illustrates the gains or losses generated from an option.

(continued)

EXHIBIT 11.1A   Payoff Diagram for a Call Option on Gamma Stock

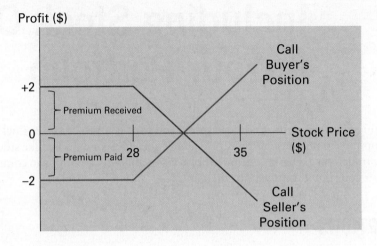

Recall that you paid a premium of $2 per share, or $200, to purchase the call option on Gamma stock. Suppose that the price of Gamma stock increases from $28 to $35 per share by the end of November. You can exercise the option and then sell the stock in the market at its prevailing price of $35. Your gain is:

Amount Received from Selling the Stock ($35 × 100 shares)	$3500
Amount Paid for Gamma Stock ($30 × 100 shares)	−3000
Amount Paid for the Call Option ($2 × 100 shares)	−200
Net Gain	=$ 300

Since you paid $200 for the call option and your net gain was $300, your return can be derived as your net gain divided by the amount of your investment:

Return = Net Gain / Amount of Investment

= $300/$200

= 1.5 or 150%

Joan does not own shares of Gamma stock, so she has to buy it in the market at $35 per share before selling it to you at $30 per share. Thus, her net gain (or loss) is:

Amount Received from Selling the Stock ($30 × 100 shares)	$3000
Amount Paid for Gamma Stock ($35 × 100 shares)	−3500
Amount Received for the Call Option ($2 × 100 shares)	= 200
Net Loss	=−$ 300

Notice that the dollar amount of your gain is equal to the dollar amount of Joan's loss.

When investing in a call option on a stock rather than the stock itself, you can magnify your return. If you had purchased Gamma stock on September 10 at a price of $28 per share, your gain would have been $7 per share. The return from investing in the call option (150 percent) is much higher.

PUT OPTIONS

A **put option** on a stock provides the right to sell 100 shares of a specified stock at a specified exercise price by a specified expiration date. You place an order for a put option in the same way that you place an order for a call option. The put option locks in the price at which you can sell the stock and also gives you the flexibility to let the option expire if you wish. You buy a put option when you expect the stock's price to decline.

put option
Provides the right to sell 100 shares of a specified stock at a specified exercise price by a specified expiration date.

EXAMPLE

On January 18, you pay a premium of $3 per share, or $300, to purchase a put option on Winger stock with an exercise price of $50 that expires at the end of March. The stock price is currently $51 per share. The put option gives you the right to sell 100 shares of Winger stock at the exercise price of $50 at any time up until the end of March. Thus, no matter how much Winger's stock price decreases before the end of March, you can still sell the stock at $50 per share.

For every buyer of a put option, there must be a seller who is willing to sell the put option. The seller of a put option is obligated to buy the shares of the specified stock from the buyer for the exercise price if and when the buyer exercises the option.

Exhibit 11.2A illustrates the payoff diagram for a put option on Winger stock. Notice that at a stock price of $50, the buyer will have a net loss of $3 per share, whereas the seller will have a profit of $3 per share. However, as the stock price decreases, the buyer's position will turn toward a profit and the seller's position will turn toward a loss. With respect to a put option, the profits and losses of the buyer and seller are capped as the difference between the exercise price and the option premium. At a stock price of $0 per share, the option buyer is able to sell the worthless stock for $50 per share for a profit of $47 per share (calculated as $50 − $3).

EXHIBIT 11.2A   A Payoff Diagram for a Put Option on Winger Stock

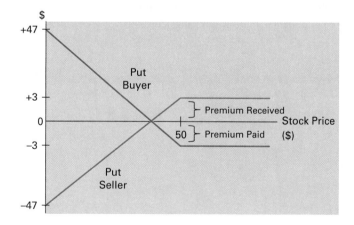

THE ROLE OF STOCK OPTIONS IN ASSET ALLOCATION

Although stock options have become a popular investment for individual investors who want to achieve very high returns, options are still very risky and should therefore play only a minimal role (if any) in asset allocation. Since asset allocation is normally intended to limit exposure to any one type of investment, any allocation to stock options should be made with caution. Many stock options are never exercised, which means that the investment generates a return of –100 percent. According to the Options Clearing Corporation, statistics for 2008 indicate that only 11.6 percent of options were exercised for that year.

EXAMPLE

You invested in 100 shares of Dragon.com stock a year ago. Although the stock has performed well, you think it may perform poorly in the near future. The present price of the stock is $40 per share. You decide to pay a premium of $3 per share, or $300, for a put option on Dragon.com stock with an exercise price of $38. If the stock price stays above $38 per share, you will not exercise the put option. Conversely, if the stock price falls below $38 per share, you can exercise the put option by selling the shares you are holding for $38 per share.

---

protective put strategy
An option strategy where you purchase a put option to protect against a decrease in the price of an underlying stock.

covered call strategy
Selling call options on stock that you own.

In this example, your purchase of a put option locked in a minimum price at which you could sell a stock you were holding, no matter how much that stock's price declined. Thus, you were able to reduce your portfolio's risk by limiting your potential loss on this stock. A **protective put strategy** refers to an option strategy where you purchase a put option to protect against a decrease in the price of an underlying stock.

You can also reduce your risk by selling call options on stock that you own. Doing so is referred to as a **covered call strategy** because the call option you purchase is covered by stock that you already own. This strategy will also generate a premium for the seller of the option.

EXAMPLE

Assume once again that you are concerned that the price of Dragon.com stock may decline in the near future. There is a call option available with an exercise price of $42 and a premium of $2. You decide to sell a call option on Dragon.com stock and receive a premium of $200 (calculated as $2 × 100 shares). If the price of Dragon.com stock rises above $42 per share, the call option will be exercised, and you will have to sell the stock to fulfill your obligation. Yet you at least will sell the stock for a gain. Conversely, if the stock price remains below $42, the call option will not be exercised. In this case, the $200 that you earned from selling the call option can help to offset the stock's poor performance, thereby reducing your potential losses from holding it.

Investing in Bonds

V. J. Matthew/Shutterstock

Neal wanted to invest in bonds because he knew that they could provide periodic interest payments that would serve as a source of income. He knew that he could buy bonds issued by the Government of Canada. However, these bonds offered a yield of only 2 percent. Neal wanted to earn a higher yield.

His broker suggested that he invest in high-yield bonds, which are issued by companies whose financial condition is weak. Neal noticed that some of these bonds offer a yield of 6 percent, triple that provided by Government of Canada bonds. He also noticed that these bonds provided very high returns to investors over the previous five years while the economy was strong, much higher than Government of Canada bonds. He decided to invest in high-yield convertible and extendible bonds issued by one particular company that were presently offering a yield of 7 percent.

QUESTIONS:

What does it mean for a bond to be convertible and extendible?

1. What other types of bonds and fixed-income products could Neal invest in?
2. What are the risks associated with investing in high-yield bonds? Are there any other risks associated with bonds that Neal should be aware of?

BACKGROUND ON BONDS

bonds
Long-term debt securities issued by government agencies or corporations that are collateralized by assets.

Recall that investors commonly invest some of their funds in **bonds,** which are long-term debt securities issued by government agencies or corporations that are collateralized by assets. Bonds frequently offer more favourable returns than bank deposits. In addition, they typically provide fixed coupon (interest) payments that represent the regular periodic interest income paid to a bondholder.

debentures
Long-term debt securities issued by corporations that are secured only by the corporation's promise to pay.

Debentures are similar to bonds, except that these long-term debt securities issued by corporations are secured only by the corporation's promise to pay. Debentures are therefore riskier than bonds issued by the same company. All other aspects of bonds discussed in this chapter also apply to debentures. For simplicity, the term *bond* will be used throughout this chapter.

par value
For a bond, its face value, or the amount returned to the investor at the maturity date when the bond is due.

The **par value** of a bond is its face value, or the amount returned to the investor at the maturity date when the bond is due. A bond's market price, which is its selling price, is generally expressed as a percentage of the bond's par value. For example, a bond that matures or comes due next year that has a $1000 par value may be quoted as selling for $95.21. That does not mean you can buy the bond for $95.21. It means that the bond is selling in the secondary market for $95.21 percent of its par value, which is actually $952.10, calculated as $1000 × 95.21. At maturity next year, the bondholder will receive the par value of $1000 and the bond will be terminated.

The coupon interest rate on a bond represents the annual rate of interest to be paid out on a bond calculated as a percentage of the par value. When a bond has a par value of $1000, a coupon rate of 6 percent means that $60, calculated as 6 percent × $1000, is paid annually to investors. The coupon payments are normally paid semi-annually (in this example, $30 every six months).

term to maturity
The date at which a bond will expire and the par value of the bond, along with any remaining coupon payments, is to be paid back to the bondholder.

A bond's **term to maturity** refers to the date at which a bond will expire and the par value of the bond, along with any remaining coupon payments, is to be paid back to the bondholder. Bond maturities may vary between 1 and 30 years. Investors provide the issuers of bonds with funds (credit). In return, the issuers are obligated to make interest (or coupon) payments and to pay the par value at maturity. Initially, some bonds are issued by firms to investors at a price below par value; in this case, investors who hold the bonds until maturity will earn a return from the difference between par value and what they paid for the bond. This income is in addition to the coupon payments earned. The principal, or face value, of the bond will likely be paid back to the investor on the maturity date.

You should consider investing in bonds rather than stock if you wish to receive periodic income from your investments. As explained in Chapter 10, many investors diversify among stocks and bonds to achieve their desired return and risk preferences.

EXAMPLE	Abigail purchased a $10 000 bond that has a coupon rate of 4 percent, payable semi-annually. She purchased the bond at a quoted selling price of 97.37. In other words, she paid $9737 for the bond, calculated as $10 000 × 97.37 percent. The bond matures in three years, at which time the par value of $10 000 will be returned to her. If Abigail holds the bond to maturity, she will earn a return of $263, calculated as $10 000 − $9737. In addition, Abigail will receive semi-annual coupon payments from owning the bond. The amount of this semi-annual coupon payment is $200, calculated as $10 000 × (0.04 ÷ 2).

Bond Characteristics

Bonds that are issued by a particular type of issuer can offer various features, such as a call feature or convertibility.

Call Feature. A **call feature** on a bond allows the issuer to repurchase the bond from the investor before maturity. This feature is desirable for issuers because it allows them to retire existing bonds with coupon rates that are higher than the prevailing interest rates.

Investors are willing to purchase bonds with a call feature only if the bonds offer a slightly higher return than similar bonds without a call feature. This premium compensates the investors for the possibility that the bonds may be repurchased before maturity. Call features also may add to the feeling of security in the investment, as part of the debt is paid off prior to maturity. Investors should look at how the call feature is set up.

Sinking Fund. In some cases, corporations will create a sinking fund that will require them to call a certain number of bonds over time. A **sinking fund** is a pool of money that is set aside by a corporation or government to repurchase a set amount of bonds in a set period of time. The sinking fund acts like a mandatory call feature. The main difference between the two is that a call feature normally allows the issuer the opportunity to repurchase the entire issue, whereas a sinking fund provision usually places a limit on how much of an issue can be repurchased at the sinking fund price.

call feature
A feature on a bond that allows the issuer to repurchase the bond from the investor before maturity.

sinking fund
A pool of money that is set aside by a corporation or government to repurchase a set amount of bonds in a set period of time.

EXAMPLE

Five years ago, Cieplak Inc. issued $10 million of 15-year callable bonds with a coupon rate of 9 percent. The corporation also created a sinking fund provision that would require them to set aside $500 000 every year in order to retire this amount of debt. As a result, Cieplak Inc. has retired $2 million worth of bonds in the past four years. In addition, interest rates have declined since then. Today, Cieplak could issue new bonds at a rate of 7 percent. It decides to retire the remaining bonds by repurchasing them from investors and to issue new bonds at a 7 percent coupon rate. By calling the old bonds, Cieplak has reduced its cost of financing. However, call features do not usually allow the company to call all outstanding bonds at one time. In addition, there is usually a call premium to compensate investors for the call.

Convertible Feature. A **convertible bond** allows the investor to convert the bond into a stated number of shares of the issuer's stock at a specified price. This feature enables bond investors to benefit when the issuer's stock price rises. Because convertibility is a desirable feature for investors, convertible bonds tend to offer a lower return than non-convertible bonds. Consequently, if the stock price does not rise to the specified trigger price, the convertible bond provides a lower return to investors than alternative bonds without a convertible feature. If the stock price does rise above the trigger price, however, investors can convert their bonds into shares of the issuer's stock, thereby earning a higher return than they would have earned on alternative non-convertible bonds. Convertible bonds offer investors a two-for-one investment suitable for those with a higher risk tolerance and reduced need for the income offered by this type of bond.

convertible bond
A bond that can be converted into a stated number of shares of the issuer's stock at a specified price.

Extendible Feature. An **extendible bond** allows an investor to extend the maturity date of a short-term bond. This feature enables bond investors to benefit when interest rates are decreasing. If interest rates decrease, investors can extend the maturity of their bonds at a slightly higher rate than what is available in the bond market. Because extendibility is a desirable feature for investors, extendible bonds tend to offer a lower return than non-extendible bonds.

extendible bond
A short-term bond that allows the investor to extend the maturity date of the bond.

put feature
A feature on a bond that allows the investor to redeem the bond at its face value before it matures.

Go to:
www.investopedia.com/calculator/aoytm.aspx

This website provides an estimate of the yield to maturity of a bond based on its par value, market value, coupon rate, and maturity. Thus, you can determine the rate of return the bond will generate from today until it matures.

yield to maturity
The annualized return on a bond if it is held until maturity.

discount bond
A bond that is trading at a price below its par value.

premium bond
A bond that is trading at a price above its par value.

Put Feature. A **put feature** on a bond allows the investor to redeem the bond at its face value before it matures. This feature is desirable for investors who are unsure whether interest rates will increase. If interest rates increase, investors can redeem the bonds and invest their money at a higher rate elsewhere.

Investors who are willing to purchase bonds with a put feature will receive a slightly lower return than similar bonds without a put feature. This discount compensates the issuer for the possibility that the bonds may be redeemed before maturity. This type of bond is also known as a retractable bond.

Yield to Maturity

A bond's **yield to maturity** is the annualized return on the bond if it is held until maturity. Consider a bond that is priced at $1000 and has a par value of $1000, a maturity of 20 years, and a coupon rate of 10 percent. This bond has a yield to maturity of 10 percent, which is the same as its coupon rate. Since the price paid for the bond equals the principal that will be received at maturity in 20 years, the yield to maturity will be the amount that is earned in the form of coupon payments.

As an alternative example, if this bond's price was lower than its par value, its yield to maturity would exceed the coupon rate of 10 percent. A bond that is trading at a price below its par value is said to be a **discount bond**. The bond would also generate income in the form of a capital gain because the purchase price would be less than the principal amount to be received at maturity. Conversely, if this bond's price was higher than its par value, its yield to maturity would be less than the 10 percent coupon rate because the amount paid for the bond would exceed the principal amount to be received at maturity. A bond that is trading at a price above its par value is said to be a **premium bond**.

EXAMPLE

Courtney Anderson purchased a $10 000 par value bond at a quoted price of 90. The discounted purchase price is $9000, calculated as $10 0000 × 90 percent. The bond has a coupon rate of 4 percent payable semi-annually. Therefore, Courtney will receive a payment of $200 every six months, calculated as $10 000 × (0.04 ÷ 2) = $200. The bond matures in exactly three years. What is the yield to maturity (*I/Y*) for this bond if interest is compounded semi-annually?

The calculator key strokes are as follows:

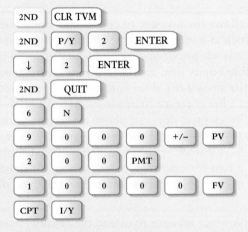

The yield to maturity for this bond is 7.8 percent. Notice that the yield to maturity is greater than the coupon rate of 4 percent. This occurs because Courtney not only earns coupon payments of 4 percent from owning the bond for 3 years, but also receives a capital gain of $1000 in 3 years' time when she receives the par value of $10 000.

Bond Calculator

Application:

The Bond Calculator app allows you to calculate the intrinsic price or yield to maturity of a bond to find out if the bond is worth investing in. A slide bar provides for quick adjustment of required yield to find out the price of a bond.

Bond Trading in the Secondary Market

Investors can sell their bonds to other investors in the secondary market before the bonds reach maturity. Bond prices change in response to interest rate movements and other factors. Bonds are traded in an over-the-counter market. Many investors sell their bonds in the secondary market to raise funds to cover upcoming expenses or to invest in other, more attractive types of securities. Investors buy or sell bonds from a brokerage firm's bond inventory. If the firm does not own the bond that the investor would like to buy, it may purchase the bond from another firm and then sell it to the investor at a higher price.

Go to:
http://stockcharts.com/freecharts/yieldcurve.php

This website provides an interactive look at the history of yield curve movements.

Term Structure of Interest Rates

Understanding how bond yield to maturities change over a bond's maturity is important for investors who want to actively manage their bond portfolio. The **term structure of interest rates** refers to a graph that shows the relationship between bond yield to maturity and time to maturity. The term structure is created by looking at bonds of different terms to maturity and plotting them against various maturities. Exhibit 12.1 displays the term structure of interest rates for Government of Canada yields. The resulting curve is known as a yield curve. The shape of the yield curve, it is believed, reflects the market's sentiment about the direction for interest rates over the short, medium, and long term. The yield curve in Exhibit 12.1 is known as a normal yield curve because it shows that yields rise over longer maturities, which is what is normally expected. The normal curve

term structure of interest rates
A graph that shows the relationship between bond yield to maturity and time to maturity.

EXHIBIT 12.1 Term Structure of Interest Rates for Government of Canada Yields

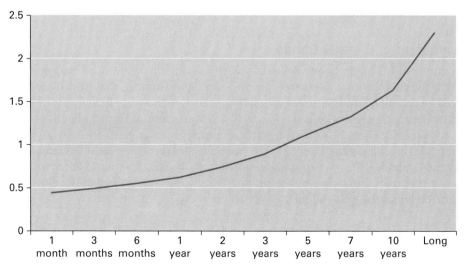

Source: Based on Bank of Canada, Government of Canada Bond & T-Bill Yield Rates as of March 27, 2017.

is upward sloping. Other yield curve shapes include steep, inverted, and flat yield curves. The name of the curve suggests the shape of bond yield over time.

> **myth** or **fact**   An inverted yield curve is always followed by an economic slowdown. Therefore, they should never be ignored.

A number of theories have been proposed to determine why it is that the term structure of interest rates is shaped the way that it is. The three most common theories are the liquidity preference theory, the pure expectations theory, and the market segmentation theory. The **liquidity preference theory** suggests that investors require a premium for investing in longer-term bonds. As the time to maturity increases, the required rate of return increases. The **pure expectations theory** suggests that the shape of the yield curve is a reflection of the market's expectation for future interest rate movements. For example, an investor who would like to invest in a bond for two years should be indifferent between investing in a two-year bond and two successive one-year bonds. In effect, the two-year bond should be a time-weighted average of the two one-year bonds. If the yield curve is sloping upward—that is, the rate for a two-year bond is higher than the rate for a one-year bond—the expectation of the market is that interest rates will rise. The rate for a one-year bond after one year will be higher than the initial one-year bond rate. The time-weighted average of these two bonds should be the same as the initial two-year bond rate. The **market segmentation theory** suggests that the shape of the yield curve is determined by the supply and demand of bonds for various market players in different segments of the yield curve. Corporations and governments that need short-term liquidity will increase the yield of short-term debt securities. Similarly, if the demand for long-term bonds is relatively higher than supply, the long end of the yield curve will rise sharply.

The relationship between the return on bonds and the term structure of interest rates is discussed later in this chapter.

---

liquidity preference theory
Suggests that investors require a premium for investing in longer-term bonds.

pure expectations theory
Suggests that the shape of the yield curve is a reflection of the market's expectation for future interest rate movements.

market segmentation theory
Suggests that the shape of the yield curve is determined by the supply and demand of bonds for various market players in different segment of the yield curve.

L.0.1

TYPES OF BONDS

Bonds can be classified according to the type of issuer, as follows:

- Government of Canada bonds
- Federal Crown corporation bonds
- Provincial bonds
- Municipal bonds
- Corporate bonds

Government of Canada Bonds

Government of Canada bonds
Debt securities issued by the Canadian government.

Government of Canada bonds are debt securities issued by the Canadian government. Because the payments are guaranteed by the federal government, they are not exposed to the risk of default by the issuer. These bonds are issued with a term to maturity of between 1 and 30 years. Interest is paid semi-annually. Government of Canada bonds are a very safe investment and can be sold easily in the secondary market. Since this class of Government of Canada bonds can be sold in the secondary market, they are often referred to as **marketable bonds**. Unlike corporate bonds that are backed by the corporation's assets, government bonds are backed by the ability to raise funds through taxation. Government of Canada bonds are non-callable.

marketable bonds
Government of Canada bonds that can be sold in a secondary market.

Federal Crown Corporation Bonds

Federal Crown corporation bonds
Debt securities issued by corporations established by the federal government.

Federal Crown corporation bonds are debt securities issued by corporations established by the government. The major Crown corporations that are active in the bond market are the Export Development Corporation (EDC), the Canada Mortgage and Housing

Corporation (CMHC), the Farm Credit Corporation (FCC), and the Business Development Bank of Canada (BDBC). Because the payments are guaranteed by the federal government, they are not exposed to the risk of default by the issuer. These bonds are issued with a term to maturity of between 2 and 10 years. Interest is paid semi-annually. These bonds are a relatively safe investment and can be sold easily in the secondary market. Even though the payments are guaranteed by the federal government, these bonds offer a slightly higher return than Government of Canada bonds. This gives investors enough incentive to invest in these corporations instead of just buying Government of Canada bonds.

Go to:
www.globeinvestor.
com/servlet/Page/
document/v5/data/
bonds

Used with permission from
Globe and Mail.

This website provides quotations of yields offered by various types of bonds with various terms to maturity. Review this information when considering purchasing bonds.

Provincial Bonds

Provincial bonds are debt securities issued by the various provincial governments. Interest and principal payments are guaranteed by the provincial government that issued the bonds. The risk of default by the issuer will differ depending on the province from which you purchased the bond. For example, the prosperity enjoyed in Alberta, mainly as a result of high oil prices, will likely result in a lower default risk for that province relative to other provinces. Since the risk of an Alberta bond is lower, the yield to maturity will also be lower. These bonds are issued with a term to maturity of between 1 and 30 years. Interest is paid semi-annually. Provincial bonds are a very safe investment and can be sold easily in the secondary market.

provincial bonds
Debt securities issued by the various provincial governments.

Municipal Bonds

Municipal bonds are long-term debt securities issued by local government agencies and they provide the funds necessary for municipal projects such as parks or sewage plants. In some cases, municipal bonds are not free from the risk of default. Nevertheless, most municipal bonds have a very low default risk. To entice investors, municipal bonds that are issued by a local government with a relatively high level of risk offer a higher yield than other municipal bonds with a lower level of risk. Municipal bonds are uncommon investments in Canada for individuals and tend to suit the needs of certain institutional investors. The terms and conditions of a municipal bond will vary with the needs of the municipality.

municipal bonds
Long-term debt securities issued by local government agencies.

Corporate Bonds

Corporate bonds are long-term debt securities issued by large firms. The repayment of debt by corporations is not backed by the federal government, so corporate bonds are subject to default risk. At one extreme, bonds issued by corporations such as Ontario Hydro and National Bank of Canada have very low default risk because of the companies' proven ability to generate sufficient cash flows for many years. At the other extreme, bonds issued by less stable corporations are subject to a higher degree of default risk. These bonds are referred to as **high-yield bonds**. Many investors are willing to invest in high-yield bonds because they offer a relatively high rate of return. However, they are more likely to default than other bonds, especially if economic conditions are poor. Given the potential to lose money in a high-yield bond, most individual investors should buy these higher-risk investments only through the purchase of a high-yield bond mutual fund. The terms and conditions of a corporate bond will vary with the needs of the corporation.

corporate bonds
Long-term debt securities issued by large firms.

high-yield bonds
Bonds issued by less stable corporations that are subject to a higher degree of default risk.

Corporate Bond Quotations. Corporate bond quotations are provided in financial newspapers, such as *The Globe and Mail*, and online at numerous financial websites. To illustrate how the bond quotation information can be used, review the information disclosed for Enbridge Pipeline Inc. in Exhibit 12.2. The bond has a coupon rate of 6.55 percent payable semi-annually. The maturity date of this bond is November 17, 2027. The last price at which these bonds were traded on the previous day was 127.06, which means that the bond was selling at a premium. The yield of 3.64 percent represents the yield that will be earned by investors who purchase the bond at the latest price and hold it until maturity.

EXHIBIT 12.2   An Example of a Corporate Bond Quotation

Company	Coupon	Maturity	Price	Yield
Enbridge Pipeline	6.55%	November 17, 2027	127.06	3.64%

Source: An in-depth look at Canadian and U.S. market data, retreived from http://www.globeinvestor.com/servlet/Page/document/v5/data/bonds?type=corp

---

FREE APPS for Personal Finance

Obtaining Bond Quotations

Application:

The CNBC Real-Time app provides bond quotations.

---

myth or **fact**   Junk bonds are just that: junk. The majority of investors should not have them in their portfolios.

OTHER FIXED-INCOME PRODUCTS

In addition to the bond classifications discussed above, a number of other fixed-income products offer special features or are characterized by a short-term maturity. These investments include:

- T-bills
- Banker's acceptances (BAs)
- Commercial paper
- Canada Savings Bonds (CSBs)
- Mortgage-backed securities (MBSs)
- Strip bonds
- Real return bonds

Short-Term Debt Securities

T-bills
Short-term debt securities issued by the Canadian and provincial governments and sold at a discount.

banker's acceptances (BAs)
Short-term debt securities issued by large firms that are guaranteed by a bank.

commercial paper
A short-term debt security issued by large firms that is guaranteed by the issuing firm.

T-bills are short-term debt securities issued by the Canadian and provincial governments and sold at a discount (less than the par value). T-bills do not make coupon payments. Instead, the return that an investor receives is based on the rise in the value of the investment as it reaches maturity. Similar to T-bills, banker's acceptances and commercial paper are short-term debt securities issued by corporations that are sold at a discount. These investments can be differentiated by the issuer of the security and the entity that guarantees the investment. **Banker's acceptances (BAs)** are short-term debt securities issued by large firms that are guaranteed by a bank. **Commercial paper** is a short-term debt security issued by large firms that is guaranteed by the issuing firm.

As a result of their differences, these short-term investments have different risk and return characteristics. The yield to maturity will be lowest for T-bills because they are issued and guaranteed by the Government of Canada. T-bills are the safest investment available to Canadian investors. The yield to maturity of BAs will be higher than it is for T-bills because BAs are riskier since they are issued by a firm. However, since BAs are guaranteed by a bank, commercial paper will have the highest yield to maturity because it is only guaranteed by the issuing corporation. Although no interest is paid, interest must be recognized every year. The recognition of interest may result in tax being payable even though no income has been received. As a result, tax planning is an important consideration when deciding whether to purchase these investments outside registered tax shelters, such as registered retirement savings plans (RRSPs), tax-free savings accounts (TFSAs), and registered education savings plans (RESPs).

Recall from Chapter 5 that money market funds (MMFs) invest in securities that have short-term maturities, such as one year or less. T-bills, BAs, and commercial paper are important parts of an MMF's investment portfolio. Although some high-net-worth investors may purchase T-bills, BAs, and commercial paper as individual securities, MMFs are ideal for most investors who want to invest in short-term debt securities.

Canada Savings Bonds (CSBs)

Canada Savings Bonds (CSBs) are 10-year debt securities issued by the Canadian government. Since the bonds are issued by the federal government, they are fully guaranteed by them. In addition, these bonds can be purchased as a simple interest bond or a compound interest bond. CSBs can be redeemed at any time before maturity. The Canada Premium Bond (CPB) is similar to the CSB. The main difference between these two bond types is that a CPB can be redeemed only on its anniversary date and 30 days afterwards. CSBs and CPBs are available for purchase from early October to April 1. Since these bonds cannot be traded, CSBs and CPBs are not considered marketable bonds.

In its March 22, 2017, federal budget release, the Government of Canada announced that the sale of CSBs and CPBs would be discontinued as of November 2017. Unmatured CSBs and CPBs will be honoured at the time of redemption or maturity.

Mortgage-Backed Securities (MBSs)

Mortgage-backed securities (MBSs) represent a pool of CMHC-insured residential mortgages that are issued by banks and other financial institutions. The CMHC guarantees the mortgages in the pool in the event of default. An MBS is a guaranteed flow-through investment. The mortgage payments made on the pool of mortgages in an MBS represent principal and interest payments. The principal and interest are flowed through to MBS investors. If mortgage payments are missed, CMHC guarantees the payment of principal and interest to the pool. This steady flow of interest and principal makes MBSs a secure and attractive investment for investors looking for debt securities that offer a slightly higher yield than Government of Canada bonds. They are particularly attractive to investors seeking income (e.g., retirees). Similar to most other bonds, MBSs are marketable since they can be sold in the secondary market. MBSs are issued with a term to maturity of between 1 and 10 years. One unique risk with MBSs is that of prepayment. Mortgages are sometimes paid back before the end of the term because homeowners may refinance at a lower rate or sell their homes. Prepayment is more likely to occur when interest rates fall or there is an active real estate market.

mortgage-backed securities
Represent a pool of CMHC-insured residential mortgages that are issued by banks and other financial institutions.

Strip Bonds

Strip bonds are long-term debt securities issued by the Government of Canada (and some provinces), that do not offer coupon payments. Instead, the coupon payments are stripped from the bond and sold separately. The strip bond is valued at the present value of the future principal amount. When the time to maturity is long, this present value can be very low. The strip bond is sold at a very deep discount. As it moves toward maturity, the present value should rise, assuming that interest rates remain the same. However, rates are not static, and movement in interest rates affects strip bonds to a greater extent than it does other bonds. The longer the term to maturity, the greater the price movement will be. The original bonds are issued with a term to maturity of 18 months to 30 years. Although no interest is paid, interest must be recognized every year. The recognition of interest may result in tax being payable even though no income has been received. As a result, tax planning is an important consideration when deciding whether to purchase these investments

strip bonds
Long-term debt securities issued by the Government of Canada (and some provinces), that do not offer coupon payments.

outside a registered portfolio. Strip bonds are a very safe investment in terms of default risk and can be sold in the secondary market. However, they have a *very* high interest rate risk.

Real Return Bonds

Real return bonds are long-term debt securities issued by the Government of Canada that protect an investor from inflation risk. All other bonds are exposed to inflation risk. For example, if inflation is 4 percent in 2015 and a bond makes interest payments based on a 3 percent coupon rate, the approximate inflation-adjusted return is –1 percent. Real return bonds eliminate inflation risk by adjusting the par value of the bond for changes in the inflation rate (as measured by the consumer price index). As a result, the par value at maturity will be higher and the coupon payments will increase with each increase in the face value if inflation has occurred.

EXAMPLE

You buy a $1000 real return bond that has a coupon rate of 5 percent. Assume that inflation increases by 2 percent in the next six months. Interest is paid semi-annually. The bond's par value and coupon payment will increase as follows:

Inflation-adjusted par value $= \$1000 \times (1 + 0.02) = \$1020$

Inflation-adjusted semi-annual coupon payment $= \$1020 \times (0.05 \div 2) = \$25.50$

The actual amount of interest paid during the year will be based on the initial par value. In the example above, the semi-annual interest payment will be calculated as $\$1000 \times (0.05 \div 2) = \$25.50$. At maturity, the accumulated difference between the inflation-adjusted coupon payment and the regular coupon payment will be paid to the investor, along with the inflation-adjusted par value. These bonds are issued with a term to maturity of between 1 and 30 years. They are a very safe investment and can be sold easily in the secondary market.

RETURN FROM INVESTING IN BONDS

L.O.2

If you purchase a bond and hold it until maturity, you can earn the yield to maturity specified when you purchased it. As mentioned, however, many investors sell bonds in the secondary market before they reach maturity. Since a bond's price changes over time, your return from investing in a bond depends on the price at the time you sell it.

Another risk that investors must consider when investing in bonds is reinvestment risk. When the price of a bond is calculated, one of the assumptions is that all interest received through the years will be reinvested at the current interest rate. While it is believed that the yield quoted is what the investor will receive, the assumption that rates will remain static for any period of time is somewhat simplistic.

Impact of Interest Rate Movements on Bond Returns

Your return from investing in a bond can be highly influenced by interest rate movements over the period you hold the bond. To illustrate, suppose that you purchase a bond at par value that has a coupon rate of 8 percent. After one year, you decide to sell the bond. At this time, new bonds being sold at par value are offering a coupon rate of 9 percent. Since investors can purchase a new bond that offers higher coupon payments, they will not be willing to buy your bond unless you sell it to them for less than par value. In other words, you must offer a discount on the price to compensate for the bond's lower coupon rate.

If interest rates had declined over the year rather than increased, the opposite effect would occur. You could sell your bond for a premium above par value because the coupon rate of your bond would be higher than the coupon rate offered on newly issued bonds. Thus, interest rate movements and bond prices are inversely related. Your return from investing in bonds will be more favourable if interest rates decline over the period that you hold the bonds.

Go to:
https://ca.finance.
yahoo.com/news/
category-bonds

This website provides a summary of recent financial news related to the bond market, which you may consider before selling or buying bonds.

You purchase $10 000 face value newly issued bonds for $9700. The bonds mature in 10 years and pay a coupon rate of 8 percent, or $800 (computed as 0.08 × $10 000) per year. The coupon payments are made every six months, so each payment is $400. Exhibit 12.3 shows your return and the tax implications for four different scenarios.

EXHIBIT 12.3 Potential Tax Implications from Investing in Bonds

Scenario	Implication
1. You sell the bonds after eight months at a price of $9800.	You receive one $400 coupon payment six months after buying the bond, which is taxed at your marginal income tax rate; you also earn a capital gain of $100, which equals a taxable capital gain of $50. The taxable capital gain is a part of your income and is subject to tax at your marginal tax rate.
2. You sell the bonds after two years at a price of $10 200.	You receive coupon payments (taxed at your marginal income tax rate) of $800 in the first year and in the second year; you also earn a capital gain of $500 in the second year, which equals a taxable capital gain of $250. The taxable capital gain is a part of your income and is subject to tax at your marginal tax rate.
3. You sell the bonds after two years at a price of $9500.	You receive coupon payments (taxed at your marginal income tax rate) of $800 in the first year and in the second year; you also incur a capital loss of $200, which equals an allowable capital loss of $100. The allowable capital loss can be used to offset any taxable capital gains for the year. Any remaining allowable capital loss can be carried back three years or carried forward indefinitely.
4. You hold the bonds until maturity.	You receive coupon payments (taxed at your marginal income tax rate) in each year over the 10-year life of the bond. You also receive the bond's principal of $10 000 at the end of the 10-year period. This reflects a capital gain of $300, which equals a taxable capital gain of $150. The taxable capital gain is a part of your income and is subject to tax at your marginal tax rate.

Tax Implications of Investing in Bonds

When determining the return from investing in a bond, you need to account for tax effects. The interest income you receive from a bond is taxed as ordinary income for federal income tax purposes. Tax on interest income is the same as other forms of income and must be paid in the year it is earned. This may not coincide with the interest payments.

Selling bonds in the secondary market at a price different than what you originally paid for them results in a capital gain (or loss). The capital gain (or loss) is the difference between the price at which you sell the bond and the initial price you paid for it. Recall from Chapter 4 that only 50 percent of a capital gain is taxable as income. In addition, only 50 percent of a capital loss is deductible as an allowable capital loss.

VALUING A BOND

Before investing in a bond, you may wish to determine its value using a time value of money analysis. A bond's value is determined as the present value of the future cash flows to be received by the investor, which are the periodic coupon payments and the principal payment at maturity. The present value of a bond can be computed by discounting the future cash flows (coupon payments and principal payment) to be received from the bond. The discount rate used to value the cash flows should reflect your required rate of return.

If you pay the price that is obtained by this valuation approach and hold the bond to maturity, you can earn the return that you require. A financial calculator, such as the TI BA II Plus, can be used to determine how much you should pay for a bond given your required rate of return.

TVM EXAMPLE

Victor is planning to purchase a bond that has 7 years remaining until maturity, a par value of $1000, and a coupon rate of 6 percent, compounded semi-annually. Therefore, Victor will receive a coupon payment of $30 every six months, calculated as $1000 × (0.06 ÷ 2). Furthermore, he is willing to purchase this bond only if he can earn a return of 8 percent because he knows that he can earn 8 percent on alternative bonds.

The calculator key strokes are as follows:

Based on this analysis, Victor is willing to pay $894.37 for this bond, which will provide his annualized return of 8 percent. If he can obtain the bond for a lower price, his return will exceed 8 percent. If the price exceeds $894.37, his return would be less than 8 percent, so he would not buy the bond.

myth or **fact**   In general, a portfolio composed of bonds is appropriate for investors who require a fixed income from their investments.

The market price of any bond is based on investors' required rate of return, which is influenced by the interest rates that are available on alternative investments at the time. If bond investors require a rate of return of 8 percent, as Victor does, the bond will be priced in the bond market at the value derived by Victor. However, if the bond market participants use a different required rate of return than Victor, the market price of the bond will be different. For example, if most investors require a 9 percent return on this bond, it will have a market price below the value derived by Victor (conduct your own valuation using a 9 percent discount rate to verify this).

L.O.3

RISK FROM INVESTING IN BONDS

Bond investors are exposed to the risk that the bonds may not provide the expected return. The main sources of risk are default risk, call (prepayment) risk, inflation risk, reinvestment risk, and interest rate risk.

EXHIBIT 12.4   Bond Rating Classes

Risk Class	Standard & Poor's	Moody's
Highest quality (least risk)	AAA	Aaa
High quality	AA	Aa
High-medium quality	A	A
Medium quality	BBB	Baa
Medium-low quality	BB	Ba
Low quality	B	B
Poor quality	CCC	Caa
Very poor quality	CC	Ca
Lowest quality	DDD	C

Default Risk

If the issuer of the bond (a firm) defaults on its payments, investors do not receive all of the coupon payments they are owed and may not receive all or any of the principal they are owed. Investors will invest in a risky bond only if it offers a higher yield than other bonds to compensate for this risk. The extra yield required by investors to compensate for default risk is referred to as the **risk premium** of the bond. Government of Canada bonds do not contain a risk premium because they are free from **default risk.**

Use of Risk Ratings to Measure the Default Risk. Investors can use ratings (provided by agencies such as Moody's Investor Service or Standard and Poor's) to assess the risk of corporate bonds. The ratings reflect the likelihood that the issuers will repay their debt over time and are classified as shown in Exhibit 12.4. Investors can select the corporate bonds that fit their degree of risk tolerance by weighing the higher potential return against the higher default risk of lower-quality debt securities.

Relationship of Risk Rating to Risk Premium. The lower (weaker) the risk rating, the higher the risk premium offered on a bond.

Impact of Economic Conditions. Bonds with a high degree of default risk are most susceptible to default when economic conditions are weak. Investors may lose all or most of their initial investment when a bond defaults. They can avoid default risk by investing in Government of Canada bonds or can at least keep the default risk to a minimum by investing in federal Crown corporation bonds or AAA-rated corporate bonds. However, they will receive lower yields on these bonds than investors who are willing to accept a higher degree of default risk.

risk premium
The extra yield required by investors to compensate for default risk; an additional return beyond the risk-free rate you could earn from an investment.

default risk
Risk that the borrower of funds will not repay the creditors.

FOCUS ON ETHICS: Accounting Fraud and Default Risk

Bond rating services are important not only for investors, but also for creditors. Just as the interest on a loan for an individual with a poor credit history will be higher than that for an individual with a great credit history, corporations are subject to similar risk premiums. Therefore, a higher rating, such as AAA, will allow a corporation to issue debt with a lower interest rate.

Rating companies are vigilant in monitoring the state of corporations, and if they reduce a firm's rating, the firm's bond price will fall. If the firm's rating has been reduced because of questionable financial statements, the price reduction on its bonds can be quite severe. Once a debt rating agency becomes aware that a firm's financial statements are misleading, it will lower the firm's bond rating and investors will in turn reduce their demand for the firm's bonds. Investors will lose confidence in the firm's ability to repay its debt. Even if a bond does not default, its price will decline if the perception of its risk is increased by credit rating agencies and investors.

Call Risk

call (prepayment) risk
The risk that a callable bond will be called.

Bonds with a call feature are subject to **call risk** (also called **prepayment risk**), which is the risk that the bond will be called. If issuers of callable bonds call these bonds, the bondholders must sell them back to the issuer.

EXAMPLE	Two years ago, Christine Ramirez purchased 10-year bonds that offered a yield to maturity of 9 percent. She planned to hold the bonds until maturity. Recently, interest rates declined and the issuer called the bonds. Christine could use the proceeds to buy other bonds, but the yield to maturity offered on new bonds is lower because interest rates have declined. The return that Christine will earn from investing in new bonds could be less than the return she would have earned if she could have retained the 10-year bonds until maturity.

Often, there is a call premium on callable bonds to account for at least a portion of the call risk. As well, callable bonds can offer a return higher than non-callable bonds, again to offset the call risk. Investors should be aware of the circumstances that would trigger a call.

Inflation Risk

inflation risk
The risk that the purchasing power of a bond investment will diminish due to a relative increase in inflation.

All bonds are subject to **inflation risk**, which is the risk that the purchasing power of a bond investment will diminish due to a relative increase in inflation. Purchasing power refers to how much goods and services can be purchased with a given level of money. Inflation decreases purchasing power because it reduces the real value of your investments. For example, if you purchased a bond that yielded 5 percent when inflation was at 2 percent, your real rate of return is approximately 3 percent. If inflation increases to 4 percent, your real rate of return diminishes to approximately 1 percent. In real terms, the return you earn, and therefore the total value of your bond, has decreased.

Reinvestment Risk

reinvestment risk
The risk that the income earned from a bond cannot be reinvested at the same or a higher rate of interest as was being earned from the original bond.

All bonds are subject to **reinvestment risk**, which is the risk that the income earned from a bond cannot be reinvested at the same or a higher rate of interest as was being earned from the original bond. For example, Paul purchased a bond at par value that pays a 6 percent annual coupon. One year later, interest rates have decreased and Paul is only able to reinvest his annual coupon payment at 5 percent.

Interest Rate Risk

All bonds are subject to interest rate risk, which is the risk that a bond's price will decline in response to an increase in interest rates. A bond is valued as the present value of its future expected cash flows. Most bonds pay fixed coupon payments. If interest rates rise, investors will require a higher return on a bond. Consequently, the discount rate applied to value the bond is increased and the market price of the bond will decline. Inflation risk and interest rate risk are closely related because interest rates tend to increase when inflation increases.

EXAMPLE	Three months ago, Rob Suerth paid $10 000 for a 20-year Government of Canada bond that has a par value of $10 000 and a 7 percent coupon rate. Since then, interest rates have increased. New 20-year Government of Canada bonds with a par value of $10 000 are priced at $10 000 and offer a coupon rate of 9 percent. Therefore, Rob would earn 2 percentage points more in coupon payments from a new bond than he does from the bond he purchased three months ago. He decides to sell his bond and use the proceeds to invest in the new bond. However, he quickly learns that no one in the secondary market is willing to purchase his bond for the price he paid. These investors avoid his bond for the same reason he wants to sell it; they would prefer to earn 9 percent on the new bonds rather than 7 percent on his bond. The only way that Rob can sell his bond is by lowering the price to compensate for the bond's lower coupon rate (compared to the new bonds).

Impact of a Bond's Maturity on Its Interest Rate Risk. Bonds with longer terms to maturity are more sensitive to interest rate movements than bonds that have short terms remaining until maturity. To understand why, consider two bonds. Each has a par value of $1000 and offers a 9 percent coupon rate, but one bond has 20 years remaining until maturity while the other has only one year remaining until maturity. If market interest rates suddenly decline from 9 to 7 percent, which bond would you prefer to own? The bond with 20 years until maturity becomes very attractive because you would be able to receive coupon payments reflecting a 9 percent return for the next 20 years. Conversely, the bond with one year remaining until maturity will provide the 9 percent payment only over the next year. Although the market price of both bonds increases in response to the decline in interest rates, it increases more for the bond with the longer term to maturity.

Now assume that, instead of declining, interest rates have risen from their initial level of 9 percent to 11 percent. Which bond would you prefer? Each bond provides a 9 percent coupon rate, which is less than the prevailing interest rate. The bond with one year until maturity will mature soon, however, so you can reinvest the proceeds at the higher interest rates at that time (assuming that the rates remain high). Conversely, you are stuck with the other bond for 20 more years. Although neither bond would be very desirable under these conditions, the bond with the longer term to maturity is less desirable. Therefore, its price in the secondary market will decline more than the price of the bond with a short term to maturity.

Selecting an Appropriate Bond Maturity. Since bond prices change inversely in response to interest rate movements, you may wish to choose maturities on bonds that reflect your expectations of future interest rates. If you prefer to reduce your exposure to interest rate risk, you may consider investing in bonds that have a maturity that matches the time when you will need the funds. If you expect that interest rates will decline over time, you may consider investing in bonds with longer maturities than the time when you will need the funds. In this way, you can sell the bonds in the secondary market at a relatively high price, assuming that your expectations were correct. However, if interest rates increase instead of declining over this period, your return will be reduced.

BOND INVESTMENT STRATEGIES

L.O.4

If you decide to invest in bonds, you need to determine a strategy for selecting them. Most strategies involve investing in a diversified portfolio of bonds rather than in one bond. Diversification reduces your exposure to possible default by a single issuer but may not reduce your interest rate and reinvestment risks. If you cannot afford to invest in a diversified portfolio of bonds, you may consider investing in a bond mutual fund with a small minimum investment (such as $1000). Additional information on bond mutual funds is provided in Chapter 14. Whether you focus on individual bonds or bond mutual funds, the bond investment strategies summarized here apply.

| **myth** or **fact** Bond investments increase in value when stock investments decrease in value.

Interest Rate Strategy

With an **interest rate strategy**, you select bonds based on interest rate expectations. When you expect interest rates to decline, you invest heavily in long-term bonds whose prices will increase the most if interest rates fall. Conversely, when you expect interest rates to increase, you shift most of your money to bonds with short terms to maturity to minimize the adverse impact of the higher interest rates.

interest rate strategy
Selecting bonds based on interest rate expectations.

Investors who use the interest rate strategy may experience poor performance if their guesses about the future direction of interest rate movements are incorrect. In addition, this strategy requires frequent trading to capitalize on shifts in expectations of interest rates.

Some investors who follow this strategy frequently sell their entire portfolio of bonds so that they can shift to bonds with different maturities in response to shifts in interest rate expectations. This frequent trading results in high transaction costs but may generate more short-term capital gains. This is a strategy that should be attempted only by sophisticated and risk-tolerant investors.

Passive Strategy

passive strategy
Investing in a diversified portfolio of bonds that are held for a long period of time.

With a **passive strategy**, you invest in a diversified portfolio of bonds that are held for a long period of time. The portfolio is simply intended to generate periodic interest income in the form of coupon payments. The passive strategy is especially valuable for investors who want to generate stable interest income over time and do not want to incur costs associated with frequent trading.

A passive strategy does not need to focus on high-quality bonds that offer low returns; it may reflect a portfolio of bonds with diversified risk levels. The diversification is intended to reduce the exposure to default from a single issuer of bonds. To reduce exposure to interest rate risk, a portfolio may even attempt to diversify across a wide range of bond maturities. This passive strategy is known as bond laddering.

One disadvantage of this strategy is that it does not capitalize on expectations of interest rate movements. Investors who use a passive strategy, however, are more comfortable matching general bond market movements than trying to beat the bond market and possibly failing.

Maturity Matching Strategy

maturity matching strategy
Selecting bonds that will generate payments to match future expenses.

The **maturity matching strategy** involves selecting bonds that will generate payments to match future expenses. For example, parents of an eight-year-old may consider investing in a 10-year bond so that the principal can be used to pay for the child's university or college education at maturity. Alternatively, an older couple may invest in a bond portfolio just before retirement so that they will receive annual income (coupon payments) to cover periodic expenses after retirement. The maturity matching strategy is conservative in that it is intended simply to cover future expenses, rather than to beat the bond market in general.

MyLab Finance   Visit MyLab Finance for additional study and practice tools. Select Financial Planning Problems are available in the Study Plan. Create your own study plan, generate personal cash flow statements and balance sheets, and set personal financial goals.

SUMMARY

L.O.1   Identify the different types of bonds

Bonds are long-term debt securities and can be classified by their issuer. The common issuers are the Government of Canada, federal Crown corporations, provinces, municipalities, and corporations. Other types of bonds include short-term debt securities (T-bills, banker's acceptances, commercial paper), mortgage-backed securities, strip bonds, and real return bonds.

L.O.2   Explain what affects the return from investing in a bond

A bond's yield to maturity is the annualized return that may be earned by an investor who holds the bond until maturity. This yield is composed of interest (coupon)

payments as well as the interest earned over time on that interest and the difference between the principal value and the price at which the bond was originally purchased.

L.O.3   Describe why some bonds are risky

Bonds can be exposed to default risk, which reflects the possibility that the issuer will default on the bond payments. Some bonds are exposed to call risk, which is the risk that the bond will be called before maturity. Bonds are also subject to interest rate risk, which is the risk of a decline in price in response to rising interest rates. This leads to reinvestment risk. Inflation, closely associated with interest rates, poses another risk for bond investors.

L.O.4 Identify common bond investment strategies

One bond investment strategy is the interest rate strategy, where the selection of bonds depends on the expectation of future interest rates. An alternative strategy is a passive strategy, in which a diversified portfolio of bonds is maintained. A third bond strategy is the maturity matching strategy, in which the investor selects bonds that will mature on future dates when funds will be needed.

REVIEW QUESTIONS

1. Define and differentiate between a bond and a debenture.

2. What is par value? Describe how a bond's market price is determined based on its par value.

3. What does the coupon interest rate represent? How frequently is a coupon payment normally made?

4. What is a bond's term to maturity?

5. What are the two ways in which you can earn a return from a bond?

6. Define and describe the call feature on a bond.

7. What is a sinking fund? What is the main difference between a sinking fund and a call feature?

8. Define and describe a convertible bond.

9. Define and describe an extendable bond.

10. Define and describe the put feature on a bond.

11. What is a bond's yield to maturity?

12. What is the difference between a discount bond and a premium bond?

13. Describe the relationship between a bond's yield to maturity and the price paid for a bond.

14. Describe how bonds are sold on the secondary market.

15. What is the term structure of interest rates? What does the yield curve tell us about the market's sentiment regarding interest rates?

16. Define and describe the liquidity preference theory.

17. Define and describe the pure expectations theory.

18. Define and describe the market segmentation theory.

19. What are Government of Canada bonds? What are the characteristics of Government of Canada bonds?

20. What are federal Crown corporation bonds? Which major Crown corporations issue these types of bonds? What are the characteristics of federal Crown corporation bonds?

21. What are provincial bonds? Do all provincial bonds offer the same default risk? Explain.

22. Define and describe municipal bonds.

23. What are corporate bonds? Do all corporate bonds offer the same default risk? Explain.

24. What are high-yield bonds? Why would investors purchase high-yield bonds?

25. Define and describe T-bills.

26. Define and differentiate between banker's acceptances (BAs) and commercial paper.

27. Define and describe a Canada Savings Bond (CSB). What is the difference between a CSB and a Canada Premium Bond?

28. Define and describe mortgage-backed securities.

29. What are strip bonds? Are strip bonds sold at a premium or a discount to their maturity value? Explain.

30. Why is it important to consider taxes when purchasing a strip bond?

31. What is a real return bond?

32. Describe how a real return bond protects an investor against inflation risk.

33. When an investor sells a bond in the secondary market before the bond reaches maturity, what determines the return on the bond? How do interest rate movements affect bond returns in general?

34. Discuss the effect of taxes on bond returns.

35. How is the value of a bond determined? What information is needed to perform the calculation?

36. List the main sources of risk for a bond.

37. Discuss default risk as it relates to bonds. How may investors use risk ratings? What is the relationship between the risk rating and the risk premium? How do economic conditions affect default risk?

38. What is call risk? What additional features are associated with a bond that is exposed to call risk?

39. What is inflation risk? What is the relationship between inflation risk and the real rate of return on a bond?

40. What is reinvestment risk?

41. What is interest rate risk? How does a rise in interest rates affect a bond's price?

42. How is interest rate risk affected by a bond's maturity? How can investors use expectations of interest rate movements to their advantage?

43. Describe how the interest rate strategy for bond investment works. What are some of the potential problems with this strategy?

44. How does the passive strategy for bond investment work? What is the main disadvantage of this strategy?

45. Describe the maturity matching strategy of investing in bonds. Give an example. Why is this strategy considered conservative?

FINANCIAL PLANNING PROBLEMS

MyLab Finance Financial Planning Problems marked with a 🌐 can be found in MyLab Finance.

🌐 **1.** Bernie purchased 20 bonds with par values of $1000 each. The bonds carry a coupon rate of 9 percent, payable semi-annually. How much will Bernie receive at his first interest payment?

🌐 **2.** Sandy has a choice between purchasing $5000 in Government of Canada bonds paying 5 percent interest, compounded semi-annually, or purchasing $5000 in BB-rated corporate bonds with a coupon rate of 7.2 percent, compounded semi-annually. What is the risk premium on the BB-rated corporate bonds?

🌐 **3.** Bonnie paid $9500 for corporate bonds that have a par value of $10 000 and a coupon rate of 9 percent, payable quarterly. Bonnie received her first interest payment after holding the bonds for three months and then sold the bonds for $9700. If Bonnie is in a 35 percent marginal tax bracket for federal income tax purposes, what are the tax consequences of her ownership and sale of the bonds?

4. Fran is evaluating ATT Ltd. Bonds using the following information: $25 000 par value, maturity Dec 22, 2023, semi-annual coupon 7.75 percent, price $105.50, and yield 7.4 percent. How much interest would this bond pay Fran on an annual basis?

5. Delia purchases a $10 000 real return bond that has a coupon rate of 4.25 percent with interest payable semi-annually. If inflation increases by 1.5 percent in the next six months, what is the effect on the bond's par value and the semi-annual coupon payment?

🌐 **6.** Katie paid $9400 for an Ontario Hydro bond with a par value of $10 000 and a coupon rate of 6.5 percent, compounded semi-annually. Two years later, Katie sold the bond for $9700. What are her total tax consequences if she is in a 25 percent marginal tax bracket?

🌐 **7.** Timothy has an opportunity to buy a $1000 par value municipal bond with a coupon rate of 7 percent and a maturity of five years. The bond pays interest quarterly. If Timothy requires a return of 8 percent, compounded quarterly, what should he pay for the bond?

🌐 **8.** Mia wants to invest in Government of Canada bonds that have a par value of $20 000 and a coupon rate

of 4.5 percent. The bonds have a 10-year maturity and Mia requires a 6 percent return, compounded semi-annually. How much should Mia pay for the bonds, assuming that interest is paid semi-annually?

🌐 **9.** Emma is considering purchasing bonds with a par value of $10 000. The bonds have an annual coupon rate of 8 percent, and six years to maturity. They are priced at $9550. If Emma requires a 10 percent return, compounded quarterly, should she buy these bonds?

🌐 **10.** Mark has a Government of Canada bond that has a par value of $30 000 and a coupon rate of 6 percent, payable semi-annually. The bond has 15 years to maturity. Mark needs to sell the bond, and new bonds are currently carrying coupon rates of 8 percent, payable semi-annually. At what price could Mark sell the bond?

🌐 **11.** What if Mark's Government of Canada bond (from Problem 8) had a coupon rate of 9 percent, payable semi-annually, and new bonds still had interest rates of 8 percent, payable semi-annually? What price could Mark sell the bond for in this situation?

🌐 **12.** Melissa purchases a one-year $10 000 Government of Canada real return bond that has a coupon rate of 6 percent, payable semi-annually. Inflation increases 2 percent over the next six months and then 1.5 percent in the following six-month period. Determine the value of the first semi-annual coupon payment. Then determine the final coupon payment and the par value of the bond at maturity.

🌐 **13.** What is the annual yield on a $10 000, 10-year, 7.5 percent bond that makes annual coupon payments and was purchased at 101.5? The bond has 8 years remaining until maturity.

14. Brady purchased a $25 000, 10.5 percent bond redeemable at par with semi-annual coupon payments. He purchased the bond 10 years before maturity to yield 12 percent compounded semi-annually. Six years after purchasing the bond (four years before maturity), what would be his selling price if the yield to maturity has not changed?

CHALLENGE QUESTIONS

1. A company purchased $200 000 in bonds that were issued by another company. The bonds were paying an 8 percent coupon rate, payable semi-annually, and the bond matured in 10 years. Five years after purchasing the bond, the company required money urgently so they sold the bond in the market when the yield was 9.5 percent compounded semi-annually. How much did they sell the bond for and what was the discount or premium on the bond at the time of sale?

2. A municipality required immediate funding so they issued a $500 000 bond paying a 4 percent semi-annual coupon. When the yield was 3.5 percent compounded semi-annually, the bond had seven years left to maturity and an investor purchased it. However, three years later, the investor required money and sold the bond. If the yield at the time of the sale was 5 percent compounded semi-annually, how much did the investor gain or lose on this investment?

3. A $10 000 bond was cleared in four years by setting up a sinking fund that was earning 5.5 percent compounded semi-annually. If deposits were made to the fund at the end of every six months, calculate the size of the periodic payments deposited and the total interest earned in the fund.

ETHICAL DILEMMA

John is a relatively conservative investor. He has recently come into a large inheritance and wishes to invest the money where he can get a good return but not worry about losing his principal. His broker recommends that he buy 20-year corporate bonds in the country's largest automobile company, United General. The broker assures him that the bonds are secured by the assets of the company and the interest payments are contractually set. He explains that although all investments carry some risk, the risk of losing his investment with these bonds is minimal. John buys the bonds and over the next two years enjoys a steady stream of interest payments. During the third year, United General posts the largest quarterly loss in its history. Although the company is far from bankruptcy, the bond rating agencies downgrade the company's bonds to high-yield status. John is horrified to see the decline in the price in his bonds, as he is considering selling a large portion of them to buy a home. When he discusses his dissatisfaction with his broker, the broker tells him that he is still receiving interest payments and if he holds the bonds until maturity he will not sustain a capital loss. The broker reiterates that in their initial meeting John's concerns were safety of principal and interest payments and that the investment still offers both of these features.

a. Was the broker being ethical by not informing John of the other risks involved in the purchase of bonds? Why or why not?

b. What could John have done differently with his bond investments if he anticipated buying a home in the next three to five years?

FINANCIAL PLANNING ONLINE EXERCISES

1. Go to http://personal.fidelity.com/products/fixedincome/ladders.shtml.

   a. This website describes three different bond building strategies. Describe the impact of each strategy on default risk and interest rate risk. In your view, when would each strategy be appropriate?

   b. What is the risk inherent in each strategy? How can you overcome the risk involved with buying individual bonds?

2. Go to www.investopedia.com/calculator/aoytm.aspx.

   a. This website allows you to calculate the yield to maturity of a bond based on changes in its market value, annual coupon rate, time to maturity, and coupon payment frequency.

Assume that you own a $1000 bond that has a current market value of $900. The bond pays a 6 percent semi-annual coupon. The bond matures in five years. What is the current yield to maturity of the bond? What is the new yield to maturity if the bond's price decreases to $850? Explain why the yield to maturity has changed. Confirm the answers provided by the bond calculator using your financial calculator.

b. Decrease the maturity by two years and repeat Part a. What is the impact of a shorter maturity?

c. Increase the annual coupon rate by 1 percent and repeat Part a. What is the impact of increasing the coupon rate on the yield to maturity? Explain.

PSYCHOLOGY OF PERSONAL FINANCE: Buying Risky Bonds

1. Investors expect that their return on a risky bond will be higher than their return on bonds with less risk. They enjoy the thrill of the gamble of investing in risky bonds and when these bonds perform well. However, investors must understand that risky bonds are more likely to default than safer bonds. Describe your behaviour toward buying risky bonds.

2. Read one practical article of how psychology affects decisions when buying bonds on margin. You can easily retrieve possible articles by doing an online search using the terms "psychology" and "buying risky bonds." Summarize the main points of the article.

MINI-CASE 1: Bond Ratings and Calculations

About six months ago, Jennie inherited a portfolio that included a number of bonds. Jennie knows very little about investing in general, and practically nothing about bonds specifically. She put together the following chart for your review. All Jennie knows for sure is that she owns seven bonds, ranging in maturity from 3 to 20 years. The chart below indicates the bond, its Standard & Poor's Rating, its maturity, and its current yield.

Bond Rating Chart

Bond	Standard & Poor's Rating	Years to maturity	Current yield
ABC Corp.	AAA	3	4.00%
XYX Industries	AA	5	3.25
INTL Limited	A	7	2.00
MED Corp.	BBB	10	4.00
SPEC Inc.	BBB	12	2.00
LAM Corp.	CCC	15	5.00
BAD Inc.	CC	20	6.00

After a cursory review of the yields, do you see anything that should cause Jennie to worry? In terms of bond maturity dates and the Standard & Poor's ratings, is Jennie being adequately compensated for the risk she is taking? Based on the information provided, which bond should offer the highest current yield? The lowest? What is the present value of Jennie's bond portfolio? Assume that each bond has a par value of $10 000 and that each pays a coupon of 6 percent payable quarterly. Interest is compounded quarterly.

MINI-CASE 2: Purchasing Bonds

While waiting for a plane recently you had the opportunity to meet Marcel, a recent college graduate. Once Marcel heard that you knew something about investing, he immediately began to ask you questions about bonds. Marcel indicated that from what he had heard from his friends, the stock market was overvalued and bonds were a safer place to invest. Marcel admitted he really did not know much about either stocks or bonds, but that he hoped to start saving so that he could purchase a house in the next five years. Answer the following questions in a way that will help Marcel learn about bond investment concepts.

Explain which bond features would be important for Marcel to consider. If Marcel thought that interest rates were going to rise, what type of bond should he purchase? Why? Describe at least five risks involved with investing in bonds.

Study Guide

Circle the correct answer and then check the answers in the back of the book to chart your progress.

Multiple Choice

1. Which of the following is not a bond feature that is desirable for bond investors?
   a. Put feature
   b. Convertible feature
   c. Call feature
   d. Extendible feature

2. An investor may be interested in investing in a Government of Canada bond because:
   a. They are a safe investment.
   b. They are available with a term to maturity of anywhere between 1 and 30 years.
   c. They can be sold easily in the secondary market.
   d. All of the above.

3. Bonds that may be exchanged for common stock at the option of the bondholders are called:
   a. Option bonds.
   b. Convertible bonds.
   c. Callable bonds.
   d. Stock bonds.

4. Which of the following short-term debt securities is issued by the Government of Canada?
   a. Banker's acceptances
   b. Strip bonds
   c. Commercial paper
   d. T-bills

5. Real return bonds protect you from inflation risk by:
   a. Increasing your coupon payments every six months.
   b. Adjusting the par value of the bond for changes in the inflation rate.

   c. Offering a term to maturity that will result in a very safe, low-risk investment.
   d. All of the above.

6. Jan buys a bond with a face value of $1000 at a purchase price of $109.40. The bond has a semi-annual coupon payment of 10 percent. If she holds the bond until maturity in six years, find its yield to maturity if interest is compounded semi-annually?
   a. 10.0 percent
   b. 8.0 percent
   c. 8.6 percent
   d. 9.0 percent

7. The risk that you will be forced to sell your bond back to the issuer prior to maturity is referred to as:
   a. Call risk.
   b. Default risk.
   c. Interest rate risk.
   d. Economic risk.

8. The amount returned to the investor when a bond matures is called:
   a. Principal.
   b. Interest gain.
   c. Capital gain.
   d. Terminal value.

9. With respect to bond valuation, which of the following statements is true?
   a. A bond's value is determined as the future value of the future cash flows to be received by the investor, which are the periodic coupon payments and the principal payment at maturity.

b. A bond's value is determined as the future value of the future cash flows to be received by the investor, which are the periodic coupon payments.

c. A bond's value is determined as the present value of the future cash flows to be received by the investor, which are the periodic coupon payments and the principal payment at maturity.

d. A bond's value is determined as the present value of the future cash flows to be received by the investor, which are the periodic coupon payments.

10. Calculate the present value of a $1000 par value bond that has five years until maturity and a coupon rate of 8 percent, payable semi-annually. New $1000 par value bonds offer a coupon rate of 6 percent.
   a. $1085.20
   b. $915.48
   c. $1045.79
   d. $1084.25

11. What is the purchase price of a $10 000, 3.5 percent bond with semi-annual coupons redeemable at 108 in 7 years if the bond is bought to yield 2.5 percent compounded semi-annually? HINT: The bond will be redeemed prior to maturity at 108.
   a. $10 011.39
   b. $11 310.82
   c. $10 800.00
   d. $10 638.53

12. How much interest does an ATT Ltd. bond pay annually, given the following information? $1000 par value, maturity Dec 22, 2023, semi-annual coupon 7.75 percent, price $105.50, and yield 7.4 percent.
   a. $7.50
   b. $77.50
   c. $7.40
   d. $74.00

13. High-yield (junk) bond funds focus on relatively risky bonds issued by firms. These funds are most susceptible to what kind of risk?
   a. Management risk
   b. Exchange rate risk
   c. Default risk
   d. Market fluctuation risk

14. To minimize the effects of default risk, an investor should choose which one of the following corporate bonds?
   a. AAA-rated corporate bonds with the shortest term to maturity
   b. AA-rated short-term corporate bonds with the shortest term to maturity
   c. AAA-rated long-term corporate bonds with the longest term to maturity
   d. AA-rated long-term corporate bonds with the longest term to maturity

15. Darvin and Kim would like to purchase a portfolio of bonds that will mature when their children are ready to attend a post-secondary institution. What would be the most appropriate bond investment strategy given their objectives?
   a. Interest rate strategy
   b. Passive strategy
   c. Bond laddering strategy
   d. Maturity matching strategy

True/False

1. True or False? The coupon payments for a bond are normally payable quarterly.

2. True or False? A bond that is trading at a price below its par value is said to be trading at a discount.

3. True or False? Crown corporation bonds are guaranteed by the province in which they are issued.

4. True or False? Bonds are long-term debt securities secured only by a promise to pay.

5. True or False? The risk of default by the issuer of a provincial bond will vary depending on the province that issued the bond.

6. True or False? Banker's acceptances are short-term debt securities issued by large firms that are guaranteed by the issuing firm.

7. True or False? A sinking fund is a pool of money that is set aside to repurchase a set amount of bonds in a set period of time.

8. True or False? Strip bonds are always sold at a discount to their par value.

9. True or False? If you wish to sell a bond that has a coupon rate of 8 percent when new bonds being sold at par value are offering a coupon rate of 9 percent, you will have to sell your bond for less than par value in order to attract investors.

10. True or False? A put feature allows an investor to redeem the bond at its face value before it matures.

11. True or False? Real return bonds protect an investor from real interest rate risk.

12. True or False? A bond is more likely to be exposed to call risk when interest rates are rising.

13. True or False? Bonds with longer terms to maturity are more sensitive to interest rate movements than bonds that have short terms remaining until maturity.

14. True or False? Reinvestment risk increases as interest rates decrease.

15. True or False? With respect to an interest rate strategy, you would select long-term bonds if you expect interest rates to increase.

Investing in Mutual Funds

CHAPTER 13

PhotoAlto Agency RF Collections/ Getty Images

There is an old saying: "Do not put all of your eggs in one basket." Consider the case of Nicki and Jack Saizon. The Saizons worked for the same company in the telecommunications field. From that vantage point, they had seen the tremendous rise in telecom stock in past years. They invested all of their savings, which up to that time had been invested conservatively in a guaranteed investment certificate (GIC), into a telecommunications mutual fund.

Within two years, their fund was worth half of their original investment. Nicki and Jack thought they had a good understanding of the telecommunications industry. What appeared to be a sure thing turned out to be a lot less than what they had expected.

QUESTIONS:

1. What are the advantages and disadvantages of investing mutual funds?
2. In addition to telecommunications mutual funds, what other funds should Nicki and Jack consider?
3. What other investment options will provide Nicki and Jack with benefits similar to those provided by mutual funds?

BACKGROUND ON POOLED INVESTMENT FUNDS

pooled investment fund
An investment vehicle that pools together money from many investors and invests that money in a variety of securities.

A **pooled investment fund** is an investment vehicle that pools together money from many investors and invests that money in a variety of stocks, bonds, or indexes of stocks and/ or bonds. An individual investor has limited resources with which to buy investments. For example, if you wish to purchase a board lot (100 shares) of a stock that is currently trading at $20 per share, you would need to spend $2000, calculated as $20 × 100 shares. Pooled investments are arranged such that you are able to pool your money with other investors in order to purchase many types of stock and bond investments throughout the world. Every pooled investment is unique in some way with respect to the securities it purchases and/or the features it offers investors.

There are many different types of pooled investments. As an individual investor, the types of pooled investments that you are most likely to come across include mutual funds, Exchange-Traded Funds (ETFs), and segregated funds. Although there are some differences among these pooled investments, they share many common features that appeal to investors.

marketability
The ease with which an investor can convert an investment into cash.

equity mutual funds
Funds that sell units, or shares, to individuals and use this money to invest in stocks.

bond mutual funds
Funds that sell units, or shares, to individuals and use this money to invest in bonds.

balanced mutual funds
Funds that sell units, or shares, to individuals and use this money to invest in a combination of stocks and bonds.

Pooled investments provide diversification, economies of scale, and marketability. **Marketability** refers to the ease with which an investor can convert an investment into cash. Recall from Chapter 10 that diversification with respect to stocks can be achieved by investing across industries and countries. In addition, an investor could purchase government bonds, such as federal, provincial, or municipal bonds, and/or corporate bonds. These bonds can also be purchased with a short, medium, or long term to maturity. Pooled investment funds are able to provide economies of scale because of their buying power. Since a pooled investment fund is able to accumulate a lot of money, the individual securities that are purchased within the fund on behalf of investors can be purchased at lower fees than what an individual investor could do for themselves. Finally, the pooled investment funds discussed in this chapter provide marketability in that they can be sold back to the issuer of the fund or to another investor. The following sections discuss the characteristics that are unique to mutual funds, ETFs, and segregated funds.

BACKGROUND ON MUTUAL FUNDS

Mutual funds can be broadly distinguished according to the securities in which they invest. **Equity mutual funds** sell units, or shares, to individuals and use this money to invest in stocks. **Bond mutual funds** sell units, or shares, to individuals and use this money to invest in bonds. **Balanced mutual funds** sell units, or shares, to individuals and use this money to invest in a combination of stocks and bonds. **Money market mutual funds** sell units, or shares, to individuals and use this money to invest in cash and investments that can be converted to cash quickly (very liquid investments). Money market funds were discussed in Chapter 5. Mutual funds employ portfolio managers who decide which securities to purchase; the individual investors do not select the investments themselves. The minimum initial investment in a mutual fund is usually between $500 and $5000, depending on the fund. Many mutual funds are subsidiaries of other types of financial institutions.

money market mutual funds (MMFs)
Funds that sell units, or shares, to individuals and use this money to invest in cash and investments that can be converted to cash quickly (very liquid investments).

Advantages of Investing in Mutual Funds

In addition to providing an investor with diversification, economies of scale, and marketability, mutual funds offer the added advantages of professional management, simple record keeping, and ease of access relative to other types of investments. First, mutual funds provide professional money management. Your investments reflect the decisions of experienced professionals who have access to the best research available. Second, mutual funds simplify the process of record keeping because the mutual fund company will send you a statement on a regular basis. The statement will show a list of the mutual funds you own as opposed to a list of all of the investments within those mutual funds. Therefore, instead of evaluating each individual stock or bond, you only have to evaluate the performance of the mutual fund relative to your goals. Finally, mutual funds are available everywhere. You can make an appointment with your bank representative to invest in mutual funds. Furthermore, almost all financial advisers and planners are licensed to sell mutual funds.

Go to:
www.mfda.ca

This website provides information about the national self-regulatory organization for the distribution side of the Canadian mutual fund industry.

Disadvantages of Investing in Mutual Funds

There are a number of potential disadvantages of investing in mutual funds. First, the management fees and other costs associated with a mutual fund vary substantially among funds. It is important to understand the fees charged by any fund you invest in. Mutual fund fees are discussed later in this chapter. Second, the investment decisions for a mutual fund are made by the portfolio manager. As a mutual fund investor, you will have no control over the investments that are purchased and/or sold within the mutual fund. This lack of control over when you buy and sell your investments may lead to an unexpected tax liability. For example, if a portfolio manager decides to sell an investment within a mutual fund, the sale may result in a capital gain. Although the money received from the sale may be reinvested in another investment, the original capital gain is passed on to the investors who have invested in the fund. This investment income has to be reported by the investors on their tax returns. Many investors are surprised by this tax effect because they have not actually received any capital gain since the money was reinvested. However, they do have to pay the tax on these gains. Third, although they are professional money managers, portfolio managers are only human. It is possible that you could invest in a well-diversified mutual fund that is invested in a group of poorly performing investments. Finally, other than with money market funds, liquidity can be very low. **Liquidity** refers to the ease with which the investor can convert the investment into cash without a loss of capital. You may need to redeem your shares when the market conditions are not favourable. Many investors buy and sell mutual funds as a short-term investment. With the exception of money market funds, mutual funds are designed to be medium- to long-term investments and should not be used as a part of your emergency fund or other short-term needs.

liquidity
Access to ready cash, including savings and credit, to cover short-term or unexpected expenses; also, the ease with which an investor can convert an investment into cash without a loss of capital.

myth or **fact** Mutual funds do not perform as well as individual stocks.

Net Asset Value per Share

Each mutual fund's value can be determined by its **net asset value (NAV)**, which represents the market value of the securities that it has purchased minus any liabilities and fees owed. For example, suppose that a mutual fund owns 100 different stocks, including 10 000 shares of Canadian National Railway (CNR) that are currently worth $60 per share. This mutual fund's holdings of CNR are worth $600 000 (computed as $60 × 10 000 shares) as of today. The value of the other 99 stocks owned by the fund is determined in the same manner, and all values are totalled. Then, any liabilities, such as expenses owed to the mutual fund's managers, are subtracted to determine the NAV.

The NAV is commonly reported on a per share basis, although some refer to the shares as units, and it can be reported on a per unit basis as well. The **net asset value per share (NAVPS)** is calculated by dividing the NAV by the number of shares in the fund. Each day,

net asset value (NAV)
The market value of the securities that a mutual fund has purchased minus any liabilities and fees owed.

net asset value per share (NAVPS)
Calculated by dividing the NAV by the number of shares in the fund.

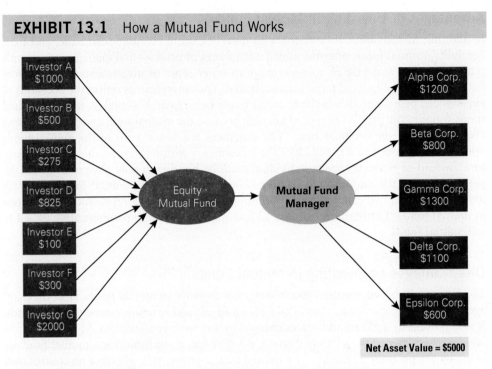

EXHIBIT 13.1   How a Mutual Fund Works

Source: Alberta Securities Commission, The Basics of Investing Presentation, 2007.

the market value of all of the mutual fund's assets is determined. Any interest or dividends earned by the fund are added to the market value of the assets, and any expenses (such as mailing, marketing, and portfolio management) that are charged to the fund and any dividends distributed to the fund's shareholders (investors) are deducted. As the value of the mutual fund's portfolio increases, so does the fund's NAVPS.

Exhibit 13.1 shows how a mutual fund works. In this exhibit, an equity mutual fund receives $5000 from new investors. The mutual fund manager uses this money to purchase shares of stock. To help them to keep track of their investment, each investor is given shares in the mutual fund. Assume that the mutual fund issues 500 total shares. The NAVPS would be calculated as:

$$\text{NAVPS} = \text{Net Asset Value (NAV)} \div \text{Number of Shares Outstanding}$$

$$= \$5000 \div 500$$

$$= \$10$$

Since one share is worth $10 and Investor G invested $2000, this investor would receive 200 shares. An increase in NAV will result in an increase in NAVPS. A decrease in NAV will result in a decrease in NAVPS.

Open-End versus Closed-End Funds

Mutual funds are classified as either open-end funds or closed-end funds.

open-end mutual funds
Funds that sell shares directly to investors and will redeem those shares whenever investors wish to "cash in."

Open-End Funds. Open-end mutual funds sell shares directly to investors and will redeem those shares whenever investors wish to "cash in." The funds are managed by investment companies that are commonly subsidiaries of a larger financial conglomerate. CIBC, Royal Bank, Great-West Life, and many other financial institutions have investment company subsidiaries that operate open-end mutual funds. Many investment companies operate a family, or group, of separately managed open-end mutual funds. For example, Fidelity, AGF, and CI Investments manage several different open-end funds, each of which has its own investment objective or purpose. By offering a diverse set of mutual funds, these investment companies satisfy investors with many different investment preferences.

Consider an open-end equity mutual fund that receives $5 million today as new investors purchase shares of the fund. In addition, today some investors who had previously purchased shares decide to redeem them, resulting in $3 million in redemptions in the fund. In this example, the equity mutual fund has a net difference of $2 million of new money that its portfolio managers will invest.

On some days, the value of redemptions may exceed the value of new shares purchased. Mutual fund managers typically maintain a small portion of the fund's portfolio in the form of cash or liquid securities so that they have sufficient liquidity when redemptions exceed new share purchases. Otherwise, they may be required to sell some stocks in their portfolio to obtain the necessary money for redemptions.

Closed-End Funds. **Closed-end funds** issue shares to investors when the funds are first created, but do not redeem those shares. Unlike an open-end fund, shares of a closed-end fund are traded on a stock exchange. Thus, the fund does not sell new shares on demand to investors and does not allow investors to redeem shares. The market price per share is determined by the demand for shares versus the supply of shares that are being sold. The price per share of a closed-end fund can differ from the fund's NAVPS. A closed-end fund's share price may exhibit a **premium** (above the NAVPS) in some periods and a **discount** (below the NAVPS) in other periods.

Load versus No-Load Funds

Open-end mutual funds can be either load funds or no-load funds. **No-load mutual funds** sell directly to investors and do not charge a fee. Conversely, load mutual funds charge a fee (or load) when you purchase them. The load charge can be either a front-end load or a back-end load. With a **front-end load mutual fund**, a fee is paid at the time of purchase to stockbrokers or other financial service advisers who execute transactions for investors. With a **back-end load mutual fund**, a fee is charged if shares are redeemed within a set period of time. The amount of the fee is based on a **declining redemption schedule**, which is a fee schedule where the back-end load charge reduces with each year an investor holds the fund. Exhibit 13.2 provides an example of a declining redemption schedule. In this exhibit, if a fund is redeemed within the first year after purchase, a fee of 6 percent is charged. The fee may be based on the original amount purchased or the value of the fund when it is redeemed. If this same investor had waited until the fund was in its fifth year, the fee would have been 2 percent. A declining redemption schedule may be anywhere from 5 to 10 years in length. Since no-load funds do not pay a commission to brokers, brokers are less likely to recommend them to investors.

Investors should recognize the impact of loads on their investment performance. In some cases, the difference in loads is the reason one mutual fund outperforms another.

closed-end funds
Funds that issue shares to investors but do not redeem those shares; instead, the fund's shares are traded on a stock exchange.

premium
The amount by which a closed-end fund's share price in the secondary market is above the fund's NAVPS.

discount
The amount by which a closed-end fund's share price in the secondary market is below the fund's NAVPS.

no-load mutual funds
Funds that sell directly to investors and do not charge a fee.

front-end load mutual funds
Mutual funds that charge a fee at the time of purchase, which is paid to stockbrokers or other financial service advisers who execute transactions for investors.

back-end load mutual funds
Mutual funds that charge a fee if shares are redeemed within a set period of time.

declining redemption schedule
A fee schedule where the back-end load charge reduces with each year an investor holds the fund.

EXHIBIT 13.2 Declining Redemption Schedule

Year Funds Are Redeemed	Deferred Sales Charge
Within the first year	6%
In the second year	5%
In the third year	4%
In the fourth year	3%
In the fifth year	2%
In the sixth year	1%
After the sixth year	0%

Source: The Canadian Securities Institute, *The Canadian Securities Course: Volume 2*, page 10-9, 2004. Reprinted with permission of CSI Global Education Inc.

EXAMPLE

You have $5000 to invest in a mutual fund. You have a choice of investing in a no-load fund by sending your investment directly to the fund or purchasing a mutual fund that has a 4 percent front-end load and has been recommended by a broker. Each fund has an NAV of $20 per share and their equity portfolios are very similar. You expect each fund's NAVPS will be $22 at the end of the year, which would represent a 10 percent return on the prevailing NAV of $20 per share (assuming that there are no dividends or capital gain distributions over the year). You plan to sell the mutual fund in one year. If the NAVPS for each fund changes as expected, your return for each fund will be as shown in Exhibit 13.3.

Notice that you would earn a return of 10 percent on the no-load fund versus 5.6 percent on the front-end load fund. While the load fund's portfolio generated a 10 percent return, your return is less because of the load fee. Based on this analysis, you decide to purchase shares of the no-load fund.

Studies on mutual funds have found that no-load funds perform at least as well as load funds on average, even when ignoring the commission paid on a load fund. When considering the commission, no-load funds have outperformed load funds on average.

Given this information, why do some investors purchase load funds? They may believe that specific load funds will generate high returns and outperform other no-load funds, even after considering the commission that is charged. Or, perhaps some investors who rely on their brokers for advice do not consider no-load funds. Some investors may purchase load funds because they do not realize that no-load funds exist or do not know how to invest in them. To invest in no-load funds, you can simply call a 1-800 number for an application or print the application off of a fund's website. As with any funds, though, the investor should review the fee structure, as there are many differences in how no-load funds charge fees.

EXHIBIT 13.3   Comparison of Returns from a No-Load Fund and a Front-End Load Fund

No-Load Fund

Invest $5000 in the mutual fund	$5000
	– $0
Your investment converts to 250 shares	$5000
	÷ $20
$5000 / $20 per share = 250 shares	250 shares
End of Year 1: You redeem shares for $22 per share	× $22
Amount received = 250 shares × $22 = $5500	$5500
Return = ($5500 – $5000) / $5000 = 10%	10%

Front-End Load Fund

Invest $5000; 4% of $5000 (or $200) goes to the broker	$5000
	– $200
The remaining 96% of $5000 (or $4800) is used to purchase 240 shares	$4800
	÷ $20
$4800 / $20 per share = 240 shares	240 shares
You redeem shares for $22 per share	× $22
Amount received = 240 shares × $22 = $5280	$5280
Return = ($5280 – $5000) / $5000 = 5.6%	5.6%

Management Expense Ratio (MER)

As mentioned earlier in this chapter, mutual funds incur expenses, including administrative, legal, and clerical expenses, and portfolio management costs. Some mutual funds have much higher expenses than others. These expenses are incurred by the fund's shareholders because the fund's NAVPS (which is what investors receive when redeeming their shares) accounts for the expenses incurred. Investors should review the annual expenses of any mutual funds in which they invest. In particular, they should focus on each fund's **management expense ratio (MER)**, which measures the annual expenses incurred by a fund on a percentage basis, calculated as annual expenses of the fund divided by the net asset value of the fund; the result of this calculation is then divided by the number of shares outstanding. An expense ratio of 1 percent means that shareholders incur annual expenses amounting to 1 percent of the value of the fund. The higher the expense ratio, the lower the return for a given level of portfolio performance. Mutual funds that incur more expenses are worthwhile only if they offer a high enough return to offset the extra expenses. MERs for no-load funds can be higher than those for load funds.

On average, mutual funds have an MER of about 2.5 percent. The MERs of mutual funds can be found in various financial newspapers and on many financial websites.

management expense ratio (MER)
The annual expenses incurred by a fund on a percentage basis, calculated as annual expenses of the fund divided by the net asset value of the fund; the result of this calculation is then divided by the number of shares outstanding.

Reported Components of MERs. The components of MERs include management expenses, dealer/adviser compensation, administrative costs, and GST/HST. The management expenses represent the costs incurred for investment research, portfolio management, marketing costs, and profit. The dealer/adviser compensation includes, among other things, fees paid to advisers and salespeople. Included in these fees is a trailing commission which represents the ongoing fee paid to the mutual fund representative to provide ongoing services and advice to investors. The third component of the expense ratio, administrative costs, includes general business expenses such as transaction processing, client reporting, and audit and legal fees. MERs do not include brokerage commissions and related expenses, as they are incurred with the purchase and sale of the investment of the portfolio and are already accounted for in the NAV.

myth or **fact** Owning a sufficient number of mutual funds will result in an adequate level of portfolio diversification for an investor.

Relationship between Expense Ratios and Performance. Research has shown that mutual funds with relatively low expenses tend to outperform other funds with similar objectives. This finding suggests that mutual funds with higher expenses cannot justify their MERs.

Some funds will have higher costs than others because of their objectives. An equity fund with the objective of aggressive growth will have higher costs than an equity fund with an income. Global and international funds are often the most expensive of all funds because of additional research costs and currency costs.

TYPES OF MUTUAL FUNDS

L.0.2

Investors can select from a wide array of mutual funds, including money market funds, equity mutual funds, and bond mutual funds. Money market funds were briefly discussed in Chapter 5. Each category includes many types of funds to suit the preferences of individual investors.

Types of Equity Mutual Funds

Open-end equity mutual funds are commonly classified according to their geographic location and their investment objectives. For example, a growth fund could be characterized as a Canadian Equity Growth Fund or a U.S. Equity Growth Fund. If you consider investing in an equity mutual fund, you must decide on the type of fund in which you wish to invest. Some of the more common investment objectives are described here.

Growth Funds. Growth funds focus on stocks that have potential for above-average growth.

Small Capitalization (Small-Cap) Funds. Small capitalization (small-cap) funds focus on firms that are relatively small. Smaller firms tend to have more potential for growth than larger firms.

Mid-Size Capitalization (Mid-Cap) Funds. Mid-size capitalization (mid-cap) funds focus on medium-size firms. These firms tend to be more established than small-cap firms, but may have less growth potential. Mid-cap firms may have more growth potential than large-cap firms.

Dividend Funds. Dividend funds focus on firms that pay a high level of dividends. These firms tend to exhibit less growth because they use a relatively large portion of their earnings to pay dividends rather than reinvesting earnings for expansion. The firms normally have less potential for high capital gains and exhibit less risk. These large-cap firms represent mature industries.

Balanced Growth and Income Funds. Balanced growth and income funds contain both growth stocks and stocks that pay high dividends. This type of fund distributes dividends periodically, while offering more potential for an increase in the fund's value than a dividend fund.

sector funds
Mutual funds that focus on stocks in a specific industry or sector, such as technology stocks.

Sector Funds. **Sector funds** focus on stocks in a specific industry or sector, such as technology stocks. Investors who expect a specific industry to perform well may invest in a sector fund. Sector funds enable investors with a small amount of funds to invest in a diversified portfolio of stocks within a particular sector. Sector funds are more risky, as they are less diversified. Sector funds should be used with discretion.

An example of a sector fund is a technology fund that focuses on stocks of internet-based firms. Most of these firms are relatively young. They have potential for very high returns, but also exhibit a high degree of risk because they do not have a consistent record of earnings. Another example of a sector fund is a financial services fund, which focuses on stocks of banks and insurance and financial services companies.

index funds
Mutual funds that attempt to mirror the movements of an existing equity index.

Index Funds. **Index funds** are mutual funds that attempt to mirror the movements of an existing equity index. Investors who invest in an index fund should earn returns similar to what they would receive if they actually invested in all stocks in the index. For example, CIBC offers a mutual fund containing a set of stocks that moves in the same manner as the S&P/TSX Composite Index. It may not contain every stock in the index, but it is still able to mimic the index's movement.

Index funds have become very popular because of their performance relative to other mutual funds. They incur fewer expenses than a typical mutual fund because they are not actively managed. The index fund does not incur expenses for researching various stocks because it is intended simply to mimic an index. In addition, the fund's portfolio is not frequently revised. Consequently, index funds incur very low transaction costs, which can enhance performance. Index funds have relatively lower MERs when compared to other mutual funds. However, there can be tracking errors, and any fees or costs will affect the return of these funds. **Tracking error** refers to how closely an index fund mirrors the movements of the existing index it is benchmarked against. A relatively high tracking error suggests that the index fund manager has not been successful in mimicking the existing index's movement.

tracking error
Refers to how closely an index fund mirrors the movements of the existing index it is benchmarked against.

Index funds can also offer tax advantages. Since they engage in less trading than most other mutual funds, they generate limited capital gains (which must be distributed to shareholders). Index funds composed of stocks that do not pay dividends are especially valuable because they do not have dividend income that must be distributed to shareholders.

Much research has found that the performance of portfolios managed by portfolio managers is frequently lower than the performance of an existing equity index. Thus, investors may be better off investing in an index fund rather than investing in an actively managed portfolio.

EXAMPLE

You consider investing in either a no-load mutual fund that focuses on growth stocks or an index mutual fund. When ignoring expenses incurred by the mutual funds, you expect that the growth fund will generate an annual return of 9 percent versus an annual return of 8 percent for the index fund. The growth fund has a MER of 2.5 percent, versus a MER of 0.85 percent for the index fund. Based on your expectations about the portfolio returns, your returns would be:

	Growth Fund	Index Fund
Fund's portfolio return (before expenses)	9.0%	8.0%
Expense ratio	2.5%	0.85%
Your annual return	6.5%	7.15%

The comparison shows that the index fund can generate a higher return for you than the other fund even if its portfolio return is lower. Based on this analysis, you should invest in the index fund.

International Equity Funds. International equity funds focus on firms that are based outside Canada. Some of these funds focus on firms in a specific country, while others focus on a specific region or continent. Funds with a country or regional concentration are attractive to investors who want to invest in a specific country but prefer to rely on an experienced portfolio manager to select the stocks. The expenses associated with managing a portfolio are higher for international mutual funds than for other mutual funds because monitoring foreign firms from Canada is expensive. In addition, transaction costs associated with buying and selling stocks of foreign firms are higher.

Some mutual funds invest in stocks of both foreign firms and Canadian firms. These are called "global mutual funds" to distinguish them from international mutual funds. Any fund that invests outside of Canada incurs a special risk in foreign currency. While choice in investments may be spectacular, gains can be wiped out because of changes in the value of the Canadian dollar relative to those currencies.

Ethical Funds. Ethical funds screen out firms viewed as offensive by some investors. For example, they may not invest in firms that produce cigarettes or guns or that pollute the environment.

Other Types of Equity Funds. The types of mutual funds described here can be further subdivided, as funds have proliferated to satisfy the preferences of investors. As an example, some growth equity funds focus on small firms while others concentrate on large ones. Investors who desire stock in large firms that are expected to grow would consider investing in large-cap growth funds. Investors who desire stock in small firms that are expected to grow would consider investing in small-cap growth funds.

Types of Bond Mutual Funds

Investors can also select a bond fund that satisfies their investment objectives. The more popular types of bond funds are identified here.

Canadian Bond Funds. Canadian bond funds focus on investments in Canadian bonds. The types of investments held within a Canadian bond fund vary significantly. Some bond funds focus on bonds issued by the federal government or a federal Crown corporation. Other bond funds will have a large portion of their portfolio invested in bonds issued by provincial governments or municipalities. Still other bond funds will focus on bonds issued by high-quality firms that tend to have a low degree of default risk, while others focus on high-risk bonds.

High-Yield Bond Funds. High-yield bond funds focus on relatively risky bonds issued by firms that may have a higher default risk. These bond funds tend to offer a higher expected return than Canadian bond funds because of the high yields offered to compensate for the higher potential default risk.

Index Bond Funds. Index bond funds are intended to mimic the performance of a specified bond index. For example, Barclays Global Investors offers six different Canadian bond index funds:

- A Canadian bond index fund that tracks an aggregate (broad) bond index
- A Canadian corporate bond index fund that tracks a corporate bond index
- A Canadian government bond index fund that tracks a government bond index
- A Canadian short-term bond index fund that tracks an index representing bonds with one to five years until maturity
- A Canadian real return bond index fund that tracks an index representing real return bonds
- A Canadian long-term bond fund that tracks an index representing bonds with more than 10 years until maturity

global bond funds
Mutual funds that focus on bonds issued by non-Canadian firms or governments.

exchange rate risk
The risk that the value of a bond may drop if the currency denominating the bond weakens against the Canadian dollar.

Global Bond Funds. **Global bond funds** focus on bonds issued by non-Canadian firms or governments. Some global bonds are attractive to Canadian investors because they offer higher yields than Canadian bonds. They are subject to **exchange rate risk** along with the other risks associated with bonds. If the currency denominating a foreign bond weakens against the Canadian dollar, the value of the foreign bond is reduced and the global bond fund's performance is adversely affected. Also, expenses incurred by global bond funds tend to be higher than those of domestic bond funds because of costly international transactions. Although the emphasis in a global bond fund is to invest in bonds issued by non-Canadian firms and governments, most global bond funds invest a portion of their assets in Canadian bonds.

Like other bond funds, global bond funds are exposed to interest rate risk. Foreign bond prices are influenced by the interest rate of the country denominating the bond in the same way that Canadian bond prices are influenced by Canadian interest rate movements. When the interest rate of the country denominating the bonds increases, bond prices decline. Conversely, when the interest rate of the country decreases, prices of bonds denominated in that country increase.

Maturity Classifications. Each type of bond fund can be segmented further by the range of maturities held in the fund. For example, some Canadian bond funds are classified as short term (1 to 5 years), medium term (5 to 10 years), or long term (10+ years). Other bond funds may also be segmented in this manner.

RETURN AND RISK OF A MUTUAL FUND

Investors purchase shares of a mutual fund so that they can receive a reasonable return on their investment. However, you must balance the expected return with the fund's risk, which reflects the uncertainty surrounding the expected return. Before you purchase a mutual fund you should set your objectives in terms of expected return and the risk you can tolerate.

Return from Investing in a Mutual Fund

A mutual fund can generate returns for its investors (shareholders) in four different ways: interest income distributions, dividend distributions, capital gains distributions, and capital gains from redeeming shares. A mutual fund that receives interest income, dividends, or capital gains must distribute these payments to its investors in the same year. However, investors are normally given the opportunity to choose whether to receive these distributions in the form of a cash payment or as additional shares (which means that the distributions are reinvested to buy more shares of the fund).

myth or **fact** Top-performing mutual funds tend not to be top-performing mutual funds in the following year.

Capital Gain from Redeeming Shares. You earn a capital gain if you redeem shares of a mutual fund when the price exceeds the price at which you purchased the shares. For example, if you purchased 200 shares of an equity mutual fund at a price of $25 per share and sell them for $30 per share, your capital gain will be:

$$\text{Capital Gain} = (\text{Selling Price per Share} - \text{Purchase Price per Share})$$
$$\times \text{ Number of Shares}$$
$$= (\$30 - \$25) \times 200$$
$$= \$1000$$

Determining your capital gain is more difficult when you have reinvested distributions into the fund, because each distribution results in the purchase of more shares at the prevailing price on that day. In addition, the NAVPS will decrease. Since the number of shares outstanding and the NAVPS will be adjusted with every distribution, the cost base for the shares that each shareholder owns will also have to be recalculated. The new adjusted cost base is used to determine the capital gain when you redeem shares. Many investors rely on the mutual fund to report their capital gain after they redeem the shares. Now that many mutual fund companies allow you to review your account online, finding price information is easy. Recall from Chapter 4 that only 50 percent of a capital gain is taxable.

Returns vary among equity mutual funds in any particular period. While they are normally affected by the general stock market conditions, equity mutual funds' returns could vary with the specific sector or industry in which the stocks are concentrated. For example, technology stocks performed better than other types of stocks in the late 1990s, so mutual funds focusing on technology stocks performed well at that time. In the 2001 to 2003 period, stocks as a group did not perform well. Because of the significant rise in price that technology stocks had experienced in the 1990s (resulting more from speculation than from actual increases in earnings), the price declines were even greater than for non-technology stocks. The same mutual funds whose performance was enhanced in the 1990s by focusing on technology stocks now suffered the greatest decline in performance.

Since the returns are highly dependent on the performance of the sector in which the equity mutual fund is concentrated, be careful when comparing mutual funds. The difference between the performances of two equity mutual funds during a particular period may be attributed to the sector rather than to the skill of the funds' managers. Some investors tend to invest in whatever equity mutual fund performed well recently because they presume that the fund has the best portfolio managers. However, if the fund performed well simply because its sector performed well, it would be a mistake to judge the management based on past performance.

Risk from Investing in an Equity Mutual Fund

Although different types of equity mutual funds experience different performance levels in a given time period, they are all influenced by general stock market conditions.

market risk
The susceptibility of a mutual fund's performance to general market conditions.

The performance of an equity mutual fund depends on the general movements in stock prices. When the stock market is weak, prices of stocks held by an equity fund decrease and the NAVPS of the fund declines as well. This susceptibility of a mutual fund's performance to general market conditions is often referred to as **market risk**.

FOCUS ON ETHICS: Risk from Investing in Hedge Funds

hedge funds
Limited partnerships that manage portfolios of funds for wealthy individuals and financial institutions.

Hedge funds are limited partnerships that manage portfolios of funds for wealthy individuals and financial institutions. They sell shares and use the proceeds to invest in various securities. In this way, they serve a similar purpose to mutual funds, yet they are often structured as limited partnerships in which investors have little or no control of the company's management. An investor must be classified as either an accredited investor or a sophisticated investor to invest in a hedge fund. The investor's income level, net worth, and investment knowledge are used to determine whether they fit one of these two classifications. Hedge funds are not regulated by a securities commission. While they strive to earn very high returns, they tend to make very risky investments that can lead to extremely poor returns. Hedge funds may invest not only in risky stocks, but also in a wide variety of investments, including silver or other metals. They may engage in short selling, the practice of selling securities not currently owned and buying these securities back at a later date. This strategy is designed to take advantage of overvalued securities. If the security's price declines, the funds will earn a high return, but if the security's price rises, they will experience a large loss. Hedge funds also commonly buy stocks on margin by supporting their investment with borrowed funds. This strategy will increase the magnitude of the gain or the loss on the investment. The number of hedge fund strategies available to qualified investors is difficult to quantify. In general, hedge fund investing should not be a part of your core investment strategy.

Trade-off between Expected Return and Risk of Equity Funds

Some investors are willing to tolerate risk from investing in an equity mutual fund when they expect that the mutual fund may offer a very high return. The trade-off between the expected return and the risk of an equity mutual fund is shown in Exhibit 13.4. On the conservative side, a dividend fund represents firms that pay a high level of dividends. As mentioned earlier, these firms tend to exhibit less growth because they use a relatively large portion of their

EXHIBIT 13.4   Trade-off between Expected Return and Risk

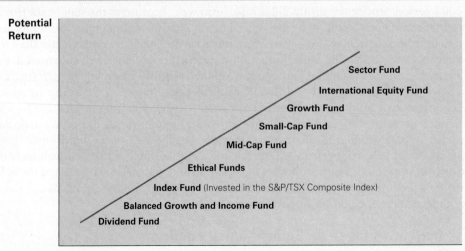

earnings to pay dividends rather than reinvest earnings for expansion. As a result, the fund's expected return is somewhat limited, but so is its risk. However, income funds such as dividend funds are subject to interest rate risk. A growth equity fund offers potential for higher returns than a dividend fund, but it also has more risk (more potential for a large decline in value). On the aggressive side, a fund that invests only in growth stocks of small firms has potential for a very high return, but it also exhibits high risk. A fund that invests within one sector (such as a technology fund) has even more potential return and risk.

Risk from Investing in a Bond Mutual Fund

Although different types of bond mutual funds will experience different performance levels in a given time period, they are all influenced by general bond market conditions. The performance of a bond mutual fund depends on the general movements in interest rates. When interest rates rise, prices of bonds held by a bond fund decrease, and the NAVPS of the fund declines. This susceptibility to interest rate movements is often referred to as **interest rate risk**.

The prices of all bonds change in response to interest rate movements, but the prices of longer-term bonds are the most sensitive. Thus, investors who want to reduce exposure to interest rate movements can select a bond fund that focuses on bonds with short terms to maturity. Conversely, investors who want to capitalize on an expected decline in interest rate movements can select a bond fund that focuses on long-term bonds.

The performance of many bond mutual funds also depends on the default risk of the individual bond holdings. Bond funds that invest most of their money in bonds with a high degree of default risk tend to offer a higher potential return to investors but also exhibit a high degree of risk. Under favourable economic conditions, the issuers of those bonds may be able to cover their payments, and the bond funds will consequently perform very well. If economic conditions are weak, however, some of the bond issuers may default on their payments, and these bond funds will provide relatively low or even negative returns to their shareholders.

Some bond funds, such as those that invest primarily in bonds issued and guaranteed by the federal government or a Crown corporation, have no (or low) default risk and a high level of interest rate risk. Other bond funds, such as short-term high-yield bond funds, have a low level of interest rate risk and a high level of default risk. Some bond funds, such as long-term high-yield bond funds, are highly exposed to both default risk and interest rate risk.

interest rate risk
The risk that occurs because of changes in the interest rate. This risk affects funds that invest in debt securities and other income-oriented securities.

Trade-off between Expected Return and Risk of Bond Funds

On the conservative side, a bond fund that holds Government of Canada bonds with a short term remaining until maturity has no exposure to default risk and limited exposure to interest rate risk. Thus, the prices of the bonds it holds are not very sensitive to external forces, so the NAVPS of the fund will not be very sensitive to these forces. The expected return on this fund is relatively low compared to that of other funds. A high-yield bond fund that invests only in high-yield bonds with long terms to maturity has the potential for a very high return. Its value is subject to default risk, however, because the high-yield bonds could default. It is also subject to a high level of interest rate risk because of the long-term maturities. A bond fund that invests in bonds issued by risky firms in a foreign country has even more potential return and risk.

DECIDING AMONG MUTUAL FUNDS

L.O.3

Your decision to purchase a specific mutual fund should be made once you determine your investment objectives, evaluate your risk tolerance, and decide on the fund characteristics you want. The final step is to search for mutual funds that exhibit those desired characteristics.

Determine whether you are interested in an equity mutual fund or a bond mutual fund. If you want your investment to have high potential for increasing in value over time, you should consider growth funds. If you want periodic income, you should consider bond funds. Some types of funds are segmented according to whether they focus their investment in stocks of mid-size firms (mid-cap) or small firms (small-cap). The mutual fund's Fund Facts will help you with this decision-making process.

Reviewing a Mutual Fund's Fund Facts

Fund Facts
A document designed to give investors key information about a mutual fund, in a language they can easily understand, at a time that is relevant to their investment decision.

For any mutual fund that you consider, you should obtain a **Fund Facts**, which is a document that is designed to give investors key information about a mutual fund, in a language they can easily understand, at a time that is relevant to their investment decision. Effective July 15, 2014, when you initially purchase a mutual fund, a Fund Facts document must be provided to you within 48 hours of your purchase. Previously, a simplified prospectus was provided to investors within 48 hours of a mutual fund purchase. The simplified prospectus will continue to be available to investors upon request. In many cases, you may be able to download the Fund Facts from the internet. The Fund Facts document contains considerable information.

Filing Date. The filing date is the date that the Fund Facts document was filed with the securities regulator.

Quick Facts. The quick facts for the fund include:

- the date on which the fund was established and available for sale;
- net asset value of the fund as of the date indicated;
- MER;
- name of the company providing portfolio management services;
- expected frequency and date at which any income or capital distributions are paid out; and
- minimum initial and subsequent investment amounts.

What Does the Fund Invest In? The Fund Facts will provide a description of what types of investments the fund invests in. In addition, a list of top 10 investments, the total number of investments, and the investment mix is included.

How Risky Is It? The Fund Facts will provide a description of how volatility can affect the returns and the chance of losing money in the fund. A risk rating scale is used to provide investors with guidance on the risk of the fund. Finally, a clear statement about what guarantees are offered by the fund is included.

How Has the Fund Performed? This section of the document informs the investor of how the fund has performed over the past 10 years. Specifically, a bar chart of year-by-year returns, the best and worst three-month returns, and the average return are included.

Who Is This Fund For? This section of the document provides a description of the type of investor that this fund is suitable for.

A Word about Tax. The Fund Facts informs the investor about the tax implications of holding the mutual fund in a non-registered versus a registered account, such as a tax-free savings account.

How Much Does It Cost? Sales charges, fund expenses and other fees are described in this section. A sales charge refers to the type of load — no-load, front-end, or back-end load — that the fund charges investors. Load versus no-load funds were discussed earlier in the chapter. The fund's expenses refer to the MER and its components. Other fees include short-term trading fees, switching fees, and change fees.

What If I Change My Mind? This section outlines the rights of the investor. In particular, the investor has the right to withdraw from the purchase agreement within two days of receiving the simplified prospectus or Fund Facts, or the right to cancel the purchase within 48 hours after receiving confirmation of the purchase.

myth or **fact** The best way to diversify is to buy as many different mutual funds as possible.

FREE APPS for Personal Finance

Performance of Investment Funds

Application:

The Invesco Canada app provides access to the latest pricing, performance, and ranking data for all mutual funds and ETFs for one of Canada's largest and most successful investment management firms.

QUOTATIONS OF MUTUAL FUNDS

L.O.4

Financial newspapers publish price quotations of open-end mutual funds, as shown in the sample Exhibit 13.5 As the internet has grown in popularity, financial market data have found their way out of the printed page and onto newspaper websites. For example, the *Financial Post* publishes the majority of its mutual fund data and related analysis tools on its website at www.financialpost.com (click on Markets). In Exhibit 13.5, each fund's NAVPS is shown in the second column, the net dollar change in the NAVPS is shown in the third column, and the percent return over the year is shown in the fourth column. The last column displays the three-year return for the two funds listed.

In any particular period, some types of mutual funds perform better than others. For example, in some years large-cap equities perform well while small-cap equities perform poorly. In other years, smaller-cap equities perform better than large-cap equities. When investors want to assess the performance of a mutual fund, they compare the return on that fund to the average return for the same type of fund. In this way, investors can determine whether their mutual fund was managed effectively.

Various information sources indicate the benchmark performance levels you can use to evaluate your mutual funds. For example, the *Financial Post* indexes provide benchmark information on the performance of growth (FPX Growth), balanced (FPX Balanced), and income-oriented (FPX Income) portfolios. In addition, the newspaper's FP Markets section provides information on various North American and international indexes.

Go to:
www.theglobeandmail.com

Click on:
Investing, then Funds & ETFs

This website provides pooled fund information, including articles, newsletters, testimonials, and much more.

EXHIBIT 13.5 An Example of Mutual Fund Price Quotations

Blazer Funds	NAVPS ($)	Net Change ($)	YTD Annual Return	Three-Year Return
Growth Fund	32.23	+0.15	8.26%	22.51%
Equity Income Fund	45.10	+0.22	9.78%	26.34%

L.O.5

EXCHANGE-TRADED FUNDS (ETFs)

Exchange-traded funds (ETFs) are a type of pooled investment fund that shares many of the same benefits of a mutual fund. Recall from the beginning of this chapter that the benefits of pooled investment funds include diversification, economies of scale, and marketability. Although ETFs and mutual funds are similar with respect to these benefits, there a number of differences. Unlike mutual funds, ETFs do not have a NAVPS. Instead, they trade on the stock exchange and have a share price much like a stock does. Similar to a stock, ETFs are purchased in real time, whereas mutual funds are purchased at the end of the day.

Fee Structure. Recall that mutual funds are sold with a back-end, front-end, or no-load fee structure. ETFs do not have a load structure and the initial fee you pay is the brokerage commission for completing the transaction when you buy or sell an ETF. However, similar to a mutual fund, there is an ongoing MER. The MER for an ETF is generally lower than what you would find for a mutual fund. This is because ETFs, like index mutual funds, track specific indexes.

Tax Efficiency. Since ETFs are designed to track an index, there is not as much active trading in an ETF as compared to a mutual fund. For investors, this means that ETFs tend to be more tax efficient since the portfolio manager is not creating capital gains and/or losses by actively selling stock.

Types of ETFs. The types of ETFs an investor may purchase are similar to the types of equity and bond mutual funds available for purchase. The difference between ETFs and mutual funds is that there are many more mutual fund companies than there are companies that sell ETFs.

FREE APPS for Personal Finance

Monitoring Exchange-Traded Funds

Application:

The ETF Central gives you instant access to all TSX-listed ETFs. ETF Central acts as a one-stop shop for all Canadian-listed ETFs including 15-minute delayed ETF pricing updates and complete news coverage of the ETF landscape.

L.O.6

SEGREGATED FUNDS

Segregated funds are insurance products. However, the advantages and disadvantages of mutual funds that were discussed earlier in this chapter also hold true for segregated funds. In fact, it is very easy for an investor to mistake a segregated fund for a mutual fund. Since segregated funds are regulated through the insurance legislation of the province in which they are sold, there are a number of unique features that may make segregated funds an attractive alternative to mutual funds.

Principal Protection

Unlike mutual funds, segregated funds offer a guarantee on your deposits when the contract matures. A segregated fund contract usually matures 10 years after the date of purchase. At the time of maturity, the policy owner is guaranteed to receive at least 75 percent of his or her deposits back. In some cases, the deposit guarantee may be as high as 100 percent.

Carla invested $10 000 in a Canadian equity segregated fund on July 13, 1997. The maturity guarantee clause in her contract indicates that she will receive at least 100 percent of her deposits back at the end of the maturity period, which is 10 years. During these 10 years, the Canadian equity market fluctuated in value. At maturity, the market and the fund have decreased in value relative to where they were 10 years earlier. Carla's investment is now worth $8900. She will receive her remaining deposit of $8900 plus $1100 from the insurance company to cover the maturity guarantee. Notice that if Carla's maturity had been 75 percent, she would not receive any additional money from the insurance company unless her fund had decreased in value by more than $2500. If Carla leaves her money on deposit with the insurance company, a new 10-year guarantee period will start.

Death Benefit Guarantee

This feature of a segregated fund also offers principal protection. However, the determination of the value of the guarantee is made at the time of death of the policy owner instead of at the maturity date of the policy. The death benefit is usually between 75 and 100 percent of the amount invested. This benefit is particularly advantageous for older investors who still want to hold stocks in their portfolio. The segregated fund contract indicates the beneficiary of the policy. As a result, the death benefit can be paid directly to the beneficiary, thereby avoiding probate fees.

Creditor Protection

Since segregated fund contracts are legally considered insurance policies, they are normally exempt from seizure by creditors in the event that the policy owner declares bankruptcy. The money invested in a segregated fund is an asset of the insurance company, not of the policy owner. The policy owner owns a contract that outlines his or her rights with respect to the money that has been invested with the insurance company. Creditor protection can be a valuable benefit for business owners who deal with creditors on a regular basis.

Assessing the Value of Protection

On the surface, segregated funds offer investors the best of both worlds. Conservative investors can purchase an equity segregated fund with the knowledge that they will receive at least their deposit back at maturity. In the event of death, the segregated fund contract will contain a death benefit provision that may return up to 100 percent of the money invested to the policy owner's beneficiaries. In addition, business owners can protect their investment assets from creditors by investing their money in a segregated fund or a portfolio of segregated funds. Since a segregated fund is regulated by provincial insurance legislation, probate fees can be avoided. Exhibit 13.6 compares the effect of different guarantees on the MER for segregated funds and mutual funds. Although the fund names in Exhibit 13.6 are fictitious, the MERs reflect the actual costs that an investor would incur if they considered mutual and/or segregated fund investments offered by a leading Canadian manufacturer of investment funds. For example, the Canadian Value Segregated Fund that offers a 100 percent maturity and death benefit guarantee has an MER of 5.13 percent, whereas the same segregated fund with a 75 percent guarantee has an MER of only 4.11 percent. The Canadian Value Fund, which is the mutual fund equivalent for these segregated funds, has an MER of 2.51 percent. As mentioned, mutual funds with relatively low expenses tend to outperform other funds with similar objectives. Exhibit 13.6 clearly shows that any segregated fund will underperform its mutual fund equivalent as a result of the difference in MERs. It is up to the individual investor to determine whether the benefits of owning a segregated fund outweigh the added costs. In addition, the term of the contract can be a detriment, reducing liquidity.

EXHIBIT 13.6   Effect of Different Guarantees on Management Expense Ratios

Investment Fund	100% Maturity & Death Benefit Guarantee Option MER	75% Maturity & Death Benefit Guarantee Option MER	Underlying Mutual Fund MER (no guarantee)
International Equity Segregated Fund	5.46	4.18	2.75
U.S. Equity Segregated Fund	5.26	4.40	2.76
Canadian Equity Segregated Fund	5.09	3.60	2.48
Canadian Value Segregated Fund	5.13	4.11	2.51
Money Market Segregated Fund	1.92	1.39	1.06

MyLab Finance   Visit MyLab Finance for additional study and practice tools. Select Financial Planning Problems are available in the Study Plan. Create your own study plan, generate personal cash flow statements and balance sheets, and set personal financial goals.

SUMMARY

L.O.1   Describe the advantages and disadvantages of mutual funds

The main advantages of mutual funds include diversification, economies of scale, marketability, professional management, simple record keeping, and ease of access. The main disadvantages of mutual funds include varying management fees and costs, less control over your investment decisions, potential for poor portfolio management, and low liquidity.

L.O.2   Identify the types of mutual funds

The common types of equity mutual funds include growth funds, small-cap funds, mid-cap funds, dividend funds, balanced growth and income funds, sector funds, index funds, and international equity funds. Income funds typically have a lower expected return than the other funds and a lower level of risk. Growth funds tend to have a higher potential return than the other funds and a higher level of risk.

The common types of bond mutual funds are Canadian bond funds, high-yield bond funds, index bond funds, and global bond funds. Canadian bond funds with short maturities have low potential return and low risk. High-yield bond funds have higher potential return and high risk (because some of their bonds may default). Any bond funds that invest in long-term bonds are subject to a high level of interest rate risk.

L.O.3   Explain how to choose among mutual funds

When choosing a mutual fund, you should select a fund with an investment objective that satisfies your needs,

and a relatively low management expense ratio (MER). The Fund Facts of each fund provide information on these characteristics.

L.O.4   Describe quotations of mutual funds

Mutual fund quotations are provided in the *Financial Post* and other business periodicals. These quotations can be used to review the prevailing prices, net asset value per share (NAVPS), MERs, and other characteristics. The quotations can also be used to assess recent performance.

L.O.5   Explain the differences between ETFs and mutual funds

An ETF is an exchange-traded pooled investment fund that, like stocks, can be bought and sold in real time. These types of investments do not have a load structure and are designed to track a particular index. As a result, the fees for ETFs tend to be lower than those for mutual funds. Since they are passively managed, ETFs tend to be more tax efficient than your average mutual fund.

L.O.6   Explain the differences between segregated funds and mutual funds

A segregated fund is an insurance product that is often mistaken for a mutual fund because these types of funds share many of the same advantages and disadvantages. The features that distinguish a segregated fund from a mutual fund include principal protection, a death benefit guarantee, and creditor protection. When assessing the value of these features, it is important to consider the additional costs associated with them. In general, a segregated fund will underperform its mutual fund equivalent as a result of the difference in MERs.

REVIEW QUESTIONS

1. What is a pooled investment fund? Provide some examples of the types of pooled investment funds.

2. List and describe the benefits of pooled investment funds? What is marketability?

3. Define and differentiate among equity, bond, and balanced mutual funds.

4. What is a money market fund? How is it different from equity, bond, and balanced mutual funds?

5. In addition to diversification, economies of scale, and marketability, list and describe three other advantages of mutual funds.

6. List and describe four disadvantages of investing in mutual funds.

7. What is liquidity? What is the difference between marketability and liquidity?

8. What is net asset value (NAV)? What is the formula for net asset value per share (NAVPS)?

9. What is an open-end mutual fund? What types of companies usually manage open-end funds? Describe how these funds work on a day-to-day basis.

10. What is a closed-end fund? Describe how closed-end funds function.

11. Define and differentiate among no-load, front-end load, and back-end load mutual funds. What is a declining redemption schedule?

12. How do loads affect a fund's return? Why do some investors purchase load funds? How does an investor purchase a no-load fund?

13. What is the management expense ratio (MER)? How is it calculated?

14. List and describe the components of the MER.

15. Differentiate among growth, small-cap, mid-cap, dividend, and balanced growth and income funds.

16. Define and describe sector funds.

17. What are index funds? Why has their popularity increased?

18. What is tracking error? What does a relatively high tracking error suggest?

19. Explain how index funds can also offer tax advantages.

20. Define and describe international funds. What is the difference between a global fund and an international fund?

21. Describe the types of investments that may be held in a Canadian bond fund.

22. Why may a high-yield bond fund offer a higher than expected?

23. What is an index bond fund? What types of indices are tracked by an index bond fund?

24. What are global bond funds?

25. What is exchange rate risk? How does it impact the value of a global bond fund for a Canadian investor?

26. What are the different maturity classifications for bond mutual funds?

27. List the four ways in which a mutual fund can generate returns for investors. In what two ways can these distributions be given to investors?

28. How do you calculate the capital gain from redeeming shares?

29. Is an equity mutual fund's past performance necessarily an indicator of future performance?

30. What is market risk?

31. Describe the trade-off between the expected return and risk of equity funds.

32. What is interest rate risk? What type of bond is the most sensitive to interest rate risk?

33. What is default risk? What types of bond funds are the most sensitive to default risk?

34. Describe the trade-off between the expected return and risk of bond funds.

35. What three things should an investor determine before choosing mutual fund investments?

36. What is a Fund Facts document? How soon must a Fund Facts document be provided to an investor who has invested in a mutual fund?

37. What nine categories of information are covered in a Fund Facts document?

38. Where can an investor find price quotations for open-end funds? What information will be provided in a quotation for open-end funds?

39. List the similarities and differences between ETFs and mutual funds.

40. Describe the three unique features of segregated funds relative to mutual funds.

FINANCIAL PLANNING PROBLEMS

MyLab Finance Financial Planning Problems marked with a 🌐 can be found in MyLab Finance.

1. The market value of securities and the current liabilities for a mutual fund are $483 450 000 and $18 070 900, respectively. What is the net asset value per share (NAVPS) for this mutual fund if there are 40 million shares outstanding?

2. Calculate the NAVPS for a mutual fund with the following values:

Market value of securities in the portfolio	$1.2 billion
Liabilities of the fund	$37 million
Shares outstanding	60 million

🌐 3. Hope invested $9000 in a mutual fund at a time when the price per share was $30. The fund has a load fee of $300. How many shares did she purchase?

🌐 4. If Hope (from Problem 3) had invested the same amount of money in a no-load fund with the same price, how many shares could she have purchased?

🌐 5. Hope later sells her mutual fund for $37 per share. What would her return be in each of the above cases (Problems 3 and 4)?

🌐 6. Hunter invested $7000 in a load mutual fund. The load is 7 percent. When Hunter purchased the shares, the NAVPS was $70. A year later, Hunter sold at a NAVPS of $68. What is Hunter's return from selling his mutual fund?

7. Almost three years ago, Forrest purchased shares in Numera Canadian Equity Fund, a back-end load mutual fund. Forrest's investment is currently worth $34 400. He has decided that he would like to sell his shares. Using the declining redemption schedule provided in Exhibit 13.2, determine the back-end load fee that Forrest will have to pay and how much he will receive after paying the fee. NOTE: The amount of the fee is based on the value of the fund when it is redeemed.

🌐 8. Mark owns a mutual fund that has an NAVPS of $45.00 and expenses of $1.45 per share. What is the management expense ratio for Mark's mutual fund?

🌐 9. Rena purchased 200 shares of an equity mutual fund. During the year she received $3 per share in dividend distributions, $2 per share in capital gain distributions, and capital gains of $1100 when she sold the fund after owning it for eight months. What are the tax consequences of Rena's ownership of this equity fund? Rena is in a 40 percent marginal tax bracket.

CHALLENGE QUESTIONS

1. Tamara purchased 500 shares of an international equity mutual fund at $9.00 per share. During the past year, the mutual fund paid dividends of $0.88 per share and had a capital gains distribution of $0.65 per share. The fund is currently trading at $9.70 per share. If Tamara does not sell the mutual fund, what is the return on her investment, including her unrealized capital gain, on a before-tax basis? If Tamara sells the mutual fund, what is the return on her investment on an after-tax basis? Tamara is in a 40 percent marginal tax bracket.

2. At the beginning of last year, Thomas purchased 200 shares of the Web.com fund at a NAVPS of $26 and automatically reinvested all distributions. Because of reinvesting, Thomas ended the year with 265 shares of the fund with a NAVPS $32.20. What was his total percentage return for the year on this investment?

ETHICS   ETHICAL DILEMMA

To obtain more business, mutual fund companies have made it easier for investors to switch between mutual funds within the same family. For example, if you buy the XYZ Equity Growth Fund, you are able to switch to the XYZ Equity

Value Fund at no charge. This feature is particularly beneficial for investors who purchase funds that have a back-end load, since these funds normally charge a fee if you redeem the investment within a certain period of time. In many cases, the same fund may be redeemed as a no-load fund or as a back-end load fund. Investment advisers normally earn more commission for selling a back-end load fund. However, the regular annual service fee on a no-load fund is higher than it is on a back-end load fund. As a result of the free switching rule, some advisers have recommended a back-end load fund and then transferred a portion of the investment during the following year into an identical fund that has a no-load fee structure. By doing this, the adviser is able to maximize his or her commission at the beginning of the trade and during the period that the investor owns the investment.

a. Discuss the ethics of this practice.
b. As a consequence of this practice, what is the impact on the MER over the long term? Discuss fully.

FINANCIAL PLANNING ONLINE EXERCISES

1. Go to www.fundlibrary.com

   a. Under Tools, click on Fund Grade A List. This tool shows all funds that have an "A" fund grade rating. Click on one of the funds in the list. What information is displayed for this fund? Describe how each piece of information can be used to help determine whether this fund is an appropriate investment for various types of investors

   b. Record the name of one of the funds from the list. Under Tools, click on Chart Maker. Type in the full or partial name of the mutual fund you selected and click on Search. Then click on Chart it beside your fund's name. A chart will be created comparing the performance of the fund you selected against a similar index benchmark and the average performance for all other similar funds. How does your fund compare? Change the chart period to five years. How does your fund compare in the last five years?

   c. Under Tools, click on Drawdown Charts. Type in the full or partial name of the mutual fund you selected and click on Search. Then click on Chart it beside your fund's name. What does this chart tell you? How can you use this information to determine whether you should invest in this fund?

2. Go to www.globefund.com.

   a. This website provides research tools to help you select among mutual funds. You can choose a fund based on any number of criteria. Click on Fund Filter. Select mutual funds based on the following two criteria: Asset Class: Canadian Equity and MER = 2.0%. Click on Get Results. How many funds match your criteria?

   b. Refine your search criteria. Return to the main page. After re-entering the above two criteria, add the following criterion: Load Type: No Load. Click on Get Results. How many funds match your criteria?

   c. Click on the Long-term tab. Put a check mark in the box beside those mutual funds that have a 15-year performance history. Click on Update Fundlist. Return to the main page. Under Tracking Tools, click on View Fundlist. A list of the funds you have selected for further analysis will be generated.

PSYCHOLOGY OF PERSONAL FINANCE: Investing in Mutual Funds

1. Investors are naturally attracted to mutual funds and similar investments that perform well. However, they should be suspicious when a fund reports consistently superior performance, even when many other types of investment funds are struggling. The high performance may be due to fraudulent reporting. Investors want to believe that the reports are true even when they should be suspicious. Describe your behaviour when investing. Are you suspicious when a fund suggests that its performance is always better than that of other funds?

2. Read one practical article of how psychology affects decisions when investing in mutual funds. You can easily retrieve possible articles by doing an online search using the terms "psychology" and "investing in mutual funds." Summarize the main points of the article.

MINI-CASE 1: Types of Mutual Funds

Match the following types of mutual funds to the appropriate investments that would be found in each portfolio.

1) Growth funds	a) Stocks of foreign companies
2) Canadian bond funds	b) Stocks of companies that are environmentally aware
3) Balanced growth and income funds	c) Market basket that represents the S&P/TSX
4) Sector funds	d) 65 percent of stocks from the technology stocks
5) High-yield bond funds	e) Dividend paying blue-chip stocks
6) Index funds	f) Mix of stocks, bonds, and money market securities
7) Dividend funds	g) High growth and high P/E companies
8) International equity funds	h) Income investments that are subject to exchange rate risk
9) Global bond funds	i) Government of Canada bonds and other securities
10) Small-cap funds	j) Stocks that trade on the TSX Venture exchange
11) Ethical funds	k) Low investment grade bonds

MINI-CASE 2: Mutual Fund Selection

Rick recently received $15 000 for the movie rights to his new book. He has always been interested in investing, but until now lacked sufficient resources. Rick has followed several telecommunications stocks over the past year. The share prices have fluctuated dramatically, but Rick is definitely interested in this type of stock. He feels that telecommunication companies offer great possibilities. When you asked Rick whether he was comfortable with the risk associated with such an investment, he indicated that he was if superior returns could be obtained. Given the fact that Rick has only $15 000 to invest, explain why he should consider investing in mutual funds rather than individual stocks. Instead of mutual funds, should he consider ETFs? Explain. What type(s) of equity mutual fund(s) would you recommend Rick invest in? Why?

Study Guide

Circle the correct answer and then check the answers in the back of the book to chart your progress.

Multiple Choice

1. All of the following are advantages of owning a mutual fund, except:
   a. You can invest in a broadly diversified portfolio with a small initial investment.
   b. Your investments reflect the decisions of experienced professionals who have access to the best research available.
   c. Mutual funds simplify the process of record keeping because the mutual fund company

   will send you a statement on a regular basis.
   d. Mutual funds are designed for sophisticated investors seeking short-term capital gains only.

2. Mutual funds, which sell units directly to investors and repurchase units from investors who want to sell, are called:
   a. Open-market funds.
   b. Open-end funds.

c. Closed-end funds.

d. Fair value funds.

3. Which of the following is true about MERs?

a. MERs only include manager and sales expenses.

b. Mutual funds with lower MERs tend to outperform those with higher MERs.

c. All types of mutual funds have similar MERs.

d. You need to subtract the MER from the posted return to figure out performance.

4. A mutual fund that aggressively seeks capital growth:

a. Will have an MER that is approximately the same as a T-bill fund.

b. Will have an MER that is higher than a global fund.

c. Will have an MER similar to that of a fixed-income fund.

d. Will have an MER that reflects the increased costs of research.

5. _____mutual funds sell shares directly to investors and redeem those shares whenever investors wish to redeem them.

a. Open-end

b. Equity

c. Bond

d. Closed-end

6. "Since they engage in less trading than most other mutual funds, they generate a limited amount of capital gains that must be distributed to shareholders." This statement refers to which of the following types of funds?

a. Bond funds

b. Dividend funds

c. Index funds

d. Growth funds

7. If Raymond does not want to pay any fees to invest in mutual funds, he should pick:

a. No-load mutual funds.

b. Front-end load mutual funds.

c. Back-end load mutual funds.

d. Zero-fee mutual funds.

8. If Rebecca's mutual fund has a sales charge schedule saying that if the fund is sold within the first year, the sales charge is 6 percent and if it is sold in the third year, the sales charge becomes 4.5 percent, Rebecca's mutual fund has a:

a. Low load.

b. Discount fee.

c. Broker commission.

d. Declining redemption schedule.

9. When you initially purchase a mutual fund, a Fund Facts document must be provided to you within _____of your purchase.

a. 24 hours

b. three business days

c. seven days

d. 48 hours

10. In order to select appropriate mutual funds for yourself, you should determine your investment objectives and evaluate your risk tolerance. Then, the final step is to:

a. Review and compare key information from the relevant Fund Facts documents.

b. Review and compare key information from the simplified prospectuses.

c. Open an account with a broker.

d. Consult a certified financial planner.

11. A mutual fund that invests only in shares of gold mining companies would be called a:

a. Growth fund.

b. Small-cap fund.

c. Canadian equity fund.

d. Sector fund.

12. Given the following mutual fund price quotation, determine which of the following statements most accurately reflects the data.

Fund	$ NAVPS	$ Ch	Yr %Ch
ABC Health Care Fund	21.95	+0.11	−1.1

a. ABC Health Care Fund has a net asset value per share of $21.95. The net change in the NAVPS during the previous day was +0.11. The fund has generated a return of −1.1 percent since the start of the calendar year.

b. ABC Health Care Fund has a net asset value of $21.95. The net change in the NAVPS during the previous day was +0.11. The fund has generated a return of −1.1 percent since the start of the calendar year.

c. ABC Health Care Fund has a net asset value per share of $21.95. The net change in the NAVPS during the previous week was +0.11. The fund has generated a return of −1.1 percent since the start of the calendar year.

d. ABC Health Care Fund has a net asset value of $21.95. The net change in the NAVPS during the previous week was +0.11. The fund has generated a return of −1.1 percent since the start of the calendar year.

13. Your return from investing in _____ is primarily affected by _____.
    a. a Canadian equity fund; Canadian interest rates
    b. an Australian bond fund; Australian interest rates and the value of the Australian dollar
    c. a European equity fund; European stock markets and the value of the Canadian dollar
    d. a Canadian equity fund; Canadian money markets

14. What is the most important difference between an index mutual fund and an exchange traded fund (ETF)?
    a. ETFs are better managed.
    b. ETFs trade like stocks.
    c. There are more types of ETFs.
    d. ETFs have higher MERs.

15. The potential benefits of investing in a segregated fund include all of the following, except:
    a. Segregated funds offer a guarantee on your deposits when the contract matures.
    b. Segregated funds offer a guarantee on your deposits when the policy owner dies.
    c. Segregated fund contracts are normally exempt from seizure by creditors in the event that the policy owner declares bankruptcy.
    d. Segregated funds are more expensive than similar mutual funds.

True/False

1. True or False? One disadvantage of mutual funds is that you could invest in a well-diversified mutual fund that is invested in a group of poorly performing companies rather than good ones.

2. True or False? The NAVPS is determined by dividing the number of shares outstanding by the NAV.

3. True or False? Unlike an open-end fund, shares of a closed-end fund are purchased and sold on stock exchanges.

4. True or False? A declining redemption schedule is associated with a back-end load mutual fund.

5. True or False? Recent studies on mutual funds have found that no-load funds outperform load funds on average, even when ignoring the fees paid on a load fund.

6. True or False? Mutual funds with relatively lower expenses tend to outperform other funds.

7. True or False? Index funds have become more popular because of very low transaction costs.

8. True or False? Exchange rate risk is the result of a decrease in the value of a foreign bond because the currency denominating the bond weakens against the Canadian dollar.

9. True or False? Short-term bonds are more sensitive to changes in interest rates than long-term bonds.

10. True or False? Equity mutual funds that have a lower expected return are also likely to have lower expected risk.

11. True or False? The most important expense statistic mentioned in the Fund Facts document is the back-end load.

12. True or False? When investors want to assess the performance of a mutual fund, one technique is to compare the return on that mutual fund to the average return for the same type of mutual fund.

13. True or False? Diversification among bond funds is not an effective means of reducing exposure to interest rate risk.

14. True or False? Similar to a mutual fund, ETFs are purchased in real time.

15. True or False? With respect to segregated funds, the determination of the value of the death benefit guarantee is similar to that of the maturity guarantee.

PART 4 BRAD MACDONALD—A CONTINUING CASE

Between watching a financial news network on cable, reading articles in some business magazines, and listening to a co-worker recount his story of doubling his portfolio in six months, Brad is now convinced that his financial future lies in the stock market. His co-worker's windfall was in internet stocks, so Brad has focused his modest portfolio on a highly speculative internet stock. Although owning one stock does not provide adequate diversification, Brad believes that this stock will maximize his growth potential.

He has heard that it might be a good idea to buy bonds and/or mutual funds for diversification purposes, and recently, a friend suggested that Brad consider purchasing exchange traded funds (ETFs) instead of mutual funds. Brad is unfamiliar with these investments. Besides, he finds investments like bonds, mutual funds, or similar types of investments boring and their returns too low.

P Pearson

| MyLab | Finance

Although ETFs are unfamiliar to Brad, he did read an article on how trading online can increase his return, and he's interested in your opinion. Brad admits that he has virtually no knowledge of investing or time to do research, but a broker gives him many "hot tips." He believes that is all he really needs. As such, Brad thinks that ETFs may not be the best option for him.

Brad has heard about misleading financial statements issued by some firms, but believes that even if companies misstate their financial condition, this will not affect their stock price.

Brad would like to hear what you think of his plan.

Case Questions

1. Comment on each of the following elements of Brad's plan:

   a. Level of diversification

   b. View on bonds and not including them in his portfolio

   c. View on mutual funds and/or ETFs, and not including them in his portfolio

   d. Trading online

   e. Source of information ("hot tips")

2. Given Brad's lack of knowledge of investing and his limited time to learn or do research, what might be the best option for Brad to pursue and still get the benefit of the potential growth in the internet sector?

3. What factors will influence Brad's asset allocation? Based on these factors, what might be a suitable sample portfolio for Brad?

4. How would your answer to the sample portfolio part of Question 3 be affected if Brad were

   a. 50 years old?

   b. 70 years old?

5. Explain to Brad why misleading financial statements may be more common than he believes and why misleading financial statements can negatively affect a stock's price.

Use the worksheets available on MyLab Finance to complete this case.

PART 5

Retirement and Estate Planning

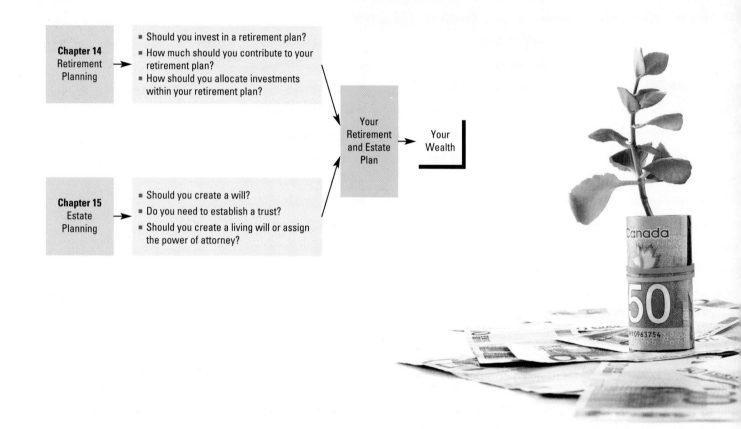

Chapter 14
Retirement
Planning

- Should you invest in a retirement plan?
- How much should you contribute to your retirement plan?
- How should you allocate investments within your retirement plan?

Chapter 15
Estate
Planning

- Should you create a will?
- Do you need to establish a trust?
- Should you create a living will or assign the power of attorney?

Your
Retirement
and Estate
Plan

Your
Wealth

The chapters in this part explain how you can protect the wealth you accumulate over time through effective financial planning. Chapter 14 explains how to plan effectively for your retirement so that you can maintain your wealth and live comfortably. Chapter 15 explains how you can pass on as much of your estate as possible to your heirs.

Retirement Planning

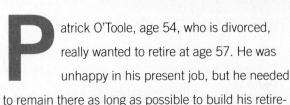

Monkey Business Images/Shutterstock

Patrick O'Toole, age 54, who is divorced, really wanted to retire at age 57. He was unhappy in his present job, but he needed to remain there as long as possible to build his retirement account. Even if he did build his retirement account, he was unsure as to whether or not retirement at age 57 was even possible.

First, his mortgage still had 15 years of payments remaining. Second, after his divorce, he had only $225 000 accumulated in his registered retirement savings plan (RRSP) and $20 000 in his tax-free savings account (TFSA). Third, he had no idea as to what sort of retirement income he could generate from government benefit programs and his personal savings.

Three years later, at age 57, Patrick had refinanced his mortgage and had only 10 years of payments remaining. In addition, his RRSP had accumulated to $315 000 and his TFSA stood at $25 000. He now felt that he was in a position to begin withdrawing money from the Canada Pension Plan (CPP).

> ### QUESTIONS:
> 1. At what age could Patrick begin withdrawing money from the CPP? Old Age Security (OAS)? What is the financial impact, if any, of withdrawing money early from either, or both, of these government programs?
> 2. What are the advantages and disadvantages of using RRSPs and/or TFSAs as retirement savings alternatives?
> 3. If Patrick's RRSP and TFSA each grow at 5.5 percent per year, compounded monthly, how much can he withdraw in equal monthly instalments from each plan from age 57 to age 85? Assume Patrick makes no new contributions.

THE LEARNING OBJECTIVES OF THIS CHAPTER ARE TO:

1. Describe the role of Old Age Security

2. Describe the role of the Canada Pension Plan

3. Explain the difference between defined-benefit and defined-contribution retirement plans

4. Describe types of individual retirement savings plans

5. Describe types of retirement income conversion options

6. Present the key decisions you must make regarding retirement plans

7. Illustrate how to estimate the savings you will have in your retirement account at the time you retire

OLD AGE SECURITY

L.O.1

Recall from Chapter 4 that Old Age Security (OAS) is a federal program, funded by income tax and other tax revenues, that makes payments to you upon retirement (subject to age and other requirements). In addition to this program, the federal government sponsors a contribution-based public pension system known as the Canada Pension Plan (CPP). Together, these federally sponsored programs are intended to ensure that you receive some income once you retire, regardless of whether you have personally saved for your retirement. As such, OAS and CPP can be thought of as the foundation of retirement planning. However, on their own, these programs do not provide sufficient income to support the lifestyles of most individuals. Therefore, additional retirement planning is necessary to ensure that you can live comfortably when you retire. Before discussing other means of retirement planning, we will describe how the public pension systems function.

Old Age Security (OAS) Program

Old Age Security (OAS) Pension. The first level of Canada's public retirement income system consists of a group of benefits that are funded by general tax revenues. The fact that these benefits are funded by general tax revenues and are not based on personal contributions is an important distinction to make. Since you do not have to contribute to the Old Age Security (OAS) program, the only qualifying criteria are age and residency requirements. To receive the OAS pension, a pensioner must have attained the age of 65. You may defer your OAS pension for up to 60 months, or 5 years. In this case your monthly pension payment would be increased by 0.6 percent for every month that you defer your payment, up to a maximum of 36 percent at age 70. For example, Tarlochan turned 65 in December 2017. If he decides to delay his OAS pension for 5 years, his monthly income will increase by 36 percent. If he was eligible for a monthly payment of $578.53, his increased monthly payment would be $786.80, calculated as 578.53×1.36.

With respect to residency, if you have lived in Canada for at least 40 years since turning age 18, you will receive the full OAS pension. You may be eligible to receive a partial pension if you have lived in Canada for fewer than 40 years but more than 10 years since turning age 18. In general, the partial pension is equal to the number of years you have lived in Canada since turning 18 multiplied by 0.025 (or 1/40) multiplied by the OAS maximum monthly benefit. For example, Sheliza immigrated to Canada when she was 40 years old. By age 65, she will have lived in Canada for 25 years since turning age 18. Exhibit 14.1 highlights the payment rates for the different benefits available under the OAS program. The maximum monthly OAS pension for the period April 2017 to June 2017 was $578.53. Therefore, Sheliza is eligible for a partial OAS pension of $361.58, calculated as $25 \times 0.025 \times \$578.53$. The OAS system, which was created in 1952, represents Canada's largest public pension system. Over time, the rules for the OAS pension have become more complex. However, the general rules outlined above provide a foundation on which you can reliably approximate how much OAS pension you will receive in the future.

EXHIBIT 14.1   Old Age Security Benefit Payment Rates (April–June 2017)

Type of Benefit	Recipient	Maximum Monthly Benefit	Maximum Annual Income
OAS Pension	All recipients	$ 578.53	See OAS Clawback
GIS	Single person	$ 864.09	$17 544
	Spouse of pensioner	$ 520.17	$23 184
	Spouse of non-pensioner	$ 864.09	$42 048
	Spouse of allowance recipient	$ 520.17	$42 048
Allowance	All recipients	$1098.70	$32 448
Allowance for the survivor	All recipients	$1309.67	$23 616

Source: Data from Government of Canada, "Old Age Security Payment Amounts," https://www.canada.ca/en/services/benefits/publicpensions/cpp/old-age-security/payments.html (accessed May 25, 2017).

OAS Clawback. All of the benefits available under the OAS program are subject to a "means test." That is, if your net income exceeds a certain amount, the benefits you will receive from the OAS program will be reduced. With respect to the OAS pension, this reduction in benefits is referred to as an OAS clawback. In 2017, the OAS pension was reduced by $0.15 for every dollar of net income above $74 788 that you earned. If your net income exceeded $119 615 in 2017, you would have to repay all of your OAS pension.

Guaranteed Income Supplement (GIS). In addition to the OAS pension, low-income pensioners may qualify for supplemental benefits. In general, a single, divorced, or widowed pensioner who is at least 65 years of age and whose sole source of income is the OAS pension will also receive the full GIS benefit of $864.09 (see Exhibit 14.1). If a pensioner receives any income other than the OAS pension, the GIS benefit is reduced by $0.50 for every $1 of additional income. This is referred to as the GIS clawback. Exhibit 14.1 illustrates that the GIS benefit will be reduced to nothing if other income reaches $17 544. Otherwise, for 2017, the combined OAS pension and GIS benefit would result in a monthly pension of $1442.62, or $17 311.44 on an annual basis.

For married couples where both spouses are receiving OAS pensions, each spouse may be eligible for a maximum GIS benefit of $520.17.

EXAMPLE	Martha is a 66-year-old OAS pensioner married to Fred, who is a 65-year-old OAS pensioner. Both of them were born and raised in Canada. They have no other sources of income besides their respective OAS pensions. Martha's total income for the month would be $1098.70 ($578.53 + $520.17). Similarly, Fred's total income for the month would be $1098.70. As a result, their combined annual income from OAS and GIS would be $26 368.80 (calculated as [$1098.70 × 12] × 2). The maximum annual income column in Exhibit 14.1 indicates that if either Martha or Fred has annual income other than OAS pension that is greater than $23 616, she or he would not be eligible to receive the GIS. This maximum annual income figure applies to each of them individually.

In Exhibit 14.1, "spouse of non-pensioner" refers to a situation in which both spouses are over age 65 but one spouse does not receive either an OAS pension or the GIS. "Spouse of allowance recipient" refers to a situation in which one spouse receives the OAS pension, while the other spouse is between the ages of 60 and 64 and receives the allowance benefit, which is discussed next.

Allowance Benefit. The allowance benefit is available to the spouse or common-law partner of a pensioner who is receiving or is eligible to receive the OAS pension and the GIS. To be eligible for the allowance benefit, the spouse or common-law partner must be between the ages of 60 and 64. In the previous example, if Fred was only 63, he would not be eligible to receive the OAS pension or the GIS. In this case, Martha and Fred would only receive half of the $26 368.80 benefit amount above, or $13 184.40. The allowance benefit was designed to reduce the financial burden that would result from only one low-income pensioner being eligible to receive OAS program benefits. Notice that if Fred is only 63 and is receiving the maximum monthly allowance benefit of $1098.70, the total amount of income the couple receives is $26 368.80, which is the same amount they would have received if Fred was over age 65 and receiving both the OAS pension and the GIS.

Allowance for the Survivor Benefit. The allowance for the survivor benefit is available to the spouse or common-law partner of a deceased pensioner who was receiving the OAS pension. To be eligible for the allowance for the survivor benefit, the surviving spouse or common-law partner must be between the ages of 60 and 64. This benefit was designed to provide benefits to the surviving spouse of a low-income senior.

Applying for Benefits. OAS program benefits do not automatically start once you have attained the appropriate age to receive benefits. You must apply to receive these benefits.

Inflation Protection. The OAS pension, GIS, and the allowance benefit are adjusted for inflation every January, April, July, and October.

Taxation of Benefits. The OAS pension is a taxable benefit. The GIS, allowance benefit, and allowance for the survivor benefit are tax-free.

| **myth** or **fact** | I don't make enough money to save for my retirement.

Go to:
www.cppib.com/en/home.html

This website provides information on the CPP Investment Board and its policies and the financial highlights of the performance of your federal pension plan.

CANADA PENSION PLAN

L.O.2

Canada Pension Plan (CPP) Program

Canada Pension Plan. The second level of Canada's retirement income system consists of a contributory pension plan program called the Canada Pension Plan (CPP). The amount of CPP benefit you are eligible to receive is based on the dollar value of your contributions and the number of years you contribute to the plan. You may apply to receive benefits as early as age 60 and as late as age 70. Under the CPP, normal retirement is considered to be age 65. In 2017, your CPP will be reduced by 0.60 percent for each month you take it earlier than normal retirement. On the other hand, your CPP will be increased by 0.70 percent for each month you take it later than normal retirement. If the amount of CPP you are eligible to receive is different than the amount your spouse is eligible to receive, you may benefit from a pension assignment. A **pension assignment** occurs when a married or common-law couple decides to share their CPP retirement pensions in order to reduce their income taxes. To apply for a pension assignment, both individuals must be at least 60 years old and be receiving a CPP pension. In addition to the CPP retirement benefit, the survivors of a CPP contributor who has passed away may be eligible to receive survivor benefits.

   In general, individuals over the age of 18 who earn more than $3500 in a calendar year must contribute to the CPP. Under CPP rules, the first $3500 of annual income, also known as your year's basic exemption (YBE), is exempt from the CPP contribution calculation. Once your income rises above the YBE, the contribution rate is 9.9 percent of pensionable earnings. **Pensionable earnings** refers to the amount of income you earn between the YBE and the year's maximum pensionable earnings (YMPE). For the 2017 calendar year, the YMPE was $55 300. The CPP contribution rate is split between employees and their employers. As a result, the CPP contribution rate for employees and employers is 4.95 percent each. Self-employed individuals must contribute to the

pension assignment
Occurs when a married or common-law couple decides to share their CPP retirement pensions in order to reduce their income taxes.

pensionable earnings
The amount of income you earn between the year's basic exemption (YBE) and the year's maximum pensionable earnings (YMPE).

CPP based on the full contribution rate of 9.9 percent. In recent years, the YBE has remained at $3500. The YMPE increases every year based on a formula that takes into account the growth in average income in Canada.

EXAMPLE

Colleen works as an employee for Dynamex Industries. During 2017, she earned income of $60 000. Her spouse, Chris, is a self-employed carpenter. His earned income in 2017 was $38 000.

Colleen's CPP contribution amount would be calculated as follows:

(The lesser of Annual Income or YMPE − YBE) × 4.95%
= ($55 300 − $3500) × 4.95%
= $2564.10

Chris's CPP contribution amount would be calculated as follows:

(The lesser of Annual Income or YMPE − YBE) × 9.9%
= ($38 000 − $3500) × 9.9%
= $3415.50

CPP contributions are deducted by your employer at each pay period. Your employer sends your contribution, along with its matching contribution to the Canada Revenue Agency (CRA). Investment decisions with respect to the money deposited in the CPP are made by the CPP Investment Board.

CPP Benefit Amount. As mentioned, the amount of CPP benefit you are eligible to receive is based on the dollar value of your contributions and the number of years you contribute to the plan. Since the dollar value of your contributions will fluctuate during the course of your career, you are allowed to exclude 17 percent of your lowest earnings years from the final calculation. In addition, you are allowed to exclude those years of employment during which you were raising children under the age of seven and any months during which you were collecting a CPP disability pension.

After taking into account these excluded periods, your CPP benefit is calculated. Although the CPP calculation is beyond the scope of this text, you can request a Statement of Contributions from the federal government. In addition to providing you with a history of your CPP contributions, this statement provides individuals who have reached age 30 with an estimate of their CPP retirement pension. For 2017, the maximum monthly CPP retirement pension was $1114.17, or $13 370 per year.

Applying for Benefits. CPP retirement benefits do not automatically begin once you have attained the appropriate age to receive benefits. You must apply to receive these benefits. As mentioned, you may apply to receive benefits as early as age 60 and as late as age 70. The decision to apply for CPP retirement benefits should not be taken lightly. Depending on your personal circumstances, you may wish to apply early or to delay application to some point in the future. Exhibit 14.2 highlights the amount of total CPP benefits you would receive under three different scenarios.

Go to:
www.servicecanada.gc.ca/
eng/services/pensions/
cpp/index.shtml

This website provides
an online form you can use to
request your CPP Statement
of Contributions.

EXAMPLE

Mark has decided to apply for early CPP benefit, Janet will apply for CPP at the normal retirement age, and Bob will apply for CPP at age 70. The annual CPP benefit amount is calculated using the 2017 maximum monthly CPP retirement pension of $1114.17. Inflation is assumed to be 2 percent per year. Exhibit 14.2 illustrates that Janet will receive an annual CPP benefit of $13 370 when she turns age 65. This represents 100 percent of the amount she is eligible for, calculated as $1114.17 × 12 = $13 370. Notice that Mark receives less than this amount ($8557) and that Bob receives more than this amount ($18 985). As mentioned earlier, in 2017, benefits are reduced by 0.60 percent for every month that you take benefits early and are increased by 0.70 percent for every month that you take benefits late, up to age 70. Mark is taking his CPP at age 60, which is 60 months earlier than the normal retirement age of 65. As a result, his CPP benefit is reduced by 36 percent, calculated as 0.60×60 months. Bob is taking his CPP at age 70, which is 60 months later than the normal retirement age of 65. As a result, his CPP benefit is increased by 42 percent, calculated as 0.7×60 months.

Exhibit 14.2 shows that even though Janet and Bob start receiving CPP benefits later than Mark, the total CPP retirement pension received by Janet and Bob will eventually be greater than the amount received by Mark. In Janet's case, her total CPP benefit will exceed that of Mark by age 75. Bob will exceed Mark's total CPP benefit by age 80, and he will pass Janet by age 84. The amount of CPP you will collect over a period of time should not be the only consideration as to when you apply for CPP benefits. Exhibit 14.2 implies that Mark, Janet, and Bob will each live until at least age 86. Although this may not be the case, Exhibit 14.2 does illustrate that if you have other retirement income options, you should carefully consider the timing of your CPP retirement pension application.

EXHIBIT 14.2 Accumulated CPP Retirement Pension

Age	Mark Early Retirement	Janet Normal Retirement	Bob Late Retirement
60	$ 8 557	—	—
61	17 285	—	—
62	26 187	—	—
63	35 268	—	—
64	44 530	—	—
65	53 978	13 370	—
66	63 614	27 007	—
67	73 443	40 918	—
68	83 469	55 106	—
69	93 695	69 578	—
70	104 126	84 340	18 985
71	114 765	99 397	38 351
72	125 617	114 755	58 103
73	136 686	130 420	78 251
74	147 977	146 398	98 801
75	**159 493**	**162 696**	**119 763**
76	171 240	179 320	141 143
77	183 222	196 277	162 952
78	195 443	213 572	185 196
79	207 908	231 214	207 885
80	**220 623**	**249 208**	**231 029**
81	233 593	267 562	254 635
82	246 821	286 283	278 713
83	260 315	305 379	303 273
84	**274 078**	**324 857**	**328 323**
85	288 116	344 724	353 875
86	302 435	364 989	379 938

Inflation Protection. CPP retirement pensions are adjusted for inflation every January.

Taxation of Benefits. The CPP retirement pension is a taxable benefit. Employee contributions to the CPP can be claimed as a non-refundable tax credit. Employer contributions are a deductible business expense and are not considered a taxable benefit for the employee. Self-employed individuals can claim both the tax credit and the expense deduction.

Concern about Retirement Benefits in the Future

The ongoing success of OAS and the CPP is critical to many Canadians. According to Statistics Canada, these public pension plans represented more than 40 percent of seniors' total income in 2010. Based on 2017 benefit payout rates, a single pensioner who retires with no private savings will receive approximately $23 996.92 per year in retirement income. This calculation assumes that a single pensioner receives 100 percent of the OAS and CPP amounts and a portion of the GIS, which would be reduced as a result of having received CPP income. For many Canadians, the amount of income provided from these programs is simply not enough. A June 2007 study completed by the University of Waterloo suggested that "two-thirds of Canadian households expecting to retire in 2030 are not saving at levels required to meet necessary living expenses." By themselves, the OAS and CPP programs provide only a modest income base and are not intended to replace personal retirement savings plans.

The concern with respect to retirement benefits should be based on two important questions:

- Will government-sponsored benefits, such as the OAS and CPP programs, be available to future generations?
- What other retirement income options are available to Canadian employees?

Fortunately, any individual who has a savings ethic should be able to reach his or her retirement goals. First, given the expected reliance of so many Canadians on the OAS and CPP programs, it is hard to imagine a situation where either of these federally sponsored programs will cease to exist or substantially reduce benefits to retirees. In addition, reforms to the CPP that were announced in June 2016 will provide this program with enhanced long-term stability. First, starting in 2019, a five-year phased-in increase to the CPP contribution rate will result in an increase to employee contributions from 4.95 percent up to 5.95 percent. Second, the year's maximum pensionable earnings (YMPE) will be extended more quickly up to 2025. These changes will allow for a larger CPP retirement benefit payout for future retirees.

The more important question that needs to be addressed by today's employee is this: What other retirement income options are available? OAS and CPP do provide a base, but it would be difficult for most people to have the retirement lifestyle they would like on an income of a little more than $20 000 per year. For this reason, it is important to understand Canada's private pension system so that you can implement a savings program that will build on the benefits you receive from government-sponsored plans. Canada's private pension system is composed of two parts: employer-sponsored retirement plans and individual retirement savings plans.

FREE APPS for Personal Finance

Estimating Your Time Until Retirement

Application:

The Retirement countdown app indicates how much time (to the second) you have left until retirement.

EMPLOYER-SPONSORED RETIREMENT PLANS

Employer-sponsored retirement plans are designed to help you save for retirement. In a non-contributory pension plan, your employer contributes money to a retirement account at each pay period. In a contributory pension plan, both the employer and the employee make contributions to the plan. According to pension legislation, your employer is required to fund at least 50 percent of the pension benefits that you earn. This money is not taxed until you withdraw it from the account. Any money you withdraw from the retirement account after you retire is taxed as ordinary income.

myth or **fact** You should be able to replace between 60 and 85 percent of your current income in retirement.

Employer-sponsored retirement plans are classified as defined-benefit or defined-contribution pension plans.

Defined-Benefit Pension Plans

Defined-benefit pension plans are employer-sponsored retirement plans that guarantee you a specific amount of income when you retire, based on your salary and years of employment. These plans may be contributory or non-contributory. The amount of contribution is based on actuarial values. Actuarial values are determined based on a set of assumptions, including that employees will retire at age 65, the retirement account will grow at 7 percent per year, and salaries will increase at 5.5 percent per year. These assumptions must be made in the case of a defined-benefit pension plan because the benefit at retirement is guaranteed. By making these assumptions, an actuary is able to work backwards and provide the employer with an assessment of how much must be contributed to fulfill the commitments made to employees. Since these assumptions are subject to change, an actuary reassesses the plan every three years. If there has been a substantial change in assumptions, the employer may have to increase their contributions; and, in the case of a contributory plan, the contributions of the employee.

At retirement, an employee will receive a pension benefit based on a specific formula. Exhibit 14.3 illustrates the specific formulas that are applied to defined-benefit pension plans. A flat benefit plan does not take into account the salary of the employee. Instead, a fixed benefit amount is earned by the employee based on the number of years of service. For example, an employee who earns a pension of $40 per month for each month of service during a 30-year career would receive annual pension income of $14 400, calculated as $40 × 12 months × 30 years. In general, the amount of pension income earned under a flat benefit plan is lower than the amount that may be earned under a unit benefit plan.

A unit benefit plan takes into account the earnings of an employee as well as years of service. There are three types of unit benefit plans: final average earnings plans, best average plans, and career average plans. All three types provide a pension that is usually expressed as a fixed percentage of earnings. Pension legislation requires that an employee cannot earn an annual pension income of more than 2 percent of their current earnings. In addition, the amount of current earnings that can be used to calculate the maximum annual pension income is restricted. For 2017, the maximum annual earnings for this calculation was $145 722. For example, if your 2017 income is $150 000, the maximum amount of pension you can earn for this year of employment is $2914, calculated as $145 722 × 0.02. If you work for the same employer for 30 years without any additional increases in income or changes to the pension plan, you will receive an annual pension income of $87 433 at retirement, calculated as $145 722 × 0.02 × 30. This is an example of a career average plan because your annual income for each year of your career is used to determine your pension income.

L.O.3

defined-benefit pension plan
An employer-sponsored retirement plan that guarantees you a specific amount of income when you retire, based on your salary and years of employment.

EXHIBIT 14.3   Registered Pension Plans

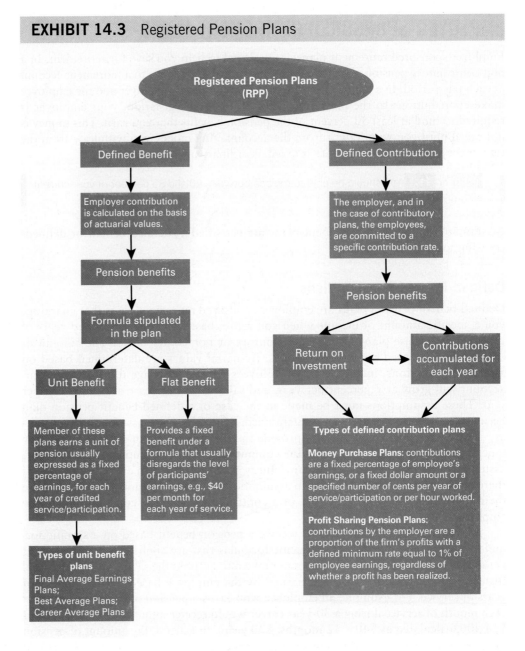

Bridgette is retiring after 30 years of employment with Barney, Smith, and Caulfield. Her employer-sponsored defined-benefit pension plan uses a best average earnings calculation to determine her benefit amount. For each year of service, Bridgette earns an annual pension income of 1.5 percent of her best average earnings. To calculate Bridgette's pension income, her best three consecutive years of income are taken into account. Bridgette's best earnings years occurred at the end of her career. The table below displays her income for the last five years of her career.

	2013	2014	2015	2016	2017
Annual Earnings	$55 000	$70 000	$90 000	$100 000	$65 000

Bridgette's best earnings years were 2014, 2015, and 2016. Her average earnings for this period were $86 667, calculated as ($70 000 + $90 000 + $100 000) ÷ 3. Her annual pension income will be $86 667 × 0.015 × 30 = $39 000.

In contrast, a final average earnings plan usually calculates your pension income based on your last three to five years of employment. Normally, your income will increase throughout your career. As a result, the final average earnings plan generally will result in a higher pension income than a career average plan. A variation of the final average earnings plan is the best average plan. Under this type of unit benefit plan, your employer will take into account your best three to five consecutive years of income when determining your pension benefit.

Pension legislation determines when employees are **vested**, which means that they have a claim to the money that has been reserved for them upon retirement, even if they leave their company. Contributions within an employer-sponsored retirement plan must be vested with the employee no later than two years after the employee has become a member of the pension plan. Once you are fully vested, the employer and employee contributions must be used to provide you with a retirement income at retirement. Vested pension benefits may be:

vested
Having a claim to the money in an employer-sponsored retirement account that has been reserved for you upon your retirement, even if you leave the company.

- Left in your former employer's pension account
- Transferred to your new employer, if it has an employer-sponsored pension plan that permits the transfer, or
- Transferred to an individual locked-in retirement account (LIRA)

One major advantage of a defined-benefit pension plan is that the benefits accumulate without the initiation of the employees. This helps employees who are not good savers and would spend this money if they were given it in the form of salary. Therefore, it ensures that these people save for their retirement. In this respect, a defined-benefit pension plan is similar to the CPP. Contributions are made by the employer in an amount that will ensure a predetermined future benefit. If the plan is a contributory plan, a deduction from your paycheque is made at every pay period. The funds in the pension plan are invested on your behalf. In its most basic interpretation, a defined-benefit pension plan is a retirement plan on automatic pilot because the employee does not have to make any retirement planning decisions. As well, such plans put the risk on the employer, as any shortfall in the plan with regard to benefit payments must be paid by the employer.

Taxation of Benefits. As discussed, pension plan income provides a taxable benefit. Employee contributions are tax deductible by the employee. Employer contributions are a deductible business expense and are not considered a taxable benefit for the employee.

Defined-Contribution Pension Plans

Defined-contribution pension plans are employer-sponsored retirement plans where the contribution rate, not the benefit amount, is based on a specific formula. Similar to defined-benefit pension plans, these plans may be contributory or non-contributory. As shown in Exhibit 14.3, the pension benefits you ultimately receive are determined by the return on investment and the contributions accumulated for each year. In most cases, you can decide how you want the money to be invested and whether to change your investments over time.

defined-contribution pension plan
An employer-sponsored retirement plan where the contribution rate, not the benefit amount, is based on a specific formula.

Since employers are not obligated to provide a predefined benefit amount, defined-contribution pension plans have become very popular. In the last 10 years, many employers have shifted from defined-benefit to defined-contribution pension plans. This places more responsibility on the employees to contribute money and to decide how the contributions should be invested until their retirement. Therefore, you need to understand the potential benefits of a defined-contribution pension plan and how to estimate the potential retirement savings that can be accumulated within this plan. The various aspects of retirement planning you must consider are covered in the next section of this chapter.

There are two types of defined-contribution pension plans: money purchase plans and profit sharing pension plans. In a money purchase plan, contributions are a fixed percentage of employee earnings, a fixed dollar amount, or a specified number of cents per year of service or per hour worked. In a profit sharing pension plan, contributions by the employer are a proportion of the firm's profits, with a defined minimum rate equal to 1 percent of employee earnings, regardless of whether a profit has been realized. Profit sharing defined-contribution pension plans are not very popular since contributions must be made even when the employer does not realize a profit during the year.

> **myth** or **fact** A college student should focus on paying off student loans and/or saving for a down payment on a first home before he or she considers saving for retirement.

The Decision to Contribute. Some people who have defined-contribution pension plans make the mistake of waiting too long before they join the plan and begin saving for retirement. They do not worry about saving for retirement when they are younger because they believe that they can save later. With this rationale, they may spend all the money that they earn. Then, as they get older, they may be forced to catch up on investing for retirement, which could severely cut their funds available for spending. However, many people who do not have the discipline to start saving for retirement at a young age do not save for retirement as they get older. The flexibility to postpone saving for retirement is one disadvantage of a defined-contribution pension plan for those people who lack the discipline to save on their own.

Go to:
www.rbcroyalbank.com/
cgi-bin/retirement/
retirementexpense/
start.cgi

This website provides
an annual retirement expense worksheet that can be used to estimate your expenses at retirement based on your current level of expenses.

Benefits of a Defined-Contribution Pension Plan. A defined-contribution pension plan provides you with many benefits. Any money contributed by your employer is like extra income paid to you above and beyond your salary. In addition, being involved in a defined-contribution pension plan can encourage you to save money at each pay period by directing a portion of your income to the pension account before you receive your paycheque. Your contributions to the plan are tax deductible. The income generated by your investments in a retirement account is not taxed until you withdraw the money after you retire. This tax benefit is very valuable because it provides you with more money that can be invested and accumulated. Finally, by the time you are taxed on the investments (at retirement), you likely will be in a lower tax bracket because you will have less income. However, because there is no guarantee with regard to the retirement benefit, the risk of shortfall rests on the employee's shoulders.

Investing Funds in Your Retirement Account. Most defined-contribution pension plans sponsored by employers allow some flexibility on how your retirement funds can be invested. You typically can select from a variety of stock mutual funds, bond mutual funds, or even money market funds. The amount of money you accumulate until retirement will depend on how your investments in the retirement account perform. In contrast, the accumulation of investment income inside a defined-benefit pension plan is not as much of a concern for each individual employee. Although you want the investments in the retirement account to perform well, the fact that you are guaranteed your final pension puts pressure on the employer to ensure that pension benefits are being managed well.

pension adjustment
Calculates the remaining annual contribution room available to an individual after taking into account any employer-sponsored pension plan contributions.

Pension Adjustment. To maintain fairness in the private pension system, the federal government restricts the ability of employees who are members of employer-sponsored pension plans from contributing to individual retirement savings plans. A **pension adjustment** calculates the remaining annual contribution room available to an individual after taking into account any employer-sponsored pension plan contributions. If an individual does not belong to an employer-sponsored pension plan, the pension adjustment is zero. With respect to a defined-contribution pension plan, the pension adjustment calculation is straightforward. Every dollar that you or your employer contributes to a defined-contribution pension plan reduces the amount you have available to contribute to an individual retirement savings plan by one dollar.

Barney has a salary of $50 000. His company's defined-contribution pension plan allows him to contribute 5 percent of his annual salary to the plan. This contribution is matched by the company. Barney's pension adjustment would be calculated as:

(Annual Salary × Contribution Rate) × 2
= ($50 000 × 0.05) × 2
= $5000

As a result of this pension adjustment, the amount that Barney can contribute to an individual retirement savings plan for the following year is reduced by $5000.

With respect to a defined-benefit pension plan, the pension adjustment amount is estimated using the pension earnings rate and the employee's pensionable earnings for the year. From the example above, if Barney was a member of a defined-benefit pension plan that provided a maximum annual pension income of 2 percent of his current earnings, the pension adjustment calculation would be:

$$(\$9 \times \text{Earnings Rate} \times \text{Pensionable Earnings}) - \$600$$
$$= (\$9 \times 0.02 \times \$50\ 000) - \$600$$
$$= \$8400$$

How do we interpret this number? Recall from the discussion of defined-benefit pension plans that the amount of pension Barney has earned would be calculated as $50 000 × 0.02 = $1000. In other words, at age 65, Barney would receive an annual pension of $1000 for this one year of service to the company. The next question to ask is this: Approximately how much money would have to be contributed to a pension plan during Barney's working years to provide a $1000 annual pension at retirement? Using mathematical calculations and various retirement assumptions, the federal government determined that multiplying a pensioner's annual pension by $9 and then subtracting $600 gives a good estimate of the pension adjustment that results from a defined-benefit pension plan. In this example, the $8400 pension adjustment represents an estimate of the lump sum contribution required to provide a $1000 annual pension during Barney's retirement. The amount that Barney can contribute to an individual retirement savings plan for the following year is reduced by $8400.

Receiving Retirement Income from Your Employer-Sponsored Retirement Plan. Under pension legislation, every registered pension plan provides an age, referred to as the **normal retirement age,** by which employees are entitled to receive 100 percent of the pension income for which they are eligible. In many plans, the normal retirement age is 65. Some plans use a combination of age and years of service to determine normal retirement age. As discussed earlier, the amount of pension income an employee will receive under a defined-benefit pension plan is based on factors such as salary and years of employment. Pension legislation requires that a pension be paid for the life of the employee. In the event of the employee's premature death, a reduced pension is often paid to a surviving spouse. At the normal retirement age, an employee will be offered several options with respect to pension income.

    Retirement income from an employer-sponsored pension plan will be paid as a single life income or as a joint-and-survivor life income. If the employee does not have an eligible spouse or common-law partner, a single life income is paid until the employee dies. In most cases, a retiring employee can choose a pension guarantee that will provide a pension income for a certain number of years. If the employee dies before the end of the guaranteed period, any remaining pension payable will be paid to a named beneficiary or to the employee's estate. Most provinces require that employer-sponsored retirement plans provide a pension income on a joint and survivor basis if the employee has an eligible spouse or common-law partner. As a result, if the pensioner should die before his or her spouse,

normal retirement age
The age by which employees are entitled to receive 100 percent of the pension income for which they are eligible.

the spouse will continue to receive a portion of the pension. A joint-and-survivor pension usually provides options that provide for a guaranteed benefit period. If the employee and spouse both die before the end of the guaranteed benefit period, any remaining benefits are paid to the named beneficiary or estate of the spouse who died last. With respect to a defined-contribution pension plan, the calculation for the amount of pension income that an employee will receive is similar to the calculation used to determine the regular payment received when a registered life annuity is purchased. Registered life annuities are discussed later in this chapter. Defined-contribution pension plans tend to be more flexible in the retirement income options offered to employees. In many cases, a retiring employee may transfer the assets from a defined-contribution pension plan into an individual locked-in account, such as a LIRA.

Pension Splitting. Beginning with the 2007 taxation year, pensioners receiving income that is eligible for the pension income tax credit, discussed in Chapter 4, may split their pension income with their spouse or common-law partner. As a result, pensioners should be able to reduce their overall tax burden. For individuals aged 65 years and older, the major types of qualifying income that can be allocated to a spouse or common-law partner are:

- a pension from a registered pension plan (RPP);
- income from an RRSP annuity; and
- payments from or under a registered retirement income fund (RRIF).

For individuals under 65 years of age, the major type of qualifying income that can be allocated to a spouse or common-law partner is a pension from an RPP. RRSPs and RRIFs are discussed later in this chapter.

EXAMPLE

Dominic, age 65, has been a member of a defined-benefit pension plan for the past 35 years. Now that he has reached normal retirement age, Dominic would like to receive his regular pension income. His employer calculates his pension benefit to be $3000 per month. In addition, if Dominic dies before his spouse, Lisette, she will receive 60 percent of the pension that Dominic was receiving. Prior to 2010, Dominic's pension benefit of $36 000 per year would have been recorded as his pension income and taxed accordingly. Under the new guidelines for the taxation of pension income, half of the pension income received by Dominic may be deducted from his tax return and included on Lisette's tax return. Assuming that they have no other income, Dominic and Lisette will each pay tax based on an annual income of $18 000.

L.O.4

INDIVIDUAL RETIREMENT SAVINGS PLANS

The second part of Canada's private pension system is composed of individual retirement savings plans. There are three main types of individual registered accounts that can be used as retirement savings plans: registered retirements savings plans (RRSPs), tax-free savings accounts (TFSAs), and locked-in retirement accounts (LIRAs), which are referred to as locked-in RRSPs in British Columbia and Nova Scotia.

Registered Retirement Savings Plans (RRSPs)

registered retirement savings plan (RRSP)
A type of private pension that enables you to save for your retirement on a tax-deferred basis.

A **registered retirement savings plan (RRSP)** is a type of private pension that enables you to save for your retirement on a tax-deferred basis. This type of plan, introduced in 1957, is registered with the CRA. As a result of registration, individuals who contribute to a RRSP receive a tax deduction for their contributions. In addition, the income earned on your investments within the RRSP is not taxed until you withdraw money at retirement. Any Canadian citizen aged 71 years or younger with an earned income can contribute to an RRSP. Although RRSP withdrawals can be made at any time, the purpose of an RRSP is to provide you with income at retirement. Any withdrawal you make is considered regular income and is subject to income tax. To assist you with tax payments, the RRSP plan sponsor will withhold some of the money you withdraw as a withholding tax. This should be considered a down payment on the total taxes payable. When you file your tax return, you claim the amount that is withheld as partial payment of the taxes you must pay on your RRSP withdrawal. Almost all financial institutions in Canada can act as an RRSP plan sponsor. As a result, many options are available to you when deciding which financial institution you want to use.

myth or **fact** It is unlikely that government benefits, such as the Canada Pension Plan, will exist when I am ready for retirement, so I better start saving.

RRSP Account Types. There are three main types of RRSP accounts: an individual RRSP, a self-directed RRSP, and group RRSPs. When you open an individual RRSP account, you can invest your money in the investment instruments offered by the financial institution with which you opened the account. For example, if you open an individual RRSP with Alpha Investments mutual fund company, you can invest in any of the mutual funds offered by Alpha Investments. An individual RRSP is sufficient for the needs of investors who are opening their first accounts or who have all of their RRSP assets in the mutual funds of a single company.

A self-directed RRSP allows you to hold a variety of investments within one plan. Within this type of RRSP, you may hold any number of investments that qualify under the rules set by the CRA (covered in the following section). Because of their nature, self-directed RRSP accounts are more costly to administer and will result in direct fees being charged to the individual investor. In general, self-directed RRSP accounts should be opened only by investors who own shares in a variety of mutual funds from different companies and/or investors who prefer to invest in an individual portfolio of stocks and/or bonds.

A group RRSP represents a series of individual RRSPs that are administered through one employer or association. Contributions to a group RRSP are normally made through payroll deductions. This type of plan provides employers with an opportunity to offer their employees another alternative to the employer-sponsored pension plans discussed earlier. Many employers prefer group RRSPs because they do not require employer contributions but still offer employees an opportunity to have a retirement savings plan through their employer. The costs to employers are substantially reduced and some companies will match the employee's contributions.

Qualified Investments. Investments that are qualified to be held within an RRSP account include:

- cash, guaranteed investment certificates (GICs), and other short-term deposits;
- individual stocks and bonds that are listed on an exchange;
- mutual and index funds;
- annuities;
- warrants, rights, and options;
- royalty and limited partnership units;
- mortgages (under specific circumstances); and
- investment-grade bullion, coins, bars, and certificates.

How Much Can I Contribute? If you were not a member of an employer-sponsored pension plan in 2016 or 2017, your maximum RRSP contribution limit for 2017 is $26 010. To determine the specific limit that applies to you for 2017, multiply your 2016 income by 18 percent. For example, Francesca has earned income of $35 000 for 2016. In addition, she has never been a member of an employer-sponsored pension plan. Her RRSP contribution limit for 2017 is $6300, calculated as $35 000 × 0.18. If you are or were a member of an employer-sponsored pension plan, you must take into account your 2016 pension adjustment in addition to some other factors. The annual RRSP contribution limit is increased based on the increase in the average industrial wage, as determined by Statistics Canada.

If Francesca does not contribute the full amount she is eligible to contribute to her RRSP, she can carry forward the balance and contribute this amount in future years. The extent to which Canadians do not contribute to their RRSPs is surprising. According to Statistics Canada, only 22.9 percent of eligible Canadian tax filers made contributions to their RRSPs in 2015. Although Canadians contributed nearly $39.2 billion to their RRSPs in 2015, this figure represents less than 5 percent of the total contribution room available after taking into account the RRSP carry forward balance. Based on these estimates, the total RRSP carry forward balance is around $800 billion. This figure represents a significant amount of money that has not been invested in individual RRSP accounts. You can contribute to your RRSP up to and including the year in which you turn age 71.

spousal RRSP
A type of RRSP where one spouse contributes to the plan and the other spouse is the beneficiary, or annuitant.

Spousal RRSPs. A **spousal RRSP** is a type of RRSP where one spouse contributes to the plan and the other spouse is the beneficiary, or annuitant. A spousal RRSP offers a number of advantages. First, it allows the higher-income spouse to receive a tax deduction for contributions, which results in greater tax savings for the couple. Second, spousal RRSP contributions may provide a useful income-splitting tool by allowing the couple to equalize their RRSP assets. In addition, since RRSP contributions can be made up to and including the year in which an individual turns age 71, a spouse who has passed age 71 can still contribute to a spousal RRSP for his or her younger spouse.

EXAMPLE

Pasquale is a 40-year-old self-employed accountant. His 2016 earned income was $150 000. Based on this income, Pasquale is eligible to contribute $26 010 to his RRSP in 2017. Pasquale's spouse, Roberta, is a 35-year-old stay-at-home mom. Prior to 2016, Roberta also worked as an accountant for a public firm. After the birth of their second child, the couple decided that Roberta should stay at home until this youngest child starts kindergarten. At present, they each have $200 000 in their RRSP plans, and neither of them has any carry-forward room. To maintain similar-sized retirement plans, Pasquale has decided to open a spousal RRSP. He will split his 2017 contribution in half by contributing $13 005 to his personal RRSP and $13 005 to a spousal RRSP. Once he has completed this transaction, Pasquale will have $213 005 in his RRSP plan while Roberta will have $200 000 in her RRSP plan, plus an additional $13 005 in a spousal RRSP. As a result of these transactions, Pasquale will have a $26 010 tax deduction and the couple will maintain RRSP accounts of similar size. They will continue to use this strategy until Roberta returns to the workforce. In the year that Pasquale turns age 72, he will still be able to make spousal RRSP contributions since Roberta will only be 67 years old.

Tax-Free Withdrawals from an RRSP

Home Buyers' Plan (HBP)
A tax-free RRSP withdrawal option that is available to Canadians who would like to buy their first home.

There are two circumstances under which money can be withdrawn tax-free from a RRSP. The **Home Buyers' Plan (HBP)** is a tax-free RRSP withdrawal option that is available to Canadians who would like to buy their first home. You are considered a first-time home buyer if you or your spouse or common-law partner has not owned a home as a principal residence in the four years preceding the year of withdrawal. The maximum withdrawal allowed is $25 000 per person. Although the withdrawal is tax-free, it must be paid back into the RRSP over a 15-year period, with payments beginning the second year after withdrawal at the latest. If you do not meet the minimum annual payment requirement of one-fifteenth of the amount withdrawn, this amount will be added to your taxable income for the year. You can also pay back all or a portion of the withdrawal before it is required by the CRA. In addition, this loan from your RRSP is interest-free. The HBP allows you to save more quickly because of the tax-sheltered RRSP environment and because, by having a larger down payment on your home, you may be able to negotiate a better mortgage rate.

A tax-free withdrawal from your RRSP may also be made under the **Lifelong Learning Plan (LLP)**, which is available to full-time students who temporarily would like to use an RRSP to finance their education. The withdrawal can be made from an RRSP owned by you and/or your spouse or common-law partner. The maximum annual withdrawal is $10 000. The total withdrawal allowed during the period you are participating in the LLP is $20 000. Although the withdrawal is tax-free, it must be paid back into the RRSP over a 10-year period, with payments beginning the fifth year after your first withdrawal at the latest.

Lifelong Learning Plan (LLP)
A tax-free RRSP withdrawal option that is available to full-time students who temporarily would like to use an RRSP to finance their education.

Before using the withdrawal options available under the HBP and the LLP, it is important to consider carefully the long-term effect of withdrawing funds from your RRSP. Any funds withdrawn from an RRSP will no longer be earning tax-sheltered income. As you will see later in this chapter, the long-term growth that results from the compounding of interest inside an RRSP account can be quite significant. Recall that an RRSP is your personal pension plan. If you had a company pension plan with your employer, would you withdraw funds to purchase a home or go back to school? Every financial planning decision you make or choose not to make will have an opportunity cost that may affect you for many years into the future.

Tax-Free Savings Accounts (TFSAs)

Recall from Chapter 4 that a TFSA is a registered investment account that allows you to purchase investments, with after-tax dollars, without attracting any tax payable on your investment growth. Exhibit 14.4 provides a comparison of RRSPs and TFSAs. The first

EXHIBIT 14.4 Comparison of RRSPs and TFSAs

	RRSP	TFSA
Eligibility	Canadian citizens aged 71 or younger with an earned income	Canadian residents aged 18 or older
Primary Purpose	Retirement income	Short- and long-term savings
Annual Contribution Limit	18% of earned income, up to a maximum of $26 010 in 2017; indexed thereafter (pension adjustment may apply)	$5500 in 2017; indexed thereafter ($500 increments)
Unused Contribution Carry Forward	Yes	Yes
Tax Deductible Contributions	Yes	No
Tax-Deferred Savings	Yes	Yes
Withdrawals are Taxable	Yes, considered earned income	No, not considered earned income
Withdrawal Recontribution	No, unless part of HBP or LLP	Yes, the following year
Withholding Tax	Yes	Not applicable
Plan Termination	Plan must be converted or collapsed in the year you turn age 71	Not applicable
Qualified Investments	Cash, GICS, other short-term deposits, stocks, bonds, mutual and index funds, annuities, warrants, right, options, royalty and limited partnership units, mortgages, investment-grade bullion, coins, bars, and certificates	

thing to note about TFSAs is that there is no income requirement for this type of savings plan. Any Canadian resident over the age of 18 is eligible to open a TFSA account. If you do not have income to open a TFSA account, money can be gifted to you by someone who does. The 2017 contribution limit for a TFSA is $5500. The contribution limit will only increase once the cumulative annual effect of inflation justifies a $500 incremental increase. Similar to RRSPs, unused contributions can be carried forward to the next year and the growth on contributions is tax deferred. Unlike RRSPs, contributions into a TFSA account are not tax deductible. TFSAs can be used for short-term as well as long-term goals. For example, you can withdraw money from a TFSA to meet short-term goals such as making a down payment on a house, purchasing a car, or paying for a vacation. This is because, unlike RRSPs, withdrawals from a TFSA are tax-free. In addition, when you make a withdrawal one year, you can recontribute the money you withdrew the following year. With RRSPs, once you make a withdrawal, you cannot make up for it by recontributing the amount withdrawn at a later date, unless you are making the recontribution to pay back an HBP or LLP withdrawal.

EXAMPLE	Jordan turned 18 on January 17, 2016. In January 2016, Jordan opened a TFSA account and deposited the maximum annual contribution limit of $5500. In December 2016, he decided to withdraw $4000, tax-free, to cover travel expenses for a Caribbean vacation and to pay for Christmas presents for friends and family. Jordan's contribution limit for the following year, 2017, is $5500. However, he will also be able to recontribute the $4000 he withdrew in December 2016. As a result, Jordan has an available 2017 contribution room of $9500. If he decides not to make any contributions in 2017, Jordan can carry forward his $9500 of contribution room to 2018.

TFSAs are ideal for long-term savings as well. First, growth on contributions in a TFSA is tax deferred. Second, a TFSA account can be held open until you die, whereas an RRSP plan must be collapsed or converted in the year you turn age 71. Retirement income conversion options for an RRSP are discussed later in this chapter. Third, qualified investments for TFSAs include long-term investment, such as stocks, bonds, and mutual funds. Since the withdrawals from a TFSA account are not considered earned income, TFSA withdrawals do not lead to the clawback of OAS or GIS benefits.

TFSA Account Types. Initially, many financial institutions set up TFSA accounts that allowed individuals to invest in high-interest savings accounts, term deposits, and GICs. As TFSAs have grown in popularity, other TFSA account types, such as mutual fund, self-directed, and group TFSAs have become available so that investors can take advantage of the tax-deferred growth and qualified investment choices that are available within this registered savings vehicle.

Locked-in Retirement Accounts (LIRAs)

locked-in retirement account (LIRA)
A private pension plan that is created when an individual transfers vested money from an employer-sponsored pension plan.

A **locked-in retirement account (LIRA)**, also known as a locked-in RRSP in some jurisdictions, is a private pension plan that is created when an individual transfers vested money from an employer-sponsored pension plan. The main purpose of a LIRA is to provide an opportunity for employees who leave a company pension plan to take the value of their pension plan assets with them. The characteristics of a LIRA are very similar to those of an RRSP and a TFSA. The plan can be established as an individual LIRA or as a self-directed LIRA. In addition, the qualified investments for a LIRA are similar to those for an RRSP and a TFSA. However, unlike these two options, LIRAs do not provide an opportunity to make regular contributions. In addition, the money in a LIRA is subject to the rules that govern pension plans, and therefore funds cannot be withdrawn at any time. At retirement, the money in a LIRA or locked-in RRSP must be used to provide a retirement income. In contrast, the money in an RRSP and/or a TFSA may be cashed in at any time.

RETIREMENT INCOME CONVERSION OPTIONS

L.O.5

Retirement Income Conversion Options for RRSPs and TFSAs

As discussed earlier, you can contribute to your RRSP up to and including the year in which you turn age 71. By the end of the year in which you turn age 71, you must cash in your RRSP or transfer your RRSP assets into an income-producing plan. In general, cashing in your RRSP is a bad option because of the immediate tax consequences. Any money withdrawn from your RRSP, aside from money withdrawn as part of the HBP or LLP, is subject to income tax as regular income. If you cash in a $200 000 RRSP, the amount will be taxed as if you had earned a salary of $200 000 in that year. On the other hand, you can cash in your TFSA without any tax consequences.

A more commonly used alternative is to transfer all of your RRSP assets into a registered retirement income fund (RRIF). RRSPs and RRIFs are similar in many ways, including the types of investments that qualify to be held within each plan. As a result, transferring money from an RRSP into an RRIF is an exercise in paperwork. Assets do not have to be sold when moving from one plan to the other. Since an RRIF may hold similar investments to an RRSP, there is always the risk that you are investing in assets that may decrease in value. For example, if you own a portfolio of stock mutual funds in your RRSP and subsequently transfer this portfolio into an RRIF, you are still exposed to the risks that come with investing in stocks. If your stock mutual funds decrease in value, your RRIF will decrease in value. This may have a negative impact on your retirement income. The main difference between an RRSP and an RRIF is that a certain percentage of the assets held within an RRIF must be taken into income each year after the year in which the RRIF was established, and any money so taken will be taxed at the prevailing income tax rates. Although TFSA assets cannot be transferred into an RRIF, the owner of a TFSA account invested in stocks or stock mutual funds is exposed to the risk that these investments may decrease in value.

EXAMPLE

Vicky Zhao turns 71 in 2017. Before the end of the year, she must either collapse her RRSP for its cash value or transfer her RRSP assets into an income-producing plan. Vicky decides to transfer her RRSP to an RRIF on November 15, 2017. As a result of this transfer, Vicky must make a withdrawal from her RRIF before December 31, 2018.

The amount that must be withdrawn from an RRIF is prescribed by the CRA in an RRIF table. Exhibit 14.5 shows an RRIF table highlighting the minimum amount that must be withdrawn. Assuming that Vicky is age 71 on January 1, 2017, she will have to withdraw 5.28 percent of her non-qualifying RRIF assets during 2018. The amount that she has to withdraw will be based on the value of her RRIF assets on January 1. The RRIF table represents only minimum withdrawal amounts. Vicky has the option to cash in her RRIF at any time.

In addition to cashing in your RRSP or TFSA or transferring RRSP assets to an RRIF, you can consider investing in an annuity. There are two types of annuities. A **term annuity** is a financial contract that provides a fixed sum of money at regular intervals until a specified year. A **life annuity** is a financial contract that provides a fixed sum of money at regular intervals for one's lifetime. Annuities that are created using assets from an RRSP are referred to as **registered annuities**. The main advantage of a registered annuity over an RRIF is that you are no longer exposed to the risk that your investment may decrease in value. By definition, an annuity can be set up using the assets in a TFSA simply by withdrawing fixed amount at regular intervals. TFSAs are still in their infancy. Therefore, retirement income conversion options are limited. As this registered investment vehicle evolves, retirement income options are likely to be designed to meet the needs of retirees who have saved significant amounts within their TFSAs. An annuity can also be designed such that the regular payment you receive is indexed to inflation.

term annuity
A financial contract that provides a fixed sum of money at regular intervals until a specified year.

life annuity
A financial contract that provides a fixed sum of money at regular intervals for one's lifetime.

registered annuities
Annuities that are created using assets from an RRSP.

EXHIBIT 14.5   CRA Prescribed Factors Expressed as Percentages of the January 1 RRIF Value

Age of RRIF owner or spouse or common-law partner at January 1	RRIF Factor	Age of RRIF owner or spouse or common-law partner at January 1	RRIF Factor	Age of RRIF owner or spouse or common-law partner at January 1	RRIF Factor
63	0.037037	74	0.0567	85	0.0851
64	0.038462	75	0.0582	86	0.0899
65	0.040000	76	0.0598	87	0.0955
66	0.041667	77	0.0617	88	0.1021
67	0.043478	78	0.0636	89	0.1099
68	0.045455	79	0.0658	90	0.1192
69	0.047619	80	0.0682	91	0.1306
70	0.050000	81	0.0708	92	0.1449
71	0.0528	82	0.0738	93	0.1634
72	0.0540	83	0.0771	94	0.1879
73	0.0553	84	0.0808	95 or older	0.2000

Source: http://www.taxtips.ca/rrsp/rrif minimum-withdrawal-factors.htm. Reproduced with the permission of TaxTips.ca. (Accessed May 29, 2017).

EXAMPLE

Vicky could have used her RRSP assets to purchase an annuity. For example, if she expects to need income that would be produced by her RRSP until age 91, she could use her RRSP to purchase a 20-year registered term annuity. Of course, there is always the concern that Vicky may live past age 91. To avoid the risk that her annuity income will stop at age 91, she could use her RRSP to purchase a registered life annuity, which would guarantee her an income for life. On the other hand, what happens if Vicky dies the year after purchasing the life annuity? In this case, Vicky will lose most of her investment since the RRSP assets were used to purchase the annuity. To reduce this risk, Vicky could purchase a registered term certain annuity for 20 years. This type of annuity will guarantee an income payable to Vicky or her estate for 20 years.

Retirement Income Conversion Options for a LIRA

The retirement income conversion options for a LIRA are more limited than those for an RRSP since a LIRA is required to provide an income for life. As a result, the two main conversion options for a LIRA are a registered life annuity and a life income fund (LIF). A LIF is a restricted form of an RRIF. Unlike an RRIF, the annual withdrawal from a LIF is subject to a maximum amount, which means that the investments in a LIF cannot be cashed in. In addition, in the year that the owner of the LIF account reaches age 80, any remaining assets in a LIF must be used to purchase a registered life annuity. In some provinces, the assets from a LIRA or locked-in RRSP may be transferred to a locked-in retirement income fund (LRIF). In general, a LIF and an LRIF are identical retirement income options. However, there are two main differences between them: the formula used to calculate the maximum withdrawal from an LRIF is different, and an LRIF does not have to be converted to a life annuity at age 80. Exhibit 14.6 provides a summary of the retirement income conversion options available for RRSPs, TFSAs, and LIRAs.

EXHIBIT 14.6 Retirement Income Conversion Options

Plan Type:	Cash In	RRIF	LIF/LRIF	Registered Term Annuity	Registered Life Annuity
RRSP	Yes	Yes	No	Yes	Yes
LIRA/Locked-In RRSP	No	No	Yes	No	Yes

Reverse Mortgages

According to Statistics Canada, more than 70 percent of Canadians age 65 or older owned a home in 2011. In fact, a significant proportion of a senior's net worth is home equity. As such, for many elderly Canadians, the most important source of retirement income will be the equity they have in their homes. In many cases, the ideal solution for unlocking home equity is to use a reverse mortgage. A **reverse mortgage** is a secured loan that allows older Canadians to generate income using the equity in their homes without having to sell this asset. To apply for a reverse mortgage, an applicant must be 60 years of age or older. Depending on various criteria, a homeowner can borrow up to 40 percent of the value of his or her home or $500 000 using a reverse mortgage. The largest provider of reverse mortgages in Canada is the Canadian Home Income Plan (CHIP, www.chip.ca).

reverse mortgage
A secured loan that allows older Canadians to generate income using the equity in their homes without having to sell this asset.

Even though it is a loan, a reverse mortgage does not have to be repaid immediately. Instead, a reverse mortgage provider, such as CHIP, allows the interest to accumulate during the period of the loan. In many cases, a reverse mortgage does not have to be paid back until the death of the borrower. The proceeds from a reverse mortgage may be paid in a single lump sum, set up as a line of credit, or used to purchase an annuity for the borrower.

There are two major drawbacks to a reverse mortgage. First, the setup costs, which include appraisal, legal, and closing costs, may be as high as $2000 to $2500. Second, the interest that accumulates on the reverse mortgage loan will reduce the value of your estate over time. As a result of these drawbacks, the decision to use a reverse mortgage should be considered carefully. It can be an ideal product for seniors who wish to remain in their home but do not have sufficient retirement income from the other income sources discussed in this chapter. However, a sound financial plan may reduce or eliminate the need for a reverse mortgage and its associated setup costs.

YOUR RETIREMENT PLANNING DECISIONS

L.O.6

Your key retirement planning decisions involve choosing a retirement plan, determining how much to contribute, and allocating your contributions. Several websites, such as www.bmo.com/home/personal/banking/investments/retirement-savings/retirement-planning, provide useful calculators that can help you to make these decisions. Using these calculators can help you to understand the trade-offs involved so that you can make the retirement planning decisions that fit your specific needs.

Which Retirement Plan Should You Pursue?

The retirement benefits from an employer-sponsored retirement plan vary among employers. Some employer-sponsored plans allow you to invest more money than others. If your employer offers a retirement plan, it should be the first plan you consider, because your employer will make at least 50 percent of the contributions toward it. Employee contributions to a defined-benefit pension plan are usually mandatory. In the case of a defined-contribution pension plan, employee contributions may be optional. However, most defined-contribution pension plans are set up such that every dollar contributed by the employee is matched dollar-for-dollar by the employer, usually to a predetermined percentage of salary. For example, if you contribute 5 percent of your salary to the company defined-contribution pension plan, your employer will also contribute 5 percent. Employer contributions are a taxable benefit to the employee but are fully tax deductible when the employee files an income tax return.

> **myth** or **fact** If I haven't saved enough for retirement, I will be able to work part-time to make up the shortfall in my retirement income needs.

If you do not have an employer-sponsored retirement plan, you will have to consider investing in an individual retirement savings plan, such as an RRSP or a TFSA. RRSPs were specifically designed to help you save for retirement. As shown in Exhibit 14.4, one of the distinguishing advantages of an RRSP is that the contributor receives an income tax deduction equal to the amount of their contribution. With a TFSA, there is no deduction permitted for income tax purposes. In addition, the annual contribution limit for RRSPs is much higher than the limit for TFSAs. On the other hand, RRSP withdrawals are taxable as earned income, while TFSA withdrawals are tax-free. The difference in the tax treatment of withdrawals can be significant because some government benefits, such as OAS, GIS, and the age amount (discussed in Chapter 4), are subject to clawback if a retiree's income exceeds a minimum threshold.

RRSP or TFSA? Since there are both advantages and disadvantages to investing in an RRSP or a TFSA, which retirement plan should you choose? The correct answer to this question depends on your personal circumstances. In general, an RRSP is more likely to be the better savings alternative under the following circumstances: You are in a very high tax bracket and can take advantage of the large RRSP contribution limits. You plan to reinvest your RRSP tax refund into your RRSP account. You expect that your marginal tax bracket during your working years will be higher than that during your retirement years. You may be tempted to withdraw money from your retirement savings account. Recall that withdrawals from an RRSP cannot be recontributed, whereas withdrawals from a TFSA can. A TFSA is better in situations where (1) you are in a low to modest tax bracket and do not have a large RRSP contribution limit, (2) you spend your tax refund, (3) your marginal tax bracket at retirement will not be lower, and (4) you are not likely to tap into your TFSA for income. It is important to note that RRSP withdrawals are considered earned income. As a result, some government benefits you receive may be cut back or eliminated entirely. This reduction in benefits will have a significant impact on your total income from investing in an RRSP or a TFSA. Many individuals would benefit from splitting their contributions between an RRSP and a TFSA. This will reduce the size of your RRSP, which will subsequently reduce the amount of earned income you would have to take from your RRIF. You will be able to maintain more of your government benefits and, if you need additional income, you can make a withdrawal from your TFSA.

How Much Should You Contribute?

As explained above, many defined-contribution pension plans allow you to determine how much money (up to a specified maximum level) to contribute to your retirement account. Similarly, individual retirement savings plans provide you with an opportunity to save for retirement if you do not have an employer-sponsored pension plan. A first step is to determine your potential savings from contributing to your retirement plan. This requires you to make assumptions about how much you could contribute per year, the return you will earn on your investments, and the number of years until your retirement, as illustrated in the following example.

Eric Lilley is considering whether he should start saving toward his retirement. Although his retirement is 30 years away, he wants to ensure that he can live comfortably at that time. He decides to contribute 5 percent of his income, or $200 per month, to his retirement through his employer's defined-contribution pension plan. His employer will provide a matching contribution of $200 per month. Therefore, the total contribution to his retirement account will be $400 per month at the end of the first month. As a result of contributing to his retirement, Eric will have less spending money now and will not have access to these savings until he retires in about 30 years. However, his monthly contribution helps to reduce his taxes now because the money he contributes is not subject to income taxes until he withdraws it at retirement.

Eric wants to determine how much money he will have in 30 years based on the total contribution of $400 per month. He expects to earn a return of 10 percent compounded monthly on his investment. The calculator key strokes required to estimate his savings at the time of his retirement are:

Eric realizes that he will be able to accumulate more than $900 000 by the time he retires.

The amount that you try to save by the time you retire partially depends on the retirement income you will need to live comfortably. There are various methods of determining the amount you should save for your retirement. Among the important variables to consider are the levels of your existing assets and liabilities, whether you will be supporting anyone other than yourself at retirement, your personal needs, the expected price level of products at the time of your retirement, and the number of years you will live while retired. Various online calculators that take into consideration these factors are available.

Given the difficulty of estimating how much income you will need at retirement, a safe approach is to recognize that OAS and the CPP will not provide sufficient funds and to invest as much as you can on a consistent basis in your retirement plan. After maintaining enough funds for liquidity purposes, you should invest as much as possible in retirement accounts, especially when the contribution is matched by your employer. A common rule of thumb is to save at least 10 percent of your after-tax earnings in a combination of retirement accounts.

How Should You Invest Your Contributions?

When considering investment alternatives within a retirement account, you do not need to worry about tax effects. With the exception of a TFSA, all of the money you withdraw from your retirement account at the time you retire will be taxed at your ordinary income tax rate, regardless of how it was earned. Most financial advisers suggest a diversified set

EXHIBIT 14.7   Typical Composition of a Retirement Account Portfolio

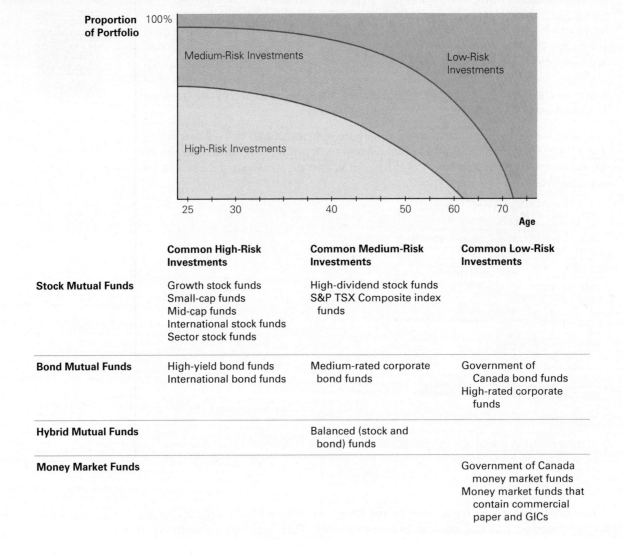

	Common High-Risk Investments	Common Medium-Risk Investments	Common Low-Risk Investments
Stock Mutual Funds	Growth stock funds Small-cap funds Mid-cap funds International stock funds Sector stock funds	High-dividend stock funds S&P TSX Composite index funds	
Bond Mutual Funds	High-yield bond funds International bond funds	Medium-rated corporate bond funds	Government of Canada bond funds High-rated corporate funds
Hybrid Mutual Funds		Balanced (stock and bond) funds	
Money Market Funds			Government of Canada money market funds Money market funds that contain commercial paper and GICs

of investments, such as investing most of your funds in one or more stock mutual funds and the remainder in one or more bond mutual funds.

Your retirement plan investment decision should take into account the number of years until your retirement, as shown in Exhibit 14.7. If you are far from retirement, you might consider mutual funds that invest in stocks with high potential for growth (such as a growth fund, a sector fund, and perhaps an international stock or bond fund). If you are close to retirement, you might consider balanced growth and income funds, Canadian bond funds, and a large-cap stock that pays high dividends. Remember, however, that any investment is subject to a possible decline in value. Some investments (such as a money market fund focused on T-bills or GICs) are less risky, but also offer less potential return. Most retirement plans allow a wide variety of investment alternatives to suit various risk tolerances.

If you are young and far from retirement, you are in a position to take more risk with your investments. As you approach retirement, however, your investments should be more conservative. For example, you may shift some of your investments to Canadian bonds so that your retirement fund is less exposed to risk. Most people invest at least part of their retirement money in mutual funds. Regardless of the specific mutual funds in which you invest, one of the most important tips for accumulating more wealth by retirement is to avoid mutual funds with high management expense ratios (MERs). If you start saving for your retirement by age 30, you can accumulate an extra $200 000 or more by the time of retirement simply by choosing low-expense mutual funds. Put another way, the odds that you will run out of retirement savings is much higher if you choose high-expense mutual funds because your retirement savings likely will not accumulate to the same degree. However, the return on the fund is very important as well. Buying a fund with low expenses is not very wise if the return is not appropriate to the fund's risk level. Investors should always look at historical returns to ensure that the fund's management is skilled. Sometimes, choosing a fund with a higher-than-average MER is warranted if management has performed well over time.

Some individuals focus too heavily on risky investments in their retirement account, because they get a psychological boost from investments that have the potential to generate very high returns. However, these investments could cause very large losses. Thus, some investors end up gambling their retirement money in risky investments, and possibly risking major losses that they cannot afford. Many risky investments may end up being worthless causing major losses. Consequently, investors' retirement accounts may lack sufficient funds to support their retirement, which might force them to work additional years.

FREE APPS for Personal Finance

Estimating Your Tax

Application:

The Retire Calc app by Scotchware Inc. calculates how much you need to save each year in order to reach a retirement income goal. This app, which considers the impact of inflation on your required yearly income in retirement, also provides you with a table of retirement cash flows.

ESTIMATING YOUR FUTURE RETIREMENT SAVINGS

L.0.7

To determine how much you will have accumulated by retirement, you can calculate the future value of the amount of money you save.

Estimating the Future Value of One Investment

Using the TI BA II Plus calculator, the future value of a registered investment today can be computed if you have the following information:

- The amount of the investment
- The annual return you expect on the investment
- The term of the investment

Relationship between Amount Saved Now and Retirement Savings. Consider how the amount you save now can affect your future savings. As Exhibit 14.8 shows, if you invested $10 000 instead of $5000 today, your savings would grow to more than $450 000 in 40 years. The more you save today, the more money you will have at the time of your retirement.

EXHIBIT 14.8 Relationship between Savings Today and Amount of Money at Retirement (in 40 Years, Assuming a 10 Percent Annual Return)

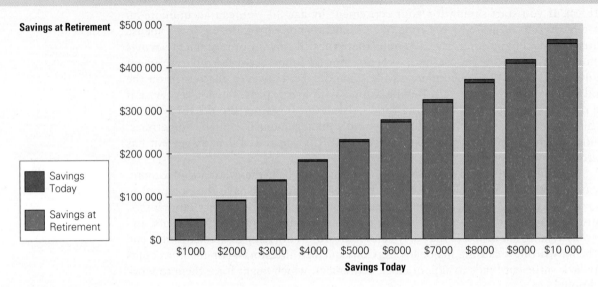

TVM EXAMPLE

You consider investing $5000 this year, and this investment will remain in your account for 40 years until you retire. You believe that you can earn a return of 10 percent per year, compounded annually, on your investment. Based on this information, you expect the value of your investment in 40 years to be:

The future value of your $5000 investment is $226 296.28. It may surprise you that $5000 can grow into more than a quarter of a million dollars if it is invested over a 40-year period. This should motivate you to consider saving for your retirement as soon as possible.

Relationship between Years of Saving and Your Retirement Savings. The amount of money you accumulate by the time you retire also depends on the number of years your savings are invested. As Exhibit 14.9 shows, the longer your savings are invested, the more they will be worth (assuming a positive rate of return) at retirement. If you invest $5000 for 25 years instead of 40 years, it will be worth approximately $54 175.

Relationship between Your Annual Return and Your Retirement Savings. The amount of money you accumulate by the time you retire also depends on your annual return,

EXHIBIT 14.9 Relationship between the Investment Period and Your Savings at Retirement (Assuming a $5000 Investment and a 10 Percent Annual Return)

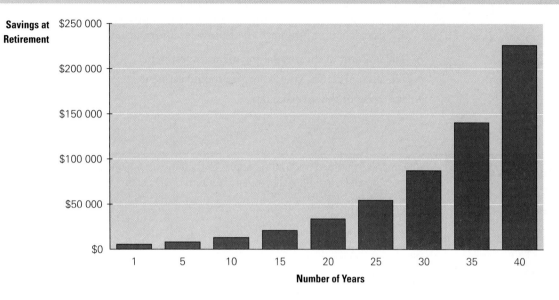

as shown in Exhibit 14.10. Notice the sensitivity of your savings at retirement to the annual return. Two extra percentage points on the annual return can increase the savings from a single $5000 investment by hundreds of thousands of dollars. Assuming annual compounding, a 12 percent return on your $5000 would be worth approximately $465 300 in 40 years, as compared to approximately $226 300 based on a 10 percent return. A decline in return rates would have a similar effect but, of course, on the negative side. Another consideration is the reinvestment rate. Return calculations assume that the interest earned through the time period can be reinvested at the same rate as the original investment, which may not be possible.

EXHIBIT 14.10 Relationship between the Annual Return on Your Investment and Your Savings at Retirement (in 40 Years, Assuming a $5000 Initial Investment)

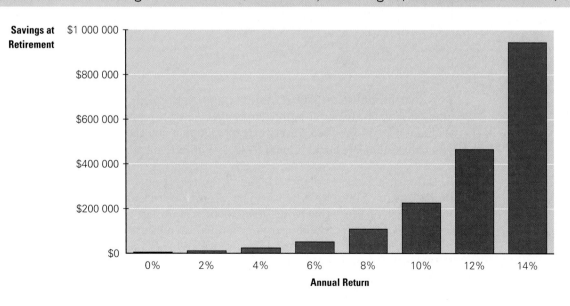

Estimating the Future Value of a Set of Annual Investments

If you plan to save a specified amount of money every year for retirement, you can easily determine the value of your savings by the time you retire. Recall that a set of annual payments is an annuity. The future value of an annuity can be computed using your TI BA II Plus calculator. You need the following information:

- The amount of the annual payment (investment)
- The annual return you expect on the investment
- The term of the investment

TVM EXAMPLE

You consider investing $5000 at the end of each of the next 40 years to accumulate retirement savings. You anticipate that you can earn a return of 10 percent per year, compounded annually, on your investments. Based on this information, you expect the value of your investments in 40 years to be:

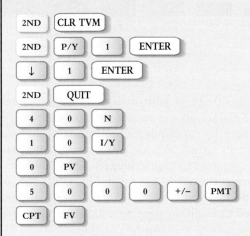

The future value of your $5000 annual investment is $2 212 962.78. This is not a misprint. You will have more than $2 million in 40 years if you invest $5000 each year for the next 40 years and earn a 10 percent annual rate of return. The compounding of interest is very powerful and allows you to accumulate a large amount of funds over time with relatively small investments. Set aside income for your retirement as soon as possible so that you can benefit from the power of compounding.

Relationship between Size of Annuity and Retirement Savings. Consider how the amount of your savings at retirement is affected by the amount that you save each year. As Exhibit 14.11 shows, for every extra $1000 that you can save by the end of each year, you will accumulate an additional $442 593 at retirement.

Relationship between Years of Saving and Retirement Savings. The amount of money you accumulate when saving money on an annual basis also depends on the number of years that your investment remains in your retirement account. As Exhibit 14.12 shows, the longer your annual savings are invested, the more they will be worth at retirement. If you plan to retire at age 65, notice that if you start saving $5000 per year at age 25 (and therefore save for 40 years until retirement), you will save $857 840 more than if you wait until age 30 to start saving (and therefore save for 35 years until retirement).

EXHIBIT 14.11   Relationship between Amount Saved per Year and Amount of Savings at Retirement (in 40 Years, Assuming a 10 Percent Annual Return)

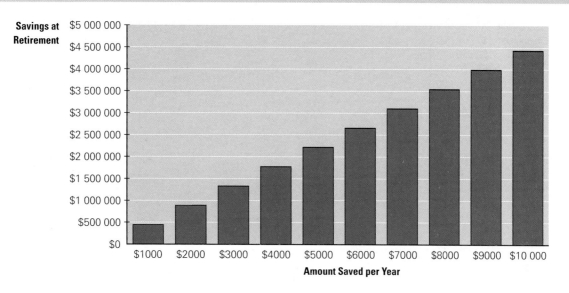

EXHIBIT 14.12   Relationship between the Number of Years You Invest Annual Savings and Your Savings at Retirement (Assuming a $5000 Investment and a 10 Percent Annual Return)

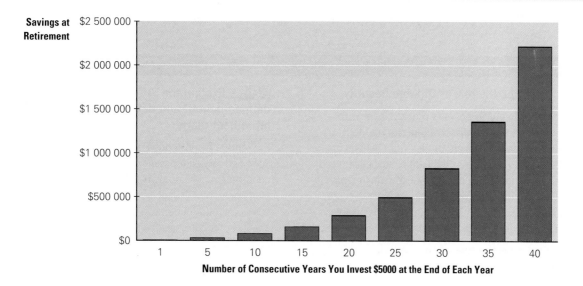

Relationship between your Annual Return and Your Savings at Retirement. The amount you will have at retirement also depends on the return you earn on your annual savings, as shown in Exhibit 14.13. Notice how sensitive your savings are to the annual return. Almost $1 million more is accumulated from an annual return of 10 percent than from an annual return of 8 percent. An annual return of 12 percent produces about $1.6 million more in accumulated savings than an annual return of 10 percent. Remember, too, the reinvestment risk discussed earlier. To achieve the results used in these examples, you must be able to obtain that same rate on all earnings.

EXHIBIT 14.13   Relationship between the Annual Return on Your Annual Savings and Your Savings at Retirement (in 40 years, Assuming a $5000 Annual Investment)

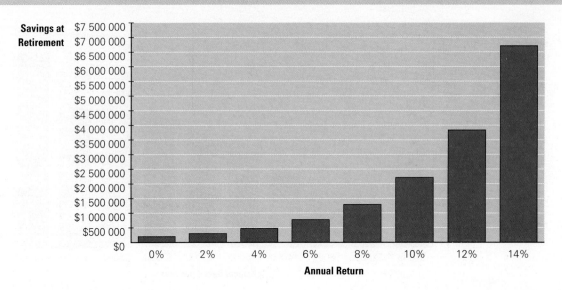

MyLab Finance   Visit MyLab Finance for additional study and practice tools. Select Financial Planning Problems are available in the Study Plan. Create your own study plan, generate personal cash flow statements and balance sheets, and set personal financial goals.

SUMMARY

L.O.1   Describe the role of Old Age Security

Old Age Security (OAS) benefits provide income to qualified individuals to support them during their retirement. These benefits are funded from general tax revenues. OAS consists of the OAS pension, the guaranteed income supplement (GIS), the allowance benefit, and the allowance for the survivor benefit. OAS benefits are subject to a "means test." The OAS pension is taxable, whereas the other benefits are received tax-free.

L.O.2   Describe the role of the Canada Pension Plan

The Canada Pension Plan (CPP) is a government-sponsored contributory plan that provides a retirement pension to most working Canadians. The amount of benefits will be different depending on when you apply. CPP benefits are taxable. The income provided by the CPP and OAS programs is not sufficient for most individuals to live comfortably. Therefore, individuals engage in retirement planning so that they will have additional sources of income when they retire.

L.O.3   Explain the difference between defined-benefit and defined-contribution retirement plans

Retirement plans sponsored by employers are normally classified as defined-benefit pension plans or defined-contribution pension plans. Defined-benefit pension plans guarantee a specific amount of income to employees upon retirement, based on factors such as their salary and number of years of service. Defined-contribution pension plans provide guidelines on the maximum amount that can be contributed to a retirement account. With respect to a defined-contribution pension plan, individuals usually have the freedom to make decisions about how much to invest and how to invest for their retirement. In most jurisdictions, an employer will match or exceed the employee contribution to a defined-contribution pension plan. However, the defined-benefit pension plan does offer security for pensioners in that the final benefit can be calculated and the risk is borne by the employer if the plan does not have enough funds to pay these benefits.

L.O.4 **Describe types of individual retirement savings plans**

In addition to retirement accounts offered by employers, individuals can establish a registered retirement savings plan (RRSP) and/or a tax-free savings account (TFSA). Many individuals own a locked-in retirement account (LIRA), which is an individual retirement plan that results from the transfer of pension plan assets from an employer-sponsored pension plan.

L.O.5 **Describe types of retirement income conversion options**

At retirement, a number of retirement income conversion options are available. With respect to an RRSP, an individual may cash in or transfer plan assets to a registered retirement income fund (RRIF). The assets from an RRSP can also be used to purchase various types of annuities, including registered term annuities and registered life annuities. With respect to a TFSA, investors can cash in the investment and/or withdraw money from the TFSA as required. Assets from a LIRA may be transferred to a LIF or an LRIF. The equity in your home can be used to generate an Income through a reverse mortgage.

L.O.6 **Present the key decisions you must make regarding retirement plans**

Three key retirement planning decisions are which retirement plan you should pursue, how much to contribute to your retirement plan, and how to invest your contributions. When an employer is willing to match your retirement contribution, you should always contribute enough to take full advantage of the matching. With respect to individual retirement savings, both RRSPs and TFSAs offer advantages and disadvantages. The decision as to which plan to pursue depends on your personal circumstances. You should try to contribute the maximum amount allowed, even if doing so means that you will have fewer funds to invest in other ways. Most financial advisers suggest investing most of your contribution in one or more diversified stock mutual funds and putting the remainder in a diversified bond mutual fund. The specific allocation depends on your willingness to tolerate risk and your overall financial position.

L.O.7 **Illustrate how to estimate the savings you will have in your retirement account at the time you retire**

Your future savings from investing in a retirement account can easily be measured based on information regarding the amount you plan to invest each year, the annual return you expect, and the number of years until retirement. The future savings reflect the future value of an annuity.

REVIEW QUESTIONS

1. What two programs can be thought of as the foundation of retirement planning?

2. What are the qualifying criteria for Old Age Security (OAS)? At what age do you become eligible to receive OAS retirement benefits?

3. Does your benefit increase if you defer your OAS pension? Explain.

4. In order to receive a full OAS benefit, how long must you have lived in Canada after turning age 18? What is the minimum number of years that you must have lived in Canada after turning age 18 in order to receive a partial OAS pension?

5. What is an OAS clawback?

6. Who may qualify for a Guaranteed Income Supplement (GIS)?

7. Who is eligible for the allowance benefit? What is the purpose of the allowance benefit?

8. What is the purpose of the allowance for the survivor benefit?

9. Do OAS benefits begin automatically once you reach age 65?

10. How frequently are OAS benefits adjusted for inflation? Which OAS program benefits are taxable and which ones are tax-free?

11. What are the qualifying criteria for the Canada Pension Plan (CPP)? At what age do you become eligible to receive CPP retirement benefits?

12. Does your benefit decrease and/or increase if you receive your CPP pension sooner and/or later? Explain.

13. What is a pension assignment?

14. In general, at what age and at what level of income must you start making CPP contributions?

15. What is the year's basic exemption (YBE)?

16. What are pensionable earnings? What is the year's maximum pensionable earnings (YMPE)?

17. At what rate does an employee make CPP contributions? At what rate does a self-employed person make CPP contributions?

18. In determining the dollar value of your contributions, do you have to include all of the contributions you have made starting at age 18? Explain.

19. Do CPP benefits begin automatically once you reach retirement age?

20. How frequently are CPP benefits adjusted for inflation? Are CPP retirement benefits taxable?

21. What is a defined-benefit pension plan? Are these plans contributory or non-contributory?

22. Explain why a set of actuarial assumptions are used to determine the amount of contributions for a defined-benefit pension plan.

23. What is the pension formula for a flat benefit plan?

24. What are the three types of unit benefit plans? What is the difference among the three types of unit benefit plans?

25. What is the pension formula for a unit benefit plan?

26. What does it mean for an employee to be vested? What is the longest period of time an employee has to work for their employer before they become fully vested?

27. If an employee leaves their employer and is fully vested, what are their options with respect to their pension benefits?

28. Describe the tax treatment of a defined-benefit pension plan.

29. What is a defined-contribution pension plan? Are these plans contributory or non-contributory?

30. In a defined-contribution pension plan, who makes the investment decisions?

31. Why are defined-contribution pension plans increasing in popularity?

32. List the two types of defined-contribution pension plans. What are the differences between these two types of plans?

33. Describe the benefits of contributing to a defined-contribution pension plan.

34. What is a pension adjustment?

35. How is a pension adjustment determined for a defined-contribution pension plan? How is a pension adjustment determined for a defined-benefit pension plan?

36. What is normal retirement age?

37. What is the difference between a single life income pension payment and a joint-and-survivor life income pension payment?

38. What is the benefit of a pension guarantee?

39. What is pension splitting? What income can be split for individuals over 65 years of age? Under 65 years of age?

40. What is a registered retirement savings plan (RRSP)? Describe the tax treatment for deposits and withdrawals.

41. List and describe the three main types of RRSP accounts?

42. List the investments that qualify to be held inside an RRSP account?

43. Describe how you calculate the contribution limit for an RRSP?

44. What is a spousal RRSP? What are the advantages of a spousal RRSP?

45. Define and describe the Home Buyers' Plan (HBP)?

46. Define and describe the Lifelong Learning Plan (LLP)?

47. What is a tax-free savings account (TFSA)? What are the similarities and differences between RRSPs and TFSAs?

48. What is a locked-in retirement account (LIRA)? What is the main purpose of a LIRA?

49. List the retirement income conversion options for an RRSP account?

50. What is the main purpose of a registered retirement income fund (RRIF)?

51. What is the difference between a registered term annuity and a registered life annuity?

52. List the retirement income conversion options for a LIRA account?

53. What is the difference between a life income fund (LIF) and a locked-in retirement income fund (LRIF)?

54. What is a reverse mortgage? What are the advantages and disadvantages of a reverse mortgage?

55. List the three key retirement planning decisions.

56. Why is it beneficial to first consider investing in your employer's defined-benefit or defined-contribution pension plan?

57. Should you use an RRSP or a TFSA as a retirement planning option? Explain.

58. Describe a safe approach for determining how much you should contribute towards your retirement.

59. Describe how you may want to change your investment allocation as you move towards retirement.

60. When estimating the future value of a retirement investment, what factors will affect the amount of funds available to you at retirement? Explain.

61. When estimating the future value of a set of annual investments, what factors will affect the amount of funds available to you at retirement?

FINANCIAL PLANNING PROBLEMS

MyLab Finance Financial Planning Problems marked with a 🌐 can be found in MyLab Finance.

1. Collette is an employee of Dynamex Industries Inc. and earned $51 000 in 2017. How much will her employer deduct in CPP contributions based on an employee contribution rate of 4.95 percent? The YMPE and YBE for 2017 are $55 300 and $3500, respectively.

2. Anita currently has 30 years of service with her employer and is ready to retire. Her average best five consecutive years of income are used to calculate her annual pension. Her earnings for the past seven years, which represent her best earnings years, are listed in the table below. What will be her annual pension if she earns a pension based on a rate of 2 percent?

2010	2011	2012	2013	2014	2015	2016
$56 000	$64 000	$67 000	$67 000	$61 000	$72 000	$75 000

3. You have earned income of $46 000 for 2016. You have a defined-contribution plan to which your employer contributes $4600 in 2016. How much of an RRSP contribution can you make in 2017, assuming you had no accumulated RRSP room?

4. The balance of your RRSP at retirement is $453 382. You would like to receive a monthly income, at the end of each month, for 20 years. What will be your monthly income if you can earn a rate of return of 4.5 percent compounded monthly?

🌐 5. Barry has just become eligible for his employer-sponsored retirement plan. Barry is 35 years old and plans to retire at age 65. He calculates that he can contribute $300 per month at the end of the month to the plan. Barry's employer will match this amount. If Barry can earn an 8 percent return, compounded monthly, on his investment, how much will he have at retirement?

🌐 6. How much would Barry (from Problem 5) have at retirement if he had started contributing to this plan at age 25?

🌐 7. How much would Barry (from Problem 5) have if he could earn a 10 percent return, compounded monthly, on his investment beginning at age 35?

🌐 8. Assuming an 8 percent return, compounded monthly, how much would Barry (from Problem 5) have if he could invest an additional $1000 per year that his employer would match beginning at age 35?

🌐 9. How much will Marie have in her retirement account in 10 years if her contribution is $7000 per year at the end of the year and the annual return on the account is 6 percent, compounded monthly? How much of this amount represents interest?

10. Sandra intends to retire in 25 years and would like to receive $2000 at the end of each month in retirement for 25 years. How much must she deposit at the beginning of each month before retirement in order to accomplish her goal if she can earn a rate of return of 6 percent compounded monthly on her investments before and during retirement?

🌐 11. Lloyd and his wife, Jean, have no retirement plan at work but they contribute a total of $4000 each year to an RRSP. They are in a 30 percent marginal tax bracket. What tax savings will they realize for these contributions annually?

🌐 12. In need of extra cash, Troy and Lilly decide to withdraw $8000 from their RRSP. They are in a 30 percent marginal tax bracket. What will the tax consequences of this withdrawal be?

🌐 13. Lisa and Mark married at age 22. Each year until their thirtieth birthdays, they put a total of $4000 at the end of the year into their RRSPs. At age 30, they bought a home and started a family. They continued to make contributions to their employer-sponsored retirement plans (they no longer contribute to their respective RRSPs). If they receive an average annual return of 8 percent, compounded monthly, how much will they have in their RRSPs by age 60? What was their total investment?

🌐 14. Ricky and Sharon married at age 22, started a family, and bought a house. At age 30, they began making an annual contribution of $4000 to an RRSP. They continued to make these contributions until age 60. If the average return on their investment was 8 percent, compounded monthly, how much was in their RRSP at age 60? What was their total investment?

🌐 15. Tilly would like to invest $2500 of before-tax income each year in an RRSP account or in alternative stock investments. She likes the alternative investments because they provide her with more flexibility and a potentially higher return. She would like to retire in 30 years. If she invests money in an RRSP account, she can earn 7 percent per year, compounded monthly. If she invests in alternative stock investments, she can earn 9 percent per year, compounded monthly. Tilly is in the 30 percent marginal tax bracket.

   a. If Tilly invests all of her money in the RRSP account and withdraws all of her income when she retires, what is her income after taxes?

   b. If Tilly invests all of her money in alternative stock investments, what are her savings at retirement? (Hint: Remember that the income is taxed prior to investment.)

c. Assuming a marginal income tax rate of 30 percent, what is the after-tax value of the alternative stock investment?

d. Should Tilly invest her money in the RRSP account or in the alternative stock investments?

 16. Anita currently has 25 years of service and a final average annual salary of $37 000 over her last five years of employment. She was looking forward to retirement, but has been offered a promotion. If she continues to work for five more years and increases her average annual salary to $47 000, how will her monthly pension benefit from her defined-benefit plan change? Anita earns an annual pension income of 2 percent for her average annual salary.

CHALLENGE QUESTIONS

1. Reece is comparing defined-contribution pension plans with prospective employers. ABC Ltd. is offering a salary of $38 000, and will match 75 percent of his monthly contributions up to 10 percent of his salary, which also happens to be his maximum contribution limit. XYZ Company is offering a salary of $35 000 and will match 100 percent of his contribution up to 6 percent of his salary. Reece can make monthly contributions of up to 15 percent of his salary starting at the end of the month to the defined-contribution plan offered by XYZ Company. If Reece assumes that he will contribute the maximum amount allowed each year and keep these amounts invested for 30 years with a 7 percent return, compounded monthly, how much will his account be worth at each company? How can he use this information in making his employment decision? Assume that his annual salary at either company will remain unchanged.

2. Gurmeet and Sunny recently reviewed their future retirement income and expenses projections. They hope to retire in 25 years. They have determined that they will have a retirement income of $67 000 in today's dollars, but they will actually need $86 000 in retirement income in today's dollars. Calculate the total additional amount that Gurmeet and Sunny must save if they want to meet their income projection. Assume a 3 percent inflation rate and an 8 percent rate of return, compounded monthly.

3. Over the years, Katrina, 43, has accumulated $400 000 in her RRSP but took a $90 000 withdrawal to build a new home. Calculate the amount of taxes Katrina must pay when she files her tax return if her marginal tax rate is 39 percent and she did not take advantage of the Home Buyers' Plan (HBP). If she did take advantage of the HBP, how much must she pay back each year? What amount of income has she lost by withdrawing the funds for the HBP assuming she pays the minimum back to the RRSP and she can earn 7.5 percent, compounded monthly, in the RRSP?

 ETHICAL DILEMMA

Nancy and Al have been planning their retirement since they married in their early twenties. In their mid-forties and with two children in college, they are finding it harder to save and fear that they will fall short of the savings needed to reach their retirement goals. Nancy's rich Uncle Charlie assures her that she has nothing to worry about: "You are my favourite niece and because you are so good to me, I am leaving my entire estate to you." Nancy and Al begin to devote considerable time and energy to making Uncle Charlie's golden years as enjoyable as possible. Factoring in their anticipated inheritance, Nancy and Al look forward to a comfortable retirement.

Ten years later, Uncle Charlie passes away. At the reading of his will, Nancy is surprised to learn that Uncle Charlie made the same comment to her four cousins. As the will is read, all five of them are horrified to learn that Uncle Charlie left his entire estate, valued at more than $2 million, to a home for stray cats.

a. Fully discuss your views on the ethics of Uncle Charlie's actions.

b. Looking at Nancy and Al's experience, what lessons about retirement planning can be learned?

FINANCIAL PLANNING ONLINE EXERCISES

1. How you invest your contributions will have a major impact on your annual return and the amount of money you will save toward retirement. Go to www.retirementadvisor.ca/retadv/apps/tools/tools.jsp. Under Investment Tools, click on Portfolio Rates of Return.

   a. Select the GRAPHS tab. What is the difference in the annual return among the three asset mixes? Which asset mix shows the highest annual return? Which shows the lowest annual return? Which asset mix is the most diversified? Record the asset mix under each scenario on a piece of paper.

   b. Return to the main page. Under Investment Tools, click on Portfolio Accumulations. Change the asset mixes so that they are the same as in part a. Enter $1000 for Amount invested at beginning of period. Now select the GRAPHS tab. Which asset mix results in the highest return? Which asset mix would you choose? Why?

2. Go to www.mackenzieinvestments.com. Click on Tools & Calculators. Then click on RIF/LIF Illustrator. This tool can be used to determine how retirement income will be received from an RRIF, LIF, or LRIF. Under Assumptions, select yes for Deduct Withholding Tax, select your province of residence, and select yes for New Funds After 1992. Input a Current Plan Value of $100 000, a Plan Type of RRIF, an Annual Rate of Return of 5.00%, a Birth Date of 06/21/1949, and an Issue Date and First Payment Date of 07/14/2014. Payment Type should be Minimum and Payment Frequency should be Monthly.

   a. Click on Next. What is the total amount of payments received from the RRIF? Select Graph. How long do RRIF payments last? What is the plan's value at age 80 and at age 100?

   b. Compare the total payments and graph from the RRIF calculation to those of the LIF and LRIF, respectively.

3. Go to www.retirementadvisor.ca/retadv/apps/tfsaRrsp/tfsaRrsp_inputs.jsp?toolsSubMenu=preRet. Complete the General Inputs section using the following information:

Planned Contribution this Year, before tax:	$5000
Current Age:	25
Planned Age to Withdraw Proceeds:	65
Expected Annual Return:	6%
Expected Inflation Rate:	2.5%

   Next, select your province of residence and enter a current income of $40 000 and an expected income in retirement of 70 percent. Click Compute.

   a. Which account type has the higher Accumulated Balance by Age 65? Which account type has the higher Proceeds after Income Tax?

   b. Does an RRSP withdrawal lead to a reduction in government benefits? Explain.

   c. Go back to the main page and click on Assumptions behind this Calculator. Describe the major income-tested benefits in Canada. Why is it important to understand these income-tested benefits?

PSYCHOLOGY OF PERSONAL FINANCE: Your Retirement

1. Some people find that it is much easier to save for retirement when they request that their employer automatically direct a portion of their income to their retirement account. Describe your strategy to invest in your retirement. Are you presently investing in a retirement account? If so, do you use a defined-benefit or a defined-contribution pension plan for this purpose? If not, which retirement account option would you prefer? Explain.

2. Read one practical article about how psychology affects decisions when investing in your retirement. You can easily retrieve possible articles by doing an online search using the terms "psychology" and "investing in retirement." Summarize the main points of the article.

MINI-CASE 1: Calculating Retirement Income

Nanci, age 42, and Serge, age 39, residents of Saint John, New Brunswick, have become increasingly worried about their retirement. Nanci, an office manager, dreams of retiring at age 62 so that they can travel and visit family. Serge, a self-employed benefits consultant, is unsure their current retirement plan will allow them to achieve that goal. He is concerned that the cost of living in New Brunswick, along with their lifestyle, has them spending at a level they cannot maintain. Although they have a combined income of well above $100 000 per year, they got a late start planning for retirement, which is now just 20 years away. Nanci has tried to plan by contributing to her RRSP, but she is currently investing only $3500, at the end of each year, of her before-tax income of $52 000. Serge does not have a set amount he contributes to his RRSP and puts money in it whenever he can. He currently earns $72 000 per year. In retirement, the couple would like to be able to cover their current annual expenses of $70 000. They project that they will each receive $1400 at the end of each month, in today's dollars, from OAS and CPP. This amount will increase at an effective rate of 2 percent per year. Nanci and Serge have RRSP accounts currently valued at $20 000 and $47 800, respectively. Their RRSPs will grow at an annual rate of 6 percent per year, compounded annually, from now until the end of their retirement. Their marginal tax rate is 36.82 percent. The couple would like to plan for a retirement that lasts until Nanci reaches age 90. Use this information to help them prepare for a prosperous retirement.

Assuming an inflation rate of 3 percent, calculate the present value, at retirement, of their retirement income need. Calculate the present value, at retirement, of their OAS and CPP pension income. Calculate the present value, at retirement, of their RRSPs. Assume that Serge will match Nanci's annual contribution amount. How much, if any, will they need to invest annually to make up for any shortfall? Nanci and Serge are considering reducing their expenses in retirement to $60 000 per year. How will this affect the amount they have to save in retirement? Assume that they make their annual investment at the end of the year and that they withdraw their retirement income need at the beginning of each year.

Study Guide

Circle the correct answer and then check the answers in the back of the book to chart your progress.

Multiple Choice

1. Which of the following benefits is not subject to a clawback?
   a. Old Age Security (OAS)
   b. Canada Pension Plan (CPP)
   c. Guaranteed Income Supplement (GIS)
   d. Allowance for the survivor benefit

2. Old Age Security benefits:
   a. Can be deferred five years, which would increase your benefit by 36 percent.
   b. Are not subject to a "means test."
   c. Can be claimed at age 60, but at a reduced amount.
   d. Are a nontaxable benefit.

3. Eleanor is a 63-year-old pensioner who has asked for advice with respect to what government benefits she may be eligible to apply for. Given no further information, which of the following government benefits is Eleanor not eligible to apply for?
   a. Allowance benefit
   b. Canada Pension Plan (CPP)
   c. Guaranteed Income Supplement (GIS)
   d. Allowance for the survivor benefit

4. For each resident of Canada, their CPP entitlement is calculated based on the:
   a. Number of years they were a working adult resident of Canada with income under $70 000.
   b. Dollar value of their contributions and the number of years they contributed to the plan.
   c. Number of years up to age 65 they were an adult resident of Canada.
   d. Income they earned above the YMPE each year.

5. For retirees, the most important difference between CPP and OAS is that:
   a. Only OAS is indexed for inflation.
   b. Only OAS is based on income earned each year relative to the YMPE.
   c. Only CPP can be taken early at a reduced amount.
   d. Only CPP can be deferred to receive an increased monthly amount.

6. Francis is an employee of Hybrid Pipeline. His income for 2017 was $52 000. Determine the amount of CPP contribution he would make for the year. The year's maximum pensionable earnings (YMPE) and employee contribution rate for 2017 are $55 300 and 4.95 percent, respectively.
   a. $2737.35
   b. $2574.00
   c. $1905.75
   d. $2336.40

7. The retirement benefit you receive from a money purchase defined-contribution plan will be based on:
   a. A certain percentage of your income in the later years of employment.
   b. A formula that guarantees a set amount to support a modest retirement lifestyle.
   c. The performance of the funds contributed on your behalf.
   d. The performance of your company's shares.

8. Serena belongs to a defined-benefit pension plan. For each year of service, she earns an annual pension income of 1.4 percent on her first $35 000 of annual income and 1.7 percent on any remaining income for the year. In 2017, Serena earned income of $65 000. Calculate the amount of annual pension income she has earned based on her 2017 income.
   a. $1007.50
   b. $1000.00
   c. $1105.00
   d. $910.00

9. Which of the following is an important factor to consider in deciding between saving in a TFSA account or an RRSP account?
   a. Your tax bracket
   b. The appropriate risk level
   c. Tax sheltering of investment income
   d. The types of investment vehicles

10. Which of the following is true about RRSPs?
    a. You can withdraw funds tax free once you are over age 71.
    b. There is no limit on the dollar amount you can contribute.
    c. Your investment income is tax-sheltered in the plan.
    d. You can transfer the funds to your children tax-sheltered.

11. Which of the following is true regarding employer-sponsored pension plans?
    a. A defined contribution pension plan is the same as an RRSP.
    b. A defined-contribution plan guarantees you a specific amount of income when you retire.
    c. In a defined-benefit plan, the risk of a shortfall in benefit payments must be covered by the employee.
    d. You should take advantage of them because the employer must contribute at least half the funding.

12. When you leave an employer prior to retirement age, your options with your vested defined-benefit plan are all of the following, except:
    a. Leave it with your former employer.
    b. Transfer it to your new employer's pension plan.
    c. Transfer it to a LIRA.
    d. Transfer it to your RRSP within 30 days.

13. If you invested $10 000 in an RRSP 30 years ago and it has a value today of $100 000, what amount will you pay tax on when you withdraw it during your retirement years?
    a. Only on the initial $10 000.
    b. Only on the $90 000 growth.
    c. On all $100 000 as it is withdrawn.
    d. There is no tax to be paid in retirement.

14. Which is a key difference between RRSPs and TFSAs?
    a. TFSA withdrawals are taxed.
    b. RRSPs' contribution limit accumulates.
    c. TFSAs give tax deductions on contributions.
    d. RRSP withdrawals are taxed.

15. If you qualify, the maximum withdrawal allowed under the Home Buyers' Plan (HBP) is:
    a. $20 000 per person.
    b. $25 000 per person.
    c. $25 000 per couple.
    d. $40 000 per couple.

True/False

1. True or False? A "means test" refers to the concept that if your income exceeds a certain amount, the amount you will receive from any of the OAS program benefits will be reduced.

2. True or False? The only qualifying criteria for OAS benefits are age and residency.

3. True or False? Olga expects to live to age 100 and would like to maximize the amount she will receive

from the CPP. Assuming that her retirement income needs are being met by other sources, she should apply for CPP benefits at age 65.

4. True or False? Your CPP benefits are based on all of your contributions from age 18 to age 65.

5. True or False? In a defined-benefit pension plan, the contribution rate is based on a specific formula.

6. True or False? A pension adjustment will reduce the amount that you can contribute to individual retirement savings plans.

7. True or False? If you are young and far from retirement, you are in a position to take more risk with your investments.

8. True or False? A self-directed RRSP is sufficient for the needs of investors who are opening their first account or have all of their RRSP assets in the mutual funds of a single company.

9. True or False? The amount that you can contribute to your RRSP is 18 percent of your previous year's income less your previous year's pension adjustment.

10. True or False? TFSAs can be used for short-term and long-term goals.

11. True or False? Money withdrawn from a TFSA cannot be recontributed.

12. True or False? The main advantage of a registered annuity over a RRIF is that you are no longer exposed to the risk that your investments may decrease in value.

13. True or False? The need to take out a reverse mortgage is reduced if you actively participate in sound financial planning.

14. True or False? The longer annual savings are invested, the more they may be worth at retirement.

15. True or False? The income generated inside a retirement account is not taxed until you withdraw the funds.

Estate Planning

Keith Bell/Shutterstock

Damaris managed to accumulate an estate of more than $1.5 million, including a house worth $500 000 and investment assets of approximately $1 million. Her two children were aware of the value of their mother's estate, but were surprised to learn that her will was no longer valid after her marriage to Paul, her widower.

Although it appeared that the children would have inherited the estate assets on a 50–50 basis, this was no longer the case. Since Damaris did not have a valid will at her death, her estate assets will be distributed according to the intestacy provisions of the province in which she lived.

QUESTIONS:

1. What does it mean to die intestate?
2. Under what circumstances should you revise an existing will?
3. What other estate planning tools could Damaris have used to distribute her estate assets?

1. Explain the use of a will
2. Describe the common types of wills
3. Describe the key components of a will
4. Describe probate fees and taxes at death
5. Explain the types of estate planning strategies
6. Introduce other aspects of estate planning

L.0.1

BACKGROUND ON WILLS

estate
The assets of a deceased person after all debts are paid.

will
A legal document that describes how your estate should be distributed upon your death. It can also identify a preferred guardian for any surviving minor children.

beneficiary
A person specified in a will to receive part of an estate (also known as an heir); also, the named individual who receives life insurance payments upon the death of the insured.

executor
The person designated in a will to pay off any debts that the testator may have and carry out the instructions regarding the distribution of the testator's assets to beneficiaries.

intestate
The condition of dying without a will.

preferential share
The dollar value of estate assets that will be distributed to the surviving spouse before assets are distributed among all potential beneficiaries.

An **estate** represents a deceased person's assets after all debts are paid. At the time of a person's death, the estate is distributed according to that person's wishes as set out in his or her will. *Estate planning* is the act of planning how your wealth will be allocated on or before your death. One of the most important tasks in estate planning is the creation of a **will**, which is a legal document that describes how your estate should be distributed upon your death. The individual who makes a will is commonly known as a testator; although the term testatrix may be used when referring to a female. As the testator, a will gives you an opportunity to ensure that your estate is distributed in the manner you desire. Once you have a positive net worth to be distributed upon your death, you should consider creating a will. In it you can specify the persons you want to receive your estate, referred to as your **beneficiaries** (or heirs). A will can also identify a preferred guardian for any surviving minor children that you have and the age at which the children will receive their inheritance. Any beneficiary that is under the age of 18 is not entitled to receive his or her inheritance directly. In this case, the inheritance is held in trust for the beneficiary. The uses of trusts will be discussed later in this chapter. A beneficiary can be of any age and in fact can be unborn at the time the will is made. The instructions in your will are carried out by an executor. The **executor** is the person designated in your will to pay off any debts that you may have and carry out the instructions regarding the distribution of your assets to beneficiaries. A female executor may also be referred to as an executrix. An executor is sometimes referred to as a personal representative.

If you die **intestate** (without a will), the court will appoint a person (called an administrator) to distribute your estate according to the laws of your province. In that case, one family member may receive more than you intended, while others may receive less. In most provinces, the surviving spouse will receive a **preferential share**. The preferential share refers to the dollar value of estate assets that will be distributed to the surviving spouse before assets are distributed among all potential beneficiaries. Depending on the circumstances of an individual case, the surviving spouse may receive more than the preferential share provided under provincial legislation. Exhibit 15.1 highlights the dollar value of the preferential share in each province. Notice that the amount that may be received varies by province. If there is no surviving spouse, the administrator decides who will assume responsibility for any minor children. Having an administrator also results in additional costs being imposed on the estate.

Creating a Valid Will

To create a valid will in most provinces, you must be at least the age of majority, which is 18 or 19 depending on the province in which you live. Some provinces permit individuals younger than the age of majority to create a legal will in the case of military duty or marriage. In all provinces, you must be mentally competent and should not be subject to undue influence (threats) from others. A will is more likely to be challenged by potential heirs if there is some question about your competence or about whether you were forced to designate one or more beneficiaries in the will.

myth or **fact**   Estate planning is only for people who have assets to distribute to heirs or children that need a guardian.

EXHIBIT 15.1 Provincial Summary of Preferential Share Amounts

	Preferential Share Amount	Remaining Assets (Spouse + 1 child)[4]
Alberta	$150 000	All to spouse[2]
British Columbia	$300 000[1]	Split 50:50
Manitoba	The greater of $50 000 or 1/2	All to spouse[3]
New Brunswick	Marital property	Split 50:50
Newfoundland & Labrador	$ 0	Split 50:50
Northwest Territories	$ 50 000	Split 50:50
Nova Scotia	$ 50 000	Split 50:50
Nunavut	$ 50 000	Split 50:50
Ontario	$200 000	Split 50:50
Prince Edward Island	$ 0	Split 50:50
Quebec	$ 0	1/3 to spouse 2/3 to child
Saskatchewan	$100 000	Split 50:50
Yukon	$ 75 000	Split 50:50

[1]The surviving spouse receives $300 000 if the child is also the child of the surviving spouse. Otherwise, the surviving spouse receives the first $150 000 plus one-half of any remainder.

[2]The entire estate goes to the surviving spouse if the child is also the child of the surviving spouse. Otherwise, the surviving spouse receives the greater of the first $150 000 or 1/2, plus 1/2 of any remainder.

[3]The entire estate goes to the surviving spouse if the child is also the child of the surviving spouse. Otherwise, the surviving spouse receives the greater of the first $50 000 or 1/2, plus 1/2 of any remainder.

[4]In all provinces, except Manitoba and Alberta, if there is more than 1 child, 1/3 of remaining assets go to the surviving spouse and 2/3 of remaining assets go to the children. In Manitoba and Alberta, the provisions for more than 1 child are the same as those described for when there is only 1 child.

English form will
A will that contains the signature of the testator as well as the signatures of two witnesses who were present when the testator signed the will.

COMMON TYPES OF WILLS

L.O.2

The most common type of will in Canada is the **English form will**, which contains the signature of the testator as well as the signatures of two witnesses who were present when the testator signed the will. The will may be handwritten or typed. In Quebec, this type of will is known as a will made before witnesses. To be valid, a will must be dated and signed. Normally, witnesses to a will do not inherit anything under the will. If this is not the case, witnesses will be denied their status as beneficiaries of the will. Although you are not required to hire a lawyer, you should consider doing so to ensure that your will is created properly. A **notarial will** is a formal type of will that is commonly used in Quebec and is completed in the presence of a notary (lawyer). In most cases, only one witness to this type of will is required. The original copy of the will is left with the notary. A **holograph will** is a will that is written solely in the handwriting of the testator and that does not require the signature of any witnesses. This type of will is not recognized in all provinces.

notarial will
A formal type of will that is commonly used in Quebec and is completed in the presence of a notary (lawyer).

holograph will
A will that is written solely in the handwriting of the testator and that does not require the signature of any witnesses.

KEY COMPONENTS OF A WILL

L.O.3

Exhibit 15.2 provides an example of a will that names either one or two alternate executors in case the intended executor is unwilling or unable to do the job of carrying out the will. This sample will leave almost everything to one beneficiary, but allows for an alternate beneficiary should the original intended beneficiary predecease the person writing the will. In addition, a specific bequest is made to one beneficiary. The will also provides instructions in case the alternate beneficiary also predeceases the testator. The key components of a will are described next.

EXHIBIT 15.2   A Sample Last Will and Testament

Last Will and Testament

THIS IS THE LAST WILL of me, **James T. Smith**, presently of the City of Brampton, in the Province of Ontario.

1. **I REVOKE** all former wills and codicils.
2. **I APPOINT** my Spouse, Karen A. Smith, as sole Executrix and Trustee of this my Will, but if my Spouse should predecease me, or shall refuse or be unable to act or continue to act as Executrix and Trustee or die before the trusts created in this Will shall have terminated, then I APPOINT Edward J. Smith of Brampton, Ontario to be the Executor and Trustee of this my Will in the place of my Spouse.
3. If my Spouse predeceases me, then **I APPOINT** Edward J. Smith of Brampton, Ontario and Marie S. Smith of Toronto, Ontario, or the survivor of them, to be the Guardian of the persons of my infant children during their respective minorities.

Disposition of Estate

4. **I GIVE AND APPOINT** to my Trustee all my property wherever located including any property over which I may have a power of appointment, upon the following trusts:
   a. To pay my legally enforceable debts, funeral expenses and all expenses in connection with the administration of my estate and the trusts created by my Will as soon as convenient after my death.
   b. To deliver, transfer and pay to Edward J. Smith of Brampton, Ontario, if he shall survive me, for his own use absolutely, the following: my gold watch.
   c. To transfer the residue of my estate to my Spouse, if she survives me for Thirty (30) full days, for her own use absolutely.
   d. If my Spouse should predecease me or should survive me but die within a period of thirty (30) days after my death, I DIRECT my Trustee to hold in trust the residue of my estate for my child: Cheryl D. Smith of Brampton, Ontario, if that child is alive at my death, and to keep that share invested and to pay the whole or such part of the net income derived therefrom and any amount or amounts out of the capital that my Trustee may deem advisable to that child or for the maintenance, education, or benefit of that child until he or she reaches the age of 25 years and thereupon to pay and transfer the remainder of the part of that share to that child.

Administration of Estate

5. **TO CARRY OUT** the terms of my Will, I give my Trustee the following powers to be used in his or her discretion at any time namely:
   a. Subject to my express direction to the contrary to use his or her discretion in the realization of my estate, with power to my Trustee to sell, call in and convert into money any part of my estate not consisting of money at such time or times, in such manner and upon such terms, and either for cash or credit or for part cash and part credit as my Trustee may in his or her uncontrolled discretion decide upon, or to postpone such conversion of my estate or any part or parts thereof for such length of time as he or she may think best and I HEREBY DECLARE that my Trustee may retain any portion of my estate in the form in which it may be at my death (notwithstanding that it may not be in the form of an investment in which trustees are authorized to invest trust funds, and whether or not there is a liability attached to any such portion of my estate) for such length of time as my Trustee may in his or her discretion deem advisable and my Trustee shall not be held responsible for any loss that may happen to my estate by reason of so doing.
   b. Except as otherwise provided, to set aside the share of any minor beneficiary, keep such share invested, pay the income or capital or as much of either or both as my Trustee considers advisable for the maintenance, education, advancement or benefit of that minor beneficiary and pay or transfer the capital of that share or the amount remaining to that beneficiary when he or she reaches the age of majority, or during the minority of such beneficiary to pay or transfer such share to any parent or guardian of such beneficiary, subject to like conditions, and the receipt of any parent or guardian discharges my Trustee.
   c. To make any payments or disburse any bequests for the benefit of any person entitled to receive funds from my estate while under the age of majority to a parent or guardian (acting or appointed) of such person, whose receipt shall be sufficient discharge to my Trustee.
   d. To make any division of the assets of my estate or set aside or pay any share or interest in them, either wholly or in part, and my Trustee shall determine the value of my assets or any part thereof for the purpose of making such division, setting aside or payment and his or her determination shall be final and binding upon all persons concerned.
   e. Upon any distribution of my estate to determine to whom or to which trust specified assets shall be given or allocated and to distribute the same subject to the payment of such amount as shall be necessary to adjust the shares of the various beneficiaries or trusts.
   f. To raise money on the credit of my estate, either without security or by mortgage or charge on any part of my estate.
   g. To make expenditures for the purpose of repairing, improving and rebuilding any property.

(continued)

EXHIBIT 15.2 continued

   h. To continue and renew any bills, notes, guarantees or other securities or contracts relating to them, but only for the purpose of facilitating an orderly liquidation of those obligations.

   i. To make any investments for my estate, including the trusts established hereunder, which my Trustee in his or her absolute discretion considers advisable without being limited to investments authorized by law for trustees.

   j. To sell, mortgage, exchange, lease, or give options without being limited as to term, or otherwise dispose or deal with any real estate held by my Trustee and to pay, alter, improve, add to or remove any buildings thereon and generally to manage such real estate.

   k. To continue, discontinue, or wind-up any ownership, business, partnership, contract or transaction in force or pending at the time of my death and to participate in the amalgamation, reorganization or recapitalization of any corporation or firm in which I may have any share or interest, and generally to deal with any and all shares and securities belonging to my estate in the fullest and most unrestricted manner without any responsibility on the part of my Trustee other than that imposed by law and my Trustee may act as an employee or officer of any such company and receive remuneration from it.

   l. Instead of acting personally, to employ and pay any other person or persons, including a body corporate, to transact any business or to do any act of any nature in relation to my Will and trusts including the receipt and payment of money, without being liable for any loss incurred. And I authorize my Trustee to appoint from time to time upon such terms as he or she may think fit any person or persons, including a body corporate, for the purpose of exercising any trusts or powers herein expressed or impliedly given to my Trustee with respect to any property belonging to me.

   m. To employ a body corporate as a custodian of all or any part of my estate and to transfer or assign all or any part of my estate to such custodian upon such terms and conditions as my Trustee may determine and such custodian may be my Trustee.

   n. Without the consent of any persons interested in my estate or trusts established hereunder to compromise, settle or waive any claim or claims at any time due to or by my estate in such manner and to such an extent as my Trustee may deem to be in the best interests of my estate and the beneficiaries or trusts thereof, and to make an agreement with any other person, persons or corporations in respect thereof, which shall be binding upon my estate and such beneficiaries.

   o. To make or not make any election, determination, designation or allocation required or permitted to be made by my Trustee (either alone or jointly with others) under any of the provisions of the Income Tax Act (Canada) or any other taxing statute, including the Excise Tax Act (Canada), in such manner as my Trustee, in his or her absolute discretion, deems advisable, and each such election, determination, designation or allocation when so made shall be final and binding upon all persons concerned.

   p. To either distribute capital property to any beneficiary or terminate any trust established under this my Will and in either case to distribute to the beneficiaries thereof the trust property immediately prior to the 21 year deemed realization period established under the provisions of the Income Tax Act (Canada).

   q. To pay any income taxes payable by my estate in installments as permitted by the Income Tax Act (Canada) if my Trustee considers such deferment to be in the best interests of my estate and its beneficiaries and to give security from my estate for such installment payments.

6. Subject to the terms of this my Will, I DIRECT that my Trustee shall not be liable for any loss to my estate or to any beneficiary resulting from the exercise by him or her in good faith of any discretion given him or her in this my Will.

IN WITNESS WHEREOF I, James T. Smith, the within named Testator, have to this my last will contained on this and the preceding pages, set my hand at the City of Brampton, in the Province of Ontario this 13th day of June, 2007.

SIGNED, PUBLISHED AND DECLARED

by James T. Smith,	)
as and for his Last Will and Testament in the	) _____
presence of us, both present at the same	) James T. Smith
time, who at his request and in his presence	)
and in the presence of each other have hereunto	)
subscribed our names as witnesses.	)

_____	_____
(Witness' signature)	(Witness' signature)
Name _____	Name _____
Address _____	Address _____
City/Province _____	City/Province _____

Source: Adapted from LawDepot.com, www.lawdepot.com. Reprinted with permission of LawDepot. (accessed July 26, 2007).

Testator Identification. The initial part of the will in Exhibit 15.2 identifies the person who made the will. In this case, the testator is James T. Smith.

Revocation of Previous Wills. To avoid confusion if more than one will exists, a standard will contains a clause revoking all other wills and declaring this will to be the last will. If two wills are later found to exist, the will with the most recent date will be the valid will.

Appointment of Executor (Personal Representative). Recall that in your will you name an executor to pay off any debts that you may have and to carry out the instructions regarding the distribution of your assets to beneficiaries. As such, an executor may be required to collect any money owed to the estate, pay off any debts owed by the estate, sell specific assets (such as a home) that are part of the estate, and then distribute the proceeds as specified in the will. The executor must notify everyone who has an interest or potential interest in the estate. Most people select a family member, a friend, a business associate, a bank trust company employee, or a lawyer as executor. You should select an executor who will serve your interests in distributing the assets as specified in your will, who is capable of handling the process, and who is sufficiently organized to complete the process in a timely manner. The executor is entitled to be paid by the estate for services provided, but some executors elect not to charge the estate. In many cases, the executor and trustee is the same individual. A **trustee** is an individual or organization that is responsible for the management of assets held in trust for one or more of the beneficiaries of a will. Recall that any beneficiary under the age of 18 is not entitled to receive his or her inheritance directly. In this case, the inheritance is held in trust by the trustee for the beneficiary. In Exhibit 15.2, the executrix and trustee is the spouse, Karen A. Smith. The alternate executor and trustee is the testator's brother Edward J. Smith. Of course, the executrix/executor can be a beneficiary as well.

Appointment of Guardian for Minor Children. If you are a parent, you should name a guardian who will be assigned the responsibility of caring for your children and of managing any estate left to them. You should ensure that the person you select as guardian is willing to serve in this capacity. Your will may specify an amount of money to be distributed to the guardian to care for the children. Section 3 of Exhibit 15.2 indicates that the guardian will be either the spouse, Karen A. Smith, or the uncle and aunt, Edward J. Smith and Marie S. Smith. The guardian does not necessarily have custody of the children. The guardian can choose another for custodial care, but would retain the legal responsibility.

Authorization to Pay Debts. Prior to the distribution of any assets, the debts and expenses of the deceased must be paid. Section 4a of Exhibit 15.2 gives the executor the legal authority to pay the debts and expenses of the deceased.

Authorization to Make Bequests. In the example will, a specific bequest of a gold watch is made to Edward J. Smith. A **bequest** is a gift that results from the instructions provided in a will. There is no limit to the number of bequests that can be made in a will. A bequest is often made in circumstances where the deceased would like to leave some personal property of sentimental value to a specific individual.

Distribution of Residue. A will details how the estate should be distributed among the beneficiaries. Since you do not know what your estate will be worth, you may specify your desired distribution according to percentages of the estate. For example, you could specify that two people each receive 50 percent of the estate. Alternatively, you could specify that one person receive a specific dollar amount and that the other person receive the remainder of the estate. **Residue** refers to the amount remaining in an estate after all financial obligations, such as the payment of debts, expenses, taxes, and bequests, have been fulfilled. This clause ensures that all remaining assets of the deceased are accounted for and distributed. As such, it is important to ensure that the individual(s) who will receive the residue of the estate have not predeceased the testator. In Exhibit 15.2, Section 4c transfers the residue of the estate to the spouse. If the spouse is predeceased,

trustee
An individual or organization that is responsible for the management of assets held in trust for one or more of the beneficiaries of a will.

bequest
A gift that results from the instructions provided in a will.

residue
Refers to the amount remaining in an estate after all financial obligations, such as the payment of debts, expenses, taxes, and bequests, have been fulfilled.

the residue is held in trust for the child of the testator. If the child is predeceased, the residue is shared equally between the testator's brother and sister. If either the brother or the sister is predeceased, their share of the residue is shared among their descendants.

Administration of the Estate. The instructions with respect to the administration of an estate can be very detailed or very simple. In Exhibit 15.2, a single clause is used to provide the trustee with complete authority in dealing with the assets of the estate. Every province provides a set of guidelines for how an estate is to be administered by a trustee. If the testator would like to give the trustee more discretion to deal with estate assets than what is provided for in provincial legislation, it is important to include clear instructions in the will. As a result, a will may contain a number of clauses that deal with the administration of an estate.

> **myth** or **fact** I'm married. If I die, everything goes to my spouse, so I don't need an estate plan.

Liability. A trustee executor can be held legally liable for any mistakes made in administering a will. As a result, it is common to include a clause in a will, such as the one in Section 6 of Exhibit 15.2, that limits the liability of a trustee who acts in good faith.

Signatures. A will must be signed by the testator and by two witnesses in order to be valid. This helps to ensure that someone else does not create a fake will.

Letter of Last Instruction. Some individuals may also wish to prepare a **letter of last instruction,** a supplement to a will that describes preferences regarding funeral arrangements and indicates where any key financial documents, such as mortgage and insurance contracts, are stored.

letter of last instruction
A supplement to a will that describes preferences regarding funeral arrangements and indicates where any key financial documents are stored.

FOCUS ON ETHICS: Undue Influence on Wills

By now, you have learned to be aware of fraudulent or unethical behaviour in all components of financial planning. Fraud and unethical behaviour can even occur during the creation of a will. Consider the following examples:

- Christine, a 60-year-old mother of 2, asks her oldest son for estate planning advice. He pressures her to leave much of the estate to him.
- Marguerite has already completed a will which specifies that most of her estate will go to charity. She becomes terminally ill. Brooke, a frequent visitor at the hospital, pressures Marguerite to include her in the will.
- Jarrod asks his son Jim (who is a lawyer) for advice on creating a will. Jim misrepresents the rules about estates, which causes Jarrod to create a will that leaves a disproportionate amount of the estate to Jim.
- Tamara, a widow, has created a will that leaves her estate to her children and grandchildren. However, she recently met Jim, who has proposed marriage. Jim suggests that she leave her estate to him since he will be her husband.

These types of situations occur more frequently than you might think. If the court determines that there is fraud or some form of undue influence on the creator of the will, it may prevent the person who used fraudulent or unethical behaviour from receiving any benefits. However, someone has to contest the will to have the court pursue an inquiry.

Consider creating a will without consulting potential beneficiaries. Meet with a financial planner or lawyer who specializes in wills and explain how you wish to allocate the estate among your heirs or others. The financial planner can design the will in a manner that achieves your goals. You can include all of your wishes in a will without discussing any of them with persons who are (or are not) named in the will.

Changing Your Will

A will should be updated every two to three years. In addition, specific events should trigger a review of your will. These events include:

- Birth or adoption of a child
- Marriage
- Undertaking of a common-law relationship
- Separation from a spouse or common-law partner
- Receipt of an inheritance
- Death of a child
- Relocation to a new province of residence
- Changes to provincial legislation
- Illness or death of an executor or trustee named in the will
- Illness or death of a significant beneficiary

With the exception of British Columbia, Alberta, and Quebec, the act of marriage will automatically cancel all wills dated prior to the date of marriage in all provinces. If you do not update your will, your estate will be subject to the intestate succession laws of the province in which you reside. The distribution of your assets will be determined, in part, based on the information provided in Exhibit 15.1.

In some cases, a common-law relationship will not trigger the preferential spouse's share under laws of intestacy. If you are in a common-law relationship, you should consider a will to make your intentions clear.

If you wish to make major changes to your will, you will probably need to create a new one. The new will must specify that you are revoking your previous will, so that you do not have multiple wills with conflicting instructions. When you wish to make only minor revisions to your will, you can add a **codicil**, which is a document that specifies changes in an existing will.

codicil
A document that specifies changes in an existing will.

L.O.4

PROBATE FEES AND TAXES AT DEATH

Executing the Will during Probate

probate
A legal process that declares a will valid and ensures the orderly distribution of assets.

Probate is a legal process that declares a will valid and ensures the orderly distribution of assets. The probate process ensures that when people die, their assets are distributed as they wish and the guardianship of children is assigned as they wish. To start the probate process, the executor files forms in a local probate court, provides a copy of the will, provides a list of the assets and debts of the deceased person, pays debts, and sells any assets that need to be liquidated. The executor typically opens a bank account for the estate that is used to pay the debts of the deceased and to deposit proceeds from liquidating the assets. If the executor does not have time or is otherwise unable to perform these tasks, a lawyer can be hired to complete them. The courts will also appoint the guardian for minor children. If family members dispute the intended guardian for cause, the court may appoint another. Exhibit 15.3 displays the amount of probate fees that are payable in each province and territory for different estate values. Probate fees vary significantly by province. In general, probate fees are very low in Canada. For example, an estate valued at $5 million in Ontario will have an associated probate fee of $74 500, or approximately 1.5 percent of the entire estate value. In Ontario, probate fees are known as estate administration taxes. Estate planning strategies that help to reduce or eliminate probate fees will be discussed in the next section.

EXHIBIT 15.3 Example of Provincial/Territorial Probate Fees for Various Estate Asset Values

	Estate Values		
	$100 000	**$1 000 000**	**$5 000 000**
Alberta	$ 275	$ 525	$ 525
British Columbia	$ 850	$13 450	$69 450
Manitoba	$ 700	$ 7000	$35 000
New Brunswick	$ 500	$ 5000	$25 000
Newfoundland & Labrador	$ 654	$ 6054	$30 054
Northwest Territories	$ 200	$ 400	$ 400
Nova Scotia	$1003	$16 258	$84 058
Nunavut	$ 200	$ 400	$ 400
Ontario	$1000	$14 500	$74 500
Prince Edward Island	$ 400	$ 4000	$20 000
Quebec (natural person/legal person)	$106/$119	$106/$119	$106/$119
Saskatchewan	$ 700	$ 7000	$35 000
Yukon	$ 140	$ 140	$ 140

Source: http://www.taxtips.ca/willsandestates/probatefees.htm, accessed November 26, 2017.

The Final Tax Return

When a taxpayer dies, a final tax return must be filed with the Canada Revenue Agency (CRA). A deceased taxpayer may have to pay taxes because, for tax purposes, he or she is deemed to have disposed of his or her assets on the date of death. This deemed disposition does not mean that the estate must sell the deceased's assets. Instead, the estate will be responsible to pay the deceased's taxes on income, investment income, and capital gains. The payment of taxes based on the filing of a final tax return is not the same as paying probate fees. Probate fees are determined based on the value of assets transferred to the estate, whereas taxes payable by the deceased are determined using deemed disposition rules and represent the amount of tax to be paid by the estate on behalf of the deceased.

All capital property is deemed to be disposed of when a person dies. This is not an actual sale, but the deemed disposition will trigger capital gains or losses for which the estate will be liable. Such gains or losses can be deferred in some cases. However, the taxpayer must plan ahead to this tax deferral. The amount of tax payable on estate assets is calculated using the difference between the fair market value of the assets at the date of death and the acquisition cost of the assets.

The amount of tax that Canadians pay upon death is relatively low. First, the increase in value of your principal residence is not subject to tax. Second, registered retirement savings plans (RRSPs) and other registered retirement accounts can be easily rolled over to a surviving spouse, thereby temporarily delaying taxes payable. Combined, these two asset types usually represent the bulk of most Canadians' net worth. As a result, taxes at death tend not to be a concern for the average Canadian taxpayer.

myth or **fact** Everything else being equal, it is more important for a couple living in a common-law relationship to have a will than it is for a married couple.

Optional Tax Returns

rights or things
Income that was owed to the deceased taxpayer but not paid at the time of death, but that would have been included in income had the taxpayer not died.

The final tax return is normally filed within six months of the date of death or on April 30 of the following year, whichever is later. In addition, the executor may be able to reduce the taxes payable by filing separate returns for "rights or things," business income, and income from a testamentary trust. **Rights or things** is income that was owed to the deceased taxpayer but not paid at the time of death, but that would have been included in income had the taxpayer not died. For example, a bond coupon payment that was earned by the taxpayer while alive that had not been paid by the time of death would qualify as a "right or thing." A deceased taxpayer's share of business income from a partnership or proprietorship that had not been paid by the time of death can be reported on a separate tax return. Finally, if the deceased taxpayer was receiving income from a testamentary trust, the deceased's share of any unallocated income can be reported on a separate tax return. The ability to split income and report it on separate tax returns will reduce the amount of tax payable by the deceased. In addition, some of the non-refundable tax credits available on the final return can be used again on each optional return. The option to use tax credits on each tax form will further reduce the amount of taxes payable by the deceased.

L.O.5

ESTATE PLANNING STRATEGIES

Joint Tenancy with Rights of Survivorship (JTWROS)

joint tenancy with rights of survivorship (JTWROS)
A form of joint ownership where the death of one joint owner results in an asset being transferred directly to the surviving joint owner.

Estate planning tools are effective when they allow assets or property to be passed directly to someone else without the asset first becoming a part of the estate of the deceased. **Joint tenancy with rights of survivorship (JTWROS)** is a form of joint ownership where the death of one joint owner results in an asset being transferred directly to the surviving joint owner, thereby avoiding the deceased's estate and probate fees. Joint tenancy does have disadvantages that may make it more worthwhile to simply pay the probate fees on the asset. First, there is a loss of control since any decisions regarding the property have to be made jointly between the owners. Second, the deceased's other beneficiaries may argue over the ownership legitimacy of the surviving joint owner. Third, the transfer of property into a joint tenancy arrangement can trigger immediate capital gains tax. Fourth, creditors and/or the spouse of either joint owner may also have a claim to the assets in a joint tenancy arrangement. Since the potential conflicts, taxes, and other issues that can arise out of a JTWROS are significant, it is important to consult a lawyer and tax accountant before entering into any joint tenancy arrangements. Remember that the principal residence of a taxpayer will not trigger capital gains or losses. If the house is owned jointly (with rights of survivorship), it will pass to the co-owner without tax consequences. RRSPs can be rolled over to a spouse with no tax consequences if the spouse is listed as the designated beneficiary. RRSPs also can be rolled over to a dependent child if the dependent child is physically or mentally impaired. In this case, RRSP proceeds may be rolled over to an RRSP, RRIF, a qualifying annuity, or a RDSP, if the child is eligible for the Disability Tax Credit. If the dependent child is not physically or mentally impaired, the taxes owing on the RRSP can be spread out by purchasing a fixed-term annuity for the dependent child for a period of 18 minus the dependent's child's age at the time of the fixed-term annuity purchase. Other assets that are owned jointly with rights of survivorship, such as investments, will simply transfer to the survivor.

EXAMPLE

Quang completed a will in 2002 that indicated that his children, Linh and Jackson, would be equal beneficiaries of his estate. In 2014, Quang purchased a cottage for $450 000. To avoid probate fees on this asset, Quang entered into a JTWROS with his daughter, Linh. One year later, Quang died and the cottage, which has not increased in value, passed directly to Linh. Quang's son, Jackson, is upset because, according to his father's will, he should have an equal share in his father's estate. Linh argues that since the cottage is not part of the estate, it belongs to her only. Furthermore, the assets in the estate should be split equally, in accordance with the will. Jackson goes to court, claiming that his father set up the JTWROS with Linh only to avoid the probate fees on the cabin. Jackson argues that his father intended for the children to split the estate equally. Linh is very angry with Jackson. The children reach an out-of-court settlement that gives Linh ownership of the cabin and allows Jackson to keep all of the assets, which are equal in value to the cabin, from his father's estate.

Beneficiary Designations

In addition to naming beneficiaries in your will, you will also complete beneficiary designation forms for your insurance policies, RRSPs, registered retirement income funds (RRIFs), and pensions. Policies and accounts for which you have named a beneficiary do not form part of your estate, thereby reducing the value of your estate subject to probate fees. It is important to update beneficiaries on a regular basis. If your beneficiary predeceases you, the proceeds that would have been payable to him or her upon your death will now pass into your estate. This may increase the amount of probate fees you will have to pay. To avoid these types of situations, you may want to name a contingent beneficiary. A **contingent beneficiary** is an individual who is entitled to receive benefits, when they become payable, because the primary beneficiary is not able to for some reason.

contingent beneficiary
An individual who is entitled to receive benefits, when they become payable, because the primary beneficiary is not able to for some reason.

> **myth** or **fact** One of the main reasons to make a will is to reduce the probate fees you pay in your province.

Trusts

Trusts are an effective estate planning tool that can be used during or after the taxpayer's lifetime to meet a number of different needs. A **trust** is a legal document in which one person, called a **settlor**, transfers assets to a trustee, who manages them for designated beneficiaries. The settlor must select a trustee who is trustworthy and capable of managing the assets being transferred. If a suitable individual cannot be found to act as a trustee, various types of investment firms can be hired to serve as trustees. Property transferred to a trust before a person dies is no longer considered owned by the individual. As a result, trust assets do not form part of the estate and are not subject to probate fees when the individual dies.

trust
A legal document in which one person, the settlor, transfers assets to a trustee, who manages them for designated beneficiaries.

settlor
The person who creates a trust.

Inter Vivos Trusts. An **inter vivos trust** is a trust in which you assign the management of some or all of your assets to a trustee while you are living. You identify a trustee that you want to manage the assets (which includes making decisions on how to invest cash until it is needed or how to spend cash). In addition to reducing probate fees, this type of trust is also a useful estate planning tool if you feel that someone will contest your will when you die, because the assets transferred into an inter vivos trust do not form part of your estate when you die. By using a trust, you can maintain some control over how assets are used. In particular, an inter vivos trust may be set up to take care of dependent children or others, to control the use of assets such as a cottage or vacation property, and to maintain control of business interests. Inter vivos trusts are private arrangements and therefore have no public accountability. If you wish to distribute assets to individuals while maintaining a high level of privacy, inter vivos trusts may be used. Similar to the situation when a taxpayer dies, assets transferred to an inter vivos trust are deemed to be disposed of at fair market value at the time of transfer. As a result, an immediate capital gains tax will be incurred by the settlor. Income earned on the assets inside an inter vivos trust is taxed at the highest combined federal and provincial marginal tax rate. To avoid having the trust pay taxes at the highest marginal tax rate, inter vivos trusts normally distribute any income to the trust beneficiaries annually.

inter vivos trust
A trust in which you assign the management of your assets to a trustee while you are living.

revocable inter vivos trust
An inter vivos trust that can be dissolved at any time.

Revocable Inter Vivos Trust. With a **revocable inter vivos trust**, you can dissolve or revoke the trust at any time because you are still the legal owner of the assets. For example, you may revoke an inter vivos trust if you decide that you want to manage the assets yourself. Alternatively, you may revoke an inter vivos trust so that you can replace the trustee or beneficiaries. In this case, you would create a new inter vivos trust with a newly identified trustee.

By using a revocable inter vivos trust, you can still avoid the probate process. However, the assets are still considered part of your estate, which will reduce some of the tax benefits that would otherwise be available if you set up an irrevocable inter vivos trust.

irrevocable inter vivos trust
An inter vivos trust that cannot be changed, although it may provide income to the settlor.

Irrevocable Inter Vivos Trust. An **irrevocable inter vivos trust** cannot be changed. This type of trust is a separate entity. It can provide income for you, the settlor, but the assets in the trust are no longer legally yours. If the settlor is one of the beneficiaries of the assets, this type of trust will be treated as a revocable inter vivos trust.

alter ego trust
A trust that contains assets that have not been subject to immediate deemed disposition, thereby deferring any capital gains tax.

Alter Ego Trust. An **alter ego trust** is a trust that contains assets that have not been subject to immediate deemed disposition, thereby deferring any capital gains tax. Recall that assets transferred into an inter vivos are deemed to be disposed of at fair market value at the time of transfer. As a result, any capital gain on the asset is subject to tax. With an alter ego trust, asset transfers occur on a tax-deferred basis. Taxes are payable when the settlor dies or when the assets in the trust are sold, whichever is earlier. To qualify as an alter ego trust, the settlor must be at least 65 years of age, a resident of Canada, and the income and capital beneficiary of the trust during his or her lifetime. A similar type of trust, called a joint partner trust, can be used in place of an alter ego trust if you have a spouse or a joint partner that you would like to include as a beneficiary of the trust. The assets in an alter ego trust or joint partner trust are owned by the trust and are not subject to probate fees.

testamentary trust
A trust created by a will.

Testamentary Trust. A **testamentary trust** is a trust created by a will. It is popular because it can be used to provide for the needs of dependent children or parents in a manner somewhat similar to the inter vivos trust. Income earned on assets inside a testamentary trust is taxed in a manner similar to that of an individual taxpayer at that same level of income. Since a testamentary trust is created by a will, assets that transfer to a testamentary trust have already been through the probate process. As such, a testamentary trust cannot be used to reduce probate fees.

Contributions to Charitable Organizations

Contributions to charitable organizations, in addition to being effective tax planning tools, can be used to provide for charities that are important to the taxpayer or the taxpayer's family. Contributions to charitable organizations made in the year a taxpayer dies or designated to be made by their will are provided special tax incentives. Normally, charitable contributions up to and including 75 percent of a taxpayer's net income may be claimed against net income. In the year of death, the amount of charitable contributions that may be claimed against net income increases to 100 percent of net income. In addition, any over-contribution to a charitable organization may be used to write off up to 100 percent of the previous year's net income.

EXAMPLE

In 2014, Ruthie donated $200 000 to the local hospital, a registered charity. That same year, Ruthie earned net income of $63 000. If Ruthie died in 2014, how much of the $200 000 donation can her executor claim for charitable donations?

The executor can claim $63 000 (100 percent of her net income) for 2014 on her final tax return and can carry back $137 000 to claim on her 2013 tax return up to a maximum of her net income claim. If Ruthie's net income for 2013 is also $63 000, her executor can claim 100 percent of her net income for 2013 as well.

OTHER ASPECTS OF ESTATE PLANNING

L.O.6

In addition to wills and trusts, estate planning involves some other key decisions regarding a living will and power of attorney.

Living Will

A living will, also known as a personal care directive or a health care directive, is a simple legal document in which individuals specify their preferences if they become mentally or physically disabled. A living will speaks for you when you are unable to speak for yourself. For example, many individuals have a living will that expresses their desire not to be placed on life support if they become terminally ill. Without a living will, there may be added conflict and uncertainty as your family members attempt to make a decision regarding your personal well-being.

living will
A simple legal document in which individuals specify their preferences if they become mentally or physically disabled.

myth or **fact** I verbally discussed my estate plan with my spouse and other relatives. Since everybody knows my wishes, I don't need an estate plan.

Power of Attorney

A limited (non-continuing) power of attorney is a legal document that grants a person the power to make specific decisions for you in the event that you are temporarily incapacitated. The decision-making power granted is relative to a specific or defined task. For example, you may name a family member or a close friend to make decisions regarding paying your bills on time while you are out of the country. Once you return, the limited (non-continuing) power of attorney document expires. This type of power of attorney document is automatically revoked if you become mentally incapacitated. You should name someone who you believe would act to serve your interests.

A general power of attorney is a legal document that grants a person the immediate power to make any decisions or commitments for you. Normally, the only restriction placed on the appointed attorney is the inability to make a will or another power of attorney document on your behalf. Otherwise, this document is effective immediately, once it is signed and witnessed.

A general power of attorney document terminates automatically if:

- The grantor dies
- The attorney dies
- The grantor becomes incapacitated due to mental illness

The addition of an enduring or continuing clause to a general power of attorney allows the power of attorney to continue even if the grantor becomes incapacitated due to mental illness. This type of document is often referred to as an enduring (continuing) power of attorney since it grants a person the immediate power to make any decisions or commitments for you, even when you are mentally incapacitated. An enduring power of attorney can also be created such that it is triggered by a specific event, such as the mental incapacity of the grantor, instead of being added as a clause to a general power of attorney document.

A durable power of attorney for health care is a legal document that grants a person the power to make specific health care decisions for you. Unlike a living will, a durable power of attorney ensures that the person you identify has the power to make specific decisions regarding your health care in the event that you become incapacitated. While a living will states many of your preferences, a situation may arise that is not covered by it. A durable power of attorney for health care means that the necessary decisions will be made by someone who knows your preferences, rather than by a health care facility. By appointing one or more people to make these decisions, you are reducing the possibility of court involvement with regard to these decisions.

limited (non-continuing) power of attorney
A legal document that grants a person the power to make specific decisions for you in the event that you are temporarily incapacitated.

general power of attorney
A legal document that grants a person the immediate power to make any decisions or commitments for you, with specific limitations.

Go to:
www.rbcds.com/estate-planning-guide.html

This website provides a helpful guide to estate planning.

enduring (continuing) power of attorney
A legal document that grants a person the immediate power to make any decisions or commitments for you, even when you are mentally incapacitated.

durable power of attorney for health care
A legal document that grants a person the power to make specific health care decisions for you.

Maintaining Estate Planning Documents

Go to:
https://www.estateplanning.
com/Estate-Planning-
Glossary/

This website provides
a special glossary of estate
planning terms.

Key documents, such as your will, living will, and power of attorney, should be kept in a safe, accessible place. You should tell the person (or people) you named as executor and granted power of attorney where you keep these documents so that they can be retrieved if and when they are needed. Medical or personal care documents may be copied and provided to your health care professionals. Other copies of such documents may be kept with your lawyer.

A checklist of the important documents you should keep together follows:

- Estate planning information, such as a will, living will, and power of attorney
- Life insurance policies and other insurance policies
- RRSP and other retirement account information
- Home ownership and mortgage information
- Information on ownership of other real estate
- Information on personal property, such as cars or jewellery
- Personal loans
- Credit card debt information
- Information on ownership of businesses
- Personal legal documents
- Most recent personal tax filing
- Bank account information
- Investment information

MyLab Finance   Visit MyLab Finance for additional study and practice tools. Select Financial Planning Problems are available in the Study Plan. Create your own study plan, generate personal cash flow statements and balance sheets, and set personal financial goals.

SUMMARY

L.O.1 Explain the use of a will

A will is intended to ensure that your wishes are carried out after your death. It allows you to distribute your estate, name beneficiaries, select a guardian for your children, and select an executor to ensure that the will is executed properly.

L.O.2 Describe the common types of wills

The most common type of will in Canada is the English form will. Other types include a notarial will, which is a will form commonly used in Quebec, and a holograph will, which is a will written solely in the handwriting of the testator.

L.O.3 Describe the key components of a will

Key components of a will include clauses that identify the testator, revoke previous wills, appoint an executor and a trustee, appoint a guardian for minor children, authorize the payment of outstanding debts, authorize bequests, direct distribution of the residue of the estate, provide instructions with respect to estate administration, and limit the liability of a trustee who has acted in good faith.

L.O.4 Describe probate fees and taxes at death

Probate fees are the fees incurred by an estate during the probate process. Probate fees are low in Canada. Taxes at death are determined based on the deceased's final tax return. Taxes at death are an issue for individuals who have assets that have increased in value above their acquisition cost. A spousal rollover can effectively delay the amount of tax payable when a taxpayer dies. In addition, your principal residence is exempt from any type of estate tax. Optional tax returns provide an additional opportunity to reduce taxes at death.

L.O.5 Explain the types of estate planning strategies

Joint tenancy with rights of survivorship can be used to transfer assets outside of your estate. Consult a lawyer before entering a joint tenancy arrangement since this method of reducing probate fees can lead to significant conflicts, taxes, and other issues. Beneficiary designations provide additional opportunities to reduce probate fees. Various types of trusts can be structured so that a large estate can be passed to the beneficiaries without being subjected to estate taxes. A deceased taxpayer's contributions to charity receive favourable tax treatment in the year of death and in the year prior to death, relative to the normal non-refundable tax credit that is provided by charitable contributions.

L.O.6   Introduce other aspects of estate planning

In the event that you someday may be incapable of making decisions relating to your health and financial situation, you should consider creating a living will and power of attorney. A living will is a legal document that allows you to specify your health treatment preferences, such as life support options. A power of attorney is a legal document that allows you to assign a person the power to make specific decisions for you if and when you are no longer capable of making these decisions. The availability of a number of different types of power of attorney provides you with some flexibility to choose how this legal document can work for you.

REVIEW QUESTIONS

1. What is an estate? What is estate planning?

2. What is a will? What does a will give you the opportunity to do?

3. What is a beneficiary? What happens if a beneficiary is under the age of 18 and inherits assets?

4. What is an executor?

5. What does it mean to die intestate? Who will distribute your estate if you die intestate?

6. What is a preferential share? Do all provinces have a provision for a preferential share? Explain.

7. List the requirements for a valid will.

8. Define and describe an English form will.

9. Define and describe a notarial will.

10. Define and describe a holograph will.

11. What is the purpose of the revocation of previous wills clause?

12. What are the duties of the executor?

13. What is a trustee?

14. Describe the responsibilities of a guardian for minor children.

15. What is a bequest?

16. What is the residue of an estate? What is the purpose of the distribution of residue clause?

17. Describe the purpose for the administration of the estate clause.

18. What is the purpose of the liability clause?

19. What is a letter of last instruction?

20. Which events should trigger a review of your will?

21. What is the impact of the act of marriage on your will?

22. What is a codicil?

23. What is probate? Describe the probate process. What are probate fees?

24. With respect to taxes, what is deemed to have happened to your assets when you die?

25. How is the tax payable on estate assets determined?

26. What is the deadline for filing a final tax return?

27. In addition to a final tax return, what three optional tax returns may be filed? Explain.

28. What are rights or things? Provide an example.

29. What is joint tenancy with rights of survivorship (JTWROS)? What are its disadvantages?

30. On what types of legal documents would you find beneficiary designations? Why is a contingent beneficiary important?

31. What is a trust? Describe the role of the settlor of a trust.

32. What is an inter vivos trust? Describe the advantages and disadvantages of an inter vivos trust.

33. Define and differentiate between a revocable inter vivos trust and an irrevocable inter vivos trust.

34. What is an alter ego trust? What are the benefits of creating an alter ego trust? What are the qualifying criteria for an alter ego trust?

35. Define and describe a testamentary trust.

36. How can contributions to charitable organizations help in estate planning?

37. What is a living will? What is the purpose of a living will?

38. Define and describe a limited (non-continuing) power of attorney.

39. Define and differentiate between a general power of attorney and an enduring (continuing) power of attorney.

40. What is a durable power of attorney for health care? Why is it needed even if you have a living will?

41. Describe how you should maintain estate planning documents.

ETHICAL DILEMMA

In the nineteenth century, people travelled the country selling tonics that were guaranteed to cure all ailments of mankind. In the twenty-first century, these "snake-oil salesmen" have been replaced by individuals who make professional presentations on estate planning. At the conclusion of the presentation, they are prepared to sell you, for many hundreds of dollars, a kit that will show you how to do everything they have discussed without the expense of a lawyer or tax professional.

One such group extols the virtues of a device called a charitable remainder trust (CRT). It tells you how you can establish one using the boilerplate template provided in its booklet. The CRT will allow you to make tax-deductible contributions to it during your lifetime and upon your death will pass to a family foundation managed by your children. This will allow the assets to avoid estate taxes and probate. The presenter describes this as a cost-effective way to pass your

assets to your children. All of what is said in the presentation concerning CRTs is true.

However, what the presenter does not explain is that distributions from the family foundation can be made only to recognized charities. In other words, your children will own the estate but will not have access to it. These devices work well for a small percentage of the population, but will not serve the purpose that the presenter has alluded to for the majority of people.

a.   Discuss how ethical you believe the presenter is being by not telling the full story about CRTs. Keep in mind that what the presenter says is true, but not the whole truth.

b.   If these presenters are the modern-day version of snake-oil salesmen, who should you go to for estate planning advice?

FINANCIAL PLANNING ONLINE EXERCISES

1. Go to www.tdcanadatrust.com/planning/tools/index.jsp.

   a. Under Estate Planning, click on Executor's Tool. Taking this quiz will enable an executor to determine the amount of assistance he or she will need in administering an estate.

   b. Return to the first page. Under Estate Planning, click on Executor Selection Tool. Taking this quiz will help you to determine whom you should select as an executor for your estate.

   c. Using the information from these two quizzes, what are some of the important considerations when determining the complexity of an estate and the process of selecting an executor?

PSYCHOLOGY OF PERSONAL FINANCE: Your Will

1. Some people put off creating a will because they do not want to think about financial planning for their death. In addition, they might struggle with the decision of how to distribute their respective estates. They may believe that it is too early to deal with estate planning because their plans for distributing their estate will change over time. What is your view on estate planning? Do you think it is too early for you to engage in estate planning?

2. Read one practical article about how psychology affects estate planning decisions. You can easily retrieve possible articles by doing an online search using the terms "psychology" and "estate planning." Summarize the main points of the article.

MINI-CASE: Estate Planning

Cindy and Nate were recently married, each for the second time. Both are concerned about leaving assets to the adult children from their previous marriages and are reluctant to combine their individual assets. Together, they have an estate valued at $1 million, of which $750 000 is in Cindy's name. They live in Cindy's $300 000 home, which she received in her divorce settlement.

Planning for incapacitation is another concern. Cindy's 86-year-old mother and 84-year-old uncle both have Alzheimer's disease, and Cindy is concerned that it may be hereditary. Nate recently lost his father to a long-term illness and has vowed never to be kept alive only by machines. Cindy, on the other hand, believes all steps should be taken to prolong a person's life. Neither Cindy nor Nate has revised their wills since their marriage. The wills still name their previous spouses as executor and beneficiary of their respective estates. What type of trust is appropriate for Cindy and Nate? What can they do to address their concerns about estate planning in the event of incapacitation? Should the couple revise their wills? If so, what changes should they make?

Study Guide

Circle the correct answer and then check the answers in the back of the book to chart your progress.

Multiple Choice

1. The reasons for having a will may include the following:
   a. A will helps to ensure that your estate is distributed in the manner you desire.
   b. You can use a will to specify the persons you want to receive your estate, referred to as your beneficiaries (or heirs).
   c. A will can be used to specify the age at which your children will receive their inheritance.
   d. All of the above are reasons for having a will.

2. Which of the following is necessary for an English form will to be valid?
   a. It must be written in the testator's handwriting.
   b. It must be dated within 10 years of death.
   c. It must be signed by the testator and two witnesses.
   d. The person writing the will must be over age 21 at the time the will is written.

3. What is the primary problem with dying intestate?
   a. An administrator will be appointed to distribute the estate according to law.
   b. Any children will become wards of the state.
   c. Medical personnel will be responsible for decisions about your care.
   d. Your estate will flow to the government.

4. Which of the following statements best describes the role of an executor?
   a. An executor may be required to collect any money owed to the estate, personally pay off any debts owed by the estate, sell specific assets (such as a home) that are part of the estate, and then distribute the proceeds as specified in the will.
   b. An executor may be required to collect any money owed to the estate, pay off any debts owed by the estate, sell specific assets (such as a home) that are part of the estate, and then distribute the proceeds as specified in the will.
   c. An executor may be required to collect any money owed to the estate, personally pay off any debts owed by the estate, sell specific assets (such as a home) that are part of the estate, appoint a guardian for minor children, and then distribute the proceeds as specified in the will.
   d. An executor may be required to collect any money owed to the estate, pay off any debts owed by the estate, sell specific assets (such as a home) that are part of the estate, appoint a guardian for minor children, and then distribute the proceeds as specified in the will.

5. Which clause in a will ensures that all remaining assets of the deceased are accounted for and distributed?
   a. Administration of the estate
   b. Letter of last instruction

c. Distribution of residue

d. Authorization to distribute remainder

6. In choosing a guardian for your children, you should:

a. Ensure he or she is also prepared to be the custodian.

b. Be sure to include this in the last letter of instruction.

c. Ensure that the person you select is willing to serve in this capacity.

d. Authorize this in a power of attorney.

7. A document that specifies changes to an existing will is:

a. A letter of instruction.

b. A codicil.

c. An amendment.

d. An addendum.

8. The purpose of probate is to ensure:

a. The will is valid to and for orderly distribution of assets.

b. Payment of liabilities are prioritized accurately.

c. Provinces collect the requisite probate fees.

d. Fair jurisprudence of all financial matters.

9. The amount of tax that Canadians pay upon death is relatively low. This statement can be supported because:

a. The increase in value of your summer cottage is not subject to tax.

b. RRSPs are only subject to tax when a taxpayer is alive and withdrawing money from them.

c. Most Canadians would count their principal residence and registered retirement accounts, such as an RRSP, as their largest assets.

d. The tax payable on RRSPs and other registered retirement accounts can be delayed using a spousal rollover.

10. Which of the following is not a characteristic of a testamentary trust?

a. It is a type of trust that is created by a will.

b. The income earned on the assets inside it is taxed in a manner similar to that of an individual taxpayer at that same level of income.

c. The income earned on the assets inside it is taxed at the highest combined federal and provincial marginal tax rate.

d. It is a popular type of trust because it can be used to provide for the needs of dependent children or others.

11. If Mary is not sure her primary beneficiary will survive her, she should:

a. Name a contingent beneficiary.

b. Name joint beneficiaries.

c. Change her beneficiary.

d. Name her estate as beneficiary.

12. Contributions to charitable organizations in the year that a taxpayer dies are provided special tax incentives. Which of the following statements most accurately reflects the tax treatment of charitable contributions in the year of death?

a. In the year of death, the amount of charitable contributions that may be claimed against net income increases to 100 percent of net income. In addition, any over-contribution to a charitable organization may be used to write off up to 100 percent of the previous year's net income.

b. In the year of death, the amount of charitable contributions that may be claimed against net income increases to 100 percent of net income. In addition, any over-contribution to a charitable organization may be used to write off up to 75 percent of the previous year's net income.

c. In the year of death, the amount of charitable contributions that may be claimed against net income remains at 75 percent of net income. However, any over-contribution to a charitable organization may be used to write off up to 100 percent of the previous year's net income.

d. In the year of death, the amount of charitable contributions that may be claimed against net income remains at 75 percent of net income. In addition, any over-contribution to a charitable organization may be used to write off up to 75 percent of the previous year's net income.

13. A(n) _____ is a legal document that grants a person the power to make specific decisions for you in the event that you are temporarily incapacitated.

a. general power of attorney

b. limited (non-continuing) power of attorney

c. durable power of attorney for health care

d. enduring (continuing) power of attorney

14. If John is going to have his first child, which of the following should he do for his estate planning?

a. Add a codicil to his will.

b. Review his will.

c. Update his will.

d. Review his power of attorney.

15. A(n) _____ is a legal document that grants a person the immediate power to make any decisions or commitments for you, even when you are mentally incapacitated.

a. general power of attorney

b. limited (non-continuing) power of attorney

c. durable power of attorney for health care

d. enduring (continuing) power of attorney

True/False

1. True or False? An estate represents a deceased person's assets, including any debts that are outstanding.

2. True or False? If you die intestate in Canada, your surviving spouse will receive a preferential share of estate assets before assets are distributed among all beneficiaries.

3. True or False? In order to create a valid will, you must be mentally competent and should not be subject to undue influence from others.

4. True or False? To avoid confusion, a standard will contains a clause revoking all other wills and declaring this latest will to be the last will.

5. True or False? A guardian appointed through a will may choose someone else to provide custodial care.

6. True or False? In Alberta, the act of marriage will automatically cancel all wills dated prior to the date of marriage.

7. True or False? The purpose of the probate process is for the court to declare a will valid, make any necessary changes to ensure the validity of the will, and ensure the orderly distribution of assets.

8. True or False? A final tax return is normally filed within six months of the date of death or on April 30th of the following year.

9. True or False? Under normal circumstances, a deemed disposition means that a deceased taxpayer has to sell his or her assets and pay any tax owing once the assets are sold.

10. True or False? A spousal rollover does not eliminate or reduce the amount of tax payable by the taxpayer; it only delays the payment of tax until the surviving spouse dies.

11. True or False? An inter vivos trust is a trust in which you assign the management of your assets to a trustee while you are living.

12. True or False? An irrevocable inter vivos trust will be treated as a revocable inter vivos trust if the settlor is one of the beneficiaries of the assets of the trust.

13. True or False? Assets transferred to an alter ego trust are subject to a deemed disposition.

14. True or False? A living will, also known as a personal care directive or a health care directive, is a simple legal document in which individuals specify their preferences if they become mentally or physically disabled.

15. True or False? A durable medical power of attorney is similar to a living will in that it ensures that the person you identify has the power to make specific decisions regarding your health care in the event that you become incapacitated.

PART 5 BRAD MACDONALD—A CONTINUING CASE

Pearson
| MyLab | Finance

Brad tells you that he has revised his retirement plans. He thinks it may be more realistic to retire in 30 years as opposed to the original 20 years he had mentioned earlier. His goal is to save $1.5 million by that time. Brad's employer offers a defined-contribution pension plan; however, Brad is not taking advantage of this plan. Brad's employer will match pension plan contributions up to $300 per month.

Factoring in the employer match, Brad could have a possible total annual pension contribution of $7200.

Brad is wondering if he would still be able to contribute to an RRSP and/or a TFSA if he eventually starts contributing to the defined-contribution pension plan.

Brad also unveils his plans to provide for the post-secondary education of his two nephews in the event of his death. He does not have a will and wonders if one is necessary.

Case Questions

1. With regard to Brad's revised retirement plans:

   a. How much will he have in 30 years if he takes full advantage of his employer's defined-contribution pension plan and invests $300 per month at an annual interest rate of 8 percent, compounded monthly? Recall that his employer will match his contribution.

b. How much will he have to save per month at an annual interest rate of 8 percent, compounded monthly, to reach his $1 million goal in 20 years? In 30 years?

c. What impact could retiring 10 years earlier have on Brad's current standard of living? In other words, compare Brad's monthly income if he retires in 20 years to his monthly income if he retires in 30 years. Brad expects to live until age 90. Assume that the annual interest rate remains at 8 percent, compounded monthly.

2. Will Brad meet his $1.5 million goal if he takes full advantage of his employer's defined-contribution pension plan and retires in 30 years?

3. Assuming that Brad participates in the defined-contribution pension plan, what will his pension adjustment be? How will this affect his RRSP contribution room for the following year?

4. To reach his goal of $1.5 million in savings by the time he retires in 30 years, could Brad save any additional funds inside an RRSP, tax-free savings account (TFSA), or other type of retirement account? Explain.

5. If Brad really wishes to provide for his nephews' post-secondary education, how can a will help him to achieve that goal? What else might Brad consider to assure his nephews' post-secondary education?

6. Not taking into account his nephews' post-secondary education needs, should Brad consider writing a will? Explain.

Use the worksheets available on MyLab Finance to complete this case.

Synthesis of Financial Planning

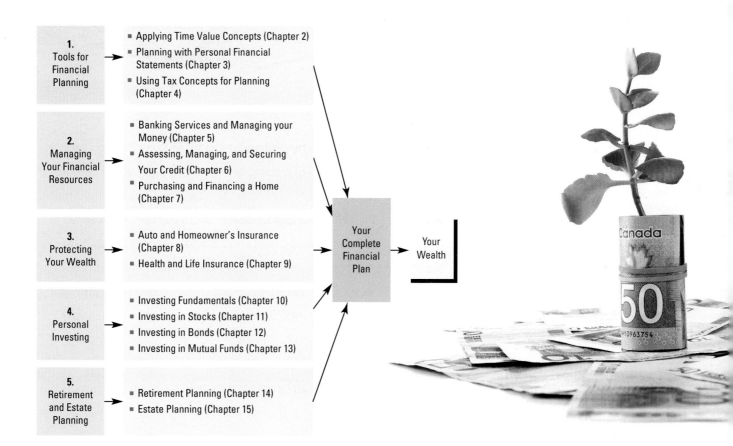

1.
Tools for Financial Planning
- Applying Time Value Concepts (Chapter 2)
- Planning with Personal Financial Statements (Chapter 3)
- Using Tax Concepts for Planning (Chapter 4)

2.
Managing Your Financial Resources
- Banking Services and Managing your Money (Chapter 5)
- Assessing, Managing, and Securing Your Credit (Chapter 6)
- Purchasing and Financing a Home (Chapter 7)

3.
Protecting Your Wealth
- Auto and Homeowner's Insurance (Chapter 8)
- Health and Life Insurance (Chapter 9)

4.
Personal Investing
- Investing Fundamentals (Chapter 10)
- Investing in Stocks (Chapter 11)
- Investing in Bonds (Chapter 12)
- Investing in Mutual Funds (Chapter 13)

5.
Retirement and Estate Planning
- Retirement Planning (Chapter 14)
- Estate Planning (Chapter 15)

Your Complete Financial Plan

Your Wealth

This part serves as a capstone by summarizing the key components of a financial plan. It also illustrates the interrelationships among the segments of a financial plan by highlighting how decisions regarding each component affect the other components.

Integrating the Components of a Financial Plan

Now that you have completed your journey through the components of a financial plan, it is time for you to compile all of this information and the many decisions you have made. Regarding your own personal financial situation, you have been asked to complete a number of assignments and online exercises throughout the previous chapters. Your first step is to determine the status of your personal finances. Establish your personal balance sheet, prepare your cash flow statement, establish your financial goals, and address your concerns. From there you can analyze each part of the financial plan—your taxes, insurance, investments, retirement planning, estate planning—and establish a plan of action to help you accomplish your financial goals.

Digital Vision./Photodisc/
Getty Images

As explained throughout this text, each component of a financial plan affects your ability to build wealth and achieve your goals. You have now learned many of the fundamentals relating to each component of a financial plan. This capstone chapter will help you to integrate that knowledge into a cohesive financial plan.

THE LEARNING OBJECTIVES OF THIS CHAPTER ARE TO:

1. Review the components of a financial plan
2. Illustrate how a financial plan's components are integrated

REVIEW OF COMPONENTS WITHIN A FINANCIAL PLAN

`L.0.1`

A key to financial planning is recognizing how the components of your financial plan are related. Each part of this text has focused on one of the six main components of your financial plan, which are illustrated once again in Exhibit 16.1 The decisions you make regarding each component of your financial plan affect your cash flows and your wealth. The six components are summarized next, with information on how they are interrelated.

Budgeting

Recall that budgeting allows you to forecast how much money you will have at the end of each month so that you can determine how much you will be able to invest in assets. Most importantly, budgeting allows you to determine whether your expenses will exceed your income so that you can forecast any shortages in that month. Your spending decisions affect your budget, which affects every other component of your financial plan. Careful budgeting can prevent excessive spending and therefore help you to achieve financial goals.

Budgeting Trade-off. The more you spend, the less money you will have available for liquidity purposes, investments, or retirement saving. Therefore, your budgeting decisions involve a trade-off between spending today and allocating funds for the future. Your budget should attempt to ensure that you have net cash flows every month for savings or for retirement. The more funds you can allocate for the future, the more you will be able to benefit from compounded interest and the more you will be able to spend in the future.

Managing Finances

You can prepare for anticipated cash shortages in any future month by ensuring that you have enough liquid assets to cover the deficiencies. Even if you do not have sufficient liquid assets, you can cover a cash deficiency by obtaining short-term financing (such as using a credit card). Long-term financing allows you to make purchases now without having the full amount of cash on hand. Therefore, financing can increase the amount

EXHIBIT 16.1   Your Financial Transactions

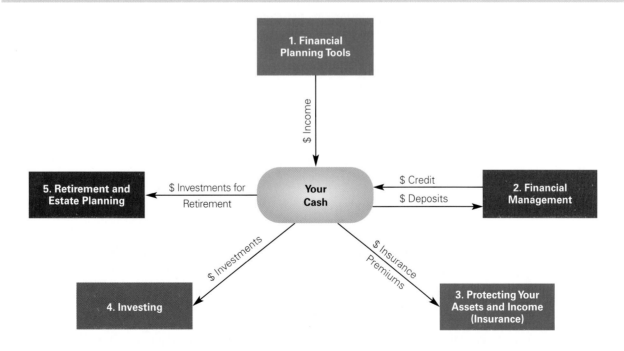

of your assets. It is especially useful for large purchases such as a car or a home. If you maintain adequate financial resources, you will not need to borrow every time you need money. In this way, you can avoid major financial problems and therefore be more likely to achieve your financial goals.

Financing

Financing Trade-off. One of the disadvantages of borrowing funds for a mortgage or home equity line of credit is that financing can cause budgeting problems. When you borrow to pay for a car, to purchase a home, or even to pay off a credit card balance, you affect your future budget because the monthly loan payment means that you will have less cash available at the end of each month. Although a loan allows you to make purchases now, it restricts your spending or saving in future months while you are paying off the loan. Therefore, an excessive amount of financing can prevent you from achieving your financial goals, even if your consumer needs are met. In addition, excessive financing may prevent you from paying off your loans on time and therefore could damage your credit rating or cause you to file for bankruptcy.

It is easier to cover monthly loan payments if you select financing with a relatively long maturity. However, the longer the maturity, the longer the loan will be outstanding and the more interest you will pay.

You may want to consider paying off a loan before its maturity so that you can avoid incurring any more interest expense, especially if the interest rate charged is relatively high. You should not use all of your liquid funds to pay off a loan, however, because you will still need to maintain liquidity. Paying off loans rather than making additional investments is appropriate when the expected after-tax return you could make on the investments is lower than the interest rate you are paying on the loan. Borrowing money should be done with discretion. Saving up for consumer purchases is a wiser choice.

Protecting Your Assets and Income

You can protect your assets and income by purchasing insurance. Recall from Chapters 8 and 9 that property and casualty insurance insures your assets (such as your car and home) and health insurance covers health expenses and provides financial support if you become disabled, critically ill, or incapacitated. Life insurance provides your family members or other named beneficiaries with financial support in the event of your death. Therefore, insurance protects against events that could reduce your income or your wealth.

Insurance Trade-off. Any money that is used to buy insurance cannot be used for other purposes such as investing in liquid assets, paying off loans, or making investments. Yet your insurance needs should be given priority before investments. You need to have insurance to cover your car and your home. You may also need life insurance to provide financial support to family members.

Managing Investments

When making investments, recall that your main choices are stocks, bonds, and mutual funds. If you want your investments to provide periodic income, you may consider investing in stocks that pay dividends. The stocks of large, well-known firms tend to pay relatively stable dividends as these firms are not growing as fast as smaller firms and can afford to pay out more of their earnings as dividends. Bonds also provide periodic income. If you do not need income and would prefer to see your money grow, you may consider investing in stocks of firms that do not pay dividends. These firms often are growing at a fast pace and therefore offer the potential for a large increase in the stock value over time.

Investment Trade-off. By investing in the stocks of large, well-known firms, you will receive dividend income. You may be able to sell the stocks easily if you need money, but may risk a loss of capital. Government of Canada bonds or highly rated corporate bonds provide periodic income and can be sold easily if you need money. Again, there may be a loss of capital. However, these investments typically do not generate as high a return as investments in growth-oriented companies.

If you try to earn high returns by investing all of your money in stocks of smaller firms, you forgo liquidity because the prices of these stocks are volatile and you may want to avoid selling them when prices are relatively low. If you have sufficient liquid assets such as chequing and savings accounts, however, you do not need additional liquidity from your investments.

Another concern about the stocks of smaller firms is that they can be very risky and are more likely to result in large losses than investments in stocks of large, well-known firms. You can invest in small stocks without being exposed to the specific risk of any individual stock by investing in a mutual fund that focuses on small stocks. When market conditions are weak, however, such funds can experience large losses, although not as much as a single stock of a small firm.

Whenever you use money for investments, you forgo the use of that money for some other purpose, such as investing in more liquid assets, paying off existing debt, or buying insurance. You should make investments only after you have sufficient liquidity and sufficient insurance to protect your existing assets. Investments are the key to building your wealth over time. By investing a portion of your income consistently over time, you are more likely to achieve your financial goals. This can be applied to your retirement planning as well.

Retirement Planning

Retirement planning can ensure that you will have sufficient funds at the time you retire. As discussed in Chapter 14, there are a variety of plans available and many tax advantages to retirement savings.

Retirement Account Trade-off. The more money you contribute to your retirement account now, the more money you will have when you reach retirement age. However, you should ensure that you can afford whatever you decide to contribute. You need to have enough money to maintain sufficient liquidity so that you can afford any monthly loan payments before you contribute to your retirement.

When deciding whether to invest your money in current investments or in your retirement account, consider your goals. If you plan to use the investments for tuition or some other purpose in the near future, you should not put this money in your retirement account. Funds invested in a retirement account are not necessarily liquid. Any money withdrawn from a registered retirement savings plan (RRSP) must be taken into income in the year of withdrawal and will be taxed at your marginal tax rate. The withdrawal is subject to a withholding tax of up to 20 percent, which should be considered as a down payment on the total tax liability. If you need to withdraw money from your RRSP, calculate your total tax payable and save this money for tax owing. Two exceptions are withdrawals with respect to the Home Buyers' Plan and the Lifelong Learning Plan. On the other hand, the introduction of the tax-free savings account (TFSA) in 2009 provides another option for saving for the long term. Withdrawals of principal and interest from a TFSA are tax-free. In addition, there is flexibility to replace contribution withdrawals in future years. If your goal is to save for retirement, you should allocate money to a retirement account, such as an RRSP or a TFSA. Contributions to an RRSP are tax deductible and you are not taxed on the growth of your contributions, as long as you leave the money in the account. Although contributions to a TFSA are not tax deductible, there is no tax payable on the growth of your contributions.

Go to:
https://midineromifuturo.com/

This website provides useful information about financial planning that can help you to complete and refine your financial plan.

Maintaining Your Financial Documents

To monitor your financial plan over time, you should store all finance-related documents in one place, such as in a safe at home or in a safe deposit box. The key documents are identified in Exhibit 16.2.

EXHIBIT 16.2   Documents Used for Financial Planning

Liquidity
- Guaranteed Investment Certificates
- Bank account balances
- Any other money market securities owned

Financing
- Credit card account numbers
- Credit card balances
- Personal loan (such as car loan) agreements
- Mortgage loan agreement

Insurance
- Insurance policies
- Home inventory of items covered by homeowner's insurance

Investments
- Account balance showing the market value of mutual funds
- Account balance showing the market value of stocks
- Account balance showing the market value of bonds
- Stock certificates
- Bonds

Retirement and Estate Plans
- Retirement plan contracts
- Retirement account balances
- Will
- Trust agreements

L.O.2

INTEGRATING THE COMPONENTS

At this point, you have sufficient background to complete all components of your financial plan. As time passes, however, your financial position will change and your financial goals will change as well. You will need to revise your financial plan periodically to meet your financial goals. The following example for Stephanie Spratt illustrates how an individual's financial position can change over time, how a financial plan may need to be revised as a result, and how the components of the financial plan are integrated.

EXAMPLE

In 2017, Stephanie Spratt established the following goals:

- Purchase a new car within a year
- Buy a home within two years
- Make investments that will allow her wealth to grow over time
- Build a large amount of savings by the time of her retirement in approximately 40 years

In the past few years, Stephanie purchased her new car and new home. She also made some small investments. She has clearly made progress toward her goal of building a large amount of savings by the time she retires.

In 2017, Stephanie had a relatively simple personal balance sheet. Her assets amounted to $9000 and she had credit card debt of $2000 as her only liability. Therefore, her net worth was

$7000 at that time. In the past few years, her assets, liabilities, and net worth have changed substantially.

In Exhibit 16.3, Stephanie's current personal balance sheet is compared to her personal balance sheet from 2017. Notice how her personal balance sheet has changed:

1. She purchased a new car for $18 000 that currently has a market value of $15 000.

2. She purchased a home for $265 000 that still has a market value of $265 000.

3. She recently used $2000 of income to invest in two mutual funds, which are now valued at $2100.

4. She recently started investing in her RRSP and has $800 in it.

5. She recently invested $2600 in a money market fund inside a TFSA.

EXHIBIT 16.3 Stephanie Spratt's Personal Balance Sheet

	2017 Personal Balance Sheet	Personal Balance Sheet (as of Today)
Assets		
Liquid Assets		
Cash	$ 500	$ 200
Chequing account	3 500	200
TFSA investment (MMF)	0	2 600
Total liquid assets	4 000	3 000
Household Assets		
Home	0	265 000
Car	1 000	15 000
Furniture	1 000	1 000
Total household assets	2 000	281 000
Investment Assets		
Stocks	3 000	3 100
Mutual funds	0	2 100
RRSP investment	0	800
Total investment assets	3 000	6 000
TOTAL ASSETS	$9 000	$290 000
Liabilities and Net Worth		
Current Liabilities		
Credit card balance	$2 000	$ 1 000
Total Current Liabilities	2 000	1 000
Long-Term Liabilities		
Car loan	0	15 000
Mortgage	0	223 750
Total Long-Term Liabilities	0	238 750
TOTAL LIABILTIIES	$2 000	$239 750
Net Worth	$7 000	$ 50 250

The main changes in her liabilities are as follows:

1. Her purchase of a home required her to obtain a mortgage loan, which now has a balance of $223 750.

2. Her purchase of a car required her to obtain a car loan (she made a down payment of $1000, has paid $2000 of principal on the loan, and still owes $15 000).

3. She has a $1000 credit card bill that she will pay off soon.

As Exhibit 16.3 shows, Stephanie's total assets are now $290 000. She increased her assets primarily by making financing decisions that also increased her liabilities. Exhibit 16.3 shows that her liabilities are now $239 750. Therefore, her net worth is:

$$\begin{aligned} \text{Net Worth} &= \text{Total Assets} - \text{Total Liabilities} \\ &= \$290\ 000 - \$239\ 750 \\ &= \$50\ 250 \end{aligned}$$

The increase in her net worth since the beginning of the year is mainly attributable to a bonus from her employer this year, which helped her to cover the down payment on her house. Now that she has a car loan and a mortgage, she uses a large portion of her income to cover loan payments and will not be able to save much money.

As time passes, Stephanie hopes to invest in more stocks or other investments to increase her net worth. If the value of her home increases over time, her net worth will also grow. However, her car will likely decline in value over time, which will reduce the value of her assets and therefore reduce her net worth.

Budgeting

Stephanie's recent cash flow statement is shown in Exhibit 16.4. The major change in her income is that her disposable income is now higher as a result of a promotion and salary increase at work. The major changes in her expenses are as follows:

1. She no longer has a rent payment.

2. As a result of buying a new car, she now saves about $100 per month on car maintenance because the car dealer will do all maintenance at no charge for the next three years.

3. Primarily by discontinuing her health club membership and exercising at home, she has reduced her recreation expenses to about $500 per month (a reduction of $100 per month).

4. She now has a car loan payment of $412 each month.

5. She now has a mortgage loan payment, including property tax and homeowner's insurance, of $1348 per month.

6. She just started paying for life insurance ($30 per month).

7. She just started contributing $300 per month to her RRSP.

Budgeting Dilemma. While Stephanie's monthly income is now $600 higher, her monthly expenses are $810 higher. Therefore, her monthly net cash flows have declined from $330 to $120. This means that, even though her salary increased, she has less money available after paying her bills and recreation expenses.

Budgeting Decision. Stephanie reviews her personal cash flow statement to determine how she is spending her money. Some of her cash flows are currently being invested in assets. Even if she does not invest any of her net cash flows now, her net worth will grow over time because she is paying down the debt on her home and on her car each month and is contributing to her retirement account.

Overall, she decides that she is pleased with her cash flow situation. However, she decides to reassess the other components of her financial plan (as discussed below) that could affect her budget.

EXHIBIT 16.4 Stephanie's Spratt's Monthly Cash Flow Statement

	Initial Cash Flow Statement	Most Recent Cash Flow Statement	Change in the Cash Flow Statement
Income			
Disposable (after-tax) income	$3 500	$4 100	+$600
Interest on deposits	0	0	No change
Dividend payments	0	0	No change
Total income	3 500	4 100	+600
Expenses			
Rent	1 100	0	−1 100
Cable TV	80	80	No change
Electricity and water	80	100	+20
Telephone	100	100	No change
Groceries	300	300	No change
Disability insurance expenses	110	110	No change
Clothing	100	100	No change
Car insurance and maintenance	200	100	−100
Recreation	600	500	−100
Entertainment	500	500	No change
Car loan payment	0	412	+412
Mortgage payment (includes property taxes and insurance)	0	1 348	+1 348
Life insurance payment	0	30	+30
RRSP contribution	0	300	+300
Total expenses	$3 170	$3 980	+$810
Net cash flows	$ 330	$ 120	−$210

Long-Term Strategy for Budgeting. Some of Stephanie's budgeting is based on the bills she incurs as a result of her car and home. Other parts of the budget are determined by the other components of her financial plan:

- The amount of cash (if any) allocated to liquid assets depends on her plan for managing liquidity
- The amount of cash allocated to pay off existing loans depends on her plan for personal financing
- The amount of cash allocated to insurance policies depends on her insurance planning
- The amount of cash allocated to investments depends on her plan for investing
- The amount of cash allocated to her retirement account depends on her retirement planning

Managing Finances

Every two weeks, Stephanie's paycheque is direct-deposited to her chequing account. She has set up pre-authorized withdrawals for some of her bills and covers the rest of her expenses using her debit card or credit card. She pays her credit card bill in full each month. She normally has about $100 at the end of the month after paying her bills and recreation expenses. Stephanie wants to ensure that she has sufficient liquidity. Her most convenient source of funds is her

(continued)

chequing account; since her paycheque is deposited there, she knows she will have enough funds every month to pay her bills. If she had any other short-term debt, she would use her net cash flows to pay it off. She recently invested $2600 in a money market fund inside a TFSA. This account is her second most convenient source of funds; it allows her quick access to cash in the event that unanticipated expenses occur.

Stephanie has a car loan balance of $15 000 and a mortgage loan balance of $223 750. She has no need for any additional loans. She considers paying off her car loan before it is due (about three years from now).

Financing Dilemma. Stephanie wants to pay off the car loan as soon as she has saved a sufficient amount of money. She realizes that to pay off this liability, she will need to reduce some of her assets. She outlines the following options for paying off her car loan early.

Stephanie's Options for Paying Off Her Car Loan Early	Advantage	Disadvantage
Withdraw funds from money market fund	Would be able to reduce or eliminate monthly car loan payment	Will no longer have adequate liquidity
Withdraw funds from retirement account	Would be able to reduce or eliminate monthly car loan payment	Will no longer have funds set aside for retirement
Sell stock	Would be able to reduce or eliminate monthly car loan payment	Would forgo the potential to earn higher returns on the stock
Sell mutual funds	Would be able to reduce or eliminate monthly car loan payment	Would forgo the potential to earn higher returns on the mutual fund

Financing Decision. Stephanie needs to maintain liquidity, so she eliminates the first option. She also eliminates the second option because she believes that those funds should be reserved for retirement purposes.

The remaining options deserve more consideration. Stephanie's annual interest rate on the car loan is 7.60 percent. Once she has a large enough investment in stocks and mutual funds that she can pay off the car loan (perhaps a year from now), she will decide how to use that money as follows:

- If she thinks that the investments will earn an annual after-tax return of less than 7.60 percent, she will sell them and use the money to pay off the car loan. In this way, she will essentially earn a return of 7.60 percent with that money because she will be paying off debt for which she was being charged 7.60 percent.

- If she thinks that the investments will earn an annual after-tax return greater than 7.60 percent, she will keep them. She will not pay off the car loan because her investments are providing her with a higher return than the cost of the car loan.

Long-Term Strategy for Financing. Once Stephanie pays off her car loan, she will have an extra $412 per month (the amount of her car loan payment) that can be used to make more investments. She does not plan to buy another car until she can pay for it with cash. Her only other loan is her mortgage, which has a 25-year amortization period. If she stays in the same home over the next 25 years, she will have paid off her mortgage by that time, assuming that interest remains the same. In this case, she will have no debt after 25 years. She may consider buying a more expensive home in the near future and would likely obtain another mortgage amortized over a long period of time.

Insurance

Stephanie presently has automobile, homeowner's, group health, disability, and life insurance policies.

Insurance Dilemma. Stephanie recognizes that she needs insurance to cover her car, home, and health. In addition, she wants to protect her existing income in case she becomes disabled. She also wants to make sure that she can provide some financial support to her two nieces in the future.

Insurance Decision. Stephanie recently decided to purchase disability insurance to protect her income in case she becomes disabled. She also decided to purchase life insurance to fund her nieces' post-secondary education if she dies. She is pleased with her current employer-provided health insurance policy.

Long-Term Strategy for Insurance. Stephanie will maintain a high level of insurance to protect against liability resulting from owning her car or home. If she decides to have children in the future, she will purchase additional life insurance to ensure future financial support for her children. She will continue to review her policies to search for premium savings.

Managing Investments

Stephanie currently has an investment in one stock worth $3100 and an investment in two mutual funds worth $2100.

Investing Dilemma. If the one stock that Stephanie owns performs poorly in the future, the value of her investments (and therefore her net worth) could decline substantially. She expects the stock market to do well but is uncomfortable having an investment in a single stock. She considers the following options.

Stephanie's Options If She Changes Her Investments	Advantage	Disadvantage
Sell stock; invest the proceeds in bonds	Lower risk than from her stock	Lower expected return than from her stock
Sell stock; invest the proceeds in her money market fund	Lower risk and improved liquidity	Lower expected return than from her stock
Sell stock; invest the proceeds in a stock mutual fund	Lower risk	Lower expected return than from her stock

Investing Decision. All three possibilities offer lower risk than the stock, but given that Stephanie expects the stock market to perform well, she prefers a stock mutual fund. She is not relying on the investment to provide periodic income at this time and wants an investment that could increase in value over time. She decides to sell her 100 shares of stock at the prevailing market value of $3100 and to invest the proceeds in her stock mutual fund to achieve greater diversification. This transaction reflects a shift of $3100 on her personal balance sheet from stocks to mutual funds. She incurs a transaction fee of $20 for selling the shares.

Long-Term Strategy for Investing. Stephanie considers using most of her $120 in net cash flows each month to purchase additional units of the stock mutual fund in which she recently invested. She does not specify the amount she will invest because she recognizes that in some months she may face unanticipated expenses that will need to be covered. Once her car loan is paid off, she will have an additional $412 in net cash flows per month that she can invest in the stock mutual fund or in other investments.

Protecting and Maintaining Wealth

Stephanie recently started to contribute to an RRSP. This account is beneficial because her contributions will not be taxed until the funds are withdrawn during retirement. In addition, this account will provide tax-deferred growth for any future contribution to it, as long as she selects investments that appreciate in value over time.

(continued)

Retirement Contribution Dilemma. Recently, Stephanie started contributing $300 per month to her RRSP. She could also use her TFSA as a long-term savings vehicle. Stephanie is not likely to use any of the contributed funds until she retires. She considers the following options.

Stephanie's Options Regarding Her Retirement Account	Advantage	Disadvantage
Do not contribute any funds to retirement account	Can use all net cash flows for other purposes	Forgo tax benefits of RRSP contributions; will have no money set aside for retirement
Continue to contribute $300 per month to an RRSP	Tax benefits will result from a tax deduction on contributions and tax-deferred growth; future benefits are taxable upon withdrawal	Could use the $300 for other purposes
Contribute $300 per month to a TFSA	No immediate tax benefits; however, growth is tax deferred and future benefits are not taxable upon withdrawal	Could use the funds for other purposes

Retirement Contribution Decision. Stephanie prefers the tax deduction afforded by the RRSP contribution over the tax-free withdrawal benefit of the TFSA. Currently, she is using her TFSA to shelter her short-term savings in a money market fund. Once she feels comfortable with her liquidity, she may consider using her TFSA as a long-term savings vehicle. She feels that the TFSA is a good complement to an RRSP because she can supplement the required withdrawals from a registered retirement income fund (RRIF) with tax-free withdrawals from a TFSA. This will help to reduce the possibility of any clawbacks she may incur on her Old Age Security (OAS) and other old age benefits that she may be eligible to receive in the future. Stephanie also wants to know how much more she will have in 40 years (when she hopes to retire) if she saves an additional $100 per month ($1200 per year). She expects to earn an annual return of 10 percent per year, compounded monthly, if she invests in an RRSP. The following calculator graphic displays that she will be able to save an extra $632 408. This amount is in addition to any savings she will have from her current $300 monthly contribution.

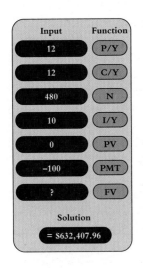

Input	Function
12	P/Y
12	C/Y
480	N
10	I/Y
0	PV
−100	PMT
?	FV

Solution

= $632,407.96

She decides to save the additional $100 per month since it will result in $632 408 more at retirement. She also realizes that contributing the extra amount will provide present-day tax benefits. Contributing the extra $100 will reduce her net cash flows, however, so she may have more difficulty meeting her liquidity needs, will be less likely to pay off her existing car loan quickly, and will have less money to spend on recreation. Yet by accepting these disadvantages in the short term, she can receive major tax benefits and ensure a high level of wealth when she retires. Stephanie's view is that any dollar invested in a retirement account is more valuable than a dollar invested in a non-retirement account because of the tax advantages.

Long-Term Strategy for Retirement Contributions. Stephanie plans to invest the maximum allowed in her RRSP so that she can take full advantage of the tax benefits. The maximum annual limit on her RRSP depends on her income. As her income increases over time, she will be able to increase her monthly contribution up to the maximum limit. She would also like to contribute the maximum amount possible to her TFSA, but cannot afford to contribute that amount right now. She will reconsider the total dollar value and asset allocation mix of her RRSP and TFSA assets on a regular basis.

MyLab Finance   Visit MyLab Finance for additional study and practice tools. Select Financial Planning Problems are available in the Study Plan. Create your own study plan, generate personal cash flow statements and balance sheets, and set personal financial goals.

SUMMARY

L.O.1 Review the components of a financial plan

A financial plan consists of a budget (Part 1), a plan for managing your financial resources (Part 2), an insurance plan (Part 3), an investment plan (Part 4), and a plan for retirement and estate planning (Part 5). The budget determines how you will spend or invest your money. Your financing plan is used to ensure that you can cover any unanticipated expenses and that you can finance large purchases. Financing also involves decisions that affect the interest rate you are charged and the duration of any loans. Your plan for protecting your assets and income involves decisions as to what types of insurance to purchase, how much insurance to buy, how much to invest periodically in your retirement account, and how to distribute your estate to your heirs. Your investment plan determines how much you allocate toward investments and how you allocate money across different types of investments.

L.O.2 Illustrate how a financial plan's components are integrated

The components of a financial plan are integrated in that they depend on each other. The budget plan depends on the other components of the financial plan. The amount of money available for any part of the plan depends on how much money is used for liquidity purposes, to make loan (financing) payments, to make investments, to buy insurance, or to contribute to retirement accounts. The more money you allocate toward any part of the financial plan, the less money you have for the other parts. Therefore, a key aspect of financial planning is to decide which components of the financial plan deserve the highest priority, because the decisions made about those components will influence the decisions for the others.

REVIEW QUESTIONS

1. Why is it important to integrate the components of your financial plan?

2. How does budgeting fit into your financial plan? How is your financial plan affected by your spending? What is the budgeting trade-off?

3. Describe some advantages and disadvantages of using financing to achieve your financial goals. What is the financing trade-off?

4. How does managing your investments fit into your financial plan? What is the investment trade-off?

5. Discuss some methods for maintaining and protecting your wealth. What is the insurance trade-off? What is the retirement account trade-off?

6. How does time affect your financial plan?

7. What do you think happens to your budget when your financial position changes?

8. You have a $7000 balance on your car loan at 11 percent interest. Your favourite aunt has just left you $10 000

in her will. You can put some of the inheritance in a money market fund at your bank as well as pay off your car loan, or you can invest it in mutual funds. What factors must you consider in making your decision?

9. In the previous question, you decide to pay off the car loan and invest the difference. Now you no longer have a monthly $350 car payment. Suggest some ways you might use these additional funds.

10. You have some extra cash in your budget that you wish to invest. You have narrowed your choices to a single stock, Government of Canada bonds, or stock mutual funds. What characteristics of each investment alternative should you consider in making your decision?

11. How does purchasing car insurance and homeowner's insurance help to protect and maintain your wealth?

12. How does purchasing sufficient health insurance help to protect and maintain your wealth?

13. How does life insurance protect your wealth? Who needs life insurance?

FINANCIAL PLANNING PROBLEMS

MyLab Finance Financial Planning Problems marked with a can be found in MyLab Finance.

 1. Judy has just received $12 500 as an inheritance from her uncle and is considering ways to use the money. Judy's car is one year old and her monthly payment is $304. She owes 48 more payments. The amount needed to pay off the loan is $12 460. How much will Judy save in interest if she pays off her car loan now?

2. Judy (from Problem 1) is also considering investing the $12 500 in a guaranteed investment certificate (GIC). She is guaranteed a return of 4 percent, compounded annually, on a four-year GIC. How much would she earn from the GIC? Which of the two alternatives (Problem 1 versus Problem 2) offers the better return?

3. Judy (from Problem 1) pays off her car loan and now must decide how she wants to invest the extra $3648 per year that she budgeted for car payments. She decides to invest this additional amount in her RRSP. Currently, the plan is averaging a 12 percent annual rate of return, compounded monthly. Judy has 15 years until retirement. How much more money will she have at retirement if she invests this additional amount?

4. Judy (from Problem 1) believes that another benefit of investing the extra $3648 per year in her RRSP is the tax savings. Judy is in a 32 percent combined provincial/federal marginal tax bracket. How much

will investing in this manner save her in taxes annually? Assuming that she remains in a 32 percent marginal tax bracket until she retires, how much will it save her in total over the next 15 years, ignoring the time value of the tax savings?

5. Maria, a 22-year-old recent college graduate, wants to retire a millionaire. How much will she need to set aside annually to achieve her goal, assuming she will retire at age 67 and earns an 8 percent rate of return, compounded annually, on her investment?

6. Referring to Question 5, what other factors should Maria consider with regard to her retirement goal? What recommendations would you give Maria regarding her goal?

FINANCIAL PLANNING ONLINE EXERCISES

1. Go to www.moneymentors.ca/learning-centre.html. This website provides a number of online and interactive tools, as well as a variety of tip sheets to help you develop your financial literacy. After reviewing the tip sheets, determine which of these tips can you put into action in the next month to begin the process of establishing a plan to improve your financial health.

PSYCHOLOGY OF PERSONAL FINANCE: Your Financial Plan

1. Do you dedicate a sufficient amount of time and money toward financial planning activities such as saving, insurance, investing, and your retirement? Explain how you could revise your spending now so that you would have more income that could be used for financial planning purposes.

2. Your financial plan should include plans for managing your liquidity, financing, insurance, investments, and retirement planning. Which of these plans causes you the greatest concern? Which of these plans will be most difficult for you to achieve? Explain.

MINI-CASE: Financial Planning

Your sister Chris and her boyfriend Doug recently announced plans to be married after graduation in May. Although you are extremely fond of both of them and want their relationship to succeed, you are concerned about their financial future. Neither Chris nor Doug completed a personal finance course while in school. Chris is a spender who has known few limits on her wants since she was a teenager. Doug, on the other hand, has worked, saved, and invested since he was a teenager to help provide for his post-secondary education. He will complete school with approximately $12 600 in student loans. But their income the first year out of school will total $90 000, in large part because of Doug's choice of major and practical work experience during school. Chris, who admits to having no financial skill or interest, is content to let Doug handle all those matters because he seems to be good at it and will always earn more than she does. Why is it dangerous for Chris to assume that Doug will always be there to take care of her? Identify three essential actions that Chris should take to ensure her financial future. Help Chris and Doug consider the issues of joint or separate chequing accounts and credit cards. Why are these important issues to resolve before the marriage?

Study Guide

Circle the correct answer and then check the answers in the back of the book to chart your progress.

Multiple Choice

1. The six main components of the financial plan include:
   a. Budgeting, managing liquidity, financing, protecting your assets and income, personal investing, and retirement and estate planning.
   b. Budgeting, managing liquidity, financing, protecting your assets, personal investing, and retirement and estate planning.
   c. Budgeting, managing liquidity, financing, protecting your assets and income, personal investing, and retirement and will planning.
   d. Budgeting, managing liquidity, financing, protecting your assets, personal investing, and retirement and will planning.

2. Which of the following statements regarding the budgeting trade-off are true?
   a. The more you spend, the more money you will have available for liquidity purposes, investments, or retirement saving.
   b. Your budgeting decisions involve a trade-off between spending today and allocating funds for the past.
   c. Your budget should attempt to ensure that you have net cash flows every month for savings or for retirement.
   d. The more funds you can allocate for the future, the less you will be able to benefit from compounded interest and the more you will be able to spend in the future.

3. Which of the following would not be considered a liquid asset?
   a. Savings account
   b. Stock mutual fund
   c. Term deposit
   d. Money market fund

4. Which of the following statements with respect to the financing trade-off is incorrect?
   a. An excessive amount of financing can prevent you from achieving your financial goals.
   b. It is easier to cover the monthly loan payment if you select financing with a relatively short maturity.
   c. You may want to consider paying off a loan before its maturity so that you can avoid incurring any more interest expense.
   d. Paying off loans rather than making additional investments is appropriate when the expected after-tax return on the investments you could make is lower than the interest rate you are paying on the loan.

5. While playing tennis with a friend, you suffer a debilitating stroke. After three weeks, you are discharged from the hospital. Which of the following types of insurance would have been of the least benefit to you and your family?
   a. Life insurance
   b. Disability insurance
   c. Long-term care insurance
   d. Critical illness insurance

6. You would like to build a portfolio that will provide periodic income. Which of the following investments may not be appropriate for the portfolio you are trying to create?
   a. An investment in stocks that pay dividends
   b. The stocks of large, well-known firms
   c. An investment in bonds
   d. An investment in the stock of a firm that is growing at a fast pace

7. All of the following would be concerns with respect to investing money in the stocks of smaller firms, except which one?
   a. An investment in stocks of smaller firms will require you to forgo some liquidity.
   b. An investment in stocks of smaller firms is more likely to result in large losses than investments in stocks of large, well-known firms.
   c. By investing in a mutual fund that focuses on small stocks, you can reduce the risk associated with being exposed to the specific risk of any individual small stock.
   d. By investing in a mutual fund that focuses on small stocks, you can reduce the risk associated with weakening market conditions.

8. With respect to your investments, which of the following documents should be stored in a safe at home or in a safety deposit box?
   a. Stock certificates
   b. Will
   c. Personal loan (such as car loan) agreements
   d. Insurance policies

9. Which of the following is a consequence of reducing your liquidity position by transferring money from a GIC to a growth mutual fund?
   a. You will earn a higher return on your assets.
   b. You may have a smaller amount of liquid funds to cover unanticipated expenses.
   c. You may have a smaller amount of liquid funds to cover anticipated expenses.
   d. All of the above.

10. To pay off a car loan, you have decided to reduce the value of one or more of your assets. Which of the following actions is most likely to have the greatest negative impact on your net worth over a period of time?
    a. Withdrawing funds from a GIC.
    b. Withdrawing funds from a retirement account composed of balanced growth and income investments.
    c. Selling a bond mutual fund.
    d. Selling shares of one of the growth stocks in your non-registered portfolio.

True/False

1. True or False? Budgeting allows you to determine whether your expenses will exceed your income so that you can forecast any shortages in that month.

2. True or False? The liquidity trade-off refers to the idea that you should maintain as much money as possible in an emergency fund to satisfy your liquidity needs.

3. True or False? Financing can increase the amount of your assets.

4. True or False? Your investment needs should be given priority before insurance.

5. True or False? You should make investments only after you have sufficient liquidity and sufficient insurance to protect your existing assets.

6. True or False? The more money you contribute to your retirement account now, the more money you will have when you reach retirement age.

7. True or False? Without exception, any money withdrawn early from a retirement account is subject to a penalty.

8. True or False? As time passes, your financial goals should remain the same.

9. True or False? To lower your overall portfolio risk and improve your liquidity, you could sell shares from a stock portfolio and invest the proceeds in a money market fund.

10. True or False? You should continuously re-evaluate your financial plan.

APPENDIX A
Projects

The following pages include projects for you to complete relating to specific aspects of personal finance.

- Assessing Your Credit
- Career Planning Project
- Leasing an Apartment
- Stock Market Project
- Comparison Shopping: Online versus Local Purchases
- Mortgage Case Project
- Mutual Fund Comparison Project

ASSESSING YOUR CREDIT

If you do not own a credit card, answer the following questions based on how you think you would use a credit card.

1. **Credit Spending.** How much do you spend per month on your credit card?

2. **Number of Credit Cards.** Do you have many credit cards? Are all of them necessary? Do you spend more money than you would normally as a result of having extra credit cards?

3. **Credit versus Cash.** Would you make the most of your purchases if you used cash instead of a credit card? Do you feel like purchases have no cost when you use a credit card instead of cash?

4. **Pay Off Part or All of Balance.** What is your normal strategy when you receive a credit card bill? Do you only pay the minimum amount required? Do you typically pay off your entire balance each month? If you do not pay off the entire balance, is it because you cannot afford to pay it off or because you would prefer to have extra cash on hand? If you have a positive balance, how do you plan to pay off that balance: pay all of it off next month or pay only the minimum amount required next month?

5. **Credit Limit.** Consider the limit on the amount you can spend using your credit cards. Does the limit restrict your spending? Would you benefit if the limit were increased or reduced?

6. **Obtaining Your Consumer Disclosure.** A consumer disclosure provides a complete account of all information on your credit report. Go to the TransUnion Canada website (www.transunion.ca/product/consumer-disclosure) to obtain your free consumer disclosure. If you recently obtained your consumer disclosure, review that report rather than obtaining a new one. Notice the types of companies that requested information on your credit. Is your consumer disclosure accurate? If not, you can write to the credit bureau to have the wrong information corrected, as explained in the text. You can, and should, obtain a free credit report by filling out the online form located at www.annualcreditreport.com/index.action.

7. **Assessing Your Credit Report.** Are you satisfied with your existing credit rating? If not, what steps do you plan to take to improve your credit rating? For example, could you reduce some debt in the future? See Chapter 6 for more ideas on improving your credit rating.

CAREER PLANNING PROJECT

Personal financial planning involves how you budget your money, manage your liquidity, finance purchases, protect your assets, invest your money, and plan your retirement and estate. All of these activities are focused on your money. A related task is career planning, which determines the amount of money that you can earn over time. Furthermore, your career determines your quality of life. Most people think about their ideal career (such as rock star, professional athlete, movie star) but do not spend enough time planning a realistic career. This project allows you to learn about possible career opportunities in which you might have an interest. Your instructor may offer you additional instructions regarding the deadline date and length of the project.

Information on Career Planning

Many websites, including the following, can guide you toward careers that may fit your interests or skills.

- www.canada.ca/en/services/youth.html
- www.tru.ca/distance/services/careers.html
- careerhub.uwaterloo.ca

These sites are general, and do not focus on a particular industry. However, once you narrow your alternatives toward a specific career, you can do an internet search for information about that career. For example, if you have an interest in health care, you can conduct a search using terms such as *health care careers*. Within the field of health care careers, you can obtain more detailed information by using more specific search terms such as *nursing career* or *lab tech career*.

The structure of this project allows you to consider a variety of alternative careers, to select one particular career, and to learn more in detail about that career.

You can insert the information you obtain into the file and save it on your computer for future reference.

1. **Career Goal.** What is your career goal? You can select a goal that requires more training, experience, or education than you presently have. However, it should be a goal that you believe is achievable. You should only select a goal that requires credentials that you are willing to obtain.

2. **Job Description.** What is the job description of the career you selected? What are the specific tasks involved in that career? What is the annual income you would expect to earn when starting this career? The website www.jobbank. gc.ca/occupation_search-eng.do?lang=eng may offer useful information that can help you to answer this question.

3. **Skills Required.** What types of skills are critical to excel in the career that you wish to pursue? For example, do you need specific technical skills, computer skills, communication skills, or managing skills for the career that you selected?

4. **Reasons for Your Career Goal.** Explain your career selection. Why would this career be ideal for you? What tasks are involved in this career that you would enjoy? Identify the specific tasks that you may be able to perform better than other people, once you have the proper training. Explain your answer.

5. **Concerns about Your Career Goal.** Any career might involve some tasks that are not desirable. Are there any tasks involved in this career that you may not like? Are there specific tasks that you may not be able to perform as well as other people, even with the proper training? Explain.

6. **Educational Background Required.** What is the typical educational background held by people with the career that you wish to pursue?

7. **Work Experience Needed.** What is the typical work experience required for people with the career that you wish to pursue? Do you have any work experience that is related to your career goal?

8. **Developing Your Resumé.** Consider your existing work experience. Create a resumé that summarizes your existing work experience in a manner that emphasizes its relationship to your career goals. For example, if your career goal is to be involved in management, make sure that your resumé emphasizes any experience you have managing employees, even if your title was not Manager.

9. **Steps to Achieve Your Goal.** Given your existing education and work experience, what additional education (if any) do you need in order to qualify for your desired career? Do you need to complete specific courses? Do you need a specific degree? Do you need specific work experience? If so, do you need any additional education to complete the work experience required? Explain.

10. **Conclusion about Your Ideal Career.** Now that you have researched your ideal career, do you still believe that it is your ideal career or have you changed your mind? If you no longer think this career is ideal, what alternative career might be more suitable for you?

LEASING AN APARTMENT

At some point in time, almost everyone will lease a place to live. Whether meeting a temporary or long-term housing need, leasing is a viable option for many individuals and families. In this project, you will explore the rights and responsibilities of leasing an apartment and compare it with other housing alternatives.

1. Look through the newspapers, the local apartment guide, or other online sources to find a potential apartment to rent. Write down your reasons for selecting this particular place to live. When making your selection, you will want to consider its distance from work or school, its proximity to family or friends, the availability of public transportation or snow routes, and so on. You might also want to consider the desirability of the neighbourhood, the amenities it offers, and other features that attracted you to this location.

2. You can obtain detailed information about apartments in a local newspaper, a local apartment guide, or on related websites.

   a. Determine the total monthly cost of living in the apartment.

      Monthly Rent   _____

      Utilities (phone, gas, electric, cable, etc.)   _____

      Parking Fees   _____

      Tenant's Insurance   _____

      Other Required Fees   _____

      Other Optional Fees   _____

   b. Determine the approximate cost of moving into the apartment.

      Application Fees   _____

      Deposit on Apartment   _____

      Deposits on Utilities   _____

      Cleaning Fees   _____

      Other Fees   _____

      Moving Costs (rental truck, gasoline, etc.)   _____

   c. Determine the cost of moving out of your current home.

      Cleaning Fees   _____

      Carpeting Cleaning Fees   _____

      Other Fees   _____

3. Review your legal rights and responsibilities as outlined in the lease agreement. Review the landlord's rights and responsibilities as outlined in the lease agreement.

     Your lease agreement should address several important factors, such as:

- What happens to your deposit when you decide to move out? Is it returned to you or held to cover other costs?
- What happens if you break the lease?
- What is the policy on subleasing the apartment?
- What other restrictions, if any, are in place for tenants?

4. Research the tenant laws in your province. Some provincial laws tend to favour the landlord over the tenant, while others tend to favour tenant rights. What conclusions can you draw about the tenant laws in your province? What surprised you the most when researching the laws regarding property rental in your province?

5. Leasing an apartment is only one option available when renting a place to live. You may decide that leasing a house is a better alternative for you and your family. What factors would influence your decision on what type of residence to lease? How does leasing an apartment compare to leasing a house?

Most universities and many colleges offer on-campus living options for their students. You can obtain information about university on-campus living options from various websites. Compare the terms of a university/college housing contract with a standard apartment lease. How is it similar? How is it different?

STOCK MARKET PROJECT

This project allows you to gain experience in making investment decisions, which are a key aspect of personal financial planning. Assume that you have $10 000 to invest. You will learn how to monitor your stock portfolio and measure your investment performance. You will also learn about the factors that affect a stock's performance over time.

Obtaining Stock Price and Dividend Information

Go to Google's Canadian financial website (www.google.ca/finance). Each stock has a ticker symbol. For example, the ticker symbol of Canadian National Railway is CNR. Insert the ticker symbol of the stock you select in the box that says "Get quotes." You will see the stock price quoted, along with other financial information. Notice that the quarterly dividend is listed within the financial details, if the stock pays a dividend. The dividend quoted on the Google finance site reflects the dividend provided per quarter.

Enter the Stock Information

1. Name of the stock in which you wish to invest   _____
2. Ticker symbol of stock   _____
3. Price per share of your stock at the time of purchase $_____ per share
4. Number of shares that you purchased ($10 000/Price per share of the stock)   _____ shares
5. Dividend per share paid per quarter $_____ per share

Your professor may ask you to submit this information at the beginning of the school term.

Determine Your Gain over the School Term

Near the end of the semester, you can determine your gain (or loss) from your investment in a stock.

6. Price per share of your stock on a date specified by your professor $ _____ per share

7. Total dollar value of your stock near the end of the school term. This is calculated as the number of shares purchased (from #4) multiplied by the price per share of your stock near the end of the school term (from #6). $ _____

8. Total dollar amount of dividends received. This is calculated as the dividend received per share (from #5) multiplied by the number of shares purchased (from # 4). $ _____

9. Total dollars that you have at the end of the school term (#7 × #8) $ _____

10. Return on your investment = (Total dollars based on #9 − $10 000) / $10 000 _____ %

Your professor may ask you to compare your results with those of other students in the class.

Comparing Your Stock to the General Market

Go to Google's Canadian financial website (www.google.ca/finance) and enter your stock's ticker symbol in the "Get quotes" box. A common benchmark used to measure general stock market conditions is the S&P/TSX Composite Index. Click on 3m in the stock price chart to review a three-month period and then check the small S&P TSX box just above the chart. The website will provide a trend of the S&P/TSX Composite Index on the same chart as your stock. This allows you to compare the performance of your stock to the stock market in general. Did your stock move in the same direction as the market for most of the school term? Did your stock perform better or worse than the market in general?

Team Project

If students are divided into teams of equal size, each team can determine its average return on investment and compare it against other teams.

COMPARISON SHOPPING: ONLINE VERSUS LOCAL PURCHASES

Today's consumers have many options when deciding to make a purchase. Online commerce, or buying online, continues to grow and create more competition for local merchants. Online purchases were approximately $168 million in 2005 and were expected to triple in size by 2010. The internet is an important source of product information for many consumers, even those who may not make online purchases. Online searches allow consumers to compare product features, prices, and availability, often saving time and energy when comparison shopping. This project will allow you to explore the advantages and disadvantages of buying online versus buying locally.

1. Select a product that you would be interested in buying. Identify possible online sources and local sources where you can get reliable information about the product you want to buy. Remember, just because something is printed or posted on the internet does not mean that the information is accurate.

2. Identify online sellers and local merchants where the product is available for sale. Generally, seller credibility is a bigger issue when shopping online because the seller may be located anywhere, and can be very difficult to track down if there are problems with the sale. For the most part, buyers have very limited knowledge about an online seller unless it is a well-branded company. Local merchants, however, can also pose a credibility risk, especially if they are small, single-location businesses that are new to the area.

3. Compare the cost of making the purchase online versus buying the product from a local merchant. List the costs associated with buying online, such as shipping and handling, potential postage for returning the product, restocking fees, website membership fees, and so on. List the costs associated with buying a product locally, such as transportation (mileage/gasoline), time, restocking fees, membership fees, sales tax, and so on.

4. Compare the benefits of making online purchases versus buying the product locally. Some of these may include time, personal contact, ability to ask questions, and so on.

5. Online shopping is probably having an impact on local governments and local merchants. Prepare a presentation on the possible short-term and long-term costs and benefits of online shopping on your local area.

   Option 1. Talk with a local representative from the Chamber of Commerce or with a local or provincial government official about the impact of online shopping on local tax revenues or local sales tax. How is online shopping affecting the number of jobs or the funds available to support local services such as schools, roads, and police?

   Option 2. Investigate a business that you follow (perhaps where you work or shop). Is it losing business to online competitors or is it using the internet to increase its appeal to consumers?

   Option 3. Conduct an internet search to research your province's policy on online sales and possible loss of tax dollars. Is it attempting to recover some of the dollars lost to online sales?

MORTGAGE CASE PROJECT

Purchasing and financing a home involves a number of steps. First, you must select a home. Second, you must choose a financial institution with which to finance your home purchase. Third, you must qualify for the home purchase based on your financial institution's maximum allowable gross debt service (GDS) and total debt service (TDS) ratios. Fourth, you must consider the transaction costs involved in closing a home purchase. Use the information provided below to help Harry and Sally determine one possible solution to their housing need.

Harry (age 27) and Sally (age 26) wish to purchase a house in the fall. They have accumulated a total of $30 000 in savings to pay for the costs associated with buying a single-family home. They have a four-year-old daughter and intend to have another child in about two years. They are first-time home buyers and are only interested in buying a house.

Harry, a graduate from a prestigious engineering program, has a job with ABC Construction. He has been on the job for two years and has an annual salary of $77 500. Sally has worked as a program administrator at a local law firm for the past three years and earns $48 500 annually.

Their debts consist of a monthly car payment of $469, with payments to continue for one more year. They have already decided that, in order to buy a house, they will require a mortgage insured by the Canada Mortgage and Housing Corporation (CMHC) due to their eligible income currently available and the expenses associated with buying a home.

1. **Suitable House.** Use the internet, local newspapers, and real estate magazines to determine and select a suitable house for Harry and Sally. Compare at least two houses that would be suitable for the couple. The criteria used to select a home will be different from couple to couple. It is important to consider not only the home itself, but also the features of the property and the surrounding neighbourhood and community. Internet research can be conducted using resources such as www.realtor.ca. Indicate which house is most suitable for Harry and Sally, and why it is most suitable.

2. **Suitable Financial Institution.** Compare the mortgage rates, application fees, mortgage options (including accelerated payment features), and any current promotions being offered by at least two financial institutions. Indicate which financial institution is most suitable for Harry and Sally, and why it is most suitable.

3. **Mortgage Calculations.** Using the $30 000 down payment and assuming that the maximum GDS and TDS ratios for the financial institution you have chosen are 32 and 40 percent, respectively, determine the monthly mortgage payment the couple can afford and the maximum value of the mortgage they can afford. For the GDS and TDS ratio calculations, use the monthly heating costs and property taxes that are appropriate for the city or town in which you live. CMHC insurance premiums will be added to the mortgage.

4. **Transaction Costs.** In addition to the down payment, the couple will incur closing costs. These closing costs include a home inspection fee, an appraisal fee, a real property report/land survey, legal fees and disbursements, title insurance, and homeowner's insurance. How much of the $30 000 down payment should the couple set aside to cover closing costs? If Harry and Sally do not reduce their down payment, how else might they cover these closing costs? What are the pros and cons of reducing their down payment?

Note: Material for the Mortgage Case Project was adapted from information provided by the Northern Alberta Institute for Technology's (NAIT's) business program.

MUTUAL FUND COMPARISON PROJECT

There are many ways to analyze a mutual fund. The following project will show you one such method. For this exercise, you will analyze four mutual funds in the Canadian equity category. In order to compare mutual funds, go to www.theglobeandmail.com, click on Investing, then Funds & ETFs, and finally click on Fund Filter. Under Asset Class, select Canadian Equity and click on Get Results. Notice that there are many mutual funds from which you can choose. To simplify your comparison, select Canadian equity mutual funds managed by the larger financial institutions, such as BMO, Scotiabank, RBC, TD, and CIBC. You could also choose to compare Canadian equity mutual funds from large, well-known mutual fund companies. Once you have selected four funds, choose the fund that you would most likely purchase. You *must* pick a winner. You can also analyze mutual funds from other categories, such as Canadian Money Market, Canadian Bond, U.S. Equity, and Foreign Equity.

You will use five criteria to pick your winning fund:

1. **Annualized Rate of Return.** The average annual compound rate of return on a fund or portfolio, including the effects of income on income. To provide a greater measure of consistency of performance over time, annual rates of return should be considered as well.

2. **Annual Rate of Return.** The absolute annual return on a fund or portfolio, including reinvested dividends.

The example below highlights the difference between annualized rate of return and annual rate of return.

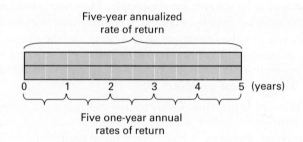

3. **Volatility.** A measure and/or statement of risk. Generally, the lower the volatility (given an equal level of return for two similar investments), the better the investment is on a risk-adjusted basis.

4. **Management Expense Ratio (MER).** The sum of management fees paid to the mutual fund administrator to manage the fund and operating expenses associated with a fund (e.g., filing, legal, and audit fees). The MER is an annualized figure expressed as a percentage of the net asset value of the fund. MERs eat into returns; however, many investors are willing to pay a higher MER for superior performance.

5. **Manager Tenure.** Consider the consistency of fund management. A change in fund manager can be positive or negative, depending on the circumstances. Is past performance attributable to the current manager? For example, if a fund has performed very well for the past five years but a new manager was hired last year, should you still buy the fund? That is, can you expect the new manager to perform as well as the previous manager?

Category: Canadian Equity

Key Indicators	Fund #1	Fund #2	Fund #3	Fund #4
Annualized Rate of Return (Five years)				
Annual Rate of Return (Years 1, 2, 3, 4, 5)				
Volatility				
MER				
Manager Tenure				

And the winner is . . .

Winner	
Runner-up	

Your Career

DETERMINING YOUR CAREER PATH

What career path is optimal for you? Review the factors described here that you should consider when determining your career path. Then, access the sources of information that are identified below to help make your selection.

Factors That May Affect Your Career Path

Perhaps the obvious first step in determining your career path is to consider your interests, and then identify the careers that fit those interests. Most people identify several possible career interests, which makes the decision difficult. However, you may be able to screen your list based on the following factors.

Educational and Skill Requirements. Some jobs may seem interesting but require more education and training than you are prepared to acquire. For example, the training required to be a doctor may be too extensive and time consuming. In addition, the entrance requirements are very high. Review the education and skills needed for each career that appeals to you. From your list of possible career paths, focus on those for which you already have or would be willing to achieve the necessary background, education, and skills.

Job Availability. There are some career paths that people think they would like to follow and could do so successfully, but the paths have a limited supply of open positions relative to applicants. For example, many people want to be actors or actresses, or waiters at very expensive restaurants. Consider the number of job positions available compared to the number of applicants pursuing those jobs.

Compensation. Most people consider compensation to be an important criterion when considering job positions. Some career tracks may be enjoyable but do not provide sufficient compensation. Information on compensation for various types of jobs is available on many websites. For example, at www.workopolis.com you can insert the type of job position you are curious about and obtain salary ranges for that position in a particular location in Canada.

Sources of Information That Can Help You to Select Your Career Path

Consider the following sources of information as you attempt to establish your list of career options from which to select your optimal career path.

Books on Careers. There are many books that identify careers and describe the necessary skills for each one. Some books provide a broad overview, while others are more detailed. A broad overview is usually ideal when you are first identifying the various types of careers that exist. Then, once you narrow down the list, you can find a book that focuses on your chosen field, such as medicine, engineering, social work, and so on.

Courses. Your college or university courses are a vital source of information about related careers. Courses in finance can help you to understand the nature of the work in the financial services industry, accounting classes provide insight into the nature of the work that accountants do, and courses in entrepreneurship may help you to understand the job skills required of a self-employed individual. Even courses that are broader in scope (for example, courses in management) may be applicable to many different types of jobs, including those of financial advisers, accountants, and entrepreneurs. If you enjoyed your basic management course, you may like a job in which you are involved in managing people, production processes, or services.

Job Experience. Management trainee positions allow some exposure to a particular type of job and allow you to learn what tasks people in a field do as part of their daily work. Such experience is especially useful because many jobs are likely to differ from your perception of them.

Contacts. For any specific job description in which you are interested, identify people who you know in that field. Set up an informational interview so that you can ask detailed questions about the job.

The Internet. A great deal of information on careers is available on the internet. To explore the types of careers that are available, and the skills needed for each, go to www. monster.ca. There you can learn about jobs in numerous fields, including finance, law, management, construction, health, agriculture, and broadcasting. Be careful, however, to note the size of the pool of applicants for any type of job in which you are interested. It is much easier to land the job you want (assuming that you have the requisite skills) when the number of openings is large compared to the number of qualified people interested in that position. Your expectations with respect to your first job should be reasonable given your knowledge and experience.

At some point, you have to narrow your choices so that you can focus more time on the careers that intrigue you the most. The internet is very valuable in offering insight even after you narrow your choices.

Personality Tests. You can get feedback on the type of career that fits you based on a personality test. Some of these tests are expensive, and there are mixed opinions about whether they can more accurately pinpoint a job that fits your personality than if you simply use the criteria described above. Some tests are offered for free online, such as the personality test at www.typefocus.com. Be aware that free tests normally do not offer as detailed an analysis as tests for which you pay.

GETTING THE SKILLS YOU NEED

Once you decide on the type of position you want, your next step is to determine the training and education you will need to qualify for it.

Training

To gather general information, go to websites such as Service Canada's Jobs Bank site (www.jobbank.gc.ca). There you can learn about the training needed for a specific job description and how to obtain it.

Be careful when reviewing information about various training courses that are available. Much information found on websites specifically devoted to training is provided by companies that want to sell you training. For this reason, carefully evaluate whether the training offered will get you the job that you want. As an extreme example, some companies provide training for modelling or acting. People are well aware of celebrities who became very rich by modelling or acting. However, taking a few courses is unlikely to lead to major success in those fields. Try to determine whether the market truly rewards people who pay for training by a particular company before you pay for it.

The training offered by some companies may be certified, which could distinguish it from others. However, a certificate does not always mean that the training is valuable or will lead to employment. In some cases, there may simply be fewer jobs than the number of people who are properly trained. In other cases, the training might not qualify you for a specific job position.

Education

A degree in a career-oriented major, such as accounting or business, will prepare you for a job in that specific field. A liberal arts degree, on the other hand, will allow you to choose from a broad range of careers in areas such as marketing, journalism, teaching, and publishing.

The reputations of post-secondary institutions vary substantially, and some schools may be much more credible than others in preparing you for a specific job position. Some jobs require that your degree be acquired from an accredited university, while other jobs require you to have the applied training that is available from a technical institute. It may be important to learn about the accreditation standards of any post-secondary institution that you wish to attend. Because there are different accreditation agencies, it is important to determine the type of accreditation that would be important for the specific type of job you plan to pursue.

Learn as much as you can about the college or department of the university in which you are considering taking courses. What percentage of recent graduates passed a standardized exam that must be taken after graduation (for fields such as financial services and accounting)? Are recent graduates being hired in the field that you wish to enter when you graduate? You may be able to get answers to these questions from the department where you would be taking courses.

Expanding Your Education

A master's degree or a doctorate provides you with additional knowledge and skills that may allow you to qualify for better jobs. However, there are costs associated with pursuing such degrees, and you must weigh them against the potential benefits.

Costs. The cost of a graduate degree is substantial, and should be estimated carefully before you make your decision to pursue one. Because the cost varies substantially among programs, you may find a program that is less expensive than others and yet satisfies your needs. Consider tuition and fees, room and board, and the opportunity cost of pursuing the degree. If you enrol in a full-time program, your opportunity cost is the salary you could have earned if you had worked during that time. You may also find it necessary to give up some social activities.

Benefits. Individuals often pursue a master's degree or doctorate to increase their marketability. There are many job positions that require a degree beyond a bachelor of arts or a bachelor of science. If your goal is to increase your marketability, determine whether an additional degree truly results in better job opportunities. In addition, determine what type of degree would make the biggest difference. For example, engineers commonly obtain a master's in business administration (MBA) rather than a master's in engineering because the MBA is intended to give them stronger management skills.

If you decide to pursue a master's degree or doctorate, determine whether the university you select would make a big difference in your marketability. Some programs have a national or international reputation, while others are known only within a local area.

CHANGING YOUR CAREER

Many people do not realize what career would make them happy until they have pursued the wrong one. In some cases, they can use their existing experience in a new career, while in other cases they must be retrained. The obvious barrier to switching careers is the amount of time already invested in a particular career. In addition, if training is necessary, the costs involved in changing careers may be high. Nevertheless, people should seriously consider switching if they truly believe that a different career would be more satisfying, but first they should obtain detailed information about the new job description.

Be realistic in assessing any career switch; look closely at your expectations. Would you really be more satisfied? How much training is involved? Would you have to stop working while you are retrained? How long will it take you to get a job once you are retrained? Is the compensation higher or lower in the new career versus your existing career? Are there more chances for advancement? Is there more job security?

Self-Employment

At some point in your life, you may decide that you want to leave your current job to become self-employed. There are millions of people who started their own businesses and are much more satisfied than when they were employed by a firm or government agency. Self-employment, however, is not for everyone; some people are excellent workers but are not effective at creating business ideas or running a business.

To start your own business, you need a business plan that will be successful. Normally, this requires the creation of a product or service that is more desirable to customers than other products or services already offered in the marketplace. Your advantage may be creating a product that you can offer at a lower price than similar products in the marketplace. Alternatively, your advantage may be higher quality. Keep in mind that competitors may be quick to adjust once you start your business and it may be more difficult than you anticipated to gain market share. A business is accountable to its customers; if it does not satisfy customers, it will not survive.

CRITERIA USED TO ASSESS APPLICANTS

When you pursue a job, you will likely be competing against many other applicants. By recognizing what the employer is seeking, you may be able to distinguish yourself from the other applicants. Understanding the criteria that employers use to assess applicants will help you to determine whether you possess the right qualifications for the job.

Your Application

An application may request general information about your education background, such as the schools you attended and your major and minor in university or college. It may also request information about your previous work experience. Applications are used to determine whether applicants have the knowledge and the experience necessary to perform well in the job position.

Your Resumé

Your resumé should provide your educational background and work experience. Companies receive numerous resumés for job positions, so it helps to describe succinctly the skills that may help you stand out from other applicants. If you obtain the skills and training that you need to pursue the job you desire, creating a resumé is relatively easy. Most career websites offer tips on how you can improve your resumé (e.g., under Career Resources on www.monster.ca). You can also post your resumé on many job websites, such as www.monster.ca and www.careerbuilder.ca.

Job Interviews

The interview process helps an employer to obtain additional information such as how you interact with people and respond to specific situations. Various personality traits can be assessed, such as:

- Your punctuality
- Your ability to work with others
- Your ability to communicate
- Your ability to grasp concepts
- Your listening skills
- Your ability to recognize your limitations

- Your ability to take orders
- Your ability to give orders
- Your potential as a leader

There are numerous books and websites that offer advice about various aspects of job interviews, such as grooming, body language, etiquette, and even answering tough questions about deficiencies in your resumé. Another source of up-to-date information on interviewing is the career centre at your college or university, which often offers seminars on effective interview techniques.

You may be asked to provide references during the interview process. You should be prepared to provide a list of business and personal references with addresses and contact numbers upon request. You should ask your references for permission before using them and be sure to thank them if they are contacted.

Conclusion

You have control over your career path. If you follow guidelines such as those described in this appendix, you can increase your chances of achieving the job and career path you want. However, keep in mind that your career aspirations and opportunities change over time. Therefore, your career planning does not end with your first job but continues throughout your career path, and even plays a role in your decision to retire someday.

GLOSSARY

accident benefits coverage Insures against the cost of medical care for you and other passengers in your car.

accumulated income payment (AIP) The taxable amount paid to a subscriber from an RESP.

actual cash value policy Pays you the value of the damaged property after considering its depreciation.

all perils coverage Protects the home and any other structures on the property against all events except those that are specifically excluded by the policy.

alter ego trust A trust that contains assets that have not been subject to immediate deemed disposition, thereby deferring any capital gains tax.

amortization The expected number of years it will take a borrower to pay off the entire mortgage loan balance.

amortize To repay the principal of a loan (the original amount borrowed) through a series of equal payments. A loan repaid in this manner is said to be amortized.

annuity The payment of a series of equal cash flow payments at equal intervals of time.

annuity due A series of equal cash flow payments that occur at the beginning of each period.

ask price The price at which a seller would like to sell a stock.

asset allocation The process of allocating money across financial assets (such as mutual funds, stocks, and bonds) with the objective of achieving a desired return while maintaining risk at a tolerable level.

asset turnover ratio A measure of efficiency, computed as sales divided by average total assets.

assets What you own.

auto insurance policy Specifies the coverage provided by an insurance company for a particular individual and vehicle.

automated banking machine (ABM) A machine that individuals can use to deposit and withdraw funds at any time of day.

average collection period A measure of efficiency, computed as accounts receivable divided by average daily sales.

average tax rate The amount of tax you pay as a percentage of your total taxable income.

back-end load mutual fund Mutual funds that charge a fee if shares are redeemed within a set period of time.

balance sheet A financial statement that indicates a firm's sources of funds and how it has invested those funds as of a particular point in time.

balanced mutual funds Funds that sell units, or shares, to individuals and use this money to invest in a combination of stocks and bonds.

banker's acceptances (BAs) Short-term debt securities issued by large firms that are guaranteed by a bank.

beneficiary A person specified in a will to receive part of an estate (also known as an heir); also, the named individual who receives life insurance payments upon the death of the insured.

bequest A gift that results from the instructions provided in a will.

beta Measures the systematic risk of an investment relative to a benchmark index.

bid price The price at which a buyer would like to purchase a stock.

board lot Shares bought or sold in multiples of typically 100 shares. The size of the board lot depends on the price of the security.

bodily injury liability coverage Protects you against liability associated with injuries you cause to others.

bond mutual funds Funds that sell units, or shares, to individuals and use this money to invest in bonds.

bonds Long-term debt securities issued by government agencies or corporations that are collateralized by assets.

budget A cash flow statement that is based on forecasted cash flows (income and expenses) for a future time period.

budget method (needs method) A method that determines how much life insurance is needed based on the household's future expected expenses and current financial situation.

budget planning (budgeting) The process of forecasting future income, expenses, and savings goals.

buy-stop order An order to buy a stock when the price rises to a specified level.

call (prepayment) risk The risk that a callable bond will be called.

call feature A feature on a bond that allows the issuer to repurchase the bond from the investor before maturity.

call option Provides the right to purchase 100 shares of a specified stock at a specified price by a specified expiration date.

Canada Health Act Establishes the criteria and conditions related to insured health care services that provinces and territories must meet to receive money from the federal government for health care.

Canada Health Transfer (CHT) The largest federal transfer of money to the provinces and territories, providing them with cash payments and tax transfers in support of health care.

Canada Savings Bonds (CSBs) Short-term to medium-term, high-quality debt securities issued by the Government of Canada.

capital asset Any asset that is acquired and held for the purpose of generating income.

capital gain Money earned when you sell an asset at a higher price than you paid for it.

capital loss Money lost when you sell an asset at a lower price than you paid for it.

captive (or exclusive) insurance agent Works for one particular insurance company.

cash value The portion of the premium in excess of insurance-related and company expenses that is invested by the insurance company on behalf of the policy owner.

certified cheque A cheque that can be cashed immediately by the payee without the payee having to wait for the bank to process and clear it.

chartered banks Financial institutions that accept deposits in chequing and savings accounts and use the funds to provide business and personal loans. These banks are federally incorporated.

cheque register A booklet accompanying your chequebook where you record the details of each transaction you make, including deposits, cheques written, withdrawals, and bill payments.

clawback Used to reduce (that is, claw back) a particular government benefit provided to taxpayers who have income that exceeds a certain threshold amount.

closed mortgage Restricts your ability to pay off the mortgage balance during the mortgage term unless you are willing to pay a financial penalty.

closed-end funds Funds that issue shares to investors but do not redeem those shares; instead, the fund's shares are traded on a stock exchange.

codicil A document that specifies changes in an existing will.

collateral Assets of a borrower that back a loan in the event that the borrower defaults. Collateral is a form of security for the lender.

collision insurance Insures against costs of damage to your car resulting from an accident in which the driver of your car is at fault.

commercial paper A short-term debt security issued by large firms that is guaranteed by the issuing firm.

common stock A certificate issued by a firm to raise funds that represents partial ownership in the firm.

compound interest The process of earning interest on interest.

comprehensive coverage Insures you against damage to your car that results from something other than a collision, such as floods, theft, fire, hail, explosions, riots, vandalism, and various other perils.

consumer price index (CPI) A measure of inflation that represents the increase in the prices of consumer products such as groceries, household products, housing, and gasoline over time.

consumer proposal An offer made by a debtor to his or her creditors to modify his or her payments.

contingent beneficiary An individual who is entitled to receive benefits, when they become payable, because the primary beneficiary is not able to for some reason.

conventional mortgage A mortgage where the down payment is at least 20 percent of the home's appraised value.

conversion option Allows you to convert your term insurance policy into a whole life policy that will be in effect for the rest of your life.

convertible bond A bond that can be converted into a stated number of shares of the issuer's stock at a specified price.

convertible mortgage Allows you to renew your mortgage before the end of the current mortgage term without paying a penalty.

corporate bonds Long-term debt securities issued by large firms.

correlation A mathematical measure that describes how two securities' prices move in relation to one another.

cost of insurance The insurance-related expenses incurred by a life insurance company to provide the actual death benefit, sometimes referred to as the pure cost of dying.

covered call strategy Selling call options on stock that you own.

credit Funds provided by a creditor to a borrower that the borrower will repay with interest or fees in the future.

credit management Decisions regarding how much credit to obtain to support your spending and which sources of credit to use.

credit reports Reports provided by credit bureaus that document a person's credit payment history.

credit unions/caisses populaires Provincially incorporated co-operative financial institutions that are owned and controlled by their members.

creditor An individual or company to whom you owe money.

creditor insurance Term life insurance where the beneficiary of the policy is a creditor.

current liabilities Personal debts that will be paid in the near future (within a year).

current ratio The ratio of a firm's short-term assets to its short-term liabilities.

day traders Investors who buy stocks and then sell them on the same day.

death benefit The total amount paid tax-free to the beneficiary on the death of the policy owner.

debentures Long-term debt securities issued by corporations that are secured only by the corporation's promise to pay.

debit card A card that not only is used as identification at your bank, but also allows you to make purchases that are charged against an existing chequing account.

debt ratio A measure of financial leverage that calculates the proportion of total assets financed with debt.

declining redemption schedule A fee schedule where the back-end load charge reduces with each year an investor holds the fund.

decreasing term insurance A type of creditor insurance, such as mortgage life insurance, where the life insurance face amount decreases each time a regular payment is made on debt that is amortized over a period of time.

deductible A set dollar amount that you are responsible for paying before any coverage is provided by your insurer.

deduction An item that can be deducted from total income to determine taxable income.

default Occurs when a company borrows money through the issuance of debt securities and does not pay either the interest or the principal.

default risk Risk that the borrower of funds will not repay the creditors.

defined-benefit pension plan An employer-sponsored retirement plan that guarantees you a specific amount of income when you retire, based on your salary and years of employment.

defined-contribution pension plan An employer-sponsored retirement plan where the contribution rate, not the benefit amount, is based on a specific formula.

demutualization Refers to the transformation of a firm from a member-owned organization to a publicly owned, for-profit organization.

depository institutions Financial institutions that accept deposits from and provide loans to individuals and businesses.

disability income insurance A monthly insurance benefit paid to you in the event that you are unable to work as a result of an injury or an illness.

discount The amount by which a closed-end fund's share price in the secondary market is below the fund's NAVPS.

discount bond A bond that is trading at a price below its par value.

discount brokerage firm A brokerage firm that executes transactions but does not offer investment advice.

discounting The process of obtaining present values.

disposable (after-tax) income Income minus applicable income taxes and other payroll deductions, such as CPP and EI contributions.

dividend discount model (DDM) A method of valuing stocks in which a firm's future dividend payments are discounted at an appropriate rate of interest.

dividend income Income received from corporations in the form of dividends paid on stock or on mutual funds that hold stock. Dividend income represents the profit due to part owners of the company.

dumpster diving Occurs when an identity thief goes through your trash looking for discarded items that reveal personal information that can be used for fraudulent purposes.

durable power of attorney for health care A legal document that grants a person the power to make specific health care decisions for you.

economic growth The growth in a country's economy over a particular period.

educational assistance payment (EAP) The amount paid to a beneficiary from an RESP.

effective interest rate The actual rate of interest that you earn, or pay, over a period of time.

efficient stock market A market in which stock prices fully reflect information that is available to investors.

eligible deposits Includes those deposits that are payable in Canada and in Canadian currency.

emergency fund A portion of savings that you have allocated to short-term needs such as unexpected expenses in order to maintain adequate liquidity.

Employment Insurance (EI) Government benefits that are payable for periods of time when you are away from work due to specific situations.

enduring (continuing) power of attorney A legal document that grants a person the immediate power to make any decisions or commitments for you, even when you are mentally incapacitated.

English form will A will that contains the signature of the testator as well as the signatures of two witnesses who were present when the testator signed the will.

equity The market value of your home less any outstanding mortgage balance and/or debts held by others that are secured against your property.

equity mutual funds Funds that sell units, or shares, to individuals and use this money to invest in stocks.

estate The assets of a deceased person after all debts are paid.

estate planning Determining how your wealth will be distributed before and/or after your death.

exchange rate risk The risk that the value of a bond may drop if the currency denominating the bond weakens against the Canadian dollar.

excise taxes Special taxes levied on certain consumer products such as cigarettes, alcohol, and gasoline.

exclusions A term appearing in insurance contracts or policies that describes items or circumstances that are specifically excluded from insurance coverage.

executor The person designated in a will to pay off any debts that the testator may have and carry out the instructions regarding the distribution of the testator's assets to beneficiaries.

exercise (strike) price The price at which a call option is exercised.

extendible bond A short-term bond that allows the investor to extend the maturity date of the bond.

face amount The amount stated on the face of the policy that will be paid on the death of the insured.

Facility Association Ensures that drivers unable to obtain insurance with an individual company are able to obtain the coverage they need to operate their vehicles legally.

Federal Crown corporation bonds Debt securities issued by corporations established by the federal government.

finance and lease companies Non-depository institutions that specialize in providing personal loans or leases to individuals.

finance charge The interest and fees you must pay as a result of using credit.

financial conglomerates Financial institutions that offer a diverse set of financial services to individuals or firms.

financial leverage A firm's reliance on debt to support its operations.

Financial Planning Standards Council (FPSC) A not-for-profit organization that was created to benefit the public through the development, enforcement, and promotion of the highest competency and ethical standards in financial planning.

fiscal policy How the government imposes taxes on individuals and corporations and how it spends tax revenues.

fixed-rate mortgage A mortgage in which a fixed interest rate is specified for the term of the mortgage.

front-end load mutual fund Mutual funds that charge a fee at the time of purchase, which is paid to stockbrokers or other financial service advisers who execute transactions for investors.

full-service brokerage firm A brokerage firm that offers investment advice and executes transactions.

Fund Facts A document designed to give investors key information about a mutual fund, in a language they can easily understand, at a time that is relevant to their investment decision.

fundamental analysis The valuation of stocks based on an examination of fundamental characteristics such as revenue, earnings, and/or the sensitivity of the firm's performance to economic conditions.

future value interest factor (FVIF) A factor multiplied by today's savings to determine how the savings will accumulate over time.

future value interest factor for an annuity (FVIFA) A factor multiplied by the periodic savings level (annuity) to determine how the savings will accumulate over time.

general power of attorney A legal document that grants a person the immediate power to make any decisions or commitments for you, with specific limitations.

global bond funds Mutual funds that focus on bonds issued by non-Canadian firms or governments.

Government of Canada bonds Debt securities issued by the Canadian government.

grace period The period the insurance company extends to the policy owner before the policy lapses due to nonpayment.

gross debt service (GDS) ratio Your monthly mortgage-related debt payments—including mortgage loan repayments, heating costs, property taxes, and half of any condominium fees—divided by your total monthly gross household income.

gross domestic product (GDP) The total market value of all products and services produced in a country.

group term insurance Term insurance provided to a designated group of people with a common bond that generally has lower-than-typical premiums.

growth stocks Shares of firms with substantial growth opportunities.

guaranteed investment certificate (GIC) An instrument issued by a depository institution that specifies a minimum investment, an interest rate, and a maturity date.

health insurance A group of insurance benefits provided to a living individual as a result of sickness or injury.

hedge funds Limited partnerships that manage portfolios of funds for wealthy individuals and financial institutions.

high ratio mortgage A mortgage where the down payment is less than 20 percent of the home's appraised value.

high-yield bonds Bonds issued by less stable corporations that are subject to a higher degree of default risk.

holograph will A will that is written solely in the handwriting of the testator and that does not require the signature of any witnesses.

Home Buyers' Plan (HBP) A tax-free RRSP withdrawal option that is available to Canadians who would like to buy their first home.

home equity line of credit A loan in which the equity in a home serves as collateral.

home inspection A report on the condition of the home.

home inventory Contains detailed information about your personal property that can be used when filing a claim.

homeowner's insurance Provides insurance in the event of property damage, theft, or personal and third-party liability relating to home ownership.

household assets Items normally owned by a household, such as a car and furniture.

identity theft Occurs when an individual uses personal, identifying information unique to you, such as your social insurance number, without your permission for their personal gain.

income method A general formula that determines how much life insurance is needed based on the policyholder's annual income.

income statement A financial statement that measures a firm's revenues, expenses, and earnings over a particular period of time.

income stocks Stocks that provide investors with periodic income in the form of large dividends.

income trust A flow-through investment vehicle that generates income and capital gains for investors.

indemnification The concept of putting an insured individual back into the same position he or she was in prior to the event that resulted in insurance benefits being paid.

independent insurance agent Represents many different insurance companies.

index funds Mutual funds that attempt to mirror the movements of an existing equity index.

individual investors Individuals who invest funds in securities.

inefficient stock market A market in which stock prices do not reflect all public information that is available to investors.

inflation The increase in the general level of prices of products and services over a specified period.

inflation risk The risk that the purchasing power of a bond investment will diminish due to a relative increase in inflation.

initial public offering (IPO) The first offering of a firm's shares to the public.

insider information Non-public information known by employees and other professionals that is not known by outsiders. It is illegal to use insider information.

insolvent A person who owes at least $1000 and is unable to pay his or her debts as they come due.

instalment loan A loan provided for specific purchases, with interest charged on the amount borrowed. It is repaid on a regular basis, generally with blended payments.

institutional investors Professionals responsible for managing large pools of money, such as pension funds, on behalf of their clients.

insurance agent Represents one or more insurance companies and recommends insurance policies that fit customers' needs.

insurance companies Non-depository institutions that sell insurance to protect individuals or firms from risks that can incur financial loss.

insurance planning Determining the types and amount of insurance needed to protect your assets.

insurance policy Contract between an insurance company and the policy owner.

insurance premium The cost of obtaining insurance.

insured health care services Medically necessary hospital, physician, and surgical-dental services provided to insured persons.

insured person An eligible resident of a province.

inter vivos trust A trust in which you assign the management of your assets to a trustee while you are living.

interest The rent charged for the use of money.

interest adjustment Occurs when there is a difference between the date you take possession of your home and the date from which your lender calculates your first mortgage payment.

interest income Interest earned from investments in various types of savings accounts at financial institutions: from investments in debt securities such as term deposits, GICs, and CSBs, and from loans to other individuals, companies, and governments.

interest rate risk The risk that occurs because of changes in the interest rate. This risk affects funds that invest in debt securities and other income-oriented securities.

interest rate strategy Selecting bonds based on interest rate expectations.

intestate The condition of dying without a will.

intrinsic valuation model A model that attempts to find the value of an investment by focusing on the amount of future cash flows generated by the investment, the timing of these cash flows, and the rate of return required on the investment.

inventory turnover A measure of efficiency, computed as the cost of goods sold divided by average daily inventory.

investment dealers Non-depository institutions that facilitate the purchase or sale of various investments by firms or individuals by providing investment banking and brokerage services.

investment risk Uncertainty surrounding not only the potential return on an investment but also its future potential value.

irrevocable inter vivos trust An inter vivos trust that cannot be changed, although it may provide income to the settlor.

joint tenancy with rights of survivorship (JTWROS) A form of joint ownership where the death of one joint owner results in an asset being transferred directly to the surviving joint owner.

letter of last instruction A supplement to a will that describes preferences regarding funeral arrangements and indicates where any key financial documents are stored.

liabilities What you owe; your debt.

Licensed Insolvency Trustee A person licensed to administer consumer proposals and bankruptcies and manage assets held in trust.

life annuity A financial contract that provides a fixed sum of money at regular intervals for one's lifetime.

life insurance Insurance that provides a payment to a specified beneficiary when the insured dies.

life insured The individual who is covered in the life insurance policy.

Lifelong Learning Plan (LLP) A tax-free RRSP withdrawal that is available to full-time students who temporarily would like to use an RRSP to finance their education.

limit order An order to buy or sell a stock only if the price is within limits that you specify.

limited (non-continuing) power of attorney A legal document that grants a person the power to make specific decisions for you in the event that you are temporarily incapacitated.

liquid assets Financial assets that can be easily converted into cash without a loss in value.

liquidity Access to ready cash, including savings and credit, to cover short-term or unexpected expenses; also, the ease with which an investor can convert an investment into cash without a loss of capital.

liquidity preference theory Suggests that investors require a premium for investing in longer-term bonds.

living benefits (accelerated death benefits) Benefits that allow the policyholder to receive a portion of the death benefits prior to death.

living will A simple legal document in which individuals specify their preferences if they become mentally or physically disabled.

loan contract A contract that specifies the terms of a loan as agreed to by the borrower and the lender.

locked-in retirement account (LIRA) A private pension plan that is created when an individual transfers vested money from an employer-sponsored pension plan.

long-term care insurance Covers expenses associated with long-term health conditions that cause individuals to need help with everyday tasks.

long-term liabilities Debt that will be paid over a period longer than one year.

management expense ratio (MER) The annual expenses incurred by a fund on a percentage basis, calculated as annual expenses of the fund divided by the net asset value of the fund; the result of this calculation is then divided by the number of shares outstanding.

margin call A request from a brokerage firm for the investor to increase the cash in their account in order to return the margin to the minimum level.

marginal tax rate The percentage of tax you pay on your next dollar of taxable income.

market makers Securities dealers who are required to trade actively in the market so that liquidity is maintained when natural market forces cannot provide sufficient liquidity.

market order An order to buy or sell a stock at its prevailing market price.

market risk The susceptibility of a mutual fund's performance to general market conditions.

market segmentation theory Suggests that the shape of the yield curve is determined by the supply and demand of bonds for various market players in different segment of the yield curve.

marketability The ease with which an investor can convert an investment into cash.

marketable bonds Government of Canada bonds that can be sold in a secondary market.

maturity or term With respect to a loan, the life or duration of the loan.

maturity matching strategy Selecting bonds that will generate payments to match future expenses.

medicare An interlocking system of 10 provincial and 3 territorial health insurance plans provided by the governments, including the federal government.

monetary policy Techniques used by the Bank of Canada (central bank) to affect the economy of the country.

money management Decisions regarding how much money to retain in liquid form and how to allocate the funds among short-term investment instruments.

money market funds (MMFs) Accounts that pool money from individuals and invest in securities that have short-term maturities, such as one year or less.

money market mutual funds Funds that sell units, or shares, to individuals and use this money to invest in cash and investments that can be converted to cash quickly (very liquid investments).

money orders and drafts Products that direct your bank to pay a specified amount to the person named on them.

mortality rate The number of deaths in a population or in a subgroup of the population.

mortgage companies Non-depository institutions that specialize in providing mortgage loans to individuals.

mortgage refinancing Paying off an existing mortgage with a new mortgage that has a lower interest rate.

mortgage term The period of time over which the mortgage interest rate and other terms of the mortgage contract will not change.

mortgage-backed securities Represent a pool of CMHC-insured residential mortgages that are issued by banks and other financial institutions.

Multiple Listing Service (MLS) An information database of homes available for sale through realtors who are members of the service.

municipal bonds Long-term debt securities issued by local government agencies.

mutual fund companies Non-depository institutions that sell units to individuals and use the proceeds to invest in securities to create mutual funds.

mutual funds Investment companies that sell shares to individuals and invest the proceeds in an overall portfolio of investment instruments such as bonds or stocks.

named perils coverage Protects the home and any other structures on the property against only those events named in the policy.

net asset value (NAV) The market value of the securities that a mutual fund has purchased minus any liabilities and fees owed.

net asset value per share (NAVPS) Calculated by dividing the NAV by the number of shares in the fund.

net cash flows Disposable (after-tax) income minus expenses.

net income The amount remaining after subtracting deductions from your total income.

net profit margin A measure of profitability that measures net profit as a percentage of sales.

net worth The value of what you own minus the value of what you owe.

no-fault auto insurance Allows policy owners in all provinces to receive immediate medical payments through their own insurance policy, regardless of who is at fault for causing the accident.

no-load mutual funds Funds that sell directly to investors and do not charge a fee.

nominal interest rate The stated, or quoted, rate of interest.

non-depository institutions Financial institutions that do not offer federally insured deposit accounts but provide various other financial services.

non-forfeiture options The options available to a policy owner who would like to discontinue or cancel a policy that has cash value.

non-participating policy A life insurance policy that is not eligible to receive policy dividends.

non-refundable tax credit The portion of the credit that is not needed to reduce your tax liability will not be paid to you and cannot be carried forward to reduce your tax liability in the future.

normal retirement age The age by which employees are entitled to receive 100 percent of the pension income for which they are eligible.

notarial will A formal type of will that is commonly used in Quebec and is completed in the presence of a notary (lawyer).

odd lot Less than a board lot of that particular stock.

on margin Purchasing a stock with a small amount of personal funds and the remainder of the funds borrowed from a brokerage firm.

online banking A service offered by financial institutions that allows a customer to check the balance of bank, credit card, and investment accounts, transfer funds, pay bills electronically, and perform a number of administrative tasks.

on-stop order An order to execute a transaction when the stock price reaches a specified level; a special form of limit order.

open mortgage Allows you to pay off the mortgage balance at any time during the mortgage term.

open-end mutual funds Funds that sell shares directly to investors and will redeem those shares whenever investors wish to "cash in."

operating profit margin A firm's operating profit divided by sales.

opportunity cost What you give up as a result of a decision.

ordinary annuity A stream of equal payments that are received or paid at equal intervals in time at the end of a period.

overdraft protection An arrangement that protects customers who write cheques for amounts that exceed their chequing account balances; it is a short-term loan from the depository institution where the chequing account is maintained.

over-the-counter (OTC) market An electronic communication network that allows investors to buy or sell securities.

par value For a bond, its face value, or the amount returned to the investor at the maturity date when the bond is due.

participating policy A life insurance policy that is eligible to receive policy dividends.

passive strategy Investing in a diversified portfolio of bonds that are held for a long period of time.

payday loan A short-term loan provided in advance of receiving a paycheque.

payment frequency The frequency with which you make a mortgage payment.

payoff diagram A graph that illustrates the gains or losses generated from an option.

pension adjustment Calculates the remaining annual contribution room available to an individual after taking into account any employer-sponsored pension plan contributions.

pension assignment Occurs when a married or common-law couple decides to share their CPP retirement pensions in order to reduce their income taxes.

pensionable earnings The amount of income you earn between the year's basic exemption (YBE) and the year's maximum pensionable earnings (YMPE).

per capita debt The amount of debt each individual in Canada would have if total debt (consumer debt plus mortgages) was spread equally across the population.

peril A hazard or risk you face.

permanent insurance Life insurance that continues to provide insurance for as long as premiums are paid.

personal balance sheet A summary of your assets (what you own), your liabilities (what you owe), and your net worth (assets minus liabilities).

personal cash flow statement A financial statement that measures a person's income and expenses.

personal finance (personal financial planning) The process of planning your spending, financing, and investing activities, while taking into account uncontrollable events such as death or disability, in order to optimize your financial situation over time.

personal financial plan A plan that specifies your financial goals and describes the spending, financing, and investing activities that are intended to achieve those goals and the risk management strategies that are required to protect against uncontrollable events such as death or disability.

personal income taxes Taxes imposed on income earned.

personal property floater An extension of the homeowner's insurance policy that allows you to itemize your valuables.

pharming Similar to phishing, but targeted at larger audiences, it directs users to bogus websites to collect their personal information.

phishing Occurs when pretexting happens online.

policy dividend A refund of premiums that occurs when the long-term assumptions the insurance company made with respect to the cost of insurance, company expenses, and investment returns have changed.

policy owner The individual who owns all rights and obligations to the policy.

pooled investment fund An investment vehicle that pools together money from many investors and invests that money in a variety of securities.

portfolio A set of multiple investments in different assets.

pre-approval certificate Provides you with a guideline on how large a mortgage you can afford based on your financial situation.

preferential share The dollar value of estate assets that will be distributed to the surviving spouse before assets are distributed among all potential beneficiaries.

preferred stock A certificate issued by a firm to raise funds that entitles shareholders to first priority to receive dividends.

premium The amount by which a closed-end fund's share price in the secondary market is above the fund's NAVPS.

premium bond A bond that is trading at a price above its par value.

premium of a call option The price paid when purchasing a call option.

prepayment privileges Features that allow borrowers to increase their monthly mortgage payment and to pay off a lump sum of the original mortgage balance during the course of each mortgage year.

present value interest factor (PVIF) A factor multiplied by the future value to determine the present value of that amount.

present value interest factors for an annuity (PVIFA) A factor multiplied by a periodic savings level (annuity) to determine the present value of the annuity.

prestige cards Credit cards, such as gold cards or platinum cards, issued by a financial institution to individuals who have an exceptional credit standing.

pretexting Occurs when individuals access personal information under false pretenses.

price–earnings (P/E) method A method of valuing stocks in which a firm's earnings per share are multiplied by the mean industry price–earnings (P/E) ratio.

primary market A market in which newly issued securities are traded.

prime rate The interest rate a bank charges its best customers.

probate A legal process that declares a will valid and ensures the orderly distribution of assets.

property damage liability coverage Protects against losses that result when the policy owner damages another person's property with his or her car.

protective put strategy An option strategy where you purchase a put option to protect against a decrease in the price of an underlying stock.

provincial bonds Debt securities issued by the various provincial governments.

publicly traded stock indexes Securities whose values move in tandem with a particular stock index representing a set of stocks.

pure expectations theory Suggests that the shape of the yield curve is a reflection of the market's expectation for future interest rate movements.

put feature A feature on a bond that allows the investor to redeem the bond at its face value before it matures.

put option Provides the right to sell 100 shares of a specified stock at a specified exercise price by a specified expiration date.

range of returns Returns of a specific investment over a given period.

real estate Principal residence, rental property, and land.

real estate investment trusts (REIT) An income trust that pools funds from individuals and uses that money to invest in real estate.

real return bonds Long-term debt securities issued by the Government of

Canada that protect an investor from inflation risk.

refundable tax credit The portion of the credit that is not needed to reduce your tax liability (because it is already zero) may be paid to you.

registered annuities Annuities that are created using assets from an RRSP.

registered disability savings plan (RDSP) A savings plan to help parents and others save for the long-term financial security of a person who is eligible for the disability tax credit.

registered retirement savings plan (RRSP) A type of private pension that enables you to save for your retirement on a tax-deferred basis.

reinstatement The process of completing a reinstatement application to restore a policy that is in lapse status.

reinvestment risk The risk that the income earned from a bond cannot be reinvested at the same or a higher rate of interest as was being earned from the bond.

relative valuation model A model that attempts to find the value of an investment by comparing it to other similar investments.

renewability option Allows you to renew your policy for another term once the existing term expires.

rental property Housing or commercial property that is rented out to others.

replacement cost policy Pays you the cost of replacing the damaged property with an item of a similar brand and quality.

residue Refers to the amount remaining in an estate after all financial obligations, such as the payment of debts, expenses, taxes, and bequests, have been fulfilled.

retail (or proprietary) credit card A credit card that is honoured only by a specific retail establishment.

retirement planning Determining how much money you should set aside each year for retirement and how you should invest those funds.

return on assets A measure of profitability, computed as net profit divided by total assets.

return on equity A measure of profitability, computed as net profit divided

by the owners' investment in the firm (shareholders' equity).

reverse mortgage A secured loan that allows older Canadians to generate income using the equity in their homes without having to sell this asset.

revocable inter vivos trust An inter vivos trust that can be dissolved at any time.

revolving open-end credit Credit provided up to a specified maximum amount based on income, debt level, and credit history; interest is charged each month on the outstanding balance.

riders Options that allow you to customize a life insurance policy to your specific needs.

rights or things Income that was owed to the deceased taxpayer but not paid at the time of death, but that would have been included in income had the taxpayer not died.

risk Exposure to events (or perils) that can cause a financial loss.

risk management Decisions about whether and how to protect against risk.

risk premium The extra yield required by investors to compensate for default risk; an additional return beyond the risk-free rate you could earn from an investment.

risk tolerance A person's ability to accept risk, usually defined as a potential loss of return and/or loss of capital.

safety deposit box A box at a financial institution in which a customer can store documents, jewellery, and other valuables. It is secure because it is stored in the bank's vault.

second mortgage A secured mortgage loan that is subordinate (or secondary) to another loan.

secondary market A market which facilitates the trading of existing securities.

sector funds Mutual funds that focus on stocks in a specific industry or sector, such as technology stocks.

secured loan A loan that is backed or secured by collateral.

sell-stop order An order to sell a stock when the price falls to a specified level.

settlor The person who creates a trust.

shoulder surfing Occurs in public places where you can be readily seen or heard by someone standing close by.

simple interest Interest on a loan or investment computed as a percentage of the loan or investment amount, or principal.

sinking fund A pool of money that is set aside by a corporation or government to repurchase a set amount of bonds in a set period of time.

skimming Occurs when identity thieves steal your credit card or debit card number by copying the information contained in the magnetic strip on the card.

spousal RRSP A type of RRSP where one spouse contributes to the plan and the other spouse is the beneficiary, or annuitant.

standard deviation The degree of volatility in an investment's returns over time.

stock exchanges Facilities that allow investors to purchase or sell existing stocks.

stock option An option to purchase or sell stocks under specified conditions.

stocks Certificates representing partial ownership of a firm.

stop payment A financial institution's notice that it will not honour a regular monthly automatic withdrawal; usually occurs in response to a request by the account owner.

strip bonds Long-term debt securities issued by the Government of Canada (and some provinces) that do not offer coupon payments.

student loan A loan provided to finance a portion of a student's expenses while pursuing post-secondary education.

systematic risk Risks that affects all companies, industries, and countries.

T4 slip A document provided to you by your employer that displays your salary and all deductions associated with your employment with that specific employer for the previous year. Your employer is required to provide you with a T4 slip by February 28 each year.

T5 statement of investment income (slip) A document provided to you when you receive income other than salary income.

tax avoidance Occurs when taxpayers legally apply tax law to reduce or eliminate taxes payable in ways that the CRA considers potentially abusive of the spirit of the *Income Tax Act*.

tax credits Specific amounts used directly to reduce tax liability.

tax evasion Occurs when taxpayers attempt to deceive the CRA by knowingly reporting less tax payable than what the law obligates them to pay.

tax planning Involves activities and transactions that reduce or eliminate tax.

tax-free savings account (TFSA) A registered investment account that allows you to purchase investments, with after-tax dollars, without attracting any tax payable on your investment growth.

T-bills Short-term debt securities issued by the Canadian and provincial governments and sold at a discount.

technical analysis The valuation of stocks based on historical price patterns.

tenant's insurance An insurance policy that protects your possessions within a house, condominium, or apartment that you are renting.

term annuity A financial contract that provides a fixed sum of money at regular intervals until a specified year.

term insurance Life insurance that is provided over a specified time period and does not build a cash value.

term structure of interest rates A graph that shows the relationship between bond yield to maturity and time to maturity.

term to 100 insurance A form of permanent life insurance that does not build cash value.

term to maturity The date at which a bond will expire and the par value of the bond, along with any remaining coupon payments, is to be paid back to the bondholder.

testamentary trust A trust created by a will.

third party liability A legal term that describes the person(s) who have experienced loss because of the insured.

ticker symbol The abbreviation used to identify a stock for trading purposes.

timelines Diagrams that show payments received or paid over time.

times interest earned ratio A measure of financial leverage that indicates the ratio of the firm's earnings before interest and taxes to its total interest payments.

total debt service (TDS) ratio Your mortgage-related debt payments plus all other consumer debt payments divided by your total monthly gross household income.

total income All reportable income from any source, including salary, wages, commissions, business income, government benefits, pension income, interest income, dividend income, and taxable capital gains received during the tax year. Income received from sources outside Canada is also subject to Canadian income tax.

tracking error Refers to how closely an index fund mirrors the movements of the existing index it is benchmarked against.

traveller's cheque A cheque written on behalf of an individual that will be charged against a large, well-known financial institution or credit card sponsor's account.

trust A legal document in which one person, the settlor, transfers assets to a trustee, who manages them for designated beneficiaries.

trust and loan companies Financial institutions that, in addition to providing services similar to a bank, can provide financial planning services, such as administering estates and acting as trustee in the administration of trust accounts.

trustee An individual or organization that is responsible for the management of assets held in trust for one or more of the beneficiaries of a will.

umbrella personal liability policy A supplement to auto and homeowner's insurance that provides additional personal liability coverage.

underinsured motorist coverage Insures against the additional cost of bodily injury when an accident is caused by a driver who has insufficient coverage.

underwriters Employees of an insurance company who calculate the risk of specific insurance policies and decide what policies to offer and what premiums to charge.

underwriting The process of evaluating an insurance application based on the applicant's age, sex, smoking status, driving record, and other health and lifestyle considerations, then issuing insurance policies based on the responses.

uninsured motorist coverage Insures against the cost of bodily injury when an accident is caused by another driver who is not insured.

universal life insurance A form of permanent life insurance for which you do not pay a fixed premium and in which you can decide to invest the cash value portion in a variety of investments.

unsecured loan A loan that is not backed or secured by collateral.

unsystematic risk Risk that is specific to a company, an industry, or a country.

value stocks Stocks of firms that are currently undervalued by the market for reasons other than the performance of the businesses themselves.

variable-rate mortgage (VRM) A mortgage where the interest charged on the loan changes in response to movements in a specific market-determined interest rate. The rate used is usually referred to as prime. Lenders will add a percentage to prime for the total mortgage rate.

vendor take-back mortgage A mortgage where the lender is the seller of the property.

venture capital Refers to investors' funds destined for risky, generally new businesses with tremendous growth potential.

vested Having a claim to the money in an employer-sponsored retirement account that has been reserved for you upon your retirement, even if you leave the company.

waiting period The period from the time you become disabled until you begin to receive disability income benefits.

whole life insurance A form of permanent life insurance that builds cash value based on a fixed premium that is payable for the life of the insured.

will A legal document that describes how your estate should be distributed upon your death. It can also identify a preferred guardian for any surviving minor children.

yield to maturity The annualized return on a bond if it is held until maturity.

INDEX

S

ANSWERS TO STUDY GUIDE QUESTIONS

CHAPTER 1
Multiple Choice

1. c 2. b 3. d 4. b 5. c 6. d 7. d
8. b 9. a 10. d 11. a 12. b 13. c
14. a 15. d

True/False

1. T 2. F 3. F 4. F 5. T 6. F 7. F
8. F 9. F 10. T 11. T 12. F 13. T
14. T 15. T

CHAPTER 2
Multiple Choice

1. c 2. a 3. a 4. d 5. a 6. c 7. b
8. d 9. b 10. c 11. a 12. a 13. d
14. c 15. a

True/False

1. F 2. F 3. T 4. T 5. T 6. F 7. T
8. T 9. T 10. T 11. T 12. F 13. T
14. T 15. F

CHAPTER 3
Multiple Choice

1. b 2. c 3. c 4. a 5. a 6. d 7. d
8. c 9. d 10. b 11. c 12. b 13. d
14. a 15. c

True/False

1. F 2. T 3. T 4. F 5. F 6. F 7. F
8. T 9. T 10. T 11. F 12. F 13. T
14. T 15. T

CHAPTER 4
Multiple Choice

1. c 2. c 3. c 4. d 5. c 6. c 7. b
8. a 9. a 10. b 11. b 12. c 13. b
14. d 15. b

True/False

1. F 2. F 3. F 4. F 5. T 6. T 7. T
8. F 9. F 10. T 11. T 12. F 13. F
14. F 15. F

CHAPTER 5
Multiple Choice

1. c 2. a 3. d 4. b 5. c 6. b 7. b
8. c 9. d 10. d 11. d 12. b 13. a
14. c 15. c

True/False

1. F 2. T 3. T 4. F 5. T 6. F 7. F
8. T 9. F 10. T 11. T 12. F 13. F
14. F 15. T

CHAPTER 6
Multiple Choice

1. b 2. d 3. c 4. a 5. d 6. b 7. a
8. c 9. d 10. a 11. b 12. b 13. a
14. a 15. c

True/False

1. F 2. T 3. T 4. F 5. T 6. F 7. T
8. T 9. F 10. T 11. T 12. F 13. T
14. F 15. F

CHAPTER 7
Multiple Choice

1. b 2. b 3. a 4. a 5. d 6. c 7. c
8. c 9. d 10. c 11. b 12. d 13. d
14. a 15. c

True/False

1. T 2. F 3. F 4. T 5. T 6. F 7. F
8. T 9. T 10. T 11. F 12. F 13. T
14. T 15. T

CHAPTER 8
Multiple Choice

1. c 2. d 3. b 4. b 5. b 6. a 7. d
8. b 9. b 10. d 11. a 12. a 13. a
14. c 15. d

True/False

1. T 2. F 3. F 4. T 5. T 6. F 7. T
8. F 9. F 10. T 11. F 12. F 13. T
14. F 15. T

CHAPTER 9
Multiple Choice

1. b 2. c 3. b 4. b 5. b 6. a 7. c
8. a 9. c 10. b 11. a 12. a 13. d
14. c 15. d

True/False

1. T 2. F 3. T 4. T 5. F 6. T 7. F
8. T 9. F 10. T 11. F 12. T 13. T
14. T 15. F

CHAPTER 10
Multiple Choice

1. a 2. c 3. c 4. b 5. c 6. a 7. d
8. d 9. a 10. d 11. b 12. c 13. b
14. c 15. a

True/False

1. F 2. T 3. F 4. T 5. T 6. F 7. F
8. T 9. F 10. F 11. T 12. F 13. T
14. T 15. F

CHAPTER 11
Multiple Choice

1. c 2. b 3. a 4. c 5. a 6. d 7. c
8. a 9. b 10. a 11. b 12. d 13. b
14. a 15. c

True/False

1. F 2. F 3. F 4. T 5. F 6. F 7. T
8. F 9. T 10. F 11. T 12. T 13. F
14. F 15. F

CHAPTER 12
Multiple Choice

1. c 2. d 3. b 4. d 5. b 6. b 7. a
8. a 9. c 10. c 11. b 12. b 13. c
14. a 15. d

True/False

1. F 2. T 3. F 4. T 5. T 6. F 7. T
8. T 9. T 10. T 11. T 12. F 13. T
14. T 15. F

CHAPTER 13
Multiple Choice
1. d 2. b 3. b 4. d 5. a 6. c 7. a
8. d 9. d 10. a 11. d 12. a 13. b
14. b 15. d

True/False
1. T 2. F 3. T 4. T 5. F 6. T 7. F
8. T 9. F 10. T 11. F 12. T 13. T
14. F 15. F

CHAPTER 14
Multiple Choice
1. b 2. a 3. c 4. b 5. c 6. c 7. c
8. b 9. a 10. c 11. d 12. d 13. c
14. d 15. b

True/False
1. T 2. T 3. F 4. F 5. T 6. T 7. T
8. F 9. T 10. T 11. F 12. T 13. T
14. T 15. T

CHAPTER 15
Multiple Choice
1. d 2. c 3. a 4. b 5. c 6. c 7. b
8. a 9. d 10. c 11. a 12. a 13. b
14. b 15. d

True/False
1. F 2. F 3. T 4. T 5. T 6. F 7. F
8. T 9. F 10. T 11. T 12. T 13. F
14. T 15. F

CHAPTER 16
Multiple Choice
1. a 2. c 3. b 4. b 5. a 6. d 7. c
8. a 9. b 10. d

True/False
1. T 2. F 3. T 4. F 5. T 6. T 7. F
8. F 9. T 10. T